Lecture Notes in Computer Science   11574

Commenced Publication in 1973
Founding and Former Series Editors:
Gerhard Goos, Juris Hartmanis, and Jan van Leeuwen

More information about this series at http://www.springer.com/series/7409

Jessie Y. C. Chen · Gino Fragomeni (Eds.)

Virtual, Augmented and Mixed Reality

Multimodal Interaction

11th International Conference, VAMR 2019
Held as Part of the 21st HCI International Conference, HCII 2019
Orlando, FL, USA, July 26–31, 2019
Proceedings, Part I

 Springer

Editors
Jessie Y. C. Chen
US Army Research Laboratory
Aberdeen Proving Ground, MD, USA

Gino Fragomeni
US Army Research Laboratory
Orlando, FL, USA

ISSN 0302-9743   ISSN 1611-3349   (electronic)
Lecture Notes in Computer Science
ISBN 978-3-030-21606-1   ISBN 978-3-030-21607-8   (eBook)
https://doi.org/10.1007/978-3-030-21607-8

LNCS Sublibrary: SL3 – Information Systems and Applications, incl. Internet/Web, and HCI

This Springer imprint is published by the registered company Springer Nature Switzerland AG
The registered company address is: Gewerbestrasse 11, 6330 Cham, Switzerland

Foreword

The 21st International Conference on Human-Computer Interaction, HCI International 2019, was held in Orlando, FL, USA, during July 26–31, 2019. The event incorporated the 18 thematic areas and affiliated conferences listed on the following page.

A total of 5,029 individuals from academia, research institutes, industry, and governmental agencies from 73 countries submitted contributions, and 1,274 papers and 209 posters were included in the pre-conference proceedings. These contributions address the latest research and development efforts and highlight the human aspects of design and use of computing systems. The contributions thoroughly cover the entire field of human-computer interaction, addressing major advances in knowledge and effective use of computers in a variety of application areas. The volumes constituting the full set of the pre-conference proceedings are listed in the following pages.

This year the HCI International (HCII) conference introduced the new option of "late-breaking work." This applies both for papers and posters and the corresponding volume(s) of the proceedings will be published just after the conference. Full papers will be included in the *HCII 2019 Late-Breaking Work Papers Proceedings* volume of the proceedings to be published in the Springer LNCS series, while poster extended abstracts will be included as short papers in the HCII 2019 *Late-Breaking Work Poster Extended Abstracts* volume to be published in the Springer CCIS series.

I would like to thank the program board chairs and the members of the program boards of all thematic areas and affiliated conferences for their contribution to the highest scientific quality and the overall success of the HCI International 2019 conference.

This conference would not have been possible without the continuous and unwavering support and advice of the founder, Conference General Chair Emeritus and Conference Scientific Advisor Prof. Gavriel Salvendy. For his outstanding efforts, I would like to express my appreciation to the communications chair and editor of *HCI International News,* Dr. Abbas Moallem.

July 2019   Constantine Stephanidis

HCI International 2019 Thematic Areas
and Affiliated Conferences

Thematic areas:

- HCI 2019: Human-Computer Interaction
- HIMI 2019: Human Interface and the Management of Information

Affiliated conferences:

- EPCE 2019: 16th International Conference on Engineering Psychology and Cognitive Ergonomics
- UAHCI 2019: 13th International Conference on Universal Access in Human-Computer Interaction
- VAMR 2019: 11th International Conference on Virtual, Augmented and Mixed Reality
- CCD 2019: 11th International Conference on Cross-Cultural Design
- SCSM 2019: 11th International Conference on Social Computing and Social Media
- AC 2019: 13th International Conference on Augmented Cognition
- DHM 2019: 10th International Conference on Digital Human Modeling and Applications in Health, Safety, Ergonomics and Risk Management
- DUXU 2019: 8th International Conference on Design, User Experience, and Usability
- DAPI 2019: 7th International Conference on Distributed, Ambient and Pervasive Interactions
- HCIBGO 2019: 6th International Conference on HCI in Business, Government and Organizations
- LCT 2019: 6th International Conference on Learning and Collaboration Technologies
- ITAP 2019: 5th International Conference on Human Aspects of IT for the Aged Population
- HCI-CPT 2019: First International Conference on HCI for Cybersecurity, Privacy and Trust
- HCI-Games 2019: First International Conference on HCI in Games
- MobiTAS 2019: First International Conference on HCI in Mobility, Transport, and Automotive Systems
- AIS 2019: First International Conference on Adaptive Instructional Systems

Pre-conference Proceedings Volumes Full List

1. LNCS 11566, Human-Computer Interaction: Perspectives on Design (Part I), edited by Masaaki Kurosu
2. LNCS 11567, Human-Computer Interaction: Recognition and Interaction Technologies (Part II), edited by Masaaki Kurosu
3. LNCS 11568, Human-Computer Interaction: Design Practice in Contemporary Societies (Part III), edited by Masaaki Kurosu
4. LNCS 11569, Human Interface and the Management of Information: Visual Information and Knowledge Management (Part I), edited by Sakae Yamamoto and Hirohiko Mori
5. LNCS 11570, Human Interface and the Management of Information: Information in Intelligent Systems (Part II), edited by Sakae Yamamoto and Hirohiko Mori
6. LNAI 11571, Engineering Psychology and Cognitive Ergonomics, edited by Don Harris
7. LNCS 11572, Universal Access in Human-Computer Interaction: Theory, Methods and Tools (Part I), edited by Margherita Antona and Constantine Stephanidis
8. LNCS 11573, Universal Access in Human-Computer Interaction: Multimodality and Assistive Environments (Part II), edited by Margherita Antona and Constantine Stephanidis
9. LNCS 11574, Virtual, Augmented and Mixed Reality: Multimodal Interaction (Part I), edited by Jessie Y. C. Chen and Gino Fragomeni
10. LNCS 11575, Virtual, Augmented and Mixed Reality: Applications and Case Studies (Part II), edited by Jessie Y. C. Chen and Gino Fragomeni
11. LNCS 11576, Cross-Cultural Design: Methods, Tools and User Experience (Part I), edited by P. L. Patrick Rau
12. LNCS 11577, Cross-Cultural Design: Culture and Society (Part II), edited by P. L. Patrick Rau
13. LNCS 11578, Social Computing and Social Media: Design, Human Behavior and Analytics (Part I), edited by Gabriele Meiselwitz
14. LNCS 11579, Social Computing and Social Media: Communication and Social Communities (Part II), edited by Gabriele Meiselwitz
15. LNAI 11580, Augmented Cognition, edited by Dylan D. Schmorrow and Cali M. Fidopiastis
16. LNCS 11581, Digital Human Modeling and Applications in Health, Safety, Ergonomics and Risk Management: Human Body and Motion (Part I), edited by Vincent G. Duffy

34. CCIS 1033, HCI International 2019 - Posters (Part II), edited by Constantine Stephanidis
35. CCIS 1034, HCI International 2019 - Posters (Part III), edited by Constantine Stephanidis

http://2019.hci.international/proceedings

11th International Conference on Virtual, Augmented and Mixed Reality (VAMR 2019)

Program Board Chair(s): **Jessie Y. C. Chen and Gino Fragomeni,** *USA*

- Tamara Griffith, USA
- Fotis Liarokapis, Czech Republic
- Joseph B. Lyons, USA
- Phillip Mangos, USA
- Amar R. Marathe, USA
- Rafael Radkowski, USA
- Maria Olinda Rodas, USA
- Michael S. Ryoo, USA
- Jose San Martin, Spain
- Andreas Schreiber, Germany
- Peter Smith, USA
- Simon Su, USA
- Daniel Szafir, USA
- Tom Williams, USA
- Denny Yu, USA

The full list with the Program Board Chairs and the members of the Program Boards of all thematic areas and affiliated conferences is available online at:

http://www.hci.international/board-members-2019.php

HCI International 2020

The 22nd International Conference on Human-Computer Interaction, HCI International 2020, will be held jointly with the affiliated conferences in Copenhagen, Denmark, at the Bella Center Copenhagen, July 19–24, 2020. It will cover a broad spectrum of themes related to HCI, including theoretical issues, methods, tools, processes, and case studies in HCI design, as well as novel interaction techniques, interfaces, and applications. The proceedings will be published by Springer. More information will be available on the conference website: http://2020.hci.international/.

General Chair
Prof. Constantine Stephanidis
University of Crete and ICS-FORTH
Heraklion, Crete, Greece
E-mail: general_chair@hcii2020.org

http://2020.hci.international/

Contents – Part I

Rendering, Layout, Visualization and Navigation

Avatars, Embodiment and Empathy in VAMR

Cognitive and Health Issues in VAMR

xx   Contents – Part I

Contents – Part II

VAMR in Learning, Training and Entertainment

VAMR in Aviation, Industry and the Military

Multimodal Interaction in VR

Presence, Immersion and Usability of Mobile Augmented Reality

Hyoenah Choi, Youngwon Ryan Kim, and Gerard J. Kim[✉]

Digital Experience Laboratory, Korea University, Seoul, Korea
judy5615@gmail.com, kyw920@gmail.com,
gjkim@korea.ac.kr

Abstract. Augmented reality (AR) is becoming truly mobile, as it was intended to be, through smartphone and embedded computer based platforms. For these computing platforms, there are three typical display systems used: (1) hand-held video see-through (smartphone) LCD as is, (2) video see-through (smartphone) LCD inserted into and isolated with the cardboard case and magnifying lenses, and (3) optical see-through (glass-like) displays. Recently, an alternative form has appeared in the market in which the magnifying lenses are simply clipped onto the smartphone. The four displays differ in few ways: e.g. wearability and convenience, image quality, size of the imagery and field of view, isolation from the outside world, the real world representation (video or actual), which all potentially can affect the levels of their usability, presence and immersion. In this paper, we examine and compare the levels of usability, presence and immersion as provided by these four different display configurations of Mobile AR. We also control another related factor, namely the amount of ambient light, which might have similar effects according to the different display types, carrying out the experiment under three different conditions: indoor (office-level lighting), outdoor (medium sun light), or outdoor (bright sun light). Our experiment first showed that the current level of technology for the optical see-through glass type displays still fall short to provide the minimum usability, display quality and presence/immersion for practical usage. The other three displays showed generally similar levels of usability and presence/immersion, which indicates that the isolation from the real world, is not important in AR unlike in virtual reality (VR). It is also thought that in the case of AR, the usability is the most important factor for users for their choice of the display type, which also affect the perceived level of immersion and presence.

Keywords: Augmented reality · Object presence · Immersion · Usability · Mobile · Display

1 Introduction

Mobile augmented reality (MAR) is a media form that "augments" the real world (or its representation) with virtual objects. Since the augmented virtual objects are situated in the "real" world, it is intended to be used as a mobile system. The recent advancement in mobile computing, spearheaded by the smartphones and similar embedded systems, has made it possible for the AR to become truly mobile. The same goes for the display

© Springer Nature Switzerland AG 2019
J. Y. C. Chen and G. Fragomeni (Eds.): HCII 2019, LNCS 11574, pp. 3–15, 2019.
https://doi.org/10.1007/978-3-030-21607-8_1

which has to be convenient to use for carry them or put on to use. There have three typical display systems used: (1) hand-held video see-though (smartphone) LCD as is, (2) video see-through (smartphone) LCD inserted into and isolated with the cardboard case and magnifying lenses, and (3) optical see-though (glass-like) displays. Recently, an alternative form has appeared in the market in which the magnifying lenses are simply clipped onto the smartphone. The four displays differ in few ways (see table below), which in turn can affect the levels of their usability, presence and immersion. Understanding of these relative qualities is important in assessing the proliferation possibility of the consumer-level AR by the right type of display and platform (e.g. cost/benefit/usability).

Table 1. Characteristics of four typical mobile AR displays

Characteristics Display	Wearability	Image FOV	Isolation	Real world representation	Convenience / Switch to smartphone
PhoneAR: video see-though smartphone	hand-held	small display: 25°, overall: human FOV	No	Live camera video	high (direct usage)
ClosedAR: video see-through smartphone inserted into cardboard case with lenses	hand-held and closely worn	medium (magnified) display: 96° overall: 96°	Yes	Live camera video	low (insert phone)
EasyAR: video see-through smartphone with flip-on lenses	hand-held and loosely worn	medium (magnified) display: 76.5°, overall: human FOV	No	Live camera video	Medium (flip on lens)
OpenAR: optical see-though (glass-like) displays	worn	large (human FOV) augmentation: 30°, overall: human FOV	No	As is	High (direct usage)

In this paper, we examine and compare the levels of usability, presence and immersion as provided by these four different display configurations of Mobile AR. We also control another related factor, the amount of environment light which is different and affects the display quality, carrying out the experiment under three different conditions: indoor (office-level lighting), outdoor (medium sun light), or outdoor (bright sun light).

Note that in this comparison, ideally, the optical see-through or glass type display would be considered as the base line with the best usability and probably the highest user experience, however, the current level of technology unfortunately does not guarantee either the wearability like the regular glasses or the augmentation image quality. Instead, the bare smartphone based AR (first row in Table 1), with the commercial success of the Pokemon Go [1] and the proven usability, could be used as the base line for the relative evaluation and comparison.

2 Related Work: User Experience in AR

The most typical platform for the Mobile AR (M-AR) is perhaps the smartphone, which now is equipped with a high resolution display and camera, sufficient computing and networking capability and other sensors to digest the needs of AR, e.g. self-contained, convenient, inexpensive, and targeted for casual use. Immersive mobile VR platform such as the Cardboard type (cheap lens equipped headset into which a smartphone can be inserted) too can serve as an alternative, which can offer the augmented imagery of different quality with the immersive isolation from the real world and magnified imagery with almost matched scale (vs. viewing the smartphone from a nominal usual arm-length distance). The recent open flip-on lenses offer similar features except for the real world isolation [2]. All of these displays are what is called the video see-through systems, which uses the live camera image as the backdrop to the augmented imagery that the user sees. Such video see-through systems generally offer, through computer vision, tracking and image processing techniques, more accurate object-augmentation registration and even image manipulation for harmonization. However, it can suffer from image quality (limited resolution and field of view), processing time (leading to latency), and focus problems.

On the other hand, the optical see-through glass has been envisioned to be the ultimate display for AR [3]. For one, it preserves the richness of the real world as seen with the right focus by the naked eyes. However, the accurate alignment and registration of the virtual objects onto the real object is difficult, and require often cumbersome calibration process. The optical and projective display systems still lack the technological sophistication to make natural looking renderings, often perceived as ghost-like images in the presence of bright environment light, not to mention seen with a fixed focus distance. Finally, the state of the art AR glasses still do not possess the ever-wished form factor of the regular vision glasses yet, being bulky and significantly heavy. Obviously, different levels of usability and user experience are expected from these displays, further compounded by the environment conditions.

There have not been much studies on the important factors that affect the user experience for AR. By contrast, there have been an extensive line of studies on what types of elements and how they affect the level of presence and immersion (the sense of the user feeling to be inside the virtual world, different than the real one that user is in [4]), one of the main objective of VR content, in the context of VR. For example, the display type is regarded one of the more important system oriented factors that affect the level of presence and usability/UX. The display type can be further characterized and explained in terms of the resolution, stereoscopy, display size, field of view (FOV), world isolation and other convenience or ergonomics related factors (e.g. headset weight). However, in AR (even though AR might be treated as one type of VR), user presence is perhaps ill-defined since AR is already used in the real world where the user is. Nevertheless, the sense of user presence or immersion can still be somewhat affected as the augmented real world, in various lighting condition, is seen through the "framed" display system. Several literatures also point to the concept of "object" presence, as a way of assessing or evaluating AR systems [5]. The object presence refers how much the virtual augmentation feels to be realistic, physical, actually part of the real world, natural and harmonious.

In our study, the focus is mainly on the effect of the display size, FOV and world isolation (and amount of ambient light) and the field of view with regards to the extent of how much and how the outer real environment is visible in the background. In VR, studies have shown that a higher level of immersion and presence is obtained through a display with a large size/FOV and high resolution, isolated from the distraction of the outer world [6]. Whether the same applies to AR remains to be seen in this study.

3   Experiment

3.1   Experiment Design

The experiment examines the levels of user felt immersion and presence and general usability in four different display configurations of mobile AR (also see Table 1): (1) hand-held video see-though (smartphone) LCD – "PhoneAR", (2) video see-through (smartphone) LCD inserted into and isolated with the cardboard case and magnifying lenses – "ClosedAR", (3) video see-through (smartphone) LCD with flip-on lenses – "EasyAR", and (4) optical see-though (glass-like) displays – "OpenAR". As we project that the environment background condition to be an important factor, we test and compare these platforms under three different lighting conditions: (1) "Indoor" at office level luminance without extreme or direct sunlight, (2) "Outdoor low" – at usual outdoor daylight luminance, but without direct sunlight toward the screen, and (3) "Outdoor high" – at outdoor daylight luminance under direct sunlight toward the screen and operating environment. In summary, the experiment was designed as a 4×3 (resulting in 12 different testing conditions) within subject repeated measure (see Table 2).

Table 2. Twelve experimental conditions from the two factors.

Lighting / Display	Indoor	Outdoor low	Outdoor high
PhoneAR	PI	POl	POh
ClosedAR	CI	COl	COh
EasyAR	EI	EOl	EOh
OpenAR	OI	OOl	OOh

To make sure the user is able to get as much sense of the augmented reality space as affected by the seam between the main display (whose video background shows part of the real space), and the rest of the real environment seen in the periphery, and the given environment light condition, we set the experimental task as a navigated viewing of the immediate environment with 8 augmentation objects scattered 360° around the initial user position (see Fig. 2). After the navigation, the user's sense of immersion, object presence, general usability and various aspects of the user experience were assessed through a survey.

We hypothesized that ClosedAR, OpenAR and EasyAR would be regarded more immersive, with higher user/object presence compared to PhoneAR. In addition, we had expected that EasyAR would show a similar level of presence and UX at least as ClosedAR, and also even higher than OpenAR under the direct sunlight (OOh).

3.2   Experimental Set-Up

PhoneAR was implemented and viewed (at a nominal arm length) on the Samsung Galaxy S8 smartphone [7] using the Unity [8] and marker recognition module from Vuforia [9]. The same went for ClosedAR and EasyAR except that the former used the Samsung GearVR [10] for the display (into which the smartphone was inserted) and the latter used the flip-on lenses from Homido [2]. OpenAR was implemented on the Microsoft Hololens (same development environment). Viewing the marker augmented objects and navigating around the test augmented reality scene with different devices are illustrated in Fig. 1. The three different lighting conditions and the scattered object placements are shown in Fig. 2.

Fig. 1. Viewing the augmented reality scene using the four different display configurations of AR (1) PhoneAR, (2) ClosedAR, (3) EasyAR and (4) OpenAR (from the left).

The AR space the user viewed and navigated were placed with 8 objects (augmented on side of the markers) in a circular fashion around the initial user position (see Fig. 2). The objects (e.g. fire hydrant, bottle, etc.) were scaled to their actual life sizes for as much realism. The markers (or augmentation objects) were put on at around 1.2 m above the ground (on chairs/boxes) so that the user could view them closely without much difficulty while standing.

One of the main differences among the four display systems were their field of view. Although the view into the real world is open in PhoneAR, the display itself, when held and viewed from the arm length, was about 23–30°. Similarly (peripheral view into the real world open), the magnified imagery of EasyAR had a much larger FOV at around 76.5°. Both of these displays, being open have the overall FOV to that of the human. ClosedAR had around 96° of FOV but the rest of the visual periphery was shut (black). OpenAR has the full human FOV, however, the portion for augmentation covered only about 30°. However, the objects were sized and augmented such that the entire object could be seen at once without being clipped. Figures 3, 4, 5 and 6 show the augmented views in the 12 different testing conditions.

Fig. 2. Three different lighting conditions for the test augmented space: Indoor (left), Outdoor low (middle) and Outdoor high (right).

Fig. 3. Looking at an augmented object (bottle) with PhoneAR, Indoor (left), Outdoor low (middle), and Outdoor high (right).

3.3   Detailed Experimental Procedure

Twelve people (mean age = 23) participated in the experiment. Most of them had prior AR experiences using the smartphone such as the Pokémon GO. We first collected the subjects' background information and had them fill out the informed consent forms. Then, the subjects were briefed about the purpose of the experiment and given instructions for the experimental task. Each participant asked to stand in the middle of the test augmented space (see Fig. 2) and was given one of the four display system (held in hand or worn) with which one went around the space and browsed through the

Fig. 4. Looking at an augmented object (bottle) with ClosedAR, Indoor (left), Outdoor low (middle), and Outdoor high (right) – p

Fig. 5. Looking at an augmented object (bottle) with EasyAR, Indoor (left), Outdoor low (middle), and Outdoor high (right).

eight augmented objects for 2.5 min with 1 min break between each treatment. The test condition was administered in the balanced Latin square fashion. The whole experiment took about an hour.

After each condition, the participant filled out survey which contained four categories of questions for evaluating the AR user experience (see Table 3): (1) user felt presence and immersion, (2) object presence, (3) basic usability and (4) preference and overall satisfaction – all answered in the 7 level Likert scale (1: negative ~ 7: positive). In particular, object presence refers how much the virtual augmentation objects felt to be realistic, physical, actually part of the real world, natural and harmonious. The preference was asked after the user experienced all the treatments.

The experiment was held in three different places according to the prescribed lighting conditions, but all located very closely for almost immediate proceeding to the next. Each participant was compensated with ten dollars.

Fig. 6. Looking at an augmented object (bottle) with OpenAR (Hololens), Indoor (left), Outdoor low (middle), and Outdoor high (right).

Table 3. The survey assessing various aspects of the AR experience, all answered in the 7 level Likert scale (1: negative ~ 7: positive).

Category	Questions
User immersion and presence	P1: How well did the overall AR environment catch your attention? P2: How much effort (mental fatigue) did you have to put into viewing the overall AR environment? P3: How naturally did the overall AR environment look and felt? P4: To what extent did the lighting condition influence the degree of immersion in the AR environment? P5: To what extent were you aware of yourself to be in the environment? P6: How much did you think you are immersed in AR environment?
Object presence	O1: To what extent did the augmented information hold your attention? O2: How much mental effort did you put into watching the augmented object? O3: How natural and harmonious (to the real world) did the augmented information look and feel? O4: To what extent did feel like you were in the real space with the augmented object(s)? O5: To what extent did the augmented objects felt realistic?

(continued)

Table 3. (*continued*)

Category	Questions
Usability	U1: How easy was this display type to use (viewing the objects and navigating)?
	U2: How confortable was this display type to use (viewing the objects and navigating)?
	U3: How suitable did you think this display for viewing and navigating the AR environment?
	U4: Did you become aware or conscious of other people around when using this display?
	U5: How fatigued are you when using this display type?
	U6: For the given display, how much were you affected by the peripheral view for viewing and navigating in the AR environment?
	U7: For the given display, how much were you affected by the lighting condition for viewing and navigating in the AR environment?
Overall satisfaction and preference	S1: How satisfied were you with this display type?
	S2: How much do you prefer this display type?
	S3: Which display type do you really want to use when taking into account the previous results and pricing? (answered after experiencing all the treatments)
	(1: OpenAR, 2: ClosedAR, 3: EasyAR, 4: PhoneAR)

4 Results

The one-way ANOVA/Tukey HSD were applied to statistically analyze for any effects of the control factors to the various AR experience survey questions. We only highlight and report the main results.

4.1 User Presence and Immersion

The effects toward overall presence and immersion scores by the display type is shown in Fig. 7. Significant differences were only found between PhoneAR, ClosedAR, EasyAR and OpenAR. Our expectation of PhoneAR to exhibit the lowest presence and immersion, while ClosedAR and EasyAR to show similar levels was validated only partially. OpenAR showed the lowest level most likely attributed to its small augmentation FOV, bad image projection quality, and low usability (see other results). The lighting condition did not produce any significant differences.

4.2 Object Presence

Figure 8 show the effects toward augmentation object presence scores among the four display types by the one-way ANOVA. The analysis indicated, similarly to the case of user presence/immersion, OpenAR exhibited significantly lower object presence than

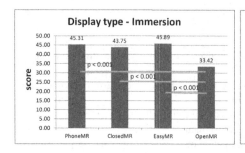
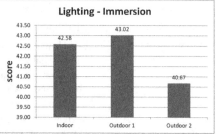

Fig. 7. A one-way ANOVA performed on the factor of display type (left) and lighting condition (right) for level of presence/immersion (P5 + P6).

the other three, possibly for the same reason. In fact, the response to O5 (object realism) is likewise significantly lower for OpenAR. The lighting conditions again had no effects.

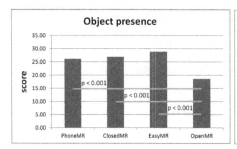
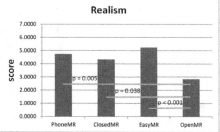

Fig. 8. A one-way ANOVA performed on the factor of display type for level of object presence (O3 + O4) and object realism (O5).

4.3   General Usability and Satisfaction/Preference

There were seven major usability questions: U1: ease of use, U2: comfort, U3: suitability, U4: social awareness/unacceptance, U5: fatigue, U6: effect of the peripheral view, U7: effect of the lighting condition. Figure 9 shows the results. Only OpenAR and ClosedAR was considered generally relatively unusable in terms of the ease of use, comfort, suitability, and fatigue (PhoneAR, EasyAR > ClosedAR > OpenAR). PhoneAR, as expected, showed the highest level of social acceptance. Peripheral view and lighting condition brought about no significant differences. Such a trend clearly points to the possibility that the user experience in AR is heavily dependent on good basic usability. User and object presence is perhaps of less importance compared to the case of VR. Again a similar trend was found with regards to the general satisfaction and relative preference, correlating to the effect of the usability of display types (Fig. 10).

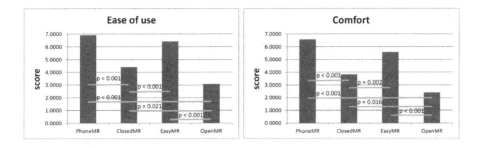

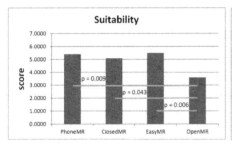

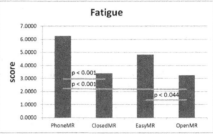

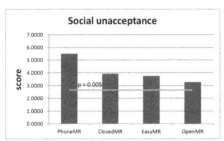

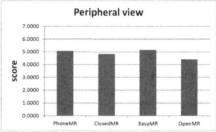

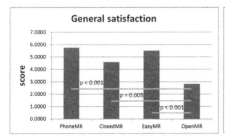

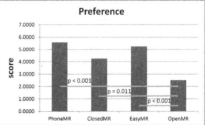

Fig. 9. A one-way ANOVA performed on the factor of display type for level of six categories of usability.

Fig. 10. A one-way ANOVA performed on the factor of display type for general satisfaction and preference.

5   Discussion and Conclusion

In this paper, we have compared the user experiences of 4 different AR displays under three different lighting conditions. The OpenAR (or Hololens) display we used was still technologically short of the user expectation in its display performance and usability form factor, leading to a very low user experience. Surely, such a result could be changed as the device becomes smaller, lighter with better image quality in the coming future. In AR, the user has to wear and use a display (or a glass as the display surface) of certain size and FOV. Depending on whether the display system is shut from the rest of the environment or not, and the seam/boundary between the display and the rest of the visible real environment (in the case of open displays) do not seem to affect the user experience all that much. This is shown by the PhoneAR being on par with EasyAR or ClosedAR in its user experience. The same argument goes with the absolute display size, for which PhoneAR is smaller, even though small absolute display size seems to induce underestimation [11]. It was rather the convenience of the PhoneAR (same as the regular smartphone) that wins the hearts of the users. Although not tested, casual usage of VR will necessitate a quick switch between the regular smartphone mode and access to the touch screen for the seamless and familiar touch based interaction. Again, in this regard, PhoneAR and EasyAR have advantages. Also there is a recent rise in the concept of Extended Reality (XR), a platform (or display) both AR and VR. EasyVR, the flip-on lens version of VR has already been proven to offer immersion and presence at the equal level of the ClosedVR [12]. Therefore, EasyAR might be the best middle ground, offering reasonable usability with higher immersion/presence (even though a statistical difference was not found), and quick and easy dual usage with the smartphone.

In addition, the user experience results can be dramatically different if interaction was involved. In particular, PhoneAR and EasyAR offers the usual touchscreen interaction, while ClosedAR and OpenAR must result to something else such as mid-air gestures and separate interaction controllers. We plan to further conduct the relative comparison considering this important user experience feature.

Acknowledgments. This work was partially supported by the Global Frontier R&D Program on <Human-centered Interaction for Coexistence> funded by the National Research Foundation of Korea grant funded by the Korean Government (MEST) (NRF-2015M3A6A3076490), and by the MSIT (Ministry of Science, ICT), Korea, under the ITRC (Information Technology Research Center) support program (IITP-2019-2016-0-00312) supervised by the IITP (Institute for Information & communications Technology Promotion).

References

1. Pokémon GO. https://www.pokemongo.com/en-us/
2. Homido mini. https://homido.com/mini/
3. Microsoft HoloLens. https://www.microsoft.com/en-us/hololens
4. Schuemie, M.J., Van Der Straaten, P., Krijn, M., Van Der Mast, C.A.: Research on presence in virtual reality: a survey. CyberPsychology Behav. **4**(2), 183–201 (2001). https://doi.org/10.1089/109493101300117884

5. Stevens, B., Jerrams-Smith, J., Heathcote, D., Callear, D.: Putting the virtual into reality: assessing object-presence with projection-augmented models. Presence Teleoperators Virtual Environ. **11**(1), 79–92 (2002). https://doi.org/10.1162/105474602317343677
6. Lin, J.W., Duh, H.B.L., Parker, D.E., Abi-Rached, H., Furness, T.A.: Effects of field of view on presence, enjoyment, memory, and simulator sickness in a virtual environment. In: Virtual Reality, Proceedings, pp. 164–171. IEEE (2002). https://doi.org/10.1109/vr.2002.996519
7. Samsung Galaxy S8. https://www.samsung.com/sec/smartphones/galaxy-s8/
8. Unity. https://unity3d.com/
9. Vuforia. https://www.vuforia.com/
10. Samsung Gear VR. https://www.samsung.com/global/galaxy/gear-vr/
11. Butchart, B.: Augmented reality for smartphones (2011)
12. Kim, Y.R., Kim, G.J.: Presence and immersion of easy mobile VR with open flip-on lenses. In: Proceedings of the 23rd ACM Symposium on Virtual Reality Software and Technology, vol. 38 (2017). https://doi.org/10.1145/3139131.3139147

Explorations in AR: Finding Its Value

Mauricio Gomes de Sá Ribeiro[✉], Isabel Lafuente Mazuecos,
Fabiano Marinho, and Alice Neves Gomes dos Santos

SIDIA, Samsung Instituto de Pesquisa e Desenvolvimento para a Informática da
Amazônia, Manaus, Amazonas, Brazil
mauricio.sr@samsung.com

Abstract. This paper presents the main findings regarding the overall effectiveness of an AR-based wearable device for different types of users performing basic, common tasks throughout a few demo scenarios, thus identifying opportunities for improvement and further investment. A series of user tests were carried out among participants using this head-mounted prototype while different aspects of their interaction and overall experience were evaluated. It was given special attention to desirability factors, as well as pain points and obstacles to completing the different scenarios.

This paper presents main insights regarding several features for an ideal head-mounted AR experience to the user, as well as their view regarding the future of digital media consumption. It also discusses some limitations and lessons learned for future work. Our results allow us to shed light onto the scope of expectations of potential end users, in order to help in the design and engineering of these devices. We argue that the value of exploratory studies of such as these lies in its potential to delve into innovative paths and their potential implications, otherwise difficult to trace.

Keywords: Mixed reality · Augmented reality · Head-mounted device ·
User research · Usability study · In-Depth interview · Gesture interaction ·
Usability

1 Introduction

Augmented Reality (AR), the technology that enables computer-generated digital information onto the user's view and interaction with the real world [13, 9], has gained extensive attention in recent years, both from the industry and the field of research. Although the adoption of AR among consumers is not yet widespread, expectations regarding its potential in terms of their transformative benefits and future market revenue are currently high [5].

Despite this promissory scenario, there is still a large range of design options that needs to be considered for these solutions to achieve sufficient maturity within a consumer market. However, in general, the research capacity within the industry is relatively small. Not only are there high levels of competitiveness and regulatory issues to surmount, but also many times the resources to carry out sounded exploratory research, both in terms of competences and time, are usually missing. And yet these

© Springer Nature Switzerland AG 2019
J. Y. C. Chen and G. Fragomeni (Eds.): HCII 2019, LNCS 11574, pp. 16–32, 2019.
https://doi.org/10.1007/978-3-030-21607-8_2

kinds of studies are particularly important when there is uncertainty about the future feasibility and user acceptance of a certain product.

Certainly, in the last years there has been a significant increase in the number of AR papers including some sort of user-centered research. The work so far has mainly focused on user interface design challenges and technology issues, whereas much less has been published regarding users' characteristics, attitude and expectations about AR solutions thus, the whole potential of user-centered theory has not been fully embraced [10].

In this regard, our research was conceived as an exploratory space where feasible future paths for AR solutions could be traced and validated. To do so, we carried out user tests using interactive proof-of-concept (POC) software on a head-mounted device to learn about users' expectations in terms of usability and utility, as well as to set out grounded steps for future explorations.

2   Theoretical Background

This section presents previous relevant studies in this field and discusses existing user-centered research on AR.

2.1   Augmented Reality (AR) and Head-Mounted Devices (HMD)

The earliest examples of AR technologies date back to 1960, when head-mounted devices were first used in military aviation, to improve pilot's ability to react to the environment in enemy fighter aircraft (REF Radical Technologies). However, it only found a niche for consumers with outspread adoption of smartphones and tablets, which bundled the kind of technology that would enable a new generation of AR-embedded applications [12]. Phone-based AR treated the handset as the display surface on top of which information and AR objects were laid.

Soon after, a new generation of AR wearable mediators emerged, with Google Glass being the first of this class to reach final consumers. Currently, the two most well-known AR HMDs are Microsoft HoloLens and Magic Leap One. Both of them integrate digital and physical environments through the use of a head-mounted device that incorporates orientation and position sensors to display digital objects into the material environment whilst allowing interaction with them. Although both of them are intended for the consumer market in the long term, their reach has been exclusively within the industry realm so far, and mainstream adoption of AR headsets is still distant.

There is a considerable number of publications related to prototypes that have been developed for research purposes in different application areas, such as industrial AR applications [1], entertainment areas [2] or commercial ends [4]. More recently, many of these proofs-of-concept have turned into full-fledged applications available for the final consumer. However, despite having an end-user perspective in mind, the amount of AR studies geared towards understanding users' needs and expectations have not increased at the same pace, which indicates a gap to be bridged in future research.

2.2 User-Centered AR Studies

The first comprehensive review of AR user studies was published in 2005 by Swan and Gabbard [6] and, among a total of 1,104 AR papers, they found only 21 related to user-centered research. All of them revolved around user task performance and usability aspects regarding perceptual and ergonomic issues. After this one, two other surveys were carried out in 2008 (Dünser et al.) and 2012 (Bai and Blackwell) respectively, both following the classification of Swan and Gabbard [11], with a few new categories being added.

The latest review of user centered research in AR was carried out by Dey et al. [3] covering AR papers published between 2005 and 2014 which contain a user study. Based on the type of display examined, their field of application and the methodology followed, the authors classified the literature to provide an overview of the state-of-the-art of the field. Different from previous surveys, they consider a wider set of sources, sifted the papers by their citational impact and broaden the classification categories to include issues experienced by the users [3].

Interestingly, they noted that despite the significant growth of AR papers published between 2005 and 2014, the relative percentage of those specifically regarding user studies had remained equally low throughout the same period [3]. The authors also suggest opportunities to explore for future user studies, such as diversifying evaluation methods and including a broader range of participant populations [3].

Another example of user-centered research involving is Olsson and Salo's work [10] which evaluates user experience with commercial applications. They measured the degree of AR technology acceptance among consumers and established a series of guidelines for developing successful applications, being curiosity and novelty among the main motivators for using mobile AR applications.

Moreover recently, Kim et al. published an extensive review of all the papers presented at ISMAR, an academic conference which is a reference in the field, from 2008 until 2017 in order to provide an overview of the AR-related research taking place worldwide and uncover emerging trends in the field [8]. One important finding of their work is that evaluation research had substantially increased as compared to a previous survey done by Zhou et al. [14] – which Kim et al. work follows on – that summarized AR work presented at the same conference in the previous ten years. According to Kim et al. [8] the increase of evaluation research in the field of AR is a signal that AR technology has achieved a maturity that brings it closer to consumers, and so there is a need to evaluate different solutions with end-users.

Although this past work provides a consistent theoretical background for AR user studies there is still room for more exploratory research in order to establish priorities, develop operational definitions and provide significant insight into identifying feasible directions for AR solutions from a user centered perspective. In this regard, this research was designed to serve as an independent project aimed at acquiring knowledge about AR user experience through validated explorations.

3   Methodology

In the present study, we developed a series of interactive proof-of-concepts on an AR head-mounted device and tested them with users to set design guidelines based on data collected during the tests. An AR wearable prototype based on Android was built for this study and five demo scenarios were designed in which participants had to perform basic, common tasks during the test. The aim was to assess the overall effectiveness, efficiency and satisfaction of the AR demo scenarios and identify obstacles to completing them. An exaggerated hand gesture was used as primary input method and several UI components were explored. We validated our hypotheses through different methods of data collection: user tests, the verbal protocol – the running commentary that participants make as they think aloud during the tests –, and short interviews with each participant at the beginning and at the end of each test, to learn about their subjective experience when using the device through the different scenarios.

3.1   Participants Sample

Recruitment for this study was conducted in an indoor environment located at the SIDIA R&D Center in Manaus, Brazil. The only requirements for participation were intermediate-level English proficiency – the software was built in this language – and smartphone ownership. A broad screener was important to have a more representative cross section of the participants sample. A total of 14 people took part in the tests, distributed as seen on Fig. 1. Among each of these three characteristics we sought an equal distribution for gender and a spectrum as wide as possible for their age distributions and area of expertise.

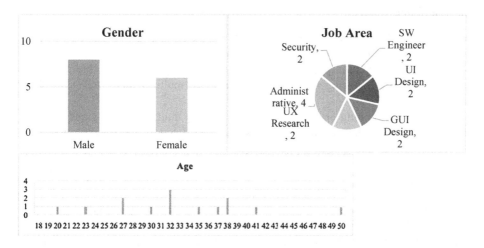

Fig. 1. Distribution of participants' gender, age, and professional background.

Among all participants, 1 had previously owned a Google Glass, 2 owned a Samsung Gear VR device, and 3 had relevant experience with mobile AR – augmented reality experiences embedded within smartphone applications, such as Pokémon Go and Snapchat lenses. Every participant had some knowledge about Virtual Reality (VR) and 5 had no prior knowledge about Augmented Reality (Fig. 2).

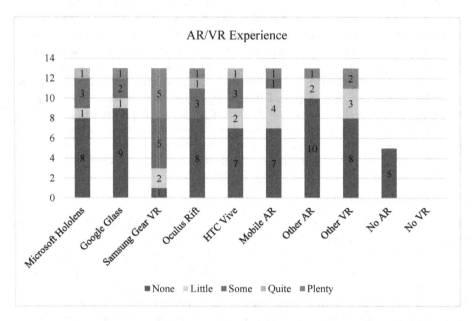

Fig. 2. Distribution of participants' previous experience with AR and VR technology.

3.2 Support Material

We used an Android-based prototype wearable device built out of a Samsung Gear VR body, with a centered world-facing camera and two round openings following the eyelines with see-through acrylic where stereoscopic images from two tiny projectors were printed after bouncing from concave mirrors to multiply their size in the short distance.

The software running on the prototype device was built using Unity and Vuforia, providing ad-hoc marker-based experiences where a printed image was responsible for the digital objects' placement.

3.3 Moderator's Role

In these tests, the moderator should never give directions or suggestions to guide the participant through the experience. The moderator should ask what the participant believes should be done and encourage he/she to follow their assumptions and think aloud throughout the entire experience – i.e. express in words all doubts and observations.

The only guidance provided by the moderator is to point to the next scenario's printed marker, so the participant can then initiate the next demo scenario.

3.4   Data Collection

The main goal for these experiments was to quickly and superficially understand people's impressions on AR, mobile computing devices – especially head-mounted ones –, and hand gestures as UI input type. Therefore, a good user experience was never intended to be achieved, instead all demo scenarios were meant to provoke reactions thus providing valuable insight to a plausible direction to which to steer augmented reality solutions in following endeavors.

Demo Scenarios: General Interactions. Once a scenario's printed marker is recognized by the device's camera, a hand animation with an upwards-pointing index finger appears, in attempt to induce the participant to repeat the gesture thus activating the beginning of that demo scenario. Once each scenario is finished, an animation with a "End of Demo... Restarting." text message appears. After the end of a scenario, the participant is directed to the starting marker for the next scenario. 2 different sequences were used split evenly among participants (Fig. 3).

Fig. 3. Close-up shot of the device showing a hand animation prompting action to initiate demo scenario.

Demo Scenario 1: Points of Interest (POI) and Navigation. The experience starts with minimized cards placed horizontally all around the participant – 360° on a horizontal plane –, each representing a different location, such as restaurants, museums or grocery stores. The card positions do not change, the participant must look around to view other cards. As a card approaches the center of the participant's Field of View (FOV), it becomes maximized. When a location nears the edge of the FOV, it minimizes into a circle through a center-distance-responsive scaling motion.

After interacting with the card through the upwards-index finger gesture, a full detail card fills the screen and, after a short timer, the participant is presented with a mini-map and directions to the location (Fig. 4).

Fig. 4. Close-up shot of the device showing a centered maximized card over the monument, and a minimized "circle card" to the right of the monument.

Main issues evaluated:

- How well do users understand there are POIs all around?
- How useful to the users the presented POI information is?
- What are the user's expectations to POI information?
- How useful to the users is the full map view?
- What are the user's expectations to navigation information?
- How do users respond to having both gesture-based and time-based actions in the same scenario?

Demo Scenario 2: Lego Shopping. The experience starts with an animation of the built Lego set with each toy interacting with each other, before presenting a "Hot Deal" badge with a discounted price tag and a shopping button with the gesture animation.

Fig. 5. Close-up shot of the device showing the animated Lego set with price and purchase information.

Interacting with the shopping button triggers a "Successfully purchased" message prior to ending the scenario (Fig. 5).

Main issues evaluated:

- Does the animation increase interest in the product?
- What are users' expectations to the presented information?
- How do users respond to having a shopping button similar to the one that triggers the start of each scenario?
- How do users feel about how long it takes for them to see the price?
- How clear it is to purchase the Lego toy set?

Demo Scenario 3: Baking. The experience consists of an animation sequence with timed steps presenting the several preparation stages of a cupcake recipe (Fig. 6).

Fig. 6. Close-up shot of the device showing an animation presenting one the cupcake recipe preparation steps.

Main issues evaluated:

- Does the animation increase interest in the product?
- How useful is the animation to understanding the product?

Demo Scenario 4: Wine Shopping. In this experience, the complementary information to the wine has been shrunk significantly to the point of minimal readability just beyond arm's length. The only way the participant can read the information is by walking towards it less than a foot away (Fig. 7).

Main issues evaluated:

- How useful is the presented information?
- Is the information layout helpful for understanding the product?
- How clear it is to purchase the wine?
- Do participants understand they can walk towards the marker to zoom in?

Demo Scenario 5: Daily Information This experience's printed marker is placed far from the participant in a way that it is difficult for it to be recognized. Regardless of the scenario sequence, this is the final demo scenario for all participants. Once initiated, 3 different dioramas are presented with a short timer triggering their replacement: weather, calendar, and music, respectively. The latter option presents the user with a

Fig. 7. Close-up shots of the device showing the downsized information (on the left) and how it appears when up close (on the right).

"Play music" button. For the first time in the entire usability test session, the moderator uses a hidden controller to discretely activate the option and initiates music playback on a mobile phone. A message "Look at the speaker" is presented and when the participant looks down at the speaker on the table, the moderator once again discretely transfers audio to the speaker via Bluetooth, thus giving the participant the impression that the music began playing on the speaker just by looking at it (Fig. 8).

Main issues evaluated:

– How useful the presented information is to the user?
– What are user expectations to this scenario's information?
– How do users feel about the timeout for each step in the scenario?

3.5   Additional Procedures

The sessions were conducted in a controlled environment, provided with a video camera to capture the participant's face and gestures. A digital voice recorder was also present at the sessions to create a set of audio recordings for backup.

During each of the evaluation sessions a standard protocol was followed. First, the participant was introduced to the user test methodology and acquainted with the equipment and recording systems in the room. Moreover, an explanation of the

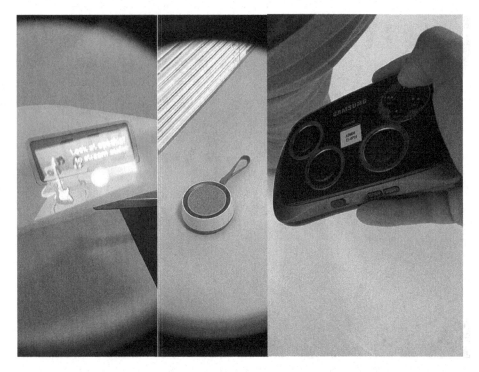

Fig. 8. Close-up shots of the device showing the music diorama (on the left), looking at the speaker (on the middle), and the moderator's hidden controller.

importance in thinking aloud when performing the usability tests so that an indicator of their confusions' moments and reasons is clearer. A particular caution to avoid entering into any details about the scenarios the participants would see was imperative as well as about any possible interactions with them, thus ensuring an experience as unbiased as possible.

Accompanying interviews with each participant happened before and after the usability tests. The former to discussing any previous experiences with augmented and virtual reality (AR/VR) and reasons for trying a new technology. The latter is preceded by a form where the participant scores each scenario. Unscripted follow-up questions were then done by the moderator to clarify participants' behavior and expectations. Finally, both moderator and observer did a debriefing together to contribute their observations about surprises and issues identified and tallied those throughout the sessions.

4   Findings and Recommendations

This section describes the main findings obtained from the study. Both quantitative and qualitative data were analyzed at the end of all the user tests and results were organized according to different categories that were evaluated during the sessions. These are:

impressions about the hardware, input controls and user experience. We also look at questions regarding the usability tests in themselves, considering main takeaways from our experience, and draw some insights that might be useful for further explorations.

4.1   Hardware

This category describes some specifics of user's acceptance and expectations regarding the head-mounted hardware. For each of them, we also give recommendations to improve future iterations of the prototype.

Focal Length. Different focal lengths between the digital projection and physical surfaces led to misconnection between the two thus resulting in little spatial interaction – i.e. little to no moving around the room to view information from other angles or distances. This suggests that in order to make use of spatial interfaces, the projection must have a focal length that matches with the real world. Virtual projections that are mismatched with the physical world's focus length don't seem to provide credible spatial behavior.

Ergonomic Device. Almost every participant complained about the device being big and uncomfortable. Even when they had enjoyed the scenarios and found the experience to be useful, the ergonomic aspect of the device in general prevailed over other considerations. This aspect of the product probed to be essential to users. Even an extremely useful software experience is quickly overshadowed by any hardware-caused discomfort. Indeed, bulky hardware was considered a main hindrance in user's acceptance of AR wearable devices. Therefore, despite its usefulness, a large and heavy hardware is not well regarded with the sole exception for where helmets or big goggles are already in use.

Small and Simple. The small form factor was also put forward as a crucial element when considering future adoption. Several participants regarded as an acceptable size, something they could carry in their pockets. Indeed, most participants found more desirable a small device that offers a simple and convenient experience, than a big, robust and powerful solution.

Modular Approach. Participants who wore prescription glasses encountered several issues when wearing the device, due to incompatibility between the available space left to fit the user's face and several larger shapes for glasses' frames. Moreover, having a touchpad on the right side of the device is an issue for left-handed individuals. This suggests that considering a modular approach might be an interesting path to explore when aiming at a consumer market. This way, the same base hardware could fit a plethora of glasses, attend to right- and left-handed individuals if using touchpads on the side, and also allow temporary upgrade to more powerful and bulky devices.

4.2   Interface

Here we present main issues that occurred during participants' interaction with the interfaces. Participants were not specified how to interact in order to learn about user's expectations of how interaction was most likely to happen by letting them spontaneously decide the appropriate response.

Useful Animations. Some participants stated that they would appreciate a more guided experience. In this regard, the use of animations to draw attention to a specific object proved to be extremely helpful. As an example, animations were successfully used to draw users 'attention to a place where the camera needs to better analyze for image recognition purposes.

Clear Design Elements. There should be a clear understanding of what is interactable and what is purely informational. Participants were confused whenever the visual representation of an interactable content differed from repeating interactive elements seen previously. Keeping the visual unity guides the user on how to interact and what to expect as a result, as well as provide context awareness through that element. Exploiting repetition and consistency of design elements, users can rapidly define mental models for greater interaction with the UI.

Feedback for Interactions. Another recurrent issue was a perceived lack of feedback whenever an interaction was initiated or ongoing. In some cases, the experience was initiated accidentally and in other situations participants tried out different gestures, stating that they felt uncertain of whether they were interacting or not. This indicates that letting users know they are being listened to or that their input is being recognized in action, matters for them. A possible solution to this difficulty is to always provide feedback for interactions – be it visual or audio –, not just for confirmation of performed action, but also for ongoing ones.

"Do not Disturb" Option. During the tests, a few participants felt overwhelmed with a continuous flow of information before their eyes. Some of them suggested having a gesture to dismiss the information at any moment during the experiences. Questions of invasiveness were also put forward during the debriefing interviews. In this regard, being mindful of an intrusive interface (e.g. providing an easily accessible 'Do not disturb' option or 'Silent mode' that could be triggered whenever the user deems necessary) can minimize this potential hindrance for user's acceptance of this kind of solutions.

Ground's Visibility. An important issue that was brought forward during the interviews with several participants, was a security concern regarding the possible risks of using an AR wearable device in public places that could potentially isolate them or even blind them against the environment. Indeed, the fact of blocking the ground's view might disguise physical obstacles, thus possibly causing accidents. Devices that have their projections positioned straight on users' eyesight, are likely to take up too much space of user's Field of View (FOV), thus getting in the way of critical information from the surroundings. This must be considered when designing wearable devices for outdoor use by consumers.

4.3   Input Controls

This category refers to questions related to how participants used the input controls during the test and presents the main insights about desires and expectations regarding those.

Hands-Free Experience. According to participants the fact of having to interact with the interface felt rather natural at times. However, it was highlighted that there would be moments where they might not be able to use their hands to interact with the UI. Another point that came to the fore, was that most participants felt shy about performing the raised finger gesture even during the user tests and most of them explicitly stated that they felt awkward while performing gestures in the air and that they would not be willing to do it in a public place. This shows a gap that can be considered in future work, by exploring real hands-free experiences for moments when interacting through gestures is not possible or in situations where social awkwardness refrains users from performing certain gestures.

Physical Surfaces. The previously mentioned social awkwardness and natural feel also speak for the possibility of using physical surfaces for more natural haptic feedback. Not only can physical surfaces make interaction feel more natural, it can also bring discretion to the experience.

Non-invasive Confirmations. During the interaction with the different scenarios, sometimes participants accidentally activated an action they were not, in fact, willing to take. The problem of false positives was a common occurrence that should be avoided. At the same time, it is important to do so, while also avoiding excessive steps for interaction (for example, a 2-step gaze interaction or temporary gesture/voice activation could be used).

Multiple Input Options. During the test, we observed a great variety of intended gestures when interacting with the interface. Indeed, natural controls and gestures depend to a great extent on existing mental models and cultural traits. One way to embrace idiosyncrasies is to allow personalization of such controls. The possibility of doing so by providing multiple options depending on the user's context and preferences, instead of only one, might be an interesting path to explore.

4.4   Experience

This section presents main findings in relation to the overall user experience, as it was described and reflected upon by participants during the interviews that followed the usability tests.

Convenience Beats Options. Throughout the accompanying in-depth debriefing interviews with participants, most of them agreed that they valued convenience in a solution, rather than a wide range of options. Therefore, it is significantly more valuable to a user an interface that, despite its simplicity and lack of options, is easy and pleasant to interact with.

Embrace User Guidance. In general, participants valued very positively user guidance during the experiences. In the study, it was realized that an introductory experience presenting the interactions works well, however other resources such as simple interaction hint animations for users to mimic proved to be highly effective. Also, using redundancy in information provides helpful guidance through the user experience (e.g. use animation, text and sound to explain an action).

IoT Controls. In several cases, participants manifested a desire to have control over objects in a seamless fashion, for instance, being able to control smart locks, lights, speakers, microwave ovens or washing machines.

5 Discussion

Our research investigated the overall user experience with an AR-focused wearable head-mounted device, thus identifying opportunities for improvement and further investment. The study was designed as an ad hoc exploration aimed at validating expectations and mental models of users towards a head-mounted display. As with any other ad-hoc reporting, the work involved a customized, small-target approach, which entails inherent limitations, especially regarding the generalizability of the findings. On the other hand, this kind of ad-hoc reporting allows to get actionable insight on specific questions that might be difficult to get from more generic reports.

We organized the recommendations in different categories that span the different aspects of the experience that we wanted to evaluate. These are: hardware, interface, input controls, and overall experience. For each of them, we identified several issues perceived during the user tests that somehow hindered the device usability and, thus, we offer some suggestions for improvement. In the case of hardware, the main takeaway is that any hardware-caused discomfort severely compromises the entire experience, regardless of how useful the software was considered. Thus, it is important to look at the AR experience as a whole, in which advances in software and hardware should walk hand in hand to get out the full potential of the technology, since the ergonomic factor seems to be a crucial element for its usage. Regarding input controls, it was observed that the range of gestures which users spontaneously came up with varied widely among participants. This suggests that a possible path that so far has remained rather underexplored is to consider input control personalization. Given that natural gestures are culturally shaped to a large extent, allowing for a degree of personalization of input controls can be one way to turn the experience with AR devices easily amenable to such diversity. A main point that the user tests revealed is that AR wearable devices should not deter user's visibility and interaction with the physical surroundings. Avoiding filling the user's field of view with a digital projection is a way out to this hindrance, as well as being mindful of an intrusive interface that might stand on the way of user's interactions with the real situations in which they find themselves.

On another level, this study discusses other questions that were encountered while carrying the usability tests that go beyond the specific purposes aimed at evaluating. In particular, some highlighted aspects perceived during the user tests are believed to certainly become opportunities for improvement in forthcoming research. These questions relate to the method used to gain insights into the usability and utility of the prototype and reveal both hits and opportunities that are worth considering regarding the user tests per se. First of all, using superficial simulations proved to work well for testing. It was observed that it allows more explorations with less effort, while facilitating any direction shift on a certain design strategy, without losing too much work. Moreover, using simulations is less prone to usage error or crashes, and bypass controls are highly effective to avoid user frustration with recurring failed attempts at interaction. Simulating the success of interactions by bypassing them with remote controls are highly effective in keeping participants engaged, while allowing for greater freedom in interactivity.

Another takeaway of this experience is that the use of repetitive elements was very helpful for participants during their navigation through the scenarios and served to conduct the sessions more easily. For example, the use of information such as "End of Scenario" upon completion of each of the demos was highly effective to keep a good pace throughout the user tests. Besides, at the moment of wearing the device, an image was immediately displayed to serve as a reference when adjusting the headset when worn for the first time. This ensured that participants could effectively see the interface as soon as it appeared and helped to create a smoother experience.

As a final note to this section, we argue that the primary value of this study lies in its exploratory character, that is, as a key step to establish priorities, develop operational insights and help improve subsequent research. Allowing for this kind of studies can provide industries with leverage to define a consistent roadmap and bring priorities into focus. In this regard, the findings reported here, although lacking statistical generalizability, still provide grounds for analytical inquiry valuable for the design of ensuing studies. In this regard, the validation presented can serve as a first step for other explorations considering a more user-centered approach to AR devices, in addition to drawing recommendations relevant to future investigations on this field.

6 Conclusion

This paper has presented main insights regarding several features for an ideal head-mounted augmented reality experience to the user, as well as their view regarding the future of digital media consumption. Among the findings, one major takeaway of our study is that hardware issues regarding the size and ergonomics of the device were given fundamental importance by participants, no matter how much utility or power they might gain through the use of a device. This means that a primary concern when designing an AR experience is first and foremost to ensure the hardware is comfortable to wear, to use, and to purchase. Through the accompanying in-depth debriefing interviews, another key finding is that convenience is much more important than options. Therefore, it is significantly more valuable to a user an interface that, despite its simplicity and lack of options, it is easy and pleasant to interact with. We have also discussed some lessons learned for future work, specifically regarding how user tests, as a method widely employed in user-centered studies, can be improved.

Our results allow us to shed light onto the scope of expectations for potential end users, in order to help in the design and engineering of AR wearable devices. We argue that the value of exploratory studies such as these lies in its potential to delve into innovative paths and their implications, otherwise difficult to trace within the industry.

References

1. Baillot, Y., Brown, D., Julier, S.: Authoring of physical models using mobile computers. In: Fifth International Symposium on Wearable Computers. IEEE, Zurich (2001)
2. Cheok, A., et al.: Human Pacman: a mobile, wide-area entertainment system based on physical, social, and ubiquitous computing. Pers. Ubiquit. Comput. **8**, 71–81 (2004)
3. Dey, A., Billinghurst, M., Lindeman, R., Swan II, J.: A systematic review of 10 years of augmented reality usability studies: 2005 to 2014. In: Frontiers in Robotics and AI (2018)
4. Dow, S., Lee, J., Oezbek, C., MacIntyre, B., Bolter, J., Gandy, M.: Exploring spatial narratives and mixed reality experiences in Oakland cemetery. In: 2005 ACM SIGCHI International Conference on Advances in Computer Entertainment Technology, pp. 51–60. ACM, New York (2005)
5. Exploring Augmented Reality for Business and Consumers. https://www.gartner.com/smarterwithgartner/exploring-augmented-reality-for-business-and-consumers/. Accessed 28 Feb 2019
6. Gabbard, J., Hix, D., Swan, J.: User-centered design and evaluation of virtual environments. IEEE Comput. Graph. Appl. **19**, 51–59 (1999)
7. Greenfield, A.: Radical Technologies: The Design of Everyday Life. Verso, London (2017)
8. Kim, K., Billinghurst, M., Bruder, G., Duh, H., Welch, G.: Revisiting trends in augmented reality research: a review of the 2nd decade of ISMAR (2008–2017). IEEE Trans. Vis. Comput. Graph. **24**, 2947–2962 (2018)
9. Olsson, T.: User Expectations and Experiences of Mobile Augmented Reality Services. Tampere University of Technology, publication 1085. Tampere University of Technology, Tampere, Finland (2012)
10. Olsson, T., Salo, M.: Online user survey on current mobile augmented reality applications. In: 10th IEEE International Symposium on Mixed and Augmented Reality, pp. 75–84. IEEE, Basel (2011)
11. Swan II, J., Gabbard, J.: Survey of user-based experimentation in augmented reality. In: 1st International Conference on Virtual Reality (2005)
12. Tredinnick, L.: Augmented reality in the business world. In: Business Information Review, vol. 35, pp. 77–80. London Metropolitan University, London (2018)
13. Wang, X., Kim, M., Love, P., Kang, S.: Augmented reality in built environment: classification and implications for future research. Autom. Constr. **32**, 1–13 (2013)
14. Zhou, F., Duh, H., Billinghurst, M.: Trends in augmented reality tracking, interaction and display: a review of ten years of ISMAR. In: 7th IEEE/ACM International Symposium on Mixed and Augmented Reality, pp. 193–202. IEEE Computer Society, Washington, DC (2008)

Designing Inclusive Virtual Reality Experiences

Matt Dombrowski, Peter A. Smith$^{(\boxtimes)}$, Albert Manero,
and John Sparkman

University of Central Florida/Limbitless Solutions, Orlando, USA
{MattD,Peter.smith}@ucf.edu,
{Albert,John.Sparkman}@limbitless-solutions.org

Abstract. Virtual Reality experiences are often touted as having the most immersive user experience possible outside of live action, yet Virtual Reality (VR) technology is often not designed to be inclusive to all users. From mild sim sickness effects to a lack of accessible controls, many users are being left out from the modern virtual reality experience. There are however tools available to the developer that will make inclusive VR design a possibility.

While many of the tools for inclusive VR experiences are physical hardware-based solution there are also what Doug Church describes as "Formal Abstract Design Tools" that are conceptual tools that can be applied in this case to allow a designer to think through making their experience design inclusive [1]. The goals of this journal paper are to provide a primer for those approaching inclusive game design. The researchers will cite current research, discuss existing accessibility forward technologies, and highlight areas that need more attention to assure a more inclusive VR experience.

Keywords: Universal Design · Inclusive design · Alternative controllers · Game design · Gamification

1 Introduction

When approaching accessible forward design, one must explore a variety of approaches, methods, and recognize past and present oversights that can occur when designing for specific communities. Though there is no "magic method" when it comes to designing for accessibility, there have been many successful utilizations of technology involving users who have disabilities. Virtual reality (VR) has been proven to be a successful tool in both rehabilitation and inclusive game design [2].

Susan Goltsman describes inclusive design as, "Inclusive design doesn't mean you're designing one thing for all people. You're designing a diversity of ways to participate so that everyone has a sense of belonging" [3]. Designs that start with assumptions that the user will have the average height, dexterity, and number of limbs as the average person are already being exclusionary. VR is a medium of which modern design patterns remain fraught with assumptions. It seems clear, however, that in many cases this could be solved by simply informing the designers that the exclusion exists and providing solutions for how to be more inclusive.

© Springer Nature Switzerland AG 2019
J. Y. C. Chen and G. Fragomeni (Eds.): HCII 2019, LNCS 11574, pp. 33–43, 2019.
https://doi.org/10.1007/978-3-030-21607-8_3

2   Background

There is a long history of accessible design, but it wasn't until wounded veterans were returning from World War II that the United States passed a law allowing free access to government buildings, with the Architectural Barriers Act of 1968 [4]. This was followed by additional legislation and a global declaration by the United Nations [5]. Of course, while access is required, ensuring the best designed access is not always the case in the physical world, and is only amplified in the virtual.

Many researchers have found positive impacts from using VR based solutions to training those with traumatic events including stroke. Laver, et. al found positive results in 8 out of 12 tests when using VR to train stroke suffers [6]. Additionally, Jack et al. found significant improvements in hand control in stroke suffers as well as positive subjective opinions of the training [7].

Phantom-limb or other phantom sensations pain is often reported from amputee populations after the loss of a limb or other innervated body part [8]. Research has investigated the role of cortical reorganization on the initiation and magnitude of phantom limb phenomena, which result in either a painful or non-painful response [9, 10]. Studies done to investigate methods of mitigating the phenomena have examined neurological and psychological influences on the underlying drivers of the phenomena [9, 11, 12]. Work by Pucher et al. [10] correlated self-perceived body image with the coping skills that may reduce phantom-limb phenomena.

New work is leveraging immersive virtual reality (IVR) as a management tool for symptomatic patients [12]. Further studies will improve the understanding of the effectiveness and statistical correlation that may have both psychosocial and psychophysiological impacts.

3   Universal Design

According to the National Disability Authority, Universal Design is, "the design and composition of an environment so that it can be accessed, understood and used to the greatest extent possible by all people regardless of their age, size, ability or disability" [13]. They also state that these design implementations should not act for the benefit of only a minority of the population. Their mantra is, "if an environment is accessible, usable, convenient and a pleasure to use, everyone benefits." The goal with universal design is to meet all user needs and maximize accessibility to the product or system.

3.1   Accessible Design

Accessible design revolves around designing for a specific disabled community the design process. In other words, the design is focused on creating an inclusive experience for a person of a specific disability. In United States, the Americans with Disabilities Act (ADA) mandates that the design of public facilities be completely accessible to people with disabilities [14].

3.2   7 Pillars of Universal Design as Related to VR Game Design

The 7 Principles of Universal Design were developed in the late 1990s by researchers at North Carolina State University. The purpose of the Principles is to act as a guide in the development of products, places involving human interaction [15]. This is the foundation for protections of equality for differently abled users that has driven much of the progress over the past decades. However, in application there are still limitations where the intentionality of inclusion is misaligned from the execution of design that can make a meaningful inclusive experience. This can be seen in the VR environments, where simulated visuals can be customized to not be limited by traditional form. This may provide empowering experiences for differently abled users, however the hardware to participate must consider a wider distribution of abilities.

Principle 1: Equitable Use
The design is useful to people with diverse abilities. Ideally the use of virtual environments can positively enhance experience for those with both cognitive, and motor skill impairments. Unfortunately, current VR systems are designed with core users in mind. Controls often require 2 hands, the ability to stand and move for long periods of time, and the ability to manipulate complex tools with the user's hands.

Identify Potential Users
It is important to identify potential users when beginning any inclusive VR game development project. Determine if the design needs to support able bodied individuals. Determine what other individuals the project will support. Will there need to be changes made of individuals with motor, cognitive, hearing, speech, vision, or other accessibility issue. The game accessibility guidelines suggest adding key remapping, text size options, colorblindness modes, and subtitle options as the easiest features to add support for [16].

Principle 2: Flexibility in Use
The design accommodates a wide range of individual preferences and abilities. While some users will be fine with 2 hand controls not all users can support that. Additionally, even if there is no exclusion for the user many users will not have the right hardware.

Identify Potential Exclusions
As consumer level VR solutions are still in an early stage the hardware individuals bring to the VR space is varied. Supporting additional hardware configurations is important from a financial perspective for many VR ventures. VR ready games on steam will often support multiple control schemes. This includes two handed controllers, the Xbox controller, or even Keyboard and Mouse. Supporting these additional interface methods allows the user to implement their own customized solution as well.

Principle 3: Simple and Intuitive Use
Use of the design is easy to understand, regardless of the user's experience, knowledge, language skills, or current concentration level. This principle is key to good user experience regardless of user's skills and abilities. Insuring a good UX/UI experience will go a long way in developing accessible games.

Unfortunately, because VR is a new interaction platform, good standard conventions are not well established. Early First-Person Shooters (FPS) were notoriously difficult to control on game consoles until the release of Halo: Combat Evolved on the original Xbox. The tutorial on Halo taught a generation how to play FPS games. This VR ready example has yet to be established. As such it is the designer's job to continue to bring the most intuitive experience to the user they can.

Mimic Real World Interaction

Most VR controllers are an attempt at mimicking what hands can do in the real world. If your player does not interact with the real world using their hands, mimic the tools they do use. This might be a prosthetic device of one form or another, a wheel chair control stick, or other implements used in the real world to interact. The closer the interaction method is for the user is in VR to what they are comfortable experiencing in reality, the better their interaction will be.

Principle 4: Perceptible Information

The design communicates necessary information effectively to the user, regardless of ambient conditions or the user's sensory abilities. This can be accomplished through the use of Heads Up Display (HUD) messages explaining things that can't be easily seen. User guidance through good game design, lighting, environmental cues will all help aid the player. Simple options like the ability to turn on subtitles, while 4th wall breaking in VR, are a necessity for those with hearing lose. While it may seem obvious that most information provided to the player would be through a graphical interface there are other ways to build the player with perceptible information.

Audio Guidance

Audio can be used to enhance a virtual experience. It can set the mood, excite action, and build a more complete immersive experience. It can also be used to help guide low vision users through an environment. Players have used audio cues only to play games like Street Fighter, and with the rise of audio assistants like Google Home and Amazon Alexa, it can be easy to integrate an audio guide into any virtual space. This can provide a deeper connection to the environment and stimulate subtle cues that can support a wider range of abilities by providing additional reaction and planning time.

Haptic Feedback

Using the haptic feedback is becoming more common in game design. It is even possible to use haptic feedback to help guide or smooth user input. The involves providing cues to the player to warn them of potential impediments in the virtual world and may have extensions to overlaid augmented reality (AR) that bridge the gaming and physical environments.

Subtitles and Other Text Cues

While there should be a standard for videogame subtitles, there is currently is not. Developers can still implement support tools for hearing lose, color blindness, and many other common disabilities. Larger successful games like Fortnite have already done so and the additional inclusion benefits a large range of users who may have long term ability differences or simply situation limitations that could be physical, interface hardware, or of the local environment.

Principle 5: Tolerance for Error
The design minimizes hazards and the adverse consequences of accidental or unintended actions. Everyone has the experience of hitting the wrong character on their cellphone when typing a message. Luckily Autocorrect features have been improving and a close miss can be corrected to the actual word required. The old saying of "close only counts in horseshoes…" no longer needs to be the case. Devices should be able to have tolerance for uneven input and do their best to interpret user intent.

Signal Smoothing
While users with less fine muscle control may input a more erratic signal then other users, smoothing algorithms can be used to interpret the input. Using smoothing for the player may not be 100% accurate or precise to the motion recorded, but this smoother interpreted motion will provide a better experience for the player.

Sensitivity Controls
Many games will offer mouse and controller sensitivity control in the options menu. This allows users to adjust the speed of their input on their own. These controls can go a long way in making a player feel comfortable with the input in the game and can easily be implemented.

Principle 6: Low Physical Effort
The design can be used efficiently and comfortably and with a minimum of fatigue. When Wii Tennis was released players thought they needed to mimic the action of actual tennis. The advertising campaign led to this belief. Players quickly learned that they could sit and flick their wrists slightly to accomplish the same effect. This of course was great for people with low upper limb dexterity.

In the case of VR games reticles can be smoothed and targeting can be sticky, so users with unsteady hands can still track and interact with objects in the virtual space. This is similar to the ability to adjust mouse sensitivity or remap controls to adjust to user preferences. A feature to engage additional levels of ability may provide additional comfort or ease for traditionally abled users.

Eye Tracking
Eye tracking is a feature that is quickly coming to VR. The basic functionality is based on shining infrared light on the pupil and then detecting it with a camera to determine the direction the eye is looking. This is commonly used to test usability on websites, but it could also be used to move a character in a virtual space. It could be used to select items or do any number of interactive tasks. Offloading the need to use hand of foot-based controls.

Hand Tracking
Some VR hardware has hand tracking built in. This is similar to eye tracking but looks at the user's hands to determine hand location and gesture. While there are multiple solutions available one common off the shelf device is the Leap Motion controller, which can be on a table or mounted to the front of a VR headset.

Standard Controller or Microsoft Xbox Adaptive Controller
While VR appears to be next level and supports free motion either with hands or with one handed controllers. Also, the standard controller might be more readily available

and easier for some users. Microsoft recently released the Xbox Adaptive Controller which connects as a standard controller and allows for custom controls to be used by a large variety of available external button controls.

Quadstick
The Quadstick is an evolution of the Sip and Puff controller found on some wheelchair controls. The Quadstick remaps all the buttons on a standard controller to a device that can be controlled 100% with facial muscles and breath.

3D Rudder and Other Foot Controls
The 3D Rudder is a foot pad that can be manipulated with feet while sitting. It is a flat platform with the bottom part of a sphere on the bottom. As the user tilts their feet their character can traverse in the virtual environment. Other foot controls are generally button based and could come in the form of individual buttons or something more similar to a Dance Dance Revolution dance pad.

Custom Controller
In many cases there will not be the perfect device available. In this situation custom controls could be considered. This is especially true when the user has expertise in a particular device. Researchers at the University of Utah have adapted a sip and puff controller to a ski simulation. Limbitless Solutions at the University of Central Florida uses a custom controller based on their prosthetic design to support their users.

Principle 7: Size and Space for Approach and Use
Appropriate size and space is provided for approach, reach, manipulation, and use, regardless of user's body size, posture, or mobility. Users will come in all shapes and sizes. The Void experience is a large room scale VR environment, that handles this situation well. It does not require users to use their hand and shows them to the player in front of them. It also supports changing the size of the avatar to match the height of the player, and even wheelchair users will find themselves with a very short avatar while in the experience.

Some VR systems may exclude specific groups of the population. For example, inside out hand tracking is inefficient for those with limb difference. One the other end of the spectrum the Vive Room Scale tracking is less effective for wheel chair users. Each type of VR experience has its own benefits and limitations and the key moving forward will be to broaden our expectations of the user profile to increase the accessibility to the virtual environment.

Room Scale
Of the three major types of consumer VR experiences Room Scale is the most complex. This form of VR has the user setup a complex set of tracking devices around their room and allows the player to walk freely in that space. This type of VR space is good for users with the ability to walk around in the space. Because tracking of the user and their hands is done from an external source this particular type of VR is well suited for people with limb difference. It can have trouble, however, for users in wheelchairs or with other types of lower limb mobility differences. The most common Room Scale VR system is the HTC Vive.

Front Facing

Another solution for VR is Front Facing. This type of VR has the user position themselves in front of a camera or multiple cameras. This type of VR works best if the user has no reason to turn around. The need to be positioned in front of the camera lends itself well to seated applications and can support tracking upper limb difference. It is also good for users with lower limb difference but does not provide the same level of freedom to move around found in Room Scale. The most common Front Facing VR systems are the Oculus Rift and PlayStation VR.

Inside Out

The new trend in VR is called Inside Out tracking. This type of tracking comes from inside the headset. The tracking looks for hand controllers in from of the headset. The issue with this type of tracking is it is not well suited for those with limb difference as it can be difficult to get the controller our far enough to see it. It can be better for wheelchair users as height of the tracked individual does not impact the tracking. Inside Out tracking can be found in the Oculus Go, and in the Microsoft Mixed Reality headsets.

4   The 6 Steps in Inclusive Game Design

When designing for accessibility it is important to recognize the various needs of your end user. Common accessibility needs revolving around remapping, text size, color blindness, and subtitle presentation. This gets more complex when dealing in a virtual or augmented space. Both virtual reality and augmented reality games can cover a large array of mechanics and user needs. These game mechanics could involve the user to utilize specific speech, hearing, vision, and other cognitive abilities. It is important that the designer recognizes these specifics and builds them into the design process.

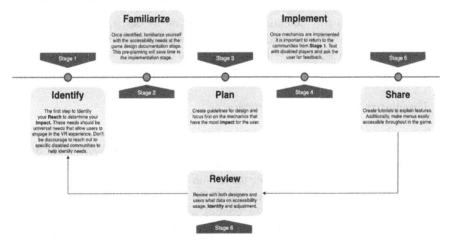

When approaching a new inclusive project, it is important to follow these steps [16]:

- Identify
- Familiarize
- Plan
- Implement
- Share
- Review

4.1   Identify Potential Exclusion

Creating an inclusive experience means avoiding unnecessary hurdles that prevent users with various impairments from fully experiencing or interacting with your game. According to the Center for Disease Control (CDC), one in every four adults has some type of disability [17]. This equates to around 61 million adults in the United States alone living with a disability. These disabilities range from highest need to lowest in mobility, cognition, independent living, hearing, vision, and self-care. A survey conducted by PopCap in 2008 [18], one in five players of casual video games have an impairment related to physical, mental or developmental disability. A study in the Netherlands revealed that around 92% of people with impairments play games despite difficulties [19].

This, however, does not mean that there has been enough done to support gameplay for this population. It is the opposite. This population is so excited about games they are figuring out personal work arounds. What should be happening is they should be supported by the developers and the player communities. Unfortunately, with the current state of competitive play, users with custom controls are often discovered as cheating, and treated as lesser then others in the community they are working hard to participate with.

This can only be truly changed with a cultural shift. Both the developers and the other players must see this potential new competition as desired. Developers must champion this to the community and hopefully the community will see how inclusion makes the playing field stronger. While this might not extend to competitive gaming in the short term, this needs to be on the horizon for all involved.

4.2   Familiarize with Current Strategies

Now that we have identified select mechanics how could one approach these mechanics to develop an accessible gaming experience. Virtual Reality and Augmented Reality games often require a large need for motor skills. Designers should take in consideration the following when designing for those with limited motor skills.

Allow controls in the game to be remapped. Do no assume that the player will have the ability to utilize the out of the box control set. Furthermore, do not limit these configuration options solely to the in-game experience. Ideally all areas of the user experience including the user interface should be able to be accessed with the alternative hardware/remapping.

When considering movement in the design process, do not assume that your user will have full dexterity of motor function. It is advised to implement calibration when needed to adjust sensitivity of controls of the experience. With that said, the designer should take a minimalist approach to designing the controller layout. The controls should be as simple as possible and have the ability to have various visual and auditory customizations to create a more inclusive experience.

When designing this type of experience the importance of a simple UI cannot be overstated. Players navigating a slew of calibration screens, menus and maps can quickly became troublesome for those utilizing a single-handed controller, especially in VR. Per the motor skill discussion above, is also a need for implementation of both customizable and easily readable typefaces in the interface. There is also a need to use simple readable fonts for users with screen readers.

4.3   Plan a Custom Solution Using a Persona or a Person

This next step in designing for inclusivity is to understand your user. This can be done in a variety of ways including creating personas or working directly with your user's community. Before the development of your VR game and even before the game design document is created designers must put themselves in the role of various gamer types. Keith Knight, a wheelchair user that streams his gameplay under the name the Aerion, recommends asking these questions that should be thought about and answer in the development of every new experience [20]:

- Does the user have the ability to physically play the game?
- What equipment do I use? What equipment with those with specific disabilities need to use to experience the game?
- Will playing the game as the designer creates it physically hurt the user?
- Will the user have to program any specialized equipment?
- Can the user be competitive (if needed) within the experience?

To answer the questions listed above, many game and user experience designers often develop user personas. The User Persona is a representation of the goals and actions of a community of hypothesized users. Of course, working directly with actual users is recommended and should be prioritized.

4.4   Implement Custom Solutions

In many cases the only solution is a custom solution. This can be in form of a combination of off the shelf products organized in appropriate configurations. It can also be with truly custom piece of hardware that allows for a specific interaction to occur. The Able Gamers Foundation has begun keeping track of specific solutions that could be implemented in a series of design patterns that will provide ways designers can change their games to meet the needs of people with various forms of disabilities. The Accessible Player Experiences (APX) is available freely on their website [21]. Further information on how to implement inclusive design in games can be found in the game accessibility guidelines [16].

While sharing what works for others is a good place to start, not all disabilities are the same. Even people with the same diagnosis can have different levels of impairment. Therefore, a single lens can not be applied universally. It is important to work closely with individual users and find what works best for them. In some cases, this might require the development of completely custom hardware solutions, in others it might be as easy as modifying an existing solution. In any case it is important to share solutions back to the community.

4.5   Share with the User and the Community

It is important that discovered or created solutions are shared back with the community. When a new solution works for one user it is likely it will help others, even if their disability is not the same. Seeing game-based solutions in action will also inspire new work.

4.6   Review and Iterate

After implementing a solution testing with real users is important. Often times developers will attempt to use a surrogate population when actual users are in low supply. This can help with general usability but will not provide enough information in ensure that a solution will work and will be accepted by the actual users. It is important to get the target population represented in the research. Able Gamers can provide access to player panels made up of game players with various disabilities.

5   Conclusions

By applying the 7 principles of universal design to the development of inclusive VR experiences, all users will benefit from a more approachable and customizable experience in the long run. This will provide a more meaningful and engaging experience. It is important to identify users with potential exclusions and find solutions that can work for them directly. In many cases off the shelf solutions, like the Microsoft Adaptive Controller, can help in the process. Modularity and the ability to interface with standard ports allows for the creation of unique tools that may translate to a larger user population after initial prototyping. Developers should not shy away from custom solutions that will help individuals participate. This will only increase the potential user base VR and improve the overall market. At the same time these solutions could easily have benefits to existing users as well.

The key to inclusive design is to not to think of inclusion as a check box that needs to be satisfied, but as a method to provide multiple paths for use. This cultural change will lead to better user experiences for everyone.

References

1. Church, D.: Formal abstract. In: The Game Design Reader: A Rules of Play Anthology. MIT Press, Cambridge (2006)
2. Dombrowski, M., Buyssens, R., Smith, P.A.: Virtual reality training to enhance motor skills. In: Chen, J.Y.C., Fragomeni, G. (eds.) VAMR 2018. LNCS, vol. 10909, pp. 393–402. Springer, Cham (2018). https://doi.org/10.1007/978-3-319-91581-4_29
3. Holmes, K.: Mismatch: How Inclusion Shapes Design. MIT Press, Cambridge (2018)
4. Williamson, B.: Accessible America: A History of Disability and Design. NYU Press, New York (2019)
5. Enable, U.N.: United Nations convention on the rights of persons with disabilities (2006). https://www.un.org/development/desa/disabilities/convention-on-the-rights-of-persons-with-disabilities.html
6. Laver, K.E., George, S., Thomas, S., Deutsch, J.E., Crotty, M.: Virtual reality for stroke rehabilitation. Cochrane Database Syst. Rev. (2) (2015)
7. Jack, D., et al.: Virtual reality-enhanced stroke rehabilitation. IEEE Trans. Neural Syst. Rehabil. Eng. 9(3), 308–318 (2001)
8. Melzack, R.: Phantom limbs and the concept of a neuromatrix. Trends Neurosci. 13(3), 88–92 (1990)
9. Flor, H., et al.: Phantom-limb pain as a perceptual correlate of cortical reorganization following arm amputation. Nature 375(6531), 482 (1995)
10. Pucher, I., Kickinger, W., Frischenschlager, O.: Coping with amputation and phantom limb pain. J. Psychosom. Res. 46(4), 379–383 (1999)
11. Hill, A.: The use of pain coping strategies by patients with phantom limb pain. Pain 55(3), 347–353 (1993)
12. Zanfir, A.-M., et al.: Immersive VR in phantom limb pain therapy of amputee patients due to critical limb ischemia. Acta Medica Marisiensis 63(3), 115–120 (2017)
13. National Disability Authority: What is Universal Design. NDA (2014). http://universaldesign.ie/What-is-Universal-Design/
14. United States Department of Justice Civil Right Division: Information and Technical Assistance on the Americans with Disabilities Act (2018). www.ada.gov
15. Story, M.F.: Principles of Universal Design. Universal Design Handbook (2001)
16. Ellis, B.: Game Accessibility Guidelines (2016). http://gameaccessibilityguidelines.com/basic/
17. Center for Disease Control: 1 in 4 US adults live with a disability. Center for Deseas Control Newsroom (2018). https://www.cdc.gov/media/releases/2018/p0816-disability.html
18. https://www.gamesindustry.biz/articles/popcap-games-research-publisher-s-latest-survey-says-that-casual-games-are-big-with-disabled-people
19. Wing, C.: Around 92% of people with impairments play games despite difficulties. Game Accessibility (2015). https://www.game-accessibility.com/documentation/around-92-of-people-with-impairments-play-games-despite-difficulties/
20. Smith, P.A., Dombrowski, M., Hassan, M., Knight, K., Stevens, K.: The importance of good user experience design for mobility accessibility across the spectrum. Electronic Arts (EA) Game UX Summit 2018, Vancouver, Canada (2019)
21. Able Gamers Foundation: Accessible Player Experiences (APX). Accessible. Games (2018). https://accessible.games/accessible-player-experiences/

Spherical Layout with Proximity-Based Multimodal Feedback for Eyes-Free Target Acquisition in Virtual Reality

BoYu Gao[1], Yujun Lu[1], HyungSeok Kim[2], Byungmoon Kim[3], and Jinyi Long[1(✉)]

[1] Jinan University, Guangzhou 510632, Guangdong, China
{bygao,jinyil}@jnu.edu.cn, yujunlu@stu2018.jnu.edu.cn
[2] Konkuk University, Seoul 05092, South Korea
hyuskim@konkuk.ac.kr
[3] Adobe Research, San Jose, CA 95110-2704, USA
bmkim@adobe.com

Abstract. Eyes-free interaction can reduce the frequency of headset rotation and speed up the performance via proprioception in Virtual Environments (VEs). However, proprioception cues make it difficult and uncomfortable to select the targets located at further distance. In VEs, proximity-based multimodal feedback has been suggested to provide additional spatial-temporal relation for 3D selection. Thus, in this work, we mainly study how such multimodal feedback can assist eyes-free target acquisition in a spherical layout, where the target size is proportional to the horizontally egocentric distance. This means that targets located at further distance become bigger allowing users to acquire easily. We conducted an experiment to compare the performance of eyes-free target acquisition under four feedback conditions (none, auditory, haptic, bimodal) in the spherical or cylinder layout. Results showed that three types of feedback significantly reduce acquisition errors. In contrast, no significant difference was found between spherical and cylinder layouts on time performance and acquisition accuracy, however, most participants prefer the spherical layout for comfort. The results suggest that the improvement of eyes-free target acquisition can be obtained through proximity-based multimodal feedback in VEs.

Keywords: Proximity-based multimodal feedback ·
Eyes-free target acquisition · Spatial layout · Virtual Environments

1 Introduction

Recent work has shown the importance and potential of eyes-free target acquisitions in Virtual Reality (VR) [1, 2]. For example, it can effectively reduce the frequency of headset rotation and greatly improve the efficiency of interaction (e.g. painting, blind typing [2]). The mostly used cue to leverage such an ability is the proprioception (*a sense of the relative position of one' own parts of the body*) [1, 3, 4]. For example, Yan et al. [1] found that the users mainly rely on proprioception to quickly acquire the

© Springer Nature Switzerland AG 2019
J. Y. C. Chen and G. Fragomeni (Eds.): HCII 2019, LNCS 11574, pp. 44–58, 2019.
https://doi.org/10.1007/978-3-030-21607-8_4

targets without looking at them in VR. However, this eyes-free interaction with proprioception cues makes difficult and uncomfortable to select the targets located at further distance. Such limitations lead to longer time performance and more efforts for eyes-free target acquisition in VR.

In this work, we focus on alleviating this issue to improve the performance of the eyes-free target acquisition in VR. Commonly, use of additional feedback to assist eyes-free interaction is a promising solution (e.g. Earpod [8]). In VR, the multimodal feedback has been suggested to provide additional temporal or spatial information [6], particularly for 3D selections. For example, Ariza et al. [11] explored the effects of proximity-based multimodal feedback (*the intensity of feedback depends on the spatial-temporal relations between input devices and the virtual target*) on 3D selections in immersive VEs, and found the feedback types significantly affect the selection movement [11]. Thus, we hypothesize that the proximity-based multimodal feedback that provides additional spatial-temporal information could further improve the performance of eyes-free target acquisition in VR. When the user's controller approaches the target, the sound or the vibration is progressively given to inform the movement or the acquisition of target (See Fig. 1).

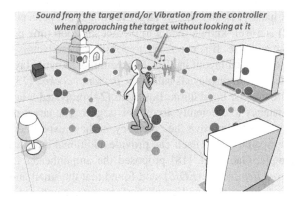

Fig. 1. This illustrates that the participant can acquire the blue target without looking at it (the participant looks at the dark cube), with the help of additional proximity-based multimodal feedback in VR (the distance between the target and the controller is mapped with the intensity of auditory and/or haptic cues). (Color figure online)

To the best of our knowledge, there is no work focusing on such investigation. We therefore create the proximity-based auditory (pitch) or/and haptic (intensity of vibration) feedback in both the spherical and the cylinder layouts. Both allow more items to display, and the items in the cylinder layout have the same horizontally egocentric distance. In the spherical layout, the item size is proportional to the horizontally egocentric distance, so that the items located at the further become larger to acquire. The items at the higher and lower locations become closer to the users so that they can acquire it easily and comfortably.

To evaluate the proposed approach, we conducted a Mixed ANOVA experimental design to measure the between-subject factor (layouts) and the within-subject factor (feedback conditions) on the eyes-free target acquisition task.

The contributions of this work are as follows:

- This is the first work to explore the proximity-based multimodal feedback (auditory, haptic, auditory and haptic) for the eyes-free target acquisition in VR.
- We designed more comfortable spherical layout and compared the performance of eyes-free target acquisition with the cylinder layout in VEs.
- Based on the results, we suggested that use of the proximity-based multimodal feedback to keep a balance between the trial completion time and the acquisition accuracy for the eyes-free target acquisition in VEs.

2 Related Work

2.1 Spatial Layouts for Target Acquisition

Target acquisition is one of the common tasks in VEs [12]. To improve the efficiency of target acquisition in VEs, it involves many factors, for example, the spatial depth between target and hand [19], the size of target [20], and the perception of the space [21]. Fitts' law [22] is a well-known model to predict selection time performance for a given target distance and size. It is necessary to consider these factors when designing the construction of the spatial layout in VEs. For example, a spatial layout for effective task switching on head-worn displays is called the *personal cockpit* [23], it allows users to quickly access the targets. In addition, Ens et al. [24] proposed a layout manager to leverage spatial constancy to efficiently access the targets. The target distance and size were carefully controlled to improve the efficiency in these experiments.

In particular, the spatial layout itself can provide additional information - the depth variation. For example, Gao et al. [18] proposed the amphitheater layout with *egocentric distance-based item sizing (EDIS)*, and found that the small and medium *EDIS* can give efficient target retrieval and recall performance, compared to circular wall layout [17]. Yan et al. [1] explored the target layout (a kind of *personal cockpit, the distance between the item and virtual camera is the same*) for eyes-free target acquisition around the body space, and found that the distance between higher/lower rows and the body make it uncomfortable to acquire the targets. In this work, we propose a spherical layout, so that participants can acquire the targets located at higher and lower rows comfortably and easily. Little work has been investigated the comparison of spherical and circular layouts for eyes-free target acquisition in the VE.

2.2 Multimodal Feedback for Target Acquisition

Previous research has shown the importance of multimodal feedback for selection guidance in 2D graphical user interfaces and gestural touch interfaces [7, 9, 10, 25]. However, increasing the quality of the visual feedback does not necessarily improve user performance [14]. In this work, we therefore mainly consider the additional auditory and haptic feedback instead of visual feedback.

Continuous auditory feedback can improve the gestural touch performance via frequency and sound [13, 25]. For example, Gao et al. [25] presented that the gradual continuous auditory feedback contributes to the performance of trajectory-based finger gestures in 2D interfaces. The distance and orientation between the target and the user can be given via the spatial auditory in VEs [6]. In addition, proximity-based multimodal feedback [11], in which the sensory stimuli intensity is matching with the spatial-temporal relationship, can provide better performance of 3D selection in VR. In particular, the binary feedback performed better than continuous feedback in terms of faster movement and higher throughput. However, the eyes-free manner is different from the eyes-engaged in terms of information perception. We believe the eyes-free target acquisition requires more information than 3D selection. We therefore focus on improving the performance of eyes-free target acquisition via continuous proximity-based multimodal feedback in the spatial layouts.

3 Target Layouts with Multimodal Feedback

In this work, we adopted the findings from Yan et al. [1] to construct the target layout. For example, the comfortable distance to acquire the target is 0.65 m for the users. The radius of the target is 0.1 m. We create three rows, each row has 12 spheres (3 × 12).

To allow better comfort when acquiring targets, we propose a spherical layout, which makes the distance between the higher/lower rows of targets and the body's chest closer. The radius is 0.45 m for both rows, and the radius of the middle row is 0.65 m. For the cylinder layout, the radius of the three rows is 0.65 m (See Fig. 2).

Fig. 2. The items size is proportional to the horizontally egocentric distance in the spherical layout (left), so that the further targets become larger and the user feels comfortable to acquire them, while the items in the cylinder layout have the same horizontally egocentric distance (right). Note that the white cube indicates the direction that the participant looked at when acquiring the target in an eyes-free way. The center of the layout is located at the user's chest.

To create the spatial-temporal relation between the location of target and movement of controller, we predefined the activation area as a sphere with 0.2 m radius for multimodal feedback (Note that the radius of blue target is 0.1 m). Such 0.2 m distance is used to give prior notification of the movement to the user. Park et al. [9] also showed that the preemptive-based continuous auditory feedback gave better performance for 3D hand gestures on circular menu selection. For example, if the controller gets closer to the center of the target (See Fig. 3: d is smaller than 0.2 m), the pitch of spatial auditory feedback from the target or the intensity of haptic feedback from the controller tends to be the larger to inform the movement. So the participant was informed that the controller is being approached to the target. When the controller intersects with the center of the target, the pitch of sound or intensity of vibration remains the largest.

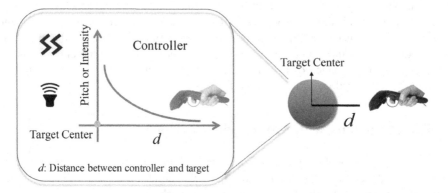

Fig. 3. The relation between the pitch of spatial auditory/the vibration intensity and the spatial distance d (between target and controller). The radius of the blue sphere (target) was 0.1 m. We defined the d as 0.2 m in the experiment. When approaching the target (smaller than 0.2 m), the pitch of sound from the target and the intensity of vibration from the controller is increased. (Color figure online)

4 Experiment

In this experiment, we utilized the 2 × 4 Mixed ANOVA experimental design, the between-subject factor was the spatial layout (cylinder layout vs. spherical layout), while the within-subject factor was the feedback condition (none, auditory only, haptic only, both auditory and haptic). The hypothesis formulated in this experiment are:

> *H1:* The spherical layout could allow the participants to have better acquisition performance and comfortable experience, compared to the cylinder layout.
> *H2:* The proximity-based multimodal feedback could assist the correct phase during eyes-free target acquisition in VR.

4.1 Participants

The 24 subjects (mean age = 22.2, SD = 2.43 years, the number of female was 12) were recruited from the local campus. All of the participants had normal or corrected-to-normal vision. None of them had experience using VR devices, and they were assigned into two groups randomly. The number of female in each group was balanced. Twenty of them have right hand for dominant and balanced into two groups. Six participants do not play games. The remaining participants play video games for 2 or 3 hour per week.

4.2   Material

The experiment was performed with HTC Vive Pro [26], which allows the user to navigate with lower-latency head tracking, and a refresh rate of 90 Hz. The device has two screens, one per eye, each one having a resolution of 1440 * 1600. The field of view of the device is 110°. The main machine has the capability of Inter core i7-8700, CPU (3.2 GHz), 16 GB RAM, Geforce GTX-1060 graphics card. The platform of development was Unity 2018 with C# language, where we implemented the cylinder and spherical layouts for eyes-free target acquisition in the VE. Target acquisition was implemented with one of the two controllers [27]. The participants were informed to press the trigger on the controller to acquire the target. The target was rendered as the blue. The selection interactions were the same in every condition.

For the assigned target, we defined the spatial distance predefined d as 0.2 m. In the program, the largest pitch value was 1, and the strongest intensity was 4000, the relationship between spatial distance and feedback intensity was illustrated in Fig. 3. As mentioned above, the radius of the circular layout, the horizontally egocentric distance between the target and the participants' main body, was 0.65 m. For the spherical layout, we reduced the radius to 0.45 m for the higher/lower rows, and the radius of middle row was 0.65 m.

4.3   Task Design

Thanks to Yan et al. [1], we adopted the similar task design and procedure with them. However, the goal of this work is to explore the effects of additional multimodal feedback on assisting the performance, it is not necessary to ask participants to acquire every target in the layout. We therefore randomly selected the representative locations (3 targets) from low, medium, and high rows respectively among 36 targets.

For each target, the participants were informed to rotate the body towards the white cube when acquiring it, twelve rotations in total (See Fig. 2). The order of rotations was random. During each rotation, the location of target was the same while the participant changed the orientation. It is important to note that the color of the target was changed to the same with other items once the experiment started, so that the participants could not notice the location of target during body rotation. The participants were asked to grasp the 3D controller with the same grip pose. To ensure the eyes-free approach, the observer was asked to look at the participant and the monitor for each acquisition. The total number of trials in the experiment were 3456 (24 subjects * 3 targets * 12 directions * 4 feedback conditions). The participants were asked to focus on acquiring the specific targets as quickly and accurately as possible with the 3D controller under each of feedback conditions in the assigned layout. The orders of the feedback conditions were randomly assigned to each participant.

4.4   Procedure

The experiment consisted of three phases. In the preparation phase, the participants were asked to fill in the personal form, and informed to get familiar with the VR environment and the interaction method, to acquire the targets several times using the controller until they felt confident.

In the experimental phase, the participant was asked to memorize the spatial location of each target, by means of practicing acquiring it in an eyes-free way several times. Then the participant started the eyes-free target acquisition. After each acquisition, the white cube was automatically rotated to the next direction randomly, which guided the participant to rotate the body towards the cube. Only the duration of acquisition was recorded as the trial completion time. The spatial and angular offset errors were also recorded. After 12 rotations for one target, they were allowed to have a 2-min break. After each of feedback conditions, they were asked to fill in the NASA-TLX questionnaire. In total, each participant finished 144 trials (3 targets * 12 directions * 4 feedback conditions).

After the experiment, the participants were informed to do a subjective interview. The whole experimental phases lasted about one hour. Each participant can obtain 4-dollar payment.

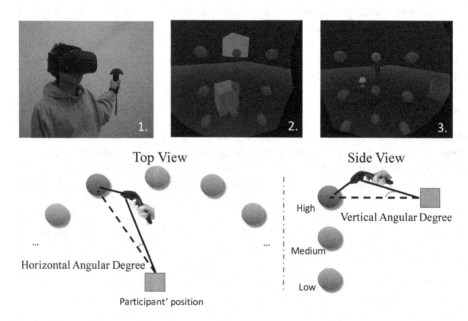

Fig. 4. The participant acquires the target without looking at it. 2: The participant looks at the white cube while acquiring the target. 3: The participant's hand approaches the target (the blue ball) using the controller. The bottom images illustrate the horizontal (from top view) and vertical (from side view) angular offset degree between controller and the target (bottom). (Color figure online)

4.5 Metrics

We utilized the following metrics, *trial completion time*, *spatial offset* [1], *angular offset* [1], and *subjective questionnaire* (NASA-TLX [5]), to measure the eyes-free target acquisition performance under the different feedback conditions. We defined the duration from the starting of acquiring each target to the acquisition confirmation as a *trial completion time. Spatial offset* was defined as the Euclidean distance between the acquisition point and the target's actual position, *Angular offset* included horizontal and vertical axis in degrees (See Fig. 4). It indicated the directions of the acquisition points were shifted from the actual location. For example, if the acquisition point was the upwards, as shown in Fig. 4, the vertical offset was positive.

5   Results

The Mixed RM-ANOVA with the post-hoc test (*Least Significant Difference*) was employed to analyze the objective measures (mean trial completion time, spatial offset, angular offset), and the *Mann-Whitney U test* and the *Kruskal-Wallis H test* for subjective rating. If the ANOVA' s sphericity assumption was violated (Mauchly's test $p < .05$), Greenhouse–Geisser adjustments were therefore performed.

5.1   Trial Completion Time

Figure 5 summarizes the mean trial completion time under four feedback conditions in both the cylinder and the spherical layouts. No significant difference was found between the cylinder (1447 ms, SD: 57) and the spherical layouts (1423 ms, SD: 57) on the trial completion time ($F_{1, 22} = .767$, $p = .09 > .05$).

As expected, there was a significant difference for four *feedback conditions* (*None*: 1145.7 ms, SD: .258; *H*: 1356.1, SD: .279; *A & H*: 1586.3, SD: .345; *A*: 1652.8, SD: .292) on the trial completion time ($F_{3,66} = 18.442$, $p < .001$). Participants spent a bit longer time under three feedback conditions than the *none* condition. The post-doc test revealed that there were significant differences ($p < .05$) for all pairs of feedback conditions except the pair (*auditory* vs. *bimodal* ($p = .423$)).

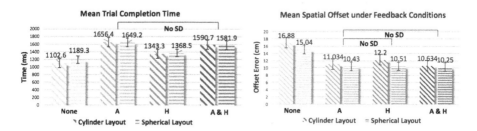

Fig. 5. Mean trial completion time under four feedback conditions (*None: no auditory and haptic feedback; A: auditory feedback only; H: haptic feedback only; A & H: both auditory and haptic feedback*) ($F_{3, 66} = 18.442$, $p < .001$) in both cylinder and spherical layouts (1447 ms vs. 1423 ms, $F_{1, 22} = .767$, $p = .09 > .05$) are illustrated, No SD represents no significant difference between two conditions, other pairs of comparisons differed significantly at $p < .05$ (Left). Mean spatial offset errors under four feedback conditions ($F_{1.968, 43.297} = 23.491$, $p < .001$, $\eta^2 = .516$) in both cylinder and spherical layouts (12.5 cm vs. 11.6 cm, $F_{1, 22} = 1.009$, $p = .326 > .05$) are illustrated (Right).

52   B. Gao et al.

Participants spent more time under the *auditory* ($p < .001$) and *bimodal* feedback condition ($p < .05$), compared to *haptic*. Most probably, the participants did not need to confirm the acquisition under *none* condition. In other words, they did not know the acquisition was correct or not. They relied on the proprioceptive cues only. In addition, there was no interaction effect for the *feedback conditions* and the *layouts* ($F_{3, 66} = .174$, $p = .914$).

5.2   Spatial Offset

As with the trial completion time, there was no significant difference between *two layouts* (*Cylinder*: 12.5 cm, SD: .006; *Spherical*: 11.6 cm, SD: .006) on the spatial offset ($F_{1, 22} = 1.009$, $p = .326 > .05$). Figure 5 shows the spatial offsets under the *feedback conditions* (*None*: 16.19 cm, SD: .051; *H*: 11.44 cm, SD: .019; *A*: 10.68 cm, SD: .025; *A & H*: 9.97 cm, SD: .019), a significant difference was found ($F_{1.968, 43.297} = 23.491$, $p < .001$, $\eta^2 = .516$). The post-hoc test showed that participants performed much better under each of three types of sensory feedback (*A, H, A & H*) than under the *none* condition ($p < .001$). The *bimodal* condition gave better spatial accuracy than the *haptic* condition ($p < .05$). However, there was no significant difference between *auditory* and *haptic* ($p = .307$), *auditory* and *bimodal* (*A & H*) feedback ($p = .224$). No interaction effect between the feedback conditions and the layouts was found ($F_{3, 66} = .033$, $p = .99$).

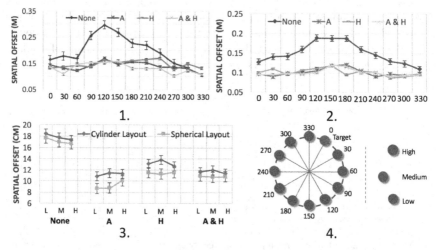

Fig. 6. 1: Mean spatial offset errors at the different horizontal degrees in the cylinder layout. 2: Mean spatial offset errors at the different horizontal degrees ($F_{11, 253} = 91.9$, $p < .001$) in the spherical layout. 3: Mean spatial offset errors at the vertical degrees (L represents targets at the low row, M represents it at the medium row, H represents it at the high row. $F_{2, 46} = 16.72$, $p < .001$) under four feedback conditions ($F_{3, 69} = 19.56$, $p < .05$) in both layouts. 4: The position of target is at 0°, when it is changed, then the 0° is changed accordingly.

However, we additionally included the mean spatial offset errors for the *horizontal rotation degrees* under the four feedback conditions in both layouts, as shown in Fig. 6 (1 and 2). We defined the position of the target as the 0°. Note that we recorded the order of rotations for each target acquisition. There was a significant difference for the horizontal rotation degree on the spatial offset ($F_{11, 253} = 91.9, p < .001$). As expected, participants performed much better under the three feedback conditions in the both layouts ($F_{3, 69} = 11.96, p < .001$), compared to the *None* condition. In particular, the additional feedback greatly improved the performance at the horizontal degree of 90, 120, 150, 180, and 210 (See Fig. 6). However, there was no significant difference among the three sensory feedback conditions (*A vs. H*: $p = .92$; *A vs. A & H*: $p = .9$; *H vs. A & H*: $p = .91$).

As with the horizontal degree, a significant difference for the vertical position (low, medium, high) on the spatial offset was also found ($F_{2, 46} = 16.72, p < .001$). Figure 6 (3) shows the mean spatial offset at the low, medium and high position under four feedback conditions in the cylinder layout and the spherical layout respectively. The participants performed much better under the additional feedback conditions ($F_{3, 69} = 19.56, p < .05$), compared to the *None* condition. No significant differences were found for the three feedback conditions with the Post-hoc test.

5.3   Angular Offset

We first calculated the absolute angular offset without considering the direction, as shown in Fig. 7. The absolute angular offset indicates the difference between target angular degree and pointing angular degree. Different from the trial completion time and spatial offset, there was a significant difference for the *layouts* (*Cylinder*: 6.316°, SD: .424; *Spherical*: 7.766°, SD: .64) on the angular offset ($F_{1, 22} = 5.848, p < .05$). Post-hoc tests showed that a significant difference was found under the haptic ($p < .001$) and the bimodal ($p < .05$) feedback conditions. Participants could greatly reduce the angular offset under the three *feedback conditions* respectively ($F_{1.364, 30.015} = 28.239, p < .001, \eta^2 = .562$). In particular, the auditory feedback gave better performance than the haptic feedback ($p < .05$).

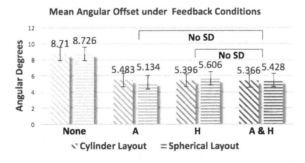

Fig. 7. Mean absolute angular offset under four feedback conditions ($F_{1.364, 30.015} = 28.239$, $p < .001$, $\eta^2 = .562$) in both cylinder and spherical layouts ($F_{1, 22} = 5.848$, $p < .05$) are illustrated.

To further understand the direction of angular offset, Fig. 8 summarizes that the horizontal rotation degree affected the horizontal angular offset of the acquisition ($F_{11, 253} = 13.23$, $p < .001$), the sensory feedback significantly reduced the horizontal angular offset in both layouts. However, no significant difference was found between two layouts ($F_{1, 23} = .103$, $p = .349$).

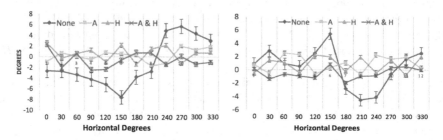

Fig. 8. Mean horizontal angular offset at the different horizontal degrees under four feedback conditions in the cylinder layout (left) and spherical layout (right) ($F_{1, 23} = .103$, $p = .349$) are illustrated.

5.4 Subjective Evaluation

The mean score of each dimension in both layouts are shown in Table 1. We found that no significant difference for the *feedback conditions* on the *temporal* ($H = 1.03$, $p < .14$) and *frustration* ($H = .146$, $p = .21$). The participants made more *effort*

Table 1. Mean subjective rating (SR) of NASA-TLX questionnaire for the four feedback conditions in both layouts (C represents the cylinder layout, and S represents the spherical layout). Note that the Mann-Whitney U test is used to compare the layouts, while the Kruskal-Wallis H test is used to compare the feedback conditions. Significant differences were marked with bold.

	None		A		H		A&H		Mann-Whitney U Test	Kruskal-Wallis H Test
	C	S	C	S	C	S	C	S		
Mental	5.3 (1.56)	4.33 (2.06)	4.8 (1.68)	4 (1.65)	4.4 (1.42)	3.5 (1.623)	4.3 (1.34)	3.45 (1.56)	**6.3** **P < .05**	**5.6** **P < .05**
Physical	5.83 (1.85)	5 (1.65)	5.75 (1.05)	5.083 (2.15)	5.5 (1.16)	4.583 (1.56)	5.25 (1.13)	4.25 (2.34)	**4.9** **P < .05**	**7.97** **P < .05**
Temporal	6 (1.15)	5.16 (1.80)	5.5 (1.43)	4.8 (1.67)	6 (2.51)	4.83 (1.85)	5.7 (1.64)	4.7 (1.84)	1.03 $p = .14$	.21 $p = .35$
Performance	5.3 (1.23)	5.6 (1.12)	6.5 (.90)	6.7 (.80)	6.37 (1.37)	6.67 (1.27)	7 (.85)	7.2 (.81)	**10.523** **p < .05**	**31.08** **p < .001**
Effort	5.67 (1.23)	5.67 (1.61)	4.67 (1.15)	4.92 (1.62)	4.17 (1.19)	5.083 (1.31)	4.083 (1.24)	4.91 (1.37)	**4.56** **p < .05**	**16.35** **p < .001**
Frustration	3.66 (1.61)	2.31 (1.25)	3.5 (1.93)	2.23 (1.09)	3.25 (1.48)	1.92 (1.03)	3.75 (1.71)	2.31 (1.03)	**11.1** **p < .001**	.146 $p = .21$

$(H = 16.35, p < .001)$ while resulted in the worst *performance* $(H = 31.08, p < .001)$ with the *none* condition. In addition, the participants required less *mental* $(H = 5.6, p < .05)$ and *physical* $(H = 7.97, p < .05)$ demand for the *bimodal (A & H)* condition to have the best performance, compared to *none* and *auditory* feedback conditions.

In terms of layouts, there was no significant difference for the *temporal* $(U = 1.03, p = .14)$. The participants reported that the spherical layout made them comfortable and easy to acquire the targets. It requires less *mental* $(U = 6.3, p < .05)$ and *physical* $(U = 4.9, p < .05)$ for the spherical layout than the cylinder layout. In the spherical layout, the horizontally egocentric distance for the targets located at low and high rows was smaller than that the targets in the cylinder layout, so participants can easily acquire them without rotating the arm or shoulder in the spherical layout. Subjectively, they can achieve better *performance* $(U = 10.523, p < .05)$ with less *effort* $(U = 4.56, p < .05)$ in the spherical layout, although there was no significant difference between two layouts on time and accuracy. Most probably, such a spherical layout can provide additional depth information, which makes the participants feel less blocking. In addition, every participant reported that they did not feel VR motion sickness after the experiment.

6 Discussion

From the experimental results, although no significant difference between two layouts, more participants preferred the spherical layout subjectively. For the feedback conditions, auditory, haptic, and auditory & haptic greatly improved the accuracy of eyes-free target acquisition in VR, rather than the trial completion time (See Figs. 5, 6, 7 and 8). Overall, the haptic feedback allowed the participants to faster acquire target than auditory feedback, while auditory feedback can provide better acquisition accuracy compared to haptic feedback. The bimodal feedback could keep a balance between the acquisition time and the acquisition accuracy basically. Subjective evaluation also reflected the result that 15 participants preferred the bimodal feedback conditions. Thus, H2 hypothesis could be accepted from the experimental results.

6.1 How to Assist Eyes-Free Target Acquisition?

From the existing work [1], the suggestion for the target UI for eyes-free target acquisition was that *"the horizontal ranges over 150 and 180 degrees (the rear region) resulted in poor performance in these dimensions [1] "*. Our results showed that with the help of auditory or bimodal feedback, the accuracy of target acquisition from such a range was significantly improved (See Fig. 6). The participant reported that *"this proximity-based feedback greatly informed the movement and correction of eyes-free target acquisition for the back side target"*.

Second, the 'area cursor' [15] and 'bubble cursor' [16] could be used to improve the acquisition accuracy according to the mean spatial offset error (around 2–20 cm). However, the proximity-based multimodal feedback can help reduce the spatial offset error to around 11 cm (See Fig. 5). This could help the designer to utilize such a guideline to decide the size of the bubble cursor.

Third, the acquisition accuracy increased under the proximity-based sensory feedback. It revealed that the proximity-based multimodal feedback can improve the correction phase, however, the trial completion time increased a bit with the help of three types of proximity-based multimodal feedback. Overall, the results suggest that the proximity-based bimodal feedback (both auditory and haptic) can keep a balance between the trial completion time and the acquisition accuracy. This is consistent with Ariza et al. [11], the bimodal is better than unimodal feedback for reduced error rates in 3D selection tasks.

6.2 Limitation and Future Work

In this experiment, we chosen the spatially continuous proximity-based multimodal feedback due to the eyes-free target acquisition requires more spatial-temporal information from the continuous feedback, while the 3D selection allows the participants to look at the target, probably less spatial-temporal information is enough. In the future, we will compare the effects of binary and continuous proximity-based multimodal feedback on eyes-free target acquisition to confirm the difference empirically. Then we will obtain the solid conclusion about the effects of the feedback type on the eyes-free target acquisition in VR.

In this work, we also leave some work to be studied in the future, for example, the effects of non-dominant hand on the eyes-free target acquisition in VR, in the real world, we always focus on performing the main task with our dominant hand, and acquiring the items using the non-dominant. We will observe how different the performance of non-dominant from the dominant hand.

7 Conclusion

This work mainly investigated the effects of proximity-based multimodal feedback on eyes-free target acquisition between two spatial layouts in VR. No significant difference was found between two spatial layouts in terms of objective measures. However, the participants preferred spherical layout subjectively over the cylinder layout for comfort (See Table 1). As expected, auditory, haptic, and bimodal feedback greatly improved the accuracy of eyes-free target acquisition in VR. The results showed that the proximity-based bimodal feedback could keep a balance between the trial completion time and acquisition accuracy basically. This research suggests the improvement of eyes-free target acquisition in VR via the proximity-based multimodal feedback.

Acknowledgements. This work was supported in part by Jinan University and the National Natural Science Foundation of China under Grant 61773179 and in part by the Bio-Synergy Research Project (NRF-2013M3A9C4078140) of the Ministry of Science, ICT and Future Planning through the National Research Foundation of Korea. Special thanks to every participant in this experiment.

References

1. Yan, Y., Yu, C., Ma, X., Huang, S., Iqbal, H., Shi, Y.: Eyes-free target acquisition in interaction space around the body for virtual reality. In: CHI 2018, no. 42, Montréal, Canada. ACM, April 2018
2. Lu, Y., Yu, C., Yi, X., Shi, Y., Zhao, S.: BlindType: eyes-free text entry on handheld touchpad by leveraging thumb's muscle memory. ACM Interact. Mob. Wearable Ubiquitous Technol. 1(2), 24 (2017). Article 18
3. Mine, M., Brooks Jr, F., Sequin, C.: Moving objects in space: exploiting proprioception in Virtual-Environment interaction. In: Proceedings of SIGGRAPH 1997, pp. 19–26. ACM Press, New York, USA (1997)
4. Chen, X., Schwarz, J., Harrison, C., Mankoff, J., Hudson, S.: Around-body Interaction: sensing and interaction techniques for proprioception-enhanced input with mobile devices. In: MobileHCI 2014, Toronto, Canada, pp. 287–290, September 2014
5. Hart, S.G., Staveland, L.E.: Development of NASA-TLX (Task Load Index): results of empirical and theoretical research. In: Hancock, P.A., Meshkati, N. (eds.) Human Mental Workload, pp. 139–183. Elsevier, Amsterdam (1988)
6. Ariza, O., Lange, M., Steinicke, F., Bruder, G.: Vibrotactile assistance for user guidance towards selection targets in VR and the cognitive resources involved. In: 2017 IEEE Symposium on 3D User Interfaces (3DUI), pp. 95–98, March 2017
7. Cockburn, A., Brewster, S.: Multimodal feedback for the acquisition of small targets. Ergonomics 48(9), 1129–1150 (2005)
8. Zhao, S., Dragicevic, P., Chigell, M., Balakrishnan, R., Baudisch, P.: earPod: eyes-free menu selection with touch input and reactive audio feedback. In: CHI, San Jose, CA, USA, pp. 1395–1404. ACM, May 2007
9. Park, Y., Kim, J., Lee, K.: Effects of auditory feedback on menu selection in hand-gesture interfaces. IEEE Multimed. 22(1), 32–40 (2015)
10. Gao, B., Kim, H., Lee, H., Lee, J., Kim, J.: Use of sound to provide occluded visual information in touch gestural interfaces. In: CHI Extended Abstracts, Seoul, South Korea, pp. 1277–1282. ACM, April 2015
11. Ariza, O., Bruder, G., Katzakis, N., Steinicke, F.: Analysis of proximity-based multimodal feedback for 3D selection in immersive virtual environments. In: IEEE Conference on Virtual Reality and 3D User Interfaces (VR), Germany, pp. 327–334, March 2018
12. Argelaguet, F., Andujar, C.: A survey of 3D object selection techniques for virtual environments. Comput. Graph. 37(3), 121–136 (2013)
13. Oh, U., Branham, S., Findlater, L., Kane, S.K.: Audio-based feedback techniques for teaching touchscreen gestures. ACM Trans. Access. Comput. 7, 9 (2015)
14. Poupyrev, I., Ichikawa, T., Weghorst, S., Billinghurst, M.: Egocentric object manipulation in virtual environments: empirical evaluation of interaction techniques. Comput. Graph. Forum 17(3), 41–52 (1998)
15. Worden, A., Walker, N., Bharat, K., Hudson, S.: Making computers easier for older adults to use: area cursors and sticky icons. In: CHI, New York, NY, USA, pp. 266–271. ACM (1997)
16. Grossman, T., Balakrishnan, R.: The bubble cursor: enhancing target acquisition by dynamic resizing of the cursor's activation area. In: CHI, New York, NY, USA, pp. 281–290. ACM (2005)
17. Gao, B., Kim, H., Kim, B., Kim, J.: Artificial landmarks to facilitate spatial learning and recalling for the curved visual wall layout in virtual reality. In: IEEE BigComp 2018, Shanghai, China, pp. 475–482, January 2018

18. Gao, B., Kim, B., Kim, J., Kim, H.: Amphitheater layout with egocentric distance-based item sizing and landmarks for browsing in virtual reality. Int. J. Hum.-Comput. Interact. **35**(10), 831–845 (2019)

19. Gerig, N., Mayo, J., Baur, K., Wittmann, F., Riener, R., Wolf, P.: Missing depth cues in virtual reality limit performance and quality of three dimensional reaching movements. PLoS ONE **13**(1), e0189275 (2018)

20. Yamanaka, S., Miyashit, H.: Modeling the steering time difference between narrowing and widening tunnels. In: CHI, San Jose, CA, USA, pp. 1846–1856. ACM (2016)

21. Loomis, J.M., Philbeck, J.W.: Measuring spatial perception with spatial updating and action. In: Behrmann, M., Klatzky, R.L., Macwhinney, B. (eds.) Embodiment, Ego-Space, and Action, pp. 1–43. Psychology Press, New York (2008)

22. Fitts, P.M.: The information capacity of the human motor system in controlling the amplitude of movement. J. Exp. Psychol. **47**(6), 381–391 (1954)

23. Ens, B., Finnegan, R., Irani, P.P.: The personal cockpit: a spatial interface for effective task switching on head-worn displays. In: CHI, Toronto, Canada, pp. 3171–3180. ACM (2014)

24. Ens, B., Ofek, E., Bruce, N., Irani, P.: Spatial constancy of surface-embedded layouts across multiple environments. In: SUI, Los Angeles, CA, USA, pp. 65–68. ACM (2015)

25. Gao, B., Kim, H., Lee, H., Lee, J., Kim, J.: Effects of continuous auditory feedback on drawing trajectory-based finger gestures. IEEE Trans. Hum.- Mach. Syst. **48**(06), 658–669 (2018)

26. HTC VIVE Pro. https://www.vive.com/us/product/vive-pro/. Accessed 20 Nov 2018

27. VRTK. https://vrtoolkit.readme.io/docs. Accessed 20 Nov 2018

A Multimodal Interface for Virtual Information Environments

Jeffrey T. Hansberger[1](✉), Chao Peng[2], Victoria Blakely[2],
Sarah Meacham[2], Lizhou Cao[2], and Nicholas Diliberti[2]

[1] Army Research Laboratory, Huntsville, AL 35816, USA
jeffrey.t.hansberger.civ@mail.mil
[2] University of Alabama in Huntsville, Huntsville, AL 35816, USA

Abstract. Continuing advances in multimodal technology, machine learning, and virtual reality are providing the means to explore and develop multimodal interfaces that are faster, more accurate, and more meaningful in the interactions they support. This paper describes an ongoing effort to develop an interface using input from voice, hand gestures, and eye gaze to interact with information in a virtual environment. A definition for a virtual environment tailored for the presentation and manipulation of information is introduced along with a new metaphor for multimodal interactions within a virtual environment.

Keywords: Multimodal interface · Gesture recognition · Virtual environment

1 Introduction

The concept of multimodal interfaces has captured the imagination of science fiction audiences and shown significant benefits among HCI researchers [1]. The mouse and keyboard, however, remain the primary method of interacting with this digital information. Continuing advances in multimodal technology, machine learning, and virtual reality are providing the means to explore and develop multimodal interfaces that are faster, more accurate, and more meaningful in the interactions they support. This paper will describe our ongoing effort to develop an interface using input from voice, hand gestures, and eye gaze to interact with information in a virtual environment.

The mouse has been a ubiquitous input device because it presents the metaphor of pointing that is known, efficient, and meaningful to the user. In conjunction with the WIMP (windows, icons, menus, and pointer) interface, the mouse provides an effective way of interacting with information. The mouse and its accompanying WIMP interface, however, afford indirect interactions with the information and goals of the user. Using a mouse, the user does not directly manipulate an object. They use a mouse on a two-dimensional horizontal surface whose movement is then translated to a two-dimensional vertical screen to manipulate elements of the WIMP interface. These steps and resulting task distance between the user and their goal has been defined as the gulf of execution by Norman [2]. A smaller gulf of execution will enable faster and more efficient task accomplishment with a smaller chance of error. Part of the potential of multimodal interactions is that it can afford a much smaller gulf of execution through the use of multiple and more direct input options.

J. Y. C. Chen and G. Fragomeni (Eds.): HCII 2019, LNCS 11574, pp. 59–70, 2019.
https://doi.org/10.1007/978-3-030-21607-8_5

Research with some of these alternative input modalities such as voice, eye gaze, and gestures has demonstrated the benefits of reducing the gulf of execution by providing faster and more efficient interactions. The use of eye gaze in place of a mouse for pointing at objects has proven to be a significantly faster technique [3]. There is also evidence that using voice commands is more efficient than activating the same option with a mouse and menu system [4].

The development and availability of multimodal systems that include two modalities has been rare and interfaces that use more than two modalities are even more scarce. Technological advancements in these multimodal domains of eye tracking, voice and gesture recognition however, has improved the accuracy, speed, and accessibility of the technologies monitoring and interpreting these modalities. We believe the technology in these areas is mature enough to develop a working prototype of a multimodal interface that has been designed from the ground up to integrate input from these three modalities: (1) eye gaze, (2) voice, and (3) hand gestures.

2 Related Work

2.1 Eye Gaze Input

One of the primary ways people direct their attention is by moving their eyes to visually explore and inspect the environment. Eye fixations have been shown to indicate what a person is currently working on or attending to and requires little cognitive effort [5]. Tracking a person's eye movement can be dated back to the late 19th century when Louis Emile Javal examined eye saccades while reading [6]. Eye tracking efforts are often used to understand what people are attending to or analyzing their scanning pattern to improve the design and effectiveness of a product [7].

Researchers have also explored the use of eye tracking as an input modality for interaction. Research has shown that eye gaze can be faster for selection than a mouse and can be particularly beneficial for hands free tasks and larger screen workspaces [3, 8]. Bolt used eye movements in user-computer dialogues [9, 10] while Glenn used them to actively track moving targets [11]. Researchers have also identified disadvantages and challenges with the use of eye tracking as an input modality.

Eye trackers have traditionally been limited in everyday use as they can be intrusive for the user, too sensitive to head movements, accuracy issues, and difficult to administer [12]. Another challenge using eye tracking as an input modality is called the Midas touch problem [13]. This problem occurs when interface elements are activated unintentionally by the user due to the fast and unintentional movement of the eyes. Potential solutions have been proposed such as limiting the use of eye gaze to selection and not activation and setting timing thresholds for dwell times before an item is activated [14].

2.2 Voice Command Input

Speech is widely regarded as the most natural method of communication and as such has been considered an important area of development for enhancing input capabilities.

With the development of larger vocabulary data sets and new algorithms, speech recognition technology has made extensive progress in the past few decades in achieving near instantaneous responses [15]. Early attention in this domain centered on human-machine performance comparisons centering on acoustic-phonetic modeling, language modeling, and error rates both in prime environments free of noise as well as degraded environments filled with noise pollution [16]. What started with simple machines recognizing only a few sets of sounds progressed to automatic speech recognition systems which use statistical models of speech derived from Hidden Markov Models [17, 18]. This technology recently has led to the development of spoken dialog systems allowing for multimodal inputs and the use of machine learning, resulting in high quality speech recognition.

Utilizing only a limited set of spoken command words can improve the accuracy and speed of a speech recognition system. Past research has shown that such spoken command word recognition systems can be faster than a keyboard and mouse interface [4, 19]. It has also been shown in some domains that even if the task takes longer to do with speech, the users prefer the speech input method over mouse interactions [19]. Current speech recognition systems require little training because they leverage commonly used vocabulary commands (i.e. using the natural command 'Stop' rather than less intuitive or longer phrases) [20]. This mode of input can both reduce cognitive load and increase system usability overall [21].

2.3   Hand Gesture Input

The use of hand gestures to communicate information is a large and diverse field. For brevity, we will reference the taxonomy work of Karam and Schraefel [22] to identify 5 types of gestures relevant to human-computer interaction: deictic, manipulative, semaphoric, gesticulation, and language gestures [23].

Deictic gestures consist primarily of a pointing gesture to spatially identify an object in the environment. Bolt's "Put-That-There" study in 1980 [24] defined and used hand gestures in this way for a graphical user interface (GUI). Manipulation with gestures controls objects by closely coupling the actions of the gesture with that object. Examples of this would be to move, relocate, or physically alter an object with a gesture [25, 26]. Semaphoric gestures are defined as a set of static and dynamic gestures that communicate a standard meaning when performed. An example of a static Semaphoric is a halt/stop gesture [27–29]. Gesticulation is one of the most natural uses of hand gestures and it consists of the gestures that accompany conversational speech [30]. The last form of gestures is language gestures, which represent the hand motions for sign language that have grammatical and lexical meaning associated with them [31].

A number of technological approaches are available to track and identify hand gestures. Optical solutions with external cameras that track the user's motion can include two basic types, a marker based system and markerless motion capture. The marker based system uses input from multiple cameras to triangulate the 3D position of the user wearing special markers while the markerless motion capture uses one or more cameras and computer vision algorithms to identify the user's 3D position. For issues of practicality, the markerless motion capture represents the optical motion capture of choice for general use. The Microsoft Kinect and the Leap Motion sensor are examples of markerless motion capture systems that are both affordable and accessible to consumers, researchers, and developers. However, these types of optical sensors must have an unobscured view of the user's hands, which can force the user's arms and hands into a high fatigue posture [27]. In addition, these sensors have shown to be limited in their gesture recognition accuracy and reliability [32, 33].

Another approach that does not use any optical devices is an inertial measurement unit (IMU) system. The IMU approach consists of several sensors placed on the user or in the clothing the user wears. Each IMU consists of a gyroscope, magnetometer, and accelerometer to wirelessly transmit the motion data of the user to a computer, where it is translated to a biomechanical model of the user. IMU gloves and suits have typically been used by the movie and special effects industry but recent crowdsourcing efforts like the Perception Neuron IMU suit have provided more affordable IMU based motion capture solutions. IMU solutions do require the user to wear the sensors in the form of gloves or straps but unlike the optical solutions, it does not provide constraints on where the user's hands must be to perform the gestures. As long as the sensors are within Wi-Fi range of the router, there are no constraints on the position, orientation, or worry of obscuring the hands from an external camera source.

2.4   Multimodal Systems

Multimodal systems involve two or more of the input modalities mentioned above and beyond. One of the primary goals of multimodal systems is to leverage naturally occurring behaviors and use them to interact with digital information. Essentially it allows the user to interact with digital information in many of the same ways they interact with everyday physical objects. Thoughtful implementation of these modalities can reduce the gulf of execution mentioned earlier to improve task efficiency.

Bolt's "Put-That-There" study was one of the earliest implementations of a multimodal system integrating speech and pointing gestures [24]. Other studies have shown that there is a strong user preference to interact multimodally when given the chance [1, 19, 34, 35]. Performance is likewise improved for many tasks that include verbal tasks [1], manipulation of 3D objects [35], and drawing tasks [36]. The flexibility of multiple modalities also allows for easier error recovery [37] and allows the user to select the modality they are most comfortable using, which provides a more customized user experience. These are all important benefits to consider when designing multimodal systems for future technology and virtual environments [38].

3   Virtual Information Environment

3.1   Virtual Information Environment (VIE) Attributes

We define a virtual information environment (VIE) as a virtual environment whose primary purpose is to facilitate information foraging and processing activities. A VIE should allow the user to (1) view information, (2) control how it is organized, and (3) allow interaction with the desired information elements. The navigation requirements are reversed for a VIE compared to typical virtual environments. In most virtual environments, the user can navigate through the environment to view and experience different aspects of the environment. With a VIE, the user is stationary and the information is moved and interacted with relative to the user's stationary position. This avoids the challenging issue of navigation within a virtual environment that many VR experiences struggle with.

The multimodal prototype developed was a digital photo management application. Fig. 1 shows the basic console with a view of the VIE from the perspective of the user. The interface allows zooming within the image collection to capture the elements of Shneiderman's visual information seeking mantra of providing an overview, while allowing the user to zoom and filter in order to obtain details on demand [39]. In order to reduce the potential for motion sickness during zooming actions with the information, the image collection is contained within the curved console. Nonmoving anchors or frames in the virtual environment help mitigate motion sickness [40]. While the images inside the console may be zooming in and out based on user input, the rest of the environment provides a nonmoving anchor.

Fig. 1. Over-the-shoulder view of the VIE and a user viewing a photo collection based on time. The timeline graph shown can be zoomed in to see that each part of the graph is composed of the images taken during that part of the timeline. The images are framed on the top and bottom by the non-moving VIE console.

Another attribute of the VIE is that most of the information visualizations, graphs, and analytics is presented primarily in a 2D fashion. Past research has found that 2D graphs are generally more accurate in presenting the intended information relative to

3D graphs [41]. Most of the graphs and information visualizations in the VIE are presented in a 2D fashion where we reserve using the third dimension for special cases where it can add new information for the user. In summary, one of the primary purposes of the VIE is to support the user in searching, manipulating, and understanding information. It does this by presenting information to the user in a virtual environment where they are stationary and most clearly presents the data, which is primarily with 2D visualizations. The second purpose of the VIE is to break the glass that separates the digital information from the user.

3.2   Bridging Digital Information with User Input Modalities

One of the most important attributes of the VIE is that it creates an environment where both digital information and multiple input modalities from the user can be directly represented. This is in contrast to WIMP interfaces where digital information is presented behind a glass monitor and interacted indirectly with a mouse and keyboard, creating a wide gulf of execution. When multiple modalities are monitored, recognized, and translated in real-time to the VIE, users have the ability to interact directly with the digital information in the same ways they interact with a physical object. This is when the full capabilities and potential of multimodal input can be realized.

3.3   A Metaphor for Multimodal Input

The use of a metaphor can help both the design and use of an interface. For design purposes, a metaphor can help identify the issues and maintain consistency. For use purposes, a metaphor can provide a schema that informs the user's current and future actions with the interface. Ware [42] and Hinckley [43] identified four control metaphors for 3D interactions:

- Eyeball-in-hand metaphor (camera metaphor): The view and perspective is controlled by the user's hand movement.
- Scene-in-hand metaphor: This is a first-person perspective view of an object where objects can be manipulated directly with a hand motion.
- Flying vehicle control (flying metaphor): This is a locomotion metaphor that covers ways to navigate through a virtual environment that includes flying, walking, jumping or riding.
- Ray casting metaphor: Object selection and navigation can occur by casting a ray at a target object or location.

We add a fifth metaphor:

- Conversation metaphor: This metaphor establishes that information elements in the virtual environment will respond to multiple input modalities of the user as if it is an active participant in a conversation. This metaphor leverages the ray casting metaphor and applies it specifically to eye gaze driven ray casting for object selection. It also expands that metaphor to include other modality inputs such as speech and hand gesture input. Each information element can respond across these different modalities, sometimes in different ways, sometimes in the same way.

The information responses are loosely based on social and conversation conventions between two humans, particularly the intent behind the action of the sender and the expected response of the receiver. The sender is the human user while the receiver is the information element in the VIE. The information element responds in a limited but similar manner as another person would. Eye gaze indicates where someone's attention is being allocated to in the environment while speech and hand gestures indicates the user's intent. The way each of these modalities supports the conversation metaphor is explored in the next section.

4 Multimodal Interactions

4.1 Eye Gaze

Technology. The technology used to monitor eye gaze in real-time is the Tobi Pro Glasses 2 installed inside an Oculus head mounted display (HMD). The eye gaze data is fed into Unity and the digital photo management application (i.e., VIE) to aid in the selection of targets and objects.

Approach. Eye gaze indicates where a person's attention is currently focused within the environment. This is typically a reliable indicator what the user is interested in or what they are currently working on. The use of eye gaze to select objects can be much faster than other selection strategies [3]. We, therefore, use eye gaze in a limited but focused manner. The eye gaze data is used purely as a selection function based on dwell time on an object. In the case of our current application, most of the objects are images, but there are other objects in the console including filters, bins the images can be sorted to, and other control devices to support the visual information seeking mantra [39]. We do not represent a cursor icon of any sort within the environment but instead, highlight the object that is currently selected based on eye gaze data.

4.2 Speech

Technology. Speech is monitored and analyzed in real-time by an open source speech recognition algorithm called Snowboy (https://snowboy.kitt.ai). Snowboy is a key word speech recognition capability that runs on raspberry pi hardware. The system requires each key word to be trained by the individual user. Training consists of repeating the key word or phrase 3 times through an online interface. The user is required to do that for each keyword to create an individual speech model that can then be loaded onto the raspberry pi hardware. Once this individual model is created and loaded, no additional changes are necessary unless new key words are added to the vocabulary list. The current key word vocabulary is around 30 words that consist of commands like "center", "home", and "activate". In order to account for terminology preferences among users, some actions are activated by more than one term such as "zoom in", "enhance", and "magnify".

Approach. The choice of using a key word approach instead of natural language processing was due to a combination of available technology, speed, and accuracy.

Based on initial testing, accuracy levels of the key word system are above 95%. In addition to the inherent speech recognition capabilities, the vocabulary list can be customized to further improve accuracy levels by selecting key words that are phonetically different from one another.

The key commands are primarily used to manipulate the view and organization of the photos in the VIE. They replace some of the functions found in the menu system of a typical WIMP interface. For example, a user can state "Filter vehicles" to apply a filter that shows only vehicles in the photo collection. Key commands can be applied generally or they can be specific to a particular photo in the VIE. Using the eye gaze input data allows the system to know which photo is being attended to and can use that location information within the VIE to zoom into when the user says a command such as, "enhance".

4.3   Gestures

Technology. Several commercial over-the-shelf motion capture systems were tested to provide real-time tracking of the user's hands and fingers. Issues arose when testing these systems regarding their accuracy, reliability, and programming flexibility. These issues motivated us to create a custom set of motion capture gloves with IMU technology. The use of IMU technology was critical in order to adopt the supported gestures described in Hansberger et al. [27] and avoid significant user fatigue. These gestures have been tested in both gaming environments [44] and with a digital photo management application [45]. A convolutional neural network was trained to recognize a set of 22 gestures. The training dataset was composed of 3D rotation data of finger joints recorded from the glove's IMU sensors. In order to meet the goal of real-time gesture recognition, we reduced the network's complexity by reducing the amount of feature layers and the number of weight parameters in the training phase of the network, and made the network find archetypal features of each gesture. As a result, the classification model produced by the network maintained a high recognition accuracy, and was able to classify new data samples by scanning a real-time stream of joint rotations during the use of the multimodal interface.

Approach. The use of hand gestures during speech is so natural and ubiquitous that people gesticulate as much whether the person they are talking to can see them or not [46]. The position of their arms and hands when they gesticulate is typically with their elbows bent at a 90-degree angle with their hands near their waist area [47]. In crafting our gesture vocabulary, we leveraged semaphoric type gestures used in the arm position that most gesticulation occurs [20, 27]. The gestures selected are commonly used semaphoric gestures that also have applicability to manipulate actions within a VIE. This results in short, familiar, and meaningful gestures that can be executed while the user is seated with their arms in a supported posture by a set of armrests (Fig. 2). Future gestures that allow for direct manipulation of VIE objects include actions such as pinching and pulling two ends of a photo to enlarge it.

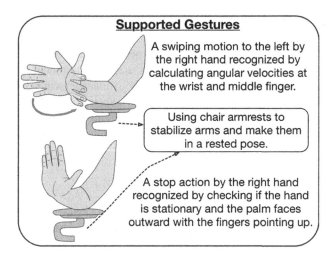

Fig. 2. Illustration of the supported gestures using an armrest of a chair as support. Two example semaphoric gestures are shown, a swipe and a stop gesture.

4.4 Multimodal Discussion

Each of these modalities offer potentially faster and more natural methods that can help reduce the gulf of execution between the user and their information related task. It is when they are integrated and designed as a single input system when the potential of a multimodal system is evident.

These modalities complement one another because we are not asking any single modality to do too much or to perform functions that they are not well suited for. Eye gaze performs the basic selection function that can then be used with either speech or gesture manipulation. With every function or task in the VIE, we have tried to provide at least two means to complete a task. For example, to zoom in on a photo, the user can look at an image and either say "zoom in" or perform a "come here" gesture. This flexibility aids in error recovery by providing alternatives for the user if one method is not effective but it also allows the user to customize their pattern of interactions within the VIE based on their individual preferences. For example, if a person, based on individual differences, prefers to interact verbally, they have the option to utilize that modality to a greater extent. This leads to greater flexibility and increased user satisfaction overall.

The application of the conversation metaphor has helped guide the multimodal system discussed here. It has motivated us to think more broadly about information and how it can be more naturally and directly manipulated in a virtual environment. More importantly, it has addressed the challenge of designing actions in the VIE that respond to multiple modalities that will help explore multimodal research questions in the future.

5   Future Directions

Future efforts in this area include a series of experiments that will examine the performance, engagement, and user experience levels that the multimodal system provides within the VIE. In addition to the VIE digital photo management application being developed, we have also developed a 2D touchscreen version that mirrors all the same functionalities. Future experiments will be able to examine the differences between unimodal and trimodal interfaces in order to better understand the advantages and disadvantages of both.

References

1. Oviatt, S.: Multimodal interactive maps: designing for human performance. Hum.-Comput. Interact. **12**, 93–129 (1997)
2. Norman, D.: Design of Everyday Things. Basic Books, New York (2013)
3. Sibert, L., Jacob, R.: Evaluation of eye gaze interaction. In: Proceedings of the SIGCHI Conference on Human Factors in Computing Systems (2000)
4. Karl, L., Pettey, M., Shneiderman, B.: Speech versus mouse commands for word processing: an empirical evaluation. Int. J. Man-Mach. Stud. **39**(4), 667–687 (1993)
5. Just, M., Carpenter, P.: Eye fixations and cognitive processes. Cogn. Psychol. **8**, 441–480 (1976)
6. Huey, E.: The psychology and pedagogy of reading. MIT Press, Cambridge (1968)
7. Donegan, M., Morris, J., Corno, F., Signorile, I., Chio, A.: Understanding users and their needs. Univers. Access Inf. Soc. **8**, 259–275 (2009)
8. Ware, C., Mikaelian, H.: An evaluation of an eye tracker as a device for computer input. In: Proceeding of ACM CHI+GI 1987 Human Factors in Computing systems Conference (1987)
9. Bolt, R.: Gaze-orchestrated dynamic windows. Comput. Graph. **15**(3), 109–119 (1981)
10. Bolt, R.: Eyes at the interface. In: Proceeding of ACM Human Factors in Computer Systems Conference (1982)
11. Glenn, F.: Eye-voice-controlled interface. In: Proceeding of 30th Annual Meeting of the Human Factors Society, Santa Monica (1986)
12. Morimoto, C., Mimica, M.: Eye gaze tracking techniques for interactive applications. Comput. Vis. Image Underst. **98**, 4–24 (2005)
13. Jacob, J.: Eye tracking in advanced interface design. In: Virtual Environments and Advanced Interface Design, pp. 258–288, June (1995)
14. Bednarik, R., Gowases, T., Tukiainen, M.: Gaze interaction enhances problem solving: effects of dwell-time based, gaze-augmented, and mouse interaction on problem-solving strategies and user experience. J. Eye Mov. Res. **3**(1), 1–10 (2009)
15. Stedmon, A., Patel, H., Sharples, S., Wilson, J.: Developing speech input for virtual reality applications: a reality based interaction approach. Int. J. Hum.-Comput. Stud. **69**(1–2), 3–8 (2011)
16. Lippmann, R.: Speech recognition by machines and humans. Speech Commun. **22**(1), 1–16 (1997)
17. Davis, K., Biddulph, R., Balashek, S.: Automatic recognition of spoken digits. J. Acoust. Soc. Am. **24**(6), 627–642 (1952)

18. Baum, L.: An inequality and associated maximization technique in statistical estimation for probabilistic functions of markov processes. Inequalities **3**, 1–8 (1972)
19. Cohen, P., Oviatt, S.: The role of voice input for human-machinge communication. In: Proceedings of the National Academy of Sciences (1995)
20. Barfield, W., Baird, K., Bjorneseth, O.: Presence in virtual environments as a function of type of input device and display update reate. Displays **19**, 91–98 (1998)
21. Hone, K., Baber, C.: Designing habitable dialogues for speech based interaction with computers. Int. J. Hum Comput Stud. **54**(4), 637–662 (2001)
22. Karam, M., Schraefel, M.C.: A taxonomy of gestures in human computer interactions. Technical report, University of Southampton (2005)
23. Quek, F., et al.: Multimodal human discourse: gesture and speech. ACM Trans. Comput. Hum. Interact. **9**(3), 171–193 (2002)
24. Bolt, R.: "Put-that-there": voice and gesture at the graphics interface. In: Proceedings of the 7th Annual Conference on Computer Graphics and Interactive Techniques (1980)
25. Rekimoto, J.: Pick-and-drop: a direct manipulation technique for multiple computer environments. In: Proceedings of the 10th annual ACM Symposium on User Interface Software and Technology (1997)
26. Rubine, D.: Combining gestures and direct manipulation. In: Proceedings of the SIGCHI Conference on Human Factors in Computing Systems (1992)
27. Hansberger, J.H., et al.: Dispelling the gorilla arm syndrome: the viability of prolonged gesture interactions. In: International Conference on Virtual, Augmented and Mixed Reality (2017)
28. Baudel, T., Beaudouin-Lafon, M.: Charade: remote control of objects using free-hand gestures. Commun. ACM **36**(7), 28–35 (1993)
29. Cao, X., Balakrishnana, R.: Visonwand: interaction techniques for large displays using a passive wand tracked in 3D. In: Proceedings of the 16th Annual ACM Symposium on User Interface Software and Technology (2003)
30. Wexelblat, A.: Natural gesture in virtual environments. In: Proceedings of the Conference on Virtual Reality Software and Technology (1994)
31. Bowden, R., Zisserman, A., Kadir, T., Brady, M.: Vision based interpretation of natural sign languages. In: Exhibition at ICVS03: The 3rd International Conference on Computer Vision Systems (2003)
32. Brown, M., Stuerzlinger, W., Filho, E.: The performance of un-instrumented in-air pointing. In: Proceedings of Graphics Interface Conference (2014)
33. Guna, J., Jakus, G., Pogacnik, M., Tomazic, S., Sodnik, J.: An analysis of the precision and reliability of the leap motion sensor and its suitability for static and dynamic tracking. Sensors **14**(2), 3702–3720 (2014)
34. Hauptmann, A.: Speech and gestures for graphic image manipulation. In: Proceedings of the SIGCHI Conference on Human Factors in Computing Systems (1989)
35. Kefi, M., Hoang, T., Richard, P., Verhulst, E.: An evaluation of multimodal interaction techniques for 3D layout constraint solver in a desktop-based virtual environment. Virtual Real. **22**(4), 339–351 (2018)
36. Leatherby, J., Pausch, R.: Voice input as a replacement for keyboard accelerators in a mouse-based graphical editor: an empirical study. J. Am. Voice Input/Output Soc. **11**(2) (2002)
37. Suhm, B.: Multimodal interactive error recovery for non-conversational speech user interfaces. Ph.D. thesis, Fredericiana University (1998)
38. Nizam, S., Abidin, R., Hashim, N., Lam, M., Arshad, H., Majid, N.: A review of multimodal interaction technique in augmented reality environment. Int. J. Adv. Sci. Eng. Inf. Technol. **8**(4–2), 1460–1469 (2018)

39. Shneiderman, B.: The eyes have it: a task by data type taxonomy for information visualizations. In: Proceedings 1996 IEEE Symposium on Visual Languages (1996)
40. Hettinger, L., Riccio, G.: Visually induced motion sickness in virtual environments. Presence Teleoperators Virtual Environ. **1**(3), 306–310 (1992)
41. Hughes, B.: Just noticeable differences in 2D and 3D bar charts: a psychophysical analysis of chart readability. Percept. Mot. Skills **92**(2), 495–503 (2001)
42. Ware, C., Osborne, S.: Exploration and virtual camera control in virtual three dimensional environments. Comput. Graph. **24**(2), 175–183 (1990)
43. Hinckley, K., Pausch, R., Goble, J., Kassell, N.: A survey of design issues in spatial input. In: Proceedings of the 7th Annual ACM Symposium on User Interface Software and Technology (1994)
44. Peng, C., Hansberger, J., Shanthakumar, V., Meacham, S., Blakely, V., Cao, L.: A case study of user experience on hand-gesture video games. In: 2018 IEEE Games, Entertainment, Media Conference (GEM) (2018)
45. Peng, C., Hansberger, J.T., Cao, L., Shanthakumar, V.: Hand gesture controls for image categorization in immersive virtual environments. In: 2017 IEEE Virtual Reality (VR) (2017)
46. Cadoz, C.: Les Realites Virtuelles. Flammarion, Dominos (1994)
47. Kendon, A.: Gesture: Visible Action as Utterance. Cambridge University Press, Cambridge (2004)

AR Assistive System in Domestic Environment Using HMDs: Comparing Visual and Aural Instructions

Shuang He[1,2,3(✉)], Yanhong Jia[2,3], Zhe Sun[3], Chenxin Yu[3], Xin Yi[1], Yuanchun Shi[1], and Yingqing Xu[2,3]

[1] Department of Computer Science and Technology,
Tsinghua University, Beijing, China
heshuang.design@foxmail.com,
{yixin,shiyc}@mail.tsinghua.edu.cn
[2] Department of Information Art and Design,
Tsinghua University, Beijing, China
jyh18@mails.tsinghua.edu.cn,
yqxu@mail.tsinghua.edu.cn
[3] The Future Laboratory, Tsinghua University, Beijing 100084, China
{sunz15,yu-cx16}@mails.tsinghua.edu.cn

Abstract. Household appliances are becoming more varied. In daily life, people usually refer to printed documents while they learn to use different devices. However, augmented reality (AR) assistive systems providing visual and aural instructions have been proposed as an alternative solution. In this work, we evaluated users' performance of instruction understanding in four different ways: (1) Baseline paper instructions, (2) Visual instructions based on head mounted displays (HMDs), (3) Visual instructions based on computer monitor, (4) Aural instructions. In a Wizard of Oz study, we found that, for the task of making espresso coffee, the helpfulness of visual and aural instructions depends on task complexity. Providing visual instructions is a better way of showing operation details, while aural instructions are suitable for presenting intention of operation. With the same visual instructions on displays, due to the limitation of hardware, the HMD-users complete the task in the longest duration and bear the heaviest perceived cognitive load.

Keywords: Augmented reality · Multimodal feedback · Assistive system · Instructions · Head mounted displays

1 Introduction

In daily life, people usually refer to printed documents while they complete tasks by using household appliance, for instance, using a coffee machine to make espresso coffee according to the manual. During the course of operation, they may skip steps, misunderstand instructions, or unable to correct mistakes in time. In part, these problems are caused by the readability of the documents. On the other hand, the gap between the paper instructions and the actual context reduces the effectiveness of

© Springer Nature Switzerland AG 2019
J. Y. C. Chen and G. Fragomeni (Eds.): HCII 2019, LNCS 11574, pp. 71–83, 2019.
https://doi.org/10.1007/978-3-030-21607-8_6

operation. We want to build an eyes-free, hands-free and non-distractive external learning environment for users. Therefore, AR assistive system providing visual and aural instructions based on head mounted displays seemed to be an ideal solution.

In this paper, we conducted a heuristic evaluation and a think aloud protocol user study based on paper manual to establish user's mental model as well as instruction design principles. We redesign the paper document according to the experimental task and develop three prototypes of assistive system, one with HMDs, one with computer monitor and one with conversational voice system. All three of the prototypes offering support to users with the same quantity of information. Through a Wizard of Oz user study with 20 participants, we compared users' performance for instruction understanding in visual and aural modality.

We have made three main contributions in this paper: (1) a diagram applied to design multimodality AR assistive system: When system providing visual or aural detailed description for each step, a simple and clear statement should contain three key information points, target objects, relative position between target objects and actions. (2) a design principle based on task complexity: For novices, when they use home appliance to perform some easy functions, there is no significant difference in helpfulness between visual and aural instructions. However, when a step contains several complex operations, visual instructions provide more helpfulness. Comparing to graphic user interface, a well-designed voice user interface is more flexible. Voice user interface is suitable for presenting intention of operation and users demand supplementary information from conversational virtual assistant expecting for better interactive experience. (3) a method applied to analyze users' decision-making process on visual and aural instructions, helping researchers to design multimodal AR assistive system.

The result of user study shows that, due to the limitation of the hardware, AR assistive system based on HMDs have theoretic feasibility on current stage. To reach the ideal state, it requires better recognition and display technology. Conversational assistive system could effectively reduce perceived cognitive loads. But when users are unfamiliar with the devices, descriptiveness of aural instructions is limited. With the accumulation of hands-on experience, there is less demand for detailed description of each step and users tend to seek support from the system for specific problems rather than being instructed.

2   Related Work

In recent years, research on AR assistive system involves varies domains, such as hospital setting [1, 2], remote work support [3], industrial manufacturing [4], education applications [5], etc.

In earlier research, AR multimodality assistive system in human settlement is usually built with in-situ projection. CounterActive is a cooking aid system used in the kitchen guiding the users with projection and aural instructions [6]. In the work of Ayaka Sato et al., the MimiCook system uses image recognition technologies to analyze user activity. With in-situ projection, Mimicook displays menu as well as supplementary information to improve users' task efficiency [7]. Yu Suzuki and

Shunsuke Morioka et al. developed a cooking support system for novices, including a conversational robot assistant "Phyno". Phyno can interact with the user via voice and gestures [8]. Meanwhile, there are some mixed modality conversational virtual assistants coming on the market, such as Siri, Amazon Echo. The aim of the research above are not to report interactive efficiency or perceived cognitive loads, but rather focus on system design, implementation, user experience and acceptance of introducing AR assistive system in domestic environment.

With the development of AR technology, the research reports task completion time, error frequency and interactive efficiency of AR assistive system in specific scenario is gradually unfolding. Markus Funk et al., compared assembly instructions based on HMDs, tablets, in-situ projections and baseline paper documents. The results show that for assembling tasks, completion time is significantly longer using HMDs. HMD-users make more error and have more perceived cognitive load [9, 10]. Markus Funk's research also involves the comparison of different visualizations, such as pictures, videos, 3D models and contour. They report that contour visualization is significantly better in perceived mental load and performance of the impaired participants [2].

For multi-modality feedbacks, Marina Cidota et al. compared audio and visual notifications in remote workspace collaboration. After analyzing the case of placing virtual objects in the shared workspace, they find that visual notifications are preferred over audio or no notifications independent from the level of difficulty of the task [11]. Youngsun Kim et al. presented an AR-based tele-coaching system for fast pace task applied to the game of tennis. They evaluate the instantaneous response rate of visual, voice, and multimodal augmented instructions. Sound show the worst performance in terms of the responsive time. AR is the most useful in stringent temporal conditions. Multimodal feedback seems to caused distraction to users [12].

Overall, previous work investigated the acceptance of AR assistive system in domestic environment. However, a comprehensive study comparing visual and aural instructions using HMDs in domestic environment has not been done yet. In this paper, we will compare baseline paper instructions, aural instructions to visual instructions based on HMDs and computer monitor. Further, we will evaluate user performance following long instructions in complex tasks in human settlement.

3   Initial Study

3.1   Evaluating Paper Document

We conducted a heuristic evaluation of paper documents in accordance with Nielson's usability principles [13, 14]. Five researchers with the background in human-computer interaction participated in the test. They evaluated the usability of original paper instruction of De'Longhi ECO 310 Icona Espresso Manual Machine (Chinese) [15]. Then, we launched a think aloud protocol test [16] involving 3 participants. They were asked to make espresso coffee according to the manual.

The results of the heuristic evaluation and the think aloud protocol test indicate that, for the task of making espresso coffee, the problems on usability and readability in original manual are found as follows: (1) The operative description in paper manual cannot be fully matched to actual operating procedure. (2) The paper documents

include terms that are not familiar to novices (i.e. filter-holder, extraction, etc.).
(3) Semantic ambiguity in descriptive text, icons, and diagrams. (4) Information
redundant: precautions, explanatory and descriptive information have been cropped up
in operating procedures. (5) User need to follow the serial number among instruction
text to look up for diagrams, which may easily lead to misreading or skipping steps.

In general, we need to select a task for experimentation, clear the procedures and
simplify the instructions. The usability and readability problems in paper manual
should be revised. Besides, related diagrams and text descriptions for each step should
be form a one-to-one correspondence and displayed on same page.

3.2   Case Study of Making Espresso Coffee

We clarified that the aim of experimental task was to "making a cup of espresso coffee
with a manual coffee machine". Operating procedure was simplified into 9 steps with
intention and specific operative descriptions (see Table 1).

The task of "making espresso coffee" was chosen because: (1) It involves the primary
operation methods for the coffee machine, helping users to understand the operating
principle. (2) It includes numerous operative steps and appliance, but makes limited use
of ingredients. Therefore, users' prior experience will not affect their performance.
(3) Concerning task complexity, operation has different levels of difficulty. Therefore,
the task is considered appropriately to be simulated in the laboratory environment.

The instructions were grouped in to two categories: (1) Simple instruction: it
describes how to interact with a single object. The spatial position or state of the object
changes such as "Position the cup under the filter holder spouts". (2) Complex
instruction: it describes how to interact with more than two objects. It involves the
changes of relative spatial position between objects and multiple physical feedback,
such as "Attach filter holder into boiler outlet. Turn right to lock into position."

Table 1. How to prepare espresso using ground coffee.

Step	Intention	Description	Complexity
1	Turn the machine on	Press the ON button	Simple
2	Install steel filter	Install steel filter cup into the filter holder	Complex
3	Filling coffee	Fill the filter with a level measuring scoop of coffee	Complex
4	Tamp the coffee	Press the coffee lightly using the coffee tamper	Complex
5	Attach filter holder	Attach filter holder in place into boiler outlet. Turn right to lock into position	Complex
6	Place coffee cup	Position the cup under the filter holder spouts	Simple
7	Extraction	Press the coffee button. (It is recommended not to run the coffee for more than 45 s). Press the same button again	Simple
8	Cleaning	Remove the cup. Turn the grip from right to left to release the filter holder	Simple
9	Turn the machine off	Press the OFF button	Simple

3.3   Tutorial Design Paradigm

In the analysis of procedures and instructions, we generalized that when assistive system providing visual or aural instruction for each step, a simple and clear statement should include three key information points: (1) Objects, what will be used in operating process; (2) Relative position between objects, where the objects should be placed; (3) Actions, how to manipulate. For example, "Attach filter holder in place into boiler outlet". The objects involved are "filter holder" and "boiler outlet", the action is "attach into", and the relative position is from separating to assembling.

In order to avoid affecting users' performance, instructions in paper document, visualization and auditory need to convey the same amount of information. In visual instructions, an object is marked with a circle. We draw lines between objects, which started with a dot and ended with an arrow, to indicate relative position and orientation. Action is described by a dynamic arrow. Orientation and acceleration of the arrow indicates how much force should be performed. Intention of each step is displayed in the lower left corner in text. In conversational voice system, aural instructions are the precise description of dynamic graphic illustrations (see Fig. 1).

Fig. 1. Example of instructions. (1) Paper manual, (2) Visual instruction, (3) Aural instruction.

4   System

For exploring visual and aural instructions in human settlement, we simulate a domestic environment in independent space in our lab. In the following, we introduce the system prototype of visualizations and auditory.

Fig. 2. AR assistive system. (1) Live stream, (2) System being used, (3) Instruction on HoloLens.

4.1 Visualizations

Visual instructions were designed according to the diagram described in Sect. 3.3. Previous works suggested that compared to video and pictorial visualization, contour instructions resulted in fewer errors and better performance. In our previous study, we tried to make contour instructions on HMDs. We used HoloLens Vuforia SDK for image recognition and built dynamic contour with Unity 3D. Because the speed of image recognition and tracing was rather slow, we decided to use video instructions instead. We photographed the standard task procedures and overlaid dynamic contour instructions on the image to simulate contour-overlapping.

Visual Instruction Based on HMDs. For HMDs implementation, the instruction system was developed with Unity 3D and C#, then implemented on HoloLens. In this system, a serial of silent video clips was provided along with the serial number of each step, the intention of the operation and minimum additional text explanation if needed (only a few steps have such additional explanation, i.e. It is recommended not to run the coffee for more than 45 s). Users could switch to the next or the previous step by interacting with buttons on the right or left side of the video clips using gestures (see Fig. 2).

Visual Instruction Based on Screen. Considering that HMDs themselves might have influence upon the study, we implemented visual instructions not only in HMDs but also on a computer monitor (27-in. screen). For visual instructions on screen, video clips are displayed on a computer monitor orderly. Each clip shows the instruction of one step out of nine (see Table 1) with the serial number and the intention of the step. Once the user complete current step, the video of next step would be played on the screen.

4.2 Aural Instructions

The conversational voice system prototype was designed according to task procedure. Conversation samples were listed and dialogue process was analyzed based on task flow. According to task procedure (see Table 1), we referred to existing voice-based interface design paradigm and developed a preset list of aural instructions and responses. Experimenter (the wizard) could select computer synthesized audio clip from the response list. We transferred text to voice instructions by Responsive Voice API[1].

After observing users' interaction in pre-test with the voice-based instruction system, we classified user behavior into five categories: Explicit next, Request, Implicit next, operation errors or timeout and undefined response. Different responses were given to the user in a Wizard of Oz study according to this classification (see Table 2).

---

[1] https://responsivevoice.org/api/.

Table 2. Example of user behavior and system response

User behavior	Response
Explicit Next: *"Okay"*, *"Next?"*	Play the instruction of next step
Request: *"What is…?" "Say it again?"*	Repeat the instruction of current step
Implicit next (complete and wait quietly)	Play the instruction of next step
Errors or timeout	Repeat the instruction of current step
Undefined response	"Sorry, I am listening"

5 Evaluation

In this work, we developed a high-fidelity Wizard of Oz simulation to evaluate user performance. We describe the protocol and apparatus below.

5.1 Procedure

We invited 20 participants to engage in our user study. The participants were aged between 20 to 33 (Avg. = 25, SD = 4.8); 9 participants were male, 11 were female. Participants were divided into four groups. Each group was asked to take one of the four evaluations: (1) Paper instructions, (2) Visual instructions based on HMDs, (3) Visual instructions based on computer monitor, (4) Aural instructions. All participants have no experience of using a manual coffee machine. Out of the 5 participants that attended HMDs evaluation, 2 reported having used HMDs within half a year, 2 reported earlier, 1 never; while among the 5 that attended aural instructions evaluation, 1 reported using a conversational assistant usually, 2 reported having used an intelligent voice system within half a year.

The experiment took place in an independent space at our research facility. Participants were briefed upon arrival, and were given 5 min to read a paper introduction about the components of the coffee machine that would be used in the following experiment. Participants of visual instruction group were guided by the same serial of looping video clips. Switching from one step to another could be done by gestures. An additional operation was provided for HMDs users to replace the video clips to wherever they prefer. Participants of conversational assistive system were informed that they could communicate with the system, either asking for step changing or instruction repeating. All participant actions were audio and video recorded.

During the experiments, lab assistants wouldn't be involved unless necessary (e.g. If users tried to do something that would probably make themselves in danger, assistants would intervene). Participants were asked to complete System Usability Scale (SUS) questionnaires [17], the NASA Task Load Index questionnaire (NASA-TLX) [18] and a semi-structured interview. The post-interview mainly focuses on: (1) Overall feelings about the system and its advantages and disadvantages; (2) Causes of errors or confusion during the experiment; (3) Open interview according to results from SUS and NASA-TLX, where participants were asked to give suggestions to better user experience.

5.2   General Impressions

All of the 20 participants completed the task. Visual instructions on screen received the highest SUS average score of 70.83 (SD = 13.91), followed by aural instructions with an average score of 69.5 (SD = 9.82) and paper instructions with an average score of 67.5 (SD = 25.74). AR assistive system based on HMDs was the least favorable, which got the lowest average score of 66.5 (SD = 9.62). All of the four prototypes were performing at the acceptable threshold level.

5.3   Task Completion Times

We accumulated users' response time and the procedure duration at each step. For the length of instructions varied a lot, we used the "point-in-time" when users started to act as the starting point for timing. When a step was completed, we stopped timing.

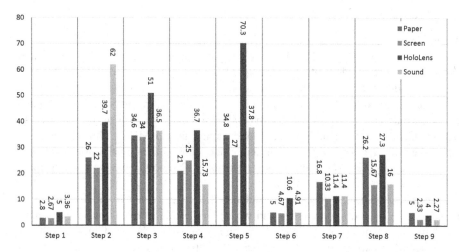

Fig. 3. Overview about the results of step completion times. Comparing (1) Paper instructions, (2) Visual instructions based on HMDs, (3) Visual instructions based on screen, (4) Aural instructions.

Participants referred to visual instructions on screen taking an average of 143.7 s (SD = 52.7) in finishing the task, which was the fastest, followed by the group using paper document with an average of 172.2 s (SD = 19.6), aural instructions with an average of 190.0 s (SD = 58.6) and visual instruction on HMDs with an average of 256 s (SD = 58.6).

For an overview of each step completion times (see Fig. 3.), participants who was supported by HMDs possessed longer procedure duration than users who was instructed by screen. When users performed some easy functions (i.e. Step1, 6, 7, 8, 9), the there was no significant difference in helpfulness between visual instructions on screen and aural instructions. However, when a step contains several complex operations (i.e. Step2, 3, 5), visual instructions seemed to improving operative efficiency.

5.4   Errors

On the whole, participants made least mistake using visual instructions on screen with an average error rate of 0.07 (SD = 0.06), followed by aural instructions with an average error rate of 0.08 (SD = 0.1), paper instructions with an average error rate of 0.18 (SD = 0.11) and visual instructions on HMDs with an average error rate of 0.36 (SD = 0.21).

We further analyzed the errors participants made while completing the task in each step. Participants supported by paper manual made errors in Step2 (error rate = 0.4), Step5 (error rate = 0.6), Step7, Step8 and Step9 (error rate = 0.2). Except for Step8, participants using the HMDs instructions made mistakes in all the other operations. Error rate for Step2 and Step5 was as high as 0.8. Users supported by visual instructions on computer monitor made mistakes mainly at Step2 (error rate = 0.4) and Step4 (error rate = 0.2). Errors occurred to conversational system users at Step2 (error rate = 0.4), Step3 (error rate = 0.2) and Step8 (error rate = 0.2).

5.5   Cognitive Load

The participants using aural instructions had the least perceived cognitive load with an average score of 6.73 (SD = 2.92). HMD-users reported the highest perceived cognitive load with an average TLX score at 10.01 (SD = 0.98). Meanwhile, visual instructions on screen caused the perceived cognitive load with a score of 8.27 (SD = 3.83). Paper instructions got the average score of 9.6 (SD = 5.48). We also analyzed the perceived cognitive load on six dimensions with each instruction techniques (see Fig. 4).

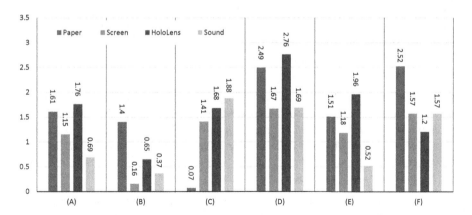

Fig. 4. Overview about the results of NASA-TLX. (A) Mental demand, (B) Physical demand, (C) Temporal demand, (D) Performance, (E) Effort, (F) Frustration.

Mental Demand. Conversational system prototype perceived the lowest mental demand score on average of 0.69. AR assistive system on HoloLens leaded to the highest mental demand of average score of 1.76, followed by paper instructions with average score of 1.61 and visual instruction on screen with average score of 1.15.

Physical Demand. The participants perceived the paper manual reported the highest physical demanding feedback with an average score of 1.4. Meanwhile, three other group's report on physical demanding was rather low.

Temporal Demand. Paper instructions leaded to the lowest temporal demand with an average score of 0.07. The other three instruction techniques were considered to a higher temporal demand.

Performance. Participants perceived their performance best using the HMDs with an average score of 2.76, followed by paper instructions with 2.49. Participants supporting by visual instruction on screen and aural instructions perceived their performance less successful with an average score of 1.67 and 1.69.

Effort. The participants perceived the lowest effort using conversational system prototype with an average score of 0.52. The group using HMDs perceived their effort the highest with an average score of 1.96.

Frustration. Surprisingly, participants using HMDs perceived least frustration with an average score of 1.2, followed by visual instruction on computer monitor and conversational system both with 1.67. Participants using paper manual perceived the highest frustration with an average score of 2.52.

5.6   Qualitative Results

Additionally, we observed the process participants interacted with the systems. Besides the quantitative results we also collected qualitative result from post interviews.

Paper Instructions. Participants who used paper manuals casually browsed through the instructions before the experiment. When they encountered with problems, they would look up the context thoroughly. Most of the participants thought that the paper manual was simple and easy to understand. *"I think this manual is better than most manuals I have ever used. For there's not much redundant information and the description is quite clear."*

Visual Instructions on Screen. Supported by visual instructions on screen, participants completed the task without much effort. The main complaint was about the motion graphic instructions. *"I didn't notice the text in the lower left corner. I was busy watching the dynamic image. Coffee tamper merged into the background, so I had some difficulties in recognize it. In addition, I hope the it could show me how much force I should use while tamping."*

Visual Instructions on HMDs. Most of the inconveniences HMDs users encountered were caused by the hardware. Due to the insensitivity of gesture recognition, participants needed to click multiple times to switch step. Furthermore, even though we had provided the function of dragging and dropping the video to a better viewing position, few participants adjusted the viewing distance. *"I was gazing at the video on HoloLens. Sometimes I lose the video instruction in my view."* *"I am short sighted. I think the line of contour better be thicker."*

Aural Instructions. Without any visual instructions, participants who was supported by sound focused on the items to be handled in the task. If they were familiar with the items mentioned in the instructions, they would operate while listening to supplementary description. Otherwise, they'd ask system to repeat. Participants found that it was interesting being instructed by a conversational virtual assistant. *"I think it would be better if the system was able to play some music for me while I was waiting for my coffee." "I'd like to know how to discern good coffee from bad. But she didn't replied."*

6 Discussion

6.1 Comparation Among Modalities

Paper Document. Participants are able to go back and forward freely through paper manual, which is natural but time consuming. Matching images and text explanations are shown on paper instructions at the same time, giving more information than the other three prototypes. As reading paper instructions is the most familiar way to absorb information of how to use a new machine, users perceived temporal demand turns out to be considerably low. For the same reason, people will get frustrated easily once failed to complete tasks.

HMDs. We suggest that the low performance of HMDs was mainly caused by the hardware, instead of the design of contour visual instructions. Although the error rate of HMDs users is the highest among the four prototypes, the TLX frustration score of which turns out to be the lowest, implying that users are willingly to explore this new device. In further study, we would introduce smartphones as another carrier and launch more comparing experiments.

Auditory vs. Visualization. Compared to visual instructions, results on aural instructions are better than expected. While user listening to aural instruction, they focus on comprehension without any distractions. We point out that appliances being used have significant influence on the users' cognition. In cases where the appliances are familiar to the users, it is easy for them to understand the intention of certain operation. It explains the result that during some steps, users using voice system performed better than those who was visually supported. In such situation, aural system shares visual perceived cognitive load. While in cases where the appliances are unfamiliar to the users (i.e. steel filter, filter holder, coffee tamper, etc.), aural system gave out worse performance than visual system. In such situation, visual system provides more effective guidance than aural system does.

6.2 Design Method for AR Tutorial

According to our study, we propose an ideal design method for multi-modal AR tutorial: (1) Define learning purpose and contents; (2) According to the contents and the design paradigm in Sect. 3.3, list steps of operations and instructions. Description of text and diagrams should be as simple and basic as possible; (3) Extract objects to be handled in each step and launch semantic tests upon these objects, to build users' mental modal; (4) Provide instruction from two aspects: On one hand, present the intention of each operation and the descriptive explanation of unfamiliar objects with voice. On the other hand, display spatial relationships between objects and tips for the operation with image. As for those complex operations, we recommend combining of visual and aural instructions.

7 Conclusion

In this paper, we explored the tutorial design method for AR assistive system applied to home appliances and evaluated different systems for providing instructions in domestic environment. We compared visual instructions on HMDs and screen to aural instructions and baseline paper instructions. Our result show that, well designed and displayed visual instructions provide helpful information. Aural instructions share visual perceived cognitive task load. Especially when users are familiar with the appliances, conversational assistive system is appropriate for building an eyes-free, hands-free and non-distractive external learning environment.

Although HMD-instructions have problems being perceived the highest cognitive loads and the longest procedure duration, with the improvement of image recognition accuracy and the acceleration of tracing speed, the results will be different. In future work, we want to investigate the effects on smartphone and portable devices by constructing multimodality assistive system, and explore users' response upon long instructions in both visual and aural modality.

References

1. Susanna, N., Björn, J.: Fun and usable: augmented reality instructions in a hospital setting. In: OzCHI 2007 Proceedings, pp. 123–130. ACM Press (2007)
2. Susanna, N., Björn, J.: Acceptance of augmented reality instructions in a real work setting. In: CHI 2008, Extended Abstracts, pp. 2025–2032. ACM Press (2008)
3. Naoya, M., TaRemote, K.: Instruction system using see-through augmented reality. In: Proceeding SA 2015, 2015 Posters (2015). Article No.31
4. Markus, F., Andreas, B.: Comparing projected in-situ feedback at the manual assembly workplace with impaired workers. In: PETRA 2015. ACM Press (2016). Article No.1
5. Yingxue, Z., Siqi, L.: ChinAR: facilitating Chinese Guqin learning through interactive projected augmentation. In: Chinese CHI 2015 Proceedings of the Third International Symposium of Chinese CHI, pp. 23–31 (2015)
6. Wendy, J., Rebecca, H.: CounterActive: an interactive cookbook for the kitchen counter. In: CHI 2001, Extended Abstracts, pp. 269–270. ACM Press (2001)
7. Ayaka, S., Keita, W.: MimiCook: a cooking assistant system with situated guidance. In: TEI 2014, pp. 121–124. ACM Press (2014)
8. Yu, S., Shunsuke, M.: Cooking support with information projection onto ingredient. In: APCHI 2012, pp. 193–198. ACM Press (2012)
9. Sebastian, B., Markus, F.: Using head-mounted displays and in-situ projection for assistive systems – a comparison. In: PETRA 2016 (2016). Article No.44

10. Markus, F., Tomas, K.: Interactive worker assistance: comparing the effects of in-situ projection, head-mounted displays, tablet, and paper instructions. In: Ubicomp 2016, pp. 934–939. ACM Press (2016)
11. Marina, C., Stephan, L.: Workspace awareness in collaborative AR using HMDs: a user study comparing audio and visual notifications. In: AH 2016. ACM Press (2016). Article No.3
12. Youngsun, K., Seokjun, H.: Augmented reality based remote coaching system. In: VRST 2016, pp. 311–312. ACM Press (2016)
13. Nielsen, J., Molich, R.: Heuristic evaluation of user interface. In: Proceedings of ACM CHI 1990 Conference on Human Factors in Computing System, pp. 249–256. ACM Press, New York (1990)
14. Nielsen, J.: Usability inspection method. In: Conference Companion on Human Factors in Computing System, vol. 25, no. 1, pp. 377–378 (1995)
15. De'Longhi Homepage. https://www.delonghi.com/zh-cn/. Accessed 24 Feb 2014
16. Jianming, D., Limin, F.: Human Computer Interaction, 5th edn. Tsinghua University Press, Beijing (2016)
17. Tom, T., Bill, A.: Measuring the User Experience, 2nd edn. Elsevier, Singapore (2016)
18. National Aeronautics and Space Administration. NASA-TLX Work Load Index. https://humansystems.arc.nasa.gov/groups/tlx/. Accessed 27 Apr 2018

KnobCollector: Custom Device Controller for Dynamic Real-Time Subjective Data Collection in Virtual Reality

Rajiv Khadka[1] and Amy Banic[2(✉)]

[1] University of Wyoming, Laramie, WY, USA
rkhadka@uwyo.edu
[2] Idaho National Laboratory, Idaho Falls, ID, USA
abanic@cs.uwyo.edu

Abstract. Real-time data collection in immersive virtual reality can be difficult due to the visual obstruction to the real-world. Furthermore, subjective data collection is conducted post-task, reducing the information of detailed user responses during a task therefore potentially missing critical events, subtle difference, or issues not obvious to a user. In this paper we present, KnobCollector, a custom device controller for dynamic real-time collection of subjective user data during an experimental. We conducted a user study with the KnobCollector to demonstrate the feasibility of use during a virtual reality task. Our results provide more rich data sets of user feedback during the virtual reality experience and could be used for future user studies in virtual reality environments.

Keywords: Real-time data collection · Immersion · Virtual reality · Device controller · Arduino prototyping · Virtual reality · User study · Evaluation

1 Introduction

Quantitative and qualitative data collection utilizing questionnaires (whether standard or specialized) during user studies for in virtual environments are conducted post-task via electronic or paper-based mediums. While this produces viable data, it lacks specificity of time and actions, rather serves more as a post-reflection. This type of data collection may miss subtitle responses on more specific actions or reactions that are less obvious to or missed by a user in real-time during their task. Particularly in a virtual environment, this becomes more difficult due to the immersive display, closing off the user from the real world. In this paper, we present the use of a custom input device controller for dynamic real-time data collection of questionnaires or other subjective inquiry for use during tasks in virtual reality using head-mounted displays. While automatic logging of user data in a virtual environment is standard practice, there is little work done to provide users with real-time input responses outside of an experimental task [1, 3, 5]. Other experiments have utilized a button on an input controller to identify a response [2], but these actions have to be done as a separate component (not in real-time during the task) and may take too long to control visual widgets.

J. Y. C. Chen and G. Fragomeni (Eds.): HCII 2019, LNCS 11574, pp. 84–95, 2019.
https://doi.org/10.1007/978-3-030-21607-8_7

Fig. 1. KnobCollector, a custom input device for real-time subjective data collection from a user.

We conducted a user study utilizing our technique and present the results of the feasibility evaluation of the data collection activity. We used two types of subjective questionnaires, a specialized questionnaire to gather a wide-range of valued responses and a 7-point standard presence questionnaire- the Witmer-Singer presence questionnaire [4]. Our findings present that is not only feasible to utilize such a device for data collection during a task in virtual reality, but that the data collected demonstrates a much more rich and detailed perspective on the feedback from users in real-time. Our results have the potential to improve subjective user data collection for user studies conducted using immersive virtual reality. This paper is organized as follows. Section 2 describes the related work and background of our work. Section 3 describes the description of our custom device controller i.e., KnobCollector. Section 4 presents our experimental study and Sect. 5 describes results of our study and Sect. 6 presents our conclusion and future work.

2 Background and Related Work

Technological advancement has introduced different methods for how quantitative and qualitative data of an experiment is collected and analyzed. In general questionnaires, observations, and interviews using a paper or an electronic medium are typically used to collect subjective data of a user experiment. This method of collecting subjective data usually fine, but in the context of virtual reality or when using immersive systems, a user must exit a virtual environment or take off an immersive system to provide the answers which might affect the response provided [6]. Researchers have designed tools and techniques for data collection while a user is within a virtual environment to maintain the level of immersion.

2.1 Button and Controllers

Researchers [7] investigated the effects of feedback delay on the qualitative subjective experience of virtual reality. They used the thumbstick on the left Oculus Touch controller [8] for scaling task as an input for data collection for scaling task. This method supported a user to provide subjective feedback of the experiment while the user is experiencing the virtual environment. This method requires the participant to train to which button in the controllers to be used, however our technique provides a dial controller where the data input is mapped more intuitively to rotate each direction to increase or decrease variable data on a scale. Furthermore, researchers [2] presented the use of a button on an input controller to provide the input for data collection. However, this use of the button to provide must be done separately and not in the real-time during the task which might affect the response of the participant.

2.2   Smartphone

Tsaramirsis et al. [9] presented navigating in virtual environments using smartphone sensors. The data collected from the smartphone sensors along with the machine learning technique is used to help the user to navigate in the virtual environments. This method only takes sensor as the data but cannot be used for the collection of the data for subjective response in real-time. Furthermore, Laaki et al. [10] showed a situation where data collected from the smartphone device is used to augment the virtual world along with the real-life data. This method of collection is different from our research work as our KnobCollector is used to provide data to the subjective questionnaire in the real-time.

2.3   Virtual Avatar

Hasler et al. [11] used a human-controlled avatar to interview the participants within the virtual world, Second Life [12], about their religion. This use of an avatar for interviewing the participants allowed the user to be within the virtual world and provide the answers to the questions. Furthermore, this provided a way for face-to-face communication, but our work is more directed towards providing input for data collection individually using a tool and is flexible move and to integrate with different immersive virtual environment.

2.4   Virtual Interface

Bell et al. [13] designed and developed a virtual data collection interface (VDCI) which used a virtual assisted self-interview (VASI) method in Second Life [12] to collect subjective data while a user is in the virtual world. This tool allowed to survey within the virtual world for collecting data while being immersed in it. Faleiros et al. [14] designed virtual questionnaire for a virtual platform to collect data of Germans diagnosed with Spina Bifida (SB). The virtual questionnaire consists of 57 questions, and it was a Likert Scale question. While these will enable real-time data collection in a virtual world, typically online virtual environments are not experienced using an immersive system so that a user can utilize standard input devices and see the virtual world as well as the devices. Our technique helps a user collect data while fully immersed in a virtual environment and cannot see the device in the real world.

3   Custom Device Controller – KnobCollector

We present our novel device, KnobCollector (see Fig. 1), that can be used to collect
subjective quantitative data in real-time while a user is experiencing a virtual environment using an immersive virtual system. To prototype the controller (see Fig. 1), we
implemented an Arduino UNO board [15], used a dial for collecting variable data, and
a laser-cut 3D printed a case for more ergonomic angle placement of the device. This
device can be used on the table (as used in this experiment) but also attached to the
body. In either case, it allows for comfortable and easy control of the device while
using a head-mounted display. This device controller is lightweight and can also be
held in a user's hand while interacting in CAVE [16], IQStation [17], HMD, or another
different immersive virtual environment while experimenting. It was important that the
user could 'feel' the knob and comfortably turn the knob left and right so as not to take
away from the virtual reality experience. As such the knob has ridges to grasp and feel
the knob better. This device currently uses a USB cable to connect and transfer the data
to the computer, however, in future we plan to add a feature for wireless connection
with the computer. The custom device controller knob was calibrated to provide a
custom range of input (calibrated by a user). We customized each rang for the standardized questionnaires that we used in this experiment: from 1 to 5 for a customized
System Usability Scale (SUS) [18] questionnaire and from 1 to 7 for the standard
Witmer-Singer Presence questionnaire [4].

Fig. 2. Virtual slider movement corresponds to a user's input change of the device controller.

4   Experimental Study

Each participant was presented with the experimental study environment and was asked
to complete the task in a virtual environment. The participant used our KnobCollector
device after each trail while they were in the virtual environment to provide their
responses as input to the SUS and Witmer-Singer questionnaire in real-time during the
experience.

4.1   Experimental Environment and Apparatus

We used the Unity3D game [19] development platform (version 5.4.0) and C# programming language to develop the experimental user study. An Arduino UNO board
[15] was used to create the custom device controller which connects to the dial for

collecting input data. A package, Ardity [22] was used to move the data from the Arduino board to Unity, bidirectionally, over a COM port. A USB cable was used to connect to the computer for transferring the data collected while rotating the dial during the experimental study. The virtual slider that is shown in the experimental environment is developed in the Unity3D which corresponds to the rotation of the dial.

4.2   Participants

We recruited participants by sending out information using emails, flyers and mouth-to-mouth information. All the participants recruited were from of the University of Wyoming. We had a total of 20 participants which included 12 females and 8 males. The participants age ranges from 19–51 years ($\mu = 25.55$, $\sigma = 8.28$)). Each participant was screened for proper 3D-vision using Butterfly Stereoscopic Test [20]. To compensate for the time, each participant was paid $5 and was entered for raffle of a $50 gift card.

4.3   Procedures

This experimental study was approved by the University of Wyoming Institutional Review Board. Each participant signed the consent form, and they were presented with the Butterfly Stereoscopic Test for proper 3D-vision. After the completion of 3D-vision test, participants completed an online pre-questionnaire (in the real-world). During the experiment, participants completed experimental task by which they each experienced a virtual environment and then provided input of their responses to each prompt during the experience using our KnobController device. After the experimental study was completed, each participant completed a post-questionnaire. The total time for the experimental study was approximately 1 h.

Fig. 3. A mock participant interacting with the experimental user study environment. The participant wears an HTC Vive to view the virtual environment and her left hand is rotating the dial to provide the input for the data collection during the experiment.

For the experimental task, participants were seated at a table with our KnobCollector device in front of them. Participants were exposed to a virtual reality environment and asked to do complete task to explore objects in the virtual reality environment. Participants were presented with the virtual environment using an HMD (HTC Vive [21]). To avoid distraction for the participants, we masked the sound of our moving apparatus by providing headphones and playing background elevator music. After each trial, the data was collected in the experimental environment with the use of the KnobCollector (combined with virtual sliders for visual feedback). The ratings were input to the experimental study environment by using the custom device controller - KnobCollector (see Fig. 1). The participants turned the dial left to select a lower value and turned it right for a higher value. As the participants turned the dial, the experimental user environment provided feedback about their current selection by showing a moving slider (see Fig. 2). Figure 3 shows a mock participant using the described setup.

5   Results and Discussion

Each participant provided their responses as input using our KnobCollector device. The participant positioned the visual slider by using a dial provided in the KnobCollector. During the experimental task the values collected could vary between 0 and 100 but participants could not see the values only the point at which the slider was on the virtual widget (Fig. 2) in the HMD. The values were then converted based on the calibrated scale for each type of questionnaire used or rating for data input. Ratings were collected during their experience and after. Without use of the KnobCollector we might only obtain a final rating for each participant, or at the very least a final rating after each trial, resulting in a summary of ratings across the trials as in Fig. 4. With data collection using KnobCollector we can gain so much more. Feasibility is demonstrated for collecting a rich amount of data over time that can show critical incidents as in Fig. 5. Additionally, as seen in Fig. 6, there is a wide variability and richness of data collected over time in the ratings for each trial.

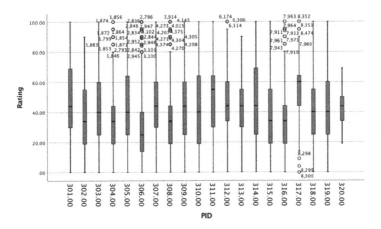

Fig. 4. User ratings after each trial, collected after a user's experience.

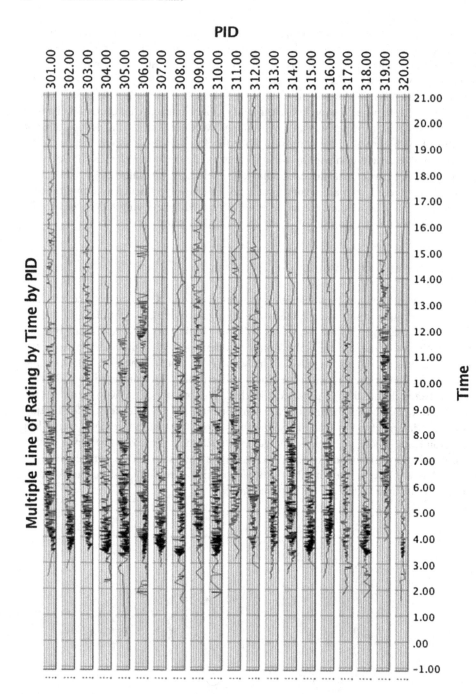

Fig. 5. User ratings over time showing critical incidents using KnobCollector during an Immersive Virtual Environment experience.

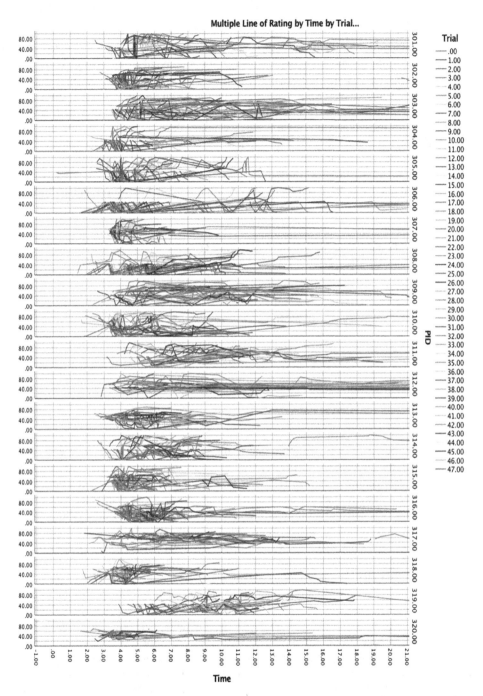

Fig. 6. User ratings over time colored by trials using KnobCollector during an Immersive Virtual Environment experience.

5.1 Witmer-Singer Presence Questionnaire

Using the standardized Witmer-Singer Presence Questionnaire, we collected the impressions of the participants while interacting and conducting the task of the experimental user study in the virtual environment. The results are listed in Table 1. These results suggest our KnobCollector using the dial did not detract from the experience of the participants, as it did not distract them from the tasks they performed; and even, from their post-study comments, we found they enjoyed using the dial for providing the input for the data collection. Questions prefixed with an asterisk are expected to have a mean close to 3 as they do not have clear applicability to our study. The highest ranked questions of the questionnaire are listed in Table 2. Conversely, the lowest ranked questions are listed in Table 3. Furthermore, below we present additional questionnaire used for the Witmer-Singer Presence questionnaire.

Table 1. Results of the Witmer-Singer Presence Questionnaire, ratings from 1 to 7.

Criteria	Mean score
Realism	5.01
Possibility to act	5.23
Quality of interface	4.62
Possibility to examine	5.53
Auto-evaluation of performance	6.11
Sounds	4.92
Haptics	5.03
Total	5.19

In our comparison, we found similar results on the sense of presence and user perception of the objects in virtual reality. Through this data, we can validate the feasibility of the technique can be used instead of or in combination with the post-task data collection. Furthermore, our paper will present the detailed results that with more rich data collection and in real-time while a user is fully immersed in a virtual environment, we were about to derive more detailed differences in presences and user response based on time. Small periods during the experience revealed interesting results in relation to user response time, user interpretation of the virtual reality environment, and user initial reactions versus reactions based on exposure over time. Our results may have implications on how designers and developers design virtual reality environments as well as a practical and useful tool for researchers conducting user experiments in virtual reality who desire more detailed data collection and critical events based on time. Furthermore, we believe KnobCollector can be used as an tool for data collection for experiences in immersive virtual environments. One idea is that the level of presence will change while a user is experiencing the virtual environment as opposed to completing the questionnaire after the experiment as he/she has completed their experiences of the virtual environment. KnobCollector will provide an effective medium to complete the pre/post-experiment data collection without having an effect of any external real-world factors (Table 4).

Table 2. Highest ranked questions of the Witmer-Singer Presence Questionnaire.

Question	Mean score	Standard deviation
How well could you concentrate on the assigned tasks or required activities rather than on the mechanisms used to perform those tasks or activities?	6.45	0.69
How quickly did you adjust to the VE experience?	6.21	1.32
How proficient in moving and interacting with the virtual environment did you feel at the end of the experience?	6.00	0.88

Table 3. Lowest ranked questions of the Witmer-Singer Presence Questionnaire.

Question	Mean score	Standard deviation
How much did the auditory aspects of the environment involve you?	3.89	2.14
How natural was the mechanism which controlled movement through the environment?	3.94	1.76
(*) How much were you able to control events?	4.25	1.60

Table 4. Additional Witmer-Singer Presence Questionnaire used for experimental user study.

Question	Mean Score	Standard deviation
How natural did your interactions with the environment seem?	4.90	1.17
How compelling was your sense of objects moving in space?	5.16	1.34
How much did your experiences in the virtual environment seem consistent with your real-world experiences?	4.53	1.12
How involved were you in the VE experience?	5.55	1.47
How responsive was the environment to actions that you initiated (or performed)?	5.39	1.69
How much delay did you experience between your actions and expected outcomes?	4.72	1.23
How much did the visual display quality interfere or distract you from performing assigned tasks or required activities?	4.50	1.76
How much did the control devices interfere with the performance of assigned tasks or with other activities?	4.63	1.67
How well could you actively survey or search the virtual environment using touch?	5.60	0.88

6   Conclusion and Future Work

We presented our custom device controller, i.e., KnobCollector, for dynamic real-time collection of subjective user data during experiences or experimental studies in real-time while in an immersive virtual environment. The KnobCollector provides rich data during an immersive virtual reality experience that can help identify critical incidents as in Fig. 5 and further breakdown of data by trials or other conditions as in Fig. 6. KnobCollector provides a practical tool for researcher and scientist while conducting a user experiment in the virtual reality to collect subjective data who desire to have their data collected while the participant is within the virtual environment. The tool has been easily mapped physically to the directionality of standardized questionnaires that can be presented virtually in the virtual environment. The results presented are promising in terms of providing confirmation of feasibility that this device can be used to provide a richer set of data. The results are exciting as the participants found the dial in KnobCollector used for collecting the input data during the experiment did not distract them from the immersive experience while doing the task. Furthermore, from the post-study feedback, we found that participants enjoyed using the KnobCollector to provide their subjective rating responses for each questionnaire during the task.

In future work, we also plan to conduct a user study to compare KnobCollector with different other methods of subjective data collection. Furthermore, we will work on developing the KnobCollector so, that it supports wireless connectivity which will help provide a user with flexibility to move around in a larger immersive virtual environment while interacting with the task.

Acknowledgement. We want to thank Daniel Wilches for developing the apparatus and data collection, who further developed Ardity [22]. We also want to thank our participants for their time to participate in the experiment.

References

1. Aggarwal, R., Ward, J., Balasundaram, I., Sains, P., Athanasiou, T., Darzi, A.: Proving the effectiveness of virtual reality simulation for training in laparoscopic surgery. Ann. Surg. **246**(5), 771–779 (2007)
2. Fox, J., Arena, D., Bailenson, J.N.: Virtual reality: a survival guide for the social scientist. J. Media Psychol. **21**(3), 95–113 (2009)
3. Lin, J.W., Duh, H.B.L., Parker, D.E., Abi-Rached, H., Furness, T.A.: Effects of field of view on presence, enjoyment, memory, and simulator sickness in a virtual environment. In: Virtual Reality, Proceedings, pp. 164–171. IEEE (2002)
4. Witmer, B.G., Singer, M.J.: Measuring presence in virtual environments: a presence questionnaire. Presence **7**(3), 225–240 (1998)
5. Yee, N., Bailenson, J.N., Urbanek, M., Chang, F., Merget, D.: The unbearable likeness of being digital: the persistence of nonverbal social norms in online virtual environments. CyberPsychology Behav. **10**(1), 115–121 (2007)
6. Bowman, D.A., Gabbard, J.L., Hix, D.: A survey of usability evaluation in virtual environments: classification and comparison of methods. Presence Teleoperators Virtual Environ. **11**(4), 404–424 (2002)

7. Van Dam, L.C., Stephens, J.R.: Effects of prolonged exposure to feedback delay on the qualitative subjective experience of virtual reality. PLoS ONE **13**(10), e0205145 (2018)
8. Facebook Technologies: Oculus Touch, 10 February 2019. https://www.oculus.com/rift/accessories/
9. Tsaramirsis, G., Buhari, S.M., Basheri, M., Stojmenovic, M.: Navigating virtual environments using leg poses and smartphone sensors. Sensors **19**(2), 299 (2019)
10. Laaki, H., Kaurila, K., Ots, K., Nuckchady, V., Belimpasakis, P.: Augmenting virtual worlds with real-life data from mobile devices. In: 2010 IEEE Virtual Reality Conference (VR), pp. 281–282. IEEE, March 2010
11. Hasler, B.S., Tuchman, P., Friedman, D.: Virtual research assistants: Replacing human interviewers by automated avatars in virtual worlds. Comput. Hum. Behav. **29**(4), 1608–1616 (2013)
12. Rymaszewski, M., Au, W.J., Wallace, M., Winters, C., Ondrejka, C., Batstone-Cunningham, B.: Second Life: The Official Guide. Wiley, Hoboken (2007)
13. Bell, M.W., Castronova, E., Wagner, G.G.: Surveying the virtual world: a large scale survey in Second Life using the Virtual Data Collection Interface (VDCI). Available at SSRN 1418562 (2009)
14. Faleiros, F., Käppler, C., Pontes, F.A.R., Silva, S.S.D.C., Goes, F.D.S.N.D., Cucick, C.D.: Use of virtual questionnaire and dissemination as a data collection strategy in scientific studies. Texto Contexto-Enfermagem, **25**(4) (2016)
15. D'Ausilio, A.: Arduino: a low-cost multipurpose lab equipment. Behav. Res. Methods **44**(2), 305–313 (2012)
16. Cruz-Neira, C., Sandin, D.J., DeFanti, T.A., Kenyon, R.V., Hart, J.C.: The CAVE: audio visual experience automatic virtual environment. Commun. ACM **35**(6), 64–73 (1992)
17. Sherman, W.R., O'Leary, P., Whiting, E.T., Grover, S., Wernert, E.A.: IQ-Station: a low cost portable immersive environment. In: Bebis, G., et al. (eds.) ISVC 2010. LNCS, vol. 6454, pp. 361–372. Springer, Heidelberg (2010). https://doi.org/10.1007/978-3-642-17274-8_36
18. Brooke, J.: SUS-A quick and dirty usability scale. Usability Eval. Ind. **189**(194), 4–7 (1996)
19. Creighton, R.H.: Unity 3D Game Development by Example: A Seat-of-Your-Pants Manual for Building Fun, Groovy Little Games Quickly. Packt Publishing Ltd. (2010)
20. Moll, A.M., Rao, R.C., Rotberg, L.B., Roarty, J.D., Bohra, L.I., Baker, J.D.: The role of the random dot Stereo Butterfly test as an adjunct test for the detection of constant strabismus in vision screening. J. Am. Assoc. Pediatr. Ophthalmol. Strabismus **13**(4), 354–356 (2009)
21. HTC Vive: HTC Vive, 10 February 2019. https://www.vive.com/us/
22. Ardity: Ardity 10 February 2019. https://ardity.dwilches.com/

CHARM: Cord-Based Haptic Augmented Reality Manipulation

Konstantin Klamka$^{(\boxtimes)}$, Patrick Reipschläger, and Raimund Dachselt

Interactive Media Lab Dresden, Technische Universität Dresden,
Nöthnitzer Str. 46, 01187 Dresden, Germany
{konstantin.klamka,patrick.reipschlaeger,raimund.dachselt}@tu-dresden.de

Fig. 1. Our *CHARM* system is a combination of a versatile retractable input device for radial AR menus (**A**) and 3D object manipulation (**B**), that is fully implemented for state-of-the-art AR glasses. The smart handle (**C**) provides additional controls.

Abstract. The recent trend of emerging high-quality Augmented Reality (AR) glasses offered the possibility for visually exciting application scenarios. However, the interaction with these devices is often challenging since current input methods most of the time lack haptic feedback and are limited in their user interface controls. With this work, we introduce *CHARM*, a combination of a belt-worn interaction device, utilizing a retractable cord, and a set of interaction techniques to enhance AR input capabilities with physical controls and spatial constraints. Building on our previous research, we created a fully-functional prototype to investigate how body-worn string devices can be used to support generic AR tasks. We contribute a radial widget menu for system control as well as transformation techniques for 3D object manipulation. To validate our interaction concepts for system control, we implemented a mid-air gesture interface as a baseline and evaluated our prototype in two formative user studies. Our results show that our approach provides flexibility regarding possible interaction mappings and was preferred for manipulation tasks compared to mid-air gesture input.

Keywords: Augmented reality · Haptic feedback · Elastic input ·
Cord input · Radial menu · 3D interaction · 3D transformation ·
Wearable computing

© Springer Nature Switzerland AG 2019
J. Y. C. Chen and G. Fragomeni (Eds.): HCII 2019, LNCS 11574, pp. 96–114, 2019.
https://doi.org/10.1007/978-3-030-21607-8_8

1   Introduction

The dissemination of high-quality head-mounted displays with augmented reality (AR) capabilities (e.g., Microsoft HoloLens) served as the foundation for the development of new AR applications in various fields. However, while the opportunities are clearly inspiring, well-known problems in interacting with these AR applications still prevail. Those issues are, e.g., interface limitations [1] and missing tactile feedback of physical surfaces [12] and references (e.g., a desk or display). This often makes it difficult and physically demanding to select or manipulate virtual objects using hand gestures. Current system control solutions often lack the support of even simple control tasks. To address the lack of haptics in AR and VR, several approaches have been proposed. Emerging technologies, including smart textiles (e.g., [8,21]), tiny wearable devices (e.g., [25]) or specialized AR devices (e.g., [9]) have been introduced for head-mounted displays and provide different forms of tactile feedback. In addition, *string-based systems* in stationary and cave-like environments connect fingers, wrists, tangible grips or even the hole body with retractable strings in a fixed interaction frame to enable force or torque feedback. However, the problem remains that these approaches often do not fulfill important needs of personal AR interaction such as mobility, eyes-free interaction, and tactile controls.

In our work, we aim to provide an unintrusive mobile controller that enables an easy and sensory-rich on-demand access to AR system control and 3D transformation tasks. In particular, we want to support interaction with AR applications by providing a frame of spatial reference. Therefore, we present *CHARM*, *C*ord-based *H*aptic *A*ugmented *R*eality *M*anipulation[1]. We see high potential in using retractable body-worn string controllers, building on mechanical wind-up mechanisms that are able to change the string length through pulling and thereby provide continuous haptic feedback. Thus, we build on our previous work Elasticcon [14], investigating its application to AR scenarios. As system control is an important aspect of AR applications, we devised an AR menu and widgets controlled by our *CHARM* device that allow to change states, modes or values. In addition, we also support *object manipulation*, which is central to most AR applications [4], by providing interaction techniques for 3D transformation. The contribution of our work is composed as follows:

- **An elastic input device** consisting of a belt-worn retractable multi Degree-of-Freedom (DoF) handle which provides a rich,cone-shaped interaction space and can be natively connected to the HoloLens.
- **A menu and interaction solution** that provides a flexible, radial widget for AR system control tasks and is controlled by our *CHARM* device.
- **Interaction techniques** for **3D object manipulation** including translation, rotation and uniform scaling of 3D content in AR environments.
- **A fully-functional software prototype** implementation of our menu and 3D transformation techniques for the Microsoft HoloLens.

---

[1] See our project website for additional information: http://www.imld.de/charm.

– **A formative, qualitative user study** investigating our menu solution regarding different interaction mapping schemes and comparing it to a baseline mid-air gesture interface.

The paper is structured along these contributions: First, we summarize and discuss previous work and thereby position our own approach. Then, we introduce the concept and realization of our mobile elastic controller for AR interaction. As a next step, we present our radial widget control concept and report about its formative evaluation. Finally, we propose a 3D transformation concept for object manipulation and conclude with a discussion and future work.

2   Background and Related Work

The related work for our approach is twofold, and we structured it into the two sections: *Interactive Controls and Menus in AR Environments* as well as *Body-worn Cord Controllers*.

2.1   Interactive Controls and Menus in AR Environments

A vast variety of interaction techniques was developed in the field of VR and AR (see [4] for an overview, [6] for menus in particular). For example, *hands-& glove-based* approaches have been used to attach menus to the user's hand and link items or interactions to different fingers [3,19]. Tinmith-Gloves [19] can be used to browse a display-referenced top menu and specify 3D input based on contacting fingers gestures. In contrast, TULIP [3] was designed to access three menu items at a time while using the fourth finger to switch to a new set. In addition, *mid-air interactions* focus on floating gestures in front of the user. For instance, Microsoft's HoloLens combines air tap gestures with a gaze cursor to confirm selections. Furthermore, *physical handheld surfaces* have been investigated to provide graspable 2D interaction surfaces that enable a familiar frame of reference for 3D interaction menus and tasks [5,13,23,26]. Szalavári introduced a two-handed Personal Interaction Panel [23] which enables pen interaction on a handheld tablet transferring the pen-and-tablet paradigm to AR menus. Further, Shake Menus [26], a menu displayed around a tracked cardboard, applies the metaphor of shaking a wrapped gift to explores menu options and thereby focus on more tangible interactions. Hyeongmook et al. [13] used a mobile phone as an interactive surface panel. *Physical controllers* provide advanced capabilities [10,17]. Gebhardt et al. [10] investigate pick ray, hand projection and hand rotation interaction techniques for extended pie menus with commercial fly sticks. Instead of pointing, Lee and Woo [17] developed a tangible spin cube for a 3D ring menu in space. In addition, the Cubic Mouse [9] and YoYo Device [22] are VR interaction devices that enable seamless 3D navigation and the application of cutting planes.

These solutions do not meet all requirements for an unobtrusive mobile AR controller as they are either not eyes-free, provide little to no tactile feedback or require large setups. In order to overcome these limitations and to provide an always-available system, we specifically focus on the promising class of body-worn retractable string controllers that have elastic and haptic properties.

2.2   Body-Worn Cord Controllers

A number of wearable and retractable cord controllers have been proposed in the literature. Some controllers build on mechanical wind-up mechanisms that are able to change the string length through pulling and thereby provide continuous haptic feedback [2,14,16,20,24]. Furthermore, cord controllers have been proposed for different positions of the body and accessories including the chest [16], wrist [2], finger [24] and belt [14,20] as well as at head-phone cables [18,21] and hoodies [15,18,21]. In addition, several degrees of freedom including the strings' traction, deflection, manipulation, and additional knobs as well as displays at the strings' end have been proposed for carrying out simple selection and navigation tasks. For example, Blasko et al. [2] presented a small wrist-worn dual-display that uses the string's length and angular deflection to provide access to a set of angular cells, while Koch and Witt [16] control a basic $3 \times 3 \times 3$ selection grid capturing the position of a chest-worn string in a cone-shaped interaction space. Pohl et al. [20] combined a retractable belt-worn system with a display badge to support indoor navigation. Furthermore, Schwarz et al. [21] propose an touch-enabled hoodie zipper, called CordInput. ARCord [15] extends the interactive hoodie cords with holographic visual overlays, while I/O Braid [18] enables visual feedback based on weaved optical fibers.

In our previous work Elasticcon [14], we introduced a design space for body-worn retractable controllers and proposed a generic belt-worn string controller with a set of exchangeable traction knobs focusing on mappings for essential interaction tasks. Although we previously already argued that body-worn retractable string controllers have a promising potential for wearable AR glasses, we conducted no detailed investigation of this scenario. In this work, we propose using a body-worn retractable string controller for *mobile AR system control and direct 3D manipulation*, which we will describe in more detail in the next sections.

3   The CHARM Input Device

First, we want to introduce our wearable *CHARM* input device (see Fig. 2) that we developed to address the lack of haptics in AR interaction by providing physical constraints. Based on our prior work Elasticcon [14], our system consists of a string-based control handle that can be smoothly pulled away from the body (see Fig. 2A) or deflected in mid-air (Fig. 2B) and thereby enables several body-relative degrees of freedom (DoF). In addition, a tangible handle (Fig. 2C) at the end of the string provides a thumb-joystick, three push- and one trigger-button, and vibro-tactile feedback. All DoFs work in synergy and create a cone-shaped interaction space (Fig. 2D).

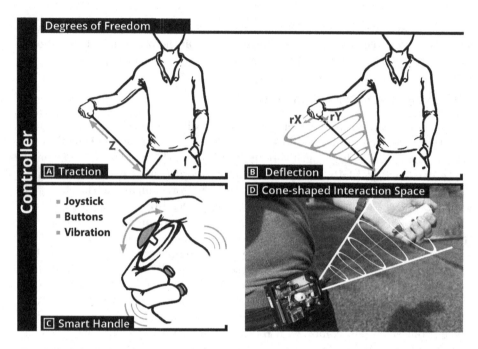

Fig. 2. Our *CHARM* controller integrates several DoF (**A–C**) including the dimensions of traction (**A**), deflection (**B**) and a multi-DoF handle control (**C**) that creates a rich cone-shaped interaction space (**D**).

3.1   Belt-Worn *CHARM* Controller

To detect the traction length (Z) and radial deflection (rX, rY) of the cord, our system needed the integration of a retractable winding and deflection mechanism as well as related sensing, processing, power and transmission components. The retractable winding mechanism (see Fig. 3A) was taken from a disassembled GameTrak[2] controller. A worm drive translates the axis of the spring-loaded spool to a potentiometer measuring the current traction length. The deflection of the corresponding pulling direction is tracked by a two-axis joint from a regular thumb-joystick using linear potentiometers. Our main logic board primarily consists of a Semiconductor nRF51822 micro-controller with built-in Bluetooth Low Energy (BLE) capabilities. We used custom BLE peripherals and implemented three sensor characteristics (traction: Z and deflection: rX, rY) based on the Generic Attribute Profile (GATT) to provide versatile wireless connectivity. In contrast to prior research, this allows us to *natively connect* our prototype to the HoloLens without other computers or mobile phones as intermediate devices. A power switch and LED were integrated in the 3D-printed casing. Small mounting rigs make it easy to clip the prototype to the belt for either right- or left-handed use. The device is powered by a 3.7 V lipo battery with 900 mAh and can be charged via an external Micro-USB connector.

---

[2] See http://en.wikipedia.org/wiki/Gametrak.

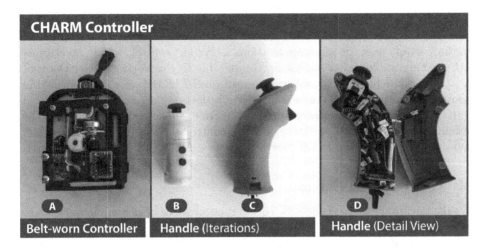

Fig. 3. Hardware prototype of our *CHARM*-Controller (**A**), showing the first (**B**) and second, ergonomic (**C**) iteration of our handle, as well as the hardware inside (**D**).

3.2 *CHARM* Handle

The *CHARM* handle went through several iterations. While at first we focused on a small and unobtrusive design (see Fig. 3B), the studies we conducted have shown that users prefer a more ergonomic handle. We addressed this issue with a refined version of the handle (see Fig. 3C). The final device uses a nRF51822 micro-controller, that handles the input of a two-axis thumb-joystick with a center button, a frontal trigger-button, two tactile push-buttons positioned left and right of the trigger, and also provides pulse-width modulated vibro-tactile feedback. The case of the *CHARM* handle consists of a custom designed, 3D-printed left and right part that hold the electronics and are held together by screws, which enables an easy access to the hardware (see Fig. 3D). All sensor values are represented in GATT characteristics and can be – depending on their type – subscribed or written via BLE.

3.3 Software Prototype

We implemented our *CHARM* Prototype for the Microsoft HoloLens[3] (as a representative of state-of-the-art AR glasses) using the Unity 3D game engine. To achieve our goal of a generic menu solution, we also designed on our software architecture to provide high flexibility and extensibility, using a modular structure and completely encapsulated the interaction functionality to offer easy support for different interaction modalities. The composition of our menus is defined by an accompanying XML-description. For 3D transformation we implemented a separate *CHARM* controlled and gesture controlled transformation widget, which can be attached to arbitrary objects and can be easily integrated into existing applications.

---

[3] See https://www.microsoft.com/en-us/hololens.

4   Our CHARM Menu-Design

One important task for most applications is system control, which we address
with a configurable radial AR menu, comparable to the works of, e.g., Davis et
al. [7]. Therefore one of our goals was to use our *CHARM* device (as described in
the previous chapter) for controlling generic widgets, that can be easily adapted
to the requirements of arbitrary applications. In the following, we introduce the
design of our AR menu and describe the control scheme using our *CHARM*
device and how its several DoFs are utilized (see Fig. 4A+B).

4.1   General Menu Design

To take advantage of the cone-shaped interaction space of our input-device (see
Fig. 2D), we decided to use a planar, hierarchical radial menu. The menu can
either be situated at a specific real world position for controlling aspects of real
or virtual objects, or in case of general menus, be situated in front of the user,
following her. Since the menu is planar, it always faces the user to prevent any
visibility issues. The segments of the menu are always distributed equally to form
a full circle (see Fig. 4A). Although our menu basically supports any number of
items, we have limited the maximum number of items in our prototype to eight
in order to ensure good visibility and interaction with each individual menu
item. The menu is hierarchical, so that a menu item can activate a sub menu
with different items, thus enabling menus of arbitrary depth and complexity (see
Fig. 4A). An additional element in the menus center displays the current menu
level and also acts as a trigger to return to the previous level.

4.2   Design of Menu Sections and Widget Controls

Since our goal is to provide a generic menu solution, we integrated common control widgets that are devised based on established graphical user interfaces. Each
menu segment consists of a description label, an icon, and widget-specific elements like, e.g., the selected element of a list (e.g., see Fig. 4C). In the following,
we describe each of the individual widget types:

Buttons are probably the most basic, but also most important type of widget for
any menu. In our solution they can activate a specific action, like switching to a
sub-menu or trigger an application-specific function (see Fig. 4A). Additionally,
we also provide toggle buttons that can be switched either on or off and are
therefore suitable for controlling boolean operations within an application, like
showing or hiding specific objects (Fig. 4B).

Sliders can be used to adjust a value within a specific range. Our slider can
be configured to handle continuous values, as well as discrete ones. The allowed
minimum and maximum values are configurable as well, and a suffix can be
defined to allow for the representation of specific units. Sliders show their current
value directly in the menu segment when inactive (see Figs. 1B and Fig. 4C).
When a slider is activated, a scale is shown above or beside the menu segment,

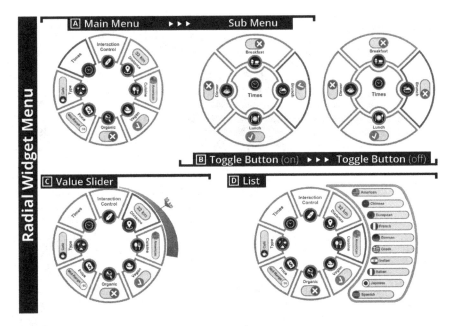

Fig. 4. Our radial AR menu consists of hierarchical sub-menus (**A**) and widget controls including toggle buttons (**B**), sliders (**C**) and lists (**D**).

which is rotated so that the original value is centered at the middle of the menu segment. This makes it easy for a user to determine if the selected value is higher or lower than the original one. During an adjustment a small red moving arrow and a respective label preview the currently selected value. In addition, the slider also supports range selections which are visualized with two arrow handles of both ends of the value range and a semi-transparent mask between them.

Lists support the selection of items from a larger data set. Each item consist of a description and a corresponding icon. Similar to the previous widgets, lists show their current selection directly in the menu segment. When a list widget is activated, a side menu is shown to the left or right, depending on the segments positions (see Figs. 1A and Fig. 4D). It shows the available items, centered on the currently selected one. To ensure optimal readability, only ten items are displayed at the same time and the list can be scrolled vertically as necessary, with a scrollbar indicating the current position.

4.3   Interaction Design for Menu Control

This section describes how the menu can be controlled with our elastic input device, *CHARM*. Simply pulling the *CHARM* handle makes the general menu appear at a fixed distance relative to the user. Object-specific menus are situated at the object's position and can be accesses by pressing the trigger-button. All menus always face the user.

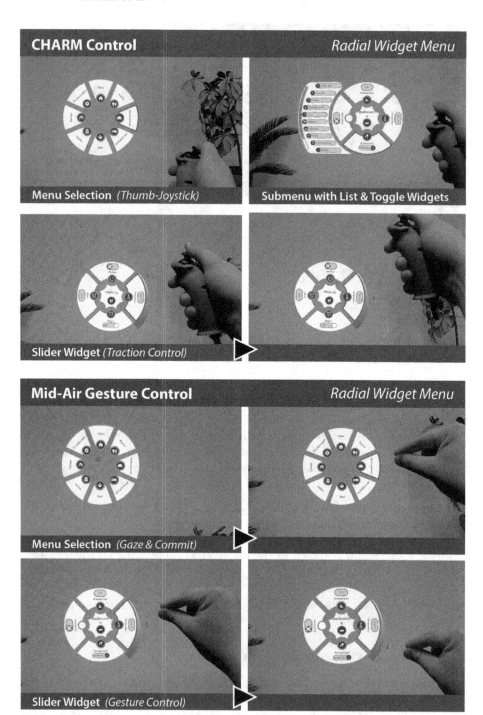

Fig. 5. Our Radial Widget Menu using our *CHARM* control and mid-air gestures.

Segment Navigation: Because of the rich input space offered by our device, the best interaction mapping for navigating the radial menu is not immediately obvious. Therefore, we propose three alternative *CHARM* interaction mappings (**C1-C3**) for the navigation: The *pulling-based browsing* mapping (**C1**) uses the string's pulling length (see Fig. 2A) to select a menu segment. When the user slightly pulls the handle and string, the menu segments are selected in clockwise order, depending on the current pulling length and symbolized by a red outline. The *deflection-based selection* (**C2**) maps the angular deflection of the string to a menu segment (see Fig. 2B). For instance, moving the handle to the left highlights the left segment in the radial AR menu. The *thumb-joystick* mapping (**C3**) uses the deflection of the thumb-joystick (see Fig. 2C) to target a specific menu segment. If the user moves the joystick to the right, the right segment in the menu is selected. While the deflection-based techniques map the finger (**C3**) or arm (**C2**) direction to a radial segment relying on two spatial dimensions, the pulling-based selection (**C1**) provides access to the radial segments by only using the one dimension of traction. Every selection change is supported by vibro-tactile feedback of the handle, which can also be deactivated if the user prefers.

Segment and Widget Control: Pressing the handle's trigger-button activates a menu-segment. Depending on the selected segment type (e.g., hierarchical sub-menu or a specific widget control), a corresponding action is executed: Changing the menu level replaces the current menu items with the ones of the corresponding sub-menu and alters the middle element accordingly. Activating a list or slider shows either the side menu with the list items or the slider scale. Since lists and sliders have only one dimension, they are manipulated by pulling the handle away from or to the body, as this offers the most haptic feedback to users. We integrate a relative mapping, using the current pulling length of the string as a starting position for sliders and lists. This makes it very easy for users to increase or decrease the current value or selection and also prevents the list or slider from immediately jumping to a new value when the section is activated as it would be the case with an absolute mapping. If a specific value is unreachable, e.g., due to physical constraints, our system provides a clutching method that allows users to hold down the trigger-button, return to a comfortable position, and release the button to continue. Lists automatically scroll when the second or second to last item is selected. In case of range sliders, the left push-button of the *CHARM* handle is used to switch between both values, which are then adjusted by pulling the handle.

5 User Feedback

To evaluate our menu concept for system control and prototype implementation, we conducted two small-scale qualitative user studies for hands-on feedback and insights. In the first study we were particularly interested in finding the most suitable interaction mapping and get general feedback to our system design. The second study improved upon our design based on the results of the first study and was focused on comparing our *CHARM* interaction to gesture interaction using the native air tap of the Microsoft HoloLens as a baseline. Both studies were conducted using our first generation handle (see Fig. 3B).

5.1   First Formative Study

The subjects of this study had to explore our menu (a restaurant finder use-case) using our *CHARM* device and perform simple menu tasks, that included all widgets. We recruited 6 participants (3 female, 3 male) between the age of 24 and 49 from students and post-doctoral personnel of our local university. Participants reported some experience with mixed reality and all except one participant had used some form of radial menu before.

Tasks and Procedure: Each participant started with a short training session to try out the menu and familiarize themselves with the interaction mappings. After that, we evaluated the three mapping conditions introduced in Sect. 4.3 (**C2**: *pulling-based*, **C2**: *string-deflection* and **C3**: *thumb-joystick*) in a counterbalanced within-subject design. Participants had to solve a continuous sequence of eight tasks for each condition, which varied between each condition to avoid learning effects. The tasks incorporated interacting with all our proposed widgets, as well as sub-menus, as we asked participants to find restaurants matching certain criteria (e.g., cuisine, price, distance, type). Participants had to accomplish these tasks without help from the experimenter and were encouraged to describe and comment on all their actions. Every interaction condition (**C1-C3**) could only be controlled with the current mapping (e.g., only thumb-joystick or deflection) with no combination of mappings. The overall duration of the study for each participant was approximately 45 min.

Measurements: We recorded the video stream from the HoloLens and a video of each participant from far away. This enabled us not only to see the user's perspective but also to reconstruct their corresponding interaction with our *CHARM* device. Of the two present investigators, one was primarily responsible for conducting the study, while the other took detailed notes of the observations of the participant. All sessions were accompanied by questionnaires after each condition that included a raw NASA-TLX [11] with seven-point scales and three open questions (general pros, cons, and comments) to get qualitative feedback.

Results: In general, our user feedback revealed that our approach has been assessed as useful and suitable for the control of AR menus. Surprisingly, no interaction mapping proved clearly superior over the others, but was instead subject to user preference. Two participants preferred the *pulling-based segment navigation* (**C1**), three participants the *string deflection* (**C2**), and one participant the *joystick-based navigation* (**C3**). Although **C3** was only rated once as the preferred interaction mapping, nearly all participants rated it as their second favorite, stating that they liked the condition in general, but did not like moving and pressing the joystick at the same time. Therefore, we have the strong assumption that this mapping would perform significantly better when the trigger button of our new handle design would be used instead of the joystick button.

Based on the feedback we also improved the mappings of all interaction styles, e.g., how much a slider value changes when the handle is pulled, and adjust a deadzone to the deflection. All participants mentioned that the tactile buttons are very helpful for interacting with Mixed Reality and much better than only getting visual feedback. Our results from the NASA-TLX test showed no conspicuous differences in the task load index (1-best; 7-worst) between our tested conditions (**C1-C3**). Participants rated *physical demand* ($A = 2.55, SD = 0.13$), *mental demand* ($A = 2.46, SD = 0.05$), *frustration* ($A = 2.55, SD = 0.10$), and *success* ($A = 2.44, SD = 0.26$) very similar between all conditions. However, the general workload was also low, which means that CHARM is useful for mobile system control tasks regardless of the used mapping condition. We were particularly pleased that participants assessed the elastic input very positively regarding haptic feedback and support for controlling the AR menu.

5.2   Second Formative Study

The goal of the second study was to compare our *CHARM* interaction concept with a suitable baseline to evaluate user satisfaction. Additionally we logged task completion times to gain first insights about user performance. We implemented a gesture interaction interface using the air tap provided by the Microsoft HoloLens in combination with a gaze-cursor. The cursor is used for selecting menu segments, while the air tap activates buttons, sliders and lists, and tap & hold manipulates slider and list values (see Fig. 5). Furthermore, we implemented two different manipulation techniques for the gesture interaction: The first is an position-based mapping, where moving the hand when performing a tap & hold gesture is directly mapped to moving the virtual slider or selected list item. The second approach uses a rate based system, where moving the hand up or down during the tap & hold gesture results in a continuous change of intensity the further the hand is moved away from the neutral position. For this study, we recruited seven participants (all male) aged between 20 and 28 from students of our local university, which did not participate in the first study. Six participants were right- and one was left-handed, all had experience with radial menus, but little experience with mixed reality.

Tasks and Procedure: To compare both interaction modalities each participant either started with the gesture interaction or the *CHARM* interaction. We alternated the order with every participant. For each modality, we again started with a short training session where participants would familiarize themselves with the current interaction scheme. After that we evaluated two different mappings for the specific modality, counterbalanced between participants. For the _Gesture_ interaction, we evaluated the position-based (**G1**) and rate-based (**G2**) mappings and for _CHARM_ interaction the thumb-joystick (**C2**) and string-deflection (**C3**) based mappings. We decided not to use mapping **C1** because results of our first study suggested that its least suitable for selecting menu segments. Participants solved two sequences of four tasks per condition, involving sub-menus and all widgets. The last task was always to activate a toggle button. Instead of the restaurant finder, we used a home automation use case were users could adjust a variety of home related values like lighting condition or temperature. Participants had to solve each tasks without help from the experimenter and were told to solve the tasks as quickly as possible (we did not encourage thinking aloud this time to not influence the time measurements). The overall duration of the study for each participant was approximately one hour.

Measurements: We again recorded the livestream from the Microsoft HoloLens and the current state of the *CHARM* device (which buttons were pressed, current deflection values, etc.), gestures recognized by the HoloLens and all events that were triggered within our menu. With this data we could accurately reproduce the actions of the users, which helped in identifying problems with the interaction mappings. Furthermore, we measured the completion times for each task sequence, taking the toggle button at the end of each sequence as completion mark. Similar to the first study, two investigators were always present, which one conducting the study and the other taking detailed notes of each participant. All sessions were accompanied by questionnaires of seven-point scales including a raw NASA-TLX [11], and questions on how easy it was to select menu items and manipulate sliders and lists with a particular interaction mapping.

Results: Somewhat surprisingly, task completion times for both gestures ($A_{G1} = 49.71$ s, $A_{G2} = 47.08$ s) and *CHARM* ($A_{C2} = 44.52$ s, $A_{C3} = 49.64$ s) were mostly the same, with *CHARM* being slightly faster overall. Due to the small number of participants we did not test for statistic significance. However, as a first indication of user performance, the results where nonetheless very interesting to us, as we did not expect this outcome. We observed that the selection of segments using the gaze cursor was a lot faster than using either **C2** or **C3**, while *CHARM* was faster manipulating sliders and lists. This is also supported by our questionnaire, were four participants stated that gestures supported them more for selection tasks, compared to two preferring *CHARM* and one undecided. For manipulation, *CHARM* was preferred by four participants and gestures by two, with one undecided. The results of the NASA-TLX (seven point scale, 1 being best and 7 being worst) showed distinctively less physical demand ($A_{G1} = 3.71, SD_{G1} = 1.16, A_{G2} = 3.71, SD_{G2} = 1.27, A_{C2} = 1.57, SD_{C2} = 0.49, A_{C3} = 2.00, SD_{C3} = 0.76$) for *CHARM* compared to gestures, and also reduced stress level ($A_{G1} = 2.86, SD_{G1} = 0.99, A_{G2} = 3.14, SD_{G2} = 1.64, A_{C2} = 1.71, SD_{C2} = 0.70, A_{C3} = 2.14, SD_{C3} = 0.63$). The other categories were very similar between both modalities, although *CHARM* scored slightly better in all categories in comparison to free hand gestures.

5.3   Discussion

Building of the insights of this study, we propose a hybrid approach of our *CHARM* concept, using the gaze cursor from our gesture interaction baseline for selecting menu items and using our *CHARM* device to manipulate them. Although we have not yet evaluated this approach, we are confident that this leads to a faster and more satisfying solution. Furthermore, we learned that users have very different preferences regarding their favored interaction mappings. Therefore, an important point for future developments is to provide customizable mappings or even their conjunction. For example, the deflection-based selection could be the default mapping, while using the thumb-joystick overrides the selection. Such a combined mapping scheme could enable a highly adaptive input device with synergetic interaction mappings that work seamlessly together and provide alternatives. Our own observations during both studies and discussions with our participants lead to the assumption that our *CHARM* device possesses a flexibility and adaptability which not only makes it suitable for system control tasks, but also as a generic input device for AR applications. This inspired us to extend our system to also incorporate an interaction scheme for the 3D transformation of objects, described in the next section.

6   3D Transformation

3D transformation is also an important aspect for AR applications and serves as an example of how our *CHARM* device can be used for the direct manipulation of objects within an application. Our concept and prototype incorporates seven degrees of freedom: Objects can be translated and rotated freely on all three axis and uniformly scaled. We decided for a uniform scale over a free scale on all three axis, because it does no distort the transformed object. Every transformation is always performed in relation to the users current position and orientation so that, e.g., moving the handle to the left always moves the object to the left as well from the perspective of the user.

Translation is activated by pressing and holding the trigger button and moving the handle in the desired direction (see upper Fig. 6). Releasing the trigger button stops the translation. We use a direct mapping between handle and virtual object, e.g., moving the handle one meter to the left also moves the transformed object one meter to the left. We also experimented with a rate-based mapping, where the rate of deflection of the handle in a certain direction determines the movement speed of the object in this direction. However, early tests with users showed that the direct mapping was preferred by users over the rate-based approach, as it was more precise and easier to understand.

Rotation is controlled by the thumb-joystick, using a rate-based quadratic transfer function to determine the speed with which the object is rotated. Since the joystick provides only two degrees of freedom, a mode switch is used to iterate through the different rotation axes. Only one rotation axis is active at a time and symbolized by a green circle around the object (see Fig. 6). The axis can be switched by pressing the joysticks push-button. Both deflection directions of the joystick result in a rotation of the object around the currently active axis. While it would be possible to map two axes at once, we found that this confuses the user more than it helps to reduce the required mode switches.

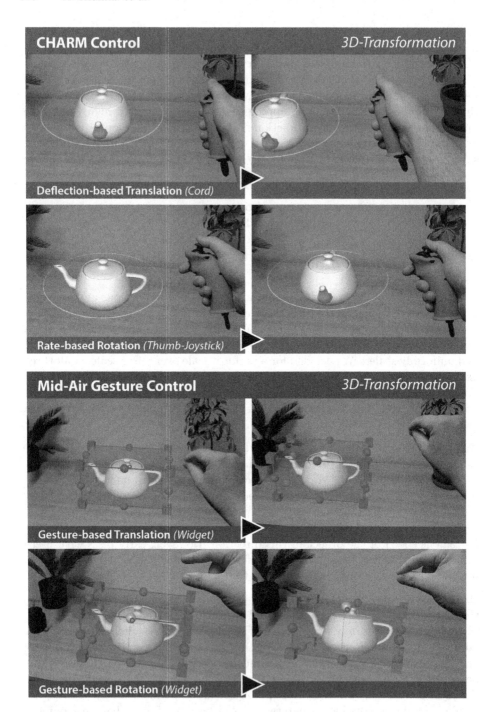

Fig. 6. 3D transformation using our cord-based techniques and mid-air gestures. (Color figure online)

Scale is activated by pressing and holding the left push-button and pulling the handle away from the body to enlarge the object and pulling it to the body to shrink it. Releasing the button stops the scale. The scale uses an linear mapping, where pulling the string 50 cm in one direction results in the object getting 50% smaller or larger. We again experimented with a rate-based mapping, but are convinced that a linear mapping works better and is more precise.

Our tests have also shown that our translation mapping is not suitable for moving objects over large distances like several meters, as this requires a lot of arm movement and is exhausting. We propose two solutions for this issue: The first is an alternative long range mode, toggled by the right push-button of the *CHARM*-device, which activates a non-uniform mapping of the deflection to the object's position. This means that moving the handle a certain distance translates into the object moving several times that amount. We made good experiences with a factor of five, but of course this can be freely configured according to the use-case. This provides our *CHARM* device with an imprecise long range mode on the direct mapping for the exact positioning of objects. The second solution is to harness the movement of the user itself by picking an object up, which results in the object moving in accordance to the user, and putting it down again, after which it can be positioned with the *CHARM* device as normal. We found the second solution to be preferable, as it enables users to pick up several objects at the same time and is also more intuitive than using a non-uniform mapping.

In addition to our *CHARM* transformation techniques, we also implemented a gesture interaction interface. The air tap supported by the HoloLens only provides three degrees of freedom. To compensate for this, our gesture interface therefore uses widgets (see lower Fig. 6). This is a contrast to the *CHARM* transformation, which makes nearly no use of widgets or additional visual feedback, with the sole exception being the circle indicating the current rotation axis. We based the widgets for the gesture interface on the ones the HoloLens itself uses, but have extended them to provide the same seven degrees of freedom *CHARM* provides. The widget can be thought of as a cube around the transformed object. It can be moved by executing a tap & hold on one of the cube's sides and moving the hand. The object will perform the exact same movement as the hand. To rotate and object on a specific axis, the corresponding handles on the edges of the cube are used. However, the object is always rotated around its center and not around the edge itself, with a green circle indicating the rotation axis. Scaling is performed by handles on the corner of the cube. Pulling the handle away from the object enlarges it, and polling the handle to the center shrinks the object. All transformations are done in relation to the users current position, e.g., moving the hand to the left always rotates the object to the left. This gesture interface acts as a baseline for a future evaluation of our 3D transformation concepts.

7 Conclusion and Future Work

In this paper, we investigated the potential of string-based elastic interaction for AR applications. Therefore, we presented *CHARM*, a retractable string-based device with a multi-DoF handle for generic tasks in AR. To demonstrate the suitability of our *CHARM* approach, we introduced a set of interaction concepts for system control (by means of AR menus) and 3D transformation. In order evaluate the feasibility of our body-centric elastic interaction approach, we built a fully-functional prototype. It can be seamlessly connected to state-of-the-art AR glasses, which we demonstrated on the example of the HoloLens. Based on mobile real-world interaction tasks, we evaluated our AR menu for system control within two small-scale user studies. Our results suggest that *CHARM* sufficiently supports generic AR interaction in a casual and easy to use way, while being useful for precise input. However, as gaze selection was rated as a promising input for rough selections, we proposed a hybrid input method of using *CHARM* in conjunction with a gaze cursor. In addition, we introduced a 3D transformation concept that allow users to translate, rotate or uniformly scale objects directly using our *CHARM* device.

For future work, our *CHARM* system needs to be miniaturized to enhance the degree of wearable integration. Furthermore, we plan to evaluate the differences between our *CHARM* and gesture interaction for the menu, as well as the 3D transformation in a future comparative quantitative user study We are confident, that *CHARM* provides a promising modality for interacting with three-dimensional content in Augmented Reality.

Acknowledgments. We would like to thank Andreas Peetz for helping us to improve the CHARM handle and Thomas Schwab as well as Paul Riedel for working on the AR menu and gesture control. This work was partly funded by the German Research Foundation (DFG, Deutsche Forschungsgemeinschaft) as part of Germany's Excellence Strategy – EXC 2050/1 – Project ID 390696704 – Cluster of Excellence "Centre for Tactile Internet with Human-in-the-Loop" (CeTI) of Technische Universität Dresden.

References

1. Azuma, R., Baillot, Y., Behringer, R., Feiner, S., Julier, S., MacIntyre, B.: Recent advances in augmented reality. IEEE Comput. Graph. Appl. **21**(6), 34–47 (2001). https://doi.org/10.1109/38.963459
2. Blasko, G., Narayanaswami, C., Feiner, S.: Prototyping retractable string-based interaction techniques for dual-display mobile devices. In: Proceedings of the SIGCHI Conference on Human Factors in Computing Systems, CHI 2006, pp. 369–372. ACM, New York (2006). https://doi.org/10.1145/1124772.1124827
3. Bowman, D., Wingrave, C.: Design and evaluation of menu systems for immersive virtual environments. In: Proceedings IEEE Virtual Reality 2001, pp. 149–156 (2001). https://doi.org/10.1109/VR.2001.913781
4. Bowman, D.A., Kruijff, E., LaViola, J.J., Poupyrev, I.: 3D User Interfaces: Theory and Practice. Addison Wesley Longman Publishing Co., Inc., Redwood City (2004)

5. Coquillart, S., Wesche, G.: The virtual palette and the virtual remote control panel: a device and an interaction paradigm for the responsive workbench(tm). In: Proceedings IEEE Virtual Reality (Cat. No. 99CB36316), pp. 213–216, March 1999. https://doi.org/10.1109/VR.1999.756953
6. Dachselt, R., Hübner, A.: A survey and taxonomy of 3D menu techniques. In: Eurographics Symposium on Virtual Environments. The Eurographics Association (2006). https://doi.org/10.2312/EGVE/EGVE06/089-099
7. Davis, M.M., Gabbard, J.L., Bowman, D.A., Gracanin, D.: Depth-based 3D gesture multi-level radial menu for virtual object manipulation. In: 2016 IEEE Virtual Reality (VR), pp. 169–170, March 2016. https://doi.org/10.1109/VR.2016.7504707
8. Dobbelstein, D., Winkler, C., Haas, G., Rukzio, E.: PocketThumb: a wearable dual-sided touch interface for cursor-based control of smart-eyewear. Proc. ACM Interact. Mob. Wearable Ubiquit. Technol. 1(2), 9:1–9:17 (2017). https://doi.org/10.1145/3090055
9. Fröhlich, B., Plate, J.: The cubic mouse: a new device for three-dimensional input. In: Proceedings of the SIGCHI Conference on Human Factors in Computing Systems, CHI 2000, pp. 526–531. ACM, New York (2000). https://doi.org/10.1145/332040.332491
10. Gebhardt, S., Pick, S., Leithold, F., Hentschel, B., Kuhlen, T.: Extended pie menus for immersive virtual environments. IEEE Trans. Visual. Comput. Graph. 19(4), 644–651 (2013). https://doi.org/10.1109/TVCG.2013.31
11. Hart, S.G.: NASA-task load index (NASA-TLX); 20 years later. Proc. Hum. Factors Ergonomics Soc. Annu. Meet. 50(9), 904–908 (2006). https://doi.org/10.1177/154193120605000909
12. Hinckley, K., Pausch, R., Goble, J.C., Kassell, N.F.: A survey of design issues in spatial input. In: Proceedings of the 7th Annual ACM Symposium on User Interface Software and Technology, UIST 1994, pp. 213–222. ACM, New York (1994). https://doi.org/10.1145/192426.192501
13. Hyeongmook, L., Dongchul, K., Woontack, W.: Graphical menus using a mobile phone for wearable AR systems. In: 2011 International Symposium on Ubiquitous Virtual Reality, pp. 55–58, July 2011. https://doi.org/10.1109/ISUVR.2011.23
14. Klamka, K., Dachselt, R.: Elasticcon: elastic controllers for casual interaction. In: Proceedings of the 17th International Conference on Human-Computer Interaction with Mobile Devices and Services, MobileHCI 2015, pp. 410–419. ACM, New York (2015). https://doi.org/10.1145/2785830.2785849
15. Klamka, K., Dachselt, R.: ARCord: visually augmented interactive cords for mobile interaction. In: Extended Abstracts of the 2018 CHI Conference on Human Factors in Computing Systems, CHI EA 2018, pp. LBW623:1–LBW623:6. ACM, New York (2018). https://doi.org/10.1145/3170427.3188456
16. Koch, E., Witt, H.: Prototyping a chest-worn string-based wearable input device. In: 2008 International Symposium on a World of Wireless, Mobile and Multimedia Networks, pp. 1–6, June 2008. https://doi.org/10.1109/WOWMOM.2008.4594882
17. Lee, H., Woo, W.: Tangible spin cube for 3D ring menu in real space. In: CHI 2010 Extended Abstracts on Human Factors in Computing Systems, CHI EA 2010, pp. 4147–4152. ACM, New York (2010). https://doi.org/10.1145/1753846.1754117
18. Olwal, A., Moeller, J., Priest-Dorman, G., Starner, T., Carroll, B.: I/O braid: scalable touch-sensitive lighted cords using spiraling, repeating sensing textiles and fiber optics. In: Proceedings of the 31st Annual ACM Symposium on User Interface Software and Technology, UIST 2018, pp. 485–497. ACM, New York (2018). https://doi.org/10.1145/3242587.3242638

19. Piekarski, W., Thomas, B.H.: The tinmith system: demonstrating new techniques for mobile augmented reality modelling. In: Proceedings of the Third Australasian Conference on User Interfaces, AUIC 2002, vol. 7, pp. 61–70. Australian Computer Society Inc., Darlinghurst (2002). http://dl.acm.org/citation.cfm?id=563985.563994

20. Pohl, N., Hodges, S., Helmes, J., Villar, N., Paek, T.: An interactive belt-worn badge with a retractable string-based input mechanism. In: Proceedings of the SIGCHI Conference on Human Factors in Computing Systems, CHI 2013, pp. 1465–1468. ACM, New York (2013). https://doi.org/10.1145/2470654.2466194

21. Schwarz, J., Harrison, C., Hudson, S., Mankoff, J.: Cord input: an intuitive, high-accuracy, multi-degree-of-freedom input method for mobile devices. In: Proceedings of the SIGCHI Conference on Human Factors in Computing Systems, CHI 2010, pp. 1657–1660. ACM, New York (2010). https://doi.org/10.1145/1753326.1753573

22. Simon, A., Froehlich, B.: The YoYo: a handheld device combining elastic and isotonic input. In: Human-Computer Interaction INTERACT 2003: IFIP TC13 International Conference on Human-Computer Interaction, 1st–5th September 2003, Zurich, Switzerland (2003)

23. Szalavári, Z.: The personal interaction panel - a two-handed interface for augmented reality. Ph.D. thesis, Institute of Computer Graphics and Algorithms, Vienna University of Technology, Vienna, Austria (1999). https://www.cg.tuwien.ac.at/research/publications/1999/Szalavari-thesis/

24. Tsai, H.R., Rekimoto, J.: ElasticVR: providing multi-level active and passive force feedback in virtual reality using elasticity. In: Extended Abstracts of the 2018 CHI Conference on Human Factors in Computing Systems, CHI EA 2018, pp. D300:1–D300:4. ACM, New York (2018). https://doi.org/10.1145/3170427.3186540

25. Weigel, M., Steimle, J.: Deformwear: deformation input on tiny wearable devices. Proc. ACM Interact. Mob. Wearable Ubiquitous Technol. **1**(2), 28:1–28:23 (2017). https://doi.org/10.1145/3090093

26. White, S., Feng, D., Feiner, S.: Interaction and presentation techniques for shake menus in tangible augmented reality. In: 2009 8th IEEE International Symposium on Mixed and Augmented Reality, pp. 39–48, October 2009. https://doi.org/10.1109/ISMAR.2009.5336500

To Speak or to Text: Effects of Display Type and I/O Style on Mobile Virtual Humans Nurse Training

Justin Loyd[1], Toni Pence[2], and Amy Banic[1,3(✉)]

[1] University of Wyoming, Laramie, USA
jloyd@uwyo.edu, abanic@cs.uwyo.edu
[2] University of North Carolina at Wilmington, Wilmington, USA
pencet@uncw.edu
[3] Idaho National Laboratory, Idaho Falls, USA

Abstract. Nursing programs are designed to teach students the knowledge, skill and attitudes needed to provide nursing care to patients of various ages, genders, cultures and religious backgrounds. Traditionally, students acquire these skills through patient interaction. There have been shown benefits to training nurses, and other medical students, via embodied virtual humans. We have designed a system to enable mobile interactive training for nursing students using an embodied conversational virtual human. Furthermore, we conducted a study to compare whether display type and interaction type have an effect on users' interactions. In this paper, we present the details of our system and results from our user study. Our results could have impact for designing and using VH training systems.

Keywords: Virtual humans · Virtual patients · Mobile · User evaluation ·
User study · Texting I/O · Speech I/O · Mobile vs Desktop · Mobility · VH

1 Introduction

Nursing programs are designed to teach students the knowledge, skill and attitude needed to provide nursing care to patients of various ages, genders, cultures and religious backgrounds [1]. Students can gain these skills through patient interaction and during a student's program of study he/she is often presented with numerous opportunities to interact with patients in a variety of environments such as hospitals, clinics, and community settings. Nursing programs provide as much patient interaction as possible however, there is a need for students to practice their skills outside of patient interaction [2]. A mobile virtual patient is a virtual human as a virtual patient that is implemented on a mobile device such as a tablet or smartphone. We designed and developed a mobile virtual patient prototype for nurse training (Fig. 1) and implemented it for two different mobile platforms, a web-based and mobile virtual patient. We also implemented two different interaction modalities, Texting I/O and Speech I/O (Fig. 2), to investigate the effects of interaction style for mobile virtual patient training. The purpose of this research was to design a prototype mobile virtual patient and

© Springer Nature Switzerland AG 2019
J. Y. C. Chen and G. Fragomeni (Eds.): HCII 2019, LNCS 11574, pp. 115–132, 2019.
https://doi.org/10.1007/978-3-030-21607-8_9

investigate the effects of mobility and screen size of the mobile virtual patient. This prototype will provide mobility and ease of access so that it can be used anywhere 24/7, without the need of specialized equipment. This paper presents the implementation details of our mobile virtual patient as well as a user study to evaluate the effects of using different mobile platforms and multi-modal input. This user study consists of investigating the effects of mobility and screen size among three devices a tablet, desktop and smartphone which will be divided between subjects as the main effect. This study will also investigate the interaction effects of I/O style within subjects using text and speech. This experimental study had a 3 × 2 mixed design with 3 device types as between-subject conditions and 2 I/O Styles as within-subject conditions. The results of this work will provide a solution for the use of mobile virtual patients as well as provide information as to how platforms and input/output modalities can affect usage in practice.

Fig. 1. A model of our Mobile Virtual Patient for Nurse Training prototype.

2 Related Work

2.1 Simulation-Based Nursing Training

The need for additional practice can be achieved through simulations techniques that represent patient interaction. "Simulation is a technique -not a technology- to replace or amplify real experiences with guided experiences that evoke or replicate substantial aspects of the real world in a fully interactive manner" [2]. There are numerous simulation models that have been used by nursing students. In paper-based cases students read scenarios that are either linear to aid in learning the interaction process [3]. Standardized patients are where an actor learns a patient scenario and acts like a real patient in order to simulate patient-nurse interaction, sometime the actor is replaced by a student [4, 5]. Mannequins allow students to train techniques that may be difficult using other simulation models [2, 5, 6]. Virtual Patients are interactive computer simulations that present students with a nursing scenario [6–14].

2.2 Virtual Patients

Virtual patients which are a computer based simulation of a virtual human modeled as virtual patient using a nursing scenario that allows for dynamic patient interaction, designed to supplement clinical training. Virtual humans are 3D and in some cases 2D computer based visual representations of humans [6–14]. Virtual humans can be autonomous agents, which are controlled by a computer, or avatars, which are controlled by a real human [6–14]. Virtual patients have the advantage of not requiring an actor, being modifiable with new scenarios, and providing standardization so that all students interact with the exact same scenario. Though most current implements are large and require an area that is dedicated to the virtual patient [7, 8, 15, 16]. With increases in technology, virtual humans are becoming widely used for marketing, education, training and research. There are a number of studies that focus on virtual patients [7–14], there have even been studies on mobile learning [17–19], however there have been few studies that focus on studying the use of virtual patients on mobile platforms.

2.3 Mobile Learning Platforms and Studies

A study conducted by Taylor et al. investigated developing a mobile learning solution for health and social care practice [17]. The program scaled over five years+ to introduce mobile learning into health and social care. Their research demonstrated that there is a potential for these platforms to be more widely used across the higher education sector to bridge the gap between the classroom and work-based learning. Another mobile learning study by Lea et al. investigated enhancing health and social care placement learning through mobile technology [18]. They conducted a three-year study of research on their mobile learning project. From this project they concluded that success in mobile learning needs to be based on a clear set of principles to ensure effective pedagogy for both staff and students.

3 Mobile Virtual Patient Prototype Design

In this section, we provide a description of our prototype. For our prototype, we based the interaction on an existing nurse-patient interaction scenario. This scenario called for a 52-year-old male with iron deficiency anemia and no defining characteristics. The scenario starts off with the practitioner asking how the patient is, and the patient replies that he is tired all the time. The practitioner asks questions about when the symptoms began, frequency, medication history, about headaches, light sensitivity, fevers, level of dehydration, weight changes, viral symptoms, breathing, swelling, lightheadedness, and pain/discomfort in stomach. The patient replies that this is a source of pain, while the practitioner asks more details about the stomach, etc. In the design of our virtual patient, while the responses of the virtual patient are designed to answer a wide range of questions in this scope of this scenario, it is designed to me more dynamic so that the student practitioner can ask questions in any order, a variety of questions, and in a variety of ways. The design of this virtual character is described in Sect. 3.3. We wanted the prototype virtual patient to serve as an interactive conversation agent [20] with animated gestures, that responded using speech or text output, further detailed in Sect. 3.4.

Fig. 2. Our Mobile Virtual Patient for Nurse Training interacting with a user through Texting I/O (left) and natural language processing or Speech I/O (right).

3.1 Pedagogical Frameworks Used in Design of the System

Nursing students need to learn the knowledge, skill and attitude to be able to provide nursing care to patients of various ages, genders, cultures and religious backgrounds. Virtual patients are simulations designed to be used as a training tool. Thus, it is important to look at the learning process that nurses follow. There are two major frameworks that we looked at these include the Miller Triangle and the RTI Triangle. The miller triangle illustrates George Millers framework for clinical assessment [21], used to evaluate, diagnose and treat patients. The pyramid's base or tier one starts with 'knows', meaning the student has the knowledge required to carry out professional function correctly. Tier two is 'knows how' refers to the competence of a student ability to perform the function that they know. Tier three is 'shows how' which represents the students' performance when interacting with a patient. Tier four is the final stage 'does' which refers to the actions of a student when they are actually working with patients. Virtual patients can be used to allow students to practice the 'knows how' tier and with modern designs of virtual patients that log interaction can allow students to demonstrate what they have learned thus completing the 'shows how' tier the miller triangle.

Another way to view the nursing learning process is by the RTI training triangle [14]. The RTI learning triangle is a learning framework designed to allow nursing students to acquire and practice skill safely in a virtual environment. The base tier of this training triangle starts with pedagogical stage where students familiarize themselves about nursing practices and interactions. The base tier is normally complete in a classroom environment. In tier two students work in a virtual environment where they acquire and practice skills that they will need to for their profession. The second tier could be completed using a virtual patient system. The last tier is on the job where student finish practicing and validating the skills which they have learned.

3.2   Platform for Mobile-Based Virtual Patient Prototype

The model and animations of the virtual patient were created using Reallusion's iClone 4 version 4.3.1928.1 [22]. A model from iClone was used but notified to match no defining characteristics (Fig. 1). The virtual patient's voice was generated using Microsoft SAPI 12 4 [23] text-to-speech generator. We used the 'Mike' voice because it sounded closer to a middle-aged man. To control the animation, we used Java's Flex Builder version 3.5 [24]. Flex Builder also provided the framework for receiving I/O interaction from the user. The Flex builder was linked to a MySQL [25] database which contained all the virtual patient's questions and responses. The database was setup using the question-resolution algorithm provided by Clemson University [REF]. This prototype virtual patient was designed to run in a web browser so that the virtual patient could be accessed via the internet. This web based virtual patient provided the foundation and idea for creating a mobile virtual patient (Fig. 2) which was implemented using a Texting I/O interaction style (left) and a natural language processing or Speech I/O interaction style (right). The mobile virtual prototype had a few challenges that we had to overcome. Due to most virtual characters' environments being created for the desktop, at the time this was developed, there were no platforms or controller methods to enable the event-driven input/output and interruption for a virtual human interaction flow to run on the web or on a mobile device. As such, we used video files in a novel way to create simulate the interactive responses of the virtual character and to enable the interaction with a web-based virtual patient. To create a realistic virtual patient that did not require as much processing power to overcome a limitation of processing power on a mobile device, we pre-rendered the virtual patients' animation responses and saved each as a video file. Each video file was played for the appropriate response using Android's media player. Another issue was having a limited screen real estate for a mobile device. To see the detail of the mobile virtual patient, the upper half of the virtual patient was only displayed (Fig. 2).

3.3 System Design of Virtual Patient

The system design consisted of the six major functions shown in Fig. 3. We implemented the input listener to listen for input provided by a user. When a user asked a question, the input listener would update the state control letting the system know that a question has been asked. The text version of the input listener functioned using android's OnClickListener API. When a user clicked the send button the input listener would fetch the input string and update the state control (Fig. 3). The speech version of the input listener functioned using androids ReconfitionListener API. The listener was on a loop waiting for user input. The current state of the listener was displayed using color coded boxes that the listener updated (Fig. 3). We set up the state control to keep track of the current state of the system and of the input and output. After a question had been asked by a user, the state control would send that user's question to the question matching algorithm. The question matching function was setup using the question resolution algorithm provided by Clemson University. The code provided by Clemson was written using C++ code that was linked to a MySQL database. The C++ code was converted to Java so that it would run on an Android Device. The MySQL database had to be converted to work as a SQLite database. This was done by taking the main SQL commands and inserting them into a java wrapper that could execute SQL code. The first part of the Question Resolution Algorithm provided by Clemson University generated a serious of synonyms from the nursing scenario questions. The synonyms created, were divided into word pairs, or bigrams. The generated files created a MySQL database that I used to create a SQLite database on an Android device. The created database is used to compare the questions asked by the user with the bigrams in the database. After the question matching algorithm matched the 'asked' question with the correct response, the system updated the state control with the response found. The virtual patient animation view was updated to display the current state of the mobile virtual patient's animation for the appropriate response to the screen. The current state of the mobile virtual patient's animation was controlled by the control thread. The control thread maintains the virtual patient in an idle state until the state control updated the state with a response that had been found. When a response was found, the control thread would update the animation so that the mobile virtual patient would respond with the correct response. When mobile virtual patient finished responding the control would default back to the idle loop until another response was returned.

3.4 I/O Styles

The user would be able to provide input to the mobile virtual patient using either text or speech input (Fig. 2). A built-in microphone was used for each device used for speech input. The speech input was then synthesized into text, and then is filtered through the question resolution algorithm. For the text-based input a QUERTY keyboard was used. We chose these input types to study whether similar training effects occur when using typing and texting. Texting with a virtual patient may be more private and less socially awkward when training in a public location. The prototype needed to be accessible so that it could be used from home, school or anywhere with an internet connection. The text interface provided the user with input and output (I/O) boxes as well as a send

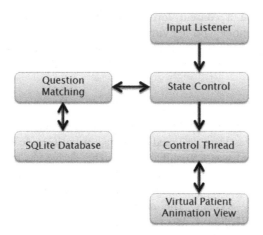

Fig. 3. Functionality of system states for our Mobile Virtual Patient prototype.

button (Fig. 2, left). The input box allowed the user to type or text a question, they would then press the send button. When the send button was pressed, the input listener received the input. After the input was processed and a response was found, the input question and output response were printed to the output box for the user to read. The mobile virtual patient's animation would also be updated to move as if he was saying the response that is displayed in the output box.

4 Experimental Design

4.1 Experimental Design and Procedure

We conducted an experiment to gather empirical data to determine how users physically interact with objects in the real-world, when asked to select a target group of objects. Our intent was to understand the actions that are more intuitive for users to inform the design of our physically-based volumetric selection technique. Our experimental study was approved by the University of Wyoming IRB. The experimental study was a 3 × 2 mixed design, with three device types as between-subjects conditions and two I/O styles (Sect. 3.4) as within-subjects conditions. The conditions were counter-balanced to reduce order effects, where each participant was randomly assigned to one order:

- Tablet-1st: Speech interaction, 2nd: Text interaction
- Tablet-1st: Text interaction, 2nd: Speech interaction
- Smartphone-1st: Speech interaction, 2nd: Text interaction
- Smartphone-1st: Text interaction, 2nd: Speech interaction
- Desktop-1st: Speech interaction, 2nd: Text interaction
- Desktop-1st: Text interaction - 2nd: Speech interaction

Participants completed a consent form and a pre-questionnaire. Each participant completed two interactions with the virtual patient in the order of conditions that was assigned. Participants completed a post-questionnaire after each interaction. Once all conditions were completed, participants answered a final debriefing interview.

4.2 Apparatus

The experiment utilized three different device types: a tablet, a smartphone, and a desktop. All the devices were designed to operate using Google's Android operating system. The tablet used was a Toshiba Thrive. The Thrive has a 10.1″, 1280 × 800 resolution, 16:10 aspect ratio screen. The tablet ran on a Tegra 2 dual-core processor with 1 GB DDR RAM and 16 GB of internal storage. The tablet ran Android 3.2, Honeycomb operating system. The smartphone used was a Motorola DROID. The DROID has a 3.7″, 854 × 480 resolution, 16:9 aspect ratio screen. The smartphone used an ARM corex A8 wih 256 MB RAM and 512 MB of internal storage. The smartphone ran android 2.3, Gingerbread operating system. The desktop setup used the same Toshiba Thrive listed above as a base though was hooked up to a mouse, keyboard and a 23″ 1920 × 1200 16:10 aspect ratio so participants were provided with a full desktop.

4.3 Measures

Demographic information was collected, such as age, gender, ethnicity, major and occupational status, by a questionnaire using a seven-point scale (1 = never used before, 7 = a great deal). The questionnaire was also used to collect information about participants' usage with virtual humans, virtual patients, and 2D or 3D applications. Examples of these questions included, but not limited to: 'To what extent have you worked in a health 26 care setting with real patients?' and 'To what extent have you been exposed to Virtual Patients.' The questions also asked how familiar users were with tablets, smartphones and computers, such as 'To what extent do you use a computer in your daily activities?'. Performance measures were automatically logged to the device during each trial. These measures include response time, time between questions asked, the question asked by the user as well as the responses provided by the virtual patient system. These measures were collected and stored to the device memory to identify trends in participant's interaction with the mobile virtual patient.

A post experiment questionnaire used a 7-point scale (1 = Not at all, 7 = A great deal) to determine the ease of use, screen size satisfaction, realism, beneficial to nursing, perception of learnability, enjoyment of use and preferred input style. Examples of these questions are 'Would you use this application as a learning tool?' and 'How much did you feel like you gained real patient-interaction experience from using this system?'. These questions provided the needed input for determining the effects of mobility and screen size has on the mobile virtual patients ease of use, screen size satisfaction, realism, beneficial to nursing, perception of learnability, enjoyment of use and preferred input style. The final stage before end of the experiment was the debriefing interview. The debriefing interview consisted of a series of questions. An example question is 'which would you prefer mobile phone, mobile tablet, laptop, pc, large screen or another device? why?'. These debriefing questions allowed for participants to provide feedback that may have been missed by the post experiment questionnaires. The purpose of these types of questions is to gain insight on participants' responses.

5 Results

This study investigated the effects of mobility and screen size using a mobile virtual patient. The qualitative data is analyzed by first summing up the measures and then calculating the mean and standard deviation. The quantitative data was analyzed using a repeated measure analyses of variance (ANOVA) statistical test for each measure.

5.1 Participants

A total of 30 students, teachers and professionals (26 females, 4 males) participated in the study. The participant's background consisted of 2 nursing instructors, 5 nursing students, 18 professionals, and 5 additional students from other disciplines that participated in this study. All participates were over 18 years of age (M = 38.2, SD = 13.22), had 20/20 or corrected 20/20 vision and used English as their first language. Volunteers were recruited from Wyoming hospitals, the University of Wyoming Fay W. Whitney School of Nursing and by word of mouth.

5.2 Performance Results

Questions Asked by Participants. The performance measures collected showed that participants asked more questions using speech (M = 11.95, SD = 8.69) than with text (M = 11.10, SD = 5.91). When comparing devices participants asked the most questions while using the tablet (M = 13.15, SD = 9.73), followed by the desktop (M = 10.67, SD = 6.96) and smartphone (M = 10.62, SD = 4.87). The performance measures collected showed that participants asked longer questions using speech (M = 4.95, SD = 1.33) than with text (M = 4.58, SD = 0.99). When comparing devices, participants asked the longest questions using the desktop (M = 5.15, 1.19), followed by the tablet (M = 4.67, SD = 0.82) and the smartphone (M = 4.32, SD = 1.20).

Error Rate of VH-Questions Having Unknown Responses. The performance measures collected showed that participants error rate, questions having unknown responses, was highest while using speech (M = 2.39, SD = 1.57) compared to text interaction (M = 1.75, SD = 1.59). When comparing devices participants had the highest error rate using the smartphone (M = 2.25, SD = 1.36), compared to the desktop (M = 1.97, SD = 1.27) and the tablet (M = 1.90, SD = 1.29). Devices by interaction style: smartphone-text (M = 2.50, SD = 1.51) had the highest error rate followed by desktop-speech (M = 2.33, SD = 1.07), tablet-speech (M = 2.30, SD = 1.89), smartphone-text (M = 2.00, SD = 1.15), desktop-text (M = 1.60, SD = 0.92) and tablet-text (M = 1.50, SD = 0.92).

5.3   Usability and User Experience Results

Ease of Use. A repeated measures ANOVA showed a significant main effect of ease of use by device type $F(2, 28.64) = 5.45$, $p = 0.01$, $\eta2 = 0.29$, Power $= 0.80$ (Fig. 6.1 and Table 6.1) and a significant interaction effect of I/O style $F(1, 27) = 15.10$, $p = 0.001$, $\eta2 = 0.0.36$, Power $= 0.96$ (Fig. 4), but no significant effect for interaction effect of I/O style by device type $F < 1$. A main effect showed that participants had the greatest ease of use with desktop (M = 6.22, SD = 0.42), followed by the tablet (M = 5.80, SD = 0.94) and the smartphone (M = 5.30, SD = 0.70). An interaction effect of I/O style showed a higher ranking of ease of use for text (M = 5.77, SD = 0.79) than speech (M = 5.37, SD = 0.95).

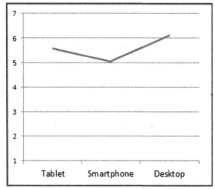

Device	Mean	Std. Deviation
Tablet	5.58	1.01
Smartphone	5.03	0.81
Desktop	6.11	0.45
I/O Style	Mean	Std. Deviation
Speech	5.37	0.95
Text	5.77	0.79
I/O Style by Device	Mean	Std. Deviation
Speech-tablet	5.35	1.08
Speech-smartphone	4.76	0.86
Speech-desktop	5.99	0.96
Text-tablet	5.80	0.94
Text-smartphone	5.30	0.70
Text-desktop	6.22	0.42

Fig. 4. Ease of Use mean ratings of Devices by Interaction Style.

Screen Size Satisfaction. A repeated measures ANOVA showed a significant main effect of screen size satisfaction between devices $F(2, 32.85) = 39.32$, $p < 0.001$, $\eta2 = 0.71$, Power $= 1.00$ (Fig. 5) and a significant interaction effect of I/O style by device type $F(2,20.05) = 5.00$, $p = 0.01$, $\eta2 = 0.768$, Power $= 0.77$, but a significant effect for interaction effect of I/O style $F < 1$. The main effect showed the highest satisfaction with the desktop (M = 6.40, SD = 0.75) followed by tablet (M = 6.25, SD = 1.02) and the smartphone (M = 3.90, SD = 1.25). When comparing interaction effect of I/O style by device type the highest was tablet-text (M = 6.70, SD = 0.48) and the lowest was smartphone-text (M = 3.50, SD = 1.08).

Learnability. A repeated measures ANOVA showed a significant main effect of participant's feeling they could learn nursing interaction skills using the virtual patient $F(2,56.63) = 14.11$, $p = 0.004$, $\eta2 = 0.33$, Power $= 0.88$ but no significant effect for an interaction effect of I/O style $F(1, 1.34) = 3.719$, $p = 0.06$, $\eta2 = 0.12$, Power $= 0.46$ nor interaction effect of I/O style by device $F(1, 1.34) = 1.38$, $p = 0.27$, $\eta2 = 0.09$, Power $= 0.27$. The main effect showed the highest rankings on the tablet (M = 5.45, SD = 0.99), followed by the desktop (M = 5.32, SD = 0.87) and smartphone (M = 3.93, SD = 1.15).

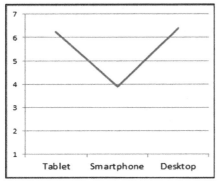

Device	Mean	Std. Deviation
Tablet	6.25	1.02
Smartphone	3.90	1.25
Desktop	6.40	0.75
I/O Style	Mean	Std. Deviation
Speech	5.53	1.41
Text	5.50	1.68
I/O Style by device	Mean	Std. Deviation
Speech-tablet	5.80	1.23
Speech-smartphone	4.30	1.34
Speech-desktop	6.50	0.53
Text-tablet	6.70	0.48
Text-smartphone	3.50	1.08
Text-desktop	6.30	0.95

Fig. 5. Satisfaction mean ratings of Devices by Interaction Style.

Enjoyable to Use. A repeated measures ANOVA showed a significant main effect of participant's enjoyment while using the virtual patient $F(2,51.48) = 14.87$, $p = 0.002$, $\eta2 = 0.37$, Power $= 0.93$ but there was no significant effect for interaction effect of I/O style $F < 1$ nor interaction effect of I/O style by device $F < 1$. The main effect showed a higher ranking of enjoyable to use for tablet (M $= 5.72$, SD $= 1.03$) followed by the desktop (M $= 5.52$, SD $= 0.74$) and the smartphone (M $= 4.13$, SD $= 1.21$).

Preference of I/O Style. A repeated measures ANOVA showed a significant inter-action effect of I/O style $F(1, 29.01) = 7.17$, $p = 0.01$, $\eta2 = 0.73$, Power $= 0.73$ (Fig. 6) but there was no significant main effect by device $F(2, 67.51) = 7.54$, $p = 0.06$, $\eta2 = 0.18$, Power $= 0.54$ nor interaction effect of I/O style by device $F(1, 29.01) = 7.17$, $p = 0.01$, $\eta2 = 0.73$, Power $= 0.42$. The interaction effect of I/O style showed a higher ranking of preference of I/O style with text (M $= 5.33$, SD $= 1.53$) than speech (M $= 4.62$ SD $= 1.30$). During the debriefing interview 14 participants responded that they preferred text compared to 10 that preferred speech and 6 that had no preference. Several comments were: "my preference would depend on my location", while many participants that preferred speech stated that "texting is slow" or "talking is easier". Some of the responses from participants that preferred text commented: "typing is easier than speaking to a computer" and "prefer texting if in a public location". During the debriefing interview, 20 participants responded that they would like to use the tablet, compared to 13 wanting to use the desktop and 7 want to use the smart-phone. (Note: users where allowed to pick more than one device) Some of the par-ticipants' responses when asked about their preferred device were: "tablet, for visual assessment" and "tablet, prefect middle ground for size and portability".

Virtual Patient as a Training Tool. For all devices, when participants were asked "how effective do you believe this system will be for training or practice?" where 30 of 30 participants responded positively. They responded with comments such as: "yes, since we currently watch boring movies for practice and training", "it would be a great tool, since we currently watch boring movies for practicing and training", "good for training", "would be really effective", "very beneficial", "would work well for specialty areas", and "really effect because, it is hard to find people to practice with".

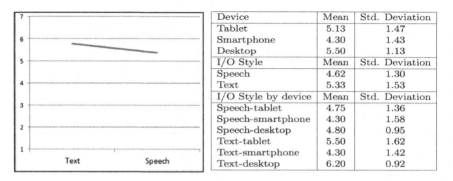

Device	Mean	Std. Deviation
Tablet	5.13	1.47
Smartphone	4.30	1.43
Desktop	5.50	1.13
I/O Style	Mean	Std. Deviation
Speech	4.62	1.30
Text	5.33	1.53
I/O Style by device	Mean	Std. Deviation
Speech-tablet	4.75	1.36
Speech-smartphone	4.30	1.58
Speech-desktop	4.80	0.95
Text-tablet	5.50	1.62
Text-smartphone	4.30	1.42
Text-desktop	6.20	0.92

Fig. 6. Preference mean ratings of I/O Type by Device.

Benefits for Nursing Students. A repeated measures ANOVA showed a significant main effect of participant's perception of the virtual patients being beneficial to nursing $F(2,40.86) = 4.98$, $p = 0.01$, $\eta2 = 0.27$, Power = 0.77 (Fig. 7) but there was no significant effect for interaction effect of I/O style $F(1,1.41) = 1.99$, $p = 0.17$, Power = 0.28, $\eta2 = 0.07$ nor an interaction effect of I/O style by device $F(2, 1.41) = 1.07$, $p = 0.37$, $\eta2 = 0.07$, Power = 0.21. The main effect showed the highest rankings on the desktop (M = 6.23, SD = 0.73) followed by the tablet (M = 6.20, SD = 0.95) and the smartphone (M = 5.15, SD = 0.89).

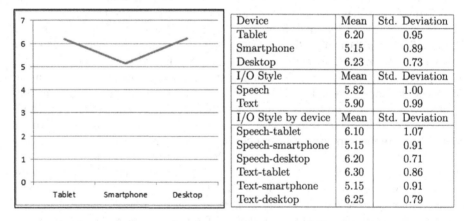

Device	Mean	Std. Deviation
Tablet	6.20	0.95
Smartphone	5.15	0.89
Desktop	6.23	0.73
I/O Style	Mean	Std. Deviation
Speech	5.82	1.00
Text	5.90	0.99
I/O Style by device	Mean	Std. Deviation
Speech-tablet	6.10	1.07
Speech-smartphone	5.15	0.91
Speech-desktop	6.20	0.71
Text-tablet	6.30	0.86
Text-smartphone	5.15	0.91
Text-desktop	6.25	0.79

Fig. 7. Benefit for Nursing Students mean ratings of Devices by Interaction Style.

5.4 Co-presence

A repeated measures ANOVA showed a significant main effect of mobile virtual patient co-presence by device, $F(2, 48.38) = 3.45$, $p = 0.046$, $\eta2 = 0.20$, Power = 0.60 (Fig. 8) and a significant interaction effect of I/O style $F(1, 9.475) = 5.747$, $p = 0.024$, $\eta2 = 0.18$, Power = 0.64 but there was no significant effect for interaction effect of I/O style by device $F < 1$. The main effect showed that participants rated co-presence the highest on the tablet (M = 5.08, SD = 1.14) followed by desktop (M = 4.13, SD = 0.69) and smartphone (M = 4.10, SD = 1.18). The interaction effect of I/O style showed higher rating of co-presence for text (M = 4.61, SD = 1.04) than speech (M = 4.25, SD = 1.16).

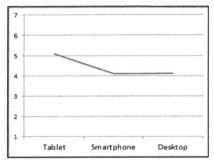

Device	Mean	Std. Deviation
Tablet	5.08	1.14
Smartphone	4.10	1.18
Desktop	4.13	0.69
I/O Style	Mean	Std. Deviation
Speech	4.61	1.04
Text	4.25	1.16
I/O Style by device	Mean	Std. Deviation
Speech-tablet	4.90	1.26
Speech-smartphone	3.90	1.29
Speech-desktop	3.95	0.59
Text-tablet	5.25	1.03
Text-smartphone	4.30	1.08
Text-desktop	4.30	0.75

Fig. 8. Co-presence mean ratings of Devices by Interaction Style.

6 Discussion

6.1 Performance Results

The performance measures collected showed that participants asked more questions using speech than with text. When comparing devices participants asked the most questions when they were using the tablet, followed by the desktop and smartphone. While this data is interesting it is hard to analyze due to a few participants asking for additional time when using a virtual patient. The increased number of questions asked with the tablet and smartphone could be due to this addition time provided. Although, it also could be related to engagement or participants enjoying the mobile virtual patient and wanting to ask as many questions as possible. In any of those cases, the virtual patient is beneficial for increased training practice. The performance measures collected showed that participants asked longer questions using speech than with text. This could be due to that is may have been easier to ask longer questions or that when using a mobile device and texting, typical texting tends to use short-handed diction. When comparing devices, participants asked the longest questions when they were using the desktop, followed by the tablet and the smartphone. Participants may have asked longer questions on the desktop because they were comfortable using that device.

The performance measures collected showed that participants error rate, or questions having unknown responses, was highest while using speech input. This could have in part due to errors in the speech recognition though it should be noted that users asked more in-depth questions while using speech, at time causing the virtual patient not to have a valid response. When comparing devices participants had the highest error rate using the smartphone, compared to the desktop and the tablet. This could be due to the smartphone being a smaller device and having a keypad that users may not have been accustomed to. It was noted that many users would move the smartphone closer to them while speaking which may have cause background noise.

6.2 Usability and User Experience

Usability: Ease of Use, Satisfaction, Learnability. On all devices and input styles participants responded positively for ease of use however, the desktop was reported as having the highest overall ease of use, followed by the tablet and the smartphone. The average age for participants in this study was 38.2 which may have attribute to all 30 participants owning a computer. Only 19 of the participants owned a mobile device with only 40% of participants that where given the smartphone device owning a smartphone. The ease of use could have also been lower on the smartphone due to it being a smaller device, with a smaller screen and a keypad that users may not have been accustomed to using, as a few smartphone participants stated: "I don't normally text" and "texting is slow". Participants responded positively about their satisfaction with the screen size on the tablet and desktop however, the smartphone the responses were neutral. The smartphone ranked the lowest is to be expected with the smartphone having the smallest screen size of 3.7″ however; it ranked noticeably lower than the tablet. Some insight on this was provided by participants' responses in the qualitative data. When asked which about device participants prefer, they responded with statements like "tablet, it is mobile and still large enough to see detail", "the smartphone might be too small" and "tablet or larger for visual assessment". These types of statements reveal that the smartphone did not show as much visual details about the virtual patient. It was also noted that, on the tablet and desktop, multiple participants reported on visual characteristic of the virtual patient, this was never reported on the smartphone.

Participants using the tablet and desktop reported positively on their perception of learnability while using the virtual patient however, users on the smartphone had a neutral response. The neutral response by participants on the smartphone may be due to is smaller screen size since attention to detail is an important aspect nurse training [1] and it can be difficult to see the mobile virtual patients detail on the small screen provided by the smartphone.

User Experience: Enjoyment and Preferences. Participants showed they enjoyed working on the tablet the most. This follows the trend of the tablet ranking highly among the previous areas of ease of use, screen size, co-presence and learnability. The participants ranked the tablet below the desktop for ease of use however; the simplest products are not always the most enjoyable. The participants ranked the smartphone lowest for enjoyable to use and this is likely due to its ranking the lowest among ease of use, screen size, presence and learnability.

Users preferred I/O style by participants across all devices was the text. This could be due several factors such as someone being present in the room with the participant while they were working with the virtual patient. Another factor could have been speech recognition and synthesis or the text-to-speech voice used. Like with all speech recognition software there are sometime errors in determining what the user is saying and the participants seemed to notice this and provided comments like "more unexpected responses with the speech version". Other users were more comfortable texting with comments like "easier to type than speaking to a computer".

Participant's responses during the debriefing interview showed that more participants preferred text than speech. There were many useful comments such as: "my preference would depend on my location" and "prefer texting if in a public location". Comments like this show that both I/O styles may be viable depending on where the mobile virtual patient is going to be used. It should also be noted that a proctor was in the room while the participants were interacting with the mobile virtual patient, this may have caused more people to prefer text since they were not using the virtual patient privately. Participants responses during the debriefing showed that the tablet was the most preferred device. This may be due to the participants ranking the tablet highly among the previous areas of ease of use, screen size, co-presence and learnability. Some participants' responses when asked about their preferred device were: "tablet, for visual assessment", "tablet, prefect middle ground for size and portability", and "I feel that a tablet is the ideal device for a mobile virtual patient as it is large enough to see detail, yet small enough to be used as a mobile device".

Benefit for Nurse Training. When participants were asked questions about the mobile virtual patient being beneficial to nursing the participants responded positively on all devices and I/O styles. The smartphone was rated the lowest may be contributed to the smaller screen size not providing as much detail of the mobile virtual patient. Noticing visual symptoms when diagnosing a patient, is an important skill for nurses to learn [1]. However, the smartphone has a hard time providing visual assessment due to its small screen. There were a lot of positive quantitative responses collected from participants. A teacher stated that it would provide "opportunities to verify practice", that "it would be useful in that students need to learn to form questions" and that it would be beneficial to "use in online classes". Another teacher stated that "it would provide a standardized scenario for students" and "it would allow us to have more off-campus practice for students". From the feedback provided shows that a mobile virtual patient would be a beneficial simulation tool for nursing students to interact with.

6.3   Co-presence

Co-presence was reported to be the highest by participants using the tablet device, which came as a surprise, as it was hypothesized that the desktop display would provide a higher co-presence with the larger screen size. The desktop had a significantly larger screen at 23″ compared to 3.7″. There are no responses that provide insight to why the co-presence was reported higher on the table than the desktop, which had a larger screen than the tablet. One theory is that the tablet is held closer to a user than the desktop monitor, which could make it seem like effective screen size larger on the tablet, creating an immersive effective. Another theory is that many people interact over video conferencing applications, such as Skype or FaceTime, and may relate to that type of interaction in a more human-to-human interaction way. There were also responses like "tablet, for visual assessment" which shows that participants liked the way the virtual patient on the tablet looked. The desktop and smartphone where rated similar by participants for co-presence. This could be that a user holding the device may increase presence however, another study would need to be done to investigate this.

7 Contributions and Conclusion

The purpose of this research was to design a mobile device-based and a web-based virtual patient with dynamic discourse interaction for nurse training to determine if mobile device platforms are sufficient to incorporate dynamic interaction of a conversational agent. We used this prototype and conducted a user experiment to investigate the effects of mobility and screen size has on a mobile virtual patient. We measured performance and participants' ratings on ease of use, screen size satisfaction, co-presence, learnability, being enjoyable to use and being beneficial to nursing students. The contributions of this evaluation can be summarized as follows:

- Mobile devices are sufficient to incorporate dynamic interaction of a virtual conversational agent or virtual human.
- Mobile virtual patients are beneficial for nursing students to provide nurse training.
- Co-presence is higher when interacting with a mobile virtual patient using a tablet.
- Speech I/O facilitates users to ask more detailed questions and engage the users more in nurse training when interacting with a mobile virtual patient.
- Text I/O is the preferred input style for interacting with mobile virtual patients.
- Ease of use was highest for interaction with a mobile virtual patient on a tablet.
- A tablet provided the highest results for interacting in a realistic manner.

The main conclusion that can be made from this study was that on all devices mobile virtual would be beneficial to nursing students and thus could be used as a learning device. All devices were acceptable platforms for interacting with a mobile virtual patient for nurse training. The tablet provided participants with the best experience with a large screen size, highest co-presence and enjoyable to use. Therefore, when training with a mobile virtual patient use a tablet with Speech I/O for the best training outcomes or Texting I/O as the more preferred method when there are people around, on the go, or when a user feels self-conscious about their training performance interacting with either a smartphone or tablet. The results from this research can be used by future researchers to continue to investigate mobile virtual patients and usage.

8 Future Work

There are several directions of research that could follow from this work. This study determines that text input is favored I/O style among users however, it does not compare different ways of implementing speech input. An extension of this work would be to run a study evaluating several versions of implementing speech input for a mobile virtual patient. Another follow-up study would be to investigate the I/O style and proxemics and density of people to users training. Another area of work for a mobile virtual patient are learning outcome associated with different scenarios for virtual patients and learnability. Another aspect would be to investigate long-term training effect and frequency of use when having access to a mobile virtual patient for training.

Acknowledgements. We would like to thank all participants who participated in this study.

References

1. Jones, M.E., Cason, C.L., Bond, M.L.: Cultural attitudes, knowledge, and skills of a health workforce. Transcult. Nurs. **15**(4), 283–290 (2004)
2. Gaba, D.: The future vision of simulation in healthcare. Simul. Healthc. **2**(2), 126–135 (2007)
3. Helfer, R.E., Slater, C.H., Goltz, L.: Measuring the process of solving clinical diagnostic problems. Med. Educ. **5**(1), 48–52 (1971)
4. van der Vleuten, C.P.M., Swanson, D.B.: Assessment of clinical skills with standardized patients: state of the art. Teach. Learn. Med. **2**(2), 58–76 (1990)
5. McKenzie, F., Garcia, H., Castelino, R., Hubbard, T., Ullian, J., Gliva, G.: Augmented standardized patients now virtually a reality. In: Third IEEE and ACM International Symposium on Mixed and Augmented Reality, ISMAR 2004, pp. 270–271, November 2004
6. Hwang, Y., Lampotang, S., Gravenstein, N., Luria, I., Lok, B.: Integrating conversational virtual humans and mannequin patient simulators to present mixed reality clinical training experiences. In: 8th IEEE International Symposium on Mixed and Augmented Reality, ISMAR 2009, pp. 197–198, October 2009
7. Triola, M., et al.: A randomized trial of teaching clinical skills using virtual and live standardized patients. J. Gen. Intern. Med. **21**(5), 424–429 (2006)
8. Johnsen, K., et al.: Experiences in using immersive virtual characters to educate medical communication skills. In: Proceedings of the Virtual Reality, VR 2005, pp. 179–186. IEEE, March 2005
9. Zary, N., Johnson, G., Fors, U.: Web-based virtual patients in dentistry: factors influencing the use of cases in the Web-SP system. Eur. J. Dent. Educ. **13**(1), 2–9 (2009)
10. Cook, D.A., Triola, M.M.: Virtual patients: a critical literature review and proposed next steps. Med. Educ. **43**(4), 303–311 (2009)
11. Zary, N., Johnson, G., Boberg, J., Fors, U.: Development, implementation and pilot evaluation of a web-based virtual patient case simulation environment - Web-SP. BMC Med. Educ. **6**(1), 10 (2006)
12. Bearman, M., Cesnik, B., Liddell, M.: Random comparison of 'virtual patient' models in the context of teaching clinical communication skills. Med. Educ. **35**(9), 824–832 (2001)
13. Triola, M., et al.: A randomized trial of teaching clinical skills using virtual and live standardized patients. JGIM J. Gen. Intern. Med. **21**(5), 424–429 (2006)
14. Hubal, R.C., Kizakevich, P.N., Guinn, C.I., West, S.L., Merino, K.D.: The virtual standardized patient-simulated patient-practitioner dialogue for patient interview training, pp. 133–138. IOS Press, Amsterdam (2000)
15. Kenny, P., Parsons, T.D., Gratch, J., Leuski, A., Rizzo, A.A.: Virtual patients for clinical therapist skills training. In: Pelachaud, C., Martin, J.-C., André, E., Chollet, G., Karpouzis, K., Pelé, D. (eds.) IVA 2007. LNCS (LNAI), vol. 4722, pp. 197–210. Springer, Heidelberg (2007). https://doi.org/10.1007/978-3-540-74997-4_19
16. Ziemkiewicz, C., Ulinski, A., Zanbaka, C., Hardin, S., Hodges, L.: Interactive digital patient for triage nurse training. In: First International Conference on Virtual Reality. Citeseer (2005)
17. Taylor, J.D., et al.: Developing a mobile learning solution for health and social care practice. Distance Educ. **31**(2), 175–192 (2010)
18. Lea, S., Callaghan, L.: Enhancing health and social care placement learning through mobile technology. J. Educ. Technol. Soc. **14**(1), 135–145 (2011)
19. Huang, G., Reynolds, R., Candler, C.: Enhancing health and social care placement learning through mobile technology. J. Educ. Technol. Soc. **82**(5), 446–451 (2007)

20. Cassell, J.: Embodied Conversation Agents. MIT Press, Cambridge (2000)
21. Rethans, J.-J., et al.: The relationship between competence and performance: implications for assessing practice performance. Med. Educ. **36**(10), 901–909 (2002)
22. iclone 4.3 (2012). http://www.reallusion.com/iclone/
23. Sapi 4 (2000). http://www.microsoft.com/
24. Adobe flex 3.5 (2012). http://www.adobe.com/products/flex.html
25. Mysql (2012). http://www.microsoft.com/

Xavier Electromyographic Wheelchair Control and Virtual Training

Albert Manero[1], Bjorn Oskarsson[2], John Sparkman[1],
Peter A. Smith[1(✉)], Matt Dombrowski[1], Mrudula Peddinti[1],
Angel Rodriguez[1], Juan Vila[1], and Brendan Jones[1]

[1] Limbitless Solutions, University of Central Florida,
4217 East Plaza Drive, Orlando, FL 32816, USA
albert@limbitless-solutions.org,
peter.smith@gmail.com
[2] Mayo Clinic Jacksonville, 4500 San Pablo Rd, Jacksonville,
FL 32224, USA
Oskarsson.Bjorn@mayo.edu

Abstract. For a variety of individuals, limited hand dexterity yields complications to independently control a power wheelchair. Neurological conditions, including quadriplegia, and traumatic brain injuries can all reduce or eliminate fine motor skills necessary to operate a joystick. For patients with progressive disorders, this acute or chronic progression can affect the hands and limbs at an early stage of the disease. In an effort to extend independence and autonomous mobility, the Xavier system was developed to utilize electromyography signals measured on the temporalis muscles on the face to enable control of a power wheelchair. This study looks to document the human to machine interaction and control scheme as well as discuss the development of a clinical trial protocol to quantify the effectiveness and meaning of the technology on patients. Patient selection in this pilot study was focused on people living with Amyotrophic Lateral Sclerosis (ALS) in conjunction with Mayo Clinic Jacksonville. A review of the clinical protocol and assessment techniques is joined with a discussion about the role of virtual training via designed vehicle simulation to develop muscle isolation and driving mechanics.

Keywords: Mobility · ALS · Electromyography

1 Introduction

Patients ailed by numerous neurologic conditions preserve mobility and function via powered wheelchairs. Their ability to use these wheelchairs can subsequently be impaired by disease progression affecting hand dexterity. The consequent limited mobility decreases independence and quality of life [12]. The state of the art technology is often limited in the extent of the autonomy and mobility that can be provided. For many patient groups challenged with progressive peripheral motor loss and other complications, autonomous wheelchair control may be lost due to limited alternative devices and remain a lower priority relative to the overall medical care.

© Springer Nature Switzerland AG 2019
J. Y. C. Chen and G. Fragomeni (Eds.): HCII 2019, LNCS 11574, pp. 133–142, 2019.
https://doi.org/10.1007/978-3-030-21607-8_10

1.1   Background

Wheelchair control and associated improved quality of life may be preserved via technology such as sip and puff pressure transducers or head mounted accelerometers [2]. However, these methods may be bulky, obtrusive, and have control systems with increased complexity [2]. For some patients with advanced disease, no independent mobility options exist that are compatible for their condition and needs. Studies [1] have assessed the effectiveness and user response to different techniques including head mouse control, speech control, and limited fine motor skill controls such as single control actuation using the Psychosocial Impact of Assistive Devices Scale (PIADS) [6]. These evaluations are discretized into three categories including: Competence (12 items), Adaptability (6 items), and Self-Esteem (8 items). The responses highlighted [1] the role of independence counteracting humiliation as well as the role of autonomy on feeling productive. This aligns with expectations patients may set for themselves from a functionalist perspective [14] and has a real impact on quality of life perceptions.

1.2   Electromyography

To attempt to preserve patient mobility in advanced disease, research has been conducted in novel control systems based on electroencephalogram (EEG) [3, 19], electrooculography (EOG) tracking [19, 20], and electromyography (EMG) [3, 4, 13, 18, 19]. These methods capture voltage signals produced in isolated muscle groups resulting from nervous system stimulation triggering an electro-chemical response during contraction. These signals can be amplified and measured sufficiently over the baseline noise bands [17].

Utilization of these modalities has been effective in capturing intentionally of motion, but has been limited by the need for more extensive on-board computers, challenges with muscle group isolation, and development of efficient control schemes and training methods. The methods have demonstrated incredible promise as these limitations continue to be mitigated. Two studies [4, 13] have both demonstrated success in isolating electromyography signals using shoulder muscle actuation and left right decoupling from a variety of muscle groups. These muscle groups include levator scapulae and sternocleidomastoid. However, for progressive diseases or high level spinal cord injuries, muscle isolation may be limited to only the muscles in the face. This, coupled with other limitations such as breathing apparatuses or head bracing, have limited control methods for use in certain populations.

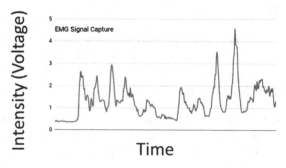

Fig. 1. Example electromyography signal featuring pattern pulse, varying magnitude (voltage over time), and long duration flexure.

Electromyographic measurements on the face have been observed to be complex, sometimes with significant artifacts. Signal processing, both hardware and software, can be done to read a more clear signal that can isolate intentionality from a variety of muscle groups. On board integrated bandpass filters can help improve the signal to noise and support more complex assessment. Further, these muscles can perform contractions of varying complexity including patterns, various magnitudes, and short activation versus long duration. This can be seen in Fig. 1 for an example reading from a bicep actuated pattern sequence. In this study's approach, muscle groups on the face including the temporalis muscles are considered for isolation. These muscles can be engaged and isolated with subtle jaw motion such as a clench of the molars. For full vehicular control, two sensors are used on opposing sides of the temporalis muscle set [5]. Additional isolation and effectiveness can be learned through practice and potentially simulation efforts. The location of the electromyography leads vary based on muscle volume and strength, but can be generalized as seen in Fig. 2.

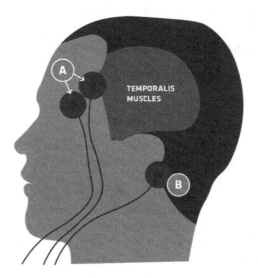

Fig. 2. Electromyographic lead placement on temporalis muscle groups for human machine interface including signal (a) and ground (b) locations

An example of the lead placement and system in use is presented in Fig. 3 during internal lab control scheme validation. It is important to note that lead placement will vary with each user and may vary with muscle composition and skin tightness. The temporalis control method permits a greater degree of independence via allowing multitasking: for example, the patient can maintain a conversation or sip from a straw while simultaneously controlling accurate wheelchair movement.

Fig. 3. Example of device in operation during internal control scheme validation

2   Clinical Assessment Design

Amyotrophic lateral sclerosis (ALS) is a heterogeneous disease involving motor neuron death, resulting in progressive weakness and disability [16]. In the limb-onset subset of ALS patients, facial muscles are often spared until late in the disease [15]. Such facial sparing makes the limb-onset subset of ALS patients candidates for significantly benefiting from our device. This initial pilot study is limited to this population, however other populations that could also significantly benefit include any afflicted by significant arm and leg weakness with preserved head muscle control, such as subsets of patients with spinal cord injury (SCI) or traumatic brain injury (TBI).

The initial pilot study was designed for patients to learn to use the hands-free wheelchair control system on a standardized 4 × 4 m indoor testing course. The course included several components such as turns, obstacle avoidance, and simulated residential obstacles. Participants are asked to perform a series of wheelchair skills in the testing course with the standard joystick system at baseline and with the Xavier hands free system. Testing will be repeated for comparison with the hands-free control system at the post-evaluation visits. Additional secondary post-evaluation visits depending on how fast proficiency is achieved.

2.1   Control Methods

The Xavier system allows users to engage and control their wheelchair or vehicle through temporalis engagement. This is more practically expressed to the patient as jaw clenching, which through coupling can isolate and engage the temporalis group for signal measurement. These instructions are presented in a user manual for new patients and clinicians. Figure 4 describes and visualizes the flex pattern required to trigger the forward and reverse actuation states by activating both left and right muscle groups simultaneously. A longer duration activation will trigger the reverse condition. At any time in the forward state, an additional dual activation flex will perform a complete vehicle stop.

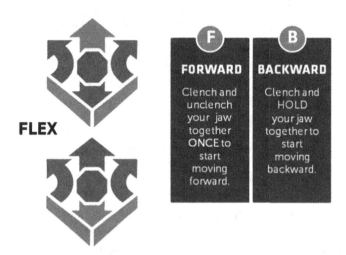

Fig. 4. Excerpt from user manual, visualizing forward and reverse control schemes for patient interaction with system.

While engaged in the forward motion, left or right translation can be activated by a single (left or right) muscle activation. This maintains the forward motion, resulting in a turning radius travel dependent on how long the muscle is engaged. This provides a direct control scheme which can also be tailored to the patient's desired control scheme, turning rate, and overall sensitivity. Figure 5 highlights this visualization of the control scheme.

Initial learning of control states is initiated while the wheelchair is in a parking mode, allowing the received gesture state actuated to be verbally or visually communicated to the patient. This is designed to provide a more comfortable learning experience. Emphasis for control is first placed on gross skills, forward and reverse, before left and right activation. For some users, decoupling the left and right temporalis muscles may prove to be complex and require additional use time before mastering. The role of visual or auditory feedback has been explored from user feedback, and noted that it may accelerate the ability to learn the control schemes.

Of interest to many is speed control of the vehicle and menu selection. This is particularly important for patients with more sophisticated or involved wheelchairs, that may include breathing support or other medical support on board. The initial pilot study only features the forward, reverse, left, and right, and their respective combinations.

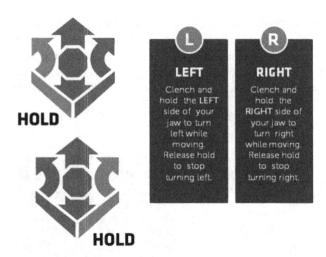

Fig. 5. Excerpt from user manual, visualizing left and right control schemes for patient interaction with system. Steering can be implemented from either the rest state or as a modifying direction while engaged in forward or reverse.

This is mainly limited by the ability to interface with many different styles of power wheelchairs and in an effort to not compromise any critical support equipment on board. Further continuation of the control schemes are in development that feature manipulation of speed with varying flex magnitude controls, but are not yet deployed. Additional 'sport' modes where turning sensitivity can be adjusted through a flex signal command to adjust for varying indoor or outdoor obstacles of different length scales are also in development.

2.2 Wheelchair Skills Test

The Wheelchair Skills test is the primary standardized assessment utilized in this study, and was developed and refined at Dalhousie University [7–11]. It is used to compare baseline function in the patient's current assistive power chair and the subsequent testing in the Xavier control system. The primary questions found in the Wheelchair Skills Test are enumerated herein. Not every question is applicable or influenced by the Xavier control system, which only interfaces with the users current chair and interacts with steering control. The clinical protocol emphasizes these control focused questions as the study team looks to understand the usability and role of training with the system.

For evaluation of the wheelchair skills, the scoring for capacity is on a 0, 1, or 2 scale. Here, a score of 0 is a failure in assessment, a score or 1 is considered pass with difficulty, and a score of 2 is identified as passing.

Wheel Chair Skills Testing Questionnaire [9]

1. Moves controller away and back
2. Turns power on and off
3. Selects drive modes and speeds
4. Disengages and engages motors
5. Operates battery charger
6. Rolls forwards short distance
7. Rolls backwards short distance
8. Turns in place
9. Turns while moving forwards
10. Turns while moving backwards
11. Maneuvers sideways
12. Reaches high object
13. Picks object from floor
14. Relieves weight from buttocks
15. Operates body positioning options
16. Level transfer
17. Gets through hinged door
18. Rolls longer distance
19. Avoids moving obstacles
20. Ascends slight incline
21. Descends slight incline
22. Ascends steep incline
23. Descends steep incline
24. Rolls across side-slope
25. Rolls on soft surface
26. Gets over threshold
27. Gets over gap
28. Ascends low curb
29. Descends low curb
30. Gets from ground into wheelchair

2.3 Patient Selection

Patient selection was established for the pilot study to provide a clear and focused population. A maximum of five patients are authorized under the pilot clinical trial protocol. While future work is designed to expand to additional patient demographics, the initial work with only a handful of patients to be included follows this inclusion criteria:

Inclusion Criteria

- ALS diagnosis by revised el Escorial criteria (definite, probable or probable laboratory supported)
- Age 18–89
- Limited mobility with use of motorized wheelchair at screening-time
- Impairment of hand function limiting the use of a standard joystick control
- Caregiver willing to assist with transfers into wheelchair and application of controllers
- Ability to attend study visits with a motorized wheelchair
- Ability to communicate and answer patient reported outcome measure questions

Exclusion Criteria

- Cognitive impairment prohibiting safe independent mobility as defined by an ALS Cognitive Behavioral Screen (ALS-CBS) score of <10 or the opinion of the investigator
- A sensory impairment prohibiting safe independent mobility in the opinion of the investigator
- Allergy to adhesives or electrode gels (required for EMG electrodes)

- Skin breakdown over the temporalis muscle that would predispose to further breakdown and/or infection with electrodes
- Severe loss of facial muscle functionality or control that would preclude EMG electrode efficacy
- Subjects who do not have the capacity to consent

3 Virtual Training Goals

During the design and prototyping phase, the need for a clear visual feedback surrounding the human to computer interaction became apparent. Because of the challenges of learning to control a vehicle in a real world environment, the study's researchers set out to create an interactive virtual simulation of the control scheme. This began with its hardware operation connecting with a computer terminal to transfer the three classes of action: isolated left flexing, isolated right flexing, and simultaneous flexing. Interfacing with a Unity® game engine, it was possible to simulate the operation of the wheelchair in a digital 3D space by setting up these states in the video game and reading the input from each separate sensor in the same way as the hardware.

Once an accurate simulation was completed where a player had the ability to navigate an avatar through a digital 3D space presented in Fig. 6, many design opportunities arose for ways to extend the experience past its current hardware limitations. This allowed the simulation team to support new functions and hardware development. Future versions of the software will allow for variable flexes based on the magnitude of the received signals. One setting allows to shift between control schemes such as vehicle gears in the simulation. Differences in the vehicle control methods and in the training methods will be tested as well to target specific training outcomes or experiences. The virtual environment will allow for advancing design goals and establishing stronger training methods to expedite learning full control of wheelchairs and vehicles.

Fig. 6. Virtual training environment built in a Unity® game engine

4   Future Work

With the designed protocol and focused patient demographic, the next step for this work is to begin the clinical assessment of the hands-free wheelchair control system. The assessment and survey instruments will provide valuable feedback and validation for the technical design, control scheme usability, and instruction or training methods. From the early developmental work, the need for a virtual training environment to support both learning the driving mechanics and proficiency has been demonstrated. Initial development findings have supported the benefit of visual or audio feedback during the calibration and early use cases. Following the conclusion of the pilot study for five ALS patients, efforts to study the role of the virtual training will be implemented in a secondary study. A comparison of the rate of training to a control group is of key interest and will demonstrate new ways to use virtual challenges and problem solving to teach mechanics or complex tasks that require longer period of training. Efforts to mask the technical learning behind a visual experience or gamified tasks will look to enhance the patient experience, affinities to the device, and overall proficiency.

Acknowledgments. The authors would like to thank the many members of the Limbitless team who have supported the project throughout its development. The authors would also like to disclose that the technology for this study is patent pending under US Application US20180147099A1 with all claims reserved [5].

References

1. Axelson, P.W., Chesney, D.A., Minkel, J.: Powered mobility device skills test. In: Proceedings of the RESNA 2000 Annual Conference: Technology for the New Millennium, 28 June–2 July 2000, Omni Rosen Hotel, Orlando, Florida, p. 450. ERIC (2000)
2. Fehr, L., Langbein, W.E., Skaar, S.B.: Adequacy of power wheelchair control inter- faces for persons with severe disabilities: a clinical survey. J. Rehabil. Res. Dev. **37**(3), 353–360 (2000)
3. Felzer, T., Freisleben, B.: HaWCos: the hands-free wheelchair control system. In: Proceedings of the Fifth International ACM Conference on Assistive Technologies, pp. 127–134. ACM (2002)
4. Han, J.S., Bien, Z.Z., Kim, D.J., Lee, H.E., Kim, J.S.: Human-machine interface for wheelchair control with EMG and its evaluation. In: Engineering in Medicine and Biology Society, Proceedings of the 25th Annual International Conference of the IEEE, vol. 2, pp. 1602–1605. IEEE (2003)
5. Jones, B., Albert, M.I., Sparkman, J.: Electromyographic controlled vehicles and chairs, US Patent App. 15/361,372, 31 May 2018
6. Jutai, J., Day, H.: Psychosocial impact of assistive devices scale (PIADS). Technol. Disabil. **14**(3), 107–111 (2002)
7. Kirby, R.L., et al.: The wheelchair skills test (version 2.4): measurement properties1. Arch. Phys. Med. Rehabil. **85**(5), 794–804 (2004)
8. Kirby, R.L., et al.: The wheelchair skills program manual. Published electronically at Dalhousie University, Halifax, Nova Scotia, Canada (2018). http://www.wheelchairskillsprogram.ca/eng/manual.php

9. Kirby, R.L., et al.: The wheelchair skills program manual. Published electronically at Dalhousie University, Halifax, Nova Scotia, Canada (2016). http://www.wheelchairskillsprogram.ca/eng/manual.php

10. Kirby, R.L., Swuste, J., Dupuis, D.J., MacLeod, D.A., Monroe, R.: The wheelchair skills test: a pilot study of a new outcome measure. Arch. Phys. Med. Rehabil. **83**(1), 10–18 (2002)

11. Kirby, R.L., et al.: Wheelchair skills capacity and performance of manual wheelchair users with spinal cord injury. Arch. Phys. Med. Rehabil. **97**(10), 1761–1769 (2016)

12. Lulé, D., Hacker, S., Ludolph, A., Birbaumer, N., Kübler, A.: Depression and quality of life in patients with amyotrophic lateral sclerosis. Deutsches Ärzteblatt International **105**(23), 397 (2008)

13. Moon, I., Lee, M., Chu, J., Mun, M.: Wearable EMG-based HCI for electric-powered wheelchair users with motor disabilities. In: Proceedings of the 2005 IEEE International Conference on Robotics and Automation, ICRA 2005, pp. 2649–2654. IEEE (2005)

14. Mooney, L.A., Knox, D., Schacht, C.: Understanding social problems: three main sociological perspectives (2007)

15. Ravits, J.M., La Spada, A.R.: ALS motor phenotype heterogeneity, focality, and spread deconstructing motor neuron degeneration. Neurology **73**(10), 805–811 (2009)

16. Ringel, S., et al.: The natural history of amyotrophic lateral sclerosis. Neurology **43**(7), 1316 (1993)

17. Silver, J.K.: Easy EMG-a Guide to Performing Nerve Conduction Studies and Electromyogra. Elsevier-Health Sciences Division (2015)

18. Tamura, H., Manabe, T., Goto, T., Yamashita, Y., Tanno, K.: A study of the electric wheelchair hands-free safety control system using the surface-electromygram of facial muscles. In: Liu, H., Ding, H., Xiong, Z., Zhu, X. (eds.) ICIRA 2010. LNCS (LNAI), vol. 6425, pp. 97–104. Springer, Heidelberg (2010). https://doi.org/10.1007/978-3-642-16587-0_10

19. Tsui, C.S.L., Jia, P., Gan, J.Q., Hu, H., Yuan, K.: EMG-based hands-free wheelchair control with EOG attention shift detection. In: IEEE International Conference on Robotics and Biomimetics, ROBIO 2007, pp. 1266–1271. IEEE (2007)

20. Yanco, H.A.: Wheelesley: a robotic wheelchair system: Indoor navigation and user interface. In: Mittal, V.O., Yanco, H.A., Aronis, J., Simpson, R. (eds.) Assistive Technology and Artificial Intelligence. LNCS, vol. 1458, pp. 256–268. Springer, Heidelberg (1998). https://doi.org/10.1007/BFb0055983

The Effect of Onomatopoeia to Enhancing User Experience in Virtual Reality

Jiwon Oh and Gerard J. Kim[(✉)]

Digital Experience Laboratory, Korea University, Seoul, Korea
{hanajitsu94,gjkim}@korea.ac.kr

Abstract. Onomatopoeia refers to a word that phonetically imitates, resembles, or suggests the sound (or motion that accompanies sound) that it describes. It is often used in comics, games, and videos, along with the actual sound in caption. This usage is a way to emphasize, exaggerate, dramatize and draw attention the situation. In this paper we explore if the use of onomatopoeia, associated with sound feedback, could also bring about similar effects and improve the user experience in immersive virtual reality. We present an experiment comparing the user's subjective experiences and attentive performance in two virtual worlds, each configured in two test conditions: (1) sound feedback with no onomatopoeia and (2) sound feedback with it. Our experiment has found that the moderate and strategic use of onomatopoeia can indeed help direct user attention, offer object affordance and thereby enhance user experience and even the sense of presence and immersion.

Keywords: Onomatopoeia · Virtual reality · Sound visualization · User experience

1 Introduction

Onomatopoeia refers to a word that phonetically imitates, resembles, or suggests the sound (or motion that accompanies sound) that it describes. Common occurrences of onomatopoeia include animal noises such as "oink", "meow", "roar" and "chirp" [16]. Onomatopoeia is much used in paper comics that have no aural feedback, to enrich the static image cuts [4]. However, it is used less in a spoken fashion especially in the Indo-European languages. The extent of use of onomatopoeia can differ between languages and cultures, and Koreans, in particular, make use of onomatopoeia in both written (not necessarily for comics) and spoken ways very frequently. It is often used even along with the actual sound in caption for entertainment shows (in Korea [6]) and games [8]) as a way to dramatize, emphasize, exaggerate and draw attention the situation [19].

On the other hand, one of the important goals to achieve in virtual reality (VR) is to provide a rich content experience by giving users a high level of immersion and presence (feeling as if situated in the [5, 13]). There are variety elements that can affect and improve the sense of presence, including the first person viewpoint, visual realism, interaction, shielding from the operating environment, and physical immersion, just to name a few.

© Springer Nature Switzerland AG 2019
J. Y. C. Chen and G. Fragomeni (Eds.): HCII 2019, LNCS 11574, pp. 143–152, 2019.
https://doi.org/10.1007/978-3-030-21607-8_11

Fig. 1. The two test virtual environments: "Animal Farm" (left) and the "Busy Kitchen" (right), "Sound-only" (above) and With-words" (below).

Based on such observations and research results, we explore if the use of onomatopoeia, associated with sound feedback. could also bring about the similar effect, i.e. enhancement in presence and immersion for VR. Note that showing of onomatopoeia is not physically possible in the real world, however, there have been many instance of purely virtual worlds or proper mixing of physically unrealistic effects (e.g. showing motion profiles of a flying ball in a tennis game [1]) such that it can still induce the suspension of disbelief and not come in the way of, or even enhance the level of immersion and presence [5, 13]. On the other hand, we can also expect overusing onomatopoeia can be distracting, too unrealistic and break the sense of immersion and illusion [12].

In the following, we present a pilot experiment (and its results) comparing the user's subjective user experience, presence and immersion in two virtual worlds, each configured in test conditions: (1) sound feedback with no onomatopoeia and (2) sound feedback with it. First, we shortly review related research in the next section.

2 Related Work

There have been several works that has artificially added "text (or glyphs)" and localized "sound word animation" to images [9] and videos [15] with the intent to add the effects of, e.g. dynamics and excitement. As for the use of onomatopoeia, perhaps due to the cultural orientation, there have been just few researches mainly from Japan, as applied to images or computer graphic contents, but not for immersive virtual reality. For example, Wang et al. developed a method for automatically transforming non-verbal video sounds to animated sound words and positioning them near the sound source objects in the video for visualization. Furthermore, they conducted a user study to show that animated sound words helped clarify the sound source and made the video watching more enjoyable [15]. Yamamoto et al. developed a method to transform the environmental sound into the corresponding onomatopoeia and visualized them in various ways (e.g. varying fonts and sizes to reflect sound qualities and loudness) [18]. In a similar vein, Fukusato and Morishima considered the estimation and depiction of onomatopoeia in computer-generated animation based on physical parameters [3]. More recently, Shimoda and Yani have applied the deep neural network in labeling an image with the appropriate onomatopoeia [12].

Among many presence enhancing elements, we take a note of the role of attention and affordance [10, 11, 17]. The use of onomatopoeia, to direct user's attention, can be regarded as a similar approach. Illusion effects and multimodal effects for enriching VR contents are also related approaches [2, 7, 20].

3   Experiment

3.1   Experiment Design

A usability experiment was carried out to assess the projected merits of the use of onomatopoeia, as an additive to the regular sound effect, towards directing user attention, affordance, and thereby to enhancing immersion and presence. The assessment was made over two different virtual reality scenes. Thus, the main factors were the use of onomatopoeia and scene type, making the experiment designed as a 2-factors x 2-levels within subject repeated measure.

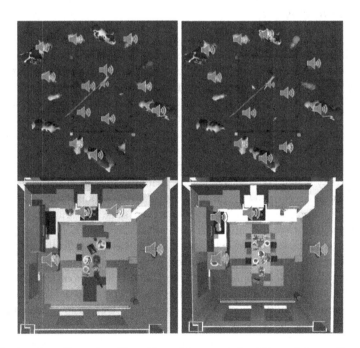

Fig. 2. The location of sound making object. (above – Animal Farm, below – Busy Kitchen)

3.2   Experiment Task

The experimental task involved the subject to experience two different scenes, "Animal Farm" and "Busy Kitchen" (see Fig. 1) and assess them guided by a subjective survey. Each scene type was configured in the two test conditions, i.e. (A) one with ordinary sound effects (denoted "*Sound-only*"), e.g. from the animals (cow, sheep, chicken, pig), cooking objects (kettle, boiling pot, operating mixer, baking oven), and other miscellaneous ones (flag on a pole, clock on the wall, running water from a faucet, ringing phone), (B) the other with the added onomatopoeia (denoted "*With-words*"). Therefore, as a within-subject experiment, there were four virtual environments for the subject to experience and assess, presented in a balanced order: (1) Farm/Sound-only, (2) Farm/With-words, (3) Kitchen/Sound-only, (4) Kitchen/With-words. To minimize any learning effect, the respective scenes (Farm and Kitchen) was slightly reconfigured between experiencing (1) and (2), and (3) and (4): as for the Farm, the number and kinds of animals making sounds were made and distributed differently (the total staying the same), and as for the Kitchen, the types of food prepared, several types of cooking apparatus and time of day (one for breakfast and other supper preparation) were changed. The total number of objects making sounds in the Farm was about 12 and 15 for the Kitchen, distributed evenly throughout the scene (see Fig. 2). For the condition (B), the onomatopoeias were positioned right next or above to the pertaining objects with sufficient contrast for visibility. The actual sound words (onomatopoeia) used in the experiment all common and registered in the standard Koreans dictionary.

3.3   Experiment Procedure

Thirty six people (18 females and males) aged between 19 and 38, (mean = 23.4, SD = 3.3) participated in the study. Each subject experienced and freely navigated around the four test VR scenes (for 5 min each) in an order balanced around the content theme (Farm/Kitchen) and the experimental factor (with or without the onomatopoeia). The subject was told to count the total number of notable objects (e.g. animals, kitchen objects) and sound making objects, and also identify which objects or how many of them were making sounds. Such measures were collected to evaluate quantitatively the effect of the onomatopoeia with respect to user focus/attention and awareness.

After experiencing the each scene (2-conditions x 2-content types), the subject answered a survey which asked of the general usability (fatigue, sickness, naturalness), content perception (liveliness, realism, affordance and attention), presence/immersion, and enjoyment/preference level, all in 7 level Likert scale (see Table 1). Finally, the subjects were asked of various situations in the respective scenes (see Table 2) and to describe the experience virtual space in words, which was linguistically analyzed for its richness in expression similar to the approach in [14].

The testing platform was implemented with Unity3D and run on a desktop PC with the HTC VIVE head-set and interaction controller (for navigation). Further experiment procedural details are omitted due to space restriction. Our basic expected outcomes

Table 1. The subjective survey assessing a variety of aspects in user experience (all answered in 7 level Likert scale).

Fatigue

F1 I am mentally tired looking around the environment

Simulation sickness

S1 I feel sick and nauseated
S2 I have a headache
S3 I feel dizzy
S4 I have a problem in concentrating

Naturalness

N1 The visual scene looks natural

Perceived Realism

R1 The visual realism is high
R2 The overall scene looks realistic

Perceived Dynamism/Liveliness

D1 The content feels to be lively and dynamic (e.g. lots of activities, things moving, sounds, etc.)

Affordance/Attention

A1 My attention is naturally drawn to various objects
A2 I am able to attend to objects making sounds

Immersion

I1 I feel immersed in the virtual space (spatially)
I2 I am immersed into the task of viewing the virtual space (mentally)

Presence

P1 I felt as if I was at the Farm/Kitchen
P2 I lost the track of time while experiencing the virtual space
P3 I felt and was drawn to act upon and interact with the objects

Enjoyment/Preference/Satisfaction

E1 I would like to experience the virtual space again if given the chance
E2 I enjoyed the virtual space

Table 2. Object attention questions (for Busy Kitchen - Breakfast scene).

What was being cooked in the pot?

What was being grinded in the mixer?

Where was the telephone?

How many different breads were there on the table?

What color was the trash can?

were that both quantitative (e.g. more accurate assessment of the objects in the scene) and subjective (e.g. preferred, helpful in perceiving the content to be rich, and leading to a higher level of awareness, presence, and immersion) performance would be better with the additive use of the onomatopoeia to sound.

148 J. Oh and G. J. Kim

4 Results and Discussion

See Fig. 3.

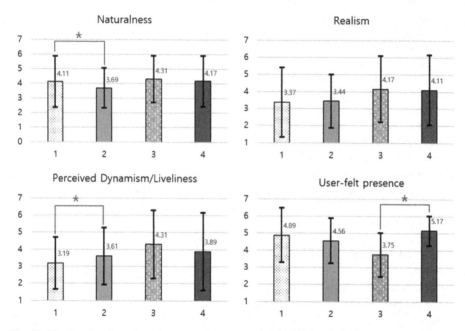

Fig. 3. The levels of various aspects of user experience for the four conditions: (1) Farm –
Sound only, (2) Farm – With words, (3) Kitchen – Sound only, (4) Kitchen – With words.

4.1 General Usability (Fatigue, Naturalness, Sickness)

ANOVA/t-test was applied for the analysis of these dependent variables (corresponding responses to the survey in Table 1). A statistically significant difference was found in the fatigue level (F1) when onomatopoeias were used (vs. not using) for the Farm scene (t(35) = −2.935, p = 0.006*), but not for the Kitchen. The Farm containing relatively more onomatopoeias per unit area (and thus also for the momentary visual span) seems to have caused this difference.

Subjects felt the scene to be, expectedly, relatively unnatural (N1) when the onomatopoeias were used for the Farm scene (t(35) = 1.898, p = 0.066), but again not for the Kitchen. Considering that the overall realism did not suffer despite the use of the sound words (see Sect. 4.2), it seems this result emanates from the scene/object specific characteristics (e.g. animals making occasional sounds/text vs. cookeries making constant sounds).

Sickness levels were low (below 2 out of 7) as the virtual environment incurred no substantial navigation (just slow-paced local exploration) and no differences were found between Sound-only and With-words.

4.2   Content Perception (Realism, Liveliness)

It was actually projected that the additive use of onomatopoeia possessed a danger of lowering the realism (R1, R2 - since obviously, such a thing does not exist in the real world). However, no significant effect was found on this variable. Aside from the usual suspension of disbelief, we attribute this partially to the fact that most people are already accustomed to using and seeing onomatopoeia in everyday living, comics and other media form (at least in Korea).

ANOVA/t-test found that users generally felt the scenes to be more dynamic and livelier (D1) when the onomatopoeias were used in the Animal Farm (t(35) = -2.076, p = .045), but not in the Busy Kitchen. Animals compared to kitchen objects moved and were expected to do so freely and onomatopoeia helped the users feel improved dynamics and liveliness. In contrast, the kitchen objects were mostly static to begin with, and the added sound words would be ineffective, and rightly so. We believe that the dynamism and liveliness can further increases for moving objects, if we also animate the words in tune with the object motion. The perceived liveliness might improve even for the non-moving objects with onomatopoeia animated in synch with the sounds made.

Even though the scenes were not interactive, users reported they were led to interact with the objects in both contents, implicating a strong sense of affordance when the onomatopoeia were used. Unfortunately, to the two relevant questions of object attention and affordance (A1 and A2), statistically significant effects were not found. However, other measures of object attention were found to be different with a statistically significant difference (see Sect. 4.4).

4.3   Immersion and Presence

ANOVA/t-test found a significant difference for the user felt immersion and presence (P1, P3 collectively) for the Kitchen scenes (Breakfast - p = .002; Supper - p = .027), but not for the Farm scenes. In the Busy Kitchen scenes, user felt immersion and presence were higher when onomatopoeias are used. Note that it was observed and found that subjects felt a substantial level of affordance and interest (for interaction possibility) through the onomatopoeia (see Sect. 4.2). This seems to have led the subjects to perceive higher immersion and presence. On the other hand, in the Farm scene, subjects felt that the animals were arranged too crowdedly and there were excessively many additive texts (in unit area), raising the level of fatigue, and eventually distracting them and breaking the sense of immersion/presence. The onomatopoeia did not help the scene to be felt interactive because of the very nature of the content type (nothing much to do with animals vs. kitchen objects having clear functional purposes). On the other hand, subjects reported that it was much easier to focus, attend and localize the objects in the less crowded Kitchen scene with the onomatopoeia (see Sect. 4.2). In fact, there are research works indicating a strong correlation between presence and affordance/attention [17] and vice versa with distraction [17].

4.4   Situation Awareness

The situation awareness was evaluated in two ways: (1) accuracy in the counting and naming objects (total or sound making) (2) linguistically analyzing the subject's scene descriptions (evaluated based on the richness of the vocabularies or expressions). In both the Animal Farm and Busy Kitchen scenarios, subjects were generally more correct in the counting and identifying objects and grasping features of objects when there was onomatopoeia either for the total or the sound making ones (we omit the exact statistical figures). In fact, when there was no onomatopoeia, the counts were significantly inaccurately less. Despite the no effect not being found for questions A1 and A2 (see Sect. 4.2), based on this result, we believe the subjects had an object-wise understanding.

Subjects were also asked to freely write out and describe the scenes they experienced. We applied the neuro-linguistic programming to code the subjective experience [14]. In general, the subject's descriptions were richer when the onomatopoeia accompanied the sound effect. For example, the descriptions were longer and changed from simple depiction to a more refined story (see Table 3). Also, the descriptions were partly imagined out with colorful vocabularies with the perceptual position changed to the first person from the third (see Table 4).

Table 3. Examples of Farm scene description from a subject (Sound-only and With-words conditions) – originally written in Korean and translated to English.

Sound-only	"Cows, pigs, chickens and sheep cry outside the fence and are observing what is going on in the fence."
With-words	"The pigs, sheep and cows have gone outside because the fence was low, but I and the chickens cannot get over it and feeling restless while, the other animals are urging us to come over."

Table 4. Examples of Kitchen scene description from a subject (Sound-only and With-words conditions) – originally written in Korean and translated to English.

Sound-only	"Based on the food on the table, it seems like it is morning time, and from the sounds, it feels like a hectic situation."
With-words	"I think I was invited for a meal and looking at the kitchen, it seems the host briefly stepped out."

4.5   Enjoyment/Preference

ANOVA/t-test found mixing results for the user enjoyment/preference as well. For example, subjects showed a significantly more willingness/preference for the content with the onomatopoeia for the Busy Kitchen, but not for the Animal Farm. As posited, this seems to relate to the difference in the object affordance and attention to them, leading the subjects to raise their interest and the desire to interact.

5   Conclusion and Future Work

In this paper we verified that using onomatopoeia as added to the sound feedback could improve the user experience in virtual reality. Our experiment result has found that the judicial use of onomatopoeia can indeed help direct user attention, offer object affordance and thereby enhance user experience and even the sense of presence and immersion, without degrading the perceived realism. Summarizing the specifics, important factors that would make an effective application of onomatopoeia to sounds were: (1) having a scene (and associated objects) that has an interactive theme and highly functional, (2) not crowding the scene with too much additive texts.

In the future, we would like to investigate in how to present the onomatopoeias in various ways, such as in their position, pose, size, animation, timings, and how they might also affect the user experience in virtual and mixed reality. Using mimetic words for emphasizing the object movement is also another consideration along this line. The ultimate goal is to derive a specific guideline for utilizing onomatopoeia in VR/MR. Finally, how onomatopoeia can help give experience to the hearing-impaired or how it can be associated with other modalities such as the haptic and visual (e.g. object animation) are another interesting future work topic.

Acknowledgements. This work was partially supported by the Global Frontier R&D Program on <Human-centered Interaction for Coexistence> funded by the National Research Foundation of Korea grant funded by the Korean Government (MEST) (NRF-2015M3A6A3076490), and by the Institute for Information & communications Technology Promotion (IITP) grant funded by the Korea government (MSIP) (No. 2017-0-00179, HD Haptic Technology for Hyper Reality Contents).

References

1. VR Tennis Online. https://colopl.co.jp/en/products/vr/vrtennis.php. Accessed 15 Aug 2018
2. Dumas, B., Lalanne, D., Oviatt, S.: Multimodal interfaces: a survey of principles, models and frameworks. In: Lalanne, D., Kohlas, J. (eds.) Human Machine Interaction. LNCS, vol. 5440, pp. 3–26. Springer, Heidelberg (2009). https://doi.org/10.1007/978-3-642-00437-7_1
3. Fukusato, T., Morishima, S.: Automatic depiction of onomatopoeia in animation considering physical phenomena. In: Proceedings of the Seventh International Conference on Motion in Games, pp. 161–169. ACM (2014)
4. Guynes, S.A.: Four-color sound: a Peircean semiotics of comic book onomatopoeia. Public J. Semiot. **6**(1), 58–72 (2014)
5. Heeter, C.: Being there: the subjective experience of presence. Presence Teleoperators Virtual Environ. **1**(2), 262–271 (1992)
6. Jung, S.-Y.: A Study on the feature and the function of TV visual character: focusing on the real variety shows. Korean J. Journal. Commun. Stud. **53**(6), 153–176 (2009)
7. Lee, J., Kim, G.J.: Visual information for inducing interactivity and presence. In: Proceedings of the Korean Society for Emotion and Sensibility Conference. The Korean Society for Emotion and Sensibility
8. Masuch, M., Röber, N.: Game graphics beyond realism: then, now and tomorrow. Level UP: Digital Games Research Conference. DIGRA, Faculty of Arts, University of Utrecht (2004)

9. Nienhaus, M., Dollner, J.: Depicting dynamics using principles of visual art and narrations. IEEE Comput. Graph. Appl. **25**(3), 40–51 (2005)
10. Norman, D.: The design of everyday things: Revised and expanded edition. Constellation (2013)
11. Norman, D.A.: The psychology of everyday things (The design of everyday things) (1988)
12. Shimoda, W., Yanai, K.: A visual analysis on recognizability and discriminability of onomatopoeia words with DCNN features. In: 2015 IEEE International Conference on Multimedia and Expo (ICME), pp. 1–6. IEEE
13. Slater, M., Usoh, M.: Presence in immersive virtual environments. In: IEEE Virtual Reality Annual International Symposium, pp. 90–96. IEEE (1993)
14. Slater, M., Usoh, M.: Representations systems, perceptual position, and presence in immersive virtual environments. Presence Teleoperators Virtual Environ. **2**(3), 221–233 (1993)
15. Wang, F., Nagano, H., Kashino, K., Igarashi, T.: Visualizing video sounds with sound word animation to enrich user experience. IEEE Trans. Multimed. **19**(2), 418–429 (2017)
16. Wikipedia. Onomatopoeia — Wikipedia, The Free Encyclopedia (2018). http://en.wikipedia.org/w/index.php?title=Onomatopoeia&oldid=854819117. Accessed 15 Aug 2018
17. Witmer, B.G., Singer, M.J.: Measuring presence in virtual environments: a presence questionnaire. Presence **7**(3), 225–240 (1998)
18. Yamamoto, T., Matsubara, M., Saito, H.: Visualization of environmental sounds using onomatopoeia and effective fonts. J. Soc. Art. Sci. **11**(1), 1–11 (2012)
19. Jick, J.Y., Seok, L.H.: The expression techniques of cartoon style in the subtitles of TV entertainment programs. J. Digit. Des. **15**(3), 779–788 (2015)
20. Yuan, Y., Steed, A.: Is the rubber hand illusion induced by immersive virtual reality? In: 2010 IEEE Virtual Reality Conference (VR), pp. 95–102. IEEE (2010)

Information Design for XR Immersive Environments: Challenges and Opportunities

Elaine M. Raybourn[1]([✉]), William A. Stubblefield[2],
Michael Trumbo[1], Aaron Jones[1], Jon Whetzel[1], and Nathan Fabian[1]

[1] Sandia National Laboratories, Albuquerque, NM 87185, USA
{emraybo,mctrumb,ajones3,jhwhetz,ndfabia}@sandia.gov
[2] Practical Tales, Albuquerque, NM 87191, USA
sfield@acm.org

Abstract. Cross Reality (XR) immersive environments offer challenges and opportunities in designing for cognitive aspects (e.g. learning, memory, attention, etc.) of information design and interactions. Information design is a multidisciplinary endeavor involving data science, communication science, cognitive science, media, and technology. In the present paper the holodeck metaphor is extended to illustrate how information design practices and some of the qualities of this imaginary computationally augmented environment (a.k.a. the holodeck) may be achieved in XR environments to support information-rich storytelling and real life, face-to-face, and virtual collaborative interactions. The Simulation Experience Design Framework & Method is introduced to organize challenges and opportunities in the design of information for XR. The notion of carefully blending both real and virtual spaces to achieve total immersion is discussed as the reader moves through the elements of the cyclical framework. A solution space leveraging cognitive science, information design, and transmedia learning highlights key challenges facing contemporary XR designers. Challenges include but are not limited to interleaving information, technology, and media into the human storytelling process, and supporting narratives in a way that is memorable, robust, and extendable.

Keywords: Transmedia learning · Storytelling · Cognitive science ·
Information design · Virtual reality · Augmented reality · Mixed reality ·
Cross reality · XR

1 Introduction

The physical world around us is well known to most of us, we spent our early years learning about space, mass, movement, and direction. We often take space for granted so much that it comprises the framework of our way of speaking [1]. A user's familiarity with real spaces makes designing virtual spaces problematic. Our innate sense of spatial orientation in the real word is undermined by cumbersome technology and the use of input/output devices when engaging in virtual environments. That said, the future looks bright—trends in games, virtual/mixed reality, robotics, and artificial intelligence promise to bring us closer to rich, technology-mediated experiences popularized by science fiction [2].

J. Y. C. Chen and G. Fragomeni (Eds.): HCII 2019, LNCS 11574, pp. 153–164, 2019.
https://doi.org/10.1007/978-3-030-21607-8_12

Designers and developers of technologies often cite popular culture and science fiction such as *Ready Player One* and *Star Trek* as sources of inspiration [3]. For example, Gene Roddenberry's *Star Trek* series—popularized by American media and Hollywood—has been a cult phenomenon in the United States celebrated for decades by scientists, artists, and technologists alike. Audiences around the world have been intrigued by the potential of Star Trek "technologies" to change our society, relationships, and abilities. The *holodeck*, first introduced in a 1974 animated episode of Star Trek called "Practical Joker," and later in the television series *Star Trek Next Generation,* has widely influenced discussions about the design and use of immersive, computationally augmented collaboration environments [4]. A holodeck is a smart virtual/architectural hybrid space that incorporates voice actuated computer interaction, artificial intelligence, storytelling, and holographic display of information. Holodeck simulations can be distinguished from reality only by their limitless programmability. The *Star Trek Next Generation* holodeck was the epitome of an interactive storyworld of illusions that could be stopped, started, redirected, recombined, and reused at will [5]. The holodeck is in fact "too good to be true."

Behind the holodeck were some highly paid Hollywood scriptwriters expert at narrative and timing. By design, the holodeck was created to stretch audience imaginations beyond their boundaries of the physically familiar and technologically possible. Usability was seamless and the technology transparent in the *Star Trek Next Generation* holodeck. Unfortunately, virtual (VR), augmented (AR), and mixed reality (MR) environments, together often referred to as XR or cross reality [6], have not yet been particularly successful at achieving the high technical ideals set by literally adopting a holodeck metaphor.

Nevertheless, science fiction and the notion of the holodeck can be useful when applied in the socio-technical context of general user expectations [7]. The holodeck introduced audiences to possible social implications of futuristic non-traditional human-computer interfaces for learning, conveying information, and collaboration. For example, by immersing oneself in the holodeck environment, crewmembers simulated problem situations, evaluated alternative solutions, employed new tools, and painlessly explored the consequences of life-altering decisions. The holodeck induced provocative changes in the behaviors of the crew of the *Starship Enterprise* while exploring what the future could hold for human communication, cognition, and creativity. In fact, the holodeck technology was so seamless, it was practically invisible. That is to say, it was not necessarily the pointer to futuristic technologies of the holodeck that inspired audiences around the globe, but rather the narratives, or stories, *created in it.*

Although the holodeck is a powerful metaphor for the way computer simulations, artificial intelligence, XR, and the design of advanced information displays can augment human learning and collaboration, like any metaphor, it must be interpreted with care. What aspects of the holodeck are most important to learning through discovery or collaborative problem solving? Possibilities from which we might have chosen include the availability of real time simulations; practically unlimited access to information, bandwidth, and artificially intelligent collaborators; and the freeing of computational power from the encumbrances of screens, head mounted displays (HMDs), smartphones, touchpads, keyboards, mice, controllers, gloves, trackers, and other 3D input devices.

More importantly, however, in the present paper the holodeck metaphor is extended to illustrate how information designers, developers, and engineers may achieve some of the *qualities* of this imaginary computationally augmented environment in order to support real life, face-to-face and virtual human learning, collaboration, and digital storytelling that is information-rich, *right now*. Information design is a multidisciplinary endeavor involving data science, communication science, cognitive science, media, and technology [8]. A brief description of the holodeck metaphor serves as a device to explore how XR information design is a social construction of narrative. Second, the Simulation Experience Design Framework & Method [9] is introduced to organize key concepts relevant to designing XR environments and their associated challenges and opportunities. The notion of carefully blending both real and virtual spaces to achieve total immersion is discussed as the reader moves through the elements of the cyclical framework. Last, the conclusions describe a solution space leveraging applied cognitive science, information design, and transmedia learning that is neither high-tech nor low-tech, but all-tech. Transmedia learning is defined as the scalable system of messages representing a narrative or core experience that unfolds from the use of multiple media, emotionally engaging learners by involving them personally in the story [10]. As previously noted by [10, 11], the challenge facing contemporary XR designers and developers is to interleave information, technology, and multiple media into the human storytelling process, and implement it in a way that is memorable, robust, and extendable.

1.1   The Social Construction of Narrative

The meaning of any metaphor emerges from an interaction between the metaphor's basis (in this case, the holodeck) and the goals, assumptions and constraints of its interpreters. In applying the holodeck metaphor to the design of collaborative XR environments, the authors' interpretive bias is to de-emphasize the advanced technologies it describes in favor of the collaborative interactions it potentially supports. One of the dangers of the holodeck metaphor is that it might steer us toward trying to replicate *Star Trek* technology, while ignoring practicality, usability, human performance, learning, ethics, and the deeper structure of human collaborative work or play. This could easily lead to the construction of yet another technical showpiece, filled with costly, soon to be obsolete, hardware that is good for little more than carefully orchestrated demonstrations. If we are to build useful and meaningful XR environments, the human dimension must drive our design decisions.

"Social construction of narrative" is the creation, by a group of people, of systematic, coherent structures for organizing shared knowledge and developing future knowledge. Although the goal of social construction of narrative is applicable to nearly all forms of collaborative information work, the emphasis on narrative as a social construction is particularly relevant to the design of information in immersive experiences. User experience (UX) design addresses the synthesis of cognitive science, human-computer interaction, communication, and design thinking. User experience design puts the human at the center of the product or service design process. As XR designers and developers create more immersive XR and persistent transmedia learning [10] experiences, it can be useful to employ a metaphor to bring to the fore initial assumptions, biases, or notions of expectations integral to the design of immersive information experiences.

Narrative plays a powerful role in virtually all forms of human problem solving, theory formation, creative work, and play [12]. For example, examining seminal work in artificial intelligence has long recognized the power of scripts and other narrative structures in creating and organizing knowledge [13, 14]. Laurel [15] has shown that human computer interfaces can be improved by paying attention to the narrative structure of the interaction activity. Narrative has even been shown to underlie the formation of scientific theory. Historical studies of scientific practice confirm the role of metaphor and analogy in theory formation [16]; these processes derive their power from their narrative-like ability to organize knowledge into a systematic structure. Landau [17] offers further support for the role of narrative in science by analyzing various versions of the theory of evolution, to show that all of them have a common narrative structure that mirrors the universal hero myth.

Therefore, the position taken in the present paper is that it is not the promise of technology that ultimately appeals to users; it is idea of *co-creating and living out stories*. More than the promise of artificial intelligence, simulation, or information visualization, it is the support for social narrative construction and creativity that is the source of the metaphor's power. This understanding gives us a basis for elaborating the holodeck metaphor in ways that may be relevant to information designers and developers of immersive transmedia learning experiences leveraging XR and other media.

2   Simulation Experience Design Framework & Method

Organizations tell stories to share learning, strategies, and knowledge. Daily operations, the communication of scientific results, and data science analyses are story-driven endeavors. Scenario and problem-based learning with simulations and games, in particular, often leverage story-driven experiential learning. The Simulation Experience Design Framework & Method [9] is a process that addresses design as a system of experiences that exists within an emergent, adaptive, cultural context that the designer shapes and facilitates throughout user engagement, before, during, between, and after the core experience has concluded. The word simulation in the name of the method refers to an experience in which the role of a human, environment, or both, can be simulated. The Simulation Experience Design Framework & Method, briefly described in the present paper, has been applied by the author and others to problem-based learning in virtual environments, serious game design [9, 18], and transmedia learning [10]. User experience design for XR (or any medium for that matter) requires that designers and developers understand what makes a good experience first, and then translate these principles, as efficiently as possible, into the desired medium without the technologies dictating the form of the experience. In simulated environments in which end users are creatively problem solving or playing together, one's experience may be unpredictable, may not have a right or wrong approach, or may not be what the designer intends. The Simulation Experience Design Framework & Method can be helpful in framing the co-creation of open-ended, rich *systems of experiences* that fosters learning, understanding, and sense-making (Fig. 1).

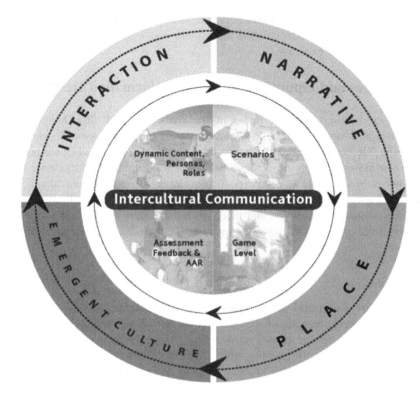

Fig. 1. Simulation Experience Design Framework [9]

The Simulation Experience Design Framework & Method suggests that supporting equitable intercultural communication and learning is comprised of several salient elements, among them (1) the *interactions* or type of communication (interpersonal, group, etc.), (2) the *narratives* that are co-created by interlocutors, (3) the *place*, or context, in which narratives occur, and (4) the *culture that emerges* from the social construction of experience [19]. Following the circular framework from upper left to upper right, design may then be considered as facilitating a journey, or *connected learning experience* from interactions to emergent culture that iteratively lead to new interactions spawned by the emergent culture. Use of the framework and method is intended to improve the quality of equitable intercultural communication and learning in collaborative, immersive environments such as XR, serious games, simulations, transmedia storytelling & learning ecosystems [9, 10].

Finally, by treating intercultural communication as a *core value*, the individual cultural backgrounds the players bring to their experiences are considered strengths, not design liabilities. As we strive to create engaging immersive XR experiences approaching the holodeck, differing cultural values of designers, developers, stake-holders, and players can create a myriad of complications and competing desires or expectations. The Simulation Experience Design Framework & Method can serve to socially construct narratives and establish a shared understanding for thoughtful analysis from which to better ground assessment and evaluation of human performance, creativity, and expertise.

3   Challenges and Opportunities in XR Information Design

The following sections describe some of the challenges and "low hanging fruit" opportunities in information design for engaging storytelling and socially constructing narratives in XR immersive environments. Challenges and opportunities are presented as the reader moves through the elements of the cyclical Simulation Experience Design Framework & Method [9]. As designers and developers strive to blend real and virtual spaces to achieve total immersion, key challenges include but are not limited to interleaving information, technology, and media into the human storytelling process, and supporting diverse cultural narratives in a way that is equitable, memorable, robust, and extendable.

3.1   Interaction

Challenge: The Communication Space. Human communication is comprised of systems of utterances, acts, and messages that are verbal, nonverbal, and incorporate each of the senses. After the novelty has worn off, virtual environments are usually less interesting and less appealing to the senses than the real world. What can we do to make XR spaces more appealing to the senses and more easily inhabitable? We know that people can make spaces more interesting, and, conversely, empty spaces may be prone to bore users—how can we make use of the emptiness often associated with virtual environments?

Opportunity: Support Quiet Reflection and Active Immersion. An immersive environment can encourage an appropriate mixing of virtual and co-present end users for public, private (alone or two), and semi-private (small group) interactions. Although we often equate immersion with activity, designing for quiet reflection can enhance learning, or problem-solving experiences. The holodeck allowed for active and reflective behavior, both physically and virtually. The "coordinated use of mind, language, and body is a fulfilling mode of being in the world" [20, p. 193]. A space that is experienced through reflection and action can enhance immersion and engagement, such that the space becomes a "*place.*" Additionally, telepresent creativity should also value the silent pauses between verbal and nonverbal communication as much as it values the communication itself. While proximity creates presence without constant communication, the telepresent space must, like the holodeck, support co-present reflection as much as co-present active communication.

Supporting XR immersion requires we be able to represent the emerging narrative (e.g., problem solution) in the shared physical space. Users may want to actively manipulate data, or quietly inhabit the same physical or virtual space while working side-by-side with colleagues. This suggests a judicious integration of both high-tech (XR or wall-size displays for AR data simulations and shared virtual spaces) and low-tech (white boards and butcher paper) representations.

For example, a review of AR research suggests its potential in the design of 3D and 2D information for quiet reflection and active immersion. AR refers to the display of virtual elements alongside those in the real world [21]. The real/virtual juxtaposition of information can be used when visualization would otherwise be difficult, such as the inclusion of 3D components alongside 2D media [22]. This combination of digital and physical elements creates immersion that facilitates critical thinking, problem solving, and communication [23]. Research further indicates that the introduction of AR can improve understanding and memory of material [24, 25] as well as raise the level of engagement during presentation of information [26].

Another potential benefit of AR is the reduction in cognitive load, or the mental effort involved in task performance [27]. Cognitive load may be divided into three types: intrinsic (related to the inherent level of difficulty in task performance), germane (the construction of schemas that facilitate task performance), and extraneous or incidental (effort required based on the method of presentation or instruction) [28]. While intrinsic cognitive load is beyond the manipulation of an instructor, and germane cognitive load is desirable as it relates to identification of problem-solving strategies, extraneous cognitive load can and should be minimized in order to reserve cognitive resources to process the intrinsic and germane aspects of a task [29]. Extraneous cognitive load is thought to be reduced with proper AR implementation [24, 27].

Using electroencephalography (EEG), theta activity can be used as an index of cognitive load [30], sustained vigilance [31], and can be used to build a classifier to detect mental fatigue [32]. Employing theta activity as an index of attention, fatigue, and cognitive load can allow for the comparison of XR versus 2D information processing in terms of how hard individuals are working to process complex information, how engaged they are attentionally, how much mental fatigue is present, and ultimately, how well information is understood and recalled. Advancements in neuroscience, data science, and communication provide the scientific foundation for information design of quiet reflection and active immersion supported by XR and environments employing transmedia learning to blend real and virtual elements.

3.2   Narrative

Challenge: The Storytelling Space. Although we think of immersion as a property of advanced computer interface technology, immersion is actually a fundamental property of narratives that goes back earlier than Homer (e.g. *The Iliad* and *The Odyssey*). All good stories can draw us in to the virtual worlds they create. How can we facilitate the simultaneous co-creation of and immersion in a shared narrative?

Opportunity: Achieve Co-created Immersion *With* and *Through* Interactivity. The medium of film has deeply immersive qualities and is both symbolic *and* spatial. Movies achieve immersion through fixed narrative, the representation of physical space and realistic audio, yet are also symbolic in that the viewer sees from a "Gods eye" view. Movies compress time to suit one's limited attention span and warp psychological and physical distances to suit narrative flow. A film is not a "true" representation of reality, but it is compelling nonetheless. However, to explore the notion of *the viewer as a co-creator of narrative* we may look at how computer game technology achieves immersion *with* and *through* interactivity. Early pioneers like Brenda Laurel and Hal Barwood pointed out that computer games are more like plays, not films [19, 33]. Like plays, scenes in computer games are often viewed from single angles and from the same distance. Additionally, as actors leave the stage, audience members know that they still exist and are not out of the context of the plot. A computer game is similar in that the player buys into a narrative of off-screen armies plotting against him or her while s/he is battling evil aliens on-screen. Thus, the action of the game takes place on and off the screen [19]. Games are stories that are co-created by the player [5]. The goal of information design of immersive narratives is to combine the symbolic narratives of movies and the co-creating nature of games into a space that support flexible creative relationships and improvisation that characterize learning and human creative problem solving. Previous research points to real spaces that support creativity and innovation [20], and the way problem solvers use objects as part of the creative process [34]. Narratives often find their way into physical spaces—via storytelling artifacts and other attempts to capture an experience in a more permanent fashion. An immersive, information-rich problem space should provide for the spatializing of narratives and artifacts necessary to facilitate innovation and creativity.

Preliminary exploration at the authors' institution in spatializing problem-solving narratives in XR environments, involves bringing legacy simulation frameworks into XR applications to create visceral experiences and provide learning takeaways unachievable through a traditional PC interface. For example, in the domain of physical security, 3D simulation frameworks have been developed for analyzing the effectiveness of security system layouts. *Dante* is a simulation framework that constructs a system-of-systems model of a facility, including accurate 3D representations of the facility along with modeling security assets [35]. *Dante* relies on its intelligent agent architecture to simulate thousands of possibilities through Monte Carlo simulation runs.

An AR prototype was developed to explore whether problem-solving "what if" narratives supported by *Dante* could become more hands-on engineering design aids with the integration of Microsoft HoloLens. The prototype enabled users to explore the placement of virtual security assets (objects) within an indoor space. Some virtual assets (e.g., simulated cameras) provided information on the sensor viewshed within the deployed space and updated the viewshed information in real-time as the objects within the physical space were moved. A viewshed is the visible area of a physical space from a sensor's vantage point. For example, a camera may be able to view a parking lot but would not see what's behind a parked car. The area in front of the parked car is within the viewshed, but the space behind the car would be outside of it. The application also supported a "what if" narrative which involved an attempt by a non-player character (NPC) to find, and take simulated objects placed by the end user in the indoor space. The NPC constructed its navigation plan based upon the physical layout instead of a human-generated 3D model of the facility. The prototype demonstrated that *Dante* agents and sensor modeling libraries may enable XR applications to access predictive simulation tools thereby adding additional dimension to the co-creation of a shared narrative to aid decision making.

3.3   Place

Challenge: The Space Isn't a Place. An immersive information space is not just a display of data; it should be a *place* where people act.

Opportunity: Achieve Immersion With Contextual Cues. Learning is situated in implicit cultural and contextual information. This includes assumptions, values, goals, meanings, and history shared by learners. This information is often implicit and comprises the tacit knowledge that is learned through interactions over time. When collaborating, especially with those who are not co-located, we should attempt to include tacit knowledge in our computational space, although much essential tacit knowledge never successfully makes it into current computational environments.

The first author and others [36] have shown that introducing subtle cultural and contextual cues into immersive environments is an effective way to encourage certain group collaboration. Cultural and contextual cues may be embedded in 3D information, simulated objects, models and data from real-world experiments, posters, or each other. Worth further exploration is a comparison of human collaboration with virtual objects or data within the XR environment, to a real-world corollary which splits attention among data in the XR environment, physical objects outside the XR environment, and a collaborator inside and/or outside of the XR environment. Being co-located in the same virtual space may allow collaborators to explore spaces intuitively, transition focus more easily, and more naturally interact with physical entities in the real world.

Designers can also carefully design places that provide clues about the unfolding narrative by stimulating memories and emotions. Research by LeDoux [37] suggests that the human brain is wired to pick up on messages crafted as stories because we feel real emotions when we connect with content or a character in a story. One potential explanation is that the brain uses two mnemonic systems to process information [37]. The brain processes information both rationally and emotionally, although emotions about rational content are usually processed by the brain split seconds before rational or logical interventions by the cerebral cortex. Put simply, LeDoux's research indicates we best remember information presented in the form of a story.

Information and user experience designers can accommodate learners' need for cultural cues and situated information through a deep understanding of social work structures, careful application of intercultural communication principles, and a willingness to accept the possibility that when faced with a choice, end users may recognize limitations of XR and prefer that some activities happen outside the immersive environment [9].

3.4   Emergent Culture

Challenge: The Space for Diversity. Immersive narrative technologies, especially simulation, have a tendency to present a single point of view so powerfully, and with such an illusion of reality, that other points of view are lost. One of the less fortunate effects of information and communication media is their tendency to homogenize different points of view. How can we ensure that learning in collaborative immersive environments celebrate creative differences and reward out-of-the-box thinking?

Opportunity: Support Multiple Points of View and Perceptions in Multiple Spaces. In parallel with our growing acceptance of virtual spaces, we can begin to explore merging a spatial and symbolic paradigm. An XR space that is populated with intelligent agents may adapt to one's perspective, cognitive perception, and indeed crucially, to specific communities and communication preferences. The *medium* may be *the message*, but we should also remember that in designing message-rich environments, the message is more important than the medium! In transmedia learning the interaction with messages communicated by each individual medium (XR, etc.) should reinforce performance improvement, reflection, and behavior change. Emergent culture is an opportunity to explore the broader story, or socially constructed narrative, in different ways to enrich the core transmedia learning experience [10]. We can use agents to tailor information and personalize the medium based on an understanding of the way learners perceive information, the narratives they co-create, and knowledge of how users juggle peripheral and focused information in multiple spaces [38].

4   Conclusion

We have captured what we believe to be the essential appeal of the holodeck metaphor, and also the essential constraints on XR environments. Recall that after the novelty has subsided, it is not the technology that appeals to users; it is idea of creating and living out stories with colleagues. This understanding provides a basis for elaborating the holodeck metaphor in ways that may be relevant to XR information design. The Simulation Experience Design Framework & Method was introduced to organize challenges and opportunities in the design of information for XR environments. The discussion of carefully blending both real and virtual spaces to achieve total immersion leveraged research from cognitive science, neuroscience, information design, and transmedia learning. Key challenges facing XR designers include but are not limited to inter-leaving information, technology, and media into the human storytelling process, and supporting diverse cultural narratives in a way that is equitable, memorable, robust, and extendable.

Acknowledgements. Sandia National Laboratories is a multimission laboratory managed and operated by National Technology and Engineering Solutions of Sandia, LLC, a wholly owned subsidiary of Honeywell International, Inc., for the U.S. Department of Energy's National Nuclear Security Administration under contract DE-NA-0003525. Image copyright NTESS LLC and reproduced with permission.

References

1. Lakoff, G., Johnson, M.: Metaphors We Live By. University of Chicago Press, Chicago (1980)
2. Bilton, N.: Disruptions: the holodeck begins to take shape. The New York Times, 26 January 2014. http://bits.blogs.nytimes.com/2014/01/26/disruptions-the-holodeck-begins-to-take-shape/. Accessed 10 Feb 2019

3. Wingfield, N.: Virtual reality companies look to science fiction for their next play. New York Times, 26 Feb 2016. https://www.nytimes.com/2016/02/17/technology/virtual-reality-companies-look-to-science-fiction-for-their-next-play.html. Accessed 10 Feb 2019

4. Zambetta, F.: Star Trek's holodeck: from science fiction to a new reality. The Conversation, 28 Mar 2017. https://theconversation.com/star-treks-holodeck-from-science-fiction-to-a-new-reality-74839. Accessed 10 Feb 2019

5. Murray, J.H.: Hamlet on the Holodeck: The Future of Narrative in Cyberspace. MIT Press, Cambridge (1997)

6. Joyce, K.: AR, VR, MR, RR, XR: A glossary to the acronyms of the future. VR Focus.com, 1 March 2018. https://www.vrfocus.com/2017/05/ar-vr-mr-rr-xr-a-glossary-to-the-acronyms-of-the-future/. Accessed 10 Feb 2019

7. Raybourn, E.M.: Learning experience design for immersive environments: future challenges and opportunities. In: Proceedings of MODSIM World, Virginia Beach, VA (2016)

8. Pettersson, R.: Information design—principles and guidelines. J. Vis. Literacy 29(2), 167–182 (2010)

9. Raybourn, E.M.: Applying simulation experience design methods to creating serious game-based adaptive training systems. Interact. Comput. 19, 207–214 (2007). https://doi.org/10.1016/j.intcom.2006.08.001

10. Raybourn, E.M.: A new paradigm for serious games: transmedia learning for more effective training & education. J. Comput. Sci. 5(3), 471–481 (2014). https://doi.org/10.1016/j.jocs.2013.08.005

11. Raybourn, E.M.: Addressing changing mindsets: transforming next generation leader development with transmedia learning. In: Hailes, T.C., Wells, L. (eds.) Changing Mindsets to Transform Security: Leader Development for an Unpredictable and Complex World. National Defense University, Washington, DC (2013)

12. Raybourn, E.M., Waern, A.: Social learning through gaming. In: CHI 2004 Extended Abstracts on Human Factors in Computing Systems (2004)

13. Schank, R.C., Abelson, R.: Scripts, Plans, Goals and Understanding: An Inquiry into Human Knowledge Structures. Lawrence Erlbaum Associates, New Jersey (1977)

14. Schank, R.C., Morson, G.S.: Tell Me a Story: Narrative and Intelligence (Rethinking Theory). Northwestern University Press, Evanston (1995)

15. Laurel, B.K.: Strange new worlds of entertainment. Compute 13(11), 102–104, November 1991. https://archive.org/stream/1991-11-compute-magazine/Compute_Issue_135_1991_Nov#page/n103/mode/2up/search/102. Accessed 10 Feb 2019

16. Hesse, M.: Models and Analogies in Science. University of Notre Dame Press, Notre Dame (1966)

17. Landau, M.: Narratives of human evolution. Yale University Press, New Haven (1993)

18. Bergin-Hill, T., Creekmore, R., Bornman, J.: Designing a serious game for eliciting and measuring simulated taxpayer behavior. McLean, VA, The MITRE Corporation. 13-1929 (2014)

19. Laurel, B.: Computers as Theater. Addison-Wesley, Reading (1991)

20. Penn, A., Desyllas, J., Vaughan, L.: The space of innovation: interaction and communication in the work environment. Environ. Planning B Planning Des. 26, 193–218 (1999)

21. Azuma, R., Baillot, Y., Behringer, R., Feiner, S., Julier, S., MacIntyre, B.: Recent advances in augmented reality. IEEE Comput. Graph. Appl. 21(6), 34–47 (2001)

22. Wu, H.K., Lee, S.W.Y., Chang, H.Y., Liang, J.C.: Current status, opportunities and challenges of augmented reality in education. Comput. Educ. 62, 41–49 (2013)

23. Dunleavy, M., Dede, C., Mitchell, R.: Affordances and limitations of immersive participatory augmented reality simulations for teaching and learning. J. Sci. Educ. Technol. 18(1), 7–22 (2009)

24. Akçayır, M., Akçayır, G.: Advantages and challenges associated with augmented reality for education: a systematic review of the literature. Educ. Res. Rev. **20**, 1–11 (2017)
25. Kamarainen, A.M., et al.: EcoMOBILE: integrating augmented reality and probeware with environmental education field trips. Comput. Educ. **68**, 545–556 (2013)
26. Liu, P.H.E., Tsai, M.K.: Using augmented-reality-based mobile learning material in EFL English composition: an exploratory case study. Brit. J. Educ. Technol. **44**(1), E1–E4 (2013)
27. Chiang, T.H., Yang, S.J., Hwang, G.J.: An augmented reality-based mobile learning system to improve students' learning achievements and motivations in natural science inquiry activities. J. Educ. Technol. Soc. **17**(4), 352–365 (2014)
28. Sweller, J., Van Merrienboer, J.J., Paas, F.G.: Cognitive architecture and instructional design. Educ. Psychol. Rev. **10**(3), 251–296 (1998)
29. Mayer, R.E., Moreno, R.: Nine ways to reduce cognitive load in multimedia learning. Educ. Psychol. **38**(1), 43–52 (2003)
30. Käthner, I., Wriessnegger, S.C., Müller-Putz, G.R., Kübler, A., Halder, S.: Effects of mental workload and fatigue on the P300, alpha and theta band power during operation of an ERP (P300) brain–computer interface. Biol. Psychol. **102**, 118–129 (2014)
31. Wei, J., et al.: The timing of theta phase synchronization accords with vigilant attention. In: 2017 39th Annual International Conference of the IEEE Engineering in Medicine and Biology Society (EMBC), pp. 2442–2445 (2017)
32. Charbonnier, S., Roy, R.N., Bonnet, S., Campagne, A.: EEG index for control operators' mental fatigue monitoring using interactions between brain regions. Expert Syst. Appl. **52**, 91–98 (2016)
33. Card, O.S.: Films can make lousy games. Compute **126**, 54 (1991). http://www.atarimagazines.com/compute/issue126/54_Films_can_make_lousy.php. Accessed 10 Feb 2019
34. Smyth, M.: The tools designers use: What do they reveal about design thinking? In: Smith, J. S., Norman, E.W.L. (eds.) Proceedings of IDATER 1998, International Conference on Design and Technology Educational Research and Curriculum Development, Loughborough University, UK, 24–26 August, pp. 146–153 (1998)
35. Hart, B., Hart, D., Gayle, R., Oppel, F., Xavier, P., Whetzel, J.: Dante agent architecture for force-on-force wargame simulation & training. In: Proceedings from the Thirteenth AAAI Conference on Artificial Intelligence and Interactive Digital Entertainment, pp. 200–206. AAAI Press, Snowbird (2017)
36. Raybourn, E.M., Kings, N., Davies, J.: Adding cultural signposts in adaptive community-based virtual environments. Interact. Comput. **15**, 91–107 (2003). https://doi.org/10.1016/S0953-5438(02)00056-5
37. LeDoux, J.E.: The Emotional Brain: The Mysterious Underpinnings of Emotional Life. Simon & Schuster, New York (1996)
38. Raybourn, E.M.: Toward culturally-aware, next generation learning ecosystems. In: Schatz, S., Hoffman, M. (eds.) Advances in Cross-Cultural Decision Making. AISC, vol. 480, pp. 173–181. Springer, Cham (2017). https://doi.org/10.1007/978-3-319-41636-6_14

Multimodal Head-Mounted Virtual-Reality Brain-Computer Interface for Stroke Rehabilitation

A Clinical Case Study with REINVENT

Athanasios Vourvopoulos$^{(\boxtimes)}$ ⓘ, Octavio Marin-Pardo,
Meghan Neureither, David Saldana, Esther Jahng,
and Sook-Lei Liew ⓘ

University of Southern California, Los Angeles, CA 90089, USA
vourvopo@usc.edu

Abstract. Rehabilitation after stroke requires the exploitation of active movement by the patient in order to efficiently re-train the affected side. Individuals with severe stroke cannot benefit from many training solutions since they have paresis and/or spasticity, limiting volitional movement. Nonetheless, research has shown that individuals with severe stroke may have modest benefits from action observation, virtual reality, and neurofeedback from brain-computer interfaces (BCIs). In this study, we combined the principles of action observation in VR together with BCI neurofeedback for stroke rehabilitation to try to elicit optimal rehabilitation gains. Here, we illustrate the development of the REINVENT platform, which takes post-stroke brain signals indicating an attempt to move and drives a virtual avatar arm, providing patient-driven action observation in head-mounted VR. We also present a longitudinal case study with a single individual to demonstrate the feasibility and potentially efficacy of the REINVENT system.

Keywords: Virtual reality · Brain-computer interfaces · Stroke rehabilitation

1 Introduction

Cerebrovascular accidents (i.e., strokes) are a leading cause of adult long-term disability worldwide [1], with up to 74% of stroke survivors requiring assistance with daily life activities due to motor impairments (e.g., an inability to move the affected side) [2]. Rehabilitation for these individuals is difficult because most current training options require some volitional movement to train the affected side. However, research has shown that individuals with severe stroke may have modest benefits from action observation, virtual reality (VR), and brain-computer interfaces (BCIs). First, in healthy subjects, action observation of motor actions has been shown to facilitate the formation of motor memories and effects of physical training. Moreover, it has been shown that action observation in association with physical training can enhance the effects of

© Springer Nature Switzerland AG 2019
J. Y. C. Chen and G. Fragomeni (Eds.): HCII 2019, LNCS 11574, pp. 165–179, 2019.
https://doi.org/10.1007/978-3-030-21607-8_13

motor training after stroke [3], eliciting motor-related brain activity on the lesioned hemisphere which leads to modest motor improvements after severe stroke [4, 5].

Second, action observation in VR through a head-mounted display (HMD) has been shown to increase motor activity in both the healthy and the post-stroke brain [6, 7]. Furthermore, gamification mechanisms, which capitalize on motivational factors that are essential for recovery and adherence to the treatment, can be built into head-mounted VR rehabilitation environments [8]. VR rehabilitation environments can also be tailored to allow for the personalization of training, self-monitoring, and monitoring by therapists. Additionally, they can enable patients to play a more active role in their rehabilitation by taking part in the development process through participatory design approaches [9].

Finally, another treatment for individuals with severe stroke is the use of neuro-feedback through BCIs, which also does not require active motor control. BCIs are communication systems capable of establishing a pathway between the user's brain activity and a computer system [10]. The most common brain signal acquisition technology in stroke BCIs is non-invasive electroencephalography (EEG) [10], as it is the most cost-effective solution for brain-computer interfacing [11]. EEG signals are distinguished by different wave patterns in the frequency domain called EEG bands or rhythms. These EEG rhythms are divided into different ranges including Delta (1–4 Hz), Alpha (8–13 Hz), Beta (13–30 Hz), Theta (4–8 Hz), and Gamma (25–90 Hz), and each rhythm or combination of rhythmic activity has been previously related with sensori-motor and/or cognitive states [12]. For example, during a motor attempt, the temporal pattern of the Alpha rhythm desynchronizes, forming a special shape which, when inverted in polarity (negativity is up), is reminiscent of the Greek letter μ (mu). This rhythm is also named Rolandic mu or the sensorimotor rhythm (SMR) because of its localization over the sensorimotor cortices of the brain. Mu-rhythms are considered indirect indications of functioning of the mirror neuron system [13] and general sensorimotor activity, and are often detected together with Beta rhythm changes in the form of an Event-Related Desynchronization (ERD) when a motor action is executed [14]. These EEG signatures are primarily detected during task-based EEG (e.g., when the participant is actively moving or imagining movement). Moreover, specific signatures from resting-state EEG activity—that is, EEG activity in the absence of a task—have been also utilized as a biomarker in research for motor deficits [15]. When combined with neural injury information, resting EEG measures, such as of frontoparietal activity, can be used to predict the efficacy of stroke therapy [16].

In EEG-based BCIs for rehabilitation, motor-related brain signals generated by the patient are reinforced by rewarding feedback, even if the patient cannot move [10]. In this way, BCI feedback can be used to strengthen key motor pathways thought to support motor recovery after stroke. Such feedback has shown modest success in motor rehabilitation for severe stroke patients [17]. The fusion of BCI and VR feedback allows for a wide range of experiences where participants can feel immersed in various aspects of their environment - either in an explicit or implicit manner-and which they can control using only their brain activity [18, 19]. This direct brain-to-VR commu-nication can induce a sensorimotor contingency between one's internal intentions and the environments responsive actions, increasing the sense of embodiment of the virtual avatar [20].

In this study, we combined the principles of action observation, virtual reality, and BCI for stroke rehabilitation to try to elicit optimal rehabilitation gains. We developed a platform called REINVENT which takes post-stroke brain signals indicating an attempt to move and drives the movement of a virtual avatar arm, providing patient-driven action observation in head-mounted VR [21].

The purpose of this study is twofold: (1) to describe the new modular REINVENT architecture that provides increased accessibility to the system, and (2) to test whether REINVENT is feasible to use across repeated sessions to strengthen motor-related brain signals in an individual after stroke.

2 Methods

2.1 Participant

For this study, a 69-year-old male stroke survivor was recruited. The participant suffered a right hemisphere middle cerebral artery stroke 9 years prior resulting in severe left hemiparesis in his upper arm. Upon inclusion in the study, the participant was unable to actively extend his wrist or fingers greater than 5°. The experimental protocol was approved by the University of Southern California Health Sciences Campus Institutional Review Board (IRB) and performed in accordance with the 1964 Declaration of Helsinki. Informed consent was obtained from the participant upon recruitment.

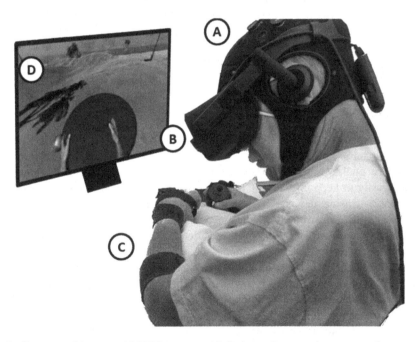

Fig. 1. System architecture: (a) EEG system with 8 electrodes over the motor and somatosensory areas, (b) Oculus Rift HMD delivering the VR feedback, (c) 4 EMG sensors over target muscles of the affected arm, (d) the dedicated desktop computer running the VR task and data acquisition.

2.2   Experimental Setup

The experimental setup was composed of a desktop computer (OS: Windows 10, CPU: Intel® Core™ i7-6700 at 4.00 GHz, RAM: 16 GB DDR3 1600 MHz, Graphics: NVIDIA GeForce GTX 1080), running the VR task, and the EEG and EMG data acquisition. For EEG acquisition, a Starstim 8 (Neuroelectrics, Barcelona, Spain) system was used. Starstim is a wearable, wireless sensor with 8 EEG channels and a triaxial accelerometer, allowing for the recording and visualization of 24-bit EEG data at 500 Hz (Fig. 1a). The spatial distribution of the electrodes followed the 10–20 system configuration [22] with the following electrodes over the somatosensory and motor areas bilaterally: Frontal-Central (FC3, FC4), Central (C3, C4, C5, C6), and Central-Parietal (CP3, CP4) (see Fig. 1 for set-up). The EEG system was connected via Bluetooth to the dedicated desktop computer for raw signal acquisition and processing. For the EMG data acquisition, a Delsys Trigno Wireless System (Delsys, MA, USA) was used, incorporating 4 differential Ag active electrodes with 16-bit A/D converter at 2000 Hz and 3-axes acceleration data at 150 Hz and 8-bit ADC resolution. The EMG sensors were placed on Extensor Digitorum Comunis (EDC), Flexor Carpi Ulnaris (FCU), Biceps Brachii (BB) and Triceps Brachii (TB) muscles of the paretic arm (Fig. 1c). The raw data was acquired from Delsys through the Lab Streaming Layer protocol [23] and processed through a custom script in Matlab (MathWorks, MA, USA). For delivering the VR feedback to the user, an Oculus Rift CV1 HMD was used (Oculus VR, Menlo Park, California, USA). The HMD has two OLED displays, 1080×1200 resolution per eye, at 90 Hz refresh rate, and 110° field of view. The HMD also features 6-DoF tracking (3-axis rotational tracking and 3-axis positional tracking), and integrated headphones with 3D spatial audio (Fig. 1b). Finally, the VR task was designed in Unity game engine (Unity Technologies, San Francisco, CA, USA) and rendered in the HMD using the Oculus SDK (Fig. 1d).

2.3   REINVENT Architecture

The goal of the software architecture design was to be able to tailor REINVENT to each participant's specific rehabilitation needs and current level of impairment. A secondary goal was to develop a flexible architecture that could integrate new hardware easily to keep up with the rapid pace of technological improvements in VR and wearable sensing devices. To do this, we upgraded the previous REINVENT system [21] with a distributed architecture, making it hardware independent. REINVENT allows for neurofeedback from a variety of interfacing devices that require different degrees of freedom from patients, including those with (1) no active movement through EEG in a direct brain-to-VR interfacing, (2) weak muscle activation through EMG in a muscle-to-VR interfacing, and (3) substantial active movement through hand tracking. The new architecture is built in an open and modular design, with the data acquisition and processing modules independent from the VR task, communicating bidirectionally over a network layer (Fig. 2). In the current study, the EMG and kinematics were only used for logging and not interaction due to the participant's ability level.

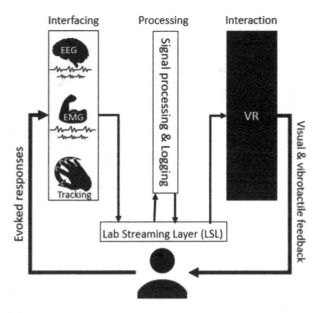

Fig. 2. REINVENT distributed architecture for a closed neurofeedback loop.

2.4   REINVENT Training Task

The VR feedback involved the rendering of two virtual hands performing a flexion/extension training task from a first-person perspective (Fig. 3). The manipulation of the virtual hand was triggered through the user's brain activity. The experimental protocol was designed for a 3-week intervention, resulting in 8 training sessions. Due to the severity of the participant's motor impairment, and positive response after the first 8 sessions, the patient participated in a second set of 8 sessions, for a total of 16 sessions with a one week break between the sessions. The duration of each session was 1.5 h during which resting state data were acquired at the beginning and end (4 min), with 4 blocks of 20 trials each of the training task in VR (80 trials total) in the middle (Fig. 4). Each task trial included a baseline rest period of 10 s, followed by a motor attempt of hand extension towards a target in VR, which lasted up to 20 s. The patient's virtual arm moved towards the target if their sensorimotor brain activity during motor attempt increased relative to baseline (e.g., increased desynchronization between 8–24 Hz under motor electrodes C3 or C4). At the end of each block of trials, a total score was calculated as a percentage of successful hand movement in VR.

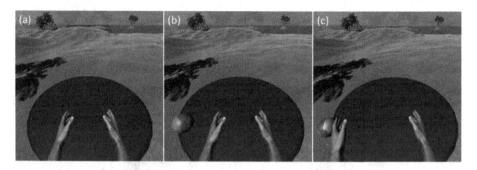

Fig. 3. VR feedback of the training task: (a) idle state during baseline measurement, (b) target onset with a ball appearing on the table, (c) motor action of wrist extension towards the target.

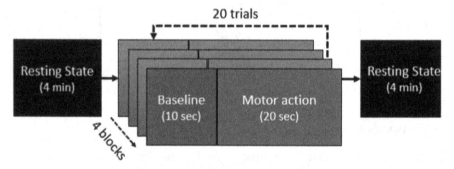

Fig. 4. Training protocol per session. In the beginning of each session, resting state data for 4 min were acquired before and after the 4 training blocks (5 min for each training block). Within each block, 20 trials of motor attempt training were performed.

2.5 Behavioral and Clinical Assessment

A set of clinical outcome measures were acquired from the patient at the beginning and the end of the intervention by a trained occupational therapist. The clinical scales included: (a) the Fugl-Meyer Assessment (FMA) for motor impairment, with 66 as the maximum score for upper limb [24] and (b) the Stroke Impact Scale (SIS), a subjective scale of the perceived stroke impact and recovery as reported by the patient with a maximum score of 100 [25].

In addition, a series of questionnaires about the VR experience were collected at three time-points: baseline (session number 1); mid (session number 8); final (session number 16). Those included the (a) Simulator Sickness questionnaire [26], (b) the Embodiment Questionnaire [27] and (c) the Presence Questionnaire [28].

The Simulator Sickness questionnaire (revised by the UQO Cyberpsychology Lab, 2013) included 16 questions on a 0 to 3 Likert scale resulting in two sub-scales: Nausea (9 questions for a maximum of 27 points) and Oculo-Motor (7 questions for a maximum of 21 points) [29]. The Presence Questionnaire was adapted from Witmer and Singer (1998) and asked participants a series of questions related to their sense of presence in VR. Responses were reported on a 1 to 7 Likert scale divided in five sub-domains: Realism, Possibility to Act, Quality of Interface, Possibility to Examine, and Self-Evaluation of Performance. The Embodiment Questionnaire included a series of questions to gauge their sense of embodiment. Responses were reported on a 1 to 10 Likert scale related to either Self Embodiment or Spatial Embodiment sub-domains.

2.6 Data Processing

EEG signals were processed in Matlab with the EEGLAB toolbox [30]. A bandpass filter was applied between 1–50 Hz, following bad channel removal. All EEG channels were re-referenced with an average reference and divided into motor-execution epochs for every trial. Finally, Independent Component Analysis (ICA) was used for removing all major artefacts related with power-line noise, eye blinking, ECG and EMG activity.

For acquiring the Power Spectral Density (PSD), the power spectrum was extracted for the following frequency bands: Alpha (8–12 Hz), Beta (12–30 Hz), Theta (4–7 Hz), and Gamma (25–90 Hz). For the current analysis, and because we were only measuring from sensorimotor areas, an Event-Related Spectral Perturbation (ERSP) analysis was performed. The ERSP is a time-frequency representation of the spectrograms of the post-stimulus EEG, divided by its pre-stimulus baseline, and then averaged across all trials (or epochs) [31]. It serves as a generalization of the Event-related synchronization/desynchronization (ERS/ERD) [32]. In our analysis, we converted all ERSP values into ERS/ERD percentages for the Mu (8–12 Hz) and Beta (12–30 Hz) bands over the C3 and C4 electrode locations in order to capture motor related activation. Finally, for assessing differences in activation from both hemispheres we extracted a hemispheric asymmetry index. Here, we defined hemispheric asymmetry as the relative power values detected at C3 and C4 for both the ERD values and Alpha power. To estimate the asymmetry, the power at the electrode contralateral to the movement side was subtracted from the ipsilateral (e.g., for left hand actions, it would be defined as C4-C3).

2.7 Statistical Analysis

Normality of the distribution of all data was assessed using the Shapiro-Wilk (S-W) normality test. A one-sample t-test was used to determine whether there was a significant difference between the patient's ERD values versus the mean ERD values of healthy population. Moreover, for comparing the means between two related score-groups of the patient on the same continuous, dependent variable (score in %), a paired-samples t-test was used. Finally, a non-parametric Spearman's rho test was used for assessing significant correlations between ERD values, EEG resting state and training scores. For all statistical comparisons the significance level was set to 5% ($p < 0.05$) and all statistical analysis were completed using IBM SPSS 20 (SPSS Inc., Chicago, IL, USA).

3 Results

3.1 Brain-to-VR Interaction

One of the major goals of the REINVENT architecture was to evoke motor-related activation from stroke participants' brains that mirrored healthy motor brain activity. Our current results show that when using REINVENT, we are able to evoke distinct patterns of sensorimotor activation during motor attempt over the lesioned area. This was achieved by extracting the level of ERD/ERS over the motor and somatosensory areas through C3 and C4 electrodes during the virtual motor training task (Fig. 5).

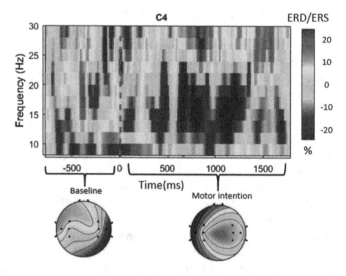

Fig. 5. Percentage of the Event-related synchronization (ERS) and desynchronization (ERD) over the lesioned area (electrode C4) between mu and Beta frequency ranges including head maps pre-post the stimulus. The blue trace 500 ms post stimulus at 12–24 Hz is the signature of the motor intention of the user over the right hemisphere as quantified by REINVENT. (Color figure online)

Although the motor intention signatures are clearly illustrated on the extracted EEG data, we also compared the patient's data with healthy population data in order to quantify how closely the patient's ERD values matched those of healthy individuals. To achieve this, we included data from two well established studies in EEG research. The first study (Study 1) from Pfurtscheller and Aranibar. included data from 10 healthy subjects performing voluntary self-paced movement [33], while the second study (Study 2) from Pfurtscheller et al. included 9 participants performing motor-imagery tasks [34]. In this way we compared the activation during stroke motor attempt to both actual motor execution and motor imagery. For consistency, we included data from the same electrode location (C4) in order to compare it with the lesioned side of the patient.

A one-sample t-test was used to determine whether there was a significant differ-ence between the patient's ERD values versus the mean ERD values of each of the two studies. Our results show that the mean ERD values of the patient data ($M = -10.8$, $SD = 21.3$) were significantly higher than those from Study 1 ($M = -70.8$, $SD = 59.7$), t (15) = 10.918, $p < 0.05$) and Study 2 ($M = -86.7$, $SD = 8.9$), t (15) = 13.813, $p < 0.05$) (Fig. 6). This suggests that although we are able to evoke motor related activation from the lesioned side, it is still far from optimal activation compared with healthy data. This distance between healthy ERD and stroke constitutes an important feature since it can be used to better quantify a stroke ERD goal amplitude during BCI-VR training.

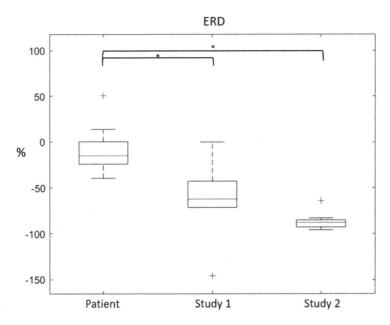

Fig. 6. ERD values of the patient with healthy population values during voluntary movement (Study 1) and motor imagery (Study 2) [33, 34]. * indicates significance of p < 0.05.

Regardless of the low ERD from the lesioned side, the VR training task scores revealed that the patient was able to voluntarily control the virtual limb by using brain signals from the lesioned side with up to 95% success ($M = 77.2$, $SD = 10.5$) (Table 1). Since the patient had two sets of training (8 sessions each), we divided the score into two sessions. Session 1 ($M = 74.2$, $SD = 5.6$) included sessions 1 to 8, and Session 2 ($M = 80.1$, $SD = 5.2$) included sessions 9 to 16 (Fig. 7). A paired-samples t-test revealed marginally significant differences between the two sessions ($t(7) = -2.2584$, $p = 0.058$).

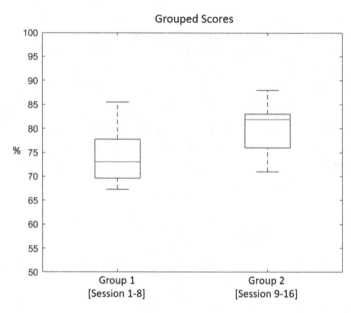

Fig. 7. Scores of Group 1 for sessions 1 and 8, and Group 2 for sessions 9 to 16.

Finally, in terms of EEG rhythmic activity during resting state, non-parametric Spearman's rho tests revealed significant correlations between resting state Alpha and performance in VR training. Specifically, Alpha rhythm during resting state each day was moderately correlated with the training score in VR that day ($r = 0.603$, $p = 0.013$). Similarly, ERD in both Mu ($r = -0.500$, $p = 0.03$) and Beta ($r = -0.541$, $p = 0.043$) during training showed significant negative correlations with resting state Alpha. That is, a higher resting state Alpha correlated with more sensorimotor activity (measured as increased negative ERD amplitude) and subsequently higher training scores. In addition, the ERD hemispheric asymmetry (that is the difference between C4-C3) of the Beta rhythm was significantly negatively correlated with the session number ($r = -0.726$, $p = 0.001$). That is, motor-related beta activity increased over the healthy hemisphere over time.

Table 1. Score table for all trials per session in %.

Trials	Sessions															
	1	2	3	4	5	6	7	8	9	10	11	12	13	14	15	16
1	92	60	91	61	81	66	46	83	79	80	92	79	83	80	78	72
2	70	91	90	71	83	68	82	93	93	65	75	74	77	67	84	79
3	58	68	83	87	59	68	76	62	95	74	79	77	79	65	89	91
4	–	88	78	72	60	67	70	77	85	76	80	83	91	72	83	87

3.2 Behavioral Data

Regarding reported presence in VR, in looking at all sub-domains extracted from the Presence Questionnaire, there was an increasing trend starting from the first session, moving to the mid-session (8th) up to the last session (16th) across four sub-domains: Realism (First: 27, Mid: 30, Last: 33), Possibility to act (First: 16, Mid: 17, Last: 20), Quality of Interface (First: 4, Mid: 5, Last: 6) and Possibility to examine (First: 12, Mid: 6, Last: 18). The Self-evaluation of performance remained stable over time (First: 14, Mid: 14, Last: 14) (Fig. 8). In terms of simulator sickness, the patient did not report any increases in either Nausea (First: Pre = 1, Post = 0, Mid: Pre = 1, Post = 0, Last: Pre = Not collected, Post = 0) or Oculo-motor sickness (First: Pre = 3, Post = 1, Mid: Pre = 3, Post = 3, Last: Pre = Not collected, Post = 1) at any of the timepoints. This suggests that the repeated VR intervention is feasible, and this was consistent over time with no increases in simulator sickness.

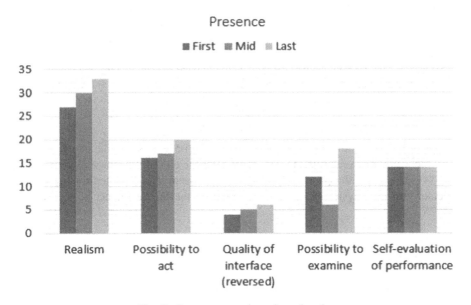

Fig. 8. Presence questionnaire subscales

Finally, in terms of embodiment, an increasing trend over time was observed concerning the participant feeling that the virtual arm was his own (real) arm (Q3), feeling that the virtual arm was him (Q4), and feeling that he was surrounded by the virtual environment (Q7). Only the question about feeling that the virtual environment seemed like the real world decreased in the last session (Q9), while the rest of the questions maintained relatively stable across all sessions (Fig. 9).

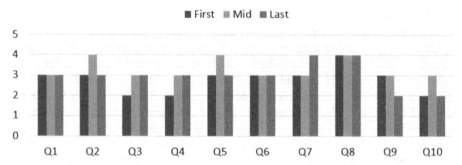

Fig. 9. Embodiment questions. Q1: To what extent was the virtual arm an extension of yourself?; Q2: To what extent did you feel if something happened to the virtual arm it felt like it was happening to you?; Q3: To what extent did you feel that the virtual arm was your own (real) arm?; Q4: To what extent did you feel that the virtual arm was yours?; Q5: How much did the virtual arm's actions correspond with your commands?; Q6: To what extent did you feel like you were really at the virtual environment?; Q7: To what extent did you feel surrounded by the virtual environment?; Q8: To what extent did you feel like you really visited the virtual environment?; Q9: To what extent did you feel that the virtual environment seemed like the real world?; Q10: To what extent did you feel like you could reach out and touch the objects in the virtual room?

3.3   Clinical Outcome

In terms of motor impairment as assessed by the Fugl-Meyer scale, the patient showed a very modest improvement in the total score after the end of the intervention (Pre: 13, Post: 14). Moreover, the patient reported an increase in stroke-related quality of life, particularly in the physical domain, as reported on the Stroke Impact Scale (Pre: 45, Post: 75).

4   Conclusions

First, the current findings illustrate that the new REINVENT architecture can be successfully used by an individual with stroke, increasing the levels of presence over time and the sense of embodiment of the virtual arm. Second, as anticipated, the stroke survivor showed sensorimotor brain activity during motor attempt from the lesioned side which resembled that of motor activity in healthy individuals, although not at the same level. This suggests that REINVENT can activate targeted motor pathways with a virtual representation of the affected arm in VR, despite lack of volitional movement. In addition, the patient was able to voluntarily control the virtual limb corresponding to the affected side with up to 95% accuracy during the VR training task and showed generally improved control over time through the increased score, suggesting that the patient was learning to modulate his own motor brain activity. Correspondingly, to examine differences in activation over time, we conducted a correlation analysis between the lesioned hemisphere and session number, showing decrease of the hemispheric asymmetry index over time. That is, motor-related beta activity increased over the healthy hemisphere. This finding is inline with stroke research showing that action observation is lateralized to the dominant, rather than ipsilesional, hemisphere [35].

Moreover, we found a positive correlation between resting state Alpha with training in VR, which was measured as sensorimotor desynchronization in Mu and Beta bands, suggesting sustained increases in motor-related brain activity. Since it is known that Mu has been associated with somatosensory information and Beta with actual motor processing [36], it is likely that the current relationship with resting state Alpha could be used as a potential predictor of training performance in VR and a potential biomarker for rehabilitation efficacy using EEG-based BCI-VR training paradigms [37, 38].

Finally, the participant reported improvements in functional measures, as captured through the Stroke Impact Scale and Fugl-Meyer following REINVENT training.

Overall, in this study, we present a new, flexible architecture for a brain-computer interface for stroke that provides neurofeedback in HMD-VR and show that it is feasible to use for individuals with chronic severe stroke across 16 sessions. Future studies may examine the use of REINVENT as a personalized training system for post-stroke individuals across varying levels of ability and should explore the impact of REINVENT training on functional activities and across additional settings (e.g., lab, clinic, home).

Acknowledgements. This research was supported by the American Heart Association through the REINVENT project (Grant #16IRG26960017) and US Army Research Office through the Cortically Coupled Computing project (W911NNF-14-D-0005).

References

1. Mozaffarian, D., et al.: American heart association statistics committee and stroke statistics subcommittee: heart disease and stroke statistics–2015 update: a report from the American heart association. Circulation **131**, e29–e322 (2015)
2. Miller, E.L., et al.: American heart association council on cardiovascular nursing and the stroke council: comprehensive overview of nursing and interdisciplinary rehabilitation care of the stroke patient: a scientific statement from the American heart association. Stroke **41**, 2402–2448 (2010)
3. Celnik, P., Webster, B., Glasser, D., Cohen, L.: Effects of action observation on physical training after stroke. Stroke J. Cereb. Circ. **39**, 1814–1820 (2008)
4. Ertelt, D., et al.: Action observation has a positive impact on rehabilitation of motor deficits after stroke. NeuroImage **36**(Suppl 2), T164–T173 (2007)
5. Garrison, K.A., Aziz-Zadeh, L., Wong, S.W., Liew, S.-L., Winstein, C.J.: Modulating the motor system by action observation after stroke. Stroke **44**, 2247–2253 (2013)
6. Ballester, B.R., et al.: The visual amplification of goal-oriented movements counteracts acquired non-use in hemiparetic stroke patients. J. Neuroeng. Rehabil. **12**, 50 (2015)
7. Vourvopoulos, A., Bermúdez i Badia, S.: Motor priming in virtual reality can augment motor-imagery training efficacy in restorative brain-computer interaction: a within-subject analysis. J. Neuroeng. Rehabil. **13**, 69 (2016)
8. Maclean, N., Pound, P., Wolfe, C., Rudd, A.: Qualitative analysis of stroke patients' motivation for rehabilitation. BMJ **321**, 1051–1054 (2000)

9. Paraskevopoulos, I., Tsekleves, E., Warland, A., Kilbride, C.: Virtual reality-based holistic framework: a tool for participatory development of customised playful therapy sessions for motor rehabilitation. In: 2016 8th International Conference on Games and Virtual Worlds for Serious Applications (VS-Games), September (2016)
10. Wolpaw, J.R.: Brain-Computer Interfaces: Principles and Practice. Oxford University Press, Oxford (2012)
11. Vourvopoulos, A., Bermudez i Badia, S.: Usability and cost-effectiveness in brain-computer interaction: is it user throughput or technology related? In: Proceedings of the 7th Augmented Human International Conference. ACM, Geneva, Switzerland (2016)
12. Schomer, D.L., Lopes da Silva, F.H.: Niedermeyer's Electroencephalography: Basic Principles, Clinical Applications, and Related Fields. Lippincott Williams & Wilkins, Philadelphia (2011)
13. Kropotov, J.D.: Chapter 2.2 - Alpha rhythms. In: Kropotov, J.D. (ed.) Functional Neuromarkers for Psychiatry, pp. 89–105. Academic Press, San Diego (2016)
14. Pfurtscheller, G., Lopes da Silva, F.H.: Event-related EEG/MEG synchronization and desynchronization: basic principles. Clin. Neurophysiol. Off. J. Int. Fed. Clin. Neurophysiol. **110**, 1842–1857 (1999)
15. Wu, J., et al.: Connectivity measures are robust biomarkers of cortical function and plasticity after stroke. Brain **138**, 2359–2369 (2015)
16. Zhou, R.J., et al.: Predicting gains with visuospatial training after stroke using an EEG measure of frontoparietal circuit function. Front. Neurol. **9**, 597 (2018)
17. Soekadar, S.R., Birbaumer, N., Slutzky, M.W., Cohen, L.G.: Brain–machine interfaces in neurorehabilitation of stroke. Neurobiol. Dis. **83**, 172–179 (2015)
18. Friedman, D.: Brain-computer interfacing and virtual reality. In: Nakatsu, R., Rauterberg, M., Ciancarini, P. (eds.) Handbook of Digital Games and Entertainment Technologies, pp. 151–171. Springer, Singapore (2017). https://doi.org/10.1007/978-981-4560-50-4_2
19. Vourvopoulos, A., Ferreira, A., Bermúdez i Badia, S.: NeuRow: an immersive VR environment for motor-imagery training with the use of brain-computer interfaces and vibrotactile feedback. In: 3rd International Conference on Physiological Computing Systems, Lisbon (2016)
20. Slater, M.: Place illusion and plausibility can lead to realistic behaviour in immersive virtual environments. Philos. Trans. R. Soc. B Biol. Sci. **364**, 3549–3557 (2009)
21. Spicer, R., Anglin, J., Krum, D.M., Liew, S.L.: REINVENT: a low-cost, virtual reality brain-computer interface for severe stroke upper limb motor recovery. In: 2017 IEEE Virtual Reality (VR), pp. 385–386 (2017)
22. Klem, G.H., Luders, H.O., Jasper, H.H., Elger, C.: The ten-twenty electrode system of the international federation. Electroencephalogr. Clin. Neurophysiol. **52**, 3–6 (1999). The International Federation of Clinical Neurophysiology
23. Kothe, C.: Lab streaming layer (LSL). https://github.com/sccn/labstreaminglayer. Accessed 26 Oct 2015 (2014)
24. Fugl-Meyer, A.R., Jääskö, L., Leyman, I., Olsson, S., Steglind, S.: The post-stroke hemiplegic patient. 1. a method for evaluation of physical performance. Scand. J. Rehabil. Med. **7**, 13–31 (1975)
25. Duncan, P.W., Wallace, D., Lai, S.M., Johnson, D., Embretson, S., Laster, L.J.: The stroke impact scale version 2.0: evaluation of reliability, validity, and sensitivity to change. Stroke **30**, 2131–2140 (1999)
26. Kennedy, R.S., Lane, N.E., Berbaum, K.S., Lilienthal, M.G.: Simulator sickness questionnaire: an enhanced method for quantifying simulator sickness. Int. J. Aviat. Psychol. **3**, 203–220 (1993)

27. Bailey, J.O., Bailenson, J.N., Casasanto, D.: When does virtual embodiment change our minds? Presence Teleoperators Virtual Environ. **25**, 222–233 (2016)
28. Witmer, B.G., Singer, M.J.: Measuring presence in virtual environments: a presence questionnaire. Presence Teleoperator Virtual Environ. **7**, 225–240 (1998)
29. Bouchard, S., Robillard, G., Renaud, P., Bernier, F.: Exploring new dimensions in the assessment of virtual reality induced side effects. J. Comput. Inf. Technol. **1**, 20–32 (2011)
30. Delorme, A., Makeig, S.: EEGLAB: an open source toolbox for analysis of single-trial EEG dynamics including independent component analysis. J. Neurosci. Methods **134**, 9–21 (2004)
31. Makeig, S.: Auditory event-related dynamics of the EEG spectrum and effects of exposure to tones. Electroencephalogr. Clin. Neurophysiol. **86**, 283–293 (1993)
32. Neuper, C., Wörtz, M., Pfurtscheller, G.: ERD/ERS patterns reflecting sensorimotor activation and deactivation. Prog. Brain Res. **159**, 211–222 (2006)
33. Pfurtscheller, G., Aranibar, A.: Evaluation of event-related desynchronization (ERD) preceding and following voluntary self-paced movement. Electroencephalogr. Clin. Neurophysiol. **46**, 138–146 (1979)
34. Pfurtscheller, G., Brunner, C., Schlögl, A., Lopes da Silva, F.H.: Mu rhythm (de) synchronization and EEG single-trial classification of different motor imagery tasks. NeuroImage **31**, 153–159 (2006)
35. Liew, S.-L., et al.: Laterality of poststroke cortical motor activity during action observation is related to hemispheric dominance. Neural Plast. **2018**, 14 (2018)
36. Ritter, P., Moosmann, M., Villringer, A.: Rolandic alpha and beta EEG rhythms' strengths are inversely related to fMRI-BOLD signal in primary somatosensory and motor cortex. Hum. Brain Mapp. **30**, 1168–1187 (2009)
37. Westlake, K.P., et al.: Resting state alpha-band functional connectivity and recovery after stroke. Exp. Neurol. **237**, 160–169 (2012)
38. Dubovik, S., et al.: EEG alpha band synchrony predicts cognitive and motor performance in patients with ischemic stroke. https://www.hindawi.com/journals/bn/2013/109764/abs/

Rendering, Layout, Visualization and Navigation

Physically-Based Bimanual Volumetric Selection for Immersive Visualizations

Angela Benavides[1], Rajiv Khadka[1], and Amy Banic[1,2(✉)]

[1] University of Wyoming, Laramie, USA
{abenavi3, rkhadka, abanic}@uwyo.edu
[2] Idaho National Laboratory, Idaho Falls, USA

Abstract. This paper presents the details of a novel selection technique, Physically-Based Volumetric Selection, to combat challenges in selecting volumes of data using immersive display spaces. We present results on a physical experiment that we used to inform design and discuss the details of our proposed technique. We also present the results of a virtual experiment to evaluate feasibility, utility, and usability. A description of user strategies and design is included. Our results will have implications for applications that use alternative rendering techniques as well as volume selection to assist with selection tasks in a physically-based manner. Our technique can be used in combination with other selection and manipulation techniques to improve the overall desired performance of volumetric selection.

Keywords: Physically-based selection · Selection technique ·
Volumetric selection · Mid-air gestures · Bimanual interaction ·
Rendering change for interaction · Volume visualizations ·
Immersive display spaces · Virtual environments

1 Introduction

Immersive display spaces, such as CAVE Automated Virtual Environments [1] and use of head-mounted displays [2], provide advantages for viewing and exploring immersive visualizations over standard desktop displays [3]. Volumetric visualizations are especially useful to explore in immersive environments to better understand spatial relationships [4]. However, when performing selection tasks in these types of environments, there are challenges that can hinder this human-visual process, such as dense data rendering, rendering ambiguity, limitations to visual channel, and/or occlusion of data points [5]. Other issues result from portions of the desired target selection to be too entangled with non-desired target areas. Typically, interaction solutions designed to solve these problems may have low learnability and require some additional instruction to use a technique. We would like to harness innate actions of reaching and grasping we well as other physical properties of objects interacting. This can be difficult to accomplish, but in this paper, we present a novel selection technique that enables users to convert the rendering to geometric-based rendering to manipulate objects using innate physical actions and seeing physics-based responses, but instead for the purpose of selection. There are known advantages to direct manipulation techniques and a

© Springer Nature Switzerland AG 2019
J. Y. C. Chen and G. Fragomeni (Eds.): HCII 2019, LNCS 11574, pp. 183–195, 2019.
https://doi.org/10.1007/978-3-030-21607-8_14

Fig. 1. A user performs mid-air gestures and movement with objects using our physically-based selection technique.

plethora of well-designed manipulation techniques. Our novel idea is to change the rendering of the objects and convert a selection task into a manipulation task. Once they are converted, users manipulate the objects to create the desired selection volume. Once completed the rendering returns to original form, position, and other spatial relationships; however, with the volume of area identified as 'selected'. Not only that, but our technique will enable selection of disjoint portions of a volume (not all of the volume in one place). In this paper, we present the details of our physically-based selection technique. We present the results of a physical experiment where observations were analyzed and used to inform design of the technique. We also present the results of an evaluation of the feasibility and usability of incorporating physically-based interaction for selection of volumes of data. The goal of this work was to determine what strategies users were able to use this technique and how this technique might be incorporated with other existing interaction techniques.

2   Related Work

2.1   Volume Tool Selection

Previous work has designed selection techniques that provide a predefined volumetric area to the user and a user manipulates that volume tool manipulation to define the selected set of points [5–9]. A predefined shape may not accommodate perfectly to the data that needs to be selected so users may have problems selecting occluded elements. Worm Selector [10] allows selecting complex shapes while providing precision. CAST [11] techniques use context-aware interactive selection to provide a faster analysis of the large datasets. Other work provides a way to refine selection from multiple objects to single sets progressively [12, 13]. However, this technique may not be suitable for dense data points in a volume visualization.

2.2   Bimanual Selection

Several of the techniques implemented uses bimanual selection techniques [8, 9]. Additionally, one technique, which has been designed for bimanual interaction, Volume Cracker [14], allows users to break open a set of data in a physical way. Users can use both hands through tracking to manipulate translation and rotation of the parts of the volume. Our technique is unique from this one in the sense that we are permitting users to change and completely manipulate and reorganize any individual or groups of data positions and other attributes of the data. We incorporate a change in rendering to ease the interaction of volume selection and treat it as a virtual environment geometric object selection task. Furthermore, Volume Cracker also does not return data to original sets as in ours but keeps track of context through use of a spine to connect the two portions [14].

2.3   Touch-Based Selection

Other techniques use interaction with 2D touch-based devices to interact with the volume data [15–17]. A few techniques do exist which combine user input and aided selection. Multi-touch touchpad [16] employs two touchpads that uses an asymmetric bimanual technique, which allows selecting a 3D region by requiring only a single action. While these are excellent solutions to reduce fatigue, our intent is to investigate the use of mid-air gestures in situations where it might be more advantageous in other ways by interacting with 6-DOF direct manipulation to solve challenges relating to rendering visibility and occlusion.

2.4   Multiple Object Selection

PORT [18] allowed selecting multiple objects using a set of actions to move and resize while defining a target object. Depth-ray technique [19] that requires two operations to specify the target uses the ray-casting technique with added depth control to select that objects that are occluded. Magic Wand [20] uses an automated procedure to select objects based upon the proximity of the other objects but is sensitive to the geometric outline, which makes it difficult to work. Balloon selection technique [15] uses the distance between two hands of a user to allow the user have control over the depth of selection in a 2D touch surface. Flower ray technique [19] uses the ray-casting technique with marking menu to select multiple target objects concurrently. However, our physical based selection technique in comparison to these works is different as we use mid-air gesture to manipulate the objects/data along with its attributes.

2.5   Semi-automated Selection

Two 3D selection techniques that use gestures for 2D volume selection are TeddySelection and CloudLasso [17]. In both techniques an initial selection is done in a 2D plane by using a Lasso tool, this shape is then extruded to form a 3D cylindrical shape, and the structure of the selected data is analyzed. These solve some of the occlusion problems in an automated way, while our technique serves to solve the issue using direct manipulation. In the future, we will compare performance differences among these techniques but are out of the scope of the work presented in this paper.

3 Physically-Based Volumetric Selection Technique

In this section, we provide a description of how the selection technique works from a user's perspective and the back-end. There are three sequential stages to this technique: Render-Swap, Manipulate-to-Select, and Transitional Return. Users are intended to use this technique with multiple types of 6-DOF devices. However, we implemented our technique with the Leap controller (Fig. 1) to use mid-air gestures and evaluate the feasibility of physical actions a user would perform in the real world.

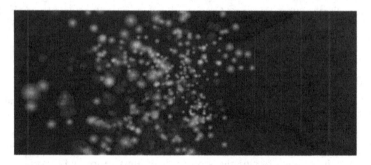

Fig. 2. Example of billboard rendering of data.

Fig. 3. Example of geometric-rendering of data.

3.1 Render Swap

This is the first of three phases. The information for volumetric data is typically rendered as billboard-based rendering, or other similar cloud-like visualizations (Fig. 2). The challenge of this rendering is such that it makes it difficult for users to perceive specific details borders of the data with what they would like to select. The first step to better volumetric selection is to swap the rendering for a geometric rendering approach (Fig. 3). The users will see data points or clusters of data points change to geometric objects. Color encoding will be retained. There is a great deal of flexibility for the user to determine what the geometric objects or glyphs should be, how many data points per cluster, clustering by data properties, and any other set of properties. For the purposes of our evaluation, we chose spherical geometric objects because they most closely matched our physical experiment (experiment one) and innate physical interaction.

3.2   Manipulate-to-Select

Once the data is represented as geometric objects, the next phase of our selection technique is engaged. The idea is that those data points or clusters of data points, easier to see and identify. We call this phase Manipulation-to-Select because users may translate, rotate, scale, or manipulate other properties of the data without penalty to the actual data properties or spatial relationship. For our prototype implementation, we implemented translational change only as per our results from our experiment one (see section Experiment 1: Physical Observations). Additionally, physics or a subset of physics aspects are applied. For the purposes of our prototype and evaluation, we enabled physics forces on collisions of the user with the objects and with other objects but did not enable gravity. The reason we did this was to retain the spatial relationships of the elements initially so that users could better begin to identify what to select.

In this phase, the rendered data is no longer locked into each position. Users can move the objects around with the intention to organize the data and separate out what elements users wish to select. There is a lot of flexibility on users' end for how they would like to organize the data. A user can collect data in a pile to indicate selection, separate out all the elements s/he does not want to select, separate out all the elements s/he does want to select, separate elements into different piles or groups for different levels of selection, etc. We discuss these user strategies, discovered from the evaluation we conducted, in more detail in the User Strategies section of the section: Experiment 2: Evaluation of Technique in Virtual Space.

Fig. 4. Example of manipulation-to-select

How the user manipulates the elements for selection could also be categorized as egocentric or exocentric. In egocentric Manipulation-to-Select, users gather the data relative to themselves. For example, a user will collect data close to the body or away from the body. In exocentric Manipulation-to-Select, users will gather elements based on spaces. For example, a user may designate a 'selection space' and then move all elements to that space or a user may identify a threshold or line through the space to push all elements to be selected across this threshold. In exocentric Manipulation-to-Select, there is an additional step for users to define the 'selection space' either by creating a volume of space through a geometric object, or by organically drawing an area or line in the space. However, once the user defines this area, that area is saved or retained in the workspace and is retrieved during the 'Render-Swap' phase.

For the purposes of our evaluation, we only implemented egocentric Manipulation-to-Select however in our evaluation is where we discovered users were performing this strategy of designating areas to put objects for selection. As such will implement support for exocentric manipulate-to-select for a future evaluation.

3.3   Transitional Return

Once users have identified the elements for selection through the task of manipulate-to-select, users may initiate the phase of Transitional Return. In this phase, the elements morph back into each element original position, individual data elements (if a Render-Swap clustered data element- see section on Render-Swap), and original rendering type. We indicate this phase as transitional, because it is important that the morph process does not occur instantaneously. This phase is a continuous animated visual change over a short period of time to maintain context in both (a) where the data points came from/ moving to but also (b) in the process a user conducts when they perform manipulation-to-select. As a user is moving the elements around in the space during manipulate-to-select, key-frames of the change in position of the elements are recorded over time. Once Transitional Return is initiated, those key-frames are loaded and played back for the user in reverse in a much quicker time. We have implemented for users to have the option to include their arm movements in the replay or not. Users also have the flexibility to adjust the speed of the replay.

4   Experiment One: Physical Observations

We conducted a qualitative experiment to determine how users physically interacted with objects when asked to select a target group of objects. We designed this experiment to understand user movement in 3-dimensional space and inform the design of our physically-based volumetric selection technique.

4.1   Experimental Design

Participants were seated at a table and presented with a volume of objects in various randomized configurations. Some of the objects were colored differently than other objects, referred to as target objects. For the objects, we chose to use cotton balls because they are lightweight, can be easily manipulated, do not easily roll away, and stay together for the most part when placed together. The task was to determine the best way for them to identify objects they would like to 'select' using physical actions. The configurations consisted of situations, which a user would encounter when interacting with volumetric data: occlusions, non-target data in-between target data, various clustering and non-clustering of data, and variety of size and shape of target volume. Participants were presented with a total of 25 trials. While configurations were assigned at random, all participants received a wide range of configurations from one end of the spectrum no occluded target object to all occluded target objects and of the spectrum from all clustered target object to zero clustered target objects. We collected data on observations, and subjective responses from participants based on questionnaires. In addition, Cyber Gloves, one for each hand, and wrists, tracked participants' hands by an optical rigid-body tracking system by Opti-Track.

4.2   Results

A total of 10 participants (6 males, 4 females; Mean age = 25.05, SD = 3.28) participated in the study. In this study, handedness was not used as a measure for exclusion, but all participants were right-handed. Video recording and hand/wrist tracking data was analyzed using 3 facilitators to independently identify patterns in participants' actions, then later came together to determine what factors would be used to inform the design of our selection technique. What we found was that participants would use actions that would separate out the target balls in some way, which related to the configuration of the target balls in relation to the non-target balls. Since the target balls were made of cotton and could be easily manipulated, we hypothesized that participants might shape or squeeze the cotton to indicate selection. However, no participants changed or manipulated the size and shape of the cotton to signal selection. The only actions participants performed were in support of translation. The following are patterns found from our observations:

Less Occluded Targets. All participants for majority of time in this situation would use their hands to divide out and separate the non-target balls from the targets. The selection configuration resulted in target balls would be left in their current positions and the non-targets spread away in new positions.

More Occluded Targets. Participants would start with larger groups of target balls and try to move other target balls closer to those groups. Any non-target balls in the way were separated out from the target balls. Any non-target balls or groups of balls were removed from the participants' view and set aside.

Widely Spread Targets. Where smaller sized groups of or more single target balls there were, the more the participants pulled together the target objects in a common area than separating away non-target objects. Therefore, in this sense, participants instead changed the position of the target balls, while non-target balls remained majority in original position.

Clustered Targets. In addition to any separation actions described in treatment of occlusion, majority of participants (N = 7 out of 10) left clusters of targets in the location of majority of target balls, while moving only single or smaller clusters towards those larger groups. Some participants (N = 3 out of 10) instead held the target balls at various times in their hands to signal each group was to be 'selected'.

5 Experiment Two: Evaluation of Technique in Virtual Space

The goal of this experiment was to evaluate the usability of our designed volumetric section technique. Our technique and three phases of 'Render-Swap', 'Manipulate-to-Select', and 'Transitional Return' are described more in detail in the earlier section: Physically-based Volumetric Selection Technique. We implemented our technique using a Leap motion controller (to enhance freedom of handedness movement) and in Unity using collision-based physics for the hands and objects. Gravity forces were disabled for all objects to help retain spatial relationships during the 'Manipulate-to-Select' phase. See Figs. 1 and 4 for an example setup and how users interacted.

5.1 Experimental Design and Procedure

Participants wore a head-mounted display (Oculus Rift) with a Leap controller attached to the front of the display. Unity 3D was used to render the task environment as well as a natural-looking hand model (male and female models were used to match the gender of the participant). Participant's hands were tracked using the Leap controller. In addition, participants' head, wrists, and elbows were tracked using a wide-area optical rigid-body tracking system provided by Opti-Track.

In the virtual environment, participants were presented with a set of volumetric data where some areas were colored different from other areas, signaling the areas as the target for selection. Initially data was rendered using billboard-based rendering where data looked like blended clouds of color. When the participant was ready, they gave a verbal command to begin the Manipulate-to-Select task. At that point, the data would become geometric spheres. While users can change this, for the purposes of the experiment we used a consistent set data point and sphere size. There was a total of 3 clusters of target balls, each one with a range of balls from 5–15. A range of configurations of occlusion and spread of these virtual objects were randomly assigned in the trials.

The task was to use their hands to identify the volumes for selection. Participants then used a voice command 'Select' to signal that they were finished with the Manipulate-to-Select task and therefore selection was complete. At that time, Transitional Return would initiate. In this study, since we used participants from a broad general subject pool, it would not make sense to evaluate retention of context in the Transitional Return phase. We plan to do this type of evaluation in the future with expert scientists who use these types of visualizations who could provide a better gradient of performance for context retention of the data. In this evaluation, our goal was to evaluate broad utility and usability of this technique. In addition to the tracking that recorded the arm/hand movements of the participants, position change of the objects in the environment were automatically logged for the Transitional Return but also for our analysis purposes. We collected data on NASA TLX workload to assess fatigue, subjective responses on a modified SUS usability questionnaire, and from an open-ended interview.

5.2   Results

Participants. Data from 14 participants was collected (mean age = 26.36, SD = 7.43). All participants had or corrected to 20/20 vision. There were 5 females and 9 males. There was one color-blind person but the distinction between target objects and non-target objects were not reported to be a problem. 7 out of 14 participants are moderately to very experienced with these types of volumetric visualizations. The remaining 4 had little to no experience. All participants completed and passed a full range of arm motion test to determine if they had any physical limitations that may influence how they were moving. All participants completed and passed the Butterfly Stereopsis Test, determining the range of stereopsis the participants could see. All 14 participants were different from the participants in experiment one. We made sure to exclude participants from experiment one because we did not want any bias or influence from their experience with the physical objects in influence their experience of the virtual selection technique. In other words, we wanted to make sure the opinions of the participants were in response to the usability and utility of our selection technique, rather than the comparison to an exact physical experience. In interaction design, it may not always be beneficial to provide an exact replicated experience to the real world and we designed the technique with this in mind. The purpose of this experiment was to identify the strengths and weakness of our proposed technique in the context of volume selection. All but one participant was right-handed. We looked at the data of the participant who was left-handed closely in comparison with our analysis and conclusion and did not find any discrepancies relating to hand dominance. In the future, we will actively recruit participants of all range of handedness to determine what differences exist for different dominance. Analysis of handedness is out of the scope for this work.

Utility, Usability, Fatigue, and Overall Workload. The mean completion time of each trial was 1.24 min (SD = 0.48) with a total of 14 trials each participant, for a total of 17.36 mean time of experience. Participants answered questions on usability, such as ease of use, usage satisfaction, own performance, comfort, and utility, and fatigue, on a scale from 1 to 7. One represents more difficulty, less satisfaction, poor performance, less comfort, higher utility, and less fatigue. Seven represents higher ease of use, higher satisfaction, better performance, more comfort, and higher fatigue. Overall usability ratings are high, as participants reported the following for ease of use (M = 5.75, SD = 1.05), performance satisfaction (M = 5.5, SD = 1.34), comfort (M = 5.62, SD = 1.53), and utility (M = 5.86, SD = 0.86). Overall, we expected much higher reports of arm fatigue, but ratings were generally low (M = 1.07, SD = 1.59).

We analyzed data on NASA TLX Overall Workload and participants reported overall workload (M = 41.26, SD = 22.34), with effort and performance being a more highly weighted contributing factor than mental and physical demand. Overall workload is lower than expected given the physical aspects of the technique.

Other positive themes are illustrated by the following positive comments (negative comments are in the limitations section):

- "I feel I completed all of the tasks as directed but had intuition with the movements"
- "I could perform and complete each task in a very comfortable way. Also, I could move comfortably throughout the room without any difficulty"

- "The Head Mounted Display was showing me almost perfectly what my moves were. It was really impressive!"

User Strategies from Movement Data and Observations

Gather. Participants often collected target balls close to them in an egocentric manner. Participants generally collected them within a short distance of themselves and then indicated selection.

Separate. Participants would move non-target balls away from target balls. In some instances, participants would separate target balls from non-target balls, but majority of those actions could be considered a gathering strategy. To be considered under a 'separating' strategy, participants removed balls away from other balls but did not collect them into one area.

Expunge Non-Targets. The ball objects move with speed relative to user's speed at which the hand is moved. As a result, the user can control the force that is applied to the balls. One strategy that users followed was to quickly and forcefully knock non-target balls out of the scene. There were a few occasions where this was not meant to happen (see Limitations section), however debriefing participants who did this often, did this as a strategy for selection. Participants did not do the reverse as we found in experiment one. No target balls were sent away to indicate selection.

Pointing. We found a number of participants would touch single objects with their finger or point at (without touching) to identify objects for selection. This is a surprising result since participants did not really do this in the physical experiment. Given this result, a Ray-Casting [21, 22] technique can then be used to select stray individual objects after the Render-Swap phase. Ray-casting has been shown to have high accuracy and fast selection completion times.

Lasso. Participants would gesture circles around groups of targets to indicate selection. This may be carry-over from other computer-based applications.

Painting. A small subset of participants used the palm of their hand to gesture strokes as if to 'paint' the objects they wished to select, typically below the balls or above the balls. This is different from LASSO because participants did not make complete or semi-complete loops.

Limitations. In this section, we outline a few themes, each illustrated by an actual comment from a participant, to facilitate discussion of the limitations of the system.

"Performance wise, however, once a ball goes the wrong way, it is impossible to get it back." We will address this limitation by implementing a snap-back feature along the translation trail of the ball. That way the user can not only 'undo' a translational change but also move to a location, as it was intended for. For example, if the user only wanted to move it to a particular location but the object(s) traveled too far.

"Occasionally it was difficult to reach some of the balls that were further away or towards the edge of the usable area." Other participants commented on unwanted body interaction as well. This limitation can be address by implementing an already useful existing technique of HOMER [21, 22], where the hand can be cast-out into space, thereby extending the physical reach of a user. We did not implement for this study since we wanted to look at how physical actions directly work as a selection technique.

"It looks like the system had trouble responding fast or sudden gestures." Other participants also reported that at times the hand models would disappear. This was a result of the tracking performance (in particular when the hands disappeared from view of the Leap system). We expect this technology will improve and that the results we are reporting in this paper would only improve with better tracking performance.

6 Discussion

The main difference in strategies found between the physical observations and the virtual evaluation is that participants in the virtual evaluation did not send target objects away from their body or away from other non-target objects. In the physical experiment, participants did this when there was less clustering of target objects as an easier way to pluck out the target objects. We speculated that this might be a result of having the desk serve as a workspace 'frame' in the physical space. In the virtual experiment, if participants sent a ball away, they could not retrieve it so that could be interpreted as a non-selection. This may be the reason why participants did not execute this strategy.

Additionally, the PAINTING strategy was an interesting and surprising result, as it was different from the physical experiment and we did not provide color change feedback for selection of the objects. We will incorporate various tools that participants can use for this manipulation phase.

We found through debriefing participants that the mean task completion time was a reasonable amount of time to complete the task. In the future, we will compare our technique to other existing techniques. We will still expect our technique to take more time however, we will expect our technique to counteract difficulty areas where other existing techniques may fail (occlusion, data spread out, non-target data too close to target data, etc.)

The results on low arm fatigue and low workload may be due to the observation that they (participants) used their arms in short bursts of actions rather than continuously holding up their arms. Given that the task was timed but not constrained to complete the task as fast as possible, perhaps users may experience more fatigue without more time to rest arms between actions.

7 Conclusion

In conclusion, we present a novel volumetric selection technique. This technique has three novel phases. The first is the phase that converts the typical volumetric rendering into geometric rendering temporarily for selection. Based on the results from our evaluation, we discovered that once in this phase, a variety of selection techniques proven high performance for virtual environments can be used for selection of these difficult to see volumes. The second is the manipulation-to-select phase. This idea is novel in the sense that you could take any manipulation technique and use it for a selection-based task. Within the scope of this paper, we only looked at translation-to-select and reported the strategies and limitations of the technique. The third idea is that the data converts back into the original rendering, position, and original state of other properties. The data travels along the path in reverse that the data took when a user manipulates the spatial relationships of the data.

This paper presents the details of a novel selection technique, a solution to combat the challenges with volumetric data selection explored using immersive display spaces. We conducted a physical experiment to inform design and then conducted a virtual experiment to evaluate feasibility utility, and usability. Overall, this technique produced high utility, usability, and satisfaction in performance ratings. Surprisingly the technique produces low fatigue and overall workload. Our results also include descriptions of strategies to incorporate and adjustments to make on our technique. Our results will be useful for applications that use alternative rendering as well as volume selection to assist with selection tasks in a physically-based manner. We view this technique to be augmented with other techniques as a way for users to use gesture-based interaction when direct manipulation is more useful.

8 Future Work

We outlined several ideas to combat weaknesses and limitations of this technique in the discussion section and throughout the paper. We plan to implement those augmentations to the technique and then conduct an evaluation to compare the performance of our technique with other existing techniques. We will investigate Transitional Return performance in relation to preserved context for expert users in selection scenarios.

Acknowledgements. We would like to thank all participants who participated in this study.

References

1. Cruz-Neira, C., Sandin, D.J., DeFanti, T.A.: Surround-screen projection-based virtual reality: the design and implementation of the CAVE. In: Proceedings of the ACM 20th Annual Conference on Computer Graphics and Interactive Techniques, pp. 135–142, September 1993
2. Forsberg, A., Katzourin, M., Wharton, K., Slater, M.: A comparative study of Desktop, Fishtank, and Cave systems for the exploration of volume rendered confocal data sets. IEEE Trans. Visual Comput. Graphics **14**(3), 551–563 (2008)
3. Sutherland, I.E.: The ultimate display. Multimedia: From Wagner to virtual reality (1965)
4. Kreylos, O., Bawden, G.W., Kellogg, L.H.: Immersive visualization and analysis of LiDAR data. In: Bebis, G., et al. (eds.) ISVC 2008. LNCS, vol. 5358, pp. 846–855. Springer, Heidelberg (2008)
5. Vanacken, L., Grossman, T., Coninx, K.: Exploring the effects of environment density and target visibility on object selection in 3D virtual environments. 3DUI'07, March 2007
6. Cabral, M., et al.: Bi-manual gesture interaction for 3D cloud point selection and annotation using COTS. In: 2014 IEEE Symposium on 3D User Interfaces (3DUI), pp. 187–188. IEEE, March 2014

7. Forsberg, A., Herndon, K., Zeleznik, R.: Aperture based selection for immersive virtual environments. In: Proceedings of the 9th Annual ACM Symposium on User Interface Software and Technology, pp. 95–96. ACM, November 1996

8. Ulinski, A., Zanbaka, C., Wartell, Z., Goolkasian, P., Hodges, L.F.: Two handed selection techniques for volumetric data. In: Symposium on 3D User Interfaces, March 2007

9. Yoganandan, A., Jerald, J., Mlyniec, P.: Bimanual selection and interaction with volumetric regions of interest. In: IEEE VR (2014)

10. Dubois, E., Hamelin, A.: Worm selector: volume selection in a 3D point cloud through adaptive modelling. Int. J. Virtual Reality 17(1), 1–20 (2017)

11. Yu, L., Efstathiou, K., Isenberg, P., Isenberg, T.: CAST: effective and efficient user interaction for context-aware selection in 3D particle clouds. IEEE Trans. Visual Comput. Graphics 22(1), 886–895 (2016)

12. Kopper, R., Bacim, F., Bowman, D.A.: Rapid and accurate 3D selection by progressive refinement. In: Symposium on 3D User Interfaces (3DUI), March 2011

13. Veit, M., Capobianco, A.: Go'Then'Tag: a 3-D point cloud annotation technique. In: 2014 IEEE Symposium on 3D User Interfaces (3DUI), pp. 193–194. IEEE, March 2014

14. Laha, B., Bowman, D.A.: Design of the bare-hand volume cracker for analysis of raw volumetric data. In: IEEE VR 2014 Workshop on Immersive Volumetric Interaction (2014)

15. Benko, H., Feiner, S.: Balloon selection: a multi-finger technique for accurate low-fatigue 3D selection. In: Symposium on 3D User Interfaces, 3DUI'07, March 2007

16. Ohnishi, T., Lindeman, R., Kiyokawa, K.: Multiple multi-touch touchpads for 3D selection. In: 2011 IEEE Symposium on 3D User Interfaces (3DUI), pp. 115–116, March 2011

17. Yu, L., Efstathiou, K., Isenberg, P., Isenberg, T.: Efficient structure-aware selection techniques for 3D point cloud visualizations with 2DOF input. IEEE Trans. Visual Comput. Graphics 18(12), 2245–2254 (2012)

18. Lucas, J.F.: Design and evaluation of 3D multiple object selection techniques (M.S. Master's Thesis, Virginia Tech) (2005)

19. Grossman, T., Balakrishnan, R.: The design and evaluation of selection techniques for 3D volumetric displays. In: Proceedings of the 19th Annual ACM Symposium on User Interface Software and Technology, pp. 3–12. ACM, October 2006

20. Stenholt, R.: Efficient selection of multiple objects on a large scale. In: Proceedings of the 18th ACM Symposium on Virtual Reality Software and Technology, December 2012

21. Argelaguet, F., Andujar, C.: A survey of 3D object selection techniques for virtual environments. Comput. Graph. 37(3), 121–136 (2013)

22. Bowman, D.A., Hodges, L.F.: An evaluation of techniques for grabbing and manipulating remote objects in immersive virtual environments. In: Proceedings of the 1997 symposium on Interactive 3D graphics, pp. 35-ff. ACM, April 1997

Integrating Historical Content with Augmented Reality in an Open Environment

Manuel Condado[1], Isabel Morais[1], Ryan Quinn[2], Sahil Patel[2], Patricia Morreale[1(✉)], Ed Johnston[2], and Elizabeth Hyde[3]

[1] School of Computer Science, Kean University, Union, NJ 07083, USA
{condadom, moraisis, pmorreal}@kean.edu
[2] Robert Busch School of Design, Kean University, Union, NJ 07083, USA
{quinryan, psahil, jedward}@kean.edu
[3] Department of History, Kean University, Union, NJ 07083, USA
ehyde@kean.edu

Abstract. Museums offer visitors a variety of historic content. However, museums still rely on traditional methods of delivering content to visitors through the use of signage to compliment an exhibit. A research study was conducted to determine the feasibility of developing Mobile Augmented Reality experiences for a museum in an open environment. Three examples of AR experiences were investigated. First, the Serpentine Path AR experience is presented, providing contextual AR, showing the development of a historically significant garden pathway with primary source historical documents, and images. The Horse Chestnut Tree AR experience follows, presenting a miniature 3D model of a tree that is a vital part of the outdoor museum grounds. The Main House AR experience illustrates AR over time, showing the contrasting progression of a home and surrounding foliage. Through mobile delivery, users are provided with an AR experience either on the physical site grounds or from a remote offsite location. Approximately two-thirds of the users (68%) considered the AR experience good for the Horse Chestnut Tree experience, with 90% of the users responding that the Serpentine Path AR experience, which included audio, provided access to historical content they would not receive anywhere else. Similarly, 96% of the users felt that the Main House AR experience provides unique access to historical content which was not available elsewhere. Evaluation of the mobile AR experience identified areas where users learned more, based on the information provided to them during their visit, with the identification of areas for future work.

Keywords: Use experience · User centered design · Mobile applications · UX evaluation

1 Introduction

Augmented Reality is distinct from Virtual Reality. In Augmented Reality (AR) the environment is real but extended with information and objects overlapping in real time. In contrast Virtual Reality fully submerges the user into a virtual environment [1].

© Springer Nature Switzerland AG 2019
J. Y. C. Chen and G. Fragomeni (Eds.): HCII 2019, LNCS 11574, pp. 196–205, 2019.
https://doi.org/10.1007/978-3-030-21607-8_15

Augmented Reality bridges the gap between the real and virtual world in a seamless way [2]. For the research presented here, three AR experiences were developed for the Liberty Hall Museum Grounds in Union, NJ. The purpose of developing these experiences was to captivate museum visitors using mobile technology. It also gives the opportunity for visitors to view historical artifacts in a non-traditional manner, integrated with the real artifact. All these experiences are suited for outdoor environments.

2   Prior Work

During the early development of Augmented Reality (AR) users wanting to take part of AR would have to wear a head-mounted display (HMD) [1]. Due to the weight of the system, the HMD was suspended from the ceiling. This headset was often bulky, and users were limited in range by the wires and components that were part of the headset.

As time progressed, advancements in technology have allowed devices to be much more powerful and smaller in size. Smartphones now contain numerous tools such as a camera, GPS, telephone, Wi-Fi support and a web browser. The widespread use of smartphones makes the smartphone a great tool for Mobile Augmented Reality (MAR), bringing new possibilities of delivering content to users. Delivery methods include virtual content such as audio, text and video which can overlap in the physical world [3].

There are countless applications for the use of AR. One venue for AR is in museums [4]. Museums are places where visitors can see hundreds of well-preserved artifacts on display. For instance, in a museum there could be skeletons of prehistoric animals such as dinosaurs. Yet visitors, mainly children do not know what an actual dinosaur looked like. In a study, museum visitors can see what a recreated dinosaur overlays on an actual skeleton [5]. This AR system allows visitors to get a better understanding of what a dinosaur may have looked like.

Another adoption of AR is the Chicago 00 Project (http://chicago00.org) by the Chicago History Museum [6], more formally known as the Riverwalk Project [7]. The Chicago 00 Project presents users with historical images and footage while users are physically present at one of their AR experience sites in an outdoor environment, which are scattered around the city of Chicago. One AR experience is the SS Eastland Disaster. Visitors have the ability to align their smartphone using the outline of an image onto the building or bridge [6]. Presenting the user with a historical image and allowing users to stand where the photograph was originally taken provides an immersive, engaging, memorable experience. Clicking on the image brings text with detailed information of what occurred, further enhancing the Chicago 00/Riverwalk experience [8]. Similar work is taking place in Montreal, as part of the Cite Memoire installation [9], with visual projections on the buildings on downtown Montreal in the evening, accompanied by information accessible through a mobile app.

AR presents museums new opportunities to place historical content that may otherwise be placed in collections or archives in an outdoor environment [10–13]. This research further explores the feasibility in developing in Mobile Augmented Reality using marker-based technology in an open space.

3 Methodology

There are two types of AR systems commonly found today: marker-less and marker-based AR. Marker-less AR uses GPS coordinates from a mobile smartphone or image recognition to determine a user's location. Mobile applications such as Snapchat currently uses marker-less AR in its platform. Users have the ability to add 3D model banners and text into their Snapchat videos, without any additional work other than the initial video recording. Marker-based AR requires an image that is used as a trigger for the AR experience to start. The image acts similar to a barcode. The user simply scans an image from their mobile smartphone and in return is presented with some form of digital content that overlaps the physical world (Fig. 1).

Mobile application detects and displays 3D content

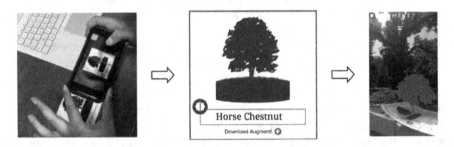

Fig. 1. Depiction of 3D content generation process.

For this research, marker-based AR was added to the Liberty Hall Museum Grounds. During the initial stage, pencil sketches of the mobile AR markers were used and were later designed digitally using the Adobe Creative Suite. This approach saved time as it allowed several versions to be made quickly. The best pencil sketch for each AR experience was later selected by the museum director and staff.

Three unique and prominent AR experiences were developed for the Liberty Hall Museum Grounds, in Union, NJ: a Serpentine Path experience, Horse Chestnut tree experience, and a Main House experience, using the Augment and Blippar AR platforms. The selection of the Augment and Blippar platforms was based on support for scaling and compatibility for mobile phones, using both the Android and iOS operating systems, and Blippar's support for the inclusion of audio clips.

3.1 Serpentine Path

The Serpentine Path (Fig. 2) is an important natural exhibit on the grounds of the Liberty Hall Museum. The path is a walk-through of the various trees, foliage and landscape of the property. The path however has been altered throughout the years.

Fig. 2. Marker for Serpentine Path

The AR experience allows visitors to explore the property back to its origin and experience the time lapse to what the property is today. Historical images were provided by Kean's History Department and from the Liberty Hall Museum staff. For the first time museum visitors would be able to see images depicting the original grounds accompanied by an audio clip (Fig. 3).

Fig. 3. AR images with audio clip options

Here is segment of the audio clipped used for this experience:

> *"Over the course of the eighteenth century, the fashion for gardens changed from the formal, geometric and symmetrical "French" aesthetic to the "English" style landscape garden. Those changes are reflected in the gardens of Liberty Hall. William Livingston owned several books on gardens, including John Evelyn's Sylva (the most important treatise on trees to be published in the seventeenth century), Philip Miller's Gardener's Dictionary (a major English reference work), and Batty Langley's Principles of Gardening, an influential volume by the noted eighteenth-century English garden designer. The same books could be found in the libraries of Livingston's American peers Robert R. Livingston, George Washington, and Thomas Jefferson, all of whom were enthusiastic gardeners ..."*

3.2 Horse Chestnut Tree

The second AR experience is the Horse Chestnut Tree experience (Fig. 4). The physical Horse Chestnut tree is currently planted in front of the Main House at the Liberty Hall Museum.

Fig. 4. Marker for the Horse Chestnut Tree

The Department of Environmental Protection in the State of New Jersey recognizes the tree has a height of 49 feet tall with a spread of 57 feet wide. It is considered the biggest in Union County and in the state of New Jersey. The tree has aged and has had parts of its trunk and branches cut off. It is believed that William Livingston's daughter Susan Livingston planted the tree. For this experience a miniature 3D model of the Horse Chestnut tree appears when the marker is scanned (Fig. 5). We felt it was important to demonstrate to the museum visitors what the tree appeared like in the past.

Fig. 5. 3D Model of Horse Chestnut besides the physical Horse Chestnut

3.3   Main House

The Main House AR experience (Fig. 6) was inspired by the works of the Chicago 00 or Riverwalk Project [6, 7], which uses marker-less Augmented Reality in which users can align their smartphones, tablets, or any other smart device with the physical world. When aligned properly, users are able to see a layered image that overlaps the physical world and displays a historical image.

For this research we proceeded with the marker-based AR route. This AR experience consists of four historical images from different points in time, taken from years 1844, 1856, 193,5 and an unspecified dated image. Images were made transparent so users can align the entire image of the Main House (Fig. 7). The transparency helps users see what property look entirely at the given year.

Fig. 6. Marker for the Main House

Fig. 7. Picture of the Main House using the Blippar platform

4 Results

A survey was conducted, and participants (n = 41) were asked a series of Augmented Reality questions. The first question asked participants if they knew what Augmented Reality (AR) was. Ninety percent of the respondents reported they did know what AR was, with only 10% reporting no. The second question asked participants if they believed AR can be used as an educational tool. All participants (97.6%) agreed that the AR can be used as education tool.

Participants were shown the Horse Chestnut experience and asked if the AR experience provided them with historical content. The majority of the survey participants (68%) did not find any historical content. Participants mentioned that there was no text to accompany the 3D model. It is possible, if a historical document were to have accompanied the 3D model, that the results may have been different.

The Serpentine Path and Main House AR experiences provided different results. Survey participants agreed there was some type of historical content to be derived from both Augmented Reality experience. The Serpentine Path AR experience, with audio, received a 90% favorable response for access to historical content that would not have

" LIBERTY HALL."[1]

Fig. 8. 1856 etching of Liberty Hall main house

otherwise been available to the participants. The Main House AR experience received a 97% favorable response for access to historical content as well.

One drawback to the AR experiences was that the transparency made it difficult to work with at certain times during the day. Environmental factors such as lighting played an important role. On cloudy days users reported that transparency made it difficult to find the anchor points or reference points with which to align the image onto the physical Main House. On one occasion a user reported that instead of aligning the virtual AR image on the physical building, simply holding the virtual image below the physical house could suffice.

Additionally, during the development of this experience, objects that were added or removed surrounding the Main House were not taken into account. For instance, in the 1856 image of the Main House (Fig. 8), the Main House and the Horse Chestnut is the focus of the image. However, on the present-day property several trees and plants have been added.

Future work would include identifying points on the property where users could stand for the best AR experience. Additionally, a narrative trail may be used to further enhance the historical context of the property. For example, audio narration could provide visitors with information about the present-day small creek beside the property which used to be a large river supporting supply ships delivering household goods from New York City and elsewhere. Understanding this commerce provides a context for the economic and social power of the residents of the home at that time. Overall, AR experiences have the potential to change the static museum-going experience, when correctly aligned with other materials, including audio narration and historical artifacts.

References

1. Elvins, T.: Augmented reality: "The future's so bright, I gotta wear (see-through) shades". ACM SIGGRAPH Comput. Graph. **32**(1), 11–13 (1998)
2. Feng Zhou, F., Duh, H., Billinghurst, M.: Trends in augmented reality tracking, interaction and display: a review of ten years of ISMAR. In: 2008 7th IEEE/ACM International Symposium on Mixed and Augmented Reality (2008)
3. Pence, H.: Smartphones, smart objects, and augmented reality. Ref. Libr. **52**(1–2), 136–145 (2010)
4. van Arnhem, J., Spiller, J.: Augmented reality for discovery and instruction. J. Web Librariansh. **8**(2), 214–230 (2014)
5. Kondo, T.: Augmented learning environment using mixed reality technology. In: Reeves, T., Yamashita, S. (eds.) Proceedings of E-Learn 2006–World Conference on E-Learning in Corporate, Government, Healthcare, and Higher Education, pp. 83–87 (2006)
6. Johnson, S.: Chicago Tribune (2018). http://www.chicagotribune.com/entertainment/museums/ct-eastland-vr-app-chicago-history-ent-1025-20161024-column.html. Accessed 7 Sep 2018
7. Chicago 00 Experience. http://chicago00.org/. Accessed 12 Oct 2018
8. Cavallo, M., Rhodes, G.A., Forbes, A.: Riverwalk: incorporating historical photographs in public outdoor augmented reality experiences. In: 2016 IEEE International Symposium on Mixed and Augmented Reality (ISMAR-Adjunct), Merida, pp. 160–165 (2016)

9. Cite Memoire. http://www.montrealenhistoires.com/en/cite-memoire/. Accessed 12 Oct 2018
10. Hunsucker, A.J., McClinton, K., Wang, J., Stolterman, E.: Augmented reality prototyping for interaction design students. In: Proceedings of the 2017 CHI Conference Extended Abstracts on Human Factors in Computing Systems, New York, NY, USA, pp. 1018–1023 (2017)
11. Hangal, S., Piratla, V., Manovit, C., Chan, P., Edwards, G., Lam, M.S.: Historical research using email archives. In: Proceedings of the 33rd Annual ACM Conference Extended Abstracts on Human Factors in Computing Systems, CHI EA 2015, pp. 735–742. ACM, New York (2015)
12. Pearson, J., Robinson, S., Reitmaier, T., et al.: Exploring the user of the physical web with resource-constrained communities. In: Proceedings of the 2017 CHI Conference on Human Computer Interaction (CHI 2017), Denver, CO (2017)
13. Hu, P., Tsai, P.: Mobile outdoor augmented reality project for historic sites in Tainan. In: 2016 International Conference on Advanced Materials for Science and Engineering (ICAMSE), Tainan, pp. 509–511 (2016)

Surface Prediction for Spatial Augmented Reality Using Cubature Kalman Filtering

Keegan Fernandes$^{(\boxtimes)}$, Adam Gomes, Cong Yue, Yousef Sawires,
and David Wang

University of Waterloo, Waterloo, ON N2L 3G1, Canada
ka3ferna@uwaterloo.ca

Abstract. Projection mapping onto non-rigid deformable objects requires highly accurate tracking of its surface position. Traditional methods of using measured deformations of the surface can be inadequate due to potential sources of time delay, such as projector lag. Previous work done by Gomes et al. [3] demonstrated a novel approach for predicting the motion of a non-rigid surface to assist in the compensation of any delays. This paper improves upon the extended Kalman filter algorithm, presented by Gomes et al., by introducing a higher order approximation using the cubature Kalman filter. This algorithm is verified using an experimental setup where an image is projected onto a deformable surface being disturbed by a "random" force. The results show a marked improvement over the extended Kalman filter. The error results demonstrate that the cubature Kalman filter can be applied to situations with low measurement capture rates as well as higher levels of occlusion.

Keywords: Spatial augmented reality · Virtual reality · Non-rigid surfaces

1 Introduction

Spatial augmented reality (SAR) is the use of projection technology for the purpose of transforming any object into a display surface. This, currently, is most often used by the entertainment industry to project large, sometimes user interactive, scenes onto walls or other rigid surfaces such as tables and buildings. Projection mapping onto non-rigid surfaces could be very useful in the entertainment and fashion industries, and the field of surgical training. Current rigid mapping algorithms, however, would not be able to function if significant deformations were to alter the surface, such as those involved with textiles, leading to a lack of realism and immersion. Current methods to solve this problem [7,10,11] involve the real-time tracking of surface geometry and projecting a warped image onto the measured surface. However, for quickly changing surfaces there is no mention of how well these techniques perform. If a surface being tracked is moving quickly the image processing and surface tracking time required may cause delays that lead to image distortions. Other solutions [6] that have been shown

© Springer Nature Switzerland AG 2019
J. Y. C. Chen and G. Fragomeni (Eds.): HCII 2019, LNCS 11574, pp. 206–220, 2019.
https://doi.org/10.1007/978-3-030-21607-8_16

to work for high speed deformations rely on highly customised and expensive projector and tracking systems. Other issues that arise due to the nature of this problem include inherent system time delays for real time purposes as well as occlusions. Projectors are notorious for having slow response times, also called input lag, which along with algorithm processing times can be a large damper on any real time effects. Occlusions occur when an object being tracked is blocked from observation and so can no longer be measured. A common occurrence when tracking non-rigid surfaces is self-occlusion where by the object itself prevents it from being fully measured. A prediction scheme can be used to approximate the position of the surface at some future time, which can smooth the overall experience. The goal of this paper is to improve upon the extended Kalman filter (EKF) algorithm presented by Gomes et al. [3] by implementing a cubature Kalman filer (CKF) process. This paper does not cover any image warping or projection techniques as it is assumed standard techniques will be used for projection. This paper is organized as follows: Sect. 2 discusses the modelling of the non-rigid surface, Sect. 3 introduces the EKF and CKF prediction based surface tracking algorithms, Sect. 4 provides a description of the experimental procedure for real-time application of the algorithm, Sect. 5 presents the results of the experiment, and Sect. 6 lists conclusions and future work.

2   System Model

The CKF algorithm requires a physically accurate deformable model that will describes the motion of the surface being tracked. Several different deformable models have been studied in the field of computer graphics ranging from aesthetically pleasing to physically accurate. This paper uses the mass-spring system used by Gomes [4] due to its simplicity, speed, and ease of construction. The mass-spring model was first developed by Provot [9], it uses an interconnection of point masses (nodes), springs, and dampers to represent a surface. Each point mass is connected to all adjacent nodes with structural springs (or dampers), diagonal nodes with shear springs (or dampers) and nodes that are two steps away with flexion springs (or dampers), as shown in Fig. 1. This allows each point mass to be connected from between 3 to 12 other nodes.

The dynamics of the system can be written in the state space form:

$$x[k + 1] = f(x[k], u[k]), \tag{1}$$

$$y[k] = Cx[k], \tag{2}$$

where $x[k]$ is the state vector containing the position and velocity information of each node at time-step k, $f(x, u)$ contains the nonlinear dynamics of the system and $u[k]$ is a vector of input forces. The matrix C in Eq. (2) selects only the position states from the state vector to be the output of the model.

To account for errors between the model and the real-life plant, a random process $w[k]$, with covariance Q_k, is added to the state equation (1) and a random

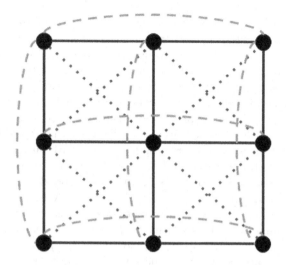

Fig. 1. Connection of point masses with structural springs (blue), shear springs (red dashed), and flexion springs (grey dashed) (Color figure online)

process $v[k]$, with covariance R_k, is added to the output equation (2). The state and output equations now become:

$$x[k+1] = f(x[k], u[k]) + w[k], \tag{3}$$

$$y[k] = Cx[k] + v[k]. \tag{4}$$

As stated in [3], the inner dynamics of the model are linear, however, the geometry of the model causes nonlinearities (similar to those of a pendulum). These nonlinearities require linearization to be used with the EKF estimation algorithm previously presented, discussed further in Sect. 3. Using the first order Taylor series expansion for linearization, the dynamics are converted to the simpler form of:

$$x[k+1] = Fx[k] + Bu[k] + w[k], \tag{5}$$

where F is the Jacobian matrix of $f(x, u)$ with respect to x and B is a matrix that selects the inputs related to the velocity states.

With the dynamics of the surface defined in a state space form, the model can easily be implemented into estimation filters; one of which will be used in the algorithm described in the next section.

3   Prediction Algorithm

A common technique to predict states of a nonlinear dynamic system is the EKF algorithm [1]. The EKF is a extension of the standard Kalman filter, which is an algorithm that uses measured outputs of a system to make state estimates, which are essentially the best guess of the internal behaviour of the system.

The Kalman filter can be used to find state estimates when measurements are corrupted with noise or when the system is not modelled perfectly, but can also be used as an algorithm for predicting what the state value will be. The standard Kalman filter produces the optimal estimate of a system under the condition that the dynamics of system are linear and any measurement or modelling error is normally distributed. The EKF extends the Kalman filter to systems that have nonlinear dynamics, in a very straightforward way. The EKF takes the nonlinear model, finds the closest linear model of the system each time a prediction is needed, and uses the standard Kalman filter algorithm to predict the states. Since the dynamics of the mass-spring system are nonlinear, the EKF is a suitable choice for predicting the motion of a non-rigid surface. However, since the EKF uses the linearized model, Eq. (5), to update the estimates of the system, it only provides a first-order approximation of system states. As a result, the EKF may only give a "near-optimal" estimate of the system. There are other filtering techniques that provide a solution to the state estimates of a system which may be more accurate than the EKF. In this paper, the Cubature Kalman filter will be used instead of the EKF to predict the position and velocity of non-rigid surfaces.

To develop a more accurate way of predicting the states of a nonlinear system, one can take advantage of the "nice" properties of Gaussian distributions. Since it is assumed that the nonlinear mass-spring system is modelled with error that is normally distributed, these properties can be exploited. It is well known that the best state prediction, $x_{k|k-1}$, of a dynamic system is given by a conditional expectation [2]. Furthermore, when the source of noise in the model is normally distributed, the state prediction can be written as an integral of the nonlinear model $f(x, u)$ and of the Gaussian density function. Since this integral may be difficult to solve, it can be approximated as

$$x_{k|k-1} \approx \sum_{i=1}^{m} \omega_i f(\zeta_i) \tag{6}$$

where ω_i are weights and ζ_i are sample points which are chosen in a specific manner. This method of approximation is called a *Gaussian quadrature rule* for solving the conditional expectation of a normally distributed random variable [2]. As already stated, the standard way of solving for a conditional expectation is to solve a complicated integral equation (which may not have a closed form solution). A Gaussian quadrature rule allows for a computationally less intensive approximation of the conditional expectation. The difficult part of finding an accurate approximation, as given in Eq. (6), is solving for the weights ω_i and sample points ζ_i. There may be many combinations weights and sample points that give a "somewhat" accurate solution of the state prediction. The Cubature Kalman filter (CKF) is a one of many approaches to finding weights and sample points that are "optimal" in a certain sense [2]. In fact, the CKF provides a solution for the state prediction that is more accurate (third order approximation of the true solution) than the solution given by the EKF (first order approximation). The CKF uses what are called *cubature rules* to solve for the weights and sample points; the mathematics of which are beyond the scope of this paper. The weights and sample points given by the cubature rules can be found by

$$\omega_i = 1/m, \quad i = 1, 2, \ldots m \tag{7}$$

and

$$\zeta_i = \sqrt{\frac{m}{2}} \{1\}_i, \quad i = 1, 2, \ldots m \tag{8}$$

where $m = 2n$, n is the number of states of the system, and $\{1\}_i$ is the ith element of the set of all n-dimensional unit axis vectors. Figure 2 provides a simple illustration of how the sample points of the CKF allows it to be a more accurate prediction algorithm than the EKF. Solving the cubature rules is only a small portion of the entire CKF algorithm which is very simply depicted in Fig. 3.

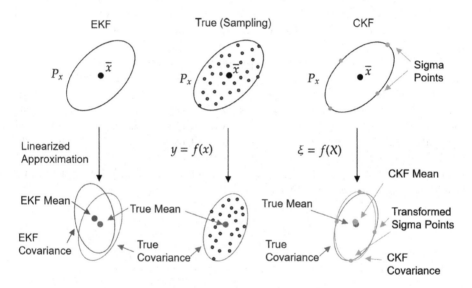

Fig. 2. Visualisation of the EKF and CKF algorithms propagation accuracy when compared to a true sampling technique

Figure 3 shows a simple flow chart of the CKF algorithm where the function $f(x, u)$ describes the dynamics of mass-spring model and the plant is the real-life system on which measurements are made. At each prediction time-step, T_m, the most recent estimate of the non-rigid surface, $x_{k-1|k-1}$ is offset by each sample point ζ_i for $i = 1, \ldots 2n$ multiplied by the square root of the most recent covariance matrix $P_{k-1|k-1}^{1/2}$ to create a set of $2n$ vectors. Each of these $2n$ offset estimate vectors are passed through the mass-spring model, Eq. (1), and are then averaged to create a prediction of the plant's position and velocity $x_{k|k-1}$. This prediction is used as the best "guess" of what the surface will look like one time-step into the future. The covariance matrix of each of the $2n$ offset vectors are sent through a simple linear transformation and are averaged to create the predicted state covariance matrix $P_{k|k-1}$. The state covariance matrix gives a description of how correlated the states of the system are to one another at each iteration of the algorithm. This entire step is known as the prediction step of the CKF. After a new measurement, y, is made from the real-world system, the state prediction $x_{k|k-1}$ is now offset by the same sample points ζ_i for $i = 1, \ldots 2n$ multiplied by the square root of the predicted covariance matrix $P_{k|k-1}^{1/2}$, is averaged again, and is subtracted from the measurement y. This "error" is then combined with the state prediction $x_{k|k-1}$ and predicted covariance matrix $P_{k|k-1}$ to produce the "near-optimal" state estimate $x_{k|k}$ and estimated state covariance $P_{k|k}$. This part of the algorithm is called the update step of the CKF. The state estimate will then be used to create a new prediction for the next time-step, and the algorithm repeats itself. An issue that can arise when measuring the position of a surface is the occlusion of markers. If only measurement data was used to determine the surface geometry, losing vision of a marker would make the projection nearly impossible. However, using this prediction algorithm, the lost marker's position can be approximated using the prediction step of the CKF, which is a very close estimate of the true position of the marker. This allows occlusion compensation to be nearly free, provided the markers are not covered for an extended period of time.

When running the CKF algorithm for SAR applications, a projector needs to project images on the predicted surface. This can pose issues as the projector takes a certain amount of time to receive and process images from a computer and an additional amount of time to draw a frame. It is well known that projectors suffer from delays when processing images and these delays usually range from 20 ms to 100 ms depending on the type of projector [5]. This delay, T_d, is troublesome when using the CKF for surface prediction in real-time. Since an image needs to be sent to the projector T_d seconds in advance to be projected at the correct time, the CKF needs to predict the geometry of the surface T_d seconds in the future at each predict step. Now, since measurements are received every T_m seconds, the CKF can only update the state estimate every T_m seconds. An issue arises when the delay time T_d and measurement time T_m do not match (i.e. are vastly different). The time of the current state prediction and the time at which the measurement is made will never be the same. This means the traditional CKF algorithm will not work, as the prediction and measurement times need to line up. To fix this issue, a further prediction, using numerical integration, is made to align the time of the current state prediction with the current measurement. At this stage, a new estimate can be made using the regular CKF algorithm.

When compensating for the delay caused by the drawing of a frame, it is imperative to consider the speed at which the surface is moving compared to the drawing rate. Surfaces that move quickly with respect to the drawing rate of the projector may incur additional image distortion because the projector is still drawing an "old" image. To compensate for the effects of surface movement during the drawing of frames, an inter-frame prediction (IFP) method is used, as proposed in [3]. Considering that the update rate of the CKF is T_m seconds, if the cloth's position changes significantly during inter-sample periods, there may be significant error between the prediction and the actual position of the cloth when a new measurement is made. To compensate for this, an interpolation approach is used. As the cloth is moving, the CKF solves for an estimate of the velocity states, and using a first-order approximation, the inter-sample position of every node is calculated. This estimation is based on the assumption that drawing horizontally is instantaneous.

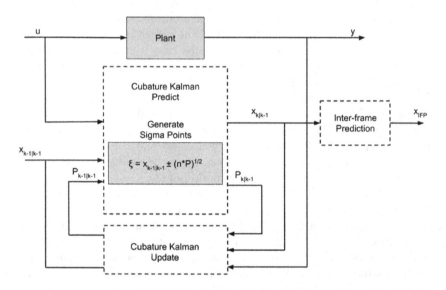

Fig. 3. Block diagram of the CKF algorithm with the mass-spring model

Using the state prediction $x_{k|k-1}$, which was solved with Eq. (1) and the corresponding time-step, $n\Delta T$, where n is the row number and the time-step ΔT is defined by

$$\Delta T = \frac{1}{\text{frame rate} \times (\#\text{rows} - 1)}, \tag{9}$$

the inter-frame prediction can be computed. First the state prediction vector is split into a position prediction vector $p_{k|k-1}$ and a velocity prediction vector $v_{k|k-1}$. The position predictions are then reordered, such that the elements are ordered based on their horizontal position with respect to the projector. More specifically, the first i elements of the position vector would contain the positional information of the first horizontal row of nodes with respect to the projector, the next j elements would contain the positional information of the second horizontal row of nodes with respect to the projector, and so on (Fig. 4).

After reordering the states, the predictions are passed through the state transition function $f(x, u)$, described by Eq. (1). This returns the derivative of the

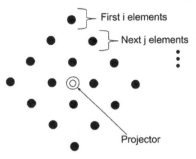

First i elements

Next j elements

Projector

Fig. 4. Orientation of cloth with respect to projector for inter-frame prediction

position state predictions, and as a result, the velocities to obtain the next position vector. The velocity vector is then multiplied by a matrix describing the time at which each row of the object is predicted. The result is added to the position estimates to obtain the inter-frame position predictions $p'_{k|k-1}$. At a time t_0, when the system receives a measurement from the cameras, the current prediction at t_0 is combined with the measurement to produce the new estimate. This is done using the aforementioned Kalman update step. Since the time between measurements, T_m, is quite large, the IFP algorithm is run at a time-step of ΔT to counteract the effects of surface motion while drawing. When each new estimate is calculated, every T_m seconds, the Kalman predict step of the CKF is run to create a prediction T_d seconds into the future. This is done to have a prediction of the surface when the projector is ready to draw a frame. This new Kalman prediction replaces the prediction from the IFP algorithm, and the whole sequence repeats itself until termination. The entire CKF-IFP algorithm, compensating for projector delay, is shown in Fig. 5.

4   Experimental Setup

Validation of the algorithm proposed in Sect. 3 will be performed using the experimental procedure proposed in [3]. The goal of the experiment is to show the effectiveness of using the CKF-IFP algorithm when compared to projecting with the EKF-IFP procedure. This will be done by projecting an image onto a perturbed surface, and using subjective measures to determine whether using the CKF-IFP algorithm is superior to using the EKF-IFP. To maintain consistency with previous measures a towel is chosen to be the surface for the experiment as it is very deformable and sensitive to external forces. Positional data of the surface of the towel is required for the prediction algorithms to function. Several choices of data capture systems can be considered, such as image processing techniques or 3D scanning systems; however, this experiment uses an infrared motion capture system for added position accuracy. The NaturalPoint OptiTrack system [8] is an infra-red (IR) camera-based motion capture system that provides positional data, both translational and rotational, within millimeter precision. For

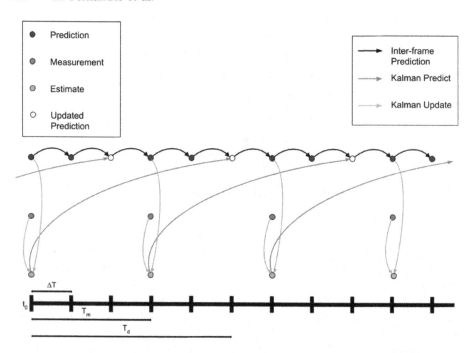

Fig. 5. Timing diagram of CKF-IFP algorithm. ΔT is the IFP time-step, T_m is the measurement time, and T_d is the delay time.

this experiment, a three camera configuration is used to measure the position of 12.7 mm diameter infra-red markers. The markers are placed on the towel to match the initial positions of the mass nodes in the model. Specifically, 20 markers are placed on the towel corresponding to a 5×4 node mass-spring system used to model the system. The towel is hung vertically, just as it would be on a standard towel rack, such that all the IR markers are visible to the cameras. An Epson VS240 short-throw projector is placed directly in front of the towel, and below the cameras as to not interfere with the cameras' view. Figure 6 shows the complete experimental setup.

Before the CKF-IFP algorithm in Sect. 3 can be used the mass-spring model parameters need to be chosen so that the simulated deformable model has similar characteristics to the real-life system. Using visual inspection, mass values of 0.025 kg for each node, spring constant values of $300\frac{N}{m}$, and damper values of $0.08\frac{N \cdot s}{m}$ for each spring and damper connection are chosen. Errors in parameter choice are considered to be process noise and lumped into the $w[k]$ term and will be handled by the CKF. The initial position states of the mass-spring model are set to be equal to the position of the IR markers on the towel and the velocity states are set to 0, as the towel is at rest. Since the initial states of the mass-spring model match the initial conditions of the real-life surface, the initial state covariance matrix is set to the zero matrix, as there is no uncertainty between the initial state and the true position of the surface. The measurement noise

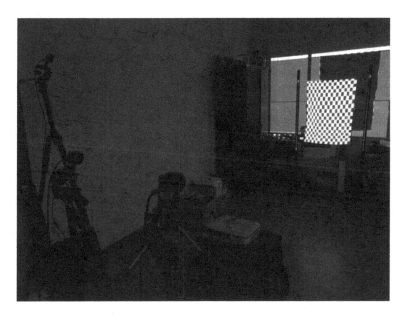

Fig. 6. Photo of experimental setup with three motion capture cameras, a projector and a towel being projected onto.

covariance matrix R_k is set so that the variance of each position state is $0.01\,\mathrm{mm}^2$, and the covariance between any two position states is $0\,\mathrm{mm}^2$ (considered independent). These values of variance are chosen based on the error specifications given by the OptiTrack system. The model noise covariance matrix Q_k is chosen to be an identity matrix, as $1\,\mathrm{m}$ can easily be assumed to be an extreme upper bound for the uncertainty in node position.

Before the experiment can be run the system needs to be properly calibrated. A still image is projected onto the towel when it is at rest, as seen in Fig. 6. The projection parameters are then adjusted so that the computer knows where the projector is relative to the surface. Finally, the timing parameters T_m and T_d are tuned so that the speed of motion of the model matches that of the towel. After the system adequately matches the mass-spring model to the towel, a rotating fan is placed behind the towel to create a "random" motion on the surface. This is done to test the robustness of the prediction algorithms under conditions of randomness. Additionally, the delay time-step is set to $30\,\mathrm{ms}$ and the rate at which the measurement are sampled is varied between $100\,\mathrm{fps}$ ($10\,\mathrm{ms}$) and $50\,\mathrm{fps}$ ($20\,\mathrm{ms}$). This is done to verify the usefulness of the algorithms on systems where data is less easily available as well its ability to deal with occlusions, as occlusions lead to fewer measurements being made available. The results of the projection method are visually inspected and predictions of the surface position states are stored to be compared to the real-world values offline.

5 Results

The effectiveness of the CKF-IFP algorithm presented in Sect. 3 is evaluated on the experimental setup described in Sect. 4, qualitative and quantitative methods are used. Qualitatively, the results of the both the EKF and CKF prediction algorithms are visually compared to each other. When the image is projected onto a flat surface (the towel at rest), both projection methods produce the exact same results. However, once the towel is disturbed by the fan, there is a noticed difference. Both algorithms perform better than no algorithm running, however, the CKF-IFP method produces slightly more true-to-life results when compared to the EKF-IFP, this is especially true with the lower 50 fps measurement sample rate. When comparing static compensation of the algorithms, both the CKF and EKF algorithms perform identically to that stated in [3] and far outperform the standard, sans algorithm, projection method, as shown in Fig. 7. In the three orientations shown in Fig. 7 the CKF and EKF algorithms both compensate identically since the towel being stationary means their solutions converge. However, the uncompensated projection produces clipped and undesirable results. Specifically, the uncompensated projection method displays parts of the image past the towel, onto the wall, while the prediction algorithms "paints" the image on the towel.

   Quantitatively, the success of the CKF-IFP algorithm is evaluated using the mean error between the measured position of the markers and the predicted position of the mass nodes. At every measurement time-step, the difference between measured position of node and the predicted position of the node are squared and then averaged. The mean error is defined as

$$E[k] = \frac{1}{N} \sum_{k=1}^{N} \|y[k] - C x_{k|k-1}\| \tag{10}$$

where N is the total number of nodes (20 in this case), $y[k]$ as defined in Eq. (2) is the output vector, and $x_{k|k-1}$ is the state prediction vector. Figure 8 shows the mean error (ME) between measured and predicted node positions over a 10 s window for both the CKF and EKF algorithms with a measurement sample rate of 100fps. It can be seen that after every large input (strong gust from the fan), the ME for both algorithms increases drastically. This is due to the non-anticipatory behaviour of real systems. After this peak in error, the ME exponentially decreases to a point where there is almost no difference between predictions and measurements. The mean error for the CKF and EKF peak at roughly 1.6 mm and 2.9 mm, respectively, when the towel is most affected by the input force, and 0.5 mm and 0.8 mm when the towel comes back to rest. These effects are even more pronounced when the measurement sampling rate is reduced to 50 fps as shown in Fig. 9. The maximum ME for the CKF and EKF in this case goes up to roughly 2.3 mm and 5.3 mm, respectively while the ME at rest is 0.6 mm for both cases. This demonstrates that CKF performs significantly better than the EKF, especially in the 50 fps measurement sample rate case. The implications of this result are that the CKF would be better suited for applications with slower measurement rates as well as in systems with higher occlusion occurrences.

(a) Standard projection: towel at rest   (b) Prediction algorithm: towel at rest

(c) Standard projection: pulled backwards (d) Prediction algorithm: pulled backwards

(e) Standard projection: pushed forward   (f) Prediction algorithm: pushed forward

Fig. 7. Visual comparison of standard projection and prediction algorithms on static deformations

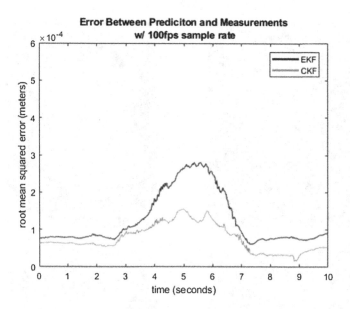

Fig. 8. Mean error graph display the average error between measured and predicted node positions over time with a 100 fps measurement sample rate.

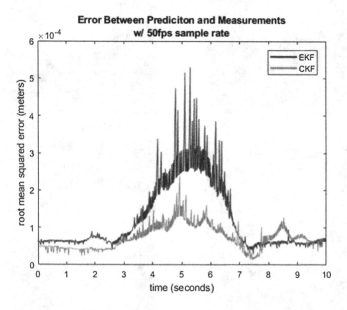

Fig. 9. Mean error graph display the average error between measured and predicted node positions over time with a 50 fps measurement sample rate.

6 Conclusion

This paper implements an improvement to the EKF techniques for predicting the motion of non-rigid surfaces for image projection specified by Gomes et al. [3]. The CKF based algorithm, named the CKF-IFP algorithm, predicts the position of a non-rigid surface by using a set of sample points to improve the accuracy of Kalman filter when applied to highly nonlinear models. The algorithm is shown to handle the delays often associated with projectors as well as handle brief occlusions of the surface far better than its EKF counterpart. Using a mass-spring system to model the dynamics of a towel, the CKF-IFP algorithm was able to improve on the position prediction of the nodes with errors ranging between 2.3 mm and less than 0.5 mm on average. The CKF-IFP algorithm was shown to outperform the EKF-IFP algorithm even when tested with a worse measurement sample rate than its counterpart. These results were observed when the non-rigid surface was being perturbed by random forces. Projection using the CKF-IFP algorithm created a more realistic and useful experience when compared to the EKF-IFP and so should be able to expand on its practical uses.

6.1 Future Work

As the mass, spring and damper parameters for the model were chosen quite arbitrarily, finding parameters that match the surface material properties would allow for more robust prediction. Future work will include using machine learning techniques for parameter identification. Additional future work includes using less obstructive motion capturing systems since the marker based motion capture system is quite expensive and sensitive to environmental conditions. A more cost-effective camera based system, combined with computer vision techniques, can instead be used to capture the position of surfaces in real-time. Although this will likely cause an increase in sensor noise in the system, the prediction algorithm should be able to compensate for the additional measurement error.

Additional work to improve the performance of the algorithm includes the distribution of the nodes on the objects surface as well as taking advantage of having access to the makeup of the surface. It is of great interest to analyse the effects of distributing the nodal masses on the mass-spring system in a way that is more optimal. Namely, to take advantage of the fact that, in the case of a hanging towel, the nodes at the top of the towel move far less than those at the bottom. Taking this information into account it would be possible to better distribute the nodal masses to improve the simulation accuracy of the areas of higher error. Additionally, by having access to the material of the non-rigid surface, it would be possible to make a surface out of interconnected masses and springs. This would allow our model of the system to be nearly perfect, instead of an approximation of the true physical system. If the model is nearly identical to the real system it would allow for far greater accuracy in prediction.

220   K. Fernandes et al.

References

1. Anderson, B.D., Moore, J.B.: Optimal Filtering. Courier Corporation, North Chelmsford (2012)
2. Arasaratnam, I.: Cubature Kalman filtering theory & applications. Ph.D. thesis (2009)
3. Gomes, A., Fernandes, K., Wang, D.: Surface prediction for spatial augmented reality. In: Chen, J.Y.C., Fragomeni, G. (eds.) VAMR 2018. LNCS, vol. 10909, pp. 43–55. Springer, Cham (2018). https://doi.org/10.1007/978-3-319-91581-4_4
4. Gomes, A.D.: Prediction for projection on time-varying surfaces (2016)
5. Livolsi, B.: What it is and why you should care, May 2015. http://www.projectorcentral.com/projector-input-lag.htm
6. Narita, G., Watanabe, Y., Ishikawa, M.: Dynamic projection mapping onto deforming non-rigid surface using deformable dot cluster marker. IEEE Trans. Visual. Comput. Graphics **23**(3), 1235–1248 (2017)
7. Piper, B., Ratti, C., Ishii, H.: Illuminating clay: a 3-D tangible interface for landscape analysis. In: Proceedings of the SIGCHI Conference on Human Factors in Computing Systems, pp. 355–362. ACM (2002)
8. Point, N.: Optitrack. Natural Point Inc. (2011). http://www.naturalpoint.com/optitrack/. Accessed 22 Feb 2014
9. Provot, X.: Deformation constraints in a mass-spring model to describe rigid cloth behaviour. In: Graphics interface, p. 147. Canadian Information Processing Society (1995)
10. Punpongsanon, P., Iwai, D., Sato, K.: Projection-based visualization of tangential deformation of nonrigid surface by deformation estimation using infrared texture. Virtual Reality **19**(1), 45–56 (2015)
11. Steimle, J., Jordt, A., Maes, P.: Flexpad: highly flexible bending interactions for projected handheld displays. In: Proceedings of the SIGCHI Conference on Human Factors in Computing Systems, pp. 237–246. ACM (2013)

Marker Concealment Using Print Color Correction and Its Application

Kanghoon Lee, Kyudong Sim, and Jong-II Park[✉]

Hanyang University, Seoul 04763, Korea
aeternalis999@gmail.com, lsh529@snu.ac.kr,
jipark@hanyang.ac.kr

Abstract. The markers used in the marker-based Augmented Reality have disadvantages that they are heterogeneous in their surroundings and difficult to detect in a dark environment. Therefore, it is necessary to study the markers that can be identified even in dark situations. We analyzed the studies that supplemented the weakness of markers and created new markers. In this method, it is produced by overlapping printing of markers and pictures based on the fact that infrared images vary depending on the type of printer. However, the printed color was darker than the original one, because the marker and the color of the picture were becoming a subtractive mixture. In order to reduce the color difference and to show a similar color, it is required to correct the picture color of the marker part and the picture color of the non-marker part. The color correction was processing by comparing the combined result of Printer-A RGB color code on the top of markers pressed by Printer-B and the sole result of Printer-A RGB color code. As a result, the color difference between the marker, the overlapping part of the picture and the picture part was reduced, and the marker was concealed so that it was not visible to the eye. The concealed markers are able to replace existing invisible markers and can be detected in dark environments. In particular, since the marker concealment method uses original ink or toner without modifying a general printer, it can be easily manufactured. Besides, given that printing work is done by a printer, it is possible to mass-produce uniform quality markers.

In this paper, we evaluated and analyzed the results of user evaluation to check the effectiveness of markers. The assessment was conducted by using the application program which was made with and without the concealed marker method. The survey results showed that there was a positive response to the AR content with the concealed marker and the rejection of the concealed marker decreased compared to the existing markers.

Keywords: Marker concealment · Color correction ·
Marker based augmented reality · Near-Infrared camera image ·
Invisible marker

1 Introduction

With the advancement of a performance of mobile and HMD devices, the application areas of AR are becoming more diverse. It is essential for AR to keep track of the position and orientation of the object in the camera image. Marker-based Augmented

© Springer Nature Switzerland AG 2019
J. Y. C. Chen and G. Fragomeni (Eds.): HCII 2019, LNCS 11574, pp. 221–234, 2019.
https://doi.org/10.1007/978-3-030-21607-8_17

Reality are most widely used in easy-to-use ways [1–3]. However, the marker is expressed in dark color and figure, hence it is heterogeneous with the surroundings. Research has been conducted to improve the disadvantages of these markers [4–8].

Additionally, it is difficult to detect the marker with the camera in a dark environment. The infrared camera has been a method for recognizing a marker in a low-light mode. This is a method of using an ink having a characteristic of absorbing infrared rays of a specific wavelength. By drawing the shape of the marker with a pen, the technique recognizes the marker. However, due to the color of the ink, we can adopt only invisible markers that are similar to the background color. Another method is to dilute the infrared absorbing ink with acetone to color the marker part.

The new markers improved the existing infrared markers, applying printing differences between printers without using infrared ink. There were differences in printed color and infrared image depending on how it works and the composition of the toner and the ink. If you print two markers on two printers with significant differences in image Infrared, you will see the markers on the infrared camera images, but the pictures are not visible. However, since the marker area is printed twice over, the color is darker than the other areas. In order to reduce the color difference and to show a similar color, it is necessary to correct the picture color of the marker part and the picture color of the non-marker part.

The color correction was processing by comparing the combined result of Printer-A RGB color code on the top of markers pressed by Printer-B and the sole result of Printer-A RGB color code. As a result, the color difference between the marker, the overlapping part of the picture and the picture part was reduced, and the marker was concealed so that it was not visible to the eye.

The characteristics of the concealed marker are as follows. First, the marker can be recognized even in the low-light mode. Second, the marker and background image look natural. Third, the mass production of uniform quality markers is possible. Lastly, it is easy to produce.

In this paper, we analyzed the description of marker concealment and the opinions and evaluation of users. The participants in the review were targeted to young 20s people who frequently use multimedia technologies such as Augmented Reality. Participants were able to directly view three samples of common markers, existing invisible markers and concealment markers, and test markers on projector-based AR applications. The majority of the users agreed with the need for invisible markers and evaluated that the markers concealment method was better than the current IR markers. A detailed analysis of user evaluation a given in Sect. 4.

The composition of this paper is as follows. Section 1 explains the need for marker concealment, its introduction, and its composition. In Sect. 2, we analyze the existing research on markers that can be used in invisible and dark places. Section 3 explains marker and image overprinting using IR image difference and printer color correction. In Sect. 4, the user evaluation process and its results are analyzed to verify the usefulness of marker concealment. Finally, conclusions and future research are discussed in Sect. 5.

2 Related Works

Previous studies on markers that can be used in the low-light mode without being visible to the naked eye use mostly Near-Infrared band. Near-Infrared rays are broadly utilized as markers because infrared objects can be seen in dark environments. Especially, considering infrared is widely used, there are many studies on Near-Infrared-based markers [4, 5].

Studies using IR cameras include using IR absorbing inks and using the infrared features of objects or prints. The IR pen has the advantage of being easy to use because it can draw the shape of the marker directly [6]. However, there is a drawback that the markers are not constant and the color of the IR pen is not transparent. IR inks are very dark in color, so when diluted with acetone, they appear to be a light, and you can draw large markers faster than pens. However, when diluted to a light color, the infrared absorption intensity is lowered, and uniform coloring is difficult [7].

The use of such inks does not show the color of the ink itself in a low-light environment but is visible to the public as a regular marker in bright light (Fig. 1).

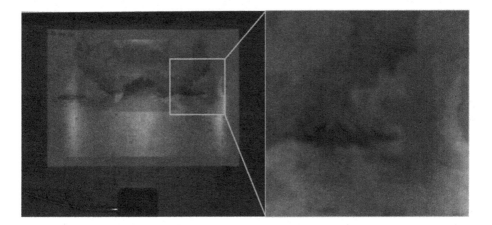

Fig. 1. Marker IR image painted with infrared absorbing ink

Some publications and printed papers are also seen in infrared images. Printing markers with printer ink with these features can be used as infrared markers. This has the advantage of being able to rapidly produce a large number of infrared markers. As it is visible, you can overlay the print marker with a different color, therefore it is similar to the surrounding tone. However, when sprayed with spray, the surface is not uniform and stains occur. These problems result in poor print quality when printing pictures (Fig. 2).

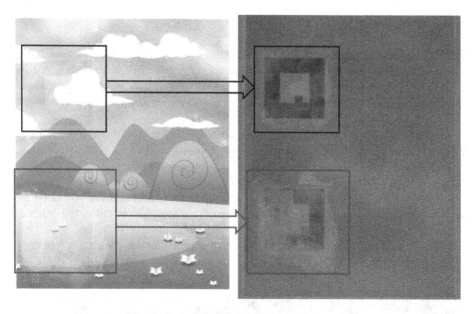

Fig. 2. Left: RGB Camera Right: IR Camera

3 Marker Concealment

The marker concealment used in this paper is a form in which a marker is inserted in the picture. Marker concealment is the use of two printers with different intensity of infrared image, not using infrared ink, to overprint the marker and the picture [8]. This section describes the process of making marker concealment.

3.1 Overprinting Pictures and Markers

If the markers printed on different printers are viewed with an infrared camera, the image intensity may be different. This difference makes it possible to achieve the same effect as using infrared ink without using infrared ink. Overprinting of markers and pictures uses two printers. Printers that print the markers use what looks good on infrared images (Printer-B). Printers that print pictures use something that is not visible in the infrared (Printer-A). We compared printers and markers printed on multiple printers with infrared cameras and chose printers for overprinting. The printer used is a regular printer and has not been deformed or reassembled.

Since the color of the marker is black, we adjusted the grayscale level from 0 to 255. Even if the grayscale level is 220, it is possible to detect the marker with the infrared camera.

3.2 Printer Color Correction

The printed color was darker than the original one, because the marker and the color of the picture were becoming a subtractive mixture. In order to reduce the color difference and to show a similar color, it is required to correct the picture color of the marker part and the picture color of the non-marker part. Figure 3(a) shows the color difference between the marker part and the non-marker part. Color correction reduces this color difference (Fig. 3(b)).

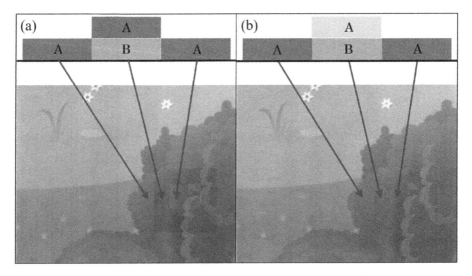

Fig. 3. Marker part color and Invisible Marker part color

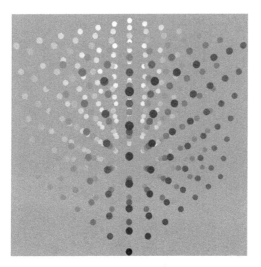

Fig. 4. Color space placement of color patch

Color patch images printed by different printers are in different colors that are caused by the printing method and the characteristics of the printing materials. For minimizing color difference between printed images, color correction algorithm is used.

For print color correction, the input color and output color of the printer must be compared, and the comparison can be performed using a color patch. Since color patches cannot be created in all colors, we used color patches that were divided into 7 spaces for all color ranges from 0–255. Figure 4 shows the color patches arranged in color spaces.

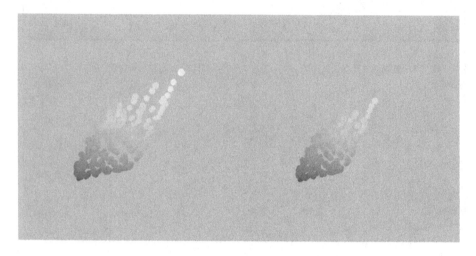

(a) Top View

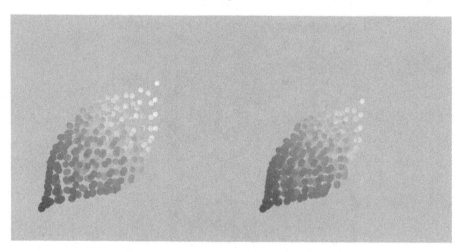

(b) Front View

Fig. 5. Left: Color patches printed on printer A, Right: Print the marker on printer-B and then print the color patch over to printer-A.

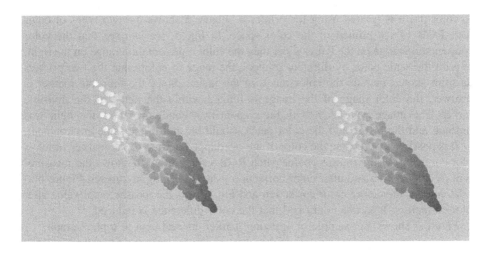

(c) Left View

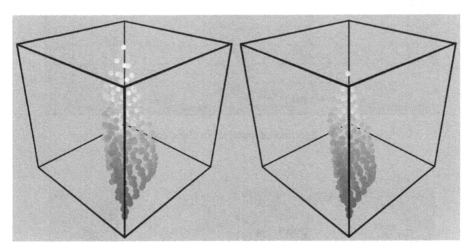

(d) Perspective View

Fig. 5. (*continued*)

The generated color patch can be printed and captured by the camera, so that the RGB values of the digital data and printed data can be used for color correction. The two RGB values correspond to each other, and when the digital data of color patch is printed, corresponding printed data indicates printed value. With the correspondence, the desired printed color can be found in digital data of color patch, and the RGB value not in the color patch can be inferred by using the color patch.

Color patches are printed in two types. The first is that the color patch is printed using the printer A, the second is that the marker is printed using the printer B, and then the color patch is printed using the printer A. Figure 5 shows the two types of color patch RGB values printed in the color space. In Fig. 5, we can see that the color representation range on the left is wider than the color representation range on the right. To print the same color by different printers, the range of colors that the two printers can print should include the color range of the image. Since the invisible marker is narrower, the color range of the image is limited within the range of the invisible marker. The image was taken with the camera in a condition where the light was constant, and the image and the color patch should be shot in the same environment.

It is possible to calculate the color of the overlapped portion of the marker which is color-corrected by the inferred color patch RGB value. Figure 6 shows the measurement of color before and after color correction using a spectrophotometer. Figure 6(a) is the color value before color correction and Fig. 6(b) is the measurement value after color correction. It can be confirmed that the color difference is reduced.

Figure 7 shows an example of applying marker concealment to a photograph.

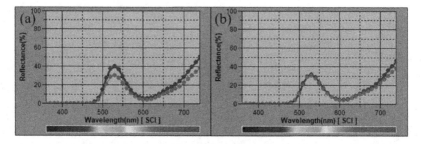

Fig. 6. Spectrophotometer color value compare

Fig. 7. Marker Concealment print comparison (Left: No Correction, Right: color correction)

4 User Evaluation

In this chapter, we conducted and analyzed user evaluations to verify the necessity and usefulness of marker concealment.

4.1 Assessment Methods and Evaluator Consist

Participants were 50 college students aged 20–22. Because they are familiar with mobile devices and frequently access multimedia technologies and contents, they will be more active in AR technology and content consumption than other age groups.

The AR system prepared for demonstration and evaluation is based on a mobile projector camera. There are four types of markers, general markers, two conventional invisible markers, and proposed concealment markers. Experiment (evaluation) was conducted in a bright environment and a dark environment so that invisible markers could be compared. The evaluation items are 10, and the necessity aspects, usability aspects are evaluated.

Figure 8(a) shows the gender of the participant. There are 33 men and 17 women. 96% (48 participants) of participants knew about AR (Fig. 8(b)). And 90% of participants (45) experienced AR (Fig. 8(c)). As shown in Fig. 8(c), no one used AR every week, and many participants experienced 1 to 3 times a year. This result shows that augmented reality is widely used but is not widely used in everyday life.

4.2 Necessity Aspects

In necessity aspects, we evaluated the problems and improvement points of the concealment markers by evaluating participants who experienced augmented reality based on concealment markers.

In Fig. 9(a), "satisfaction" and "Neutral" are large numbers because they did not experience augmented reality in various environments and form. Figure 9(b) and (c) show the reason for this. After experiencing marker based augmented reality in a dark environment, the necessity ratio was high.

4.3 Usability Aspects

In usability aspects, the interest in AR technology and the concealment marker system used in this paper are investigated.

In usability aspects, 74% of the participants rated the concealment markers in dark environments very useful (Fig. 10(a)). In addition, the quality of the concealment marker was evaluated to be higher than that of the conventional invisible markers (Fig. 10(b)). And 72% of the evaluators suggested that an augmented reality system with a concealment marker could be recommended to others (Fig. 10(c)).

The evaluators evaluated that the concealment markers used in this paper are superior in performance and quality to the conventional invisible markers. Also, as shown in Fig. 11, the markers applied to the children's storybooks used in the demonstration were evaluated very positively for the contents of the hiding augmented reality contents.

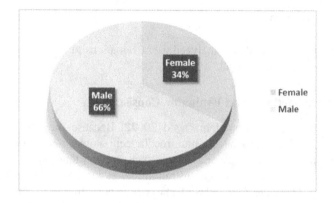

(a) Question1 Please indicate your gender

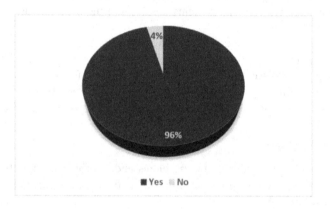

(b) Question2 Do you know about Augmented Reality?

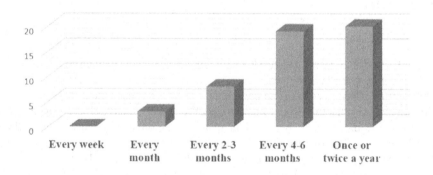

(c) Question3 How often have you used Augmented Reality?

Fig. 8. Evaluator configuration and background

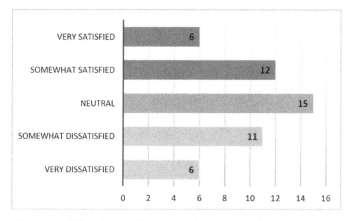

(a) Question4. What do you think about Marker-based Augmented Reality?

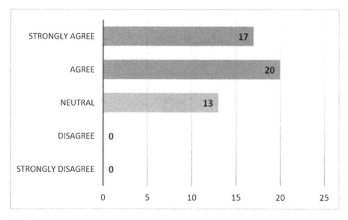

(b) Question5. Do you need AR technology that can be used in dark environments?

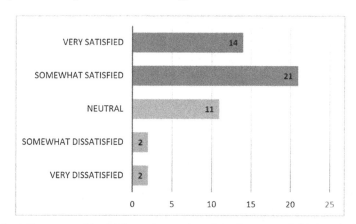

(c) Question6. Do you need invisible markers and markers that are available in a dark environment?

Fig. 9. Survey of result on necessity

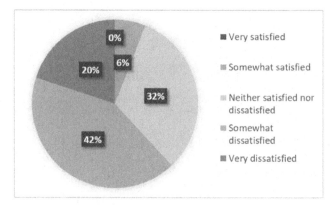

(a) Question7. Concealed markers were useful when using AR in dark environments.

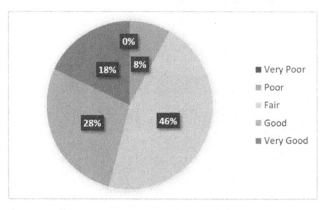

(b) Q8. What is the quality of the Concealed markers that printed the picture and the marker?

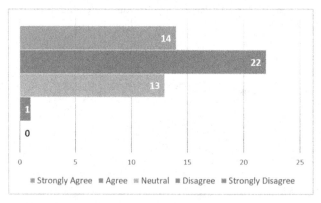

(c) Question9. Can I recommend the marker concealment system to others?

Fig. 10. Survey of result on Usability

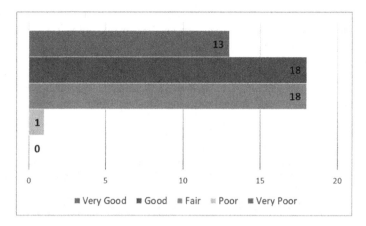

Fig. 11. Question10. What do you think of the cloaking marker augmented reality applied to children's storybooks?

5   Conclusion and Future Work

We analyzed and calibrated the printer colors of the two printers to reduce color differences, and consequently, hid the markers in the images. In this paper, a user evaluation was conducted to confirm the usefulness of a concealment marker. The user evaluations were performed to compare the proposed method with the conventional infrared absorbing ink method. And they perform evaluation and analysis on the concealment marker that we proposed. The survey results showed that there was a positive response to the AR content with the concealed marker and the rejection of the concealed marker decreased compared to the existing markers. In the future work, we plan to improve the color correction algorithm and find out how to apply it. Utilization research studies will be conducted to print pictures and concealment markers on different types of paper surfaces or clothing.

Acknowledgements. This work was supported by Institute for Information & communications Technology Promotion (IITP) grant funded by the Korea government (MSIT) (No. 2017-0-01849, Development of Core Technology for Real-Time Image Composition in Unstructured In-outdoor Environment).

References

1. Azuma, R.: A survey of augmented reality. Presence Teleoperators Virtual Environ. **6**(4), 355–385 (1997)
2. van Krevelen, D.W.F., Poelman, R.: A survey of augmented reality technologies, applications and limitations. Int. J. Virtual Reality **9**(2), 1–20 (2010)
3. Zhou, F., Duh, H.B.L., Billinghurst, M.: Trends in augmented reality tracking, interaction and display: a Review of Ten Years of ISMAR. In: Proceedings of ISMAR, Cambridge, UK, pp. 193–202 (2008)

4. Comport, A.I., Marchand, E., Pressigout, M., Chaumette, F.: Real-time markerless tracking for augmented reality: the virtual visual servoing framework. IEEE Trans. Vis. Comput. Graph. **12**(4), 615–628 (2006)
5. Nakazato, Y., Kanbara, M., Yokoya, N.: Localization system for large indoor environments using invisible markers. In: Proceedings of VRST, Bordeaux, France, pp. 295–296 (2008)
6. Park, H., Park, J.I.: Invisible marker based augmented reality system. In: Proceedings of Visual Communications and Image Processing, Beijing, China, pp. 59601I-1–59601I-8 (2005)
7. Willis, K.D., Shiratori, T., Mahler, M.: HideOut: mobile projector interaction with tangible objects and surfaces. In: Proceedings of TEI, Barcelona, Spain, pp. 331–338 (2013)
8. Lee, K., Kim, C., Park, J.I.: Infrared-camera-based metamer marker for use in dark environments. In: 2018 Proceedings of ICCE, Las Vegas, NV, USA, pp. 1–3, January 2018

Visual Effects of Turning Point and Travel Direction for Outdoor Navigation Using Head-Mounted Display

Yuji Makimura[1,3], Aya Shiraiwa[1,3], Masashi Nishiyama[1,2,3(✉)],
and Yoshio Iwai[1,2,3]

[1] Graduate School of Sustainability Science, Tottori University, Tottori, Japan
nishiyama@tottori-u.ac.jp
[2] Graduate School of Engineering, Tottori University, Tottori, Japan
[3] Cross-informatics Research Center, Tottori University,
101 Minami 4-chome, Koyama-cho, Tottori 680-8550, Japan

Abstract. We investigate the visual effects of superimposing turning points and travel directions within the user's field of view in a navigation system using a subjective assessment procedure. Existing methods were developed without conducting subjective assessments of the effects of superimposing the turning points and travel directions on the user's display while walking outdoors. We therefore designed a questionnaire-based subjective assessment of the use of these navigation methods. We developed an outdoor navigation system using a recently launched optical see-through head-mounted display (HMD) product that was compact and lightweight. We demonstrated that the subjective scores in terms of understanding of the turning points and the travel directions were significantly increased by the visual effects of superimposing these cues on the display. We confirmed that the HMD helps to increase user likeability of use of the navigation system while walking outdoors.

Keywords: Visual effect · Navigation · Superimposed image ·
Turning point · Travel direction

1 Introduction

There is considerable demand for an outdoor navigation method that can guide users intuitively while they walk. Conventional navigation methods [1] guide users by providing a route on a map to allow the user to reach their destination smoothly. Before the user walks, he or she sets the destination at the starting point and selects the route that is suggested by the navigation method. While walking, the user checks for the required turning points on the map and searches for landmarks in the real world. Figure 1 illustrates the typical process of this type of navigation method. If the user understands and can determine the turning points in the real world, he or she can then determine the required

© Springer Nature Switzerland AG 2019
J. Y. C. Chen and G. Fragomeni (Eds.): HCII 2019, LNCS 11574, pp. 235–246, 2019.
https://doi.org/10.1007/978-3-030-21607-8_18

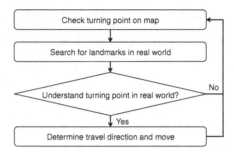

Fig. 1. Overview of conventional navigation method.

travel direction. Otherwise, the user must laboriously repeat the navigation process until he or she correctly understands both the turning points and the travel directions. Note here that a turning point is a location at which the user changes the travel direction to start the next stage of the journey, and the travel direction is a unit vector that is directed from the current position to the next turning point. A navigation method that leads to frequent repetition of the navigation process cannot guide the user intuitively. Ease of understanding of both the turning points and the travel directions for the user is therefore very important. Many researchers [2,3] have attempted to design suitable navigation methods.

To reduce repetition in the navigation process, the existing methods [4,5] often generate either a rough map or a written announcement. These existing methods can thus become a burden because they require the user to read the map or the announcement at least once. To eliminate the repetition from this process, existing methods [6–11] generally overlay the navigational information on real world images. Narzt et al. [6] overlaid routes on images that were acquired from a camera equipped in a mobile device. Mulloni et al. [7–9] developed hand-held indoor navigation systems using mobile phones. Oliveira et al. [10] overlaid the travel directions on images using a process based on recognition of markers using a mobile device. For their car navigation application, Narzt et al. [11] overlaid the route when using a head-up display for the car's driver. We believe that users can understand the routes intuitively, including the turning points and the travel directions. However, holding up a mobile device or using a head-up display while walking can prove to be very inconvenient for the user.

In this work, we discuss a method to superimpose the turning points and the travel directions directly using an optical see-through head-mounted display (HMD). As described in [12–15], an HMD helps the user to have intuitive understanding of the navigation process. In indoor navigation studies using HMDs, Rehman et al. [16] superimposed the travel directions, while Gerstweiler et al. [17] superimposed the route on the HMD. However, the existing methods assumed the case of indoor use. In addition, the existing methods did not assess whether or not the user understood the turning points and the travel directions intuitively. Recently, compact and lightweight commercial optical see-through HMDs have

Fig. 2. This study investigated whether or not the visual effects of superimposing turning points and travel directions within the user's field of view help the user's understanding of the directions given while walking outdoors.

been launched. We are now able to test outdoor navigation with these HMDs using subjective assessment processes.

In this paper, we investigate the visual effects that are used in our method for outdoor navigation and demonstrate that they help the user to understand the turning points and the travel directions intuitively while walking by superimposing these directions directly into the real world using the HMD. Note that we consider the scenario in which the user is approaching a turning point while walking. Figure 2 illustrates the overview of the outdoor navigation process. We conducted a questionnaire-based subjective assessment of the navigation methods used with the HMD. The experimental results show that there was significant agreement among the participants about the visual effects of superimposing both the turning points and the travel directions. The rest of the paper is organized as follows. Section 2 describes the user study protocol, while Sects. 3 and 4 present the results of the subjective assessment. Our concluding remarks are given in Sect. 5.

2   Design of Test for Evaluation of the Visual Effects

2.1   Overview

We aimed to evaluate whether or not the visual effects of showing the turning point and the travel direction aid the user's understanding of these aspects. We therefore developed a navigation method that superimposed both the turning point and the travel direction in the user's field of vision using the HMD. We tested four possible methods, as follows:

M1: The navigation method did not provide visual effects for the turning point or the travel direction.
M2: The navigation method provided visual effects for the turning point only.
M3: The navigation method provided visual effects for the travel direction only.
M4: The navigation method provided visual effects for both the turning point and the travel direction.

We set a walking task for each participant using each navigation method. After walking, we used a questionnaire to ask each participant about the different navigation methods. We showed a printed map that included the starting point, the turning point, and the destination point to each participant before they began walking. While the user walked, our navigation method provided the same voice guidance for each of methods M1 to M4 to inform the user of the timing of the turning point. The details of this evaluation are described below.

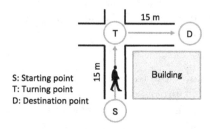

Fig. 3. Illustration showing the starting point, the turning point, and the destination point.

2.2   Walking Task

We designed a walking task in which the participant moved from a starting point to a destination point. In the general case, there is a polarity for the turning points that are used for navigation. In our evaluation, we set the number of turning points to be one to simplify the navigation issue. We used a crossroads as the turning point. When standing at the starting point, the participant was able to see the turning point, but was unable to see the destination point, which was hidden behind a building. The distance from the starting point to the destination point was 30 m. We set the turning point to be 15 m forward from the starting point. Figure 3 shows the starting point, the turning point, and the destination point. We prepared two combinations of the starting point, the turning point, and the destination point. We used the combinations of these points at random for each assessment.

2.3   Representation of the Turning Point and the Travel Direction

We used a three-dimensional virtual object composed of an arrow to represent the turning point and/or the travel direction. The arrow object is frequently used in navigation systems, as described in [18]. Use of the arrow object was intended to ensure that the experimental conditions remained the same for each of methods M1 to M4.

Figure 4 shows examples of the superimposed arrow objects used for each navigation method. In this figure, the angle of view shown in the camera images is smaller than the actual angle of view of the participant. The arrow object had identical dimensions of $28 \times 10 \times 34$ cm in each navigation system. We adjusted

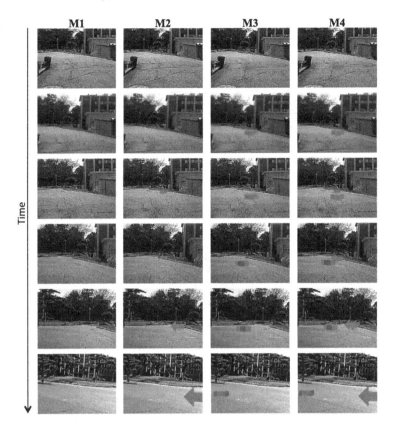

Fig. 4. Navigation methods M1 to M4 were compared to investigate the visual effects of superimposing the various combinations of the turning point and the travel direction. The participants walked wearing the HMD while using each navigation method. In this figure, we have overlaid the arrow objects on images that were acquired from a camera that was attached close to the eye level of the user.

the height of the arrow object above the floor to suit each participant within the range of the vertical angle of view of the HMD. In method M2, we superimposed the arrow object at the three-dimensional location of the turning point to inform the user of the turning direction. The navigation system varied the size of the arrow object based on the distance from the current position to the turning point. In method M3, we superimposed the arrow object to inform the user of the travel direction. We set the arrow object at a distance of 2 m in front of the user's current position. The navigation method changed the direction of the arrow when the user reached a distance of 1 m from the turning point. The arrow turns stepwise by 45° rather than turning by 90° around the turning point. We assumed that each walking human moves by 1 m over a period of 0.75 s, as described in [19]. In method M4, we superimposed arrow objects for both the turning point and the travel direction in the user's field of view by combining methods M2 and M3. Note that the arrows of methods M2 and M3 never crossed because the arrow in M3 turns stepwise around the turning point, as described above.

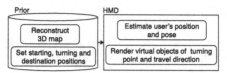

Fig. 5. Architecture of proposed navigation method using the HMD. We used an HMD (HoloLens Development Edition, Microsoft). Our method superimposed the arrow objects by rendering them on the display based on the position and the pose of the user.

Fig. 6. Participant wearing the HMD.

2.4   Optical See-Through HMD

Using the HMD, we developed navigation methods to superimpose the arrow objects within the user's field of view. Figure 5 illustrates the architecture of our navigation method. We used an HMD (HoloLens Development Edition, Microsoft) that was equipped with an optical see-through display, an inertial measurement unit, cameras and a speaker. The HMD is capable of acquiring both the position and the pose of the user in real time. Figure 6 shows a participant wearing the HMD. Our method superimposed the arrow objects that represented the turning point and the travel direction by rendering them on the display based on the position and the pose of the user. We reconstructed a three-dimensional (3D) map to represent the surroundings of the road to be navigated in advance of the experiments. Figure 7(a) shows the reconstructed 3D map. The HMD renders the arrow on the 3D map shown in part (b) in the participant's field of view, which is illustrated in part (c). We also set the locations of the starting, turning, and destination points on this map in advance. We assumed that no obstacles were present on the road during the period in which user was walking.

3   Questionnaire-Based Subjective Assessment of Turning Point and Travel Direction

3.1   Design of the Subjective Assessment

Sixteen participants (13 males and three females, with an average age of 22.3 ± 1.6 years old) participated in the study. We used Scheffe's paired comparisons

method [20] (Ura Variation [21]) in the assessment. We set various pairs of
the navigation methods 12 ($= {}_4C_2 \times 2$) times. For each pair of methods, the
participant used first the former and then the latter navigation method. We
then asked each participant the following questions:

(a) Complete 3D map from bird's-eye view   (b) 3D map with first-person view   (c) Camera image with first-person view
of participant   of participant

Fig. 7. Reconstructed 3D map of the surroundings of the road shown in part (a). The
HMD renders the arrow on the 3D map shown in part (b) in the participant's field of
view, which is illustrated in part (c).

Questions
    Q1: Which navigation method made it easy to understand the turning point?
    Q2: Which navigation method made it easy to understand the travel direc-
        tion?
Answers (four response levels)
    – Absolutely the former navigation method (-1.5)
    – Maybe the former navigation method (-0.5)
    – Maybe the latter navigation method (0.5)
    – Absolutely the latter navigation method (1.5)

We also asked the inverse questions of Q1 and Q2, i.e., to determine which
method made it more difficult to understand the travel direction and the turning
point. Each participant selected an answer for each question of each pair. We
showed the pairs of questions to the participants in random order.

3.2   Results of the Subjective Assessment

Figure 8 shows the subjective scores from the questionnaire. Yardstick Y indicates that there is a significant difference of 5% or 1% when the difference in subjective scores between the navigation methods is larger than $Y(0.05)$ or $Y(0.01)$,
respectively. In the answers to Q1 and Q2, there were significant differences
between method M4 and the other three methods. We can therefore claim that
each user found it easier to understand the turning point and the travel direction
when using method M4, as compared with methods M1 to M3. In the answers to
Q1, no significant difference was observed between methods M2 and M3. Despite
the fact that M2 superimposes the turning point in the user's field of view, we
cannot claim that the user found it easier to understand the turning point when
using M2 as compared with M3. In the answers to Q2, however, there was a significant difference between M2 and M3. We can thus claim that the user found it
easier to understand the travel direction when using M3 rather than M2 because
M3 superimposes the travel direction in their field of view.

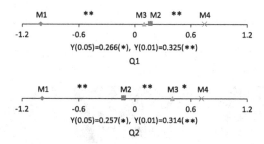

Fig. 8. Rated scores of participants' understanding obtained via comparison of navigation methods M1 to M4.

3.3 Assessment of Likeability

We also evaluated the likeability of the navigation methods that superimposed the turning point and the travel direction in the user's field of view. We used the same procedure that was described in Sect. 3.1. We asked the participants the following questions:

Q3: Which navigation method guided you intuitively?
Q4: Which navigation method guided you comfortably?

We also asked the inverse questions of Q3 and Q4, i.e., to establish which of the navigation methods guided the users less intuitively or comfortably. The answers were given with the same four response levels.

Figure 9 shows the subjective scores that were obtained from the questionnaire. In the answers to Q3 and Q4, significant differences were again found between method M4 and the other three methods. We can therefore claim that M4 increases the likeability of the navigation method for the users when compared with methods M1 to M3. We also observed that M3 obtained better subjective scores than M2. We believe that the users preferred the dynamic movement of the arrow in M3 in accordance with the movement of the users when compared with the static fixed arrow in M2.

4   Assessment of the Visual Effect of the Route

4.1   Design of the Route Navigation Method

We evaluated the visual effects of superimposing a route that contained both the turning point and the travel direction in the user's field of view using the following method:

M5: The navigation method showed the route within the range in which the user is looking.

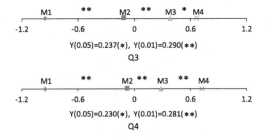

Fig. 9. Rated likeability scores obtained via comparison of navigation methods M1 to M4.

The method again used the arrow objects to represent the route. We set the arrow objects at 1 m intervals over the route from the starting point to the destination point. Figure 10 shows an example of the superimposed arrow objects used for method M5. Each participant evaluated navigation methods M4 and M5. The reason for the use of the arrow objects here was that we intended to maintain consistent experimental conditions between M4 and M5.

4.2 Results of Superimposing the Route

Ten participants (eight males and two females, with an average age of 22.9 ± 1.3 years old) participated in the study. We compared the subjective scores of the participants for methods M4 and M5 using Q1 and Q2 from the questionnaire that was described in Sect. 3.1. Each participant used methods M4 and M5 in random order and then answered the questionnaire.

Figure 11 shows the subjective scores that were obtained from the questionnaire. We used the Wilcoxon signed-rank test in this case. There were no significant differences ($p < 0.01$) between the methods for Q1. We believe that the users felt that they were able to understand the turning point that was provided by M5 in a similar manner to that provided by M4. However, there was a significant difference for Q2. We believe that the users felt that it was easier to understand the travel directions provided by M5 when compared with M4 because method M5 superimposed the future travel directions in the field of view in addition to the current travel direction.

4.3 Likeability of Superimposing the Route

We also evaluated the likeability of the navigation methods in which the route is superimposed. We used the same procedure that was described in Sect. 4.1 with questions Q3 and Q4.

Figure 12 shows the subjective scores that were obtained from the questionnaire. No significant differences were observed between M4 and M5. We therefore cannot claim that M5 increased the likeability for the users when compared with M4. After completion of the experiments, we issued a free-form questionnaire to

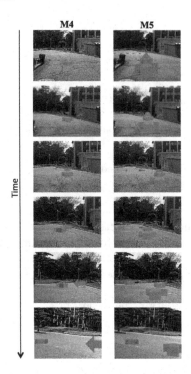

Fig. 10. Navigation method M5 for evaluation of the visual effects of a route that contains both the turning point and the travel direction.

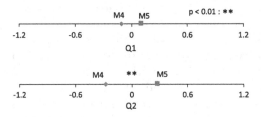

Fig. 11. Rated scores of participants' understanding obtained via comparison of methods M4 and M5.

the participants. From this questionnaire, we obtained the opinion that a single moving arrow was sufficient for navigation, while there was also the opinion that it is preferable to superimpose a number of arrows simultaneously. The results for the likeability of the route were different for each participant. We therefore need to perform a further subjective assessment of the method of displaying the route.

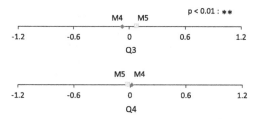

Fig. 12. Rated likeability scores obtained via comparison of methods M4 and M5.

5   Conclusions

We have demonstrated the visual effects of showing the turning point and the travel direction in navigation systems by superimposing them in the user's field of view using a commercial HMD. The combination of the turning point and the travel direction produced higher subjective scores in terms of user understanding when compared with use of only one of these directions. A route that contained the turning point and the current and future travel directions increased the subjective score in terms of both user understanding and likeability of the travel direction when compared with the simpler combination of the turning point and the travel direction.

In future work, we will expand our assessment of the system's usability, and we also intend to develop a navigation method using more complex outdoor routes.

References

1. Blades, M., Spencer, C.: How do people use maps to navigate through the world? Cartogr. Int. J. Geogr. Inf. Geovisualization **24**(3), 64–75 (1986)
2. May, A.J., Ross, T., Bayer, S.H., Tarkiainen, M.J.: Pedestrian navigation aids: information requirements and design implications. Pers. Ubiquit. Comput. **7**(6), 331–338 (2003)
3. Munzer, S., Zimmer, H.D., Schwalm, M., Baus, J., Aslan, I.: Computer-assisted navigation and the acquisition of route and survey knowledge. J. Environ. Psychol. **26**(4), 300–308 (2006)
4. Devlin, A.S., Bernstein, J.: Interactive wayfinding: use of cues by men and women. Environ. Psychol. **15**(1), 23–38 (1995)
5. Monobe, K., Tanaka, S., Furuta, H., Mochinaga, D.: Fundamental research on traffic support to the pedestrian by route giude map based on the space perception. Appl. Comput. Civ. Eng. **16**, 323–330 (2007)
6. Narzt, W., et al.: Pervasive information acquisition for mobile AR-navigation systems. In: Proceedings of the Fifth IEEE Workshop on Mobile Computing Systems and Applications, WMCSA 2003, pp. 13–20 (2003)
7. Mulloni, A., Seichter, H., Schmalstieg, D.: Indoor navigation with mixed reality world-in-miniature views and sparse localization on mobile devices. In: Proceedings of the International Working Conference on Advanced Visual Interfaces, AVI 2012, pp. 212–215 (2012)

8. Mulloni, A., Seichter, H., Schmalstieg, D.: User experiences with augmented reality aided navigation on phones. In: Proceedings of International Symposium on Mixed and Augmented Reality, ISMAR 2011, pp. 229–230 (2011)

9. Mulloni, A., Seichter, H., Schmalstieg, D.: Handheld augmented reality indoor navigation with activity-based instructions. In: Proceedings of the 13th International Conference on Human Computer Interaction with Mobile Devices and Services, MobileHCI 2011, pp. 211–220 (2011)

10. Oliveira, L.C.D., Soares, A.B., Cardoso, A., Andrade, A.D.O., Lamounier Jr., E.A.: Mobile augmented reality enhances indoor navigation for wheelchair users. Res. Biomed. Eng. 32(2), 111–122 (2016)

11. Narzt, W., et al.: Augmented reality navigation systems. Univ. Access Inf. Soc. 4(3), 177–187 (2006)

12. Feiner, S., MacIntyre, B., Höllerer, T., Webster, A.: A touring machine: prototyping 3D mobile augmented reality systems for exploring the urban environment. Pers. Technol. 1(4), 208–217 (1997)

13. Reitmayr, G., Schmalstieg, D.: Scalable techniques for collaborative outdoor augmented reality. In: Proceedings of International Symposium on Mixed and Augmented Reality, ISMAR 2004, pp. 1–10 (2004)

14. Grasset, R., Mulloni, A., Billinghurst, M., Schmalstieg, D.: Navigation techniques in augmented and mixed reality: crossing the virtuality continuum. In: Furht, B. (ed.) Handbook of Augmented Reality, pp. 397–407. Springer, New York (2011). https://doi.org/10.1007/978-1-4614-0064-6_18

15. Krevelen, D.W.F.V., Poelman, R.: A survey of augmented reality technologies, applications and limitations. Int. J. Virtual Real. 9(2), 1–20 (2010)

16. Rehman, U., Cao, S.: Augmented-reality-based indoor navigation: a comparative analysis of handheld devices versus google glass. IEEE Trans. Hum. Mach. Syst. 47(1), 140–151 (2017)

17. Gerstweiler, G., Platzer, K., Kaufmann, H.: Dargs: dynamic ar guiding system for indoor environments. Computers 7(1), 1–19 (2017)

18. Kalkusch, M., Lidy, T., Knapp, N., Reitmayr, G., Kaufmann, H., Schmalstieg, D.: Structured visual markers for indoor pathfinding. In: Proceedings of the First IEEE International Workshop of Augmented Reality Toolkit, ART 2002, pp. 1–8 (2002)

19. Sato, H., Ishizu, K.: Gait patterns of Japanese pedestrians. J. Hum. Ergol. 19(1), 13–22 (1990)

20. Scheffé, H.: The Analysis of Variance. Wiley, New York (1967)

21. Ed, J.: Sensory Evaluation Handbook. JUSE Press (1973)

Oculus Rift Versus HTC Vive: Usability Assessment from a Teleportation Task

Crystal Maraj[(✉)], Jonathan Hurter, Schuyler Ferrante,
Lauren Horde, Jasmine Carter, and Sean Murphy

Institute for Simulation and Training,
University of Central Florida, Orlando, FL 32826, USA
{cmaraj,jhurter,sferrant,lhorde,
jcarter,smurphy}@ist.ucf.edu

Abstract. Virtual Reality (VR) technology has shown impressive growth in recent years, extending to industrial, military, and rehabilitation occupations. However, despite such growth, there is little research on the usability aspects associated with different VR devices. This paper investigates subjective and objective usability differences between two commercial Head-Mounted Display (HMD) systems, the HTC Vive and Oculus Rift, using a between-subjects experimental design on three teleportation task scenarios. Each scenario had a time limit of five minutes and sequentially increased in complexity. Objective usability was evaluated through performance measures, including per scenario effectiveness, time duration, total time duration, completion rate, and time-based efficiency. Subjective usability was evaluated by users after the three scenarios, via a questionnaire formed of ease of use, comfort, effectiveness, and visual quality subscales. The results, interpreted using Mann-Whitney U Tests, indicated significant differences between the HTC Vive and Oculus Rift: in terms of objective usability, Vive's overmatch in scenario three effectiveness suggests harder tasks in the Rift may require additional aids; in terms of subjective usability, Vive's overmatch in effectiveness questionnaire items suggests it is a preferred choice for a range of applications, as well as for learning real-world skills. In terms of significant Spearman's rho correlations, more HMD comfort is aligned with completion rates, within the Vive; different contexts may lead to a reversal effect, where visual quality can either relate to negative or positive performance, depending on the headset; and overall, many different usability aspects positively relate to total time-based efficiency of the teleportation task.

Keywords: Virtual Reality · Usability analysis · Head-Mounted Displays · Usability games

1 Introduction

The purpose of this research is to compare the HTC Vive and Oculus Rift Virtual Reality (VR) systems from a human factors perspective. The research focuses on assessing subjective and objective usability differences between the two Head-Mounted Displays (HMDs), and their respective controllers, through teleportation scenarios

© Springer Nature Switzerland AG 2019
J. Y. C. Chen and G. Fragomeni (Eds.): HCII 2019, LNCS 11574, pp. 247–257, 2019.
https://doi.org/10.1007/978-3-030-21607-8_19

within a Virtual Environment (VE). Specifically, this research aims to investigate the usability of each device through statistical analysis of a usability survey and performance data.

1.1   Virtual Reality, Augmented Reality, and Mixed Reality

The Reality-Virtuality (RV) Continuum [1] serves as a guide in referencing Mixed Reality (MR), Augmented Reality (AR), Augmented Virtuality (AV), and all respective positions which fall between the Real Environment (RE) and the complete VE (see Fig. 1). In the RV Continuum, MR is defined as an environment in which aspects of real and virtual worlds are combined within a single display. AR falls to the left of the RV Continuum, with the RE composing the majority of the environment. AV, although similar to AR, falls more to the right of the RV Continuum, as the VE is supplemented with real world objects, such as people or things. The AV/AR distinction stems from the proportions of real and synthetic objects in the environment. VR, defined as being immersed within a VE that is entirely synthetic, is the focus of this paper. It can be considered colloquial to the VE, and is thus outside the range of MR due to its complete visual virtuality. The VE may mimic components of the real world, such as the constraints of gravity and time, or be entirely fabricated with no governing physical or temporal laws at play.

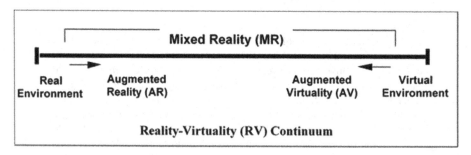

Fig. 1. Depiction of Reality-Virtuality (RV) Continuum (Milgram, P., Takemura, H., Utsumi, A., & Kishino, F. (1994). Augmented reality: a class of displays on the reality-virtuality continuum. *SPIE, 2351*, 282–292.)

1.2   Societal Applications

The use of VR has branched out into the world of entertainment, as well as more serious circles involving training and rehabilitation [2, 3]. A VR-based training system grants subjects the ability to navigate critical, sometimes dangerous situations without the real-world risk associated with the task: for example, VR-based training was reported to be effective at portraying real job hazards in a safe and controlled way for South African miners [4]. A study done by Bouchard et al. [5] concluded that VR may also be used as a preventative measure for Posttraumatic Stress Disorder (PTSD) in military occupations, as it allows individuals to better train and prepare for stressful circumstances in the real world. The controlled nature of VR lends itself to rehabilitation undertakings, in how highly realistic VEs are able to evoke therapeutic levels of anxiety, while offering complete control over an anxiety-inducing stimulus [3, 6]. Furthermore, VR has been bolstered as an economic choice in comparison to traditional training and rehabilitation methods; a company may invest less than $2500 USD and use VR technology with any number of people for years to come [6].

1.3 Related Work

VR technology has created interest in assessing different areas of performance with HMD systems. In a prior usability study, an HMD system was shown to underperform when compared to a desktop, mostly due to a lack of familiarity; there was no further data comparing the HMD system to another HMD system [7]. An additional study examined various locomotion methods, but not the same method on two different devices: the study utilized a joystick, physical walking, and a point-and-teleport method [8]. These studies illustrate the overall lack of research comparing HMD-to-HMD system usability.

HMD system comparison studies are focused on assessing technological functions, as opposed to usability. Although a study found the Vive performed slightly better than the Oculus in terms of quality of experience, this research used a small participant group in a sorting task [9]. Researchers attributed the Vive's success to its strong sensor system. Another study cited the Vive's tracking system as a positive attribute over the Oculus; yet both devices presented low visual jitter, and minimal tracked head movements [10]. In terms of visual performance, the Oculus was shown to outperform the Vive in lower distance compression, where HMD weight, field of view, and lens type were thought to be contributing factors [11].

1.4 Usability

Usability is defined as a system's level of "effectiveness, efficiency and satisfaction" [12]. In this study, the subjective usability subscales assessed by the participants were ease of use, comfort, visual quality, and effectiveness. For the purpose of this study, the following operational definitions are given:

- **Ease of use** typically refers to "the degree to which a person believes that using a particular system would be free of effort" [13].
- **Comfort** relates to physical comfort while wearing the HMD, such as how the HMD fits on the head or if it causes visual stress.
- **Visual quality** relates to how clearly the image is presented through the HMD.
- **Effectiveness** relates to whether or not the participant is able to achieve the experimental goal [14].

Objective usability data includes numerical performance acquired from the virtual scenarios. Within the simulation, several different forms of data were logged. Overall, performance data focused on how well an experimental task was completed, in terms of completion, time-to-completion, and efficiency (i.e., an equation resulting in a mix of completion and time-to-completion). The specific performance measurements will be detailed in the method section: per scenario effectiveness, time duration, total time duration, completion rate, and total time-based efficiency.

1.5   Research Questions

Below are the Research Questions (RQs) of interest, based on outcomes from the three virtual scenarios (i.e., an object collection game controlled via teleportation locomotion). There are two main research avenues: determining if differences exist between the Rift and Vive, in terms of usability; and determining if measures of objective usability (i.e., performance data) relate to measures of subjective usability (i.e., survey data).

RQ1: Is there a statistically significant difference in objective usability (i.e., per scenario effectiveness, per scenario time duration, total time duration, completion rate, and total time-based efficiency) between the Vive and Rift?

RQ2: Is there a statistically significant difference in subjective usability survey subscales (i.e., ease of use, comfort, visual quality, and effectiveness) between the Vive and Rift?

RQ3: Is there a correlational relationship between the subjective usability survey subscales and objective usability for the Vive and Rift?

2   Method

2.1   Participants

Participants were recruited from the University of Central Florida (UCF). To be considered as a participant in the study, the individual had to be a U.S. citizen, be at least 18 years-of-age, have had normal or corrected-to-normal vision, have had no previous history of seizures, and not be colorblind. For this study, there were 40 participants with an age range of 18-to-30; 14 participants were males ($M = 20.93$; $SD = 3.36$) and 26 were females ($M = 21.38$; $SD = 1.55$). After study completion, the participant was monetarily compensated up to $10 USD, for his or her time and travel.

2.2   Experimental Design

A between-subjects design, with one independent variable, was used to measure user-differences in the teleportation tasks. The independent variable was the type of HMD system, with two conditions (i.e., Vive and Rift). The dependent variable was the objective and subjective usability data of the teleportation task scenarios.

Teleportation Task Battery. All three virtual scenarios required the participant to use a handheld controller to navigate the virtual environments: either the Vive controller or the Oculus Touch controller was used exclusively for all scenarios, with its respective headset. Although the teleportation locomotion was the same per each system, the buttons for teleportation differed between controllers. In the Vive, one held down a trackpad to initiate the laser, tilted or laterally moved the controller to indicate direction of the laser, and let go of the trackpad to jump to the laser's projected location.

The Rift's Oculus Touch controller incorporated a joystick instead of a trackpad, though kept the same control scheme.

In each scenario, a usability game was given: the participant's goal was to collect a set number of objects, within a five-minute time limit. By teleporting into the desired object, it became collected. The user viewed the VE from a first-person perspective. In the first and second scenarios, a new collectable object would only appear after the current collectable was retrieved. The first scenario involved a flat-floor room filled with red-tile floors; thirty blue tiles could light up to be collected. The second scenario involved a lightly populated forest with hills; thirty blue circles could be shown as collectables. In the third scenario, which involved a small village, the collectables of twenty bright-blue spheres were presented simultaneously (see Fig. 2). As illustrated, the scenarios increased in complexity.

Fig. 2. The virtual environment of the third scenario, seen from the experimenter's monitor. The user's goal was to collect all bright blue spheres within five minutes.

2.3   Testbed

The testbed used to run the experiment and collect data for this task was one desktop computer (see Table 1 for the desktop specifications). The task scenarios were developed in the Unity game engine. Unity was selected for its high-quality graphics, user-friendly graphical interface, and capability to support different software development kits for the Vive and Rift.

Table 1. Desktop specifications.

Component	Specification
Operating system	64-bit Windows 10 Enterprise
Processor	Intel Core i7-7700K CPU @ 4.20 GHz
Installed memory (RAM)	32.0 GB
Graphics card	Intel HD Graphics 630 and NVIDIA GeForce GTX 1080 Ti
Input connectivity	USB 2.0, USB 3.0, HDMI 1.4, and Bluetooth 4.1 USB
Positional trackers	Oculus: Two constellations Vive: Two base stations
Software	Oculus App Version 1.28.0633101, Steam VR Version 1532655920, and Unity 2017.1.1 Personal (64bit)

2.4   Data Logging

As the participant completed each scenario, objective usability data was tracked and logged into an Excel file. Each individual scenario recorded two measurements: per scenario effectiveness and time duration. Per scenario effectiveness was calculated by dividing the number of objects collected by the total possible objects one could collect per a scenario. Per scenario time duration, expressed in minutes, was measured by the time it took the participant to complete the scenario, starting from the beginning of the scenario and ending either after collection of all objects, or until the maximum allotted time of five minutes passed, per each scenario.

After all scenarios were completed, three measurements were tracked and logged into the Excel file: total time duration, completion rate, and total time-based efficiency. Total time duration, expressed in seconds, was measured by combining all scenario time durations. The completion rate was found by dividing the number of successful scenarios by the total three scenarios and multiplying the quotient by 100% [14]:

$$Completion\ rate = \frac{\text{Number of scenarios completed successfully}}{\text{Total number of scenarios undertaken}} \times 100\% \qquad (1)$$

A scenario was considered complete if the participant was able to collect all objects before the allotted time ran out. Total time-based efficiency, expressed in objects collected per second, incorporated per scenario time duration and completion rate:

$$Time-based\ efficiency = \frac{\sum_{j=1}^{R}\sum_{i=1}^{N}\frac{n_{ij}}{t_{ij}}}{NR} \qquad (2)$$

For the purpose of this study, N represents the three scenarios, R represents the number of participants (which will always be one), n_{ij} is the result of object collection being successful or not (i.e., completion rate), and t_{ij} represents time spent by the user to complete the scenario (i.e., per scenario time duration) [14].

Further, participants reported their responses to a subjective usability survey at the end of the final scenario. The usability survey was developed in-house and assessed the system's utility. The survey comprised 14 statements, rated from strongly disagree (1) to strongly agree (5). There were also three additional open-form comment sections, regarding positive, negative, and freeform thoughts about each participant's given device.

2.5 Procedure

Prior to experimentation, each participant was randomly assigned to a condition (i.e., either the Vive or Rift). The participants' actions reflect the experimental procedure:

1. Signed informed consent
2. Completed color blindness test
3. Completed demographics questionnaire
4. Read interface PowerPoint training
5. Presented with scenario instructions
6. Completed the first scenario
7. Received 1-minute mandatory break
8. Presented with scenario instructions
9. Completed the second scenario
10. Received 1-minute mandatory break
11. Presented with scenario instructions
12. Completed the third scenario
13. Received 1-minute mandatory break
14. Completed usability survey
15. Completed receipt details
16. Received dismissal from the study

3   Results

3.1   Preliminary Data Analysis

Tests for normality, homogeneity of variance, and outliers were conducted for the usability data points to determine the data distribution. Specific results from the Kolmogorov-Smirnov test for normality indicated a violation of assumption for a normal distribution. Homogeneity of variance indicated no major discrepancies in the data for removal. However, a selection of non-parametric tests were used for data analysis.

The usability survey was tested for reliability using Cronbach's alpha. The Cronbach's alpha reported for the usability survey was .80, which is considered preferable [15]. As a result, the survey was included for data analysis. In total, there were 17 participants in the Vive condition, and 23 participants in the Rift condition.

3.2 Inferential Statistics

In terms of RQ1, a statistically significant difference was found between the Vive ($Md = 95$, $n = 17$) and Oculus ($Md = 90$, $n = 23$) within scenario 3 for per scenario effectiveness. The Mann-Whitney U Test reported $U = 127.5$, $z = -1.194$, $p = .056$, $r = -0.302$. There were no other reported statistically significant differences between the Vive and Oculus for usability performance.

For RQ2, there was a statistically significant difference between the Vive and Oculus Rift HMD systems on the usability survey. A Mann-Whitney U Test showed there was a significant difference between Oculus ($Md = 4$, $n = 23$) and Vive ($Md = 4.33$, $n = 17$) in the effectiveness subscale, $U = 100.5$, $z = -2.663$, $p = .008$, $r = -0.421$. Further analysis showed a statistically significant difference between the survey questions pertaining to effectiveness in the questionnaire. Regarding the system's ability for learning real-world skills (i.e., "I could use this device to learn real-world skills"), differences were found between the Vive ($Md = 4$, $S.E = .550$, $n = 17$) and Oculus ($Md = 4$, $S.E. = .935$, $n = 23$), $U = 105.5$, $z = -2.721$, $p = .007$, $r = -0.430$. Regarding the system's ability to be used for a range of applications (i.e., "This device would be beneficial for a broad range of applications"), differences were found between the Vive ($Md = 4$, $S.E = .550$ $n = 17$) and Oculus ($Md = 4$, $S.E. = .935$ $n = 23$), $U = 119$, $z = -2.314$, $p = .021$, $r = -0.366$.

For RQ3, results indicated both positive and negative relationships between the usability survey and the usability performance measures for the Vive and Rift conditions. Table 2 illustrates the Spearman's rho correlation results for the conditions.

Table 2. Correlations between the subjective and objective usability data

	Comfort	Ease of use	Effectiveness	Visual quality
First scenario time duration	_	−.500*	_	−.446*
Second scenario time duration	−.565*	−.824**	−.493*	.681**
Completion rate (Percentage)	.494*	_	_	_
Total time-based efficiency	.374	.707** .479*	.333	.528* .509*

Note. **Correlation is significant at the 0.01 level (2-tailed), *Correlation is significant at the 0.05 level (2-tailed). Italicized and bolded numbers refer to Oculus; others are Vive.

4 Discussion

4.1 HMD Differences in Usability: Research Questions 1 and 2

The usability dimensions overall favor the Vive. In terms of performance measures, participants in the Vive condition scored significantly higher in the third scenario. The per scenario effectiveness, or how many objects were collected with the Vive, speaks to the fluidity of the device, allowing one to effectively visually search and interface with a scenario. Although simpler tasks (i.e., the first and second scenarios) may not result in performance differences, more complex tasks could benefit from the Vive. Further, complex tasks using the Rift may benefit from performance aids to complete the same complex tasks at the level of Vive users. Therefore, matching a device to the complexity of a task should be considered.

The significant usability survey results were also grounded in effectiveness. The effectiveness subscale was made up of three statements, two of which were significant when sub-subscales were treated independently: "I could use this device to learn real-world skills" dealt with transference, and "This device would be beneficial for a broad range of applications" dealt with generalizability. Based on the generalizability question, it may save time and money to select the Vive if a user intends on having a broad array of applications within one device. Similarly, the Vive has an inclination to help users learn real-world skills. Given how VR is often used to train, the Vive appears to outline an actual system preference for learning. More analysis may help determine if this learning preference translates into demonstrable learning measures.

Overall, the Vive was better in terms of effectiveness. If a stakeholder were to choose the better, or more usable, device for a locomotion-by-teleportation task, Vive would be recommended. This choice is based on how all other usability aspects were equal. That is, if one was seeking a device with the best comfort, one may choose between the Vive and Rift without any comfort distinction (at least for short sessions). Yet, all measurements being equal, effectiveness matters the most: it held the only distinction between the devices.

Although more research could elaborate on the benefits leading to these improved ratings, immediate differences may relate to the controller scheme or HMD specification provided. Given the scenarios were identical between conditions, this leads to questioning the naturalness of the controller interface and the fidelity of the HMD. A future analysis would be, since the Vive is already preferable in usability, whether the Vive's effectiveness is based off the controller or other technical aspects.

4.2   HMD Correlations in Usability: Research Question 3

At a practical level, if one is interested in an HMD's role in facilitating a high completion rate within the Vive, a key indicator of performance may be comfort. Although this is a correlation, a direction of causality attributable to the system, and not performance, is plausible.

Total time-based efficiency had many correlations with subjective usability (Table 2). Note how performance does not indicate completion, but completion at a quick rate. This level of efficient performance may be suited to first responders, bomb disposal, or surgeons. At a practical level, one should consider how different layers of usability relate to performance in these domains. All aspects of subjective usability correlated significantly with efficiency in the Vive condition, whereas only two aspects correlated significantly in the Oculus condition. This overall trend shows how different aspects of usability matter in respect to performance tasks.

Two significant correlations suggested a reversal effect: visual quality was negatively related to time duration in the first scenario (with the Oculus); whereas in the second scenario, visual quality was positively related to time duration (with the Vive). In other words, Oculus participants were able to complete task one quicker as visual quality increased. This may be due to a minimal environment, with little clutter helping the user learn the initial task. The better the visual quality, the quicker one could perform the new task. However, by the second trial (here, in the Vive), the user's attention shifted more towards the compelling visuals rather than completing the task. The environment may have been a curious distraction, especially since the interface would be learned at this point. Yet, it is unclear the rationale behind the effect being device-specific.

5 Limitations

The limitations of this experiment centered on controllers and scenario instructions. Vive controllers lacked changeable batteries; when both controllers lost power, participants had to use a controller tethered to a computer. As a result, participant arm movement was restricted. When both the Vive and Oculus controllers started to lose power, positional tracking was interrupted, which may have caused the participants to accidentally teleport out of bounds. Further, although there were scenario instructions on how to complete the task objective, there were no practice tests to ensure the participants mastered the task skills. Future experiments may consider the aforementioned limits to improve experimental design.

6 Conclusion

The present research examined the HTC Vive and Oculus Rift systems from a usability perspective. Overall, the results suggest the Vive was a stronger candidate, at least within the given scenario tasks. Objectively, the most complex task was easier with the Vive. However, more research is needed to elaborate if and how the Vive is preferable for different applications (e.g., locomotion types), and especially for learning tasks, to thus confirm the subjective results.

Acknowledgments. This research was sponsored by Gino Fragomeni of the U.S. Army Research Laboratory Human Research Engineering Directorate Advanced Training and Simulation Division (ARL HRED ATSD), under contract W911QX-13-C-0052. However, the views, findings, and conclusions contained in this presentation are solely those of the author and should not be interpreted as representing the official policies, either expressed or implied, of ARL HRED ATSD or the U.S. Government. The U.S. Government is authorized to reproduce and distribute reprints for Government.

References

1. Milgram, P., Takemura, H., Utsumi, A., Kishino, F.: Augmented reality: a class of displays on the reality-virtuality continuum. Proc. SPIE **2351**, 282–292 (1994)
2. Burdea, G.C., Coiffet, P.: Virtual Reality Technology, 2nd edn. Wiley, New York (2003)
3. Schultheis, M.T., Rizzo, A.A.: The application of virtual reality technology in rehabilitation. Rehabil. Psychol. **46**(3), 296–311 (2001)

4. Wyk, E.V., Villiers, R.D.: Virtual reality training applications for the mining industry. In: 6th International Conference on Computer Graphics, Virtual Reality, Visualisation and Interaction in Africa, pp. 53–63. ACM (2009)

5. Bouchard, S., Guitard, T., Bernier, F., Robillard, G.: Virtual reality and the training of military personnel to cope with acute stressors. In: Brahnam, S., Jain, L.C. (eds.) Advanced Computational Intelligence Paradigms in Healthcare 6: Virtual Reality in Psychotherapy, Rehabilitation, and Assessment, pp. 109–128. Springer, Heidelberg (2011). https://doi.org/10.1007/978-3-642-17824-5_6

6. Robillard, G., Bouchard, S., Fournier, T., Renaud, P.: Anxiety and presence during VR immersion: a comparative study of the reactions of phobic and non-phobic participants in therapeutic virtual environments derived from computer games. CyberPsychology Behav. 6(5), 467–476 (2003)

7. Bozgeyikli, E., Raij, A., Katkoori, S., Dubey, R.: Point & teleport locomotion technique for virtual reality. In: Proceedings of the 2016 Annual Symposium on Computer-Human Interaction in Play - CHI PLAY 16, pp. 205–216. ACM (2016)

8. Santos, B.S., et al.: Head-mounted display versus desktop for 3D navigation in virtual reality: a user study. Multimedia Tools Appl. 41(1), 161–181 (2008)

9. Suznjevic, M., Mandurov, M., Matijasevic, M.: Performance and QoE assessment of HTC Vive and Oculus Rift for pick-and-place tasks in VR. In: 2017 Ninth International Conference on Quality of Multimedia Experience (QoMEX). IEEE (2017)

10. Borrego, A., Latorre, J., Alcañiz, M., Llorens, R.: Comparison of Oculus Rift and HTC Vive: feasibility for virtual reality-based exploration, navigation, exergaming, and rehabilitation. Games Health J. 7(3), 151–156 (2018)

11. Buck, L.E., Young, M.K., Bodenheimer, B.: A comparison of distance estimation in HMD-based virtual environments with different HMD-based conditions. ACM Trans. Appl. Percept. 15(3), 1–15 (2018)

12. ISO 9241-11:2018: Ergonomics of human-system interaction – Part 11: Usability: Definitions and concepts. https://www.iso.org/obp/ui/#iso:std:iso:9241:-11:ed-2:v1:en. Accessed 10 Oct 2018

13. Davis, F.: Perceived usefulness, perceived ease of use, and user acceptance of information technology. MIS Q. 13(3), 319–340 (1989)

14. Sergeev, A.: UI designer - ISO-9241 efficiency metrics - theory of usability. http://ui-designer.net/usability/efficiency.htm. Accessed 10 Oct 2018

15. DeVellis, R.F.: Scale Development: Theory and Applications. Sage Publications, Thousand Oaks (1991)

Impact of Foveated Rendering on Procedural Task Training

Rafael Radkowski$^{(\boxtimes)}$ and Supriya Raul

Virtual Reality Applications Center, Iowa State University, Ames, IA, USA
rafael@iastate.edu

Abstract. Foveated rendering (FR) is a technique for virtual reality (VR) that adapts the image quality to the user's eye fixation. The content within the user's eye fixation appears in high quality, the peripheral area in lower quality. The technique exploits the fact that the eye, the retina, in particular, has its highest density of light-sensing cells in the center, the so-called fovea. All other areas are covered with less density. Eye tracking is essential for foveated rendering since one needs to be able to determine the user's fixation. Although FR is a promising technique to reduce computer performance requirements, it is unclear whether it has an impact on the user's task performance, primarily when one uses VR as a training tool. Theoretically, the technique is invisible. However, its implementation depends on several parameters and technical hardware limitations. We conducted a study to see whether or not these limitations distract the user and reduce his/her training performance. The results indicate that the user notices the technique. However, s/he does not care, and the performance difference is insignificant, except for some outliers caused by technical eye tracking limitations.

Keywords: Virtual reality · Foveated rendering · Procedural tasks · Training

1 Introduction

Foveated rendering (FR) is an upcoming rendering technique for virtual reality (VR) application that adapts the quality of the rendered image with respect to the user's eye focus. Human eyes perceive the physical world with different fidelity and attention due to the density distribution of light-sensitive nerve cells on the retina. The density, thus the visual resolution, is at a maximum in a central pit of the retina, the so-called fovea. It decreases with increases distance to the fovea; so does the perceivable resolution or fidelity. Foveated rendering exploits this fact by decreasing the rendering quality depending on the user's eye focus, also called fixation. The visual rendering quality is high at the fixation point, and lower in the visual periphery. Figure 1 illustrates an example; Fig. 1(a) shows a regular computer graphics scene, and (b) the same scene with a fixation kernel. A round area in which content appear in high quality. The peripheral portion of the scene is rendered with lower fidelity. Here, every second pixel is discarded. FR relies on eye tracking to determine the user's fixation point in real-time so that that renderer can adapt the kernel's position depending on the user's fixation.

© Springer Nature Switzerland AG 2019
J. Y. C. Chen and G. Fragomeni (Eds.): HCII 2019, LNCS 11574, pp. 258–267, 2019.
https://doi.org/10.1007/978-3-030-21607-8_20

Head-mounted displays (HMD) need to be equipped with eye tracking hardware and sample the eye position with a high sampling rate so that the user's eye cannot outrun the tracking device.

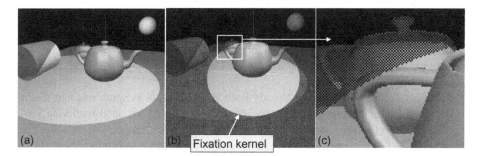

Fig. 1. (a) A regularly rendered scene. (b) with foveated rendering, the bright area shows the fixation kernel (too large here). The remaining image appears darker since the example approach (c) uses a pattern to reject every second pixel. The colors were not reconstructed for this example.

FR reduces the computational requirements to graphics hardware. Depending on the utilized algorithm, one either renders in a low-resolution buffer, skip fragments, or use another technique which reduces the number of pixels and triangles to compute. Thus, it facilitates high-quality VR on mobile devices and other systems with limited graphics performance.

Our research focuses on the user-aspect of FR, on two points in particular. First foveated rendering is not free of visual artifacts. These artifacts are noticeable [1]. Previous research reported that users see antialiasing in their peripheral vision [2], experience a sense of tunnel vision [3] or notice a screen-door effect [4]; note that these artifacts highly depend on the implementation of FR. We are interested in learning whether or not these artifacts distract the user when performing tasks in a virtual environment (VE) or if the user does not mind the artifacts. Related to the first question, we are interested to see if any artifacts or eye tracking problems reduce the user's performance when learning procedural tasks in a virtual environment. Therefore, we conducted a user study that asks the user to perform a training task. The task incorporates a virtual engine room. Volunteers were asked to operate buttons, levers, and other instruments. The paper reports about the study and the results. The remainder of this paper is structured as follows: The next section introduces the essential FR background and different implementations. Section 3 explains the VE and our FR implementation. Section 4 presents the results. The paper closes with a conclusion and an outlook.

2 Foveated Rendering Background

FR exploits the fact that the human perception is focused onto a small central area which aligns with fovea, the point of highest density of light-receptive cells on the retina. This central area covers, depending on the source, between 3°–5° of the visual field. People are mostly aware of the objects that we see in this central area. The remaining peripheral area is covered with a lower density of light receptive cells. Consequently, its recognizable visual fidelity is limited. FR exploits this and renders a scene with high quality only for the focused area. The remainder of the scene is generated with lower fidelity.

Different FR algorithms have already been introduced. In general, one can distinguish two approaches (Fig. 2): Layer-based vs. region-based foveated rendering [10]. Layer-based approaches render multiple images. Using two layers, for instance, one low-resolution layer covers the entire scene view, and a high-resolution layer shows high-quality content. The number of layers and the size of each layer can vary. User studies are essential to identify the right parameters. Region-based foveated rendering split the scene into a fixed number of regions. The inner region is rendered with the highest quality, the outer region with the lowest quality. All intermediate regions are rendered with interpolated quality. Since the field is currently very active, variations of those two approaches were also already introduced. The following paragraphs introduce some of these algorithms.

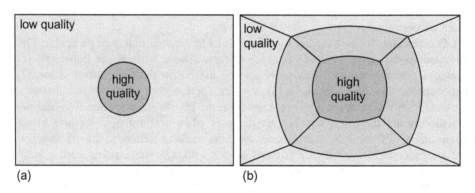

Fig. 2. (a) Layer-based approach - the different regions are rendered as individual layers and then stacked together. (b) Region-based approach - The display is split into different regions, each region is rendered with different quality.

Guenter et al. [6] introduce a layer-based approach combining three layers with three different resolutions. The inner layer is rendered with the highest quality, the outer layer - the remaining image - with the lowest quality. The second layer covers near peripheral vision. It provides an average quality.

Meng et al. [5] suggest a kernel-based foveated rendering using two pass rendering approach. The first render pass generates the low-quality images, and the second render pass augments a circular kernel area with the full image resolutions.

Patney et al. (Patney, 2016), (Patney, 2018) introduce a perceptually-based foveated rendering algorithms. The author report that the human peripheral vision is best at seeing things like color, contrast, edges, and motion in the peripheral area. Thus, the authors focus on these aspects in the peripheral area and ignore high-fidelity details. Additionally, the authors also suppress anti-aliasing artifacts. They report that the employed techniques reduce the number of artifacts so that a user does not notice any of them anymore.

Aldehayyat et al. [7] propose a foveated rendered, that first blurs the entire image and then refocuses the fovea area with a high-quality renderer.

All these techniques require eye tracking. Besides these, some authors introduced hardware solutions and techniques that work without eye tracking.

For instance, Tan et al. [4] suggest a hardware solution. They developed an HMD with two displays embedded. The first display renders the full-resolution image for the fovea area, the second one the low-quality image. An optical combiner merges both images. The authors report that this technique reduces visual artifacts successfully.

Additionally, the area is currently highly industry-driven. Head-mounted display (HMD) manufacturers and others already provide software solutions for their headsets. For instance, Oculus supports two foveated rendering techniques, both work without eye tracking: Fixed Foveated Rendering (FFR) [8] allows one to render the center portion of the display with high resolution and the edges with lower resolution. The second technique, Mask-based foveated rendering (MBFR) [9] drops every other pixel on the complete rendering. However, the pixels are reconstructed in a subsequent render pass. This approach gains the same performance win by ignoring pixels, although without the need for eye tracking and regions.

Although previous studies already demonstrate that artifacts are noticeable, depending on the utilized technique, the studies did not assess to what extent the user mind the artifacts and whether or not they affect his/her performance.

3 VR Test Environment

This section describes our VE, including the test scene, the implemented foveated renderer filter, the utilized headset along with the eye tracking system. Figure 3 shows the VE. The content of the VR scene resembles part of an engine room of size 20×30 ft, with a row of control panels and several valves and levers to operate. Figure 3(b–c) depicts a part of the control panel in detail. It incorporates three active buttons and two dials; active means they can be operated. All operational parts are within 10 ft walking distance, along one corridor of the room. The scene was prepared so that the user can reach all relevant locations by walking. Although the content of the scene appears to be old and in bad condition, we selected this content since it exhibits plenty of high-fidelity details. The application conveyed instructions via a small board in front of the user. Its position is fixed relative to the user's position, at his/her lower left side. Thus, the user has to look down and to the left to see the instructions. The entire VE was prepared with Unity.

Fig. 3. (a) The VE resembles part of an engine room. It comes with plenty of high-fidelity details and contains several buttons and lever to be operated. (b) A part of the control panel.

We implemented two different foveated rendering filter: a kernel-based foveated rendering (KFR, [5]) filter and a layer-based rendering (LBR) filter with three layers [6]. The first one renders a low-resolution image (720 × 800) depicting the entire scene. We also used a black-white pattern to ignore every other fragment. This image is upscaled and augmented with a high-fidelity rendering for the fixation area. The area is round with a radius of 300 pixels. Thus, the area covers approximately 20% of the display (1440 × 1600). The second one works similar to the first filter with the difference that three layers are used. First, the entire image is rendered with low-quality (720 × 800). Two kernels at the user's fixation with gradually decreasing quality augment the first one. Here, we first used a 300-pixel radius for the second layer and a 150-pixel radius for the first layer. We used the same size to be able to compare both techniques.

Also, all these parameters were found empirically. We internally optimized those parameters with tests within the research group until everybody was more or less satisfied with the visual result. However, it was impossible to find a parameter set that satisfied everybody completely. All filters are implemented with Cg.

Our foveated rendering implementation relies on eye tracking. We use an HTC Vive Pro HMD and a Pupils Labs eye tracking add-on for this purpose (https://pupil-labs.com). The eye tracking system needs to be mounted into the HTC Vive. It samples the eye position 120 times/s. Pupil Labs provides open source Python scripts to operate the device. Additionally, a script for Unity is available to directly process the data.

Since every user has different eyes, every user needs to calibrate the eye tracking system. Pupil Labs provides a tool for this purpose, which we adopted. It asks the user to follow a dot that jumps along the periphery of a circle. The entire calibration procedure is straightforward, requires 20-s attention, and is part of a Unity application.

Our VE uses hand tracking for user interaction. The user sees white 3d hand models. The hand models are articulated and match the user's hand postures. The application uses one set of hand models for all users. Each hand changes its color to red if an interaction or an interaction attempt is detected. This feature provides user feedback so that he or she knows that the interaction attempt is detected. We use a Leap Motion sensor for hand tracking, attached to the Vive Pro display (Fig. 4).

Fig. 4. (a) The Pupils Labs eye tracking. (b–c) It tracks both eyes with a sampling rate of 120 samples second using infrared lights (Color figure online)

4 Study

The goal of this research is to determine whether or not foveated rendering affects the user in a virtual environment. Previous studies reported that the user could notice artifacts. However, noticing artifacts and being affected, e.g., exhibiting a lower task performance, are two different aspects. We conducted a user study to determine whether or not the user notice a difference. Three modes were compared: No FR (Mode A), KFR (Mode B), and LBR (Mode C). We followed a between-subject design and asked each volunteer to repeat the tasks four times. Each user was subjected to two times to Mode A and two times either to Mode B or to Mode C. In total, 24 volunteers (m = 17, w = 7, age 21–33) perform the task. The next sections describe the procedure, explain the results, and discuss the outcome (Fig. 5).

4.1 Procedure and Measurement

Upon arrival, each user was asked to complete a pre-questionnaire pertaining to the user demographics, as well as to sign a consent form. The experimenter then briefly explained the task (follow instructions). Each user could study a printout showing the instruction panel. Additionally, the experimenter introduced the safety measures (white grid when approaching the tracking limit, curbs on the floor) to prevent the user from running into walls. Next, the user puts on the HMD (no users were allowed to wear glasses since the eye tracking device does not work with glasses) and the experimenter started the VR environment. Initially, the user calibrated the eye tracking device and verified that it is functional by directing a dot onto three targets using his/her eyes. The experimented observed this task on a screen and manually restarted the calibration if the user were not able to hit the targets or proceed to the next step. After completing the calibration task, the VR scene became active. Next, the user verified that the Leap Motion hand tracking system worked as expected. He or she were asked to observe his/her hand models and to verify that the models match the user's hand posture. Additionally, the user had to push one button and to grab a screwdriver to verify functionality. This step concluded the initialization.

Subsequently, the engine room appeared, and the first task started. Each task came with 21 interactions (operations). The user had to walk six times to different locations within a 10×10 ft area. Each user was asked to repeat the task four times. Each trial slightly changed parameters (e.g., set the lever to position A for trial 1 and to position B for trial B), so that no two trials were utterly equal. This measure should mitigate learning effects. The VR application automatically selected the modes (Mode A, B, C). All trials were administered in a random order.

Between trials, the experimenter asked the user to complete a NASA TLX and a Simulator Sickness Questionnaire (SSQ). The user needed to answer the questions verbally since we intended to keep the user in the virtual environment. The experimenter read the questions aloud and noted the volunteer's answer. The answer options were displayed in the VE. We did not expect severe simulation sickness problems since the entire scene does not contain any effects that elicit simulation sickness. However, previous studies reported that a user might experience a tunnel view, which can cause simulation sickness. Also, we do not believe that the scene and task ask too much from the user. Thus, we use the NASA TLX questionnaire to verify that frustration does not affect the user.

After the user performed the four trials, we ask each user to complete a post-assessment questionnaire. Its questions (Table 1) directly ask the user whether he or she noticed the difference between trials or artifacts. We used a 5-point Likert scale to obtain the answers. Additionally, it verifies that the application was usable and that the user did not experience any significant interaction problems. The experiment concluded after the user completed this questionnaire.

Additionally, the VR application automatically registered each user interaction, the time of interaction, and the user's head position (moving path). Also, the entire time was recorded starting when displaying the first task and ending when the user performed the last task. The application also detected user mistakes, e.g., wrong lever position, the wrong button pushed, and recorded them. All data were logged in an ASCII file, one per user.

4.2   Results

We analyzed the time the users required per mode as well as the mistakes the users made; Fig. 5 illustrates the results. Here, Mode AB means that this user experience Mode A and Mode B, every two times. Mode AC is the group that experienced Mode A and Mode C, also every two times. We performed an ANOVA for the group subject do mode A and B ($F1,11 = 0.13$, $p < .05$), A and C ($F1,11 = 0.73$, $p < .05$), and between Mode B and Mode C (F1,11 = 0.85, p < .05). However, the results do not indicate any significant differences. Figure 5(b) illustrates the mistakes the users made. The results vary between Mode A, 1.25 and 0.66 mistakes, Mode B, 3.33 mistakes, and Mode C, 2.67 mistakes, with a total number of 21 steps per trial; thus, 21 possible mistakes. We conducted an ANOVA, again for the group subjected to Mode A and B (F1,11 = 4.78, p < .05), Mode A and C (F1,11 = 9.54, p < .05). Both results show a statistically significant difference. We also analyzed the difference between Mode B and C (F1,11 = 0.53, p < .05), which does not yield any significant differences.

The NASA TLX results show no significant findings. The reported results for mental demands, physical demands, etc. are mostly low. The effort was reported to be low in general. Some users became frustrated as a result of eye tracking limitation and the extended test duration, which affected the results. Also, the procedure was monotonous, which also increased frustration; both aspects are discussed in the next sections.

Additionally, no user became severely sick in the virtual environment. Although the user spent almost 40 min in the virtual environment, the majority of users did not report discomfort, fatigue, or headaches. The only exceptions were eye strains and blurred vision. The first one reached moderate severity, and the second one affected some users severely. However, further investigation showed that this might be a result of foveated rendering. If eye tracking worked inadequately, the users just eye focused on a low-quality part of the rendering. A more significant number of users reported dry eyes. However, we do not attribute this to foveated rendering.

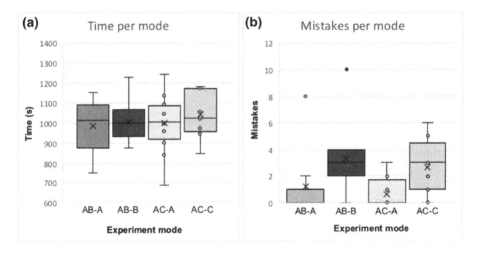

Fig. 5. (a) Time per mode, (b) Errors per mode

Table 1 summarized the results of the post-assessment questionnaire yielded per mode. The questionnaire asked ten questions aiming to render quality, interaction, and usability in general. We conducted a one-way ANOVA. The results are insignificant except for question Q1, Q4, and Q7. However, these results are most likely due to a technical limitation of the eye tracking hardware.

4.3 Discussion

The results of this experiment do not reveal essential significant difference pertaining to time. However, users that work with foveated rendering make more mistakes, although there are some reservations to this result since was most likely caused by the extended test period and user frustration.

First, we noticed a training effect between the first and the second trial as mentioned. We expected to find a training effect although the tasks slightly changed. The users remembered the general location of equipment and panels. They became familiar with the VE which allowed them to move faster. This training effect remained unnoticeable in subsequent trials.

Although the mistakes users made with FR and without FR are statistically significant, some user reported increasing frustration. The users' answer too Q5 and Q1 allow us to assume that they had problems reading the text. The eye tracking device requires thorough calibration; it did not work as expected for some of the user's, and we noticed this too late since these users also passed the initial test. Adjusting and calibrating the eye tracking device per user was challenging. Self-tests revealed that one has to carefully adjust the interpupil distance very accurately first before calibrating the eye tracking device. The calibration tool is not completely visible otherwise.

Unfortunately, we noticed an increasing frustration among some volunteers. Some users reported that they just wanted to finish the test and to be quick after trial number two or three. We attribute the increased number of mistakes to this trait.

Table 1. Questionnaire results, mean (std. deviation)

No.	Question	Mode A–B	Mode A–C
1	The scene was always clearly visible and not blurred	1.67 (0.77)	3.58 (0.79)
2	The display was free of aliasing and other artifacts	1.41 (0.51)	1.41 (0.66)
3	The field-of-view was appropriate for this scenario	1.67 (0.77)	1.91 (0.90)
4	The rendering quality of all four trials was equal	1.75 (0.86)	3.67 (0.88)
5	I was able to read the text in the virtual environment	2 (0.60)	3.92 (1.08)
6	I was able to identify all buttons, levers, and switches in the virtual environment	1.16 (0.38)	2.08 (1.16)
7	The eye tracking device and its functionality was invisible to me	2.83 (1.69)	2 (0.85)
8	All instructions were clear and easy to understand	1.5 (0.90)	2.17 (0.93)
9	I could easily interact with virtual parts using my hands	1.58 (0.90)	1.91 (0.90)
10	I would recommend this virtual reality training application to my friends	1.83 (1.11)	1,75 (0.86)

Furthermore, a more significant number of people noticed FR and its effect on the scene. Although the results are not significant, users reported that they notice some differences between the scenes, without being able to not further detailing them. However, users do not mind the differences. Also, the results let us believe that only the direct comparison of different renderers facilitates this outcome. Users who do not know about FR would not notice any difference.

4.4 Conclusion and Outlook

This research aimed to understand the impact of foveated rendering on users, especially on task performance. Foveated rendering can cause rendering artifacts, and previous studies reported that users notice them. They can distract users. Thus, we were interested to see if they have an effect on the users' performance in a training task, or if users do not mind them. User study results indicate that a significant number of users notice the different renderer since they had an opportunity to compare them, although they cannot describe the effect in detail. Moreover, users do not mind the differences. Thus, we also did not notice any significant differences when analyzing the training task results. Thus, we conclude that FR does not affect the user if correctly implemented. Nonetheless, eye tracking and display limitations can result in a suboptimal outcome, which could distract the user.

We are in the process of conducting a second user study with a focus on procedural task training with VR. The goal is to optimize the training task. This study gives us another opportunity to examine FR user impact.

References

1. Swafford, N.T., Iglesias-Guitian, J.A., Koniaris, C., Moon, B., Cosker, D., Mitchell, K.: User, metric, and computational evaluation of foveated rendering methods. In: Proceedings of the ACM Symposium on Applied Perception (SAP 2016) (2016)
2. Patney, A., et al.: Perceptually-based foveated virtual reality. In: SIGGRAPH Emerging Technologies (2016)
3. Patney, A., et al.: Towards foveated rendering for gaze-tracked virtual reality. ACM Trans. Graph. **35**, 179:1–179:12 (2016)
4. Tan, G., et al.: Foveated imaging for near-eye displays. Opt. Express **26**(19), 25076–25085 (2018)
5. Meng, X., Du, R., Zwicker, M., Varshney, A.: Kernel foveated rendering. PACMCGIT **1**, 5 (2018)
6. Guenter, B.K., Finch, M., Drucker, S.M., Tan, D.S., Snyder, J.: Foveated 3D graphics. ACM Trans. Graph. **31**, 164:1–164:10 (2012)
7. Aldehayyat, Y.: Foveated image refocusing in VR applications (2018)
8. Oculus Inc., Fixed foveated rendering. https://developer.oculus.com/documentation/unreal/latest/concepts/unreal-ffr. Accessed 11 Feb 2019
9. Oculus Inc., Masked-based foveated rendering. https://developer.oculus.com/documentation/unreal/latest/concepts/unreal-mbfr. Accessed 11 Feb 2019
10. Bastani, B., Turner, E., Vieri, C., Jiang, H., Funt, B., Balram, N.: Foveated pipeline for AR/VR head-mounted displays. Inf. Display **33**, 14–35 (2017)

User Guidance for Interactive Camera Calibration

Pavel Rojtberg[1,2]([⊠])

[1] Fraunhofer IGD, Darmstadt, Germany
`pavel.rojtberg@igd.fraunhofer.de`
[2] TU Darmstadt, Darmstadt, Germany

Abstract. For building a Augmented Reality (AR) pipeline, the most crucial step is the camera calibration as overall quality heavily depends on it. In turn camera calibration itself is influenced most by the choice of camera-to-pattern poses – yet currently there is only little research on guiding the user to a specific pose. We build upon our novel camera calibration framework that is capable to generate calibration poses in real-time and present a user study evaluating different visualization methods to guide the user to a target pose. Using the presented method even novel users are capable to perform a precise camera calibration in about 2 min.

Keywords: Augmented reality and environments ·
Interaction in virtual and augmented reality environments

1 Motivation

Camera calibration in the context of Augmented Reality (AR) is the process of determining the internal camera geometrical and optical characteristics (intrinsic parameters) and optionally the position and orientation of the camera frame in the world coordinate system (extrinsic parameters). The performance of the 3D vision algorithms which AR builds upon directly depends on the quality of this calibration. Furthermore, calibration is a recurring task that has to be performed each time the camera setup is changed. Even if a camera is replaced by an equivalent from the same series, the intrinsics will vary due to build inaccuracies.

The prevalent approach to camera calibration is based on acquiring multiple images of a planar pattern of known size [6]. In contrast to 3D calibration objects that were used earlier, 2D patterns are easy to obtain as conventional printers can produce them at high precision.

The pattern is then used to establish correspondences between known 3D world points and measured 2D image points. The point correspondences form a over-determined system of equations which constrains the camera model.

However, due to the projective nature of the transform multiple images must be acquired from different poses. Here, special pose configurations [5] that lead to an unreliable solutions and should be explicitly avoided.

© Springer Nature Switzerland AG 2019
J. Y. C. Chen and G. Fragomeni (Eds.): HCII 2019, LNCS 11574, pp. 268–276, 2019.
https://doi.org/10.1007/978-3-030-21607-8_21

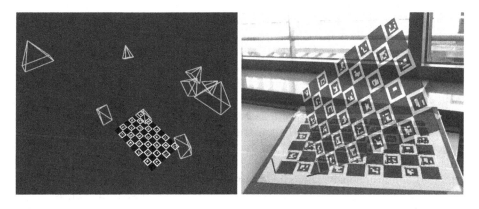

Fig. 1. Exemplary set of 9 target poses and the user guidance overlay, projecting for the bottom right camera.

Therefore a user interface is desirable which guides users through the calibration process. The guidance allows to select to a minimal set of "good" frames that result in a fast and reproducible calibration.

2 Background

The first step to camera calibration is to detect the calibration pattern. Typically chessboard patterns (Fig. 2a) are used, which have strong gradients that can be detected even under difficult lighting conditions. Additionally, the 2D points can be located with sub-pixel accuracy.

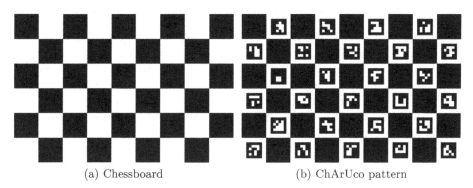

(a) Chessboard   (b) ChArUco pattern

Fig. 2. Common planar calibration patterns

However, the detection process usually involves the time consuming task of ordering the detected rectangles to a canonical topology. This slows down frame acquisition to below 30 Hz and impedes the interactivity of the method. Furthermore the board needs to be fully visible for the corner identification to work.

Therefore new methods interleave fiducial markers [2] within the chessboard pattern (Fig. 2b). The markers encode an unique id and are designed to be rotationally invariant - hence the detection of a single marker allows deducing the location and orientation of the whole board. However the marker positions become imprecise at steep view angles. Hence only chessboard corners are used, which generate measurements at sub-pixel accuracy.

The second step in calibration is to capture a calibration set of multiple images. This set needs sufficiently constrain the camera model for the calibration to succeed. For instance the pattern vies must not be all parallel to the image plane. As both pattern distance and camera focal length ("zoom level") are estimated simultaneously, there is no unique solution in this case. Consequently popular calibration toolboxes like ROS[1] or OpenCV[2] impose some heuristics on pose variance or screen space coverage to alleviate the problem (see Fig. 3).

 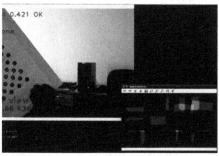

(a) The ROS toolbox showing the variance in position and size.

(b) OpenCV showing the current screen coverage

Fig. 3. User interfaces of popular, non-interactive, systems.

As these systems are not capable of generating pose suggestions, their user interfaces only visualize statistics about the data captured so far. The user is responsible to reason about an optimal next pose that would improve on the imposed heuristics. Furthermore the unreliable pose configurations are not explicitly addressed—therefore degraded performance is still possible.

In contrast, new calibration systems [3,4] are capable to guide users to specific target poses by displaying an overlay (see Fig. 1). This explicitly avoids unreliable configurations and reduces intrinsic cognitive load [1]. While both [3,4] performed user surveys, they merely showed operability of their methods by novice users.

Additionally the user interfaces implemented by each method are very different. [4] only display highlighted projection of the real pattern to tag the target pose, while [3] display an abstractly colored, wireframe of the board at the target pose and additionally overpaint the real board with squares of matching color (see Fig. 4).

---

[1] http://wiki.ros.org/camera_calibration/Tutorials/MonocularCalibration.

[2] https://docs.opencv.org/master/d7/d21/tutorial_interactive_calibration.html.

(a) Target pose wireframe and real-board (b) Target pose projection as used by [4]
overpaint as used by [3]

Fig. 4. User guidance overlays used by interactive calibration systems

Therefore this work focuses on the question how which user interface is best suited to guide users to specific calibration poses. At this we take the specific geometric properties of the calibration problem into account, namely:

– Only the relative pose between camera and pattern matters
– The pattern can be arbitrarily flipped horizontally and vertically.

Indeed, these properties make the calibration guidance significantly different from typical AR guidance use-cases where a pose needs to be matched exactly.

2.1 Calibration Poses

In general a rigid pose has six degrees of freedom (DOF); yaw, pitch, roll for the orientation and the three dimensional position. However the underlying algo-rithm [4] generates more restricted poses, based on the calibration objective. These fall in the following two categories:

Intrinsic Calibration Pose. To estimate the intrinsic camera parameters, the goal is to maximize the angular spread of the measurement points. Here the pattern is placed in the central image region and tilted along one primary axis. Additionally the board needs to be tilted and rotated along the remaining axes to avoid ambiguous configurations (see Fig. 5a). Therefore there are only three rotational DOF.

Distortion Calibration Pose. To estimate the lens distortion parameters, the pattern must be placed in regions with highest distortion which are typically the corners. Here a parallel view is used and the distance and relative position changes (see Fig. 5b). Therefore there are only three positional DOF.

Therefore a user only ever has to change 3 DOF when starting from a central, parallel view on the pattern.

(a) Intrinsic calibration pose   (b) Distortion calibration pose

Fig. 5. Exemplary view from the two pose categories

3   Method

To evaluate different user guidance options, we performed two user surveys, measuring the time the users required to match a series of target poses. The participants were students and co-workers at our lab. Most of them had never performed a camera calibration before and all users were using the tool for the first time. The pose sequence was given by our system [4].

The only instruction given was that the calibration pattern should be matched with the displayed overlay.

We triggered the time measurement only after the first target pose was reached. This explicitly discards the time the users needed to accommodate to the calibration scenario and the system setup.

For each question a separate survey was performed. The surveys were several months apart time-wise. Hence there is no overlap of participants and the pose setup varies slightly.

3.1   Relative Motion Survey

The goal of the first survey was to determine whether moving the camera or moving the calibration pattern is preferable. This takes advantage of the fact that only the relative orientation and translation between camera and pattern matters. Therefore we evaluated the following two scenarios:

1. Fixing the camera position at the screen and let the user move the pattern like in front of a virtual mirror.
2. Fixing the pattern position and let the user move the camera in a first-person-view like fashion.

There were 5 participants in this survey which successively tried both options. To exclude the effect of familiarization we randomized the order of the options.

The user guidance consisted only of the target pose overlay as shown in Fig. 5. There were 9 target poses that had to be matched.

3.2 Pattern Appearance Survey

Complementing the first survey, the second survey determined whether one can take advantage of the geometric property that the pattern can be flipped horizontally and vertically. To this end we chosen two different visualization of the calibration pattern as follows:

1. The asymmetric chessboard as in used for the preceding survey.
2. A quadrille paper visualization, which is fully symmetric yet still contains the necessary perspective cues.

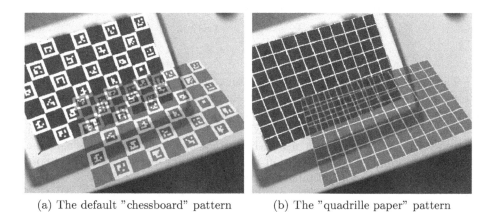

(a) The default "chessboard" pattern   (b) The "quadrille paper" pattern

Fig. 6. The two overlay patterns we evaluated in our second user survey. Note that we now do overpaint the real board in the video stream.

To keep the connection between the target pose overlay and the physical calibration board when using the new visualization, we overpaint the actual calibration target in the video stream - similarly to [3]. We also apply the over-painting to the first option (see Fig. 6) to exclude the effect of tracking imprecision from the survey.

There were 7 Participants in this survey which had to reach 10 target poses. As with the preceding survey the order of the options was randomized so 3 participants started with option 1 and 3 participants started with option 2.

We only used the "virtual mirror" setup based on the results from the first survey.

4   Results

In the following the results of our user surveys are shown. First we discuss the quantitative timings of each experiment. Then we also present some qualitative observations made during the trials.

4.1 Quantitative Results

Table 1 shows the quantitative results of the first survey, giving the per-user times as well as the overall average.

Table 1. Time the users required to reach 9 given target poses.

	t (first-person view)	t (virtual mirror)
User 1	1:39 min	1:44 min
User 2	3:17 min	1:08 min
User 3	2:46 min	1:55 min
User 4	7:22 min	1:36 min
User 5	2:22 min	1:25 min
Mean	3:29 min	1:33 min

The average calibration time of 1:33 min to complete the calibration show a strong advantage of the virtual mirror scenario over the first-person view approach with an average time of 3:29 min. Looking at the individual results we see that only User 1 is slightly faster using the first-person view, while all other Users were considerably faster using the virtual mirror approach. User 4 even struggles to complete the calibration using in the first-person view. Therefore we conclude that the virtual mirror approach is preferable.

Table 2. Time the users required to reach 10 given target poses with different visualizations

	t (chessboard)	t (quadrille paper)
User 1	2:14 min	1:00 min
User 2	2:07 min	1:20 min
User 3	3:06 min	2:11 min
User 4	3:43 min	3:20 min
User 5	1:21 min	1:44 min
User 6	1:52 min	2:00 min
Mean	2:24 min	1:56 min

Table 2 shows the results of the second survey, again giving the average as well as the per user times. There are only 6 results given as one participant failed to match the first intrinsic pose within 3 min with any method. Therefore we aborted the trial and no results are given.

The average time of 1:56 min to complete the calibration using the quadrille paper visualization shows a slight advantage over the chessboard visualization with 2:24 min. However looking at the individual results there are 2 participants being faster using the chessboard visualization. Furthermore there is strong variation between the individual users. Therefore no clear conclusion can be given.

4.2 Qualitative Results

Additionally to the times presented above we made the following qualitative observations:

- It took the participants much longer to match the intrinsic pose then the distortion pose.
- With the "quadrille paper" pattern, some users did not rotate the pattern to match the distortion calibration pose, but rather moved it out of view.
- The users reached a target pose faster if it was from the same category as the previous one; e.g. if a distortion pose followed a distortion pose. Conversely the needed to re-orient if e.g. a distortion pose followed a intrinsic pose.
- When asked about the experience users preferred the "quadrille paper" visualization - even if their calibration time was higher in this mode.

Here the time it took the participants to match the intrinsic pose was the determining factor in overall calibration time.

5 Conclusion

We have presented an evaluation of different user guidance methods for camera calibration. This allows us to give a recommendation that the "virtual mirror" setup is preferable for camera calibration. However the results of our second survey only hint that using the simplified "quadrille paper" overlay is of advantage. While the user feedback was generally positive and we measured a slight advantage in the average calibration time, there was a strong variation between the individual participants. Therefore a larger scale survey is necessary to give a definitive answer here.

However our qualitative observations indicate that larger gains are to be expected from adapting the pose sequence then from modifying the pattern visualization. Particularly the arbitrary switching between the pose categories requires physical and mental switching on the user side. Additionally we observed that matching 3 arbitrary rotations of the pattern to the target pose took considerably longer then to match the position.

Therefore the pose sequence should adapted to further improvements on user guidance. Currently the poses optimize the algorithmic constrains while neglecting the user. One option would be to find for a better compromise between these two objectives. Alternatively one could introduce "guidance only" poses that are placed between the current pattern position and the target pose. Those would not be used for calibration, but rather to give the user more hints on how to reach the target pose. Trivially one could insert the neutral pose between two calibration poses s.t. only 3 DOF change between each two displayed targets.

References

1. Chandler, P., Sweller, J.: Cognitive load theory and the format of instruction. Cogn. Instr. **8**(4), 293–332 (1991)
2. Garrido-Jurado, S., Muñoz-Salinas, R., Madrid-Cuevas, F.J., Marín-Jiménez, M.J.: Automatic generation and detection of highly reliable fiducial markers under occlusion. Pattern Recogn. **47**(6), 2280–2292 (2014)
3. Richardson, A., Strom, J., Olson, E.: AprilCal: assisted and repeatable camera calibration. In: Proceedings of the IEEE/RSJ International Conference on Intelligent Robots and Systems (IROS), November 2013
4. Rojtberg, P., Kuijper, A.: Efficient pose selection for interactive camera calibration. In: 2018 IEEE International Symposium on Mixed and Augmented Reality (ISMAR), pp. 31–36, October 2018
5. Sturm, P.F., Maybank, S.J.: On plane-based camera calibration: a general algorithm, singularities, applications. In: IEEE Computer Society Conference on Computer Vision and Pattern Recognition, vol. 1. IEEE (1999)
6. Zhang, Z.: A flexible new technique for camera calibration. IEEE Trans. Pattern Anal. Mach. Intell. **22**(11), 1330–1334 (2000)

Scaling Gain and Eyeheight While Locomoting in a Large VE

Betsy Williams-Sanders[1]([✉]), Tom Carr[2], Gayathri Narasimham[3],
Tim McNamara[3], John Rieser[3], and Bobby Bodenheimer[3]

[1] Rhodes College, Memphis, TN 38104, USA
sandersb@rhodes.edu
[2] Michigan State University, East Lansing, MI 48824, USA
[3] Vanderbilt University, Nashville, TN 37235, USA

Abstract. Virtual Environments (VEs) presented through head-mounted displays (HMDs) are often explored on foot. This type of exploration is useful since the inertial cues of physical locomotion aid spatial awareness. However, the size of the VE that can be explored on foot is limited to the dimensions of the tracking space of the HMD unless locomotion is somehow manipulated. This paper presents a system for exploring a large VE on foot when the size of the physical surroundings is small by leveraging people's natural ability to maintain spatial awareness using their own locomotion. We examine two strategies to increase the explorable size of the virtual space: scaling the translational gain of walking and scaling eyeheight. Translational gain is scaled by changing the relationship between physical and visual translation so that one step forward in physical space corresponds to several steps forward in virtual space. To scale gain higher than ten, it becomes necessary to investigate ways to minimize distracting small physical head motions. We present such a method here. We examine a range of scaling factors and find that we can expect to scale translational gain by a factor of 50. In addition to this finding, this paper also investigates whether scaling eyeheight proportionally to gain increases spatial awareness. We found that providing a map-like overview of the environment does not increase the user's spatial orientation in the VE.

Keywords: Virtual reality (VR) · Virtual environment (VE) ·
Space perception

1 Introduction

Virtual environments (VEs) provide people with opportunities to experience places and situations remote from their actual physical surroundings. Virtual reality systems potentially allow people to learn about an environment which, for reasons of time, distance, expense, and safety, would not otherwise be available. This work focuses on head-mounted display (HMD) technology because it is relatively inexpensive and readily available as compared to other immersive technologies.

© Springer Nature Switzerland AG 2019
J. Y. C. Chen and G. Fragomeni (Eds.): HCII 2019, LNCS 11574, pp. 277–298, 2019.
https://doi.org/10.1007/978-3-030-21607-8_22

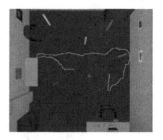

Fig. 1. This figure show a top-down view of a VE that is ≈5 m × 5 m with head motion a user "looking around" in yellow. (Color figure online)

Fig. 2. This example shows the same physical movement as Fig. 1, with virtual movement scaled by a factor of twenty.

Our work examines exploring an HMD-based VE by physically walking. By using physical locomotion, we seek to leverage the natural ability of people to maintain spatial orientation. This modality is natural for the HMD since HMD technology often uses a head tracker that measures changes in the orientation and the position of the user's head within the physical environment. Unfortunately, the finite range of the HMD tracking system, or, more importantly, the limited amount of space a commodity level user may have to devote to an HMD system, constrains the size of space that can be freely explored using bipedal locomotion. Of course, using some other type of locomotor interface such as a joystick to translate in an environment might be a solution, but bipedal locomotion results in much better spatial orientation [4].

Williams et al. [23] investigate increasing the translational gain of walking (where each step in physical space moves the user a longer distance through virtual space) as a viable method to explore a large VE. They present two experiments that show the translational gain of bipedal walking can be scaled, and this type of locomotion results in better spatial orientation compared to using a joystick. However, their experiments limit the scale of translational gain to a factor of ten, since head movements and other small movements become distracting at higher gains. This paper expands the findings of Williams et al. [23] and examines how far translational gain can be increased with the aid of engineering solutions to improve the problems of small head movements. At high translational gains small locomotive movements become disorienting, making it difficult to position oneself near stationary objects in the VE.

There are two potential issues to address when designing an algorithm to alleviate distracting head movements [7,23]. First, when people locomote at high rates of gain, a strategy must be employed to allow users to move locally in a natural way. That is, small head movements when the user is not locomoting to a new position need to be filtered or somehow minimized. For example, it is difficult and unnatural to maintain a fixed head position and rotate about that axis with the HMD. Consider the head movement of a user examining the contents of a VE from a center location as in Fig. 1 where locomotion in the physical space matches locomotion in the virtual space. In Fig. 2, this same physical movement is replicated, yet the translational gain is scaled by a factor of 20. In this example, simply turning to view the contents of the room amounts to considerable visual motion in the VE. Motions such as gazing around the room (Fig. 1) should not be scaled. Second, when users walk in an environment their heads may bob from side to side as they shift their weight. This side–to–side movement should not be scaled. Locomotion should only be scaled in the direction of intended travel. Although we did investigate this issue, we did not find it to be a problem at high rates of gain. Thus, our algorithm does not address side–to–side bob.

This work uses a nonlinear method of scaling gain to minimize the distracting effects of small head movements. The basic idea of the algorithm involves ramping to high gain when the user's speed reaches above a certain threshold. Experiments 1 and 2 aid in the creation and testing of our nonlinear scaling technique. As a second focus to this paper, we examine whether it may be advantageous to also scale eyeheight. We reasoned that scaling eyeheight could allow gain to be scaled even higher and allow us to gain more explorable space from our HMD system. Therefore, this work investigates whether a person's spatial orientation is improved when eyeheight is increased while locomoting through a virtual world at high rates of translational gain. We reasoned that increasing the eyeheight to explore a large VE could be useful when exploring an outdoor environment like a large city. Such a strategy would allow users to develop spatial orientation based on a map-like overview yet unlike virtual flying still give users the proprioceptive feedback of walking.

The main experiment of this work is found in Experiment 3 of Sect. 6. Here we directly compare linearly scaled translation gain (no correction of small head movements), nonlinearly scaled translational gain (minimizing the effects of small distracting head movements), and gain scaled proportionally to eyeheight. Specifically, we compare these three locomotion methods using four different scaling factors of translational gain: 10, 25, 50, and 100. We show that scaling gain nonlinearly is significantly superior to scaling gain linearly. Additionally, we find that people can maintain good spatial orientation with translational gains up to 50 using the nonlinear scaling technique presented in this paper. We find no significant advantage with respect to the user's spatial orientation when eyeheight is scaled.

2 Background

Much like in the real world, humans update their spatial knowledge or spatial awareness with respect to a VE as their relationship to objects in the environment change [25]. However, humans are more disoriented in VEs [4,8]. Thus, navigation, the most common way people interact with a VE [2], causes people to feel disorientated. Exploring a VE by physically walking seems to result in the best spatial awareness [4], but the size of the space that can be explored using a tracking system is limited without alternate interventions such as teleporting. Much work has looked at how best to explore a VE larger than the tracked space while maintaining spatial awareness [6,9,15,19,27,30]. These locomotion methods involve real walking, redirected walking, walking–in–place, teleporting, joystick, swimming, arm–swinging and more (for a literature review see [1]). Much of the more recent navigation work has focused on engaging the user in physical movement as it seems to result in better spatial awareness of the VE as compared to using a joystick [6,9,19,20,27].

The current work adds to the body of work on redirected walking [3,5,13,14, 19] as we are manipulating walking. Rieser et al. [16] and Mohler et al. [12] show that people can quickly recalibrate to a new mapping between their own physical translation and visual input. However, the scaling factor of the translational gain in these recalibration studies was significantly smaller than that which is investigated in this work. Kuhl [10] reports that people can also recalibrate rotations. A compelling reason to manipulate translations instead of rotations is that research shows that physical rotations are more disorienting than physical translations with respect to spatial orientation [16]. Moreover, rotations are not a problem; a user can turn through any distance of rotation in any space that is large enough to stand in. Williams et al. [23] show that the translational gain of walking can be scaled by a factor of ten and that there is no significant difference in spatial orientation when compared to exploring an environment using normal bipedal locomotion.

This work also examines the role of eyeheight when experiencing a VE. More specifically, eyeheight refers to the distance from the viewer's visual horizon to the ground (for more information, see [18]). An observer's eyeheight influences perception and action in the physical world; it is used to scale the distances of objects and to scale the height and width of apertures. In our everyday lives, we humans constantly change our viewing perspective by sitting, standing, etc., yet the perceived relative size of objects remains the same. This may be because of familiar size or previous knowledge about size and shape [28]. Additionally, the angle of declination from the horizon line to the ground also provides another source of information. People use this information to recalibrate the relative sizes of objects at different eyeheights [28]. Wraga et al. [28] compare seated, standing and ground–level prone observations and find that seated and standing observations are similar, but prone observations are significantly less accurate. Warren [21] finds that people judged whether they could sit on a surface according to whether the surface height exceeded 88% of their leg length. Moreover, people choose to climb or sit on a surface according to the relationship between the surface's height and their eyeheight [11].

3   Method for Minimizing Disorienting Head Movements

To investigate how high gain can be scaled, a method of scaling gain while minimizing these disorienting movements was devised. Informal user studies of participants at unfiltered high gain (100:1 and 50:1) revealed that small head movements were disorienting. More specifically, disorientation seemed to occur when the user's locomotion was minimal and they were simply trying to either perform a local task such as move a few feet, or observe the environment. Participants also reported that large gain factors seem more natural and much less disorienting if their own physical locomotion was above a certain rate. Thus, we sought a method to minimize this effect by targeting the problem of disorientation when gain is scaled by large factors at slow speeds.

In the experiments presented in this paper, users "ramp-up" to high gain based on the magnitude of their velocity, or speed. When users are not moving, but simply observing an environment, then their speed is low and the translational gain is also low. As they begin to locomote, their speed is increasingly scaled up to the desired gain. We refer to this method as nonlinear translational gain. In this nonlinear condition, once users reach a critical speed threshold all movements are scaled linearly by a scaling factor (or a simple linearly scaled translational gain). Speeds below the critical threshold are scaled nonlinearly according to a pre-specified function. Thus, for physical speeds between zero and the critical threshold speed, virtual speed is obtained by scaling physical speed according to this function. Suitable functions should be strictly monotonically increasing with an initial value equal to zero (for zero speeds) and value at the threshold equal to the threshold multiplied by the high gain scaling factor. An example of such a function is seen in Fig. 3 where speeds above the critical threshold of 0.5 m/s are scaled by a factor of 100. Speeds below 0.5 m/s are scaled according to a cubic function. User speed is calculated every time the graphics are updated, which was 60 Hz. Speed is defined as the distance between the user's position at the time of the graphics refresh (p_x, p_z) and the position of the preceding graphics refresh (p'_x, p'_z) divided by the refresh rate, $refreshRate$. To calculate the distance traveled we simply use the user's position in the x and z directions and ignored y direction idicating the user's viewing height. Thus, speed is calculated as follows: $speed = \frac{\sqrt{(p_x-p'_x)^2+(p_z-p'_z)^2}}{refreshRate}$. In "high gain mode" when gain is linearly scaled, calculating the new virtual position involves scaling the speed by the gain amount, $scale$. Thus, in high gain mode the virtual position in the new x and z positions in virtual space, v_x and v_z, can be obtained from

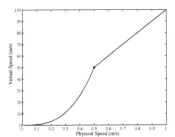

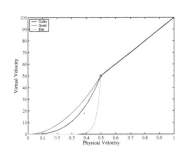

Fig. 3. This is figure shows a ramping cubic function used in Experiment 1. For speeds above 0.5 m/s gain was scaled by 100.

Fig. 4. This shows all three ramping functions evaluated in Experiment 2. For speeds above 0.5 m/s gain was scaled by 100.

the user's position at the previous and current frames: $v_x = v'_x + (p_x - p'_x) * scale$ and $v_z = v'_z + (p_z - p'_z) * scale$, where v'_x and v'_z represent virtual position from the previous frame.

There are many functions that meet the requirements for a ramping function, and beyond these requirements our goal was to select one which was pleasing from a user's perspective. Additionally, the value of the critical threshold itself needs to be determined. We evaluated the different functions using user studies. Thus, two experiments were designed to validate engineering choices for both the threshold and ramping functions. First, Experiment 1 examines the critical speed threshold at which a user should enter into linearly scaled high gain or linear gain. Experiment 2 evaluates three plausible functions used to scale speeds smaller than the critical threshold: an exponential, a cubic polynomial, and a quadratic polynomial. In the experiments there is a chicken-and-egg problem in that a ramping function cannot be derived without knowing the critical threshold, and determining a critical threshold assumes the use of some form of ramping function. In this work we do not examine this question exhaustively. Rather, we assume a cubic ramping function to determine the critical threshold, then assume this threshold is the best value for testing different ramping functions.

The mathematical details below describe the simple cubic function (Fig. 3). Below the critical threshold, the virtual speed, s_v, is described in terms of physical speed, s_p as follows: $s_v = s_p + c_1(s_p)^3$, where c_1 is a constant whose value depends on the gain level. Thus, the value of c_1 changes with each gain level. Above the critical threshold gain is scaled directly by the high gain amount. We use this simplistic form of the cubic because it has a desirable slope and has one solution. The function we use passes through (0,0). Thus, at a physical speed of $0\,m/s$, virtual speed is also $0\,m/s$. Subjects ramp up to high gain according to a function whose first derivative is not continuous. This discontinuity represents the boundary between normal walking and high gain. Interestingly, the discontinuity does not produce a noticeable artifact. We explore this idea further in Sect. 7.

Table 1. Values of the constants

Gain	Cubic	Quad	Exp
10	$c_1 = 129600$	$c_1 = 1080$	$c_1 = 1/433.794, c_2 = 433.794$
25	$c_1 = 345600$	$c_1 = 2880$	$c_1 = 1/575.341, c_2 = 575.341$
50	$c_1 = 705600$	$c_1 = 5880$	$c_1 = 1/677.594, c_2 = 677.594$
100	$c_1 = 1.4256e + 06$	$c_1 = 1.1880e + 04$	$c_1 = 1/776.954, c_2 = 776.954$

As an example we solve for c_1 at 100:1 gain and a critical threshold value of $0.5\,m/s$. The refresh rate of the graphics and tracking system has a direct impact on the values of the constants found in the above equation. For purposes of this example, let us assume that tracking updates every $1\,s$. At $0.5\,m/s$ speed should be scaled by 100, and values under $0.5\,\mathrm{m/s}$ should be scaled according to the cubic function. We know that at a physical speed of $0.5\,\mathrm{m/s}$ the virtual speed should be $50\,\mathrm{m/s}$ ($0.5\,\mathrm{m/s} * 100$). Thus, plugging in two known values, $s_p = 0.5$ and $s_v = 50$ gives us $50 = 0.5 + c_1(0.5)^3$, $c_1 = 396$. Thus, we scale gains lower than $0.5\,\mathrm{m/s}$ according to the following function: $s_v = s_p + 396(s_p)^3$, which, again, is plotted in Fig. 3. In our system, the graphics are refreshed every $60\,\mathrm{Hz}$. Therefore the constants change. Let us look again at the cubic function at 100:1 gain. Since we are updating the graphics every $\frac{1}{60}$ of a second, we would like a speed of $\frac{1}{60} * 0.5$ (or 0.0083) to map to $\frac{1}{60} * 50$ (or 0.8333) since each frame is $\frac{1}{60}$ of a second. Thus we solve for c_1 with these values $s_p = 0.0083$ and $s_v = .8333$ and find that the value of c_1 at 100:1 gain, a critical threshold of $0.5\,\mathrm{m/s}$, and a refresh rate of $60\,\mathrm{Hz}$, is $1.4256e + 06$. The constants for the quadratic and exponential ramping functions at each of the gain levels are found in a similar manner. The quadratic function we evaluated was: $s_v = s_p + c_1(s_p)^2$, and the exponential had the form $s_v = s_p + c_1 e^{c_2 s_p} - c_1$. We wanted the exponential function to be flat or have a small slope at small speeds so that gain would be scaled by a minimal amount. The values of the constants for a $1/60$ refresh rate are shown in Table 1. The three functions are plotted in Fig. 4.

4   Experiment 1: Finding the Critical Threshold

The purpose of this experiment was two-fold. First, this within–subject experiment investigates how rapidly users can switch from speed scaled by a function to the linearly scaled high-gain speed. This experiment examines two critical speed threshold values: $0.5\,\mathrm{m/s}$ and $1\,\mathrm{m/s}$ and compares these results to linearly scaled translation gain where there are no critical values and gain is simply scaled by the high-gain amount. Thus, the second objective of this experiment is to formally evaluate the use of this "ramp-up" function and investigate whether users feel that problems with disorienting small head movements have become negligible with the proposed method. In this experiment the high gain value or the highest scaled value of translational gain was fixed at 100:1. The scaling function used to scale speeds lower than the critical threshold speed value was a cubic polynomial (Fig. 3).

Six subjects participated in the experiment for compensation. Subjects were unfamiliar with the experiment and the VE. Subjects were asked to find and read three different Snellen eye charts which were arranged on the sides of buildings in a large outdoor VE. They were allowed to get as close as they liked and could readjust their position at any time. The ease of reading these charts allowed subjects to report a subjective measurement of the ease of localized movements or local locomotion in each condition. Subjects read three different charts for each condition because we wanted the subjects to get a feel for making small position changes in the VE in each condition. To understand the goal of the Snellen chart task, it is important to note the difficulty of controlling small movements when no "ramp up" function is used. When gain is simply scaled by 100, $1\,\mathrm{cm}$ of movement corresponds to $100\,\mathrm{cm}$ of virtual movement.

Therefore, it is challenging for users to position themselves in a precise location and hold their heads steady enough to read the small letters on the chart. They were also asked to find and walk to a series of seven objects in the VE that were a considerable distance apart. This task allowed subjects to report the ease of large-scale locomotion through the entire environment, which is referred to as global locomotion.

4.1 Materials

The virtual world was viewed through a full color stereo NVIS nVisor Head Mounted Display with 1280×1024 resolution per eye, a nominal field of view of $60°$ diagonally, and a frame rate of 60 Hz. The HMD weighs approximately 1 kg. An InterSense IS-900 tracker was used to update the participant's rotational movements around all three axes. Position was updated using two optical tracking cameras with an accuracy of <0.5 cm over a $3\,m \times 3\,m \times 3\,m$ volume and an update rate of 60 Hz. The size of the physical room in which the experiments were performed was approximately $5\,m \times 6\,m$, and within the room the limits of the tracking system was approximately 5 m by 5 m. The same $650\,m \times 650\,m$ large, outdoor environment was used in each of the conditions. The size of the Snellen eye charts that participants was instructed to read were approximately $0.7\,m \times 0.7\,m$ and the charts were randomly located on the sides of buildings that appeared in the environment. A ten line Snellen eye chart was randomly generated for each trial using software that is freely available [17]. The environment is pictured in Fig. 5. Buildings and other objects were scattered throughout the environment. These objects were of natural shape and size and were items that one would expect to see outdoors. Larger objects are positioned further away from the center of the environment and smaller objects were closer to the center enabling the viewing of all objects from the center of the environment. The seven target objects that the subjects had to walk to varied by trial but were such things as the front door of the cathedral, the water tower, the swing set, the entrance to the Panera building, the front of the hotel, the parking meter, the police car, etc.

4.2 Procedure

There were three conditions in this experiment: critical threshold speeds of 0 m/s (linear gain scaled by 100), 0.5 m/s, and of 1 m/s. Two conditions use a cubic polynomial to scale gain until a critical threshold speed is reached, then gain is simply scaled by 100. If speed drops below the critical value, then gain is again scaled according to the cubic function. Each of the six participants explored each environment under the three different critical thresholds (0.5 m/s, 1 m/s, and 0 m/s). Since there were six orders of three different critical threshold speeds, one subject was tested in each order in a counter-balanced fashion. The experimental procedure was explained to the participant prior to viewing the VE. Subjects were told what condition they were experiencing and were instructed to walk freely around the environment to familiarize themselves with the gain and the critical threshold of that condition. When the subject indicated to the experimenter that they felt comfortable with the environment, they were instructed to find the first Snellen eye chart and read as many lines down the Snellen chart as they felt comfortable. The subjects were allowed to position themselves as close to the Snellen chart as possible, and reading the smallest rows generally required subjects to be about two virtual feet away from the Snellen chart. After they had read as many rows as possible, they were instructed to find the second Snellen chart and read that set of letters, and continue on to the third Snellen chart.

After they had read as much of the charts as possible, participants were asked to find and locomote to seven different objects in the environment. The objects were far enough apart so that subjects were required to exceed the critical threshold speed and locomote at high gain to reach the objects. If subjects walked too slowly in the environment to reach an object, a situation could occur where they could not reach that object because they reached the limits of the tracking system first (or reached a physical wall). We refer to this error as an out-of-range target error. When this error occurred, the experimenter would slowly lead the subject backward in the physical environment so that they were moving at low gains backward in the VE. This was done until the experimenter felt that the subject had enough tracking space to reach the target object. This issue only had the potential to occur in the nonlinear conditions (or when there was a critical value equal to 0.5 m/s or 1 m/s). The frequency of this occurrence was recorded. The speed and accuracy of reading the Snellen chart was also recorded. The subject indicated to the experimenter that they were ready to read the chart. The experimenter then began timing the subject reading the Snellen chart and stopped the timer when the subject was finished reading the chart or when they indicated that they could no longer read the rest of the chart. Time was recorded using a stopwatch. After completing each condition, subjects were asked to rate the following on a scale from 1 to 10: local control, global control, sense of sickness, and sense of balance. Upon completing all three trials and the post-trial questions, subjects were asked to indicate what condition they preferred. They were also asked specifically if they found the scaling of side-to-side movement at high gain disorienting.

4.3 Results

The results of the post-condition tests are shown in Table 2. In each condition differentiated by critical threshold value, subjects were asked to rate the local control of their movement, the global control of their movement, their feeling of sickness, and their feeling of unbalancedness on a scale from 1 to 10. In the 0.5 m/s critical threshold condition, subjects felt the highest global control or sense of being able to control traveling around the environments for greater distances. They also felt control over local movements or locomotion needed to travel short distances. Participants felt the highest control over local movements with a 1 m/s critical threshold speed, yet their sense of global control was considerably less than when using the 0.5 m/s critical threshold. The linearly scaled

Table 2. Mean ratings of the post-condition test of Experiment 1

Critical threshold	Mean user ratings			
	Local control	Global control	Sickness	Unbalanced
0	1.5 (0.5)	7.2 (1.5)	5.8 (2.4)	4.1 (1.8)
0.5	7.8 (1.3)	8.2 (1.3)	1.3 (0.5)	1.8 (0.7)
1	8.1 (1.1)	6.1 (2.3)	2.1 (0.7)	2.4 (0.9)

Note: One represents "No" feeling while ten represents a strong feeling.
Standard errors are indicated by parentheses.

gain (or 0 m/s critical threshold speed) provided very little local control and reasonable global control. The linearly scaled gain condition made people feel nauseated and altered their sense of balance. People rarely felt these effects in the other two nonlinear gain conditions.

When asked to rate which method they prefer best, four of the six participants preferred a critical threshold of 0.5 m/s, while the other two preferred the 1 m/s critical threshold. One of the subjects that preferred the 1 m/s over the 0.5 m/s condition found reading the Snellen charts easier in the 1 m/s condition yet preferred 0.5 m/s for walking long distances. Overall, subjects found the 0.5 m/s felt "most natural" for doing both local and global locomotion. Interestingly, four of the six subjects in the 1 m/s condition had problems reaching their target objects in a few of their trials because they did not travel fast enough and ran out of tracking space. This out-of-range target error only occurred once in the 0.5 m/s critical threshold condition across all of the subjects. As for reading the Snellen charts, in the 0.5 m/s condition, it took participants an average of 105 s to read the chart with an average of 0.3 mistakes per chart. This means on average, subjects did not make a mistake reading the chart. However, after reading approximately three charts, they would be more likely to make a mistake. Similarly, for the 1 m/s critical threshold value, Snellen charts were read at an average of 111 s and were done so with an average of 0.28 mistakes per chart. In the linearly scaled gain condition, no subject was able to read the last three lines of the Snellen chart. On average, they could discern a few letters on the fourth to last line, but usually stopped because they felt uncomfortable. At the end of the experiment subjects indicated whether they felt side-to-side movements while walking at high gain was disorienting. None of the subjects found this disorienting or thought any method of filtering needed to be employed.

We find that a critical value of 0.5 m/s is best since it provides a nice compromise between global and local control. Users can travel longer distances with little physical space, yet small head movements are not as distracting and disorienting as the linearly scaled gain. We also found that the 0.5 m/s threshold resulted in little or no sickness. Users also had the best sense of balance as compared to the other conditions. Thus, we use a critical value of 0.5 m/s for the remainder of this paper. Future work might involve using a more exhaustive experiment to find a more precise value of the critical threshold. However, given the good user evaluations of this method, we feel that 0.5 m/s represents a reasonable critical threshold. Some of the user comments about the method were: "stepping on the gas in a car", "felt in control of their locomotion even though they were really moving fast", "Wow, this is cool." With no filtering several subjects noted that positioning themselves in front of the Snellen chart was "particularly difficult."

5   Experiment 2: Finding the "Ramping" Function

Six subjects participated in this experiment and were given compensation for their participation. The subjects were unfamiliar with the experiment and the VE. The materials used in this condition were the same as Experiment 1. The procedure for this experiment was almost the same as Experiment 1. However, the difference was that participants experienced different ramping functions in each of the three conditions. The critical threshold speed was fixed at 0.5 m/s. Additionally, in this experiment they were not told which condition they were experiencing. They were again asked to read three Snellen charts and locomote to seven target objects. After each condition, subjects rated their experiences. After completion of all three conditions, subjects indicated which condition they preferred best.

Table 3. The mean ratings of the post-condition test of Experiment 2

Ramping function	Mean user ratings			
	Local control	Global control	Sickness	Unbalanced
Quadratic	6.9 (1.9)	8.3 (1.1)	3.4 (1.8)	1.4 (0.5)
Cubic	7.9 (1.5)	8.1 (1.2)	1.4 (0.4)	1.8 (0.5)
Exponential	8.3 (1.3)	8.5 (0.9)	1.3 (0.4)	1.7 (0.5)

Note: One represents "No" feeling while ten represents a strong feeling. Standard errors are indicated by parentheses.

The results of the post-condition questionnaire are presented in Table 3. In all of the conditions, subjects felt a high amount of global control and local control. The quadratic function had the lowest local control. From observing the three functions in Fig. 4, we can see that gain is scaled higher at smaller speeds for the quadratic function than the other two functions. People felt a slight sense of sickness in the quadratic condition as well, an effect that was not observed with the cubic and exponential functions. Since subjects were not told what condition they were experiencing, they were asked which condition they like best by the order of experience. Four of the six participants preferred the exponential function, while the other two preferred the cubic function. The average time to completely read the Snellen chart in the exponential condition was 112 s and the average time to read the cubic was 109 s. On average participants were unable to completely read the last line of the chart in the quadratic condition.

Again, subjects were asked about the side-to-side movement when speed is linearly scaled in high gain and it was also not an issue in this experiment. Overall, the exponential function performs best; compared to the other two methods, it seems to give the user the highest amount of global and local control. Upon examining the functions in Fig. 4, the exponential has a smaller slope at small speeds which gives it an increased local control. Thus, our nonlinear scaling method involves an exponential "ramping" function with a 0.5 m/s critical threshold.

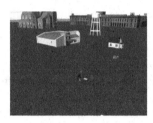

Fig. 5. This figure shows a view of the VE used in the experiments at normal eyeheight (≈1.67 m.)

Fig. 6. This figure represents 10 times normal eyeheight (≈16.7 m). Gaze is directed downward by 20°.

Fig. 7. This figure represents 25 times normal eyeheight (≈41.7 m). Gaze is directed downward by 30°.

Fig. 8. This figure represents 50 times normal eyeheight. Gaze is directed downward by 35°.

Fig. 9. This figure represents 100 times normal eyeheight. Gaze is directed downward by 40°.

6   Experiment 3

Having selected the ramping function and threshold, we are now in a position to examine the limits of scaling translational gain. Thus, in this experiment, the goal was to assess how well subjects could maintain spatial orientation when the gain of translation in the virtual environment was varied relative to translation in the physical environment. More specifically, we wanted to find the limit to which gain can be scaled under three different conditions: linearly scaled gain, nonlinearly scaled gain, and linearly scaled gain with eyeheight scaled. The subjects' spatial orientation was tested in each of the five translational gain conditions: 1:1, 10:1, 25:1, 50:1, and 100:1. To test orientation, subjects were asked to remember the location of five objects in the environment, then to move themselves to a new point of observation and instructed to turn to face the targets from memory without vision. Each subject performed the task in each of the five gain scales under one of three conditions: linearly scaled gain, nonlinearly scaled gain, and linear gain scaled proportionally to eyeheight.

Forty-five subjects participated in the experiment. Subjects were unfamiliar with the experiment and the VE. Subjects were given compensation for their participation.

6.1   Materials

The same HMD system that was used in Experiments 1 and 2 was used in this experiment. Also, the same 650 m × 650 m large outdoor VE was used in this experiment for all of the gain conditions. Figures 5, 6, 7, 8 and 9 show the VE used in this experiment. These figures give a glimpse of the VE at each of the different scaled eyeheights. The explorable region of the VE changed according to the size of the gain in each of the different conditions. The size of the explorable region in the 10:1 condition was 50 m × 50 m or 10 times the size of the explorable region in the 1:1 condition. Similarly, the virtually explorable region for the 25:1, 50:1, and 100:1 conditions was 125 m × 125 m, 250 m × 250 m, and 500 m × 500 m, respectively. In each environment, subjects were asked to memorize the location of five objects differing in shape and size. An example of one of the five objects in the 1:1 environment was a fire hydrant. Example objects in the 10:1, 25:1, 50:1, and 100:1 environments are a picnic table, an 18-wheel truck, a church, and a tall hotel, respectively. These five target objects were arranged in a particular configuration, such that the configuration in the 1:1, 10:1, 25:1, 50:1, and 100:1 conditions varied only in scale (1, 10, 25, 50, and 100, respectively), and by a rotation about the center axis. In this manner, the five objects were arranged similarly in the two environments so that the angles between the target objects were preserved.

6.2   Procedure

One-third of the subjects performed the experiment in the linearly scaled gain condition, one-third performed the experiment in the nonlinearly scaled gain condition, and the last third performed the experiment with linear gain and eyeheight scaled proportionally. Translational gain was defined as the rate of translational flow in the VE that mapped onto a given amount of motor activity. In all three conditions, rotation in the VE matched rotation in the physical environment. In the 1:1, 10:1, 25:1, 50:1, and 100:1 conditions, the translational gain of the tracker was scaled by one, scaled by 10, scaled by 25, scaled by 50 and scaled by 100, respectively. Since there were 120 orders of the five gain conditions, subjects were tested in a pseudo-balanced fashion using a Latin square design.

Given the five gain conditions and 15 subjects, we used three Latin squares to counterbalance our testing. Full details can be found in [22].

The experimental procedure was fully explained to the subjects prior to seeing the VEs. After about three minutes of study, the experimenter tested the subjects by having them walk to various targets, close their eyes, and point to randomly selected targets. This testing and learning procedure was repeated until the subject felt confident that the configuration had been learned and the experimenter agreed.

Participants' spatial orientation was tested from five different locations. A given testing position and orientation were indicated to the subject by the appearance of a tall red rod and an avatar in the environment. Subjects were instructed to locomote to the red rod, position themselves near it and face the avatar. At each testing location, the subject completed three trials by turning to face three different target objects in the environment, making 15 trials per condition. Specifically, subjects were instructed, "Close your eyes and turn to face the ⟨target name⟩." After each trial, subjects were instructed to rotate back to their starting position facing the avatar. To compare the angles of correct responses across conditions, the same trials were used for each condition. The testing location and target locations were analogous in all conditions. The trials were designed so that the angle of correct response was evenly distributed in the range of 20–180°. Once the subject reached a testing location (the red rod), they were not allowed to look at the target objects as the objects were made invisible. They were, however, encouraged to re-orient themselves after finishing each testing position and locomoting to the next test position.

In the eyeheight condition, gain was scaled proportionally to eyeheight. In the 10:1, 25:1, 50:1, and 100:1 conditions users experienced the environment from a new viewing height. The target objects appeared smaller to the user since their eyeheight was elevated. Moreover, targets were observed by looking down. In this experiment eyeheight and gain were coupled. We considered a few different potential experimental designs for this experiment. We chose to run an experiment where gain was scaled proportionally to eyeheight. Other designs are possible. We could have held gain constant, but findings would have been specific to a particular gain. Running several such conditions at different gains was considered too cumbersome. An advantage of investigating eyeheight scaled proportionally to gain is that we are not limiting ourselves to findings relative to a particular gain. Another possible experimental design was to fix eyeheight and vary the gains, but Experiment 3 already gives us results for eyeheight fixed at one eyeheight, natural eye level. Thus, we felt that we could gain the most knowledge in a practical experiment by scaling gain proportional to eyeheight. However, the disadvantage of choosing this experiment is that eyeheight and gain are confounded.

To assess the degree of difficulty of updating orientation relative to objects in the VE, latencies and errors were recorded. Latencies were measured from the time when the target was identified until subjects said they had completed their turning movement and were facing the target. Turning errors were measured as the absolute value of the difference in the subjects' actual facing direction minus the correct facing direction. The subjects indicated to the experimenter that they were facing the target by verbal instruction, and the experimenter recorded their time and rotational position. The time was recorded using a stopwatch, and the rotational position was recorded using the InterSense tracker. Subjects were encouraged to respond as rapidly as possible while maintaining accuracy.

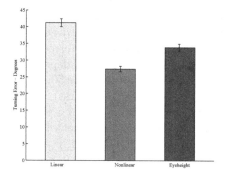

Fig. 10. This figure represents the mean turning error of each conditions: Linear, Nonlinear, and scaled Eyeheight. Error bars show standard errors of the mean.

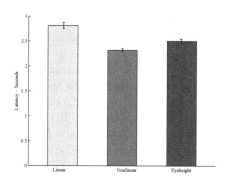

Fig. 11. This figure represents the mean latency of each condition: Linear, Nonlinear, and scaled Eyeheight. Error bars show standard errors of the mean.

6.3   Results

Figures 10 and 11 show the mean errors and latency collapsed across gain in the linearly scaled gain, nonlinearly scaled gain, and eyeheight condition. Figures 12, 13, 14, 15, 16 and 17 show the mean turning error and latency across different subjects, in the different experiment conditions (linear and nonlinear), and with different levels of translational gain (1:1, 10:1, 25:1, 50:1, and 100:1).

The linear and nonlinear gain data of this experiment were analyzed with five gain conditions. We first examine the effects of the levels of translational gain in the two different experimental conditions of linear and nonlinear gain. All subjects were tested on different levels of translational gain, hence gain was a within-subjects factor; subjects were tested in one of the three experimental conditions, hence experimental condition was between-subjects. Separate analyses were done for each of the two dependent variables, turning error and latency. A multivariate repeated measures analysis on mean turning error showed main effects of gain, $F(4, 112) = 10.6, p < .001$, experiment condition, $F(1, 28) = 13.3$, $p = .001$, and a significant interaction of the two, $F(4, 112) = 2.6, p = .05$. Participants' errors were greater in the 1:1 and 100:1 gain levels, as well as in the linear gain experiment condition, than in other gain levels or in the nonlinear gain condition. Planned comparisons revealed that in the nonlinear gain condition, turning errors in the 1:1 gain level were significantly different from errors in the 10:1, 25:1, and 50:1 levels, but not from the 100:1 level. Interestingly, in the

linear gain condition, errors at the 1:1, 10:1, 25:1, and 50:1 levels were all significantly different from errors at the 100:1 gain level. A similar within subjects
analyses on mean latency showed a main effect of gain, $F(4, 112) = 3.7$, $p < .05$,
a marginal effect of the experiment condition, $F(1, 28) = 3.9$, $p = .06$, and no
significant interaction. In both the linear and nonlinear gain, participants were
faster in the 10:1, 25:1, and 50:1 gain levels, and slower in the 1:1 and 100:1
levels. These differences were significant in the nonlinear gain condition but not
in the linear gain condition.

Analyses with order, experiment condition, and gain levels follow. We used
three Latin squares to complete a counterbalanced array for 15 subjects at 5
different conditions. Thus, three subjects from each group had performed the
experiment first in a given condition. A mixed model analysis on the dependent
variable turning error, with translational gain levels (1:1, 10:1, 25:1, 50:1, and
100:1) and order (1:1 first, 10:1 first, 25:1 first, 50:1 first, 100:1 first) within
group, and experiment condition (eyeheight, linear, nonlinear) between groups,
showed a main effect of gain $F(4, 120) = 9.7, p < .001$; a main effect of order
$F(4, 30) = 2.6$, $p = .05$, and a main effect of condition $F(2, 30) = 7.4$, $p < .005$.
Only the gain by condition interaction was significant, $F(8, 120) = 2.9$, $p < .05$.
Participants were liable to make more errors in the 1:1 and 100:1 gain levels,
more errors when they had the 10:1 gain level first in the eye-height condition
(one-way $F(4, 10) = 4.1$, $p < .05$) and the 50:1 gain level first in the linear
gain condition (one-way $F(4, 10) = 5.5$, $p < .05$). Overall participants made the
fewest errors in the nonlinear gain condition. When we repeated the analyses
without the 1:1 gain level (i.e., with only four gain levels), we obtained similar
main effects of gain, order, and condition but no interactions were significant.
A similar analysis on latency as the dependent variable showed a main effect of
gain, $F(4, 120) = 4.1$, $p = .02$, but no effect of order or condition. The gain by

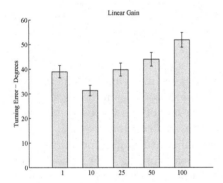

Fig. 12. This figure shows the mean
turning errors in the Linear Gain condition for each of the translational gains.
Error bars represent standard errors of
the mean.

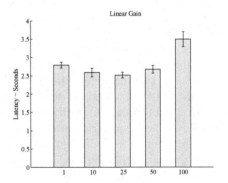

Fig. 13. This figure shows the mean
latencies in the Linear Gain condition
for each of the translational gains. Error
bars represent standard errors of the
mean.

order interaction was significant, $F(16, 120) = 3.6$, $p = .001$. There were no other significant interactions. In general participants were slower in responding to the gain levels that they first performed, however overall most participants took longer to respond when they started with the 100:1 and 10:1 gain levels. These results did not change when we removed the 1:1 gain level from the analyses.

We report the effects of three experimental conditions (linear, nonlinear, and eyeheight) analyzed without the 1:1 data in all of the conditions. We started by testing for effects of the levels of translational gain (four), in the three different experimental conditions. All subjects were tested on different levels of translational gain, hence gain was a within-subjects factor; subjects were tested in one of the three experimental conditions, hence experiment condition was between-subjects. Separate analyses were done for each of the two dependent variables, turning error and latency. A multivariate repeated measures analysis on mean turning error showed main effects of gain, $F(3, 126) = 11.4$, $p < .001$, and experiment condition, $F(2, 42) = 7.6$, $p = .002$, but no significant interaction. Participants' errors were less in the 10:1 gain level, and increased as gain increased; participants' errors were also less in the nonlinear gain condition than in the other two experimental groups. Planned comparisons revealed that errors in the 10:1 gain level were significantly lower than errors in the 50:1 ($t(44) = -2.4$, $p < .05$), and errors in the 10:1, 25:1 and 50:1 gain levels were all lower than errors in the 100:1 gain level (all $t > 3$, $p < .001$). A similar within–subjects analyses on mean latency showed a main effect of gain, $F(3, 126) = 3.9$, $p < .05$, no significant effect of the experimental condition, and no significant interaction. Similar to error, planned comparisons revealed that participants were faster to respond in the 10:1, 25:1, and 50:1 gain levels, than in the 100:1 gain level, all $t > 2$, $p < .05$.

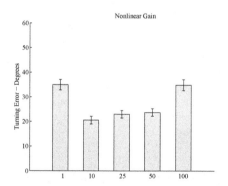

Fig. 14. This figure shows the mean turning errors in the Nonlinear Gain condition for each of the translational gains. Error bars represent standard errors of the mean.

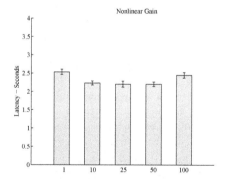

Fig. 15. This figure shows the mean latencies in the Nonlinear Gain condition for each of the translational gains. Error bars represent standard errors of the mean.

7   Discussion

This paper looks at how high gain can be scaled. Increasing the user's eyeheight proportional to gain was added as an extra factor in the experimental design. Eyeheight could potentially aid in spatial orientation and this warranted further investigation. The results of this work suggest further techniques on how best to build a virtual HMD system when the size of the tracking space is small.

Three experiments are presented in this paper. The first two experiments investigate a method of minimizing small head movements when gain is scaled higher than ten. A user study indicates two movements that were particularly distracting in high gain: simply looking around the environment and localized movements. Thus the method of ramping up to high gain discussed in this work minimizes these effects. Experiment 1 reports that subjects preferred a 0.5 m/s critical threshold because they were able to control local and global movements. This critical speed threshold is found using a cubic function to move into a linearly scaled translational gain. In Experiment 2, the critical threshold value is fixed at 0.5 m/s, and we find that subjects preferred an exponential ramping function.

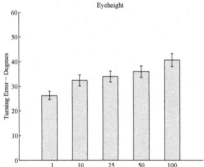

Fig. 16. This figure shows the mean turning errors in the scaled Eyeheight condition for each of the translational gains. Error bars represent standard errors of the mean.

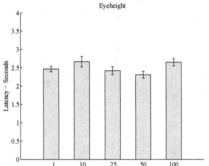

Fig. 17. This figure shows the mean latencies in the scaled Eyeheight condition for each of the translational gains. Error bars represent standard errors of the mean.

The results of Experiment 1 suggest that using this ramping function is an effective method of minimizing the visible effects of small head movements. We test this more closely in Experiment 3 using four different gain values (10:1, 25:1, 50:1, 100:1). Experiment 3 further reveals that using the ramping function results in better spatial orientation than simply scaling gain linearly. Turning errors in this condition are significantly better than the linearly scaled gain. There is also a marginal effect of nonlinearly scaling gain on latency. This marginal effect of faster responses in the nonlinear gain condition could suggest that people are more spatially oriented, but definitely shows that people were not making speed accuracy trade-offs. Experiment 3 also shows that scaling eyeheight proportionally to gain did not aid in spatial orientation as compared to linearly scaling gain.

This work shows that scaling gain nonlinearly is an effective method of exploring a large VEs for gains up to 50. According to results of Experiment 3, turning errors and latencies get significantly worse at 100:1, making 100:1 an unreasonable choice for allowing users to explore a VE and expecting them to maintain spatial orientation. At 50:1, turning errors and latencies are statistically the same as the 10:1 and 25:1 levels. Performance is better at the 50:1 gain than at the 1:1 gain. Thus, with a tracked HMD system, one can expect to explore a virtual space 50 times the size of the tracked space. For example, a 5 m by 5 m tracked HMD space allows users to explore a virtual space that is 250 m by 250 m. This increase is a huge space gain.

In Experiment 3, we also looked at spatial orientation when eyeheight was scaled proportionally to gain. Our motivation for doing this was that virtual reality allows user to experience environments in ways that they could not normally in the real world. Thus, we hypothesized that manipulating eyeheight could give the user an advantage when exploring a large city where the user would have a map-like overview of the environment. However, we found that scaling the eyeheight proportionally to gain does not result in better spatial orientation than scaling gain using the user's normal eyeheight. Raising the eyeheight did bring up an interesting issue about viewing angle with HMDs and its role on our ability to be spatially oriented in an environment.

We conjectured that the high errors in the 1:1 condition of Experiment 3 occurred because the objects appeared on the ground and users had to look downward to view and memorize the locations of the objects in this condition as opposed to more naturally viewing them in the other conditions. Williams et al. [26] looked specifically at people's ability to learn the spatial layout of objects at different viewing angles by having subjects memorize objects of different heights across conditions. They found no effect of viewing angle. Attempting to replicate this result with more controlled factors is a subject for future work.

Simply scaling translation gain is not the final answer to the problem of exploring large VEs, however. Inevitably, the physical limits of the tracking system will be reached. Our related research presents methods that were developed to intervene with users when they reach the end of their physical space by changing their location in physical space while maintaining their spatial orientation and location in the virtual environment [23,24]. This system of interventions, called resets, can be combined with the system of scaled translational gain described here [29]. Xie et al. [29] used such a system to navigate in a VE that measured 750 m by 750 m with turning errors close to those in this paper. Several factors remain to be engineered before this becomes a practical system, but this work and Xie et al. [29] may form the basis for a system that can allow users to freely explore vast VEs.

Finally, although our results regarding eyeheight were disappointing, we feel it is too early to dismiss it as a modality for navigating in a VE. Experiment 3 raises some interesting questions regarding the role of eyeheight on spatial orientation in a VE. We would like to revisit this topic in future work. Specifically, we would like to fix eyeheight relative to different gains. We feel that increasing eyeheight proportionally to gain in our experiments resulted in participants being too high in the VE.

Acknowledgements. This material is based upon work supported by the National Science Foundation under grant 1351212. Any opinions, findings, and conclusions or recommendations expressed in this material are those of the authors and do not necessarily reflect the views of the sponsors. We thank the Rhodes College Fellowship program for also supporting this research.

References

1. Boletsis, C.: The new era of virtual reality locomotion: a systematic literature review of techniques and a proposed typology. Multimodal Technol. Interact. **1**(4), 24 (2017)
2. Bowman, D., Kruijff, E., LaViola, J., Poupyrev, I.: 3D User Interfaces: Theory and Practice. Addison-Wesley, Redwood City (2004)
3. Bruder, G., Lubas, P., Steinicke, F.: Cognitive resource demands of redirected walking. IEEE Trans. Visual Comput. Graphics **21**(4), 539–544 (2015)
4. Darken, R.P., Peterson, B.: Spatial orientation, wayfinding, and representation (2014)
5. Grechkin, T., Thomas, J., Azmandian, M., Bolas, M., Suma, E.: Revisiting detection thresholds for redirected walking: combining translation and curvature gains. In: Proceedings of the ACM Symposium on Applied Perception, pp. 113–120. ACM (2016)
6. Hashemian, A.M., Riecke, B.E.: Leaning-based 360° interfaces: investigating virtual reality navigation interfaces with leaning-based-translation and full-rotation. In: Lackey, S., Chen, J. (eds.) VAMR 2017. LNCS, vol. 10280, pp. 15–32. Springer, Cham (2017). https://doi.org/10.1007/978-3-319-57987-0_2
7. Interrante, V., Ries, B., Anderson, L.: Seven league boots: a new metaphor for augmented locomotion through moderately large scale IVEs. In: IEEE Symposium on 3D UIs, pp. 167–170, March 2007
8. Kelly, J., Donaldson, L., Sjolund, L., Freiberg, J.: More than just perception-action recalibration: walking through a VE causes rescaling of perceived space. Attn. Perc. Psych. **75**, 1473–1485 (2013)
9. Kitson, A., Hashemian, A.M., Stepanova, E.R., Kruijff, E., Riecke, B.E.: Lean into it: exploring leaning-based motion cueing interfaces for virtual reality movement. In: IEEE VR, pp. 215–216 (2017)
10. Kuhl, S.A.: Recalibration of rotational locomotion in immersive virtual environments. In: APGV 2004: Proceedings of the 1st Symposium on Applied Perception in Graphics and Visualization, pp. 23–26, August 2004
11. Mark, L.: Eyeheight-scaled information about affordances: a study of sitting and stair climbing. J. Exp. Psychol. Hum. Perc. Perf. **13**, 361–370 (1987)

12. Mohler, B.J., Thompson, W.B., Creem-Regehr, S.H., Willemsen, P., Pick Jr., H.L., Rieser, J.J.: Calibration of locomotion resulting from visual motion in a treadmill-based virtual environment. ACM Trans. Appl. Percept. **4**(1), 4 (2007)
13. Nguyen, A., Rothacher, Y., Kunz, A., Brugger, P., Lenggenhager, B.: Effect of environment size on curvature redirected walking thresholds. In: 2018 IEEE Conference on Virtual Reality and 3D User Interfaces (VR), pp. 645–646. IEEE (2018)
14. Razzaque, S., Kohn, Z., Whitton, M.C.: Redirected walking. In: Proceedings of EUROGRAPHICS, vol. 9, pp. 105–106. Citeseer (2001)
15. Riecke, B.E., Bodenheimer, B., McNamara, T.P., Williams, B., Peng, P., Feuereissen, D.: Do we need to walk for effective VR navigation? physical rotations alone may suffice. In: 7th International Conference on Spatial Cognition, pp. 234–247 (2010)
16. Rieser, J.J., Pick, H.L., Ashmead, D.A., Garing, A.E.: The calibration of human locomotion and models of perceptual-motor organization. J. Exp. Psychol. Hum. Perc. Perf. **21**, 480–497 (1995)
17. Saksida, A.: Alejandro saksida's ultimate random snellen eye chart generator. http://i-see.org/random_snellen/random_snellen.html
18. Sedgwick, H.A.: The geometry of spatial layout in pictorial representation. In: Hagen, M. (ed.) The Perception of Pictures, pp. 33–90. Academic Press, New York (1980)
19. Suma, E., Bruder, G., Steinicke, F., Krum, D., Bolas, M.: A taxonomy for deploying redirection techniques in immersive VE. In: IEEE VR, pp. 43–46 (2012)
20. Waller, D., Hodgson, E.: Sensory contributions to spatial knowledge of real and virtual environments. In: Steinicke, F., Visell, Y., Campos, J., Lécuyer, A. (eds.) Human Walking in VEs, pp. 3–26. Springer, New York (2013). https://doi.org/10.1007/978-1-4419-8432-6_1
21. Warren, W.H.: Perceiving affordances: visual guidance of stair climbing. J. Exp. Psychol. Hum. Perc. Perf. **10**, 683–703 (1984)
22. Williams, B.: Design and evaluation of methods for motor exploration in large virtual environments with head-mounted display technology. Ph.D. thesis, Vanderbilt University, Nashville, Tennessee, USA (2008)
23. Williams, B., Narasimham, G., McNamara, T.P., Carr, T.H., Rieser, J.J., Bodenheimer, B.: Updating orientation in large VEs using scaled translational gain. In: ACM APGV, pp. 21–28 (2006)
24. Williams, B., et al.: Exploring large virtual environments with an HMD when physical space is limited. In: APGV 2007: Proceedings of the 4th Symposium on Applied Perception in Graphics and Visualization. ACM Press, New York (2007)
25. Williams, B., Narasimham, G., Westerman, Rieser, J., Bodenheimer, B.: Functional similarities in spatial representations between real and VEs. TAP **4**(2) (2007)
26. Williams, B., Wilson, P.T., Narasimham, G., McNamara, T.P., Rieser, J., Bodenheimer, B.: Does neck viewing angle affect spatial orientation in an HMD-based VE? In: Proceedings of the ACM Symposium on Applied Perception, SAP 2013, pp. 111–114. ACM, New York (2013). https://doi.org/10.1145/2492494.2492516
27. Wilson, P., Kalescky, W., MacLaughlin, A., Williams, B.: VR locomotion: walking > walking in place > arm swinging. In: ACM VRCAI, pp. 243–249 (2016)
28. Wraga, M.: Using eye height in different postures to scale the heights of objects. J. Exp. Psychol. Hum. Perc. Perf. **25**, 518–530 (1999)

29. Xie, X., et al.: A system for exploring large VES that combines scaled translational gain and interventions. In: APGV 2010: Proceedings of the 7th Symposium on Applied Perception in Graphics and Visualization, pp. 65–72. ACM, New York (2010)
30. Zielasko, D., Horn, S., Freitag, S., Weyers, B., Kuhlen, T.W.: Evaluation of hands-free HMD-based navigation techniques for immersive data analysis. In: IEEE 3DUI, pp. 113–119 (2016)

Emergency Response Using HoloLens for Building Evacuation

Sharad Sharma[1]([✉]) [iD], Sri Teja Bodempudi[1], David Scribner[2],
Jock Grynovicki[2], and Peter Grazaitis[2]

[1] Department of Computer Science, Bowie State University, Bowie, MD, USA
ssharma@bowiestate.edu
[2] Army Research Laboratory,
Aberdeen Proving Ground, Aberdeen, MD 21005, USA

Abstract. Emergency response in indoor building evacuation is needed for rescue and safety management. One of the challenges is to provide user-specific personalized evacuation routes in real time. Early hands-on experiences with the Microsoft HoloLens augmented/mixed reality device have given promising results for building evacuation applications. A range of use cases are tested, including data visualization and immersive data spaces, in-situ visualization of 3D models and full-scale architectural form visualization. We present how the mixed reality technology can provide spatial contextualized 3D visualization that promotes knowledge acquisition and support cognitive mapping. Our HoloLens application gives a visual representation of a building in 3D space, allowing people to see where exits are in the building. It also gives a path to the various exits; a shortest path to the exits as well as directions to a safe zone from their current position. This paper describes the system architecture and implementation of the augmented reality application to leverage the Microsoft HoloLens for emergency response during a building evacuation. The experimental results show the effectiveness of our Microsoft HoloLens application in an emergency evacuation by offering 3D visualizations of multilevel spaces while adding the spatial context that allows the individual to better understand their position and evacuation path when evacuation is necessary. We believe that AR technologies like HoloLens could be adopted by people for building evacuating during emergencies as it offers enriched experience in navigating large-scale environments.

Keywords: Augmented reality · Immersive AR · Microsoft HoloLens · Building evacuation · Mixed reality

1 Introduction

Augmented reality (AR) is an emerging technology that has the potential to transform the way we interact about the built environment during emergency response for decision making. Traditionally, 2D maps are used in the building to show users where they are and the available exits in the building. The 2D maps help the patrons form a mental representation of the building for emergency response. We hope that our research will aid in inspiring future applications of AR in emergency management to

J. Y. C. Chen and G. Fragomeni (Eds.): HCII 2019, LNCS 11574, pp. 299–311, 2019.
https://doi.org/10.1007/978-3-030-21607-8_23

replace 2D maps with 3D visualization with a better understanding of space, mitigate risk, and improve public safety. AR could be used to add spatial context in the building that will allow users to better understand their position within it. We propose that emergency response and emergency preparedness in a building is influenced by the presence of evacuation maps, the ability to display, interact with it, a cognitive mapping of a built environment, and explore the information using AR. We have introduced a series of permanent assets in the buildings (such as room numbers, boards, displays as markers) to enhance spatial perception, and situational awareness of multilevel spaces through proprioceptive affordances of situated AR evacuation displays. The permanent assets are used for finding the current location of the user if GPS and wireless are not available in emergencies. They trigger the visualization of 3D floor plans with layered situational data.

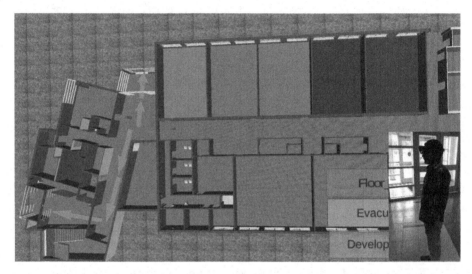

Fig. 1. View of the floor-plan from HoloLens using existing 2D plans and room numbers as markers

Figure 1 shows the floor plan from the HoloLens using existing 2D evacuation plans and room numbers in the buildings as markers to project the 3D floor plan. The 3D floor plan also shows the current and previous locations the user has navigated by offering enriched experience in navigating large-scale environments. Our proposed AR application was developed in Unity 3D for Microsoft HoloLens. It is a fast and robust marker detection technique inspired by the use of Vuforia AR library. The application offers users an enhanced evacuation experience by offering enthralling visuals, helping occupants learn the evacuation path they could use during an emergency situation where evacuation is necessary. Our aim is to enhance the evacuation process by ensuring that building patrons know all of the building exits and how to get to them. This would improve evacuation time and eradicate injuries and fatalities which occur during indoor crises such as fires and active shooter events. We have incorporated existing features in the building as markers for the HoloLens application to trigger the floor plan and subsequent location of the person in the building. This work also describes the system architecture as well as the design and implementation of this AR application to leverage the Microsoft HoloLens for building evacuation purposes. Pilot studies were conducted with the system showing its partial success and demonstrated the effectiveness of the application in an emergency evacuation. Our results also indicate that the majority of participants felt that HoloLens application can be used as a substitute for evacuation plans (2D plan) in a building. Usually, the evacuation plans are displayed as 2D plans in the buildings. Sometimes it can difficult for users to visualize a building through a 2D plan. The use of AR application gives the user the flexibility and ability to visualize the building and exits in a 3D space.

Emergency response and decision making are very important in fire safety studies as well as during active shooter events. Causalities can be reduced if occupants are successfully evacuated as soon as the emergency begins. The reasons for the failure of timely evacuation by occupants in emergency situations could be a result of improper layout of the building structure or the occupants make unreasonable choices due to unfamiliarity with the building. Evacuation training and evacuation drills are conducted in real buildings that have disadvantages such as high cost, limited response time, and failure to simulate real emergencies. The rapid rise of AR technology has made it possible to overcome these disadvantages by using AR methodologies [1–3] and VR methodologies [4, 5]. With VR, the safety professionals and the occupants of the buildings immerse themselves in the virtual building with virtual fire and smoke. Sharma et al. [6–9] have conducted virtual evacuation drills in immersive VR environments with fire and smoke. With AR, safety professionals and occupants of the building get a 3D, holographic view of building floor plans, a better perspective of the building, making it easier for them to find a way out of the building during the evacuation. Our past results and pilot studies have indicated that majority of participants felt that HoloLens application [10, 11] and AR mobile applications [12, 13] can be used as a substitute for evacuation plans (2D plan) in a building.

The objective of this paper is to present the research and development behind a series of mixed reality (MR) 3D visualization systems for communicating emergency evacuation plans within multilevel spaces using Microsoft HoloLens, tablets, and phones. The rest of the paper is organized as follows: Sect. 2 discusses previous work related to this paper; Sect. 3 describes the system architecture of the proposed application; Sect. 4 focuses on how the implementation and deployment; Sect. 5 discusses the results of the pilot study; Sect. 6 discusses the conclusions.

2   Related Work

The most common 3D perspective carrier's headsets are in Virtual reality (VR), augmented reality (AR), and mixed reality (MR). VR, AR, and MR enhance the user's sense of presence in the environment but they differ from each other. VR immerses the user in a digital space and cuts off the physical world [14]. AR presents an overlay of digital content over the physical word [15] to the user. On the other hand, MR adopts the advantages of both AR and VR by blending reality and virtuality. MR is able to transform the physical world into the virtual world in real-time [16]. Unlike AR, MR allows the user to experience depth spatial persistence, and perspective [17]. MR head-mounted display (Microsoft HoloLens) has been utilized as an example to show how to express and visualize 3D geographic information from a 3D perspective [18]. HoloLens contains stereoscopic 3D displays, gaze design, gesture design, spatial sound design, and spatial mapping [19]. Fruend et al. [20] have built an AR tool to train assembly line workers on new and complex assembly processes.

Mobile augmented reality (MAR) allows the users to effectively learn, ubiquitously, the same concepts that can be taught in the classroom [20]. Emergency evacuation is important for building evacuations in an indoor setting due to the need for safe evacuation and safety considerations. There have been several works that involve the development of Mobile augmented reality application (MARA) using the Android Software Development Kit. Meda et al. [21] have built a MARA that translates English text into another language (Telugu). In this Android-based application, the user takes a picture of English text and saves it as a jpg image file. Parhizkar et al. [22] have designed and developed an Android-based MARA to teach students general science. On the other hand, Sabri [23] have described and evaluated MARA [24] to teach users cultural heritage. Iguchi et al. [23] have implemented a MARA that features virtual children and trains adult users on how to direct children during a real-life evacuation.

3   System Architecture

The objective of this research is to demonstrate the application of MR interfaces that can provide spatial contextualized 3D visualization that promotes knowledge acquisition and support cognitive mapping within the realm of emergency management. This research builds upon the authors' previous emergency evacuation research [6–9] exploring game-engine based evacuation and HoloLens [10, 11] for evacuation in real and virtual spaces. Figure 2 shows the system architecture diagram of our built application.

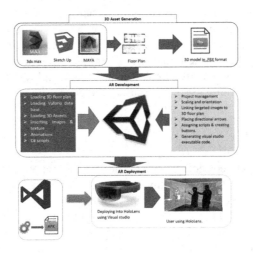

Fig. 2. System architecture diagram.

3.1   3D Assets

The AR visualizations presented in this paper focus on the visualization of 3D building models, text, and annotations using Sketch up, Maya, and 3Ds Max. The initial step for this process was to create a 3D model of each floor plan for the building. SketchUp was initially used to build the 3D assets such as walls, windows, furniture, etc. Both the 3D building and the evacuation pathways were exported as 3D Object files (.obj). The 3D model of the campus was built using 3Ds Max and then exported to FBX format. This format is acceptable by all 3D software and gaming engines. One of the main challenges of this project was to identify the user's location. During emergency situations, GPS capabilities and wifi technology might fail or not work adequately. To overcome this challenge, we incorporated existing permanent objects (images) in the physical surroundings. For example, existing 2D room numbers nameplate in the building were used for location detection as well as for superimposing 3D floor plan on top of it. Figure 3 shows the existing signboards of the room numbers in the building.

Fig. 3.   Existing signboards of different room numbers in the building (used as markers)

3.2   AR Development

The development of the mobile augmented reality (MAR) application was done using Unity 3D. The prototypes developed provided an example of image-based AR (or marker-based AR), which uses computer vision software to identify pre-defined images, subsequently rendering virtual objects according to the position and orientation of those images in real space. The development involved C# scripting, animation, 3D assets, image, texture creation, mapping, and user gaze. In this phase, the unity project is created and all necessary assets and data files are loaded into the project. In unity environment rest of the project is developed, such as inserting buttons assigning C# scripts to the objects to get effects.

3.3   AR Mobile Deployment

The 3D visualizations were developed for Android mobile devices and could be reconfigured for Apple or Windows-based devices. These prototypes were tested on two Samsung Galaxy mobile phones (S9 and Note 9). These mobile devices are typical of the compact mobile technology available in today's life. The prototypes were also tested in the HoloLens and Samsung tablet. Deploying from unity to HoloLens lead to challenges like connection issues, packets missing etc. To overcome these issues, we generated APK file from unity which can be accessible by visual studio. Later, we connected the computer and HoloLens with a USB cable. By choosing HoloLens as a targeted device in visual studio we deployed the AR application into HoloLens. After successfully deploying the project into HoloLens, the user can use the application in the HoloLens by opening the application.

4   Implementation and Deployment

The aim of this paper is to give a detailed view of the project, how HoloLens can be used for building evacuation purpose and for internal navigation. The whole lifecycle of the project can be divided into four phases.

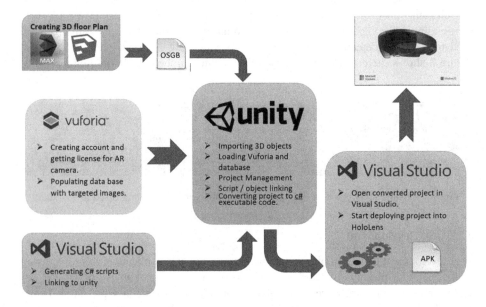

Fig. 4. The life cycle of the project.

4.1   Phase 1

During the initial phase, the aim was to build the 3D model of the floor plans in the building. By using a 2D floor plan as a reference, the 3D model was designed in sketch up. After completing the model designing, the furniture and 3D assets were added to the model. The 3D modeling of the floor plans was done using Google sketch up and 3DS Max. The file was converted into FBX format in which unity can accept. FBX enables wide options to exchange 3D data between different applications. This FBX file was imported into the unity project.

4.2   Phase 2

In this phase, Vuforia was loaded into unity. As we discussed earlier, HoloLens is not equipped with GPS. This problem was overcome by using a feature extraction through the use of Vuforia. The permanent features such as room number signs and evacuation plan boards in the building were used as targeted images or markers. Thus, markers are nothing but existing 2D assets or images in the environment. All these images (refer Fig. 3) were collected and loaded into the Vuforia database. After successfully importing Vuforia assets into the project, Vuforia data database was also imported into the unity project. This was done by dragging that file into the assets folder in the unity project. When the unity project was created, the scene was also populated with light and camera. Later the camera was replaced with the AR camera. If the Vuforia asserts are loaded properly one can find the AR camera under Vuforia options in unity. This camera needs a license key, which one can get from the Vuforia account. The license key allows the AR camera to become active and give full access to unity.

4.3   Phase 3

In this phase, scripts were written using C# language for finding user location by feature extraction method. As mentioned earlier, all the 2D targeted images were collected and loaded into the Vuforia database. Now by using the feature image targeted method, the current location of the user was extracted and the 3D marker was placed in the 3D. This was done by assigning C# code to the respective targeted image. This process was repeated for all targeted images in the database. Thus, it allowed us to populate the application with the current location and the respective path to the nearest exits in the floor plan. The arrows were assigned on all floor plans from the user's current location by writing a script using the C# programming language. The room numbers and description of the rooms were added on top of the 3D floor plan. These room numbers can be toggled on and off through the button on the GUI. These descriptions of the rooms are embedded into floor objects. So that, when the floor plan has loaded the details of the floor also popup. Later buttons were created on the GUI for controlling arrows displays and floor plan descriptions. Later fire and smoke were also added in the floor plan that can be toggled on or off. If the user would like to use the application for indoor navigation, fire and smoke can be toggled off. The color of the user location cubes from red to yellow. When the user faces the targeted image, the location cube is red. But, when the user moves to a new location current location, the previous cube becomes yellow and the new current location cube shows as red.

4.4   Phase 4

In this phase application deploying was done HoloLens, tablets, and phones. During the deployment phase, the unity application was converted into visual studio executable format. The converted code was opened in visual studio. Next, HoloLens was connected to the system for deployment. After deploying the application successfully, a new application icon appears in the HoloLens menu. Figure 4 shows the deploying steps. By tapping the new icon in HoloLens launches the MARA application. When the MARA application is launched it starts scanning the surroundings for targeted images. When the targeted image is in front of the camera, then the application pulls the respected floor plan and current location cube. If the user selects the floor info button on the GUI, then the application displays the room numbers text/description on the floor plan.

5 Simulation and Results

The AR interface presented here is a custom-designed mobile augmented reality application (MARA) that augments the evacuation plan with additional 3D geospatial data. It was developed with Unity and the AR SDK from Vuforia, and was installed on an author's smartphone (Galaxy Note 9 and S9) using the Android and visual studio development kits. A photograph of the evacuation plan was converted into an AR image-target and used as a marker. AR content is displayed on the mobile device when the user points the device camera at the evacuation plan posted on the wall (Fig. 5). The user can also enable different layers for text and annotations. Figure 5 also shows the path to the nearest exit by the use of green arrows.

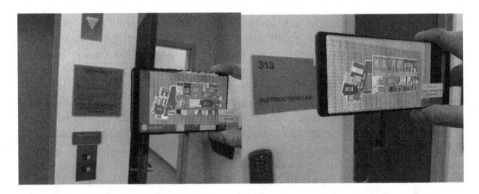

Fig. 5. The 2D evacuation plans and room number signs posted within a building serve as markers to the MARA (Color figure online)

The posted 2D evacuation plans in the building (refer Fig. 5) provide a quick overview of the evacuation plan and a limited amount of spatial information. These 2D floor plans are designed as a quick reference to help occupants of the building who are not familiar with the building or are lost during the evacuation. Without spatial context, it becomes difficult for the occupants to know where exits are and where the direct route to safety is. Figure 5 provides a visualization of 3D model of the building in MARA. The user can rotate the model, adjust its scale, shows the shortest path to the exit, show current location, enable text and annotations for room numbers through the use of buttons on the graphical user interface (GUI). The added layers of information help the user to get a better mental representation of the building and provides visual perspectives to elicit cognitive connection between data and space. The MARA allows the user to locate the exits, evacuations paths to the exit in 3D and improves their ability to evacuate the building and find safety.

A limited user study was conducted to evaluate the effectiveness of the proposed HoloLens application, mobile application, and tablet application. The study illustrates its partial success and demonstrates the effectiveness of the application in emergency response for the building evacuation. The responses were collected from 10 participants, 8 male and 2 female. The post-study questionnaire measured participant's perceptions of motivation, usability, educational and training effectiveness, of the AR applications (HoloLens, Mobile phone, and Tablet) appropriateness.

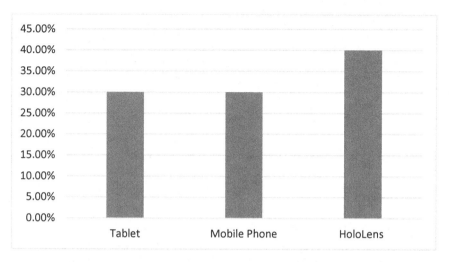

Fig. 6. Device suitability for the study.

Figure 6 shows that the majority of the users (60%) felt that HoloLens was more suitable for evacuation than with a tablet or mobile phone. The following questions were asked in the post-study questionnaire for the user study:

- Do you consider this system useful in unknown buildings with a complex structure?
- Will viewing this HoloLens App help during the real-time evacuation
- Substitute for evacuation plans (2D plan) in a building
- Used for educational or training purposes in evacuation

The HoloLens application received more positive answers regarding usability as shown in Fig. 7. All of the participants (100%) felt that this system will be useful in unknown buildings with a complex structure while 90% of the participants felt that viewing this HoloLens app will help during a real-time evacuation.

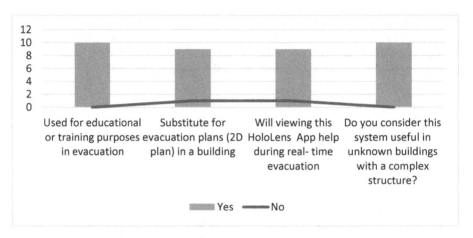

Fig. 7. Device suitability for the study.

6 Conclusions

This paper presented the research and development of a series of prototype AR visualizations for emergency evacuation using HoloLens, tablets, and mobile phones. This work highlights the ability to represent complex multilevel spaces in an inherent 3D form using AR technology. Our proposed AR applications give a visual representation of a building in 3D space, allowing people to see where exits are in the building. It also gives a path to the various exits; a shortest path to the exits as well as directions to a safe zone from their current position. We have described the system architecture and implementation of the AR application to leverage the Microsoft HoloLens for emergency response during a building evacuation. We have introduced a series of layers in the visualization to show text and annotations for each floor to enhance spatial perception and situational awareness of multilevel spaces. We have demonstrated how AR tools can support improved emergency preparedness through the use of HoloLens.

The existing posted 2D evacuation plan in the building indicates the location of the exits that are in close proximity to the viewer, but it does not provide the spatial context which would allow the viewer to make an informed decision about the safety of

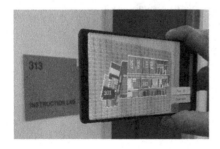 

Fig. 8. Contextualizing evacuation pathways through the use of arrows

those exits. When augmented with 3D models, the viewer is provided with that additional context as shown in Fig. 8. The spatial context is provided through the MARA for multi-level buildings. Thus, the user is able to formulate new spatial knowledge concerning their location in multilevel space and its relation to safely evacuate the building in emergencies. AR technology has the potential to transform the way we interact with the information in the built environment. The 2D maps in the buildings are traditional ways in showing the occupants where they are and where the exits are in the building. They do not give a mental representation to the users to visualize the building. However, with the use of AR technology, the users can use the existing 2D maps as markers for an enriched view of the building in 3D space with layered spatial information. A user study was conducted for the AR applications for HoloLens, tablets, and mobile phones. The experimental results show the effectiveness of our AR applications for emergency evacuation. All of the participants felt that this system would be useful in unknown buildings with a complex structure while 90% of the participants felt that viewing this HoloLens app will help them during a real-time evacuation.

Acknowledgments. The authors would like to acknowledge the support of the VR Laboratory at Bowie State University. This work is funded in part by the ARL Award: W911NF1820224.

References

1. Gamberini, L., Chittaro, L., Spagnolli, A., Carlesso, C.: Psychological response to an emergency in virtual reality: effects of victim ethnicity and emergency type on helping behavior and navigation. Comput. Hum. Behav. **48**, 104–113 (2015)
2. Moreira, S., Bernardes, F., Rebelo, F., Vilar, E., Noriega, P., Borges, T.: Methodological approaches for use virtual reality to develop emergency evacuation simulation for training, in emergency situation. Procedia Manuf. **3**, 6313–6320 (2015)
3. Sánchez, J.M., Carrera, Á., Iglesias, C.Á., Serrano, E.: A participatory agent-based simulation for indoor evacuation supported by Google Glass. Sensor **16**, 1360 (2016). https://doi.org/10.3390/s16091360
4. Shih, N.J., Lin, C.Y., Yang, C.: Virtual-reality-based feasibility study of evacuation time compared to the traditional calculation method. Fire Saf. J. **34**(4), 377–391 (2000)
5. Freund, E., Rossmann, J., Bucken, A.: Fire-training in a virtual-reality environment. In: Woods, A.J. (ed.) Proceedings of SPIE The International Society for Optical Engineering, vol. 5664, Proceedings of SPIE-IS and T Electronic Imaging Stereoscopic Displays and Virtual Reality Systems XII, San Jose, USA, pp. 388–394 (2005)
6. Sharma, S, Jerripothula, S., Devreaux, P.: An immersive collaborative virtual environment of a university campus for performing virtual campus evacuation drills and tours for campus safety. In: Proceedings of IEEE International Conference on Collaboration Technologies and Systems (CTS 2015), Atlanta, Georgia, USA, pp. 84–89, 01–05 June 2015 https://doi.org/10.1109/cts.2015.7210404
7. Sharma, S, Jerripothula, S., Mackey, S., Soumare, O.: Immersive virtual reality environment of a subway evacuation on a cloud for disaster preparedness and response training. In: Proceedings of IEEE Symposium Series on Computational Intelligence, IEEE SSCI 2014, Orlando, Florida, USA, pp. 1–6 (2014). https://doi.org/10.1109/cihli.2014.7013380

8. Sharma, S., Otunba, S.: Collaborative virtual environment to study aircraft evacuation for training and education. In: Proceedings of IEEE, International Workshop on Collaboration in Virtual Environments (CoVE-2012), as part of The 2012 International Conference on Collaboration Technologies and Systems (CTS 2012), Denver, Colorado, USA (2012)
9. Sharma, S., Otunba, S., Han, J.: Crowd simulation in emergency aircraft evacuation using virtual reality. In: Proceedings of IEEE, 16th International Conference on Computer Games: AI, Animation, Mobile, Interactive Multimedia, Educational & Serious Games, (CGAMES), Kentucky, USA, 27–30 July 2011
10. Sharma, S., Bodempudi, S.T., Scribner, D., Grynovicki, J., Grazaitis, P.: Emergency response using HoloLens for building evacuation. In: Proceeding of 21st International Conference on Human-Computer Interaction, Walt Disney World Swan and Dolphin Resort, Orlando, Florida, USA (2019)
11. Stigall, J., Bodempudi, S.T., Sharma, S., Scribner, D., Grynovicki, J., Grazaitis, P.: Building evacuation using microsoft HoloLens. In: Proceedings of 27th International Conference on Software Engineering and Data Engineering (SEDE 2018), New Orleans, Louisiana, USA, pp. 20–25, 8–10 October 2018
12. Stigall, J., Sharma, S.: Mobile augmented reality application for building evacuation using intelligent signs. In: Proceedings of ISCA 26th International Conference on Software Engineering and Data Engineering (SEDE-2017), San Diego, CA, USA, 2–4 October 2017, pp. 19–24 (2017)
13. Sharma, S., Jerripothula, S.: An indoor augmented reality mobile application for simulation of building evacuation. In: Proceedings of SPIE Conference on the Engineering Reality of Virtual Reality, San Francisco, CA, USA, 9–10 February 2015, pp. 9392–1–9392–9 (2015)
14. Frank, L.A.: Using the computer-driven VR environment to promote experiences of natural world immersion. In: Proceedings of the SPIE Engineering Reality of Virtual Reality, Burlingame, CA, USA, 4–5 February, vol. 8649, pp. 185–225 (2013)
15. Uchiyama, H., Saito, H., Servières, M., Moreau, G.: AR city representation system based on map recognition using topological information. In: Shumaker, R. (ed.) VMR 2009. LNCS, vol. 5622, pp. 128–135. Springer, Heidelberg (2009). https://doi.org/10.1007/978-3-642-02771-0_15
16. Wang, X., Dunston, P.S.: User perspectives on mixed reality tabletop visualization for face-to-face collaborative design review. Autom. Constr. **17**, 399–412 (2008)
17. Brigham, T.J.: Reality check: basics of augmented, virtual, and mixed reality. Med. Ref. Serv. Q. **36**, 171–178 (2017)
18. Wang, W., Wu, X., Chen, G., Chen, Z.: Holo3DGIS: leveraging microsoft HoloLens in 3D geographic information. ISPRS Int. J. Geo-Inf. **7**(2) (2018). Article no. 60, https://doi.org/10.3390/ijgi7020060
19. Furlan, R.: The future of augmented reality: Hololens-Microsoft's AR headset shines despite rough edges, Resources_Tools and Toys. IEEE Spectr. **53**, 21 (2016)
20. Fruend, J., Grafe, M., Matysczok, C., Vienenkoetter, A.: AR-based training and support of assembly workers in automobile industry. In: The First IEEE International Augmented Reality Toolkit Workshop, Darmstadt, Germany, 19 September 19 2002
21. bin Hanafi, H.F., Said, C.S., Ariffin, A.H., Zainuddin, N.A., Samsuddin, K.: Using a collaborative Mobile Augmented Reality learning application (CoMARLA) to improve student learning. In: IOP Conference Series: Materials Science and Engineering, vol. 160 (2016)
22. Meda, P., Kumar, M., Parupalli, R.: Mobile augmented reality application for telugu language learning. In: 2014 IEEE International Conference on MOOCs, Innovation and Technology in Education, Patiala, India, pp. 183–186 (2014)

23. Parhizkar, B., Obeidy, W.K., Chowdhury, S.A., Gebril, Z.M., Ngan, M.N.A., Lashkari, A. H.: Android mobile augmented reality application based on different learning theories for primary school children. In: 2012 International Conference on Multimedia Computing and Systems. IEEE (2012) https://doi.org/10.1109/icmcs.2012.6320114
24. Sabri, F.N.M., Khidzir, Z., Ismail, A.R., Daud, K.A.M.: Empirical study on important elements of mobile augmented reality application for heritage content. In: 2016 4th International Conference on User Science and Engineering, Melaka, Malaysia, pp. 210–215 (2016)
25. Iguchi, K., Mitsuhara, H., Shishibori, M.: Evacuation instruction training system using augmented reality and a smartphone-based head mounted display. In: 2016 3rd International Conference on Information and Communication Technologies for Disaster Management, © IEEE (2016). https://doi.org/10.1109/ict-dm.2016.7857220

A New Traversal Method
for Virtual Reality:
Overcoming the Drawbacks of Commonly Accepted Methods

Karl Smink, J. Edward Swan II[(⊠)], Daniel W. Carruth, and Eli Davis

Center for Advanced Vehicles (CAVS) - Mississippi State University, Starkville, USA
swan@acm.org

1 Introduction

One of the biggest issues facing VR as a platform is the limitation of the user's physical space. Not everyone has a lab, empty warehouse, or open space in their home or office, and even if they do, the hardware also limits the physical space the user can take advantage of. For example, the HTC Vive hardware limits the play area to $12.5\,\mathrm{m}^2$, assuming the user does not add additional lighthouses [1]. Fitting the entirety of the environment within few square meters is a strict limitation for many applications. A method of moving the user within a larger space is needed, but current methods come with a trade-off. Determining the best movement method for an application is necessary to ensure a proper experience for the user.

2 Keywords

Virtual Reality, Teleportation, Virtual Reality Sickness, Spatial Memory, Cognitive Mapping, Edit Blindness, HTC Vive, Virtual Reality Toolkit (VRTK).

3 Related Work

Related methods have focused on comparing and exploring different traversal methods in VR. A good example comes from Freedom Locomotion VR [2]. This game is a showcase demo of a virtual reality navigation system that allows a user to navigate a full scale virtual environment from within a small physical space. Freedom Locomotion VR's development goals were focused on reducing VR sickness, while allowing the user a high degree of freedom with regards to their movement. The program uses three locomotion systems: Controller Assisted

---

Electronic supplementary material The online version of this chapter (https://doi.org/10.1007/978-3-030-21607-8_24) contains supplementary material, which is available to authorized users.

J. Y. C. Chen and G. Fragomeni (Eds.): HCII 2019, LNCS 11574, pp. 312–320, 2019.
https://doi.org/10.1007/978-3-030-21607-8_24

On the Spot, Dash Step, and Blink Step. Controller Assisted On the Spot is a physical movement method that translates head bobbing and hand swinging into steps within the virtual environment. Dash Step and Blink Step are more traditional, teleportation-style systems that have been modified to help reduce the VR sickness felt by many users. Both make use of motion blur and interval-based movements, which some users claim prevents them from becoming ill.

Literature reviews comparing the cognitive aspects of different traversal methods exist, such as the investigation done by Boletsis et al. [3] and Karlson et al. [4]. Dr. Roy A. Ruddle at the University of Leeds conducted an investigation on users' ability to travel and gain mastery of different navigation systems [5].

4   Background

Common locomotion methods in VR:

- Point-and-click teleportation
- Artificial methods: sliding, dashing, and flying
- Physical methods: hand-swinging, head bobbing, and walk-in-place
- Teleportation via portal

Point-and-click teleportation is the most commonly adopted method of moving the user relative to the virtual environment. The abrupt shift in visual stimuli, referred to in film as a *mash cut*, can make some users sick; however, sickness responses from point-and-click teleportation are far less common than in other methods of movement. Point-and-click teleportation does not allow the user to maintain a constant view of their environment, or make use of translational cues, resulting in degraded spatial memory. It has been shown that for spatial tasks, users suffer a noticeable increase in error when using methods without translational components [6]. Another flaw of point-and-click teleportation is that it lacks the parity of position between the virtual and physical space, requiring the user to reposition themselves within their physical space to avoid stepping outside of the boundary. Point-and-click teleportation trades memory retention and awareness for user comfort. Not all users experience a reduction in memory or awareness, however, likely due to a well-known phenomenon referred to in the film industry as *edit blindness* [7].

Artificial interaction types such as sliding, dashing, and flying often lead to VR sickness, possibly due to the disconnect between the user's external sensory information (what they see and hear) and their vestibular system [8]. These movement paradigms are commonly well-received in fast-paced applications such as action games [9], where the user is more focused on specific objects rather than their entire field of view. In more relaxed settings with less fixation, users seem to receive these paradigms less favorably [10]. A notable exception to this trend is *Richie's Plank Experience*, where the flying mode seems to have been well accepted [11]. Artificial interaction methods can cause users to neglect their ability to freely walk within their space: the major focus of VR locomotion research since the "revival" in 2014 [3]. One thing artificial interaction methods do well is allow the user to maintain a continuous view of their environment. In film, abrupt cuts in visual stimuli have been shown to reduce cognitive representation [12], and recent research has shown that people react similarly to transitions in VR as they would in film [13]. Artificial methods trade user comfort for memory retention and awareness.

The last, somewhat-common alternative to point-and-click teleportation is physical-movement-based interpolation such as hand-swinging, walking in place, head bobbing, etc. These methods are less common, and how well they are received by users seems to vary wildly, as shown by user reviews of games on Steam that are centralized around these methods [14]. Some are received very well [15], and others very poorly [16].

Alternative methods of teleporting the user exist other than point-and-click teleportation, but are not mentioned in Boletsis's literature review of all movement types [3]. These methods often make use of a visible portal that needs to be touched or entered by the user, instantly transporting them to another location. Teleportation via portal does not seem to cause significant VR sickness, and a few well-received titles have made excellent use of the paradigm [17]. The effects of teleportation via portal on memory depend on two factors: the portal's location and its destination. Location refers to the entry point for the teleportation, and destination refers to the area that the user will arrive at once they enter the portal. The location and destination of a portal can be either fixed or dynamic (Table 1). When teleportation via portal has a fixed location and fixed destination, the user's cognitive map becomes distorted [18], and this paradigm is not very useful for navigating complex environments, because it only shortens travel between predetermined locations, and one side of the portal must remain with the virtual environment mapped to the physical boundary, otherwise the user cannot access it. When teleportation via portal has a fixed location but a dynamic destination (or vis-versa), memory retention will likely be degraded due to the impossibility of accurately integrating the wormhole into the cognitive map [18].

Table 1. Portal paradigms with literary examples

Portal location	Portal destination	Literary example
Fixed	Fixed	Mario Bros: Warp Pipes [19]
Fixed	Dynamic	Stargate: SG1 Stargate Device [20]
Dynamic	Fixed	World of Warcraft: Hearthstone item [21]
Dynamic	Dynamic	Rick and Morty: Rick's portal gun [22]

5   Methodology

5.1   New Traversal Mechanism

We have begun testing a teleportation via portal implementation where both the location and destination are dynamic, and the user has full control over both. The user pilots a remote camera using handheld controllers. This remote camera broadcasts its view to a stationary plane elsewhere in the scene, which the user can observe from a distance (Fig. 1). When the user wants to go to another area in the environment, he pilots the remote camera to that location, using the broadcast plane as a visual indicator of the camera's location (Fig. 2). Once the camera has arrived at the desired destination, the user physically steps into the broadcast plane. This causes the headset camera and remote camera's locations to be swapped, effectively transporting the user to the previous location of the remote camera (Fig. 3). The broadcast plane will appear behind the user, allowing him to step directly backwards, or turn around and step through the plane again, to return to his previous location (Fig. 4). While in the new area, the user may give commands and interact with the environment as normal, even piloting the camera to a third location.

We hypothesize that the constant visual stream provided by the broadcast plane will allow the user to build up spatial knowledge of the environment, similar to artificial methods, improving path integration. By abstracting the visual stream away from the headset and onto the plane, we are hoping to allow users' sensory information and expectations to remain in agreement, reducing the likelihood of experiencing VR sickness. Once the user becomes familiar with the system, we expect it to outperform point-and-click teleportation and artificial methods in both user comfort and cognitive mapping by providing a best of both worlds type experience.

Fig. 1. The user stands in front of the broadcast plane. The remote camera shows the user standing next to the blue cube. (Color figure online)

Fig. 2. The user pilots the remote camera to a new location. The remote camera shows the 2 slates on the blue plane, and the other location in the distance. (Color figure online)

Fig. 3. The user physically steps through the broadcast plane. The user's view will seamlessly transition to the remote camera's location.

Fig. 4. The user has swapped positions with the remote camera. The broadcast plane has appeared behind the user for continued travel or easy returning.

Video demonstration of new method. (see Supplementary Material).

6   Upcoming User Study

An interior screenshot and floor plan of the virtual environment can be seen in Fig. 5. It was modeled closely after the images of the environment shown in Ruddle et al. [5] in an attempt to reduce any effect the visual aspects of the environment might have on the results. The environment was made in Unity 2017.4. The HMD used will be a first generation HTC Vive Pro, with both controllers and two lighthouses. Participants' position and orientation in the virtual environment will be recorded for later analysis.

Fig. 5. The virtual environment for the upcoming user study.

The experiment will be done in three groups; one group for each movement method. The point-and-click teleportation group will use a traditional, trigger-operated method with a Bézier curve indicator from the VRTK library to control their movement. The artificial group will use the thumb-operated trackpad on the HTC Vive Pro controllers to control their movement. The teleportation via portal group will use the thumb-operated trackpad and menu buttons to control the movement of the camera and the broadcast portal.

6.1 Proposed Procedure

First, users will be introduced to the VR hardware and display by completing the Steam VR Tutorial, which explains the control layout and visual information displayed inside the HMD. Participants will then be asked to take a short VR sickness questionnaire before agreeing to continue the study. Then participants will be given a brief description of their movement paradigm, and allowed to test it an a large, empty virtual room for a few minutes. Participants will then be placed in the virtual environment described above, and given their task: locate eight murals within the room in a specific order, and touch them. Participants will complete this task 10 times, then complete a post-experiment VR sickness questionnaire identical to the first.

6.2 Proposed Analysis

Four aspects of participants' travel will be analyzed: time, accuracy, speed, and backtracking. This data will be manually extracted from the video footage of what is displayed to the user, as well as the footage of the user's location and actions from the perspective of the entire virtual environment.

Time will be measured from the first moment of purposeful user movement until the final image has received its trigger condition. Along with speed, time can be used as a partial measure of how confident the user is with the movement method, and we expect their time to decrease from trial to trial.

Accuracy will be measured both by correct sequence order and by collisions with scene objects. Comparing this value with speed will allow us to estimate a user's mastery of a movement method, and we expect accuracy to increase as the experiment progresses.

Speed will be measured as a ratio between idle and active user action. For the teleportation-via-portal group, idle time will be categorized as periods where neither the camera object nor the user's translational coordinates changed. For the other two groups, idle time will be categorized as periods where solely the user's translational coordinates do not change (standing still but looking around, aiming, etc). We expect individual's speed to increase as they become more comfortable with their prescribed movement method.

Backtracking will be measured by how often a user's path overlaps with itself, and by how often users spend moving away from (or at least no closer to) the next panel in the sequence. Over time, we expect backtracking to decrease if users can build an accurate cognitive map of the virtual environment.

7   Future Work

We are interested in seeing the effects that abstracted, continuous visual information has on the user while navigating their environment. During testing of the implementation, some users commented on the relative difficulty and higher learning curve of the new method compared to others. We hope this can be overcome with user mastery, otherwise these potential drawbacks may restrict the types of applications the new method could be integrated into.

We are hoping to implement seamless transitions into the paradigm before the upcoming user study. The current offset upon arrival at the new location may reduce the visual benefit and differences between the new method and point-and-click teleportation.

An HCI study comparing user's evaluation of the method under fast-paced conditions vs. less stressful stimuli would prove fruitful going forward. It's possible the method's somewhat cumbersome visuals would need to be adjusted or hidden, or perhaps it's simply not well suited for scenarios requiring fast reaction times and short response windows.

A psychological study with a more complex environment focused more exclusively on memory recall and retention might contribute to the body of work describing how visual stimuli affects human object permanence, as well as the updating and outdating processes of short term and working memory.

Comparing how different VR movement methods affect the severity of change blindness on users would be an interesting film study topic.

References

1. SteamVR FAQ. https://support.steampowered.com/kb_article.php?ref=7770-WRUP-5951
2. Projects. en-AU. https://hugerobotvr.com/projects/
3. Boletsis, C.: The new era of virtual reality locomotion: a systematic literature review of techniques and a proposed typology. In: Multimodal Technologies and Interaction, vol. 1, no. 4 (2017). ISSN: 2414–4088. http://www.mdpi.com/2414-4088/1/4/24, https://doi.org/10.3390/mti1040024
4. Karlsson, R., et al.: Virtual reality locomotion: four evaluated locomotion methods, October 2017. http://www.diva-portal.org/smash/record.jsf?pid=diva2:1144090&dswid=837
5. Ruddle, R.A., Volkova, E., Bulthoff, H.H.: Learning to walk in virtual reality. ACM Trans. Appl. Percept. **10**(2), 11:1–11:17 (2013). https://doi.org/10.1145/2465780.2465785. ISSN: 1544–3558
6. Ruddle, R.A., Lessels, S.: The benefits of using a walking interface to navigate virtual environments. ACM Trans. Comput. Hum. Interact. **16**(1), 5:1–5:18 (2009). https://doi.org/10.1145/1502800.1502805. ISSN: 1073–0516
7. Smith, T.J., Henderson, J.M.: Edit blindness: the relationship between attention and global change blindness in dynamic scenes. J. Eye Mov. Res. **2**(2) (2008). ISSN: 1995–8692, https://bop.unibe.ch/JEMR/article/view/2264
8. LaViola Jr., J.J.: A discussion of cybersickness in virtual environments. SIGCHI Bull. **32**(1), 47–56 (2000). https://doi.org/10.1145/333329.333344
9. Survios: Raw Data on Steam. https://store.steampowered.com/app/436320/
10. Virtual Reality 360° Skydive - Apps on Google Play. https://play.google.com/store/apps/details?id=com.gravityjack.skydive360&hl=en_US
11. Toast: Richie's Plank Experience on Steam. https://store.steampowered.com/app/517160/Richies_Plank_Experience/
12. Garsoffky, B., Huff, M., Schwan, S.: Changing viewpoints during dynamic events. Perception **36**(3), 366–374 (2007). https://doi.org/10.1068/p5645
13. Serrano, A., Sitzmann, V., Ruiz-Borau, J., Wetzstein, G., Gutierrez, D., Masia, B.: Movie editing and cognitive event segmentation in virtual reality video. ACM Trans. Graph. **36**(4), 47:1–47:12 (2017). https://doi.org/10.1145/3072959.3073668
14. Yore VR on Steam. en. https://store.steampowered.com/app/524380/Yore_VR/
15. Steam Community: Freedom Locomotion VR. en. https://steamcommunity.com/app/584170/reviews/?browsefilter=toprated&snr=1_5_reviews_
16. Tropical Girls VR on Steam. en. https://store.steampowered.com/app/534480/Tropical_Girls_VR/
17. Neat Corporation: Budget Cuts on Steam, July 2018. https://store.steampowered.com/app/400940/Budget_Cuts/
18. Warren, W.H., Rothman, D.B., Schnapp, B.H., Ericson, J.D.: Wormholes in virtual space: from cognitive maps to cognitive graphs. Cognition **166**, 152–163 (2017). https://doi.org/10.1016/j.cognition.2017.05.020
19. Warp Pipe. https://www.mariowiki.com/Warp_Pipe
20. Stargate. https://stargate.fandom.com/wiki/Stargate
21. Wowpedia. Hearthstone, January 2019. https://wow.gamepedia.com/Hearthstone
22. Portal Gun and Portal Technology. https://rickandmorty.fandom.com/wiki/Portal_Gun_and_Portal_Technology

Comparative Study for Multiple Coordinated Views Across Immersive and Non-immersive Visualization Systems

Simon Su[1]([✉]), Vincent Perry[2], and Venkateswara Dasari[1]

[1] US Army Research Laboratory, Aberdeen Proving Ground,
Adelphi, MD 21005, USA
simon.m.su.civ@mail.mil
[2] Parsons Corporation, Aberdeen Proving Ground, Columbia, MD 21005, USA

Abstract. Our objective is to qualitatively assess how users interact with and explore heterogeneous views of data in novel hybrid 2D and 3D visual analytic applications, and assess attitudinal responses on the usefulness of such applications. The application used for the study visualizes simulated network communication data of multiple assets over time, and shows topological, geospatial, and temporal aspects of the data in multiple views. We first perform a usability test, where the participants complete a couple of exploratory tasks: one, identifying corresponding assets in a visualization, and two, identifying patterns/relationships between particular assets. Participants perform the same tasks using several different system configurations: using only 2D visualizations, using 2D and 3D visualizations together but as separate applications, and using the 2D and 3D visualizations together with multiple coordinated views across the two systems. Afterwards, participants complete a user survey of questions that probe at user preferences and opinions about the relative effectiveness of each system towards accomplishing the given tasks. We discuss how the results of the study confirm current system design decisions, and also evaluate additional user-centric characteristics that must be considered to inform future design decisions. These results will inform hypotheses and guidelines for a future behavioral, quantitative study.

Keywords: Immersive and non-immersive analytics · User study design

1 Introduction

Effective exploration, modeling, and analysis of complex heterogeneous requires an entire toolbox of vastly different tools. Despite the dramatic increase in the complexity of data, the ability to quickly analyze the data sets generated to identify trends, anomalies, and correlations remains crucial. Without this ability, users would lose valuable exploratory data analysis capability. Thus, the development of data visualization tools enabling realtime interactive data exploration enhances a user's ability to make useful discoveries from their data.

The U. S. Army Test and Evaluation community tests and evaluates everything the Soldier touches. This includes network, application, vehicle, weapon, communication

© Springer Nature Switzerland AG 2019
J. Y. C. Chen and G. Fragomeni (Eds.): HCII 2019, LNCS 11574, pp. 321–332, 2019.
https://doi.org/10.1007/978-3-030-21607-8_25

device, data link, etc. As a result, the community is the single largest producer of 2D and 3D data in the Department of Defense Research, Development, Test and Evaluation community. The different types of data collected is challenging to analyze as the testing and evaluation process measures everything conceivable to assess its effectiveness, suitability, survivability, and safety. These requirements produce massive, heterogeneous, distributed data sets requiring new data analysis approaches to obtain usable information from the data. In addition, there is a growing number of requirements for time-critical analysis for the heterogeneous data collected throughout the larger Department of Defense Testing and Evaluation community [1]. We developed a hybrid 2D and 3D visual analytics tool to demonstrate the viability of using the underlying technologies to enable complex 2D and 3D data analysis on a Large High-Resolution Display (LHRD) system and complete-immersive Head Mounted Display (HMD) for U. S. Army Test and Evaluation heterogeneous data.

Visual analytics tools running on a LHRD and 3D complete-immersive system opens up the possibility for the users to visualize and interact with more of the data in its natural state to support complex data exploration. The data analysis process includes 2D data interaction on the LHRD and 3D data interaction using complete-immersive HMD. Our complex network simulation data can unfold in many different ways, driving the need for a hybrid 2D and 3D visualization environment. Andrews et al. described the potential benefits of using LHRD for information visualization [2], which are in many ways applicable to our data analysis and visualization requirements.

Our hybrid 2D and 3D LHRD with complete-immersive HMD interactive data visualization application is capable of supporting 2D and 3D temporal and spatial data analysis. Our LHRD data visualization application takes advantage of Scalable Amplified Group Environment2 (SAGE2) [3] support for large high-resolution visualization. SAGE2 allows multiple displays to be used as a single large high-resolution multiuser workspace resulting in a low cost LHRD system.

In our development, we extended ParaViewWeb to run on SAGE2 framework to overcome the scalability limitation of our previous visualization framework [4] in the development of a LHRD information visualization application targeting complex data visualization. Furthermore, for 3D data visualization, we developed a WebGL visualization component into the ParaViewWeb framework, a standalone Unity application running on HTC Vive, and a Unity Event Server facilitating user interaction between the LHRD and complete-immersive HMD visualization.

In the next section, we describe the related work of our paper. The following section describes our hybrid 2D and 3D visual analytics system to support heterogeneous data exploration. We then elaborate on the usability study to validate the design of our application before we conclude.

2   Related Work

The realtime interactive and hybrid 2D and 3D visual analytics application is part of our ongoing Visual Analytics Ecology research as mentioned in our Visualization In Practice workshop poster [5]. Our LHRD visualization framework, SyncVis, is a web-based data visualization tool running on SAGE2 framework. The past few years saw an explosion of web-based information visualization tools. Bostock's publication on D3 library [6] in 2001 has enabled countless innovative interactive information visualization projects. Although web-based visualization is emerging as industry standard, using them in the development of visualization applications for a LHRD environment can be challenging.

Chung's survey paper on software frameworks for cluster-based LHRD mentioned a number of software capable of supporting LHRD [7]. However, adding many existing information visualization tools to those LHRD software frameworks can be challenging as they are not compatible with a web-based visualization framework. The following subsections further describe the ParaViewWeb framework for providing web-based information visualization capability and the SAGE2 framework that provides the reconfigurable tiled display environment running our LHRD visualization framework.

2.1 ParaViewWeb Framework

ParaViewWeb is a collection of visualization modules for web-based interactive rendering of potentially large scale scientific and information visualizations. In this work, we exclusively utilize the JavaScript information visualization modules of the library, in particular because it has the support for multiple coordinated views. The library implements this coordination, as well as coordination of the data through a provider system. Each provider module is responsible for managing a particular piece of data and/or part of the application state, and notifying the views where there is a change in state. For example, the FieldProvider keeps track of which data attributes are currently being visualized across all the views, and notifies when the list of attributes changes (due to user input).

In addition, the ParaViewWeb library implements a collection of visualization components that is responsible for the rendering of particular views. They form the building blocks of the UI and are solely concerned with the rendering aspects of that particular component. In order to be a ParaViewWeb component, it must implement a small number of functions that provide the interface that ParaViewWeb expects, and so other charting libraries can be made into a component by creating this interface. As mentioned previously, they will receive events from the providers, and update their views appropriately.

In this work, we utilize some of the built-in data visualizations and provider modules that are provided to build SyncVis. To bring in additional functionality not supported by the default ParaViewWeb modules, such as the visualization of temporal data and 3D scene rendering, we integrate other existing visualization libraries by creating new ParaViewWeb compatible providers and visualization components.

2.2 SAGE2 Software Framework

SAGE2 is a software framework that uses web-browser technologies to enable data-intensive collaboration across multiple displays acting as one large desktop workspace environment. For our visualization cluster, we have three client machines driving a 24-tiled display wall, with 8 displays per machine. The SAGE2 framework combines the multiple displays to act as one large workspace, allowing multiple users to connect via a modern browser and network access.

The framework is launched on the head node of our cluster, by launching a web server with the specified configuration of the client machines to host the display clients. Once the server is started, users can connect via UI clients by typing the URL of the web server into a modern browser. The client machines of the cluster run the display clients to actually display what is to be shown on the wall. Multiple users can connect to a UI client on their own laptop or machine, with the ability to interact with what is displayed on the wall, as well as drag/drop files or open SAGE2 applications on the wall. The application may be resized, allowing viewing and interacting with web pages in a large display environment.

3   Hybrid 2D and 3D Visual Analytics System

A typical analytical workflow may involve an analyst first exploring the overview of the data set, and then zoom and filter with details on demand [8]. However, in the process, it may be necessary for the user to explore the data set using several different visualization techniques. The analyst may have to reformat the data and switch between different visualization techniques. In most cases, the analyst often times has to switch between applications, languages, or libraries/toolboxes to iterate between visualizing and tweaking the parameters and/or querying a new subset of data. This complicates the data analysis process, and also increases the cognitive load.

Our SyncVis on LHRD was designed with the visual information seeking Mantra in mind to streamline the data exploration process. LHRD visualization environment gives us the screen size to use different visualization techniques to analyze the same data set at once. In addition, taking advantage of functionality provided by Para-ViewWeb, our multiple coordinated views implementation allows different visualization modules to update interactively based on user input. Furthermore, we also incorporate visual filters for the analyst to filter out undesired data ranges.

However, SyncVis may not be suitable for all types of data visualization tasks. Some 3D spatial data visualizations are more suitable using a complete-immersive visualization system. Most visualization systems are loosely coupled systems with limited interoperability capability to support unified data analysis tasks. Therefore, we designed a hybrid 2D and 3D data visualization system to support both 2D visualization (using SyncVis running on LHRD) and 3D complete-immersive visualization (using Unity application running on HTC Vive) with support for user interaction across visualization systems. In another word, we are supporting linking and brushing across LHRD and 3d complete-immersive visualization platforms. Our data-flow-oriented hybrid visualization system gives users the ability to select a spatial range of data of interest on the 3D complete-immersive HTC Vive HMD and have the same set of data displayed on the LHRD visualization system, supporting a unified data exploration experience. Figure 1 shows our realtime interactive hybrid 2D and 3D visual analytics tool running on LHRD and HTC Vive.

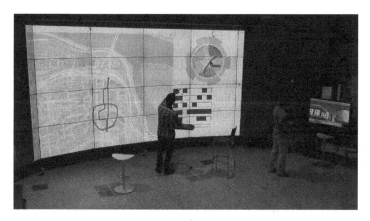

Fig. 1. Hybrid 2D and 3D network simulation data visualization.

4 Network Simulation Visualization Usability Study Design

The data set used for this study includes network link data for multiple moving assets. The data is both geospatial and temporal, such that each 3D asset has a latitude, longitude, and altitude value for each time step of the data set. In addition to asset position, there is link data that records when the network link between two assets is up, and when it is down. In all, the network simulation contains network connection data for multiple assets over time.

There are two visualizations we created for our study, one to represent 2D data, and the other to represent 3D data. The 2D visualization is a web-based application composed of 3 different components: **(A)** a geo location map, **(B)** a mutual information (chord) diagram, and **(C)** a horizon time plot diagram. This can be seen in Fig. 2.

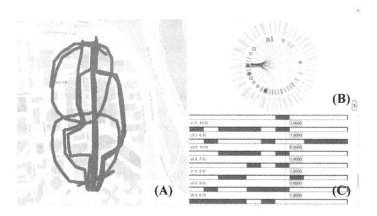

Fig. 2. 2D SyncVis geo-network visualization: **(A)** geo location map, **(B)** mutual information diagram, **(C)** horizon time plot diagram.

The geo location map shows the entire path of an asset for the entire simulation run. The chord diagram shows the uptime/downtime similarity between two links depending on the thickness of the chord connecting the two links. The horizon time plots show the actual uptime and downtime of each of the links over the length of the entire simulation run. If the link is up, it is represented by a green rectangle. When it is down, there is just white space on the plot.

For the 3D visualization, we created a Unity application that illustrates the simulation over time. Each of the assets moves according to its geo location as specified in the data file, and a line is shown between two assets whenever the link is up between them. For the 3D visualization on a 2D display, mouse and keyboard are used to interact with the 3D scene. More specifically, space bar is used to play or pause the animation, right click is to rotate, middle click is to pan, and scroll bar is to zoom. The left mouse click is reserved for selecting links and/or assets in the scene. Running the Unity application on the HTC Vive HMD, the menu button of the hand controller plays or pauses the animation, the top of the thumbpad is used for teleporting, while the right of the thumbpad is used for selecting. Figure 3 shows an omniscient view looking down on the 3D scene.

Fig. 3. 3D unity geo-network visualization.

When the 3D visualization is coordinated with the 2D visualization, any asset and/or link selected in the 3D visualization will be sent to the 2D visualization. So, if an asset is selected, the path of that asset over the entire simulation is plotted on the 2D visualization's geo location map. If a link is selected, that link's uptime/downtime data is presented on the 2D visualization's horizon time plot diagram. If other links have already been selected, then the mutual information between the previously selected and newly selected link are shown in the chord diagram of the 2D visualization. Figure 4 shows the coordination between the 2D visualization and the 3D visualization. When the visualizations are not coordinated, selection of any asset or link in the 3D visualization will have no effect on the 2D visualization. Instead, the 2D visualization will always show all of the data, including paths of all the assets in the scene, and uptime/downtime and similarity of all links in the scene.

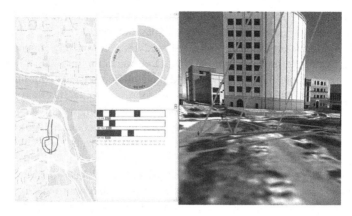

Fig. 4. 2D visualization (left) is displaying the location and link data over time for the highlighted assets and links in the 3D visualization (right).

The main goal of our informal comparative study is to gain feedback on using the hybrid visualization system for data analysis. More specifically, we wish to better understand the user's opinion on using 3D environments for analysis of 3D data, and if coordinating visualizations across dimensions enables keener insights to be drawn during the data analysis workflow. There were many design considerations involved in determining the actual environments to compare, the tasks for the users to complete in each environment, and the questions posed to users for feedback.

4.1 Environment

The first decision to make involves deciding on the environments through which to run the users. Again, our ultimate goal is to study multiple coordinated views across display devices to better understand its use in data analysis. However, we want the users to have a fair and controlled study so as not to bias the responses in favor of the 2D/3D coordinated system. To do so, we compare both multiple coordinated views to separate views, as well as 3D visualizations in a virtual environment to 3D visualizations on a 2D monitor (2.5D).

Without bringing the 3D visualization into the 2D side, we would essentially only be testing how important the 3D visualization is to the entire data exploration. In that case, we completely lose any relevance to the coordinated views and/or hybrid nature of the system components, since the 3D visualization would not be a constant factor for all tests. By bringing the 3D visualization into the 2D environment, we allow all environments to share the same components, just with different interaction capability. In addition, bringing the 3D visualization into 2D allows the users to determine if there is a benefit of visualizing 3D data in a virtual environment, or if a 2D monitor is enough. After all, most data analysts observing 3D data use a 2D display to do so.

Having a separate 2D and 3D application is very unusable for the user. Without coordinating the data, the user is unable to gain much insight from the data shown in either visualization. However, the 2D/3D coordinated application allows the user to manipulate the virtual environment and have the corresponding data appear on the 2D visualization. In doing so, the user will be able to decide if it is worthwhile to coordinate the 2D and 3D visualizations across display devices.

The only thing we are omitting from our study is a completely immersive virtual environment. Similar to how we brought the 3D visualization into 2D, we could bring the 2D visualization into 3D. Thus, we could have all components coordinated in 2D, all components coordinated in 3D, and a hybrid coordinated 2D/3D environment. This would answer the question of the true benefit of a hybrid framework, using 2D display for 2D visualization, 3D display for 3D visualization, with coordination among them. Unfortunately, we were not able to replicate the 2D visualization in the virtual environment for this study.

We ultimately decided on the three environments alluded to above. The first environment, 2D, contains the 2D visualization coordinated with the 2D display version of the 3D visualization. The mouse and keyboard are used to interact with and move around the 3D visualization, where interaction updates the 2D visualization. The second environment, 2D/3D separate, contains the 2D visualization displayed on a monitor and the 3D visualization in the virtual environment. However, the 2D visualization has all the data pre-populated, such that any interaction in the virtual environment has no effect on the visualizations in 2D. The third environment, 2D/3D coordinated, once again contains the 2D visualization displayed on a monitor and the 3D visualization in the virtual environment. For this environment, no data is pre-populated into the 2D visualization, and instead any interaction with the virtual environment updates the 2D visualization.

4.2   Tasks

For the study, the users are asked to complete tasks solely to get them interacting with the environments. Although the answers do not quite matter, the users are asked to complete tasks in each environment as if they are a data analyst using such environment to answer questions about the data set.

The ordering of environments experienced by each user is randomly assigned, and the tasks have no particular environment for which they are asked. However, each environment only involves completing two tasks, and each task has a specific reasoning. Of the two tasks asked of the user, one of them involves determining the path of an asset in the scene, and the other involves determining the similarity of two links in the scene.

In each environment, the user is required to interact a bit differently to answer the posed question. By keeping the questions of similar nature, though not quite the same, we avoid preconditioning the users in any of the environments and are able to analyze the same data for the same purpose. Thus, the interaction and data analysis process is unique to the environment of the user, with all other factors being controlled. This allows the user to compare and contrast the data analysis process for each of the environments individually.

For the 2D environment, the user has to use the mouse to zoom, rotate, and pan the 3D visualization's scene in order to find and select the correct asset. Once the correct asset is selected, the user can look to the map of the 2D visualization next to the 3D visualization to determine the path of the asset. For determining the similarity of the two links in the scene, the user interacts similarly with the 3D visualization, this time selecting links instead of assets. However, this interaction requires the user to look to the 2D visualization after each selection to determine if this is the correct link number or not. Once both the links have been selected, the user then observes the horizon time plot diagram on the 2D visualization to determine the similarity of the links' uptime.

For the 2D/3D separate environment, the user can look around the 3D scene using the headset, use the pointer to identify assets, and even teleport right up to assets if need be. However, because the visualizations are not coordinated, no selection in the 3D environment populates the 2D visualization's components. That is, the map on the 2D visualization shows all paths for all assets in the simulation, whether they are selected or not. Instead, to determine the path of an asset in this environment, the user must watch the simulation play out in the 3D visualization and try to determine the path of the requested asset. For determining the similarity between links, the user may once again try to identify and watch them play out in the 3D visualization, or the user can go to the 2D visualization, find the requested links in the horizon time plot diagram, then try to distinguish how similar they are by comparing. However, there is no way to organize the links in the horizon time plot diagram, so the user may have to compare two links that require scrolling up and/or down, with dozens of links in between them.

For the 2D/3D coordinated environment, the user can look around the 3D scene pointing at assets to select them, or teleport right up next to each asset to select them. For this environment, the selected asset in the 3D visualization updates the map in the 2D visualization. Thus, once the user selects the asset in the 3D environment, the headset may be removed to observe the path of the asset on the 2D visualization's map. For the link similarity task, again the user can look and/or transport around the virtual environment finding and selecting the links in question. Once the links have been selected, the user may remove the headset and observe how similar the link uptimes are using the horizon time plot diagram on the 2D visualization. In order to compare the links with a one-to-one correspondence, the user should only select the two links in question in the 3D visualization, deselecting any extraneous links.

4.3 Question and Analysis

For the questionnaire (as listed in the Appendix), we ask the users 10 questions total. For the first 8 questions, the users are asked to give their environment preference that they felt best answers the question. The answers were 2D, 2D/3D separate, 2D/3D coordinated, or none. The final two questions we pose are to be answered on a Likert scale from 1 to 5, with 1 representing "strongly disagree" and 5 representing "strongly agree." Of the first 8 questions, there is an equal split in questions answered in favor of 2D/3D coordinated and questions answered in favor of just 2D.

For example, the majority of people prefer the 2D/3D coordinated environment for the question "Which mode did you feel allowed you to fully understand the data?" This shows that the combination of visualizations in their natural environment provides users with a deeper understanding. Another example includes the question "Which mode allowed for the most intuitive interaction with the data?" The majority of users voted that the 2D/3D coordinated allowed the most intuitive interaction. It was commented that interacting with the 3D visualization in 2 dimensions using only a mouse was not as intuitive as 3D. However, 2D was still said to be faster and more convenient.

For the question "Which mode allowed for the quickest insights to be drawn from the data?", the majority of users voted that the 2D environment allows for the quickest insights to be drawn. Similar to the comment above, 2D is faster and more convenient considering the visualizations are side by side. With the headset, there is no way to quickly analyze the data filtering and selection across visualizations. Thus, it is quicker for a user to interact with and quickly understand what is happening when looking at the same display.

In addition, the majority of users chose the 2D environment when asked "If you had to select one mode to use for data analysis, which would you select?" The main reasoning for selecting this mode is familiarity and quicker insights. Although the 3D representation may be a better way for the user to visualize the 3D data, there is overhead in getting comfortable with virtual reality when one is used to using a mouse and keyboard on a 2D monitor. The first step is to show the overall benefit of viewing this data in 3D, then easing the interaction with that data for the user to make it as intuitive as possible.

The final two questions are answered on a Likert scale from 1 to 5. The purpose of the Likert scale is to quantify the user's opinion on using the hybrid system for data analysis. For the question "There is benefit in coordinating visualizations across 2D and 3D visualization systems?" all responses were a 4, with one 5. For the question "There is benefit in viewing 3D visualizations in an immersive environment?" all uses responded with a 5 except for one user giving a 4. In both cases, all users chose to agree with the statements posed. These responses show that the users do believe there is a benefit in viewing 3D visualizations in a 3D environment, but not necessarily in a hybrid visualization system where the user has to switch between virtual reality and a 2D display.

As alluded to above, one of the main complaints from the users is having to remove the headset to view the 2D visualization. Having to enter a virtual world to visualize the 3D data and then removing the headset to observe the 2D data is too disruptive for the data analysis workflow. However, due to the promising feedback on coordinated systems and 3D viewing, the next step is to use mixed reality to combine both environments into one system experience.

While the 2D system allows a user to seamlessly look at both types of visualizations, so too would a mixed reality experience allow a user to view both visualizations at the same time. In addition, the mixed reality system allows the 2D visualization to be viewed in 2D and the 3D visualization to be viewed in 3D. With such a hybrid approach and one central viewing system, users will be able to get the best of both 2D visualizations and 3D visualizations to interact with and analyze their data.

5   Discussion and Conclusion

In this paper, we described our realtime interactive hybrid 2D and 3D visual analytics application that allows the user to analyze and visualize the 3D network simulation. Our data centric design allows the user to set up the spatial coordinate of interest and visualize the 2D and 3D data of the data set on both the LHRD and HTC Vive visualization systems. This gives the user the capability to visualize 2D data on a 2D LHRD platform and 3D data using 3D immersive virtual reality technology.

We also described the data-flow-oriented architecture design which is used to support the development of a hybrid 2D and 3D visual analytics tool. The architecture is used to develop an application demonstrating a viable realtime interactive hybrid 2D and 3D visual analytics application for a complex network simulation. The hybrid 2D and 3D application gives the user a better understanding of the outcome of their 3D simulations. The results of our usability survey show that users agree there is benefit in using a hybrid 2D and 3D visual analytics application to support their data exploration. Furthermore, mixed-reality could be the solution to ease the interaction between 2D and 3D systems while allowing the user to view the data in its natural environment using multiple coordinated views.

Acknowledgments. This work was supported in part by the DOD High Performance Computing Modernization Program at The Army Research Laboratory (ARL), Department of Defense Supercomputing Resource Center (DSRC).

Appendix: Comparative Study Questionnaire

1. Which mode did you feel allowed you to fully understand the data? Why?
   2D   2D/3D separate   2D/3D coordinated   None
2. Which mode did you feel most appropriately represented the data? Why?
   2D   2D/3D separate   2D/3D coordinated   None
3. Which mode allowed for the most intuitive interaction with the data? Why?
   2D   2D/3D separate   2D/3D coordinated   None
4. Which mode allowed for the quickest insights to be drawn from the data? Why?
   2D   2D/3D separate   2D/3D coordinated   None
5. Which mode were you most likely to gain a better understanding of the data through interaction? Why?
   2D   2D/3D separate   2D/3D coordinated   None
6. Which mode was the most effective at updating the representation of data in response to interaction? Why?
   2D   2D/3D separate   2D/3D coordinated   None
7. Given the coordinated visualizations, which mode did you feel was easiest to understand how the data was filtered due to coordination? Why?
   2D   2D/3D separate   2D/3D coordinated   None
8. If you had to select one mode to use for data analysis, which would you select? Why?
   2D   2D/3D separate   2D/3D coordinated   None
9. There is benefit in coordinating visualizations across 2D and 3D visualization systems.
   (strongly disagree) 1   2   3   4   5 (strongly agree)
10. There is benefit in viewing 3D visualizations in an immersive environment.
    (strongly disagree) 1   2   3   4   5 (strongly agree)

References

1. Barton, J.M., Namburu, R.: Data-intensive computing for test and evaluation. ITEA J. **38**(2), 177–182 (2017)
2. Andrews, C., Endert, A., Yost, B., North, C.: Information visualization on large, high-resolution displays: Issues, challenges, and opportunities. Inform. Vis. **10**(4), 341–355 (2011). https://doi.org/10.1177/1473871611415997
3. Marrinan, T., et al.: Sage2: a new approach for data intensive collaboration using scalable resolution shared displays. In: 10th IEEE International Conference on Collaborative Computing: Networking, Applications and Worksharing, pp. 177–186, October 2014. https://doi.org/10.4108/icst.collaboratecom.2014.257337
4. Su, S., Perry, V., Cantner, N., Kobayashi, D., Leigh, J.: High-resolution interactive and collaborative data visualization framework for large scale data analysis. In: 2016 International Conference on Collaboration Technologies and Systems (CTS), pp. 275–280, October 2016. https://doi.org/10.1109/CTS.2016.005
5. Su, S., et al.: Visual analytics ecology for complex system testing. In: Visualization in Practice 2017 Workshop at IEEE Visualization 2017, Phoenix, AZ, USA, October 2017
6. Bostock, M., Ogievetsky, V., Heer, J.: D3: Data-driven documents. IEEE Trans. Visual Comput. Graphics **17**(12), 2301–2309 (2011). https://doi.org/10.1109/TVCG.2011.185
7. Chung, H., Andrews, C., North, C.: A survey of software frameworks for cluster-based large high-resolution displays. IEEE Trans. Visual Comput. Graphics **20**(8), 1158–1177 (2014). https://doi.org/10.1109/TVCG.2013.272
8. Shneiderman, B.: The eyes have it: a task by data type taxonomy for information visualizations. In: Proceedings 1996 IEEE Symposium on Visual Languages, pp. 336–343, September 1996. https://doi.org/10.1109/VL.1996.545307

Avatars, Embodiment and Empathy in VAMR

A Face Validation Study for the Investigation of Proteus Effects Targeting Driving Behavior

Corinna A. Faust-Christmann[1(✉)], René Reinhard[2,3],
Alexandra Hoffmann[1,3], Thomas Lachmann[3,4], and Gabriele Bleser[1]

[1] Junior Research Group wearHEALTH,
Technische Universität Kaiserslautern, Kaiserslautern, Germany
christmann@cs.uni-kl.de
[2] Fraunhofer ITWM, Kaiserslautern, Germany
[3] Cognitive and Developmental Psychology, Center for Cognitive Science,
Technische Universität Kaiserslautern, Kaiserslautern, Germany
[4] Facultad de Lenguas y Educación, Universidad Nebrija, Madrid, Spain

Abstract. The Proteus effect describes the phenomenon that Immersive Virtual Reality users derive identity cues from their avatar's appearance which in turn activate specific stereotypes that influence the users' behavior or attitudes. The aim of this study was to validate faces of different age groups that can be used for avatars in further studies of Proteus effects targeting driving behavior. To achieve this goal, four neutral faces were selected from the CAL/PAL face database. They were rated with established questionnaires for driving behavior and driving styles to reveal explicit driver stereotypes. Implicit stereotypes were assessed with the implicit association test.

Study 1 (N = 93) revealed explicit driver stereotypes. In line with prior research, the young man's driving style was seen as riskier, angrier, with a higher velocity, and as less careful and less patient. The opposite pattern of results was found for the old woman, who received high scores for dissociative, anxious, and patient driving styles.

Study 2 (N = 160) replicated the overall pattern of results from study 1. Moreover, there were in-group out-group effects for the implicit gender stereotypes with regard to dissociative driving style and overall driving ability.

Based on these results, observable influences upon driving behavior are expected for driving errors, violations and lapses, as well as upon driving velocity with more violations and higher velocity for the male avatars and with more errors and lapses for the old female avatar. All faces were remodeled with Autodesk 3ds Max for further experiments investigating the Proteus effect targeting driving behavior.

Keywords: Explicit stereotypes · Implicit stereotypes · DBQ · MSDI · Avatar

1 Introduction

1.1 Proteus Effects

The Proteus effect describes the phenomenon that Immersive Virtual Reality (IVR) users derive identity cues from their avatar's appearance, e.g., height or age,

© Springer Nature Switzerland AG 2019
J. Y. C. Chen and G. Fragomeni (Eds.): HCII 2019, LNCS 11574, pp. 335–348, 2019.
https://doi.org/10.1007/978-3-030-21607-8_26

which in turn activate specific stereotypes that influence the users' behavior or attitudes [1]. There are first indications that these effects can persist for a short time after leaving IVR [2]. Although driving behavior is known to be associated with strong gender and age stereotypes (see Sect. 1.2 for details), possible Proteus effects have not yet been investigated in this context. This is rather surprising as there are first indications from simulator studies that driving behavior can be modulated by activating age [3] and gender stereotypes [4]. If the choice of a specific avatar actually influences subsequent driving behavior, special attention should be given to those avatars that trigger careful, attentive and skillful driving behavior to reduce the frequency of potentially dangerous driving errors.

1.2 Driver Stereotypes Regarding Age and Gender

Generally, two types of stereotypes can be distinguished. Explicit stereotypes refer to conscious thoughts and beliefs about a certain social group, whereas implicit stereotypes refer to unconscious attitudes [5].

Explicit driver stereotypes regarding age were so far only addressed in a few studies. Here, older drivers were rated as less aggressive than younger ones [6] and they were also perceived to have a lower likelihood of getting involved in accidents compared to younger drivers [7]. Moreover, one previous simulator study showed that priming an elderly stereotype by completing a scrambled-sentence task, resulted in lower maximum speed and longer driving time compared to a control condition [3]. In contrast to these findings, the only study on implicit driver stereotypes regarding age found "old" to be associated with dangerous drivers, whereas "young" was stronger associated with safe drivers. This finding was apparent for young and old participants [8]. In this study, the terms safe and dangerous drivers referred to driving skill (capable, skilled, ability) and different driving styles (awake, aware, focused, inattentive, risky), making it hard to deduce a certain driving behavior for older drivers.

Regarding gender stereotypes, men are generally perceived as risk takers and as more aggressive compared to women [9] and therefore are believed to be at a higher crash risk [7], to not comply to traffic rules [10, 11], and to drive more aggressively and at higher speed [10, 11]. These negative stereotypes are particularly pronounced with regard to young men [7]. The impact of these stereotypes was also apparent in a driving simulator study with young men, where it was revealed that priming with masculine words resulted in increased speeding compared to feminine or neutral words [4].

In contrast, the feminine stereotype is assumed to be passive, non-competitive and careful [11]. Following this idea, women are expected to drive carefully, at low speeds and to comply with traffic rules [10]. Moreover, women were more readily described as nervous drivers [12].

Despite the assumed risky and non-compliant driving style, men are, at the same time, believed to be more skilled drivers than women [7, 10, 13]. This shows that the difference between driving and safety skills is apparent in people's perceptions [14]. The former, driving skill, refers to driving performance, whereas the latter, safety skill, is determined by the driving style which someone chooses, for example a careful, patient or risky driving style. The perception of the two skills may, however, be linked.

An expected higher driving skill level may allow drivers to take more risks, while a fast and aggressive driving style may be considered a proof of driving skill [10].

1.3   Assessment of Driver Stereotypes

To allow a quantifiable approach for the assessment of explicit driver stereotypes regarding age and gender, pre-selected faces (one young man, one young woman, one old man, and one old woman, see Sect. 2.1 for details) were rated with established questionnaires for the assessment of driving behavior [15] and driving styles [16].

In this context, driving behavior usually refers to acts of aberrant behaviors while the driver is in control of a car. In the Driving Behaviour Questionnaire (DBQ) [15] safety-relevant driving behaviors are classified into three types: lapses, errors and violations. Lapses are absent-minded behaviors that do not pose any threat to others, whereas errors and violations can both be hazardous to others, but only the latter involve deliberate contraventions of traffic rules [17].

Driving style refers to how a person habitually drives, including choice of driving speed and level of attentiveness [18]. The following driving styles can be assessed with the Multidimensional Driving Style Inventory (MDSI) [16]: risky, angry, high velocity, dissociative, anxious, distress-reduction, patient, careful.

In addition to explicit stereotypes, implicit driving-related stereotypes can be assessed with the implicit association test (IAT), for example with regard to the driver's gender [8, 19]. An IAT is a reaction time based task that measures the strength and direction of an association between two dimensions (e.g. male/female and skilled/unskilled driver). In order to increase comparability between measures of explicit and implicit stereotypes, there was one IAT for driving behavior (skilled/unskilled) and several IATs for the driving styles: attentive/dissociative for the dissociative driving style, fast/slow for the high-velocity driving style, defensive/aggressive covering the patient, careful, angry and risky driving styles, as well as relaxed/distressed representing the anxious and stress reduction driving style.

Hypotheses on Driver Stereotypes
Based on the review of literature (see Sect. 1.2 for details), the following pattern of results are expected for the ratings of the four faces (see Sect. 2.1 for details) with MDSI [16] and DBQ [15]:

1. The young man receives higher scores for the risky, angry, and high velocity driving styles compared to the other three faces.
2. The women, especially the old woman, receive higher ratings for the anxious, distress-reduction, patient, and careful driving styles compared to the men.
3. Due to the assumed differences in driving skill, the women receive higher scores for lapses and driving errors.
4. The young man receives the highest scores for violations.

In addition, implicit driver stereotypes were investigated on an explorative basis, as the current literature does not afford clear expectations.

2 Methods

2.1 Face Selection

The aim of this study was to validate faces of different age groups that can be used in the process of avatar generation, which will become the basis for future studies of Proteus effects targeting driving behavior.

To achieve this goal, four neutral Caucasian faces (one young woman, one young man, one old woman, and one old man) were selected from the CAL/PAL face databank [20]. Care was taken to choose faces that only differ in gender and age, while controlling for further properties. Previous ratings reported by Ebner and colleagues indicated these faces to be comparable regarding overall attractiveness, likeability, distinctiveness, energy and mood [21]. In detail, the four faces were selected based on the following criteria:

1. The young faces of either gender were rated as younger than 31 years.
2. The old faces of either gender were rated older than 60 years.
3. The portrayed mood was rated as neutral by at least 60% of the participants.
4. All persons were rated as similar as possible with regard to attractiveness (means: 1.77–1.85), likeability (means: 1.69–1.92) and energy (means: 1.87–2.04) on a 0–4 scale [21].

2.2 Study 1: Explicit Age and Gender Stereotypes

The complete sample consisted of 93 adults. This sample consisted of both young adults (23 males, 22 females), at a mean age of 24.00 years (SD = 2.32; range 19–30 years), and an older sample (28 males, 20 females), at a mean age of 67.13 years (SD = 6.81; range 60–83 years). The sample of young adults consisted of students, while the participants in the older group consisted of retirees (62.5%), people still in the work process (27.1%), homemakers (8.3%) and unemployed persons (2.1%).

Participants rated the four selected faces using a German version of the DBQ [15] and the MDSI [16] to reveal explicit age and gender stereotypes for driving behavior and driving styles. The sequence of faces was counterbalanced between participants.

2.3 Study 2: Explicit and Implicit Gender Stereotypes

The sample consisted of 160 adults (75 males) with a mean age of 28.2 years (SD = 9.56, range: 18–65 years). Most participants were university students (58.75%) or employed (32.5%). The rest were unemployed (5.6%), retirees (1.9%) or homemakers (1.3%).

Participants had to rate two of the four faces (young man and young woman or old man and old woman) on a German version of the DBQ [15] and the MDSI [16] to reveal explicit gender stereotypes. The sequence of faces was counterbalanced between participants.

Moreover, they performed an IAT to reveal implicit stereotypes. The first dimension was always male/female. Each participant was randomly assigned to one of the following driving related dimensions: attentive/dissociative, skilled/unskilled, relaxed/distressed, fast/slow, or defensive/aggressive.

Based on a pilot test (N = 27 German university students) regarding the proximity of words to the target categories, the following German synonyms were chosen for the driving dimensions:

aufmerksam (attentive): achtsam, fokussiert, konzentriert, wachsam

nachlässig (dissociative): achtlos, abgelenkt, verzettelt, unbedacht

begabt (skilled): gut, geübt, talentiert, kompetent

unbegabt (unskilled): schlecht, hilflos, leistungsschwach, unfähig

gestresst (stressed): angespannt, erschrocken, nervös, ruhelos

entspannt (relaxed): gelassen, unverkrampft, locker, ruhevoll

schnell (fast): fix, rasend, eilig, zügig

langsam (slow): lahm, schleichend, bummelnd, trödelnd

defensiv (defensive): besonnen, ungefährlich, vorsichtig, zurückhaltend

aggressiv (aggressive): bedrohlich, ungezügelt, waghalsig, gefährdend

The seven-block version of the IAT was used [8, 22]. The first two blocks (24 trials each) were practice blocks with the category headings male and female in the first block and the driving related categories in the second block (e.g. skilled driver and unskilled driver). In the third (24 trials) and fourth block (40 trials) both category headings were combined (e.g. male and skilled driver on the left side and female and unskilled driver on the right side). The fifth block (40 trials) consisted of practice trials with the driving related category only, but the position of the headings was changed for left and right as compared to blocks 2, 3, and 4. In blocks 6 (24 trials) and 7 (40 trials) both category headings were again presented in combination (e.g. male and unskilled driver on the left side and female and skilled driver on the right side). Thus, data from blocks 3, 4, 6, and 7 were used in later analyses.

Participants sorted the target words as belonging to the respective driving related category and faces as belonging to the category male or female. Category pairings were displayed in the upper left and right corners of the computer screen. Words (8 for each category) and photographs (the same 4 as used in study 1) appeared in the middle of the screen in random order. Participants sorted them according to the correct category label by pressing a key on the keyboard that corresponded to the spatial location of the correct category.

The stimuli pair order was counterbalanced across participants. Thus, half of the participants would for example start in blocks 3 and 4 by sorting stimuli according to the category pairing male/skilled driver and female/unskilled driver, while the other half would start with the pairings of male/unskilled driver and female/skilled driver. They were then presented with the alternate pairing during blocks 6 and 7. The target stimuli remained on the screen until a response was recorded. Afterwards, feedback was displayed during 500 ms interstimulus intervals. Following trials with correct responses no stimulus was displayed in the center of screen, while a centrally displayed error symbol (X) followed incorrect responses.

IAT D scores were calculated by using the improved IAT scoring algorithm [22, 23]. The D score represents the difference in mean reaction time between the critical conditions divided by the standard deviations across conditions. Reaction times slower than 10,000 ms and faster than 300 ms were removed from the data set prior to D score calculations. Error trials were not removed from the analysis in accordance with Greenwald, Nosek and Banaji [23].

3 Results

3.1 Study 1

The data obtained from each of the first study's questionnaires (MDSI and DBQ) were analyzed using a mixed-design multivariate analysis of variances (MANOVA) with age group and gender of the participant as between subject factors and age and gender groups of the photograph as within subject factors. For the MDSI data the MANOVA revealed a main effect of participant's age group, Wilk's $\lambda = .62$, $F(8,82) = 6.28$, $p < .01$, a main effect of photograph's age group, Wilk's $\lambda = .35$, $F(8,82) = 18.87$, $p < .01$, as well as a main effect of gender group of photograph, Wilk's $\lambda = .37$, $F(8,82) = 17.45$, $p < .01$. Moreover, there was an interaction between the participant's age group and the age group of the photograph, Wilk's $\lambda = .66$, $F(8,82) = 5.32$, $p < .01$, between participant's age group and the photograph's gender group, Wilk's $\lambda = .83$, $F(8,82) = 2.16$, $p = .04$, and lastly between the age group and gender group of the photographs, Wilk's $\lambda = .56$, $F(8,82) = 8.07$, $p < .01$.

Comparable results were found for the DBQ scales. Here, a main effect of participant's age group, Wilk's $\lambda = .78$, $F(3,87) = 8.04$, $p < .01$, a main effect of the photograph's age group, Wilk's $\lambda = .47$, $F(3,87) = 32.91$, $p < .01$, and a main effect of the photograph's gender group, Wilk's $\lambda = .36$, $F(3,87) = 51.67$, $p < .01$ were found. Additionally, the interactions between the participant's and the photograph's age group, Wilk's $\lambda = .79$, $F(3,87) = 7.60$, $p < .01$, between the participant's age group and the photograph's gender group, Wilk's $\lambda = .89$, $F(3,87) = 3.62$, $p = .02$, and between the photograph's age and gender group, Wilk's $\lambda = .72$, $F(3,87) = 11.05$, $p < .01$. All remaining main effects and interactions did not reach significance.

To further explain this pattern of results, additional univariate analyses of variance (ANOVA) were conducted for each scale of the MDSI and DBQ. Alpha level was adjusted according to the Holm-Bonferroni method to consider effects of multiple testing. The main effect of the participant's age group was found for all scales (all $p < .01$, except the MDSI's anxious driving, $p = .02$, and the DBQ's violations scale, $p = .03$) with the exception of risky ($p = .14$), and patient driving ($p = .24$). The main effect of the photograph's age group was present in all scales (all $p < .01$) apart from distress reduction driving ($p = .32$). At the same time, the main effect of the photograph's gender group was apparent in each scale (all $p \leq .02$). The interaction between the participant's and the photograph's age group was found for dissociative, risky, and patient driving, as well as for errors (all $p < .01$). The interaction between the photograph's age and gender group was apparent for dissociative driving, risky, distress reduction, and careful driving, as well as for errors and lapses (all $p < .01$).

All remaining main effects and interactions did not reach significance for any of the scales. Ratings for the four photographs were compared with post-hoc t-tests, separately for the young and old subgroup. The results for each MDSI scale, including post-hoc comparisons between photographs, are pictured in Fig. 1 for the young subsample and in Fig. 2 for the old subsample. The results of the DBQ for both the young and old groups are displayed in Fig. 3.

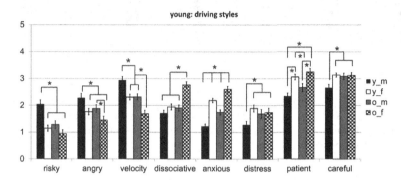

Fig. 1. Mean ratings from the young group of participants for the four faces (young male = y_m, young female = y_f, old male = o_m, old female = o_f) regarding the eight driving styles based on the MDSI. Error bars indicate standard errors of the mean.

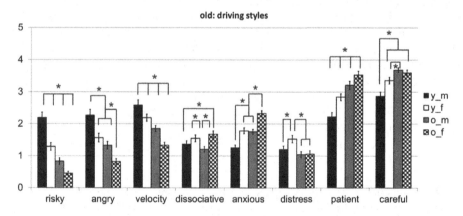

Fig. 2. Mean ratings from the old group of participants for the four faces (young male = y_m, young female = y_f, old male = o_m, old female = o_f) regarding the eight driving styles based on the MDSI. Error bars indicate standard errors of the mean.

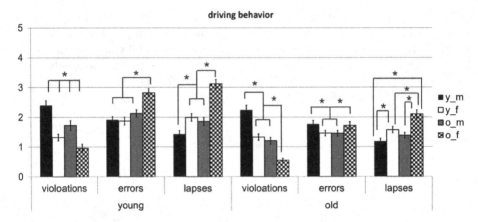

Fig. 3. Mean ratings from the young group of participants (left side) and the old group of participants (right side) for the four faces (young male = y_m, young female = y_f, old male = o_m, old female = o_f) regarding driving behavior based on the DBQ. Error bars indicate standard errors of the mean.

3.2   Study 2

Comparable with Experiment 1, a MANOVA was conducted for each questionnaire data set (MDSI and DBQ). The age group of the photograph had been introduced as a between subject factor to reduce overall testing time. For the MDSI data the MANOVA revealed a main effect of the participant's gender, Wilk's λ = .89, $F(8,149)$ = 2.40, p = .02, a main effect of the photograph's age group, Wilk's λ = .72, $F(8,149)$ = 7.23, p < .01, a main effect of the photograph's gender group, Wilk's λ = .51, $F(8,149)$ = 18.25, p < .01 and an interaction between the photograph's age and gender group, Wilk's λ = .79, $F(8,149)$ = 4.94, p = < .01. For the DBQ scales, there was a main effect of the age group of photograph, Wilk's λ = .71, $F(3,154)$ = 21.00, p < .01, as well as a main effect of the gender group of photograph, Wilk's λ = .49, $F(3,154)$ = 53.21, p < .01. The interaction between the participant's and the photograph's age group also reached significance, Wilk's λ = .84, $F(3,154)$ = 9.51, p < .01.

This pattern of results was further explored using additional univariate analyses of variance (ANOVA) for each scale of the MDSI and DBQ with Holm-Bonferroni alpha level adjustment.

The main effect of the photograph's age group was present for angry, high velocity, anxious, and careful driving, as well as for all scales of the DBQ scales (all p < .01). The main effect of the gender group of the photograph was found for all scales (all p < .01) with the exception of risky (p = .92) and distress reduction driving (p = .74). The interaction between age and gender group of the photograph was apparent for dissociative, risky, and careful driving, as well as for errors and lapses (all p < .01). The mean ratings for each MDSI scale are shown in Fig. 4 and for each DBQ scale in Fig. 5.

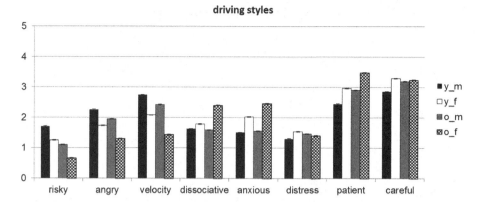

Fig. 4. Mean ratings for the four faces (young man = y_m, young woman = y_f, old man = o_m, old woman = o_f) regarding the eight driving styles based on the MDSI. Error bars indicate standard errors of the mean.

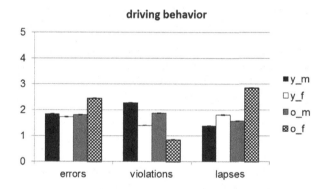

Fig. 5. Mean ratings for the four faces (young man = y_m, young woman = y_f, old man = o_m, old woman = o_f) regarding driving behavior based on the DBQ. Error bars indicate standard errors of the mean.

Significant group differences in D scores were found for the attentive/dissociative category, $t(33) = -4.57$, $p > .001$, and the skilled/unskilled category, $t(31) = -4.67$, $p > .001$, with higher D scores for female than for male participants (see Fig. 6), indicating that female participants more strongly associated attentive and skilled with female compared to male participants, who more strongly associated attentive and skilled with male.

344   C. A. Faust-Christmann et al.

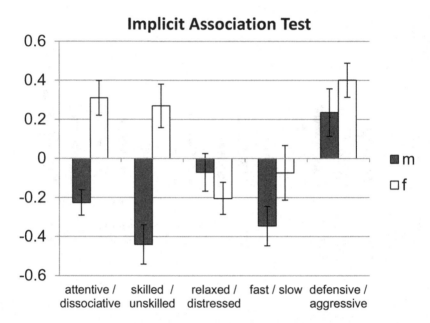

Fig. 6. Mean D scores for male (m, grey boxes) and female participants (f, white boxes). D scores above zero indicate stronger associations between the female attentive/skilled/relaxed/fast/defensive and the male-dissociative/unskilled/distressed/slow/aggressive category pairings. Error bars indicate standard errors of the mean.

4   Discussion

The goal of this study was to evaluate if pre-selected faces (see Sect. 2.1 for details) are associated with distinctive driver stereotypes related to their perceived age and gender. Study 1 dealt with explicit stereotypes on driving behavior and driving styles. Ratings were made by young and old adults. Study 2 replicated the explicit ratings with a larger sample and also included a set of IATs to reveal implicit stereotypes on driving behavior and driving styles.

4.1   Study 1

In line with the expectation that young men are perceived as risk takers (hypothesis 1), the photograph of the young man received the highest scores for the risky, angry, and high velocity driving styles. This finding was evident both in the ratings of young and old participants. Moreover, in line with the stereotype of the passive, non-competitive female driver (hypothesis 2), the women received higher ratings for the patient, and careful driving styles compared to the young man. Additionally, comparable with the previous attribution of females as nervous drivers [12], the driving style of women was described as more anxious and geared towards distress-reduction. In line with prior findings that old drivers are expected to be less aggressive [6] and to be at lower risk for accidents [7], the old man also received high ratings for the careful driving style.

In compliance with stereotypes of higher driving skills in male drivers (hypothesis 3, also see [7, 10, 13]), there was a main effect of the gender group of the photograph on ascribed lapses and errors. This pattern was particularly pronounced for ratings of the old woman. In line with hypothesis 4, the opposite pattern of results was found for violations. Here, the young man received the highest score, followed by the young woman and the old man, while the old woman received the lowest score.

By comparing the ratings of the young and old subsample two main findings become apparent. First, that the overall pattern of results is quite similar in both subsamples. The results underpin the existence of explicit stereotypes of young men as risky, angry and high velocity drivers committing a lot of violations and of especially old women as patient and anxious drivers with a lot of lapses and errors. Second, by comparing the ratings of the young and old subsample for the old man, pronounced in-group out-group effects become apparent. For the young subsample, the only difference between the young woman and the old man was found for the patient driving style (higher ratings for the young woman). By contrast, the old subsample rated the old man's driving style as less risky and dissociative, as prone to lower velocities, and to be more patient and careful compared to the young woman. The group serving bias is also apparent for the DBQ ratings. Here, the old woman received much lower scores by the old subsample compared to the young subsample. This is the first demonstration of age group specific biases. No in-group out-group effects were observed with regards to gender. This is inconsistent with previous reports of gender-specific stereotypes. Here, it had been reported that females rated men's likelihood of accidents as a higher than male raters [7].

4.2   Study 2

Explicit Stereotypes
With regard to explicit stereotypes, the second study was able to replicate the patterns observed in the first study. In line with the first study, the young man received the highest scores for the risky, angry, and high velocity driving style, whereas the old woman received the highest scores for dissociative, anxious and patient driving style. Moreover, for the pattern of ascribed errors, violations and lapses were replicated, with most errors and lapses attributed to the old woman and most violations to the young man. The second study, could again not establish any in-group out-group effects with regard to gender.

Implicit Stereotypes
In-group out-group effects with regard to gender were, however, apparent in the implicit stereotype measurements. Women were strongly associated with attentive and skilled drivers, whereas the opposite pattern of results was found for men. For defensive and slow drivers, both male and female raters showed a tendency to associate defensive drivers with female and aggressive drivers with male. The implicit association of male drivers with an aggressive and female drivers with a defensive driving style is consistent with the findings from the observed explicit driving stereotypes.

The current study is the first to reveal implicit driver stereotypes with respect to gender (but see [8] for implicit driver stereotypes regarding age). Further studies are, however, needed to substantiate the findings of implicit driver stereotypes.

4.3 Outlook

To summarize, the four faces are associated with explicit and implicit driver stereotypes. For experiments on the Proteus effect, observable influences upon driving behavior are expected for driving errors, violations and lapses, as well as upon driving velocity with more violations and higher velocity for the young male avatar and with more errors and lapses for the old female avatar.

All faces were remodeled with Autodesk 3ds Max for further experiments investigating the Proteus effect regarding walking speed [24] and driving behavior based on these results (see Fig. 7). Body models for each gender and age group were constructed based on data from a representative serial measurement campaign of German adults conducted between 2007 and 2008 by the Forschungsinstitut Hohenstein Prof. Dr. Jürgen Mecheels GmbH & Co.KG and the Human Solutions GmbH.

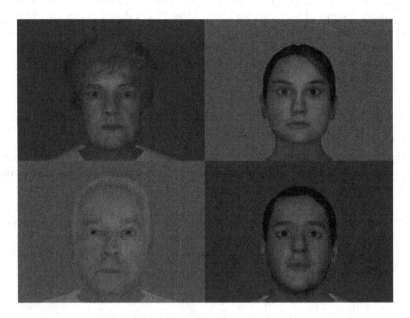

Fig. 7. Avatar faces based on the four faces.

An additional questionnaire based study (N = 50, 22−81 years) asked for ratings of both the original photos of the faces and the resulting avatars with regard to their attractiveness, likeability, energy and perceived age [21] to ensure comparability of the avatars with the original faces. Spearman's rank correlation analysis revealed systematic associations between the face and avatar ratings. The correlations were significant for all combinations of the same face and avatar (all $p \leq .05$), for the old man (attractiveness: ρ = .341, likeability: ρ = .401, energy: ρ = .423, perceived age: ρ = .396), the old woman (attractiveness: ρ = .565, likeability: ρ = .343, energy: ρ = .520, perceived age: ρ = .424), the young man (attractiveness: ρ = .499, likeability: ρ = .555, energy: ρ = .493, perceived age: ρ = .414), and the young woman (attractiveness: ρ = .324, likeability: ρ = .334, energy: ρ = .337, perceived age: ρ = .457).

In a further study, 67 young adults (18–34 years) either experienced the young (22 participants) or old avatars of their own gender (23 participants) in IVR, or did not enter IVR (22 participants). They then rated the two avatars of their own gender with regard to their anticipated walking speed. One-sample upper-tailed z-tests for dichotomous outcomes revealed that the elderly avatars were rated as slower more often than would be expected by chance. This was apparent for participants who had previously embodied the older avatar, z = 2.294, p = .022, in the ratings of participants who had embodied the young avatar, z = 1.705, p = .044, and for the control group who had not entered IVR, z = 2.558, p = .016.

The avatar's different age groups were further successful in eliciting Proteus effects on real life walking speed after participants had left IVR, as participants tended to traverse a set distance slower after embodying the older gender-matched avatars than either the group of participants who had previously embodied the younger avatars or a non-IVR control group [24]. Future studies will explore, whether the avatars can elicit similar effects on objective driving behaviors in driving simulators, e.g., on the choice of driving speed. In these studies, the temporal stability of such Proteus effects after leaving IVR, as well as the preconditions for their occurrence, will be of particular interest.

Acknowledgements. This project was supported by the Landesforschungsinitiative Rheinland-Pfalz (Germany) Potentialbereich Cognitive Science. The junior research group wearHEALTH is funded by the Federal Ministry of Education and Research (Bundesministerium für Bildung und Forschung, BMBF, reference number: 16SV7115).

References

1. Yee, N., Bailenson, J.: The proteus effect. The effect of transformed self-representation on behavior. Hum. Commun. Res. **33**, 271–290 (2007)
2. Yee, N., Bailenson, J.N., Ducheneaut, N.: The proteus effect. Commun. Res. **36**, 285–312 (2009)
3. Branaghan, R.J., Gray, R.: Nonconscious activation of an elderly stereotype and speed of driving. Percept. Mot. Skills **110**, 580–592 (2010)
4. Schmid Mast, M., Sieverding, M., Esslen, M., Graber, K., Jäncke, L.: Masculinity causes speeding in young men. Accid. Anal. Prev. **40**, 840–842 (2008)
5. Greenwald, A.G., Banaji, M.R.: Implicit social cognition: attitudes, self-esteem, and stereotypes. Psychol. Rev. **102**, 4–27 (1995)
6. Davies, G.M., Patel, D.: The influence of car and driver stereotypes on attributions of vehicle speed, position on the road and culpability in a road accident scenario. Leg. Criminological Psychol. **10**, 45–62 (2005)

7. Glendon, A.I., Dorn, L., Davies, D.R., Matthews, G., Taylor, R.G.: Age and gender differences in perceived accident likelihood and driver competences. Risk Anal. **16**, 755–762 (1996)
8. Lambert, A.E., Seegmiller, J.K., Stefanucci, J.K., Watson, J.M.: On working memory capacity and implicit associations between advanced age and dangerous driving stereotypes. Appl. Cognit. Psychol. **27**, 306–313 (2013)
9. Locksley, A., Borgida, E., Brekke, N., Hepburn, C.: Sex stereotypes and social judgment. J. Pers. Soc. Psychol. **39**, 821–831 (1980)
10. Granié, M.-A., Papafava, E.: Gender stereotypes associated with vehicle driving among French preadolescents and adolescents. Transp. Res. Part F Traffic Psychol. Behav. **14**, 341–353 (2011)
11. Simon, F., Corbett, C.: Road traffic offending, stress, age, and accident history among male and female drivers. Ergonomics **39**, 757–780 (1996)
12. Berger, M.L.: Women drivers!: the emergence of folklore and stereotypic opinions concerning feminine automotive behavior. Women's Stud. Int. Forum **9**, 257–263 (1986)
13. DeJoy, D.M.: An examination of gender differences in traffic accident risk perception. Accid. Anal. Prev. **24**, 237–246 (1992)
14. Lajunen, T., Summala, H.: Driving experience, personality, and skill and safety-motive dimensions in drivers' self-assessments. Pers. Individ. Differ. **19**, 307–318 (1995)
15. Reason, J., Manstead, A., Stradling, S., Baxter, J., Campbell, K.: Errors and violations on the roads: a real distinction? Ergonomics **33**, 1315–1332 (1990)
16. Taubman-Ben-Ari, O., Mikulincer, M., Gillath, O.: The multidimensional driving style inventory—scale construct and validation. Accid. Anal. Prev. **36**, 323–332 (2004)
17. Parker, D., Reason, J., Manstead, A., Stradling, S.: Driving errors, driving violations and accident involvement. TERG **38**, 1036–1048 (1995)
18. Taubman-Ben-Ari, O., Skvirsky, V.: The multidimensional driving style inventory a decade later: review of the literature and re-evaluation of the scale. Accid. Anal. Prev. **93**, 179–188 (2016)
19. Greenwald, A.G., McGhee, D.E., Schwartz, J.L.K.: Measuring individual differences in implicit cognition: the implicit association test. J. Pers. Soc. Psychol. **74**, 1464–1480 (1998)
20. Minear, M., Park, D.C.: A lifespan database of adult facial stimuli. Behav. Res. Methods Instrum. Comput. **36**, 630–633 (2004). A Journal of the Psychonomic Society, Inc.
21. Ebner, N.C.: Age of face matters: age-group differences in ratings of young and old faces. Behav. Res. **40**, 130–136 (2008)
22. Lane, K.A., Banaji, M.R., Nosek, B.A., Greenwald, A.G.: Understanding and Using the Implicit Association Test: IV: What We Know (So Far) about the Method. Guilford Press, New York (2007)
23. Greenwald, A.G., Nosek, B.A., Banaji, M.R.: Understanding and using the implicit association test: I. an improved scoring algorithm. J. Pers. Soc. Psychol. **85**, 197–216 (2003)
24. Reinhard, R., Shah, K.G., Faust-Christmann, C.A., Lachmann, T.: Acting your avatar's age: effects of virtual reality avatar embodiment on real life walking speed. Media Psychology (in press)

Towards a Framework to Model Intelligent Avatars in Immersive Virtual Environments for Studying Human Behavior in Building Fire Emergencies

Jing Lin and Nan Li[✉]

Department of Construction Management,
Tsinghua University, Beijing 100084, China
lin-jl7@mails.tsinghua.edu.cn, nanli@tsinghua.edu.cn

Abstract. Driven by the fast development of virtual reality (VR) technologies, immersive virtual environments (IVEs) have been frequently used to conduct human behavior experiments for studying human behavior in building fire emergencies. Avatars in these IVEs are usually used to provide social influence and improve the sense of presence experienced by participants. However, limited intelligence of avatars in prior studies significantly lowered the level of sense of presence and reality experienced by participants. Improved intelligent avatars (IAs) are needed for developing high-quality building fire IVEs. A framework for modeling IAs to support the investigation of human behavior in building fire emergencies was proposed in this study. A number of levels of IA intelligence were defined based on the characteristics of avatars in VR for studying human behavior in building fire emergencies. This study also proposed a roadmap to achieve each of these levels of intelligence. A case study was presented to demonstrate how the framework could be used to guide the design of IAs for research purpose. It was concluded that applications of IAs in VR experiments could benefit the investigation of human behaviors, crowd simulation in building fires, and even fire safety design of buildings.

Keywords: Virtual reality · Intelligence · Avatar · Human behavior · Building fire · Evacuation

1 Introduction

Human behavior in building fires, such as occupants' evacuation behavior and firefighters' relief behavior, has been studied for decades. Recently, immersive virtual environments (IVEs) have been used to conduct human behavior experiments in many studies [16, 23, 25], driven by the fast development of virtual reality (VR) technologies. These IVE-enabled experiments allow for the collection of rich behavioral data in controlled laboratory environments to support the investigation of human behavior in building fire emergencies [19]. Avatars in these IVEs, such as those used in [14, 19], are usually modeled to have limited, pre-defined behaviors that are arbitrarily set by researchers, without any autonomous responses to or interactions with experiment

© Springer Nature Switzerland AG 2019
J. Y. C. Chen and G. Fragomeni (Eds.): HCII 2019, LNCS 11574, pp. 349–360, 2019.
https://doi.org/10.1007/978-3-030-21607-8_27

participants or other elements in the IVEs. Limited intelligence of avatars significantly lowers the level of sense of presence and reality experienced by participants. As a result, the behavioral data collected in such virtual environments may be less real and valid, compromising their ability to support the investigation of human behavior. Thus, improved intelligent avatars (IAs) are needed for developing high-quality building fire IVEs. This study developed a framework to model IAs, by defining a number of levels of intelligence of IAs, and proposing a roadmap to achieve each of these levels of intelligence.

2 Definition of Intelligent Avatar

Drawing on the concept of artificial intelligence (AI) [21], IAs in IVE-based experiments should think and act like humans or rationally. To simulate the realistic social environment, IAs in IVE-based experiments for studying human behavior in building fire emergencies should act like humans. There are four types of abilities that AIs need to possess in order to perform like humans [21]: (1) communicating ability in human language; (2) memory ability to store information, such as behavioral rules; (3) response ability by using the memory and assessing the results of the responses; and (4) learning ability to adapt to new scenarios and form new memory. Accordingly, behavior target setting (BT), response to the environment (RE), response to avatars' behavior (RAB), response to participants' behavior (RPB), and learning and adaption ability (LAA) are identified as fundamental characteristics of IAs in building fire IVEs in this study, as shown in Table 1. Each of these five characteristics can be further divided into several functional levels, as described in Table 1. A higher level of a given characteristic can be reached by achieving associated new functions, in addition to those already achieved at the lower level, that are described in the rightmost column of the table. It needs to be noted that avatars with none of these characteristics cannot be called IA and are hence not considered in this study.

Table 1. Functional levels of characteristics of IA in building fire IVEs

Characteristics	Descriptions	Levels (Low to high) and associated new functions
Behavioral target (BT)	It could set and modify behavioral targets based on his/her role and perception of the environment	• BT1: Have a behavior target that could be fulfilled by its behavior; • BT2: Can choose behavior targets based on its role; • BT3: Can define behavior targets in different priorities; • BT4: Can modify behavior targets based on its perception of the environment

(continued)

Table 1. (*continued*)

Characteristics	Descriptions	Levels (Low to high) and associated new functions
Response to environment (RE)	It could respond to perceived environment by text, voice or other reactions	• RE1: Can respond one-time to a pre-defined situation, such as an occurrence of a fire; • RE2: Can respond consecutively to multiple pre-defined situations; • RE3: Can interact with perceived environment by text, voice or other reactions
Response to avatars' behavior (RAB)	It could perceive and respond to other avatars' behavior by text, voice or other reactions	• RAB1: Can respond one-time to a certain avatar's pre-defined behavior, such as calling for help; • RAB2: Can respond to a specific pre-defined behavior of any avatar; • RAB3: Can respond consecutively to multiple pre-defined behaviors of any avatar; • RAB4: Can interact with avatars by text, voice or other reactions
Response to participants' behavior (RPB)	It could respond to perceived participants' behavior by text, voice or other reactions	• RPB1: Can respond one-time to a specific pre-defined behavior of a single participant, such as his/her proximity; • RPB2: Can respond to a specific pre-defined behavior of multiple participants; • RPB3: Can respond consecutively to multiple pre-defined behaviors of a single participant; • RPB4: Can interact with participants by text, voice or other reactions
Learning and adaption ability (LAA)	It could adapt to any unexpected situations by learning from experiences	• LAA1: Can adapt to unexpected situations by trying random choices of pre-defined responses; • LAA2: Can adapt to unexpected situations by learning from its experiences; • LAA3: Can adapt to unexpected situations by observing and learning from other avatars' experiences; • LAA4: Can adapt to unexpected situations by observing and learning from participants' experiences

3   Avatars in Building Fire IVEs

Avatars in building fire IVEs that have been modeled and used in previous studies are reviewed and assessed based on the above characteristics, to summarize the state of the art of and identify the gaps in modeling IAs. A total of twelve relevant studies were found through keyword searching in *Web of Knowledge*, *Scopus*, and *Google Scholar*. These studies were published between 2008 and 2018 in nine international journals and three international conferences. A detailed review of these publications found that avatars reported in eight of them did not qualify as IAs based on the aforementioned criterion. For avatars in the remaining four studies, only two characteristics were partially achieved. Specifically, RE2 was achieved, as some avatars could avoid obstacles during evacuation wayfinding [20]. Some avatars achieved RPB1 since they could respond to the proximity of a participant with onscreen text or voice [2, 7, 9]. Avatars in prior studies did not exhibit other characteristics of IAs.

In general, the avatars in prior studies had relatively low levels of intelligence. However, it is important to note that the research objectives vary in different studies, such as studying the impact of signage [24] or social influence [12] on human behavior in building fire emergencies. Considering that modeling ideal IAs may come at considerable costs, avatars do not always have to be the most intelligent. Rather, the level of intelligence of avatars should be tailored to the needs of specific studies. Thus, this study proposed a framework that provided definitions of different levels of intelligence of avatars, which could be used to fulfill different needs in studying human behavior in building fire emergencies, as well as a roadmap that ultimately leaded to the development of the most intelligent IAs.

4   Framework for Developing IAs in Building Fire IVEs

Achieving higher levels of intelligence relies heavily on the advancement of various VR and AI technologies, such as graphical processing hardware capabilities, rendering and visualization algorithms, and cognitive and behavioral models. To pave the way for more intelligent avatars, this study classifies the intelligence of avatars in building fire IVEs at five different levels, each of which is defined based on the aforementioned five characteristics of IAs. These definitions are summarized in Table 2. IAs at every intelligence level either inherit the same characteristics of the lower level AIs, or are more advanced with regard to certain characteristics as suggested in Table 2.

Based on the proposed framework, a simple character (Level I) can respond to a specific change in the environment or from one specific avatar or participant for only once [2, 7, 9]. For instance, when a participant was near a simple character acting like a victim, another simple character acting as medical service worker would speak to the participant "*I'm taking care of him; you go to the exit*" [9]. An intelligent character (Level II) can continuously respond to a specific pre-defined behavior of multiple avatars and participants [20]. Both simple and intelligent characters would not be able to respond to scenarios that are not pre-defined. Agents, on the other hand, can respond to unexpected situations. There are simple agents, intelligent agents, and human agents, which are differentiated mainly by their different levels of learning ability. A simple

Table 2. Definitions of different levels of avatar intelligence based on levels of IAs' characteristics

Levels of avatar intelligence	Associated levels of IAs characteristics				
	BT	RE	RAB	RPB	LAA
I - Simple character	BT 1	RE 1	RAB 1	RPB 1	
II - Intelligent character			RAB 2	RPB 2	
III - Simple agent	BT 2	RE 2	RAB 3	RPB 3	LAA 1
IV - Intelligent agent	BT 3	RE 3	RAB 4	RPB 4	LAA 2&3
V - Human agent	BT 4				LAA 4

agent (Level III) can choose behavioral targets based on its role, and respond to environments, avatars, and participants continuously as pre-defined. Since human behavior in building fire emergencies has a characteristic of randomness [17], a simple agent responds to unexpected situations by randomly selecting a behavior that it can perform. An intelligent agent (Level IV) can further prioritize behavioral targets, interact with environments, avatars and participants in different ways, and learn from how it responded to the scenarios in the past and how other IAs respond to diverse scenarios. Lastly, a human agent (Level V) can modify behavioral targets and adjust behaviors to adapt to surrounding environment by pre-defined rules, and learning from its own, other IAs' or participants' experiences.

In previous studies, simple characters, intelligent characters, and simple agents have been used [2, 7, 9, 20]. Ideally, IAs should be developed in a way that they both satisfy the requirements of research and minimize time and cost for modeling. Therefore, based on a holistic review of prior research, different levels of IAs are suggested for different aims for research, as outlined in Fig. 1, which is also a roadmap that highlights the technical bottlenecks for achieving every level of IAs and demonstrates how the most intelligent IAs can be ultimately achieved.

Some of the bottlenecks highlighted in Fig. 1 need technological breakthroughs. For instance, although voice recognition has been widely used in speeches [10] and smart home systems [1], how to recognize the voice of participants and present reasonable voice feedback to participants would require advanced voice recognition technologies in building fire emergencies. What would be more challenging is to train IAs to learn, not only from its own behavior, but also from other avatars and participants. This learning process includes perception and recognition of others' expression, voice, behavior and surrounding environment, and evaluation of consequences of others' responses.

As the most intelligent IA, a human agent should perceive the changeable environment, think like humans, and behave like humans to fulfill their behavioral targets in building fire emergencies. Based on the existing literature on human behavioral response in building fires [4, 6, 11, 13, 22], the cognitive process of behavioral decision-making in response to fire emergencies is identified, based on which a conceptual model of a human agent is developed in this study (Fig. 2).

Level

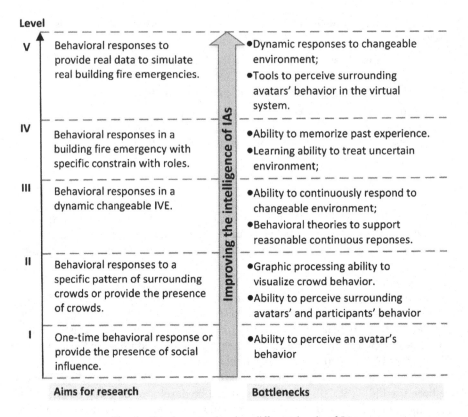

	Aims for research	Bottlenecks
V	Behavioral responses to provide real data to simulate real building fire emergencies.	•Dynamic responses to changeable environment; •Tools to perceive surrounding avatars' behavior in the virtual system.
IV	Behavioral responses in a building fire emergency with specific constrain with roles.	•Ability to memorize past experience. •Learning ability to treat uncertain environment;
III	Behavioral responses in a dynamic changeable IVE.	•Ability to continuously respond to changeable environment; •Behavioral theories to support reasonable continuous reponses.
II	Behavioral responses to a specific pattern of surrounding crowds or provide the presence of crowds.	•Graphic processing ability to visualize crowd behavior. •Ability to perceive surrounding avatars' and participants' behavior
I	One-time behavioral response or provide the presence of social influence.	•Ability to perceive an avatar's behavior

Improving the intelligence of IAs

Fig. 1. Roadmap to develop different levels of IAs

A human agent should have one or more achievable behavioral targets based on its role in a building fire [18]. For instance, a 'patient' agent should investigate whether a fire exists and set a target of successful evacuation from the hospital, whereas a 'nurse' agent should have an additional target of helping patients to evacuate. Different behavioral targets should be assigned different priorities [3, 5, 15]. Human agents would keep perceiving the surrounding environments [8], including physical environment, other human agents and experiment participants, and take actions accordingly. In the proposed model, there are two different decision-making processes for human agents' behaviors. The first one is to follow pre-defined rules for pre-defined scenarios, such as the avatars modeled in [2, 7, 9, 20]. The pre-defined scenarios and rules are usually based on existing knowledge of human behavior in building fire emergencies. If the perceived environment is different than all pre-defined scenarios, human agents would set their primary target and take actions based on learning outcomes about others' behavior and their own past experiences in similar scenarios [15]. During their evacuation process, human agents would continuously perceive environments, take actions, fulfill all targets based on priorities, until all behavioral targets are fulfilled.

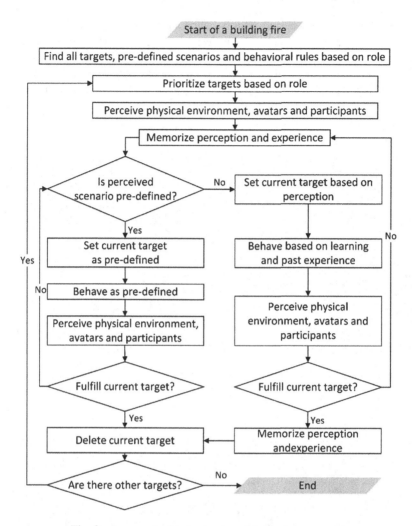

Fig. 2. A conceptual behavioral model of a human agent

5   Case Study

This paper presents a case study which used IAs in VR-based experiments for studying the effects of crowd dynamics, design visibility and residential location on people's evacuation wayfinding in building fires.

Based on the roadmap illustrated in Fig. 1, studies aiming at understanding people's behavioral responses to the wayfinding pattern of surrounding crowds should involve avatars of intelligent character (level II). Thus, the case study should model the avatars in its IVEs who could respond to a specific pre-defined behavior of any other avatars and the experiment participants.

The IVE used in the case study was based on a metro station in Beijing, China. The script of the fire scenario in the IVE was designed based on a fire accident in a metro station in Hong Kong: fire occurred in a metro train in a metro section; passengers (avatars) were initially onboard the train or waiting at the platform (Fig. 3); the burning metro train approached platform in the station (Fig. 4); and passengers (avatars) had to evacuate from the station. The participant acted as a passenger initially positioned at the platform.

Fig. 3. Intelligent characters waiting for metro train at platform in the case study

Fig. 4. Burning metro train approaching platform in metro station in the case study

There were 53 IAs in the IVE that varied in age and gender. Each IA had a visual access with a range of 270° based on its head orientation. When the burning metro train emerged within 15 m of the IAs' view, the IA would perceive the signal of a fire emergency and start to evacuate. Based on literature review, three patterns of crowd dynamics during evacuation wayfinding were modeled in the IVE: even distribution (50% vs. 50%), uneven distribution (80% vs. 20%), and binominal distribution (100% vs. 0%, as shown in Fig. 5) at each intersection. The behavioral target of every avatar was set as running through its pre-defined path that leaded to one of the exits of the station. To improve the realism of the crowd dynamics, avatars were modeled to be able to respond to collisions with other avatars and participants by scuttling away from collided avatars and participants. Specifically, the tactile sensor of IAs would continuously work to detect the distance from other objects, IAs, and participants. Once the distance was within 0.1 m, IAs would slightly adjust their orientation to avoid collisions.

Fig. 5. Intelligent characters evacuating from metro station in the case study

While the results of the case study are still being analyzed and prepared for a separate publication, there are two lessons learned from the use of avatars in the case study that are noteworthy. Firstly, the maximum number of IAs that could be modeled in the IVE was largely constrained by the capability of mainstream graphics processors (GTX 1080 was used in the study). Overloaded graphics processors could cause discontinuous or delayed display of the IVE shown to participants. This prevented the possibility of modeling a high-density crowd that would block certain points in the evacuation paths in the IVE, as it would happen in reality. Future research should consider the tradeoff between the need for more intelligence and finer-grained rendering in IAs, and the need for simply more IAs. Secondly, avatars' responses to the proximity of both virtual elements and participants were relatively easy to model. However, their abilities to respond to gestures of avatars and participants, and to learn from past experiences were still challenging to achieve. Future research requiring IAs with these characteristics would need novel solutions to address these needs.

6   Conclusion

Avatars could improve IVEs used in the investigation of human behavior in building fire emergencies. However, the intelligence of avatars used in prior studies was not always sufficient to provide a high sense of presence and social influence. This study firstly defined what an IA is and what important characteristics an IA should possess. Secondly, the IAs used in prior research on human behavior in building fire emergencies was reviewed. By identifying the state of the art in IAs development and the existing gaps, a framework for modeling IAs to better support the investigation of human behavior in building fire emergencies was proposed in this study. Different levels of avatar intelligence in building fire IVEs were defined in this framework for satisfying different research needs. Moreover, the framework includes a roadmap to achieve high intelligence in IAs, which also identifies the bottlenecks in achieving each of the five levels of IAs. While the highest level of IAs, human agent, is yet to be achieved at the moment due to technological and methodological constraints, the proposed framework provides a conceptual behavioral model of a human agent. Future research, by benefiting from the advancement of knowledge about mechanisms of human behavior in building fire emergencies as well as the development of VR and AI technologies, could improve the intelligence of avatars based on the roadmap and the conceptual behavioral model.

A case study was presented, which guided by the proposed framework utilized intelligent characters in the investigation of people's wayfinding behavior in building fire emergencies. Lessons learned from the case study were reported. As the authors envisioned and the case study demonstrated, applications of IAs in VR experiments could largely improve VR-based human evacuation behavior studies, and ultimately enable more fine-grained crowd simulation in building fires, and support reliable evaluation of fire safety design of buildings as well as various other applications.

Acknowledgments. This work was supported by the National Natural Science Foundation of China (NSFC) under Grant No. 71603145, the Humanities and Social Sciences Foundation of the Ministry of Education (MOE) of China under Grant No. 16YJC630052, and the Tsinghua University-Glodon Joint Research Centre for Building Information Model (RCBIM). The authors are grateful for the support of NSFC, MOE, and RCBIM. Any opinions, findings, and conclusions or recommendations expressed in this paper are those of the authors and do not necessarily reflect the views of the funding agencies.

References

1. Alshu'Eili, H., Gupta, G.S., Mukhopadhyay, S.: Voice recognition based wireless home automation system. In: International Conference on Mechatronics (2011)
2. Becker-Asano, C., Sun, D., Kleim, B., Scheel, C.N., Tuschen-Caffier, B., Nebel, B.: Outline of an empirical study on the effects of emotions on strategic behavior in virtual emergencies. In: D'Mello, S., Graesser, A., Schuller, B., Martin, J.-C. (eds.) ACII 2011. LNCS, vol. 6975, pp. 508–517. Springer, Heidelberg (2011). https://doi.org/10.1007/978-3-642-24571-8_64

3. Bernardini, G., Quagliarini, E., D'Orazio, M.: Towards creating a combined database for earthquake pedestrians' evacuation models. Saf. Sci. **82**, 77–94 (2016). https://doi.org/10.1016/j.ssci.2015.09.001

4. Bode, N.W.F., Codling, E.A.: Human exit route choice in virtual crowd evacuations. Anim. Behav. **86**, 347–358 (2013). https://doi.org/10.1016/j.anbehav.2013.05.025

5. Darken, R.P., Peterson, B.: Spatial orientation, wayfinding and representation. Handb. Virtual Environ. Technol. **4083**, 1–22 (2001). https://doi.org/10.1080/13506280444000058

6. Dash, N., Gladwin, H.: Evacuation decision making and behavioral responses: individual and household. Nat. Hazards Rev. **8**, 69–77 (2007)

7. Drury, J., et al.: Cooperation versus competition in a mass emergency evacuation: a new laboratory simulation and a new theoretical model. Behav. Res. Methods **41**, 957–970 (2009). https://doi.org/10.3758/BRM.41.3.957

8. Galea, E.R., Hulse, L., Day, R., Siddiqui, A., Sharp, G.: The UK WTC 9/11 evacuation study : an overview of findings derived from first-hand interview data and computer modelling, pp. 501–521 (2012). https://doi.org/10.1002/fam.1070

9. Gamberini, L., Chittaro, L., Spagnolli, A., Carlesso, C.: Psychological response to an emergency in virtual reality: effects of victim ethnicity and emergency type on helping behavior and navigation. Comput. Hum. Behav. **48**, 104–113 (2015)

10. Haderlein, T., et al.: Application of automatic speech recognition to quantitative assessment of tracheoesophageal speech with different signal quality. Folia Phoniatr. Logop. **61**, 12–17 (2008)

11. Haghani, M., Sarvi, M.: Crowd behaviour and motion: empirical methods. Transp. Res. Part B Methodol. **0**, 1–42 (2017). https://doi.org/10.1016/j.trb.2017.06.017

12. Kinateder, M., Warren, W.H.: Social influence on evacuation behavior in real and virtual environments. Front. Robot. AI **3**, 1–8 (2016). https://doi.org/10.3389/frobt.2016.00043

13. Kinateder, M.T., Kuligowski, E.D., Reneke, P.A., Peacock, R.D.: Risk perception in fire evacuation behavior revisited: definitions, related concepts, and empirical evidence. Fire Sci. Rev. **4**, 1 (2015). https://doi.org/10.1186/s40038-014-0005-z

14. Kinateder, M.T., Müller, M., Jost, M., Mühlberger, A., Pauli, P.: Social influence in a virtual tunnel fire–influence of conflicting information on evacuation behavior. Appl. Ergon. **45**, 1649–1659 (2014)

15. Kobes, M., Helsloot, I., De, V.B., Post, J.G.: Building safety and human behaviour in fire: a literature review. Fire Saf. J. **45**, 1–11 (2010)

16. Lin, J., Cao, L., Li, N.: Assessing the influence of repeated exposures and mental stress on human wayfinding performance in indoor environments using virtual reality technology. Adv. Eng. Inform. **39**, 53–61 (2019)

17. Lovreglio, R., Fonzone, A., dell'Olio, L., Borri, D.: A study of herding behaviour in exit choice during emergencies based on random utility theory. Saf. Sci. **82**, 421–431 (2016). https://doi.org/10.1016/j.ssci.2015.10.015

18. Lovreglio, R., et al.: Prototyping virtual reality serious games for building earthquake preparedness: the Auckland City hospital case study. Adv. Eng. Inform. **38**, 670–682 (2018). https://doi.org/10.1016/j.aei.2018.08.018

19. Ren, A., Chen, C., Luo, Y.: Simulation of emergency evacuation in virtual reality. Tsinghua Sci. Technol. **13**, 674–680 (2008)

20. Sharma, S., Jerripothula, S., Mackey, S., Soumare, O.: Immersive virtual reality environment of a subway evacuation on a cloud for disaster preparedness and response training, pp. 1–6 (2015)

21. Stuart, R., Peter, N.: Artificial Intelligence: A Modern Approach. Prentice Hall, Eaglewood Cliffs (1995)

22. Tong, D., Canter, D.: The decision to evacuate: a study of the motivations which contribute to evacuation in the event of fire. Fire Saf. J. **9**, 257–265 (1985). https://doi.org/10.1016/0379-7112(85)90036-0

23. Tucker, A., Marsh, K.L., Gifford, T., Lu, X., Luh, P.B., Astur, R.S.: The effects of information and hazard on evacuee behavior in virtual reality. Fire Saf. J. **99**, 1–11 (2018). https://doi.org/10.1016/j.firesaf.2018.04.011

24. Vilar, E., Rebelo, F., Noriega, P., Duarte, E., Mayhorn, C.B.: Effects of competing environmental variables and signage on route-choices in simulated everyday and emergency wayfinding situations. Ergonomics **57**, 511–524 (2014)

25. Zou, H., Li, N., Cao, L.: Emotional response-based approach for assessing the sense of presence of subjects in virtual building evacuation studies. J. Comput. Civ. Eng. **31**, 04017028 (2017). https://doi.org/10.1061/(ASCE)CP.1943-5487.0000679

The Effects of Embodiment in Virtual Reality on Implicit Gender Bias

Stephanie Schulze[✉], Toni Pence[✉], Ned Irvine[✉], and Curry Guinn[✉]

Univeristy of North Carolina at Wilmington, Wilmington, NC 28403, USA
{ss4134,pencet,irvinen,guinn}@uncw.edu

Abstract. Virtual reality allows users to have a virtual body that is different from their physical body, an idea known as embodiment. In previous research, embodiment in different types of avatars affected implicit attitudes. The purpose of this experiment was to discover how embodiment in different gendered avatars in virtual reality affects implicit gender bias. For embodiment, participants were placed in an office virtual environment with a male or female avatar. First, there was an orientation period where participants grew accustomed to their virtual body while looking at a mirror placed in front of them. Next, virtual humans of different genders walked in and out of the office with the mirror in view. Each participant completed a gender and leadership Implicit Association Test before and after the embodiment experience. The difference between post test scores and preliminary test scores indicates how implicit bias was affected.

Keywords: Virtual reality · Embodiment · Gender bias

1   Introduction and Related Work

Virtual reality has a multitude of applications. One use is to provide a virtual body in place of the physical one, known as embodiment. Whether the virtual body is similar or quite different than the physical body, it is possible for a user to transfer body ownership to the virtual body [1]. The idea of body ownership stems from the rubber hand illusion where a rubber hand is placed in front of a participant and is stroked at the same time as their real hand which remains hidden [2]. Participants reacted to the rubber hand as if it were their own [2]. In this case, ownership was achieved by synchronous visual and tactile stimulation as well as propriorception [2]. However, when a variation of the rubber hand illusion was implemented in virtual reality using a data glove, it was shown that visual and propriorception synchronicity along with motor activity created ownership [3]. Essentially, tactile information was not necessary. The illusion of ownership with a full-body avatar in virtual reality can also be created [1]. For example, adult males were able to take ownership of a female child avatar; when

Supported by University of North Carolina at Wilmington.

J. Y. C. Chen and G. Fragomeni (Eds.): HCII 2019, LNCS 11574, pp. 361–374, 2019.
https://doi.org/10.1007/978-3-030-21607-8_28

the avatar was threatened by another virtual human, heart rate accelerated [1]. In this experiment, for creating body ownership in virtual reality, having a first person perspective from the avatar was the most important condition while visuomotor synchronicity also was a key factor [1].

Being embodied and taking ownership of a virtual body can have an effect on implicit attitude and perceptions. Known as the Proteus Effect, users conform to the behavior that they believe others would expect them to have based on their avatar [4]. Exemplified in virtual reality, when embodied in a tall avatar as opposed to short, participants were more confident/aggressive in negotiation than those in the short avatar condition [4]. Because a common perception of tall people is that they are more confident, participants conformed to that behavior. Similarly, a participant approached a virtual human more closely when embodied in an attractive avatar over an unattractive avatar [4]. The perception of virtual objects within virtual reality was also shown to be affected based on the avatar [5]. In this experiment, participants were embodied in either a child avatar or an adult avatar scaled down to the same height as the avatar and asked to estimate the size of a series of virtual objects [5]. When there was strong body ownership, those embodied in the child avatar approximated the objects to be relatively twice their actual size [5]. This effect was not seen in those embodied in the adult avatar [5].

Adding to implicit attitude and perceptions, embodiment with body ownership in virtual reality can have an effect on bias. Participants who were embodied as either an elderly avatar or young avatar were asked to complete a word association task [6]. Those embodied in the old avatar were significantly more positive to the elderly than those embodied in the young avatar. There are several studies where implicit racial bias was affected by embodiment. In one in particular, the implicit racial bias against African Americans was actually higher for participants embodied in African American avatars than participants embodied in Caucasian avatars, regardless of participant race [7]. For this experiment participants engaged in an job interview in virtual reality with either an African American or Caucasian model [7]. An explanation as to why this bias occurred is because implicit racial bias typically exists in interviews [8]. Contrasting results occurred in a study also examining implicit racial body and embodiment, where the scenario was neutral. Participants were either embodied in a light skin avatar, a dark skin avatar, a purple 'alien' skin avatar, or not embodied at all [9]. While embodied, participants observed their body in a virtual mirror before a series of virtual humans, alternating in race, walked past. For those who were not embodied, or embodied in the purple skin avatar, implicit racial bias was affected less than those participants who were embodied in light skin and embodied in dark skin conditions. The implicit gender bias in participants embodied in the light skin avatar condition increased, while it decreased for those in embodied dark skin avatar condition. An extension of this experiment found that this decrease in implicit racial bias can be sustained for at least a week following embodiment experience [8].

While there is extensive research on virtual embodiment, there is a lack of research on gender embodiment and the effects on implicit gender bias in virtual reality. The intent of this experiment is to discover if users can take ownership of a virtual body of a different gender and, with this body ownership, explore how embodiment affects implicit gender bias.

2   Materials and Methods

2.1   Experiment Design

The purpose of conducting this experiment is to discover if embodiment into each gender avatar reduces implicit gender bias. A 2 × 2 between groups design of gender of participant vs. gender of avatar was used for this experiment. Within each participant gender group, the gender of the avatar assigned to the participant alternated each time. The conditions were: male participant with male avatar, male participant with female avatar, female participant with male avatar, and female participant with female avatar. A gender and leadership Implicit Association Test (IAT) was completed before and after embodiment.

2.2   Technical Details

Physical Environment. The experiment was conducted in a private room within the computer and information science graduate lab on the University of North Carolina Wilmington's campus (UNCW). Participants used HTC Vive head mounted display (HMD) and controllers. The HMD offers a field of view of 110° and a resolution of 1080 × 1200 pixels per eye. Two HTC base stations set up in opposing corners track six degrees of freedom (x, y, z, yaw, pitch, roll) for the HMD and controllers.

Virtual Environment. The virtual environment participants were put in was a manager's office pictured in Fig. 1. The environment, "Manager Office Interior" by 3D Everything, was downloaded from the Unity Asset Store. What appears to be a white plane in Fig. 1 is a working mirror for those wearing the HMD. The mirror asset was abstracted from an HTC plugins demo scene which was downloaded from the Unity Asset Store.

Virtual Humans. The virtual humans and participant avatars were created using MakeHuman 1.1.1 software. This application allows you to fine tune details of a 3D model and apply a variety of hair and clothing. The models can also be exported with a skeleton to facilitate animation in Unity. Figure 2 features the basic customization elements with a model on the left and the model with the CMU-Compliant skeleton on the right. There were a total of eight models created: four female and four male. Out of these models, one female and one male were used for participant avatars. All models are 158 cm in height and Caucasian. The virtual humans that are used, exclusive of participant avatars, can be seen in Fig. 3.

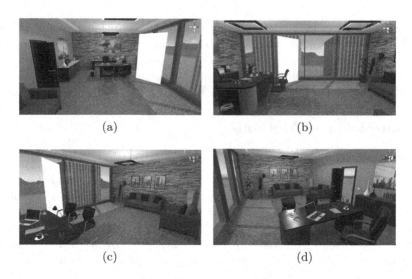

(a)   (b)

(c)   (d)

Fig. 1. The office environment

Animations. For the virtual humans in the scene, the idle neutral, walk forward, and turn short animation clips from Raw Mocap Data for Mecanim were used. These clips were used in conjunction with Unity's mecanim animation system to have each virtual human walk through the office door to the other side of the room, turn around, and walk out the office door. The first virtual human to walk through the door is a male. When he walks out, a female walks in. The animations continue like this, alternating genders, until all six virtual humans have walked out of the office.

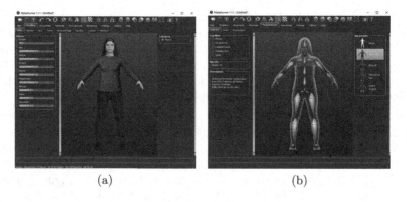

(a)   (b)

Fig. 2. MakeHuman interface

The participants' avatar is animated using FinalIK by RootMotion. FinalIK takes the bones of a humanoid skeleton so when one bone is moved, related bones are also moved creating animation that appears natural. This technique is called inverse kinematics. The position and rotation of the participants head and hands were tracked and reflected by their avatar in the virtual environment. While the exact position and rotation of the other parts of the participants body were not reflected, FinalIK calculated a relative position for corresponding bones of the virtual body.

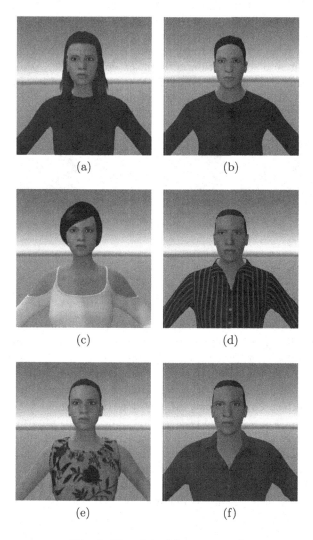

Fig. 3. The virtual humans used

2.3 Participants

A total of sixteen participants took part in this study. There were eleven males and five females. Broken down into each condition, male with male avatar had five participants, male with female avatar had six participants, female with male avatar had two participants, and female with female avatar had three participants. Fifth percent of the participants were aged eighteen to twenty-two. Thirty seven and a half percent of the participants were aged twenty-three to twenty-seven. Twelve and a half percent of the participants were over 47. Regarding race, fifteen participants were Caucasian and one participant was African American.

Participants were recruited from various classes in UNCW's computer science department and information technology department. Additional participants were acquired by asking people in the computer and information science building on UNCW's campus if they would like to participate.

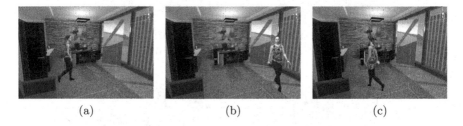

(a)   (b)   (c)

Fig. 4. Virtual humans walking in the office environment

2.4 Procedures

First, on a desktop computer, participants completed a preliminary questionnaire regarding demographics and previous experience with virtual reality. Then, also on the desktop computer, they completed a preliminary Implicit Association Test (IAT) on gender and leadership. Next, the participant put on the head mounted display (HMD) and took hold of the controllers to be placed in the immersive virtual office. In the environment, an avatar of the assigned gender is in place of the participant's physical body. The first time in this environment was the orientation period. A virtual mirror was placed in front of the participant so they could see their avatar. With controller functionality, they able were able to adjust avatar height and arm length so they corresponded with physical body proportions. The virtual mirror was placed in front of the participant as they performed a series of physical movements. The participant could look down at their virtual body to see their physical movements reflected in their avatar as well as in the mirror. Following the exercises, the participant was allowed 2 min to explore avatar movements. This process allowed the participants to become accustomed to their virtual avatar. After the orientation period, the participant was told a series of virtual humans will walk into the room. The environment remained identical to the environment in the orientation period, except the mirror was located further away to allow room for the virtual humans to walk in front of the participant. The path the virtual human took through the virtual office is pictured in Fig. 4. The participant was then removed from the virtual environment and their avatar. Next, they took the gender and leadership IAT again on the desktop computer and results were recorded. Finally, the participant completed a post questionnaire regarding body ownership and what they thought the purpose of the experiment was.

2.5 Response Variables

Body Ownership. After being embodied in an avatar, participants answered questions relating to the level of body ownership they felt (Table 1). Each statement was presented with a one to five Likert scale with one being strongly disagree and five being strongly agree. While the variable Nervous was an inquiry, it was not used to determine body ownership.

Table 1. Post experience questionnaire statements

Variable	Statement
My body	I felt that the virtual body when looking down at myself was my own body
Two bodies	I felt as if I had two bodies
Mirror	I felt that the virtual body I saw when looking in the mirror was my own body
Features	I felt that my virtual body resembled my own (real) body in terms of shape, skin tone, or other visual features
Agency	I felt that the movements of the virtual body were caused by my own movements
Nervous	I became nervous when the other avatars approached me

Implicit Association Test. To measure implicit gender bias of participants, a gender and leadership implicit association test (IAT) was used. The IAT was created using FreeIAT 1.3.3. This test required users to rapidly categorize male and female faces of virtual humans used in the environment (Fig. 3) with words associated with a leader and a supporter (Table 2). The test consisted of five different stages each with five trials. Though the participants did not know, the first stage is a learning trial where users practice categorizing the virtual human images into female and male. Similarly, in the second stage users practice categorizing different words into leader and supporter. The third stage is no longer practice. Here, users are presented with both images and words to categorize into either Female-Leader group or Male-Supporter group. Stage four is another learning trial with the images, but the female and male category labels switch sides. This is to break up any familiarity with associations. The fifth and final stage is akin to the third stage. Both images and words are presented, but this time participants must categorize into either Male-Leader group or Female-Supporter group.

Table 2. Word categoriazation for IAT

Label	Words in group
Leader	leader, ambitious, determined, dedicated, assertive, manager
Supporter	supporter, understanding, sympathetic, compassionate, follower, assistant

The scores of the IAT are related to response time and accuracy in categorization [10]. The faster the reaction time, the more biased a user is to that category pairing. A positive score indicates that the user exhibits preference for Female-Leader and Male-Supporter pairings over Male-Leader and Female-Supporter pairings. Likewise, a negative score indicates that the user exhibits preference for Male-Leader and Female-Supporter pairings over Female-Leader and Male-Supporter pairings.

To determine how the embodiment experience affects a participant, the IAT was adminstered both before and after the experience. The difference between the score after the experience and the score before the experience provides the change in IAT (changeIAT = postIAT − preIAT). In the changeIAT case, a positive score signifies a reduction in implicit gender bias. Similarly, a negative score indicates an increase in implicit gender bias.

3   Results and Discussion

3.1   Body Ownership

From the post experience questionnaire shown in Table 1, variables MyBody, Mirror, Features, and Agency are used to ascertain the degree of body ownership participants felt with their given avatar. The TwoBodies variable is not used because participants expressed confusion, which is reflected in the data. Figure 5 shows the mean of each body ownership variable per condition.

For the MyBody variable, ten participants indicated a four or five signifying they agree that the avatar body felt like their own. Three participants reported a three meaning they neither agree nor disagree the avatar body felt like their own. Finally, three participants marked a one or two, expressing that they disagree the avatar body felt like theirs. Overall, the mean response to MyBody was 3.625. Specified by condition, female with female avatar has the highest mean response of 4. Following is male with female avatar with a mean of 3.6666. Next is female with male avatar with a mean of 3.5. Lastly, those in male with male avatar condition reported a mean of 3.4.

When responding to the Mirror variable, ten participants replied with a four or a five. These participants agreed that they felt the virtual body when looking in the mirror was theirs. Neither agreeing nor disagreeing with the statement, two participants reported a 2. Four participants marked a two or a one. The mean

Body Ownership Averages vs. Condition

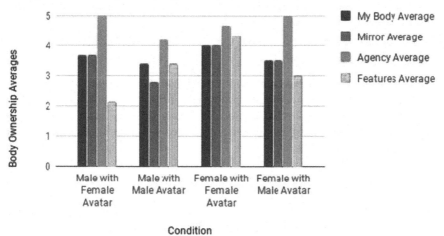

Fig. 5. Body ownership averages by condition

response for all participants for the Mirror variable was 3.4375. Having a mean over 3 are the conditions: male with female avatar, female with female avatar, and female with male avatar. Their means are 3.6666, 4, and 3.5 respectively. One thing to note is that for these three conditions, the Mirror mean is equivalent to the MyBody mean. Differing from the MyBody mean, the Mirror mean for the male with male avatar condition dips below 3 at a 2.8. This conveys that on average, male participants given a male avatar do not feel as if the virtual body they saw in the mirror was their own.

Participants responded to the Features variable to indicate to what degree they felt their virtual body resembled their physical body in terms of shape, skin tone, or other visual features. The variation of responses for Features is much more than the other variables. Six participants responded with a four or five, five participants responded with a three, and five participants responded with a two or one. However, the mean for all participants equates to 3.0625. While only slightly over three, this suggests that overall participants felt their virtual body resembled their physical one. Those in the conditions where participant gender matched their avatars, the Implicit Association Test resulted in higher means than those with mismatched gender. Female with female avatar amounted to 4.3333 and male with male avatar 3.4. The male with female avatar and female with male avatar had means 2.1667 and 3 respectively. The male with male avatar mean for Features is noticeably lower than the other conditions.

The Agency variable refers to how much a participant felt that the movements of the virtual body were caused by their own movements. Fifteen participants indicated a four or five while one participant indicated a two. Equating to 4.6875, the overall mean for Agency was higher than the overall mean for any other variable. In all conditions, the mean was above four. The mean for both the male with female avatar condition and female with male avatar condition was 5. The mean for male with male avatar condition was 4.2 and the mean for female with female avatar was 4.6667.

3.2   Implicit Association Test

To gauge the effect embodiment has on implicit gender bias, participants took a gender and leadership implicit association test prior to embodiment (preIAT) and after embodiment (postIAT). Recall that a positive score indicates an implicit bias against males while a negative score indicates an implicit bias against females. The further the score is away from zero, the stronger the bias. Subtracting preIAT scores from postIAT scores results in the change of IAT scores: either reduced or increased.

Looking at the left figure of Fig. 6, the mean postIAT score increases from the mean preIAT score for the male with female avatar, male with male avatar, and female with female avatar conditions. This means on average participants in these conditions became more biased against females. In all of these conditions, the average participant initially revealed implicit gender bias against females in the preIAT with mean scores of $-.6218$, $-.82954$, and $-.15393$ respectively. However, for the remaining condition, female with male avatar, a reduction in bias against males is seen. The mean postIAT score is reduced from the mean preIAT score. In this condition, the average participant initially revealed implicit gender bias against males in the preIAT with a mean score of $.3544$.

When analyzing the left figure of Fig. 6, the degree of bias in both conditions with male participants is noticeably greater than the degree of bias in both conditions with female participants. The right figure of Fig. 6 organizes the data by gender to more closely examine this insight. On average, female participants initially express implicit gender bias against males with a mean of $.0494$ for preIAT scores. After the embodiment, there is a switch and implicit gender bias against males is expressed with a mean of $-.077$. For the female average scores, both the preIAT and post IAT scores never exceed $\pm.1$. This is not the case for the male participant average scores. The mean preIAT score is $-.7162$ and the mean postIAT score is $-.8606$. Both of IAT mean scores for males surpasses $-.1$, implying that the male participants have stronger implicit gender biases than female participants.

The results of individual participants can be evaluated for more specification. While thirteen participants scored negative on the preIAT, indicating implicit gender bias against females, three participants scored positive on the preIAT, indicating implicit gender bias against males. For the purpose of evaluating the change in IAT scores equivalently across data, the preIAT and postIAT scores of these participants are negated. Therefore, a negative change in IAT implies an increase in implicit bias against males while a positive change in IAT implies a decrease in implicit bias against males. The other thirteen participants' change in IAT remains interpreted as increase in implicit bias against females for negative values and decrease in implicit bias against females for positive values. As the data is represented together, a negative change indicates an increase in implicit

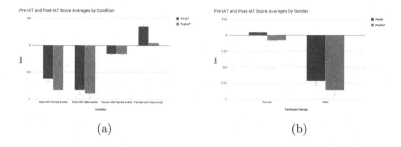

(a)   (b)

Fig. 6. Pre-IAT and Post-IAT score averages by condition and by gender

gender bias while a positive change indicates a reduction of implicit gender bias, regardless of which bias.

In Fig. 7, each participant's change in IAT score is provided. On average, the mean change in IAT was a .0976, meaning participants experienced a slight improvement in gender bias. The participants appear to be well-balanced in whether their implicit bias increased or decreased. Seven of the participants improved their IAT score after being embodied, implying a reduction in implicit gender bias. The other nine participants exemplified a worse IAT score after being embodied signifying an increase in implicit gender bias. The mean of the degree of improvement for those participants whose bias decreased was .83717. This is a larger degree of change than for those whose bias increased. Here, the mean degree of decrement was −.4776. Grouping by gender, IAT change was relatively equitable with females on average experiencing a .18536 change and males on average experiencing a .0577 change.

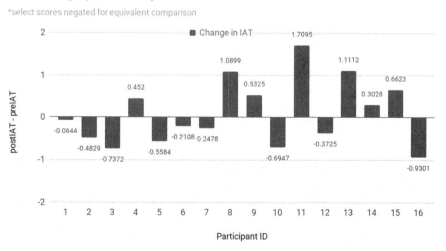

Fig. 7. IAT change per participant

4   Discussion

When discussing the results for body ownership and implicit association test, it is important to note that there were relatively few participants that took part in this study. Moreover, the genders of participants was disproportionate. There were only five female participants and eleven male participants. Therefore the results should be interpreted with caution.

4.1   Body Ownership

The effects of embodiment on implicit attitudes and perceptions are known to be stronger the more a user takes ownership of the virtual body. For example, when looking at the effects of embodiment on implicit racial bias, those who were in the not embodied condition experienced significantly lower body ownership; these participants also experienced less of a change in IAT scores compared to those who were embodied in either a light skin or dark skin avatar [9]. In this experiment, body ownership was achieved with first person perspective from the avatar and visuomotor synchronicity [9]. When comparing perspectives (first person vs. third person) as well as visual movement synchronicity (synchronous vs. asynchronous) it was discovered that first person perspective and synchronous movements were the ideal conditions for creating the body ownership illusion in virtual reality [1].

To achieve body ownership in this experiment, the participants were all placed in first person perspective and physical movements were synchronously reflected by their avatar in the virtual environment. The variable Agency, referring to how much control of the avatars movements the participant felt, was most positively responded to with an overall mean of 4.6875. This signifies that visuomotor synchronicity can be achieved using just a head mounted display and tracked controllers.

Looking at the results of body ownership pictured in Fig. 5, the mean response for the My Body variable across all conditions was slightly above 3, indicating that an average participant felt as if the virtual body were their own. However this is a relatively low mean when comparing with a study using embodiment into different races [9]. Here, the mean for embodied conditions was around 4. Given that first person perspective was used and visuomotor synchronicity was achieved for both experiments, there may be another factor affecting body ownership. One reason for why the My Body mean is lower may be the amount of time participants spent embodied. In the experiment, participants spent around four minutes in the orientation period, depending on how quickly the participant completed the exercises, and two minutes in the period where virtual humans walked by. This equates to a total embodiment time of around six minutes. In the racial embodiment experiment, participants spent five minutes in the orientation period and six and a half minutes in the approach period for a total embodiment time of eleven and a half minutes [9]. For The racial embodiment experiment with sustained effects, participants spent even longer being embodied with a five minute orientation period and a ten minute scenario period for a total embodiment time of fifteen minutes [9]. The total embodiment time for both the implicit racial bias experiments is around double of the total embodiment time for this experiment.

Overall, using first person perspective and visuomotor synchronicity, participants were able to take ownership of a virtual body even if the body was the opposite gender. Future research may want to explore how the total time spent embodied affects the degree of body ownership.

4.2   Implicit Association Test

Looking at the results of preIAT scores and postIAT scores in Fig. 6, one interesting observation is that the overall degree of implicit gender bias was noticeably different between male and female participants, regardless of what gender avatar was assigned to them. For all of the conditions, the postIAT score was one that is more bias towards males/against females than preIAT score. For those in the female with male avatar condition, this means there was actually a reduction in implicit gender bias because the preIAT scores were bias against males. For all other conditions this means there was an increase in implicit gender bias. But again, all postIAT scores in comparison to preIAT scores represent a change to favor males. Although the scenario itself remained neutral to biases, the virtual environment was a managers office which could have existing implicit gender biases associated with it. This is comparable to the experiment in which those embodied in an African American model became more biased against African Americans because the scenario was an interview which involves pre-existing bias [7]. Likewise, this could explain why those in the male with female avatar and female with female avatar conditions became more favorable to males.

Something to consider is that in this experiment, each IAT stage only had five trials. In a similar experiment, where an IAT was used to measure effects of embodiment, 20 or 40 trials were used for each stage depending on the stage. This is a considerably large amount of trials compared to this experiment. Having more trials could provide a more accurate representation of implicit gender bias and therefore better exemplify the effect of embodiment on said bias.

5   Conclusion

Virtual reality is a powerful tool that can be used to change the way people think or feel, even implicitly. Using embodiment, users can take ownership of a completely virtual body, even if it is a different size, shape, race, or gender than the physical body. Many studies have shown how being embodied in different virtual bodies can affect implicit attitudes. More specifically, there are studies addressing how embodiment can reduce, or in some cases increase, racial implicit bias or age- related implicit bias. However, there is no research examining how implicit gender bias is affected by embodiment in virtual reality. This experiment shows that users are able to take ownership of a virtual body, even one of a different gender, using visuomotor synchronization and first person perspective. With this body ownership, the average implicit gender bias of participants became more favorable to males than before the embodiment experience. Future research in this area should focus on how the total time embodied affects body ownership of different gendered avatars. In addition, replicating this study with more participants could provide more evidence that implicit gender bias is affected by gender embodiment.

References

1. Slater, M., Spanlang, B., Sanchez-Vives, M.V., Blanke, O.: First person experience of body transfer in virtual reality. PloS one **5**(5), e10564 (2010)
2. Botvinick, M., Cohen, J.: Rubber hands feel touch that eyes see. Nature **391**(6669), 756 (1998)
3. Sanchez-Vives, M.V., Spanlang, B., Frisoli, A., Bergamasco, M., Slater, M.: Virtual hand illusion induced by visuomotor correlations. PloS one **5**(4), e10381 (2010)
4. Yee, N., Bailenson, J.: The proteus effect: the effect of transformed self-representation on behavior. Hum. commun. Res. **33**(3), 271–290 (2007)
5. Banakou, D., Groten, R., Slater, M.: Illusory ownership of a virtual childbody causes overestimation of object sizes and implicit attitude changes. Proc. Nat. Acad. Sci. **110**(31), 12846–12851 (2013)
6. Yee, N., Bailenson, J.N.: Walk a mile in digital shoes: the impact of embodied perspective-taking on the reduction of negative stereotyping in immersive virtual environments. In: Proceedings of PRESENCE, vol. 24, p. 26 (2006)
7. Groom, V., Bailenson, J.N., Nass, C.: The Influence of racial embodiment on racial bias in immersive virtual environments. Soc. Influ. **4**(3), 231–248 (2009)
8. Banakou, D., Hanumanthu, P.D., Slater, M.: Virtual embodiment of whitepeople in a black virtual body leads to a sustained reduction in their implicit racial bias. Front. Hum. Neurosci. **10**, 601 (2016)
9. Peck, T.C., Seinfeld, S., Aglioti, S.M., Slater, M.: Putting yourself in the skin of a black avatar reduces implicit racial bias. Conscious. Cogn. **22**(3), 779–787 (2013)
10. Greenwald, A.G., Nosek, B.A., Banaji, M.R.: Understanding and using the implicit association test: I. an Improved scoring algorithm. J. Pers. Soc. Psychol. **85**(2), 197 (2003)

Effects of Character Guide in Immersive Virtual Reality Stories

Qinghong Xu[1(✉)] and Eric D. Ragan[2]

[1] Department of Visualization, Texas A&M University,
College Station, TX 77840, USA
qinghx39@tamu.edu
[2] Department of Computer and Information Science and Engineering,
University of Florida, Gainesville, FL 32611, USA
eragan@ufl.edu

Abstract. Bringing cinematic experiences from traditional film screens into Virtual Reality (VR) has become increasingly popular in recent years. However, striking a balance between storytelling and user interaction can cause a big challenge for filmmakers. In this paper, we present a media review on the common strategies that constructed the existing framework of computer generated cinematic VR by evaluating over 80 real-time rendered interactive experiences across different media. We summarized the most-used methods, which creators applied to maintain a relative control when presenting a narrative experience in VR, that were associated with story-progression strategies and attention guidance techniques. We then approach the problem of guiding the audience through major events of a story in VR by using a virtual character as a travel guide providing assistance in directing viewers attention to the target. To assess the effectiveness of this technique, we performed a controlled experiment applying the method in three VR videos. The experiment compared three variations of the character guide: (1) no guide, (2) a guide with a matching art style to the video, and (3) a guide with a non-matching art style. The experiment results provided insights for future directors and designers into how to draw viewers attention to a target point within a narrative VE, such as what could be improved and what should be avoided.

Keywords: Virtual Reality · Interactive storytelling · Gaze redirection · Character design · Interaction design · 3D interface

1 Introduction

Virtual Reality (VR) has become a growing entertainment medium. It incorporates multiple types of sensory feedback including visual and auditory, and sometimes even haptic. As defined by Jerald [12], VR is "a digital environment that enables users to experience and interact as if that environment were real." Because of this, VR can provide the audiences unprecedented film experience that encourages their free exploration of an immersive environment and interaction with virtual props and characters. In recent years, along the showcasing of many cutting-edge VR stories,

© Springer Nature Switzerland AG 2019
J. Y. C. Chen and G. Fragomeni (Eds.): HCII 2019, LNCS 11574, pp. 375–391, 2019.
https://doi.org/10.1007/978-3-030-21607-8_29

more and more innovative techniques have been designed and developed to experiment with storytelling in virtual spaces.

The biggest challenge directors face when telling a story through VR is determining how to best guide viewers through important events of a narrative without hindering their freedom to discover the virtual world. In traditional film-making, the directors have absolute control over the storytelling process, whereas the audience can only wait and receive a selective amount of information within a set frame of the camera. In VR, viewers are encouraged to alter their senses in relation to the Virtual Environment (VE), including their points of view, location and so on. This indicates the audience's role transition from being absolutely passive to more active in VR storytelling.

However, allowing the audience more freedom to explore and interact within a narrative scenario might lead them to getting lost following a series of events that build up a story. Hence, VR filmmakers must formulate ways to maintain relative control over story presentation in order to ensure that the audience does not miss any important information about the story. One effective option is to conditionally add guiding assistance as redirecting cues to shift the user's attention toward the relevant events and objects within the VE [17].

In this research, we first present a media review to construct a framework by summarizing the most-used storytelling strategies and attention guidance techniques. We proposed and tested a new gaze redirection technique by overlaying a guiding character on top of an existing 360-degree video. The added character would react based on the user's head-tracking data, and the user's gaze was expected to follow the guide towards the focal content of a story.

To assess the effectiveness of this technique, we conducted an experiment. We chose three different 360-degree animated videos as background stories. We then created three virtual characters, where each character has a corresponding art style to a specific video, so that we could evaluate whether the guide's art style would affect the users' gaze behavior. The experiment compared three variations of the character guide: (1) no guide, (2) a guide with a matching art style to the video design, and (3) a guide with a non-matching style.

By the end of this study, we concluded what works well and what should be avoided when directing viewers' attention to a target point in VR stories with the help of a designed character guide. Future creators can follow the resulting framework and refer the experiment outcomes to develop better VR narrative experiences that are easier to follow and more enjoyable to watch.

2   Related Work

In this section, we discuss related literature about immersive stories and methods for guiding attention in applications allowing 360-degree viewing.

2.1   VR as a Narrative Medium

Throughout history, storytelling has been developed in a variety of forms in terms of the different media that carry them; these forms range from oral expression, theatrical performances, and prints to movies. As argued by Ryan [21], immersion and interactivity, have been the main motivating forces behind some major paradigm shifts in the history of narrative and human culture. Despite the types of medium the creators use, an important trend in storytelling is to raise audiences' sensory satisfaction and level of immersion associated with the story world.

The emergence of VR, as Steuer reasoned [26], fulfilled the desire to bring greater sensory depth to traditional media content by immersing viewers in a 360-degree visual environment. For this reason, VR is perceived and studied by numerous people as a medium that possesses substantial potential for telling a story through its powerful sensory input.

Aylet and Louchart [1] maintained that VR should be considered as a specific narrative medium along other traditional narrative forms such as theater, literature, and cinema. However, they pointed out that VR narrative designers must be aware of the participants' active role within the VEs. They argued that the traditional methods of presenting a story must be manipulated to ensure that the viewers will not remain passive.

Similarly, Clarke and Mitchell [6] attempted to review certain methods used in traditional film-making in order to determine whether they can be applied and situated in the construction of a VR narrative. They suggested that VR content creators abandon the traditional reliance on the continuity of time, space, and action to focus mainly on character interaction.

Various researchers and artists began experimenting with VR storytelling medium over two decades ago. For instance, back in 1996, Pausch et al. [18] found it beneficial to provide the audience with a background story and assign them a concrete goal to accomplish in the VE. More recently, Google Spotlight's DUET [13] put together a two-line story experience based on the main characters, a boy and a girl. This design allowed the audience to follow whichever story-line they preferred and watch the story develop along that line. Oculus Story Studio's Henry [14] presented an eye-contact experience between the viewers and the main character, Henry the hedgehog, creating a more intimate connection between the audience and the story. Penrose Studio's Allumette [5] followed a more traditional approach that involves several camera cuts to transfer audiences from one space and time to another, etc.

2.2 Gaze Redirection in VR

Many researchers have conducted specific studies that explored the effects of various gaze-redirecting techniques in VR. Some of them focused on designing perceptual properties that will make visual objects stand out from their surroundings, such as luminance contrast, edge or line orientation, color, and motion. For instance, Hillaire et al. [10] constructed and evaluated models of dynamic blur that combine depth of field and peripheral blur effects to direct user navigation in the VE. Smith and McNamara [23] developed a dynamic real-time color effect stimulus to redirect the user's gaze toward points of interest. Danieau et al. [8] suggested driving the user's gaze smoothly toward a point of interest by applying fade to black and desaturation visual effects outside of the area of interest.

Some researchers focused on operating the camera to change the viewer's gaze relative to a target area within the VE. Bolte and Lappe [2] proposed rotating the camera during a rapid movement of the eye between fixation points (saccade) to a non-perceivable degree. Looking at fully automated transitions analogous to cuts in traditional film, Rahimi et al. [20] and Moghadam et al. [16] conducted studies of scene transitions in VR systems to compare how different types of cuts, fades, and interpolations affect sickness and viewer ability to keep track of spatial changes in the VE. Looking at rotational adjustments that allow the user freedom to look around, Sargunam et al. [22] investigated the use of amplified head rotation, which produces a rotation angle that allows the viewing of a 360-degree virtual world by physically turning the head through a comfortable range. They also evaluated the "guided rotation" technique, which realigns a users' head orientations as they virtually translate through the VE. Stebbins and Ragan [25] explored a scene rotation-based method in a 360-degree movie, where the rotation is triggered if the user has looked at a sufficiently extreme angle for more than a particular length of time. Brown et al. [3] studied direct scene transitions and forced camera rotation for a multi-user VR narrative experience. Particularly, the direct scene transition technique makes the camera fade out and then fade back in with the event in the center of a viewer's field of vision. The forced camera rotation technique makes the user camera rotate, independently of the user, to face the event taking place.

Besides these, others took the approach of employing animated three dimensional figures as guiding indicators. Brown et al. [3] implemented a firefly as a visual distractor. The firefly would drift into a user's field of view and flied off screen in the general direction of the active story event. It would remain in the user's field of view until he/she witnessed the story event taking place. Pausch et al. [18] built virtual characters to point at or even move toward the target scene when directing user's attention. Similarly, Wernert and Hanson [28] introduced personal "guides" to help the user focus on the target subject areas in the navigation space.

2.3 Interaction with a Virtual Character

Researchers also studied the effects of human-to-virtual-character interaction as an interface design approach in real-time systems. The characters can be designed in the form of either a human or an animal. The effects are different, but each form has its own benefits.

According to Cassell [4], the advantage of designing virtual humans as interfaces is that the user has a natural ability to recognize and respond quickly to the agent's messages as in face-to-face communications. Thus, a virtual human agent can largely increase communication efficiency. In addition, based on a research by Takeuchi et al. [27], users can accomplish tasks smoothly and effectively when the behavior of a virtual agent resembles theirs. This study supported that people's experience with real social interaction will enrich their experience with human-computer interaction. Consequently, it is likely that the users will receive more valid information from a personified virtual character.

Same as humans, animals also manifest social qualities. Virtual companions may establish an emotional connection with user similar to pets. Hofmann et al. [11]

approved that "the presence of a virtual companion (compared to being alone)" led to a higher level of cheerfulness for individuals watching a comedy film. In all, mutual dependencies and closeness can be built between a virtual companion and the user, which may reduce the users' feeling of loneliness and enhance their level of enjoyment.

3   Media Review

To situate our work in the context of existing VR storytelling framework, we conducted a media review to better characterize the key attributes and differences among different forms of relevant media. We reviewed over 80 different real-time rendered interactive content on the current market. Media was identified from a variety of sources, including the Valve Steam store, Google Spotlight Stories, Oculus Story Studio, Sony Playstation VR Catalog, and various game stores. We conducted a qualitative review of different media by identifying attributes that characterize differences among different works. Examples of attributes cataloged in the full review included: supported display/system; use of 3D input; types of interaction techniques; artistic style; degree of user control; presence of characters; character response to the user/viewer; game elements and goals; and narrative and story elements. We revised the analysis through iterative review cycles when new attributes or attribute categories were added. After an analysis of all these works, we simplified the review by distinguishing four major categories based on their design objectives, content, and methods applied during presentation. The resulting categories are: (1) Interactive Experience; (2) Game; (3) Interactive Film (Not-animated); and (4) Interactive Film (Animated).

In order to study how former creators struck a balance between story presentation and user interaction, we evaluated and summarized the common qualities from each category, including the implementation of narrative, design of guidance techniques, and level of character interaction. Table 1 shows a high-level summary of the four categories, and the following sections provide additional explanation.

Table 1. A brief comparison of the differences among the four content categories

	Medium	Narrative	Gaze-redirection	Character interaction
Interactive experience	VR	No	No	None
Game	Mixed	Yes	No	High
Interactive film (Not-animated)	VR	Yes	No	None
Interactive film (Animated)	VR	Yes	Yes	None/Low

3.1   Categories and Characteristics

We summarize the major media categories identified from the media review.

Interactive Experience. The "Interactive Experience" category comprises of the works that do not involve narratives or game tasks. These works are the most abstract out of all those reviewed, as there is often a lack of clear storylines or specific goals expected to be accomplished. For content designers, the most important thing is to demonstrate to the audience that VR can be a powerful communication tool. Due to this design objective, there are usually no gaze redirection techniques created and implemented in these experiences. Depending on the content, the level of character interaction in these experiences is mostly low, or no character interaction at all. Examples of applications falling under this category include: *THEBLU: Encounter, Longing for Wilderness, In the Eyes of the Animal,* and *The Dreams of Dali.*

Game. The "Game" group refers to the works that involve a set of specific tasks expected to be accomplished throughout the experience. There is often a clear narrative involved in most games. However, the primary design objective for a gaming experience is not to tell a story; rather, the stories are generally introduced as a background context to assist users in understanding and completing their game tasks. The most common gaze redirection techniques designed for games are quite obvious, such as a GUI element of a text box that displays instructions or a symbol such as an arrow. Occasionally, the progression of the game can be paused without affecting the user's experience negatively. The level of character interaction for this category is typically medium to high. Examples of media categorized as games include: *Call of Duty, Pokemon GO, Robinson: The Journey,* and *Back to Dinosaur Island.*

Interactive Film (Not animated). "Interactive Film (Not animated)" are categorized by a documentary film type of experience. There is often a clear narrative involved, and users do not need to complete specific tasks other than watching the story. Many experiences under this category feature either places that most audience cannot go, such as the outer space or deep in the ocean, or stories that present the aftermath of a significant disaster, such as an earthquake or military attack. Consider its primary design objective as recording and displaying something the way it is; there is no gaze redirection technique being implemented. The level of user interaction included is quite limited, entailing that the users cannot necessarily affect a virtual character's action, but can occasionally feel the eye contact. Examples falling into this category include: *Journey to the Edge of Space, The Nepal Quake Project, Welcome to Aleppo,* and *The Invisible Man.*

Interactive Film (Animated). "Interactive Film (Animated)" is categorized by animation shorts that are interactive. The biggest difference between the works falling under this category and those from the aforementioned category is that interactive animations usually include the design and implementation of various gaze redirection techniques. This is done not only because the stories and styles for most animated films are creative, which makes it reasonable and less abrupt to incorporate additional guiding elements, but also, it's easier to do so with the help of CG. Several examples falling into this category include: *Windy Day, HELP, Crow: The Legend,* and *The Rose and I.*

3.2 Storytelling Strategies

In this section, we summarize the other primary types of attributes from the media review.

We summarized some prevalent strategies associated with story progression in VR from the media review. We particularly focused on evaluating the experiences under the "Interactive Film (Animated)" category, where numerous effective story-progression strategies were established.

Story progression in VR usually involves conditionally adding in constraints or creating guiding assistance. According to Nielsen et al. [17], there are three prevalent approaches in furthering the story progression in VR. First, the story automatically pauses before the user notices a target event, and whether the user has perceived that event is deduced based on his/her head or gaze direction. The story will continue only after the user turns to a certain angle and the important events and objects in the scene have been presumed as "observed". Second, certain narrative systems would dynamically present events and objects within the user's field of view. Third, the filmmaker will use directing cues (visual or auditory) to transfer the user's attention toward relevant events within the VE.

In addition to this, below we have provided in-depth explanations and other approaches of what we have summarized from the media review:

Area Restriction. A most common technique content creators use in VR storytelling is limiting the action area that is directly related to the target event within the VE. Specifically, within a 360-degree environment, about two thirds of the areas are filled with minor actions or even no action. Therefore, the user will eventually stop exploring and focus on what is actually moving in the environment. *Rain or Shine* [15] by Google Spotlight Stories is a good example of applying this technique.

Time Extension. Another general technique involves extending the interval between each crucial plot to ensure that users have enough reaction time. This strategy is similar to what Nielsen et al. [17] summarized as "story halted before the user sees an important scene." It also includes situations wherein the story continues no matter where the viewer is looking but in a very slow pace, increasing the likelihood of the viewers catching up and following the narrative. *Colosse* [19] is a VR animation that exploits this strategy, as one of its main characters moves at a very slow pace.

Distractors. The last technique involves visual or auditory cues as attention guidance tools. The distractor technique allows the storytellers to suggest an action to the audience without forcing it on them. A good example is Crytek's *Back to Dinosaur Island* VR Demo [7]. In this demo, creators utilized a dragonfly distractor that keeps bumping into the corner of the camera along with a constant wing-flapping sound to grab the viewer's attention. Additionally, auditory distractors take the form of sounds in the VE relatively close to the target event occurring. This technique assumes that the users will hear the distractors and turn to face them. For example, *Sonaria* [24] by Google Spotlight Stories demonstrates how sound could be designed to assist story-telling in VR.

4   User Study of Character Guide

Our media review revealed key differences in how different forms of immersive media handle requirements for viewer attention to activity in the 360-degree medium and the behavior of story characters. We found that among various guidance techniques in immersive VR stories, limited examples exist regarding the application of virtual characters. Moreover, the level of character interaction in works that involved narratives is typically lower or non-existent. We therefore explore the use of supplemental characters in a way that might guide viewer attention during 360-degree experiences. We conducted a study based on animated interactive films with custom-created character guides to collect empirical data about the feasibility and limitations of such an approach.

4.1   Character Guidance

It might be useful to consider using virtual characters as a gaze redirection approach when presenting a story in VR because they were helpful in facilitating the user to focus on target subject areas within a VE [18, 28]. They may induce greater understanding and improve task accomplishments [27] by enhancing information exchanging efficiency [4]. Moreover, implementing a companion type of virtual character may create emotional bonding between the user and the character, which can lead to a higher enjoyment level. Therefore, as a part of the presented research, we chose to study the effects of character guides in directing the viewers' gaze in cinematic VR.

However, as different stories have diverse designs regarding visual styles and creative outcomes, it would be difficult to custom-create a new character guide for each specific experience. Hence, we proposed the method of overlaying a separate virtual character on top of an existing 360-degree video and allowing the added character to react based on the head-tracking data in order to guide the viewer to the focal content of the story. The benefit was that it would be more useful and convenient if a working character guide could be added to other existing applications as a part of the immersive interface. For this reason, it is important that we examine whether it works, how well it works, and other associated design factors that could influence the qualifications of this approach.

Particularly, if adding an external character guide that was not created specifically to match its background story, it might not fit with the overall visual design, and users might find it distracting for their viewing experience. On the other hand, if a character guide could be designed independently of the story (that is, without worrying about matching the art style), it would be convenient for designers or developers to easily apply add character overlays to existing immersive videos without require custom design work or additional development. For these reasons, we designed our study to also investigate whether the art style of a character guide should match the presented story and thus. We tested whether a similar art style can lead to better viewing experiences or following more of the primary story animation.

4.2   User Study

For this research, we proposed to introduce a designed guiding character to lead our users through a sequence of essential story events in VR and ensure that they do not miss core activity. To provide variability in testing, the study used multiple immersive videos. We prepared three 360-degree animated videos and set them up in Unity as the background. All three stories were presented as first-person experiences, and the camera used to display the VEs was placed at the user's eye level. Each video had a distinct art style and story development. To study different character designs and matching the stories, we created three distinct virtual character guides, where each character has a corresponding art style to the video being displayed (See Figs. 1, 2 and 3).

Fig. 1. The left image shows the style from *Rain or Shine* (Massie [15]), and the right shows the custom-created girl character guide designed with a matching art style for the experiment.

The experiment followed a three-way within-subjects design. To simplify the experimental procedure, we identified three groupings of the three VR videos and character guide conditions (See Table 2). The groupings can be considered an additional between-subjects factor in the experimental design.

Fig. 2. On the left, a single frame from *Colosse* (Pittom [19]) shows the story's art style, and the right shows the custom-created fox character with a matching style designed for the experiment.

We showed only one character guide at a time and hid the other when playing each VR experience. The implemented guiding characters were not a part of the storyline, nor did they affect the development of the story. The only function they served in the

Fig. 3. The left shows a still from *INVASION!* (Darnell [9]), and the right shows the custom-created rabbit character with matching art style for the experiment.

narrative scenario was to attract the viewer's attention to a target region within the VE where an important event took place. The user's gaze was expected to follow the character guide toward the goal area.

We animated each character with several body movements associated with different objectives (See Table 3), and we were able to trigger a specific action of the characters under a certain condition.

Table 2. Specific groupings of videos and guides used in the experiment.

	Video 1: *Rain or Shine* [15]	Video 2: *Colosse* [19]	Video 3: *INVASION!* [9]
Group 1	N/A (no guide)	Girl (non-matching)	Rabbit (matching)
Group 2	Girl (matching)	N/A (no guide)	Fox (non-matching)
Group 3	Rabbit (non-matching)	Fox (matching)	N/A (no guide)

Table 3. Animation design and objectives for each character guide.

	Gaze-redirecting (Horizontal)	Gaze-redirecting (Vertical)	Attention grabbing
Girl	Point left/right	Point up/down	Jump and wave
Fox	Turn to left/right	Jump up/dig down	Bark
Rabbit	Turn to left/right	Look up/down	Jump

Per VR video, there was a sequence of target scenes, wherein each target scene displayed a focal event along the story development time-line within the 360-degree VE. These scenes were determined based on: (1) The main character of the story is performing a major action; (2) The secondary character(s) is performing a major action, and the main character's action has become secondary; (3) The secondary object(s) is introduced in the story, and the main character's action has become secondary; and (4) The event in one scene must relate to the event occurring in the following scene. For example, if a user missed Scene 1, there is a chance that he would feel confused when watching Scene 2.

To help us assess when participants where viewing the primary story content during the movie narrative, we identified a "target" gaze direction throughout the duration of the story. This was done by determining the angle to use as approximately the center of story activity, and the target direction was adjusted over time as the story progressed. For analysis purposes, we considered a field-of-view (FoV) range around the target direction such that if the center of the viewer's gaze was contained within the FoV range, we could estimate that the viewer was following the primary story activity. For our purposes, we used a FoV range of 120° in the horizontal direction and 100° in the vertical direction (See Fig. 4).

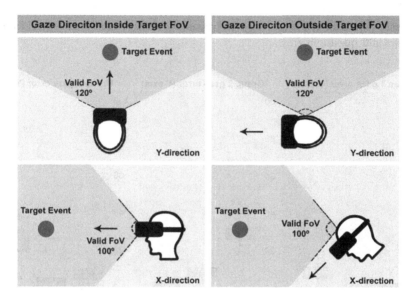

Fig. 4. The user's head orientation (gaze direction) in relation to a target event and its valid FoV along the horizontal and vertical directions.

The research was conducted with approval from our institutional review board (IRB). Each study session lasted approximately 60 min. Participants were asked to watch three animated 360-degree videos in VR, and each video lasted for approximately 4–5 min.

There were a total of 30 participants from Texas A&M University who participated in our study. Each participant completed a background questionnaire prior the study to collect information such as age, gender, education, occupation, average weekly computer usage, and experience with video games and VR.

All participants were seated during the experiment, and their interactions with the VR experiences only involved head and body rotations. We used HMDs to track their head orientation, which determined where their gazes fell throughout the experiences. We recorded and saved quantitative data every 0.2 s during the experiment, and the data included the following: (1) Run-time of each VR experience; (2) Target scene IDs for each VR experience; (3) User's head orientation (gaze direction) along X-axis and Y-axis throughout each VR experience; and (4) Guiding character's animation being triggered.

We also collected qualitative data during each study session via observing user reactions and performances. We gathered a post-study questionnaire to collect information such as preferred technique, ease of use, natural level, and sense of immersion. Lastly, we conducted an in-depth structured interview that aimed to gather detailed information about the participants' thoughts regarding their experience of interactive VR stories with a character guide. All data and findings were anonymized.

4.3   Results

Study results were analyzed based on participants' objective gaze data as well as from interviews and questionnaires.

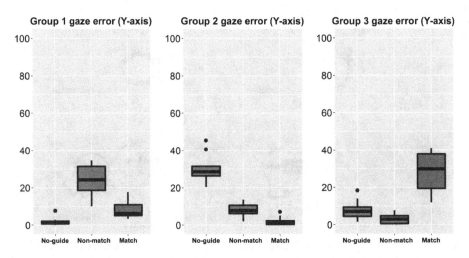

Fig. 5. Significant differences in gaze behavior for the three different VR stories, as seen in the three ordering groups.

Gaze Redirection with Virtual Character. To assess the impact of the virtual characters, we logged participant gaze data collected during the study sessions by saving head orientation from the VR tracker ever 0.2 s. We used the head orientation data with the previously described "target" directions identified for each story to determine whether the users' gazes were with the target range in a particular scene. If the user's gaze direction fell in this region during the time period that the corresponding events were occurring, we counted this as time looking at the story's target content. For analysis, we used this data to calculate the total percentage of time out of the target range, which we refer to as *gaze error*.

To simplify the presentation of results, we focus our analysis on gaze error for rotation about the vertical axis (i.e., heading or yaw), as our media review found this to be most relevant for story motion in immersive media. Significant differences were detected in gaze behavior due to different VR stories (see Fig. 5). A two-way mixed ANOVA result of the gaze error showed a significant interaction between group and character conditions with $F(4, 54) = 67.76$ and p ¡ 0.001. The results further indicate that all the guidance techniques used with *Rain or Shine* [15] had the smallest values, whereas all the guidance techniques used with *Colosse* [19] had the largest values.

This represents clear evidence that the movie assignments affected the gaze behavior. However, there were no significant primary effects for the group or condition factors individually. Due to the confounding of the groups, we could not be confident when comparing character conditions from this test.

Virtual Character and Art Style. Since the results showed previously are so heavily influenced by different videos, we considered the difference between each participant's gaze error and the median for the movie, which removed the variation based on the movie differences to allow the comparison of the character conditions more fairly. We normalized the results based on the overall median gaze error on y-axis-rotation for each video. A one-way repeated measures ANOVA found $F(2, 58) = 0.56$, indicating no evidence of differences due to character conditions; the three conditions were very similar (see Fig. 6). We found no gaze differences between added characters or matching art styles.

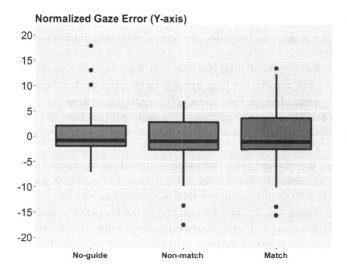

Fig. 6. Gaze differences between character conditions normalized for differences in stories.

Other than the quantitative data, we summarized some interesting results from interview responses. For example, some participants thought implementing a character guide that has a corresponding art style to the story was a contributing factor for their experience. They explained that the similar art style was more natural and made them believe that the character guide belonged to that specific story world. For these participants, if a character guide had a non-matching art style to the story, they would feel that the existence of the guiding character was unnecessary. On the other hand, some participants maintained that implementing a character guide that has a different art style to the story was more helpful, since it made the character guide stand out more from the background. In this case, the viewers felt that they were more likely to notice the guide and its redirecting actions. This was something that a guiding character with a matching art style could not achieve since it blended into the surrounding environment "too well," leading it to become indiscernible.

Level of Enjoyment. We measured the participants' ratings of level of enjoyment for each story experience. Based on the results of the post-study questionnaire, there was no concrete evidence that the participants' enjoyment level was affected by a character guide, nor did it indicate that the character's art style influenced their level of enjoyment.

According to the questionnaire and the interview, there are several possible reasons that could explain why a character guide did not contribute to the user's enjoyment: (1) The character guide made viewers less focused on the story events; (2) the character guide did not affect story development and therefore was unnecessary; (3) the character guide's art style did not match the presented story; and (4) the enjoyment level was related to whether the user understood the story regardless of the guidance condition.

Guiding Actions. As for the character guide's redirecting actions, regardless of whether the virtual character appeared in the form of a human or an animal, the guiding intentions for the horizontal direction worked well within a narrative VE. On the other hand, the guiding actions designed for the vertical direction did not work effectively as expected.

Specifically, the length of time that the user's gazes stay outside the target FoV along the x-axis was mostly not long enough to trigger the character's guidance animation for the vertical direction. Even if the guiding actions for the x-axis were triggered for a few times, many participants mentioned that they did not notice them. For instance, numerous users did not notice the fox character jumping up or digging on the ground.

Additionally, the guiding body language designed for an animal character caused certain confusion, especially for the vertical direction. For example, the majority of the users reported that they did not understand what the meaning of "jumping" or "digging" was. The reason was because we considered the character's directing actions as a part of its art style design. If we attempted to match the character's art style to its background story, the types of guiding behavior would be limited, especially for the animal characters. As a result, although the users reacted fairly quickly to certain instructional gestures such as pointing towards a direction, we could not simply have every animal character perform human-like behaviors for the purpose of our experiment. Nevertheless, we found that having the animal characters turn their bodies to face a particular direction worked well for most participants.

5   Discussion

The experiment results demonstrate that the inclusion of a virtual character that was independent from the narrative had limited effects on users' gaze performances when watching an interactive story in VR. Furthermore, the implemented character's art style, despite of whether it matched or did not match that of the background environment, made very few difference to users' gaze performance and their level of viewing satisfaction. Nevertheless, through the study we conducted, the character guide approaches still provided insights for future directors and designers into how to draw viewers' attention to a target point within a narrative VE.

One reason that no significant gaze difference was found could be due to limitation of the implementation design. Our design was to attach the character guide to the main camera's view-port; in this case, the character guide was always in sight at a fixed spot (bottom right corner) throughout the entire story-viewing experience. Even when users change their head orientation, the character guide would still follow and "float" in the corner of their vision. Although a few participants responded during the interview that they could ignore the character guide in the corner and just focused on the story content, others considered it to be quite distracting because it took their interest away from the background story. Thus, the effects of its guiding actions were restricted.

Another reason was that the guiding body language designed for an animal character posed certain challenges for us. As pointed out earlier, certain gestures and postures such as pointing are common knowledge of the human societies. However, we could not simply have every animal character perform human-like directing actions if we were to consider their actions as a part of the art style design corresponding to its background story. For these characters, the types of guiding behavior were limited. For instance, even though having the animal characters turn their bodies to face a particular direction worked for most participants, numerous users reported that they did not understand what the fox guide was trying to convey when it was "jumping" and "digging".

Lastly, ability to accurately determine gaze focal points of the users solely by tracking their head orientation. As mentioned earlier, the character guide was stuck to the bottom corner of the user's HMD view-port, and some users were able to ignore the character guide while others were not. This implied that there was a possibility that the change of some head orientation data was associated with certain story elements (such as sound cues) in the background instead of the virtual character's guiding action.

There are several alternative design factors that may help to make the character guide technique feasible for future study. One option is to create the virtual character in a form of a flying creature so that it is natural even if it is "floating" with the user's vision. In addition, we may have the character guide become less visible when the user is looking at the expected regions within the VE. For example, (1) The character may hide a portion of its body somewhere outside of the headset's view-port; (2) the character may turn to a shadow profile, as if it was an audience that the user would normally see in a theater; or (3) giving audience the choice of turning on or off the character, so that they would feel less bothered whenever they don't need it.

As for the experimental design, it is important that we train the users to understand a character's postures and its guiding intentions. This can be done by showing them a short demo with a practicing session before presenting a story. In addition, we should test the character technique with an eye-tracking system to find out the user's gaze focus more accurately. Finally, we need to further test the character guide technique in a constructed VE rather than placing it in a 360-degree video playing in the background. The guiding characters will be more natural if they can walk within the virtual space.

References

1. Aylett, R., Louchart, S.: Towards a narrative theory of virtual reality. Virtual Reality **7**(1), 2–9 (2003)
2. Bolte, B., Lappe, M.: Subliminal reorientation and repositioning in immersive virtual environments using saccadic suppression. IEEE Trans. Vis. Comput. Graph. **21**(4), 545–552 (2015)
3. Brown, C., Bhutra, G., Suhail, M., Xu, Q., Ragan, E.D.: Coordinating attention and cooperation in multi-user virtual reality narratives. In: 2017 IEEE Virtual Reality (VR), pp. 377–378. IEEE (2017)
4. Cassell, J.: Embodied conversational interface agents. Commun. ACM **43**(4), 70–78 (2000)
5. Chung, E.: Allumette. Penrose Studios (2016)
6. Clarke, A., Mitchell, G.: Film and the development of interactive narrative. In: Balet, O., Subsol, G., Torguet, P. (eds.) ICVS 2001. LNCS, vol. 2197, pp. 81–89. Springer, Heidelberg (2001). https://doi.org/10.1007/3-540-45420-9_10
7. Crytek: Back to Dinosaur Island (2015)
8. Danieau, F., Guillo, A., Doré, R.: Attention guidance for immersive video content in head-mounted displays. In: 2017 IEEE Virtual Reality (VR), pp. 205–206. IEEE (2017)
9. Darnell, E.: INVASION! Baobab Studios Inc. (2016)
10. Hillaire, S., Lécuyer, A., Cozot, R., Casiez, G.: Depth-of-field blur effects for first- person navigation in virtual environments. IEEE Comput. Graph. Appl. **28**(6), 47–55 (2008)
11. Hofmann, J., Platt, T., Ruch, W., Niewiadomski, R., Urbain, J.: The influence of a virtual companion on amusement when watching funny films. Motiv. Emot. **39**(3), 434–447 (2015)
12. Jerald, J.: The VR Book: Human-Centered Design for Virtual Reality. Morgan & Claypool, New York (2015)
13. Keane, G.: Duet. Google Spotlight Stories (2014)
14. Lopez Dau, R.: Henry. Oculus Story Studio (2015)
15. Massie, F.: Rain or Shine. Google Spotlight Stories (2016)
16. Moghadam, K.R., Ragan, E.D.: Towards understanding scene transition techniques in immersive 360 movies and cinematic experiences. In: 2017 IEEE Virtual Reality (VR), pp. 375–376. IEEE (2017)
17. Nielsen, L.T., et al.: Missing the point: an exploration of how to guide users' attention during cinematic virtual reality. In: Proceedings of the 22nd ACM Conference on Virtual Reality Software and Technology, pp. 229–232. ACM (2016)
18. Pausch, R., Snoddy, J., Taylor, R., Watson, S., Haseltine, E.: Disney's aladdin: first steps toward storytelling in virtual reality. In: Proceedings of the 23rd Annual Conference on Computer Graphics and Interactive Techniques, pp. 193–203. ACM (1996)
19. Pittom, N., C.J.B.N.D.K.G.A.H.E.K.D.L.J.S.D.S.J.T.J.: Colosse. Fire Panda Ltd. (2016)
20. Rahimi Moghadam, K., Banigan, C., Ragan, E.D.: Scene transitions and teleportation in virtual reality and the implications for spatial awareness and sickness. IEEE Trans. Vis. Comput. Graph. (2018)
21. Ryan, M.L.: Narrative as Virtual Reality: Immersion and Interactivity in Literature and Electronic Media. Johns Hopkins University Press, Baltimore (2001)
22. Sargunam, S.P., Moghadam, K.R., Suhail, M., Ragan, E.D.: Guided head rotation and amplified head rotation: evaluating semi-natural travel and viewing techniques in virtual reality. In: 2017 IEEE Virtual Reality (VR), pp. 19–28. IEEE (2017)
23. Smith, M., McNamara, A.: Gaze direction in a virtual environment via a dynamic full-image color effect. In: 2018 IEEE Conference on Virtual Reality and 3D User Interfaces (VR), pp. 1–2. IEEE (2018)

24. Stafford, S.: Sonaria. Google Spotlight Stories (2017)
25. Stebbins, T., Ragan, E.D.: Redirected scene rotation for immersive movie experiences. In: 2018 IEEE Conference on Virtual Reality and 3D User Interfaces (VR), pp. 695–696. IEEE (2018)
26. Steuer, J.: Defining virtual reality: dimensions determining telepresence. J. Commun. **42**(4), 73–93 (1992)
27. Takeuchi, Y., Katagiri, Y.: Social character design for animated agents. In: 1999 8th IEEE International Workshop on Robot and Human Interaction, ROMAN 1999, pp. 53–58. IEEE (1999)
28. Wernert, E.A., Hanson, A.J.: A framework for assisted exploration with collaboration. In: Proceedings of the Conference on Visualization 1999: Celebrating Ten Years, pp. 241–248. IEEE Computer Society Press (1999)

Cognitive and Health Issues in VAMR

Spatial Perception of Size in a Virtual World

Pritam Banik[1(✉)], Debarshi Das[2(✉)], and Si Jung Kim[3(✉)]

[1] University of Engineering and Management, Kolkata, West Bengal, India
iampbanik@gmail.com
[2] Institute of Engineering and Management, Kolkata, West Bengal, India
dasd2@unlv.nevada.edu
[3] University of Nevada Las Vegas, Las Vegas, NV, USA
sj.kim@unlv.edu

Abstract. This paper investigated the spatial perception of size in a virtual space using a wire free mobile Virtual Reality (VR). A simple game called, The Object Popping Project (OPP) that allows the user to find and pop out a 3D object in VR has been developed and used as a tool to measure human spatial perception. The purpose of the OPP is to know how our spatial cognitive abilities differ we planned to get help of VR technology. A total of 7 spheres of different sizes in a 3D space were used in the OPP and the user had to gaze at any of the spheres for 3 s to select and pop it out. A study with 30 participants revealed that there was no effect by colors or numbers in perceiving the different sizes of the object. However, there was a gender effect that on an average, male participants spent less time than female participants in all the tasks.

Keywords: Perception · Cognition · Virtual Reality · Spatial · Orientation

1 Introduction

Virtual Reality (VR) is an immersive experience taking place in a computer-generated simulated environment that can be used as a tool to measure the spatial perception of human [1]. This paper introduces an empirical study about how a human perceives spatial perception of size in an immersive virtual environment called the Object Popping Project (OPP). This OPP is based on VR, an artificial environment which is experienced through sensory stimuli such as sights and sounds provided by a computer and in which one's actions partially determine what happens in the environment. The main purpose of creating this project was to establish a connection with human spatial cognition study [2], a branch of cognitive psychology that studies how people acquire and use knowledge about their environment. It is our conjecture that using VR as an immersive game and a tool to measure spatial cognition would be easier and accountable because it takes place a three-dimensional world. The two research questions that we would like to find answers were whether people find the different sizes of one same object and how fast they do so.

© Springer Nature Switzerland AG 2019
J. Y. C. Chen and G. Fragomeni (Eds.): HCII 2019, LNCS 11574, pp. 395–402, 2019.
https://doi.org/10.1007/978-3-030-21607-8_30

2 Background

In the past decade and a half, the word "Virtual" became very common in English language. In the field of computers and information technology, VR is now-a-days one of the most sought after fields of innovative exploration that includes VR in drones [3]. A VR user these days is able to navigate themselves in 3D computer generated environments by walking, running and even flying, unlike anything possible in the real world. For a human being to experience the advancements of this technology, that person's cognitive ability and spatial perception of the virtual environment is of utmost importance.

Spatial cognition concerns the study of knowledge and beliefs about spatial properties of objects and events in the world that include location, size, distance, direction, separation and connection, shape, pattern, and movement [4]. Spence and Feng studied the ability of video games to modify processes in spatial cognition that the more video game enthusiasts spend hours at play, the intense activity has the potential to alter both brain and behavior [5]. Hubbard et al. suggested that numerical and spatial representations have been inextricably linked [6]. According to Kimberley Osberg Spatial processing skills are an important component in cognitive development [7, 8]. So our game basically includes spatial processing skills. By knowing more about our spatial processing skills and how it differs from one person to another can easily contribute in cognitive development studies.

Based on the literature review, this paper dealt with the study of spatial perception of size in VR. The research questions were how a person's cognitive ability in recognizing size is affected in a world that is not real and how the cognitive ability is affected by the factors of colors and numbers. This study will help us explore the cognitive performance and spatial understanding of a person by observing how they identify objects according to their sizes in a virtual space.

3 Methods

The method was a lab based controlled empirical experiment where participants worn a mobile VR and experienced the OPP. The research design was a two factor within subject design shown in Table 1, where the first factor was three different tasks that were performed by participants and the second factor was genders.

Table 1. A two factor within subject design

Factors	Levels	# of Levels
Task	Size, Color, Number	3
Gender	Male, Female	2

3.1 Independent and Dependent Variables

There were two independent variables that are already shown in Table 1, Gender and Task. There were two dependent variables that we collected and measured - time spent on each task and the order of the ball popping out. Taking in consideration of both dependent and independent variables we had to analyze the data which is described in the result section below.

3.2 Task and Setup

There were 3 tasks in the study and all of them were playing a simple VR game in which a participant worn a mobile VR based on a Google VR box and an Android phone with the app installed shown Fig. 1 that we made were there to carry out the experiment. Participants' role in the game was found 3D balls in a virtual space and eliminating them by gazing them for 3 s.

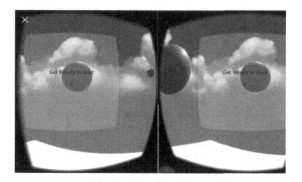

Fig. 1. A snapshot of the OPP app.

After taking several iterations of formative evaluation [9, 10] about how the game should be like, we decided to keep the number of the objects 7 and we assigned all the objects a fixed place on a 3D space because if we randomized them the outcomes would be difficult to co-ordinate. We planned 3 tasks called Size Scene, Color Scene and Number Scene. The Size Scene (Task 1) is to measure how accurately and fast participants perceive size in a virtual 3D space, and Color Scene (Task 2) and Number Scene (Task 3) were to see how color and number affect the ability to perceive size in a 3D space. Each task is described in detail.

Task 1 (Size Scene): We allocated a total of 7 Grey color 3D balls on a 360 virtual space shown in Fig. 2. The task for participants was to find and eliminate them from the smallest to the largest. In order to keep the consistency, the placement of the 7 objects didn't change and in the same place for all participant shown in Fig. 3.

Fig. 2. A snapshot of Task 1 (Size Scene).

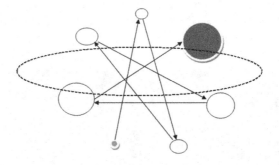

Fig. 3. Placement of the 7 ball shape objects.

Task 2 (Color Scene): The task was the same setup with Task 1 but unlike previous task all the objects had rainbow colors - Violet, Indigo, Blue, Green, Yellow, Orange, Red. To keep the consistency for all participants, the color assigned to an object had not been changed. A snapshot of Task 2 is shown in Fig. 4.

Fig. 4. A snapshot of Task 2 (Color Scene).

Task 3 (Number Scene): The task was the same that find objects from the smallest to the largest but the same was different from the previous two tasks. The placement of the 7 objects were the same as Task 1 but all the 7 spheres in the 3D space had a number on them (1, 2, 3, 4, 5, 6, 7) shown in Fig. 5.

Fig. 5. A snapshot of Task 3 (Number Scene).

3.3 Experimental Room Setup

We chose a room that is free from noise and there is nothing uncomfortable for the subject because these external factors can change the outcome. A computer was setup for pre-survey and post-survey. A swivel chair was used so that the subject can easily take a look in the 3D space while sitting.

3.4 Procedures

As the protocol used in the study, we first welcome participants and asked to fill out the pre-survey. Once they're done the survey, they were instructed on how to use the VR system as a familiarization session. After the session, we provided them a swivel chair so that they can rotate freely. Once they are ready, we started the OPP program for them to start the first task then the other two tasks. The aforementioned 3 tasks were provided to participants one by one. Once all the 3 tasks were done, the participant filled out the post-survey form. We thank their participation and adjourn.

4   Results and Discussions

A total of 30 people participated in the study. Their age ranged from 19–46 year old (mean age = 23.2, median = 21, sd = 6.4). 26 of which were males (87%) and 4 of which were females (13%).

4.1 Before the OPP Tasks

19 (63.3%) of the participants were familiar with Virtual Reality technology and the rest 11 (36.7%) were experiencing this technology for the very first time with us. It can also be a deciding factor because people who already had an idea about how spatial environment looks like (27 (90%) of the participants who used VR technology was for gaming) performed better, they were also very quick to response and understand the concept of the game while giving instructions. 25 (86%) of the participants were students. The rest included music producer, faculty members, creative director and front desk manager.

4.2   After the OPP Tasks

The 30 participants participated in the OPP Tasks shown in Fig. 6. Positive responses from them were noticeable and they were the most excited as some of them were even eager to know the plans in future with this game.

Fig. 6. A snapshot of the study in progress

Task 1 – Perception in Size
The task 1 was the easiest one because here subjects had to discriminate the sizes only without any restrictions such as color and number. But if we look at the datasheet we will see that this is the task that took maximum time to finish and the reason behind is this was the first one. Subjects took time to get accustomed to the spatial environment. This task developed their cognitive skill on that particular spatial environment which actually helped in the respective tasks. We can see that the mean of 30 participant's time spent on Task 1 is 51.6 s which more than both Task 2 and Task 3. The fastest time is 31 and the longest time is 103. 5 participants (16.7%) popped out the 7 objects in a wrong order.

Task 2 – Perception in Size with Colors
This is second task so we expected the participants performed better and the result was actually better. The mean of 30 participant's time spent on Task 2 is 45.4 s which is more than Task 3 and less than Task 1. It cannot be said that this task was the toughest one but definitely the colors were confusing to some extent but to only a few (exceptional) it was the easiest. The fastest time is 31 and the longest time is 88. In terms of how accurately the objects were popped out, 2 participants (6.7%) popped out the 7 objects in a wrong order.

Task 3 – Perception in Size with Numbers
This was the easiest one because by this time the subjects knew the position of the objects as we fixed the objects there and did not change anything in the game scene from Task 1 other than adding colors to the spheres in Task 2 and adding numbers to

the spheres in Task 3. The mean time spent on Task 3 is 42 s. The fastest time is 31 and the longest time is 60.0. All the participants popped out the 7 objects correctly.

A descriptive statistic of the time spent (in second) on Task 1, Task 2 and Task 3 is shown in Table 2. As seen in the table, the first task spent most time, then the second and third tasks in order. It seemed there was no effect by the colors or numbers in perceiving the size of the object in the experiment. However, there was a gender effect that on an average, male participants spent less time in all the 3 tasks. The table suggests that the female participants took more time to finish the same task than the male participants which directly refers to a journal by Kaveri Subrahmanyam that suggests a study on Spatial performance, measured using two subtests of a computerized spatial skills battery, was significantly better in boys than in girls during pretest assessment. Subjects then practiced on an action video game, Marble Madness, or a computerized word game, Conjecture [8].

Table 2. A summary table of the tasks.

	Task 1 (size)	Task 2 (color)	Task 3 (number)	Mean	Sd
Male	42.5	38.9	36.9	39.4	2.8
Female	60.8	51.8	47.0	53.2	7.0
Mean	51.6	45.4	42.0		
Sd	13.0	9.1	7.1		

In another case, it is also seen that color affects the perception of size more in a 3D space than number. It can be clear from the descriptive statistics of the three consecutive tasks below. Only a few of the young age participants while undergoing this test mentioned that the color task was easier. While to some the number task was easier because they were getting confused between Indigo and Blue. In this context a quote of Issac Asimov is worth mentioning "It is customary to list indigo as a color lying between blue and violet, but it has never seemed to me that indigo is worth the dignity of being considered a separate color. To my eyes it seems merely deep blue." So our experiment actually supported that statement.

5   Conclusion and Future Works

This paper shared the results of an experiment about the spatial perception of size in a virtual space called, The Object Popping Project (OPP). The study found that percepting different sizes of 3D object were not affected by colors and numbers. However, there were a gender difference and an age difference in percepting sizes in 3D space. As a limitation of the study, most of the participants were from France but we had other participants from United States, South Korea, The Netherlands, Cuba and Mexico. As an extension of the study, we will continue another user study with more participants in different places to get a diverse result, not converging on a single demographic area.

References

1. Kim, S.J., Jeong, Y., Park, S., Ryu, K., Oh, G.: A survey of drone use for entertainment and AVR (Augmented and Virtual Reality). In: Jung, T., tom Claudia, D.M. (eds.) Augmented Reality and Virtual Reality. PI, pp. 339–352. Springer, Cham (2018). https://doi.org/10.1007/978-3-319-64027-3_23
2. Burgess, N.: Spatial cognition and the brain (2008)
3. Kim, S., Jung, Y., Park, S., Ryu, K., Oh, K.: A survey of drone use for entertainment, augmented and virtual reality. In: The 3rd International AR/VR Conference, Manchester, UK
4. Montello, D.R.: Spatial cognition. Int. Encycl. Soc. Behav. Sci. (2001)
5. Spence, I., Feng, J.: Video games and spatial cognition. Rev. Gen. Psychol. **14**(2), 92–104 (2010)
6. Hubbard, E.M., Piazza, M., Pinel, P., Dehaene, S.: Interactions between number and space in parietal cortex (2005)
7. Winn, W., Hoffman, H., Osberg, K.: Semiotics, cognitive theory and the design of objects, actions and interactions in virtual environments. J. Struct. Learn. Intell. Syst. **14**(1), 29–49 (1999)
8. Osberg, K.: Spatial cognition in the virtual environment
9. Vredenburg, K., Isensee, S., Righi, C.: User Centered Design-An Integrated Approach. Prentice-Hall, Inc., New Jersey (2002)
10. Weston, C., Mcalpine, L., Bordonaro, T.: The influence of participants in formative evaluation on the improvement of learning from written instructional materials. Instr. Sci. **25**, 369–386 (1997)

Design Implications from Cybersickness and Technical Interactions in Virtual Reality

Patricia S. Bockelman(✉), Sharlin Milliard, Matin Salemirad,
Jonathan Valderrama, and Eileen Smith

Institute for Simulation and Training, University of Central Florida,
Orlando, FL 32828, USA
pbockelm@ist.ucf.edu

Abstract. The present study sought to advance understanding about the relationships among contextual, individual, and technical factors in their influence upon human responses to virtual reality (VR) environments. Within this examination, the researchers first conducted a systems analysis of the two comparable VR training environments to isolate potential cybersickness antecedents. Second, a pilot study presented both environments in randomized order to participants to examine how specific features in these environments contributed to user cybersickness responses. Finally, these results were examined considering a triadic theory of cybersickness which positions the phenomenon as a combination of task, system, and individual differences converging and interacting.

Keywords: Cybersickness · Virtual reality · User experience

1 Cybersickness Resituated

1.1 Positioning Cybersickness

Researchers traditionally have grounded examinations of cybersickness (CS) firmly in the physiological realm. This is neither surprising, nor entirely ineffective, as CS is triggered by a physiological situation (interaction with a cyber system of some sort, including virtual reality VR) and resulting in symptoms akin to those experienced in simulator sickness (regardless of whether motion is virtual or real). The reigning theory firmly lies in a bias toward the physical; a mismatch between the vestibular (balance and movement) and visual senses [7] manifests with symptoms such as nausea, disorientation, headache, sweating, and eye strain (e.g. [4]).

However, this bias toward the role of the physical body and its unique perceptual mismatch may be leading researchers to overlook more nuanced interactions between the human, the technical system, and the task [2]. In this scoping of the CS problem, the boundaries of the problem are extended so that more nuanced factors can be considered as likely contributors to CS symptoms. This triadic account then can provide insight into the relationships among symptoms and individual differences, combinatorial features of hardware and software, as well as cognitive and embodied tasks within the cyber environment.

© Springer Nature Switzerland AG 2019
J. Y. C. Chen and G. Fragomeni (Eds.): HCII 2019, LNCS 11574, pp. 403–415, 2019.
https://doi.org/10.1007/978-3-030-21607-8_31

An opportunity to examine the triadic CS model arose when two projects called for using one set of computer aided drafts to develop two different VR worlds, based on real-world oil rigs.

2   A Tale of Two Rigs

The two VR environments examined in the present study were designed from the same CAD drawings of an ADT-500 oil rig. While created from the same architectural core, the purposes of the environments were different. Rig A was designed as a multi-purpose training tool. From its inception, its end users were trainees and instructors who were the people who typically live and work in these environments. Rig B's end users were different. This environment was designed primarily to provide business personnel opportunities to conduct "walk-throughs" on a rig environment. Rig B end users navigate the space together, even if they are not co-located, and can share attention on a rig that has been labeled to assure that all users know where they are located and what they are looking at, even if they are unfamiliar with life on a rig.

As the end users required different interactions within the systems, the design decisions for Rig A varied from those for Rig B. It provides an excellent example of the inseparability between the considerations of system and task. While imperative to differentiate the rigs for these uses, these design decisions impacted the factors that are potential contributors to cyber sickness. The following section highlights some examples of design differences between these two environments, in relationship to the theoretical cybersickness factor.

2.1   Field of View

Research suggests that both internal (the virtual camera angle) and external (screen size and viewing distance) fields of view (FOVs) affect cyber sickness, but the relationship between internal FOV (iFOV) and external FOV (eFOV) is complicated [14]. Counter intuitively, congruence between eFOV and iFOV is more likely to trigger cybersickness symptoms (Fig. 1).

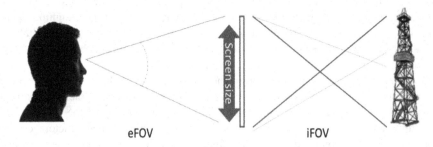

Fig. 1. eFOV provides the user access to the virtual world by externalizing the image via a display, whereas iFOV comes from the internal virtual "camera angles". Adapted from [10].

The studies by van Emmerik and colleagues [14] suggest that cybersickness symptoms may be reduced by increasing the difference between eFOV and iFOV. Further, they noted that postural stability was linked to the cybersickness symptoms, raising a concern for task-based VR contexts (as opposed to the traditional ocular-motor and gustatory symptoms raised in the SSQ).

For the Rig A and Rig B comparison, the eFOV to iFOV ratio is more pronounced in Rig B than Rig A, and consequently, Rig B introduces greater opportunity for time and attention to be given to very wide-camera angle vantages. When wearing the VR headset, the display screen is very close to the eyes yet the image upon first sight and while initial orienting is wide-angle, the exploration of the rig a priority in this environment. Simply, Rig B has a proximal eFOV: distal iFOV (see Fig. 2). Whereas the tasking assigned to Rig A holds the a stable eFOV (with the headmounted VR), but changes the camera angles with the tasks to be more frequently focused.

Fig. 2. Rig B example on ATD 500. iFOV overlaps with task, as users of the Rig B simulation system are more likely to engage in "exploration" compared to Rig A users.

As FOV presents immediate embodiment cues for navigation, regardless of whether the affordances are embedded into the system or not, it informs the experimental design described in Sect. 3.

2.2 Level of Detail

Rig A had a much higher level of detail in range of colors and textures implemented in the simulation than Rig B. Take a look at Table 1 below for images comparing the level of detail built into Rig A and Rig B.

This difference in the level of detail throughout the simulations may also affect the susceptibility of VR environment users experiencing cybersickness symptoms. Research has shown that the more realistic a VR environment is, the more likely it is to induce cybersickness [4, 10].

Table 1. Comparison of the level of detail between Rig A and Rig B simulations.

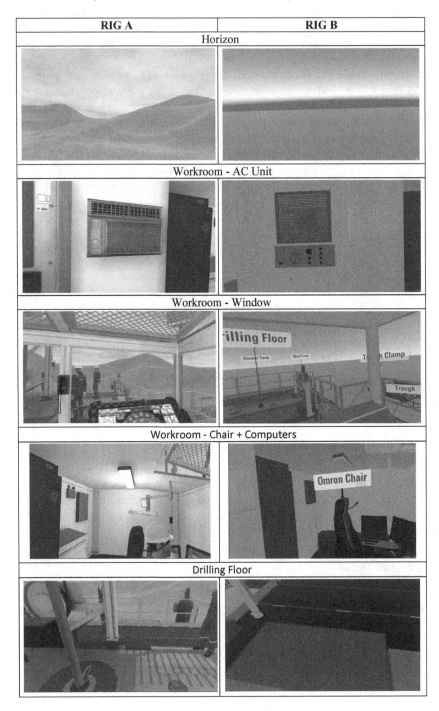

While it may seem that increased level of detail does not align with the sensory conflict theory, it potentially follows a different aspect of sensory conflict that the results of other studies also seem to follow. A dissonance triggered by a difference between what is expected of the VR environment and what is presented in the VR environment results in cybersickness symptoms. However, some studies suggest that when the difference between what is expected and what is presented decreases, the risk of inducing more cybersickness in VR users also increases. For example, the smaller the difference between the external field of view (screen size and viewing distance) and internal field of view (the virtual camera angle), the more cybersickness VR participants experienced [14]. According to these positions on realism, when there are unrealistic elements in a VR environment, such as impractical scenarios and limitations in the VR, cybersickness may occur. As realism increases, the chance of inducing cybersickness increases.

Examples of possibly cybersickness-inducing realism within Rig A include avatars, a detailed horizon, metal texture, vibrant colors, object depth, interior fluorescent lighting, shading and casting, large windows, and suspended ceiling grates. Rig B has less realistic features, such as a flat air conditioning surface, solid color texture and shading, flat objects, and boxy doghouse wall-to-ceiling structure. Furthermore, labels are an unrealistic feature in Rig B which are absent in Rig A.

2.3 Locus of Control

Both a psycho-construct and a literal form of manipulating oneself through space, the phrase "locus of control" (LOC) can mean a bevy of things when raised for an interdisciplinary audience. In such a vein, the present work embraces this holistically and includes psychological components (the study described below includes LOC metrics) as well as manual navigation from a first-person perspective within the VR worlds. The following description highlights aspects of the control and navigation experiences within the rigs.

While walking is the same in both simulations, the method of teleportation differs. Rig A teleportation was more precise than Rig B. A teleportation line appears to indicate where a user may navigate to throughout the VR simulation. The Rig A simulation casts a blue straight teleportation line (Fig. 3) that teleports users to the exact location commanded at the end of the teleportation line (as long as it was on the ground or floor). The Rig B simulation projected a green parabolic teleportation line perpendicular to the floor, (Fig. 4). However, there are restricted areas in the simulation design preventing some of these points to correctly teleport. If the teleportation line is in a restricted area, the system defaults to another teleportation location.

The teleportation line in Rig B is less accurate than the one in Rig A because the navigation was restricted to certain areas even though the user could direct the teleportation line anywhere. Thus, the VR environment user would be teleported to an entirely different area in the simulation than expected. This is an example of sensory conflict which leads to a higher risk of experiencing cybersickness. Sensory conflict theory occurs when the VR environment and reality are perceived simultaneously. The vestibular system does not sense the motion that the visual system perceives, and thus, induces cybersickness [7].

Fig. 3. The figure illustrates the straight teleportation teleport line in the Rig A simulation. (Color figure online)

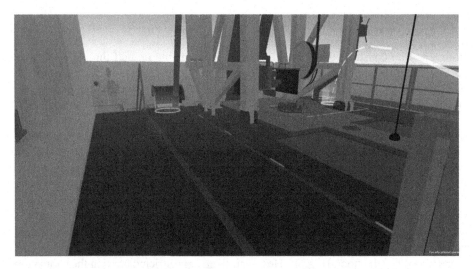

Fig. 4. The figure illustrates the parabolic teleport line in the Rig B simulation as well as the blue circles that the VR environment user can teleport to. (Color figure online)

A similar experience was examined in a study where it stated that a "mismatch between visual and vestibular cues can cause simulator sickness" [9]. For example, "as the user took one step, she was moved 10 steps in the VR environment. This causes a large mismatch between vestibular and visual cues and might be the reason for users experiencing more simulator sickness using this specific technique" [9]. The expectation of what should happen and what occurs in the VR environment is disproportionate and can cause cybersickness symptoms. This aligns with the sensory conflict theory of cybersickness which refers to the clash between the vestibular (physically senses movement from VR graphics) and visual (seeing) systems in the virtual environment [4, 7].

An early study done by Bowman, Koller, and Hodges [3] also found dissonance to relate to cybersickness symptoms when their results indicated "that motion techniques which instantly teleport users to new locations are correlated with increased user disorientation" (p. 45). This corresponds to the postural instability theory of cybersickness which occurs "whenever the environment changes in an abrupt or significant way, and where postural control strategies have not been learnt the result is postural instability" [4]. This type of change occurs in many VR environments when a visual change occurring in the VR does not match with how an individual would normally move. Instantaneous teleportation is not a natural navigation. The dissonance between normal postural control and the visual system due to "abrupt and significant" changes in the VR environment can result in cybersickness [4]. This type of change occurs in many virtual environments when a visual change occurring in the VR does not match with how an individual would normally move.

Further, it has been reported that "participants who have good control in a virtual environment can better predict future motion and are found to be less susceptible to cybersickness" [4]. Likewise, the dissonance felt when the expectation of the desired teleportation location where the VR environment user would be teleported in the SO5 simulation and where the user actually teleported to when the teleport line did not exactly match with the restricted area of teleportation is an example of dissonance of the senses in a VR environment, which can lead to cybersickness. This particular situation more closely aligns with the postural instability theory and explains why the movement in the Rig B simulation may lead to experiencing more cybersickness symptoms than movement in the Rig A simulation.

Studies on locus of control in virtual environments also observe how dissonance can lead to cybersickness. In studies on locus of control, it was found that the less control or prediction VR users had in their environment, the more cybersickness they experienced [1, 4, 8, 11]. This also aligns with the sensory conflict theory in that the mismatch between two sensory systems: visual (senses movement from VR graphics) and vestibular (senses lack of physical motion).

3 Walking in Two Worlds—A Study

To examine the impacts of these design decisions on user experiences, particularly in respect to cybersickness, participants were exposed to both VR rigs, randomized by order. They were guided in tasks by a researcher so that the time activity spent in each VR world was semi-controlled. That said, as user familiarity with gaming generally varied, as well as familiarity with this kind of environment, users were given the liberty to explore areas of the rig and take their time with navigation controls in a manner that they found comfortable.

Participants experienced two VR environments differing in level of visual detail using the HTC VIVE. The order in which the environments were presented was randomized. Participants were guided through the same 7 tasks in each environment for a total of 10 min. The total time a participant spent in each environment was recorded.

Participants were asked to complete a set of surveys administered at different points. Before experiencing the first VR environment, participants completed a personality survey and the Simulation Sickness Questionnaire (SSQ) to establish baseline cybersickness scores. The SSQ was administered after each VR experience in addition to an experience survey. After the second VR experience, participants completed the Motion Sickness Susceptibility Questionnaire (MSSQ) and a demographics survey.

The study included a total of 33 participants of which the majority (78.8%) were between the ages of 18 and 26, 12.1% were between 26 and 40, 6.1% were between 41 and 60, and one (3%) participant reported being under 18. The majority of the participants, 57.6%, were female and 42.4% were male. The average weight of participants was 162.2 lbs. with an average height of 5.6 ft. Participants' familiarity with VR headsets was very minimal as only one participant owned a device and the majority of participants (36.4%) indicated having used one once or twice. Participants' experience playing video games was also minimal; 54.5% reported rarely playing video games. With regard to participants' vision, 63% wore corrected lenses and 33% reported having an astigmatism.

3.1 Physiology of Pupillary Distance

While recent work suggests that eye position itself cannot account for ocular strain and associated symptoms in cyber contexts [13], there has been some push for more consideration of pupillary distance (PD) coming from some industry partners. While the push may be in part informed by necessary consideration of multiple genders and ethnicities in design, the empirical support for the role of PD in cybersickness experiences is debatable. Consequently, it was important for the present study to include this basic physiological consideration. The Pupillary distance (PD) of the participants ranged from 53 to 69. The majority of the participants (27.3%) had a PD of 62. The PD of the participants averaged 61.91 (M = 61.91), the SD = 3.2, and SE = .558.

Of the 33 participants:

27.3% (n = 9) had a PD of 62
15.2% (n = 5) had a PD of 64
12.1% (n = 4) had a PD of 63
9.1% (n = 3) had a PD of 61 and 9.1% (n = 3) a PD of 65
6.1% (n = 2) had a PD of 58 and 6.1% (n = 2) a PD of 60
3% (n = 1) had a PD of 53, 3% (n = 1) had a PD of 54, 3% (n = 1) had a PD of 57,
3% (n = 1) had a PD of 66, and 3% (n = 1) had a PD of 69

The PD data was divided into three groups to create low, medium, and high PD groups. The group ranges were as follows:

Low PD: PD is between 53 and 57
Medium PD: PD is between 58 and 62
High PD: PD is between 63 and 69

The majority of the participants (48.5%) had medium PDs with the least amount of participants in the low PD category (9.1%).

3.2   The Experience of Simulation Sickness Between Conditions

To understand the effect of condition on participant report of sickness, regardless of order, researchers examined the overall scores reported in the SSQs. Overall, most participants did not experience cybersickness symptoms in any of the conditions (a baseline survey to ascertain initial symptom rates, Rig A, and Rig B). At baseline, 84.8% (n = 28) of participants did not experience general discomfort and 12.1% (n = 4) experienced slight general discomfort. The same percent, 84.8% (n = 28) of participants did not experience general discomfort in the Rig A simulation, and 15.2% (n = 5) experienced slight general discomfort. After Rig B, 90.9% (n = 30) of participants did not experience general discomfort and 9.1% (n = 3) experienced slight general discomfort.

This section presents analyses for determining if there are any differences in individuals' experienced simulation sickness symptoms following baseline, Rig A, and Rig B. First, normality was tested to determine the appropriate statistical analysis test to use. This procedure and results are presented here. To account for change scores in this within-measures design, scores were calculated for nausea, disorientation, oculomotor, and total SSQ score. A Mixed Design ANOVA was run to determine if there are any differences in simulation sickness scores depending on the order of condition.

For both condition orders (Rig A first and Rig B first), the overall nausea simulation sickness scores were on average lower at baseline (mean = 3.58), and equal for Rig A and Rig B (mean = 5.37). The average nausea score for individuals who experienced Rig B first (mean = 5.09) was higher at baseline than those who experienced Rig A first (mean = 2.24). For the experience of nausea symptoms in Rig A, the average nausea score for individuals who experienced Rig B first (mean = 6.36) is higher than those who experienced Rig A first (mean = 4.49). For the experience of nausea symptoms in Rig B, the average nausea score for individuals who experienced Rig A first (mean = 5.61) is higher than those who experienced Rig B first (mean = 5.08).

In sum, the participants in the present study reported more nausea simulation sickness symptoms after their second exposure to the simulation regardless of the order in which condition was experienced. This aligns with postulations regarding cybersickness, simulator sickness, and other maladies in connection with time-in-system/exposure rates. However, these values represent trends. There was no significant effect of condition on the experience of nausea symptoms. In other words, there are no significant changes in the experience of nausea symptoms between conditions (baseline, Rig A, and Rig B); F (2,60) = 1.294, p = .282, np2 = .041. Further, there was no significant interaction between condition and condition order in terms of nausea scores. There are no differences in nausea scores between conditions and nausea scores are the same for each condition order; F (2,60) = .982, p = .380, np2 = .032. Thus, regardless of condition order, there is no difference in the experience of nausea symptoms between conditions. A two-way mixed ANOVA showed that there was no significant main effect of condition on nausea simulation sickness scores. Again, while not statistically significant, participants reported more nausea simulation sickness symptoms when their second simulation was Rig A.

To better understand condition on ocular-motor symptoms, a mixed-design ANOVA was also conducted. For both condition orders (Rig A first and Rig B first), the overall oculomotor simulation sickness scores are on average lower at baseline (mean = 6.12), and higher for Rig A (mean = 9.71) than for Rig B (mean = 7.58). The average oculomotor score for individuals who experienced Rig B first (mean = 6.70) is higher at baseline than those who experienced Rig A first (mean = 5.80). For the experience of oculomotor symptoms in Rig A, the average oculomotor score for individuals who experienced Rig B first (mean = 9.10) is lower than those who experienced Rig A first (mean = 10.26). For the experience of oculomotor symptoms in Rig B, the average oculomotor score for individuals who experienced Rig A first (mean = 8.03) is higher than those who experienced Rig B first (mean = 7.07).

As with the nausea symptoms, individuals reported more oculomotor symptoms after having experienced Rig A, regardless of condition order. The same tests were conducted statistically, and these appear to be trends and did not reach significant oculomotor symptoms between conditions (baseline, Rig A, and Rig B); F (1.5,45) = 1.715, p = .197, np2 = .054.

These symptom trends feed specifically into results regarding disorientation, particularly considering the relationship between the human interactions within the systems and the artistic designs for the system navigations. For individuals that experienced Rig A first, the disorientation scores are the same, on average, after experiencing both Rig A and Rig B (mean = 5.73).

For individuals that experienced Rig B first, the disorientation scores are higher, on average, after experiencing Rig A (mean = 13.92) than after Rig B (mean = 8.35).

Disorientation scores were lower on average for Rig B (mean = 7.04) than Rig A (mean = 9.83). These results suggest that individuals reported more disorientation symptoms after each condition if they experienced Rig B first. The reported disorientation symptoms increase drastically after having experienced Rig A second. A two-way mixed ANOVA showed that there was a significant main effect of condition on disorientation simulation sickness scores (F (1.6,46.59) = 5.041, p = .016, np2 = .144) with scores lower on average at baseline (mean = 1.86) than for Rig A (mean = 9.83) and Rig B (mean = 7.04). Additionally, there was no significant main effect of condition order on disorientation simulation sickness scores (F (1,30) = 1.709, p = .201, np2 = .054) with overall scores lower on average at baseline (mean = 1.74) than Rig A (mean = 9.57) and Rig B (mean = 6.96). Furthermore, there was also no significant interaction between condition and condition order F (1,30) = 1.709, p = .201, np2 = .054). The findings indicate that the experience of disorientation symptoms differ between conditions with individuals having experienced more disorientation in Rig A than any other condition. Furthermore, results indicate that condition order has no effect on the experience of disorientation simulation sickness symptoms in the different conditions.

3.3 Individual Differences and Psychometric Responses

Participants were asked to indicate via Likert-style survey aspects of their experiences following interactions in each condition. When asked to indicate the degree to which they found the navigation easy to use, the majority of participants (54.5%) felt very positive/good about the ease of navigation in Rig A. Individuals' satisfaction with ease of navigation was slightly lower in Rig B with 42.4% feeling very positive/good about the ease of navigation. They were also more likely to feel "very positive/good" looking at objects in Rig A (66.7%) than Rig B (54.5%), although it should be noted that no one indicated feeling negatively about looking at objects in either environment. It was of no surprise that interacting with objects garnered more positive responses in Rig A vs. Rig B (Table 2).

Table 2. Participant opinions of interactions with objects in Rigs A & B.

	Rig A		Rig B	
	Frequency	Percent	Frequency	Percent
Feel generally negative	2	6.1	3	9.1
Feel neither negative nor positive	4	12.1	10	30.3
Feel generally positive	14	42.4	10	30.3
Feel very positive/good	13	39.4	10	30.3
Total	33	100.0	33	100.0

One of the most intriguing results from the user experience survey was in regard to participant self-reported "interest" in the world (Table 3).

Table 3. Participant opinions of their interest in Rigs A & B.

	Rig A		Rig B	
	Frequency	Percent	Frequency	Percent
Feel generally negative	3	9.1	3	9.1
Feel neither negative nor positive	1	3.0	5	15.2
Feel generally positive	8	24.2	13	39.4
Feel very positive/good	21	63.6	12	36.4
Total	33	100.0	33	100.0

While an equal number of participants felt a general negative interest, the strongly "very positive/good" response was 27% higher in Rig A.

4 Discussion

There are numerous limitations to be considered in this study. First, the small sample size and use of student-body samples skewing in favor of gaming familiarity, and non-normalized data sets creates the standard cautions for generalization, especially when making assumptions about physio-sensory systems. Additionally, the data collected was non-normal and the ANOVA for examining effects by condition could not be evaluated. Beyond these obvious caveats, the research team also sees challenges in the following considerations, and offer them in the form of question for future VR design:

(1) Inherent sexism in design of hardware (e.g. rigid pupillary distance in headgear, uncomfortable coronal fit) may contribute to cybersickness physiological responses, what task-based design decisions may also be contributing to biases within whole system and consequently introducing risk?
(2) When task design influences artistic decisions which may contribute to cyber-sickness, how does that feedback into compensatory processes for hardware/software development in parallel?
(3) How can the industry contribute to authentic metrics for predicting the likelihood of cybersickness symptoms based on the triadic influence of system, task, and individual factors (as opposed to the reactive and diagnostic measures currently standard practice)?

The present study in its limited design barely scratches the surface of these larger questions. However, the hope is to position this work a part of a scholarly dialog to advance safer VR tools.

References

1. Almeida, A., Rebelo, F., Noriega, P., Vilar, E.: Virtual reality self induced cybersickness: an exploratory study. In: Rebelo, F., Soares, M. (eds.) Advances in Ergonomics in Design. AISC, vol. 588, pp. 26–33. Springer, Cham (2018). https://doi.org/10.1007/978-3-319-60582-1_3
2. Bockelman, P., Lingum, D.: Factors of cybersickness. In: Stephanidis, C. (ed.) HCI 2017. CCIS, vol. 714, pp. 3–8. Springer, Cham (2017). https://doi.org/10.1007/978-3-319-58753-0_1
3. Bowman, D.A., Koller, D., Hodges, L.F.: Travel in immersive virtual environments: an evaluation of viewpoint motion control techniques. In: Proceedings of IEEE 1997 Annual International Symposium on Virtual Reality, pp. 45–52. IEEE, March 1997
4. Davis, S., Nesbitt, K., Nalivaiko, E.: A systematic review of cybersickness. In: Proceedings of the 2014 Conference on Interactive Entertainment, pp. 8:1–8:9. ACM, New York (2014). https://doi.org/10.1145/2677758.2677780
5. Davis, S., Nesbitt, K., Nalivaiko, E.: Comparing the onset of cybersickness using the Oculus Rift and two virtual roller coasters, vol. 167, p. 12 (2015)
6. Keshavarz, B., Hecht, H.: Stereoscopic viewing enhances visually induced motion sickness but sound does not. Presence Teleoperators Virtual Environ. 21(2), 213–228 (2012). https://doi.org/10.1162/PRES_a_00102
7. LaViola, J.J.: A discussion of cybersickness in virtual environments. ACM SIGCHI Bull. 32(1), 47–56 (2000). https://doi.org/10.1145/333329.333344
8. Liu, C.L.: A neuro-fuzzy warning system for combating cybersickness in the elderly caused by the virtual environment on a TFT-LCD. Appl. Ergonomics 40(3), 316–324 (2009)
9. Nabiyouni, M.: How does interaction fidelity influence user experience in VR locomotion? pp. 1–158. Doctoral dissertation, Virginia Tech (2016)
10. Porcino, T.M., Clua, E.W., Vasconcelos, C.N., Trevisan, D., Valente, L.: Minimizing cyber sickness in head mounted display systems: design guidelines and applications. ArXiv:1611.06292 [CS] (2016). http://arxiv.org/abs/1611.06292

11. Sharples, S., Cobb, S., Moody, A., Wilson, J.R.: Virtual reality induced symptoms and effects (VRISE): comparison of head mounted display (HMD), desktop and projection display systems. Displays **29**(2), 58–69 (2008). https://doi.org/10.1016/j.displa.2007.09.005
12. Tiiro, A.: Effect of visual realism on cybersickness in virtual reality. University of Oulu, Finland (2018). http://jultika.oulu.fi/files/nbnfioulu-201802091218.pdf
13. Turnbull, P.R., Phillips, J.R.: Ocular effects of virtual reality headset wear in young adults. Sci. Rep. **7**(1), 16172 (2017)
14. van Emmerik, M.L., de Vries, S.C., Bos, J.E.: Internal and external fields of view affect cybersickness. Displays **32**(4), 169–174 (2011). https://doi.org/10.1016/j.displa.2010.11.003

Characterizing the Cognitive Impact
of Tangible Augmented Reality

Michael W. Boyce[1](✉), Aaron L. Gardony[2], Paul Shorter[3],
Carlene Horner[2], Cortnee R. Stainrod[4], Jeremy Flynn[4],
Tad T. Brunyé[2], and Charles R. Amburn[1]

[1] US Army, Combat Capabilities Development Command Solider Center,
Orlando, FL, USA
michael.w.boycell.civ@mail.mil
[2] Center for Applied Brain & Cognitive Sciences, Medford, MA, USA
[3] Human Research and Engineering Directorate, Army Research Laboratory,
Aberdeen Proving Ground, Adelphi, MD, USA
[4] University of Central Florida, Institute for Simulation and Training (UCF IST),
Orlando, FL, USA

Abstract. This study examines how cognitive processes that support mission planning are influenced by the physical ability to touch and manipulate sand, compared to passively observing the same action. It employs a systematic investigation on terrain conceptual knowledge, terrain recognition and, landmark memory using the ARES sand table. Sand tables are topographic models that support learning through the physical creation of scenarios. In the military, sand tables support strategic exercises for soldiers to practice the process of collective decision making and communication. Operational mission planning typically occurs with one person shaping the sand, followed by a larger group of individuals observing. It is the relationship between the person shaping terrain and those observing that is of specific interest. A total of 96 participants were recruited, from the University of Central Florida (UCF) and the Center for Applied Brain & Cognitive Sciences (CABCS). Results indicate that physically shaping the terrain improved recognition but did not have an effect on conceptual knowledge or recollection of landmarks compared to observers. This experiment supports the need for further investigation to determine how tangible interaction can contribute to cognitive understanding.

Keywords: ARES · Terrain recognition · Landmark identification ·
Military training

1 Introduction

The human being uses the sense of touch to assist in understanding the world. Each sensation experience of touch, also known as a tactile experience, provides information to our brain [21]. A common tactile experience in the military is to represent topography using sand tables. Rehearsal and practice with sand tables are a part of standard military curriculum. A Sand Table Exercise (STEX) is a common military practice for learning terrain features in order to facilitate collective decision making and

© Springer Nature Switzerland AG 2019
J. Y. C. Chen and G. Fragomeni (Eds.): HCII 2019, LNCS 11574, pp. 416–427, 2019.
https://doi.org/10.1007/978-3-030-21607-8_32

communication [2, 4, 30]. STEX usually consist of a group of soldiers being briefed on a table that was constructed by a single soldier who shapes the terrain on the table. Therefore, during a STEX only a single soldier will have the tactile experience of shaping the terrain while the majority observe the construction. This research looks at how the role of the individual (e.g., shaper vs. observer) impacts spatial and cognitive metrics related to terrain learning.

The role of the shaper and the role of the observer are expected to affect learning. Literature supports this in the concept of active vs. passive learning. Active learning consists of physically performing activities, while passive learning is characterized by observing those activities [19]. Active learning provides benefits of user engagement, increased motivation and higher-order thinking when synthesizing, analyzing, and evaluating information [5]. For example, research has shown that objects actively explored were recognized faster than objects that were passively viewed [17].

Activities that facilitate active learning by manipulating an interface are known as tangible interactions. The concept of tangible interaction has a foundation across the fields of computing, human-computer interaction (HCI) and product/industrial design [13]. The ability to engage physical touch during tangible interaction can provide a lower barrier to entry, increased user engagement, reduce cognitive load, and create the perception of an intuitive interface [15, 18]. However, Hornecker [14] points out that, just being intuitive is not enough to ensure learning gains. Rather it is consideration of the task, context, and user that maximizes the learning value of tangible interaction. Tangible interaction provides an opportunity for naturalistic interaction to accomplish a task at hand [7] and has been shown to increase speed and accuracy of tasks as well as increase awareness of other interaction types [10].

To support battlespace visualization for mission planning, after action review and the various types of combat interactions, the Combat Capabilities Development Command Solider Center has developed ARES, a distributed interactive visualization architecture. Of its various modalities this study used ARES real-time augmented reality-enhanced sand table. ARES sand table facilitates tangible interaction by intelligently adjusting topographic contour lines projections whiles the user shapes the sand. This is enabled by a combination of commercial, off the shelf (COTS) technologies including a Microsoft Xbox Kinect ™ sensor and a short-throw projector and software. The capabilities provided by the ARES sand table present a unique opportunity to evaluate the role of shaper versus observer, and the impact of active and passive learning during collective terrain construction.

1.1 Tangibility Metrics

As a first step to establishing a research design, we developed metrics that assess three knowledge areas; terrain conceptual knowledge, (i.e., knowing what a terrain feature is), terrain recognition, (i.e. recognizing familiar terrains, and landmark memory (i.e., recalling landmark locations relative to terrain features). Overall, three cognitive task were used working under the assumption that active learners would perform better [16]. These tasks were the Terrain Conceptual Knowledge Test (TCKT), Sketch Map Drawing, and Terrain Verification Test (TVT), which assess each of the knowledge areas respectively.

The Terrain Conceptual Knowledge Test (TCKT) assesses terrain knowledge related to terrain features. Terrain knowledge consists of fact-based material that is needed to perform a procedural task such building a terrain feature (e.g., hill). The TKCT consisted of a 40 multiple choice labeling task of pictures of terrain features (5 major, 2 minor). This task was administered prior to and following the experiment.

The Sketch Map Drawing Task involved participants drawing a sketch map of the locations of landmarks embedded in the terrain. Quantitatively analyzing sketch maps can be burdensome so we used the Gardony Map Drawing Analyzer (GMDA) software [12] to easily collect and analyze sketch maps. Participants were required to memorize the locations of eight items; and then recall them on a top-down map. The GMDA evaluates the relative and absolute position of the eight items, providing a variety of quantitative measures that can provide insight on how active versus passive participants remember specific aspects of landmark locations.

The Terrain Verification Task (TVT) evaluated the comprehension of three-dimensional terrain models. Participants were presented with several views of 3D terrain images and were tasked to decide whether the depicted terrain was the one that their group had created or whether it was different (i.e., distractors). To excel at this task, participants had to understand and translate their spatial mental representation of the terrain topography into new orientations as the TVT showed terrains from various angles.

1.2   Research Questions

The primary research questions guiding this experiment are:

1. Is there a difference in terrain conceptual knowledge gained when the shaper constructs the terrain versus passively observing someone else shaping?
2. Is there a difference in the ability to recognize terrain topography between the individual shaper and the individual observing?
3. Is there a difference in landmark memory between shapers and observers?

1.3   Hypotheses

H1: The shaper will demonstrate greater terrain knowledge gains (post vs. pre-experiments) on the TCKT compared to the observer.

H2: The shaper will demonstrate improved accuracy in recognizing the shaped terrain on the TVT over the observer.

H3: The shaper will demonstrate a faster response time on the TVT compared to the observer.

H4: The shaper will demonstrate greater landmark placement accuracy on the GMDA over the observer.

2 Method

2.1 Participants

Study trials were conducted at the University of Central Florida (UCF) in Orlando FL, and at the Center for Applied Brain & Cognitive Sciences (CABCS) in Medford, MA. A total of 96 participants ranging in age from 18 to 35 were recruited. The UCF Institute for Simulation and Training, administers a research participation program named SONA which provides volunteer research studies for students in exchange for course credit. This study awarded UCF students one credit hour for participation. Tufts University students recruited at CABCS received payment of $20.00 in exchange for their participation. All participants were randomly selected as shaper or observer upon arrival.

2.2 Apparatus and Materials

The Augmented REality Sandtable (ARES) is a proof-of-concept is a traditional sand table, augmented with a commercial, off the shelf (COTS) projector, LCD monitor, PC, Microsoft Kinect ® and Xbox Controllers. ARES allows for the construction of topographic terrain maps through projection as well as the display of tactical graphics and military icons to support real time collaboration for mission rehearsal, planning and after action review. ARES was developed internally at the Combat Capabilities Command Soldier Center, and has been used and validated in several previous experiments [1, 5, 6, 8].

3 Experimental Design

The study employed a yoked control design to investigate the effect of tangibility (i.e., independent variable) on incidentally-learned terrain knowledge and spatial memory (i.e., dependent variables). Participant were placed in dyads and randomly assigned to either of two experimental conditions described below:

1. Shaper condition: In this condition, one participant (i.e., the shaper) shapes various terrain features by hand as described and depicted in a PowerPoint presentation based on an Army Field Manual and included animated GIFs showing the motions needed to create each feature. Shapers were told that they would have someone watching them, but that this person is not assessing them.
2. Observer condition: In this condition, one participant (i.e., the observer) watches the other participant (i.e., the shaper) hand-shaping terrain features. Their goal is to pay close attention to the shapers action but to not comment or influence the shaper in any way.

The dependent variables, described below, relate to the behavioral outcomes of interest:

1. <u>Terrain Conceptual Knowledge:</u> Reaction time and accuracy, evaluated using a multiple choice classification assessment of terrain features.

2. <u>Terrain Verification Test:</u> Reaction time, accuracy, and reaction time slope and intercept, relative to view angular disparity. These variables were evaluated using a terrain verification task that employed a 3-D terrain model generated by ARES software. Participants were required to make quick decisions (i.e., "This is the terrain we made", or "This is not the terrain we made"), based on multiple pictures viewed from various angles, as well as comparable views from similar but non-identical 3-D models.

3. <u>Gardony Map Drawing Analyzer:</u> Angle and Distance Accuracy. Participants were required to memorize the locations and positions of eight items (basic colored shapes) placed in the sand; then draw a 2-D map from a top-down view. The GMDA software evaluated the relative positional information, with respect to angles and distances, of the eight items derived from the 2-D drawings.

3.1   Procedure

In this experiment two participants are run simultaneously. One participant is randomly assigned the role of shaper and the other has the role of the observer. Both participants' first sign informed consent documentation and are assessed on baseline knowledge of terrain features via computer administered surveys. Next they complete the building task in which the shaper is tasked to build basic terrain features and follow directions provided by a PowerPoint slideshow while the observer looks. The TCKT is administered prior to and immediately after the building task while the TVT and the GMDA are both administered after (see Fig. 1).

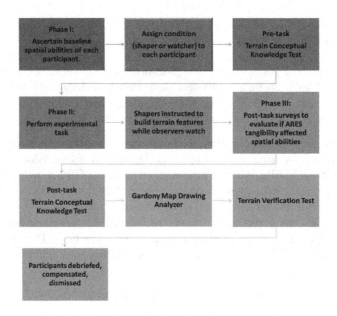

Fig. 1. Chronological table of participant procedure.

3.2   Generating TVT Stimuli

To provide terrain images for the TVT, alternative terrain features were created by the authors while participations completed the post-task TCKCT in a separate location. This involved creating alternative terrain by swapping the location of two terrain features. Before shaping the sand attention was paid to the height and orientation of the terrain features in order to make the swapped features resemble how the participant shaped them. In total three swaps were made, creating three sets of distractor terrains.

4   Results

4.1   Terrain Conceptual Knowledge

We first investigated response accuracy on the Terrain Conceptual Knowledge Test (TCKT) to determine differences in conceptual terrain knowledge acquisition between participant roles. We submitted participants response accuracy in the TCKT to a 2 (role: shaper, observer) × 2 (session: baseline, post-task) repeated-measures ANOVA.

This analysis revealed a significant main effect of session, $F(1,39) = 122.57$, $p < .0001$, $\eta_p^2 = .76$, indicating that participants response accuracy increased after the building task relative to baseline.

This main effect was qualified by a significant session by role interaction, $F(1,39) = 4.52$, $p = .04$, $\eta_p^2 = .10$. To examine this interaction further we conducted follow-up pairwise comparisons of the estimated marginal means with Bonferroni p-value adjustments. This analysis revealed no significant differences between roles in either session (all p's > .1). This finding suggests that while observers showed larger accuracy gains across sessions than shapers these gains did not result in significantly higher post-task knowledge.

We next investigated response times (RTs) on the TCKT. As is common in psychological experiments, RTs were positively skewed and so we applied the natural log transform prior to analysis. We then submitted log transformed RT to the same 2 × 2 repeated measures ANOVA. This analysis revealed a significant main effect of session, $F(1,39) = 107.23$, $p < .0001$, $\eta_p^2 = .73$, indicating that participants response time decreased across sessions. No interactions emerged.

4.2   Terrain Recognition

We next investigated response accuracy on the Terrain Verification Task (TVT). This task presented images of the constructed terrain interspersed with alternative terrains (i.e., same, different) at different rotations (i.e., angular disparities), similar to the classic mental rotation task (MRT; Shepard & Metzler, 1971). As a first step, we submitted participants response accuracy in the TVT to a 2 (role: shaper, observer) × 2 (trial type: same, different) × 5 (absolute-valued angular disparity: 0°, 45°, 90°, 135°, 180°) repeated-measures ANOVA. This analysis revealed a significant trial type x angular disparity interaction, $F(4,156) = 3.03$, $p = .02$, $\eta_p^2 = .07$. For different trials, response accuracy remained relatively stable as a function of angular disparity.

However, for same trials, accuracy increased as a function of angular disparity, peaking at 90°, and then declined. No other main effects or interactions emerged (Fig. 2).

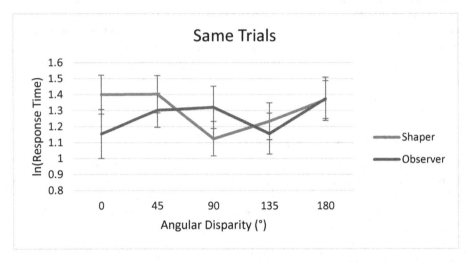

Fig. 2. Angular disparity by response time for same and different trials. Note these are estimated marginal means and standard errors of the estimated marginal means.

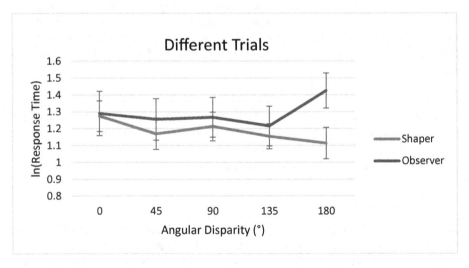

Fig. 3. Angular disparity by response time for same and different trials. Note these are estimated marginal means and standard errors of the estimated marginal means.

We next investigated RT on the TVT. As with the TCKT, RTs were positively skewed and so we applied the natural log transform prior to analysis. We then submitted log transformed RT to a $2 \times 2 \times 5$ repeated measures ANOVA. This analyses revealed a main effect of angular disparity, $F(4,36) = 2.80$, $p = .04$, $\eta_p^2 = .24$ (see Fig. 3).

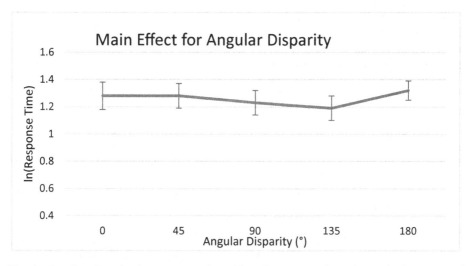

Fig. 4. Angular disparity by response time. Note these are estimated marginal means and standard errors of the estimated marginal means.

This main effect was qualified by a marginally significant condition x angular disparity interaction, $F(4,36) = 2.58$, p = .054, $\eta_p^2 = .22$. This result is reported due to its medium effect size which provides evidence against it being a false alarm (see Fig. 4).

4.3   Landmark Memory

Last we investigated landmark memory on participants' maps using GMDA. We assessed two individual landmark measures provided by GMDA, angle and distance accuracy, which reflect the accuracy of inter-landmark relationships with respect to angles and distances, respectively. We first submitted angle accuracy to a one-way repeated measures ANOVA for role. This analysis revealed a marginal main effect of role, $F(1,38) = 3.84$, $p = .06$, $\eta_p^2 = .09$. We next submitted distance accuracy to the same ANOVA which revealed a significant main effect of role, $F(1,38) = 5.79$, $p = .02$, $\eta_p^2 = .13$, indicating observers' sketch maps better represented inter-landmark distance relationships than shapers.

5   Discussion

This study investigated how physical tangible interaction during terrain construction impacted conceptual knowledge, terrain recognition and landmark memory. Research has shown that active learning through engaging with an interface leads to better understanding than passive learning. Literature supports the use of tangible interaction to facilitate learning [3, 25, 26].

Empirical results have yielded mixed findings on the role of physical touch with some advocating for the use of tangibles [17, 26] others stating no difference [24], and others saying the applicability changes based on task [11, 27]. The outcome of this experiment yielded mixed results.

With respect to conceptual knowledge gains, the hypotheses was that the shaper would gain more terrain knowledge (post vs. pre-experiments) than the observer. As it turned out, this experiment showed no difference between the two groups in terrain knowledge gains. The lack of difference could be due to the task creating a high or low workload state that, in turn, created a ceiling or floor effect respectively. It is also possible that the shapers were in a higher workload state than the observers given that they were responsible for shaping the terrain (i.e., the shapers had more work/tasking). This possibility could have created a masking situation which could not be accounted for in this experiment without a way to address workload as a covariate.

The terrain verification test demonstrates the orientation of content matters through the effect of angular disparity. Participants demonstrating highest accuracy at 90° rotation. The peaking at 90° could be due to the experimental setup where participants tended to move from a 0-degree position to a 90-degree position as the shaper was building the features, therefore providing experience at visualizing from that perspective. This advocates for future studies to carefully control participant position relative to the overall table.

The results from the GMDA were in the opposite direction than expected, with observers performing better than shapers in terms of landmark locations. This finding can be explained due to the differences between roles during the landmark placement task.

Since the observers themselves did not have to be concerned with the positioning of landmarks, they had the ability to maintain an overview of the landscape, whereas the shaper might have been focusing on the task. This focusing could change the key elements recalled, such that shapers and observers emphasized different information. This is supported in the literature through the concept of attentional narrowing. Attentional narrowing is defined as when an individual involuntarily fails to process critical information [23, 29].

If there is an assumption that the observer was experiencing less attentional narrowing and more overview related to the landmarks, this overview would provide them with an advantage on the post-assessment test. This is relevant to sketch drawing map task because the task provides a top down overview of the terrain. Therefore, when it came to taking the post-assessment using an overview image, the observer had less translation to do relative to what they witnessed during the test.

6   Future Research

The task of shaping terrain features was selected because it was a constrained space with clearly defined differences which enabled a foundation for a baseline assessment to be conducted. However, the continued focus of progressing this research to meet the needs of the operational soldier, it will be necessary to create future iterations of this research to be more representative of military sand table scenarios.

From a practical perspective, it is not going to be possible to have each solider shape their own terrain with a physical sand table. However, most soldiers do have access to mobile devices (e.g., smartphone). Since the literature already supports the value of active versus passive learning and research has demonstrated the value of mobile AR devices [16], the next logical step is to provide similar active learning experiences on a mobile device. It may be possible to run a similar experiment where instead of the participant manipulating sand, the participant shapes the terrain using pinching gestures onto a mobile device. This would provide clarity to the type of physical activity necessary to support cognitive process.

7 Conclusion

This research study established a foundation for understanding cognitive processes associated with constructing military terrain features and landmark identification. Data shows that physically shaping the terrain assisted with recognition but did not have an effect on conceptual knowledge or recollection of landmarks. Results indicate the need for further research to better understand how active learning can support recognition and memory. With the increased reliance of technology in military training, providing practical recommendations as to how to best implement tangible interaction to support knowledge acquisition is valuable for operational decision making and training. Through quantitative metrics and the evaluation of spatial representations and mod-elling, this research provides insight on the cognitive affordances of using AR for learning terrain topography, recognizing terrains, and recalling landmark locations. With the development of technologies such as ARES, determining how active learning can support cognitive processes can serve as a guide to identify appropriate technology for operational decision making and future classroom applications.

References

1. Abich, J., Eudy, M., Murphy, J., Garneau, C., Raby, Y., Amburn, C.: Use of the Augmented REality Sandtable (ARES) to enhance army CBRN training. In: Stephanidis, C. (ed.) HCI 2018. CCIS, vol. 851, pp. 223–230. Springer, Cham (2018). https://doi.org/10.1007/978-3-319-92279-9_30
2. Amburn, C., Vey, N., Boyce, M., Mize, J.: The Augmented REality Sandtable (ARES). Army Research Laboratory (2015)
3. Antle, A., Wang, S.: Comparing motor-cognitive strategies for spatial problem solving with tangible and multi-touch interfaces, pp. 65–72. ACM Press (2013)
4. Brewseter, F.W.: Using tactical decision exercises to study tactics. Mil. Rev. **82**, 3–9 (2002)
5. Bonwell, C.C., Eison, J.A.: Active learning: creating excitement in the classroom. School of Education and Human Development, George Washington University, Washington, DC (1991)
6. Boyce, M.W., et al.: The impact of surface projection on military tactics comprehension. Mil. Psychol. (American Psychological Association) **31**(1), 45–59 (2019)
7. Bouabid, A., Lepreux, S., Kolski, C.: Design and evaluation of distributed user interfaces between tangible tabletops. Universal Access in the Information Society (2017)

8. Boyce, M.W., et al.: Effect of topography on learning military tactics - integration of Generalized Intelligent Framework for Tutoring (GIFT) and Augmented REality Sandtable (ARES). Army Research Laboratory (2016)
9. Boyce, M.W., et al.: The impact of surface projection on military tactics comprehension. Mil. Psychol. **31**, 45–59 (2018)
10. Cherek, C., Brocker, A., Voelker, S., Borchers, J.: Tangible awareness: how tangibles on tabletops influence awareness of each other's actions. In: CHI Conference on Human Factors in Computing Systems (2018)
11. Clifton, P., Chang, J., Yeboah, G., Doucette, A., Chandrasekharan, S., Nitsche, M.: Design of embodied interfaces for engaging spatial cognition. Cognit. Res. Principles Implications **1**, 24 (2016)
12. Gardony, A.L., Taylor, H.A., Brunyé, T.T.: Gardony map drawing analyzer: software for quantitative analysis of sketch maps. Behav. Res. Meth. **48**, 1–27 (2015)
13. Hornecker, E., Buur, J.: Getting a grip on tangible interaction: a framework on physical space and social interaction. In: Proceedings of the CHI 2006, pp. 437–446 (2006)
14. Hornecker, E.: Beyond affordances: tangibles' hybrid nature. In: Proceedings of TEI 2012, pp. 175–182. ACM (2012)
15. Hornecker, E.: Understanding the benefits of graspable interfaces for cooperative use. In: Proceedings of Cooperative Systems Design, pp. 71–87 (2002)
16. James, K.H., Humphrey, G.K., Vilis, T., Corrie, B., Baddour, R., Goodale, M.A.: "Active" and "passive" learning of three-dimensional object structure within an immersive virtual reality environment. Behav. Res. Meth. Instrum. Comput. **34**, 383–390 (2002)
17. Kim, M.J., Maher, M.L.: The impact of tangible user interfaces on spatial cognition during collaborative design. Des. Stud. **29**, 222–253 (2008)
18. Klemmer, S.R., Hartmann, B., Takayama, L.: How bodies matter: five themes for interaction design. In: Proceedings of the DIS, pp. 140–149. ACM Press (2006)
19. Krathwohl, D.R.: A revision of Bloom's taxonomy: an overview. Theory Pract. **41**(4), 212–218 (2002)
20. Michel, N., Cater, J., Varela, O.: Active versus passive teaching styles: an empirical study of student learning outcomes. Hum. Resour. Dev. Q. **20**(4), 397–418 (2009)
21. Obrist, M., Seah, S., Subramanian, S.: Talking about tactile experiences, pp. 1659–1668 (2013)
22. Ozdemir, M., Sahin, C., Arcagok, S., Demir, M.K.: The effect of augmented reality applications in the learning process: a meta-analysis study. Eurasian J. Educ. Res. (EJER) **74**, 165–186 (2018)
23. Prinet, J.C., Mize, A.C., Sarter, N.: Triggering and detecting attentional narrowing in controlled environments. In: Proceedings of the Human Factors and Ergonomics Society Annual Meeting, vol. 60, no. 1, pp. 298–302. Sage, Los Angeles (2016)
24. Richardson, R., Sammons, D., Delparte, D.: Augmented affordances support learning: comparing the instructional effects of the augmented reality sandbox and conventional maps to teach topographic map skills. J. Interact. Learn. Res. **2**, 231 (2018)
25. Schneider, B., Blikstein, P.: Unraveling students' interaction around a tangible interface using multimodal learning analytics. J. Educ. Data Mining **7**, 3 (2015)
26. Schneider, B., Jermann, P., Zufferey, G., Dillenbourg, P.: Benefits of a tangible interface for collaborative learning and interaction. IEEE Trans. Learn. Technol. **4**(3), 222–232 (2011)
27. Skulmowski, A., Pradel, S., Kühnert, T., Brunnett, G., Rey, G.D.: Embodied learning using a tangible user interface: the effects of haptic perception and selective pointing on a spatial learning task. Comput. Educ. **92–93**, 64–75 (2016)
28. Vogel-Walcutt, J.J., Fiorella, L., Malone, N.: Review: instructional strategies framework for military training systems. Comput. Hum. Behav. **29**, 1490–1498 (2013)

29. Wickens, C. D.: Attentional tunneling and task management. In: Proceedings of the 13th International Symposium on Aviation Psychology, pp. 620–625 (2015)
30. Wildland Fire Lessons Learned Center. https://www.fireleadership.gov/toolbox/documents/TDGS_STEX_Workbook.pdf. Accessed 5 Feb 2019

Evaluation of Immersive Interfaces
for Tactical Decision Support

Mark Dennison[1]($\boxtimes$), Mark Mittrick[2], John Richardson[2],
Theron Trout[2], Adrienne Raglin[2], Eric Heilman[2],
and Timothy Hanratty[2]

[1] U.S. Army Research Laboratory West, Playa Vista, CA 90094, USA
mark.s.dennison.civ@mail.mil
[2] U.S. Army Research Laboratory, Adelphi, MD 20783, USA
{mark.r.mittrick.civ, john.t.richardson7.civ,
theron.t.trout.ctr, adrienne.raglin2.civ,
timothy.p.hanratty.civ}@mail.mil

Abstract. The benefits and limitations of immersive technologies in military decision-making are not well understood. Here, we describe the framework of an experiment which seeks to empirically determine the effects of immersive and non-immersive technology on decision-making. In this experiment, users are shown tactical spatial information about a building layout and told they must decide which of three pre-determined breach points is optimal for maximizing mission success and minimizing risk to the ground team. To ensure observable effects are related to immersion and not simply perception of depth, we deploy a between-subjects design with three viewing conditions: data shown in 2D on a desktop display, data shown in 3D on desktop display, and data shown in 3D in a head-mounted display (HMD). Dependent variables include decision accuracy, time to task completion, decision confidence, and score on the System Usability Scale. In the VR version of the experiment, full telemetry is captured to track when and for how long users interacted with specific information in the scenario environment. Pilot results suggest that tracking these metrics will allow for intricate comparison of decision-making behaviors between display types.

Keywords: Virtual reality · Mixed reality · Decision-making · User experience

1 Introduction

Future combat environments will require military analysts to utilize a common operating environment that integrates information from a complex network of interacting intelligent systems (human, robotic, and networked sensors) to support the decision-making of commanders. The integration of information originating from heterogeneous sensors and intelligence sources often requires the use of discrete systems, such as multiple computers, laptops, tablets, or even physical objects on a map. Such setups typically require significant physical and cyber resources to bring information into a unified space where collaborative decision-making can occur more effectively. Immobile command and control structures are especially at significant risk from hostile attacks.

© Springer Nature Switzerland AG 2019
J. Y. C. Chen and G. Fragomeni (Eds.): HCII 2019, LNCS 11574, pp. 428–440, 2019.
https://doi.org/10.1007/978-3-030-21607-8_33

Evaluation of Immersive Interfaces for Tactical Decision Support   429

Discovering new ways of accessing, consuming, and interacting with information from the battlefield is necessary to expedite military operational effectiveness. Mixed reality (MR) is one technology that may enable this. Two promising applications of MR may be data ingestion, visualization and collaborative analysis at standoff from the tactical edge and the ability for users to modify their perception of reality depending on their personal preferences, areas of expertise, or other mission requirements. Despite this, there is currently a limited understanding of how, when, and where using mixed reality provides explicit benefit over more traditional display systems. For example, does viewing spatial information in an immersive HMD result in faster or more accurate decisions? More so, the existing literature is dominated by studies that only compare non-immersive and immersive systems at a surface level, where reported metrics are often qualitative.

In this paper, we discuss the design of a decision-making experiment which seeks to measure how users interact with tactical information when it is displayed in 2D, 3D, and in an immersive virtual environment. We describe the technical aspects of AURORA-VR, a research system developed at ARL which enables precise tracking and analysis of military tasks across mixed reality. Finally, results from pilot data from the development team are discussed.

Existing literature outside of the military domain has shown that virtual and augmented reality may provide benefit to decision-making and understanding in certain scenarios. For example, Moran [1] showed enhanced situational awareness, cognition, data pattern detection, and that visual analytics were more efficient in an immersive system compared to a traditional 2D system. McIntire and colleagues [3, 4] showed that for most subjects, using a stereoscopic display increased performance by roughly sixty percent. However, this survey covered a broad range of tasks and devices, which makes true comparison difficult. A study by Dan and Reiner [4] measured differences in performance on simple tasks, such as a paper folding, after training occurred in 2D as viewed on a desktop monitor versus in 3D when viewed in augmented reality. The authors reported that subjects in the augmented training condition demonstrated significantly less cognitive load when learning the folds, as measured by power spectral changes in electroencephalographic (EEG) recordings. This indicated that information transfer was significantly easier when the data was viewed in an augmented environment. This decreased cognitive load may be related to the suggestion that humans are "biologically optimized" to perceive and learn in 3D [5].

Research by Donalek et al. [5] reported that in a waypoint drawing task, subjects who viewed the environment in an Oculus Rift HMD performed with less distance and angle errors than those who viewed the environment on a 2D desktop monitor. Moran et al. [1] created an immersive virtual environment where Twitter data was overlaid atop real geography to improve the experience for analysts. The authors claimed that this augmented environment enhanced situational awareness, cognition, and that pattern and visual analytics were more efficient than on traditional 2D displays. However, metrics enabling precise comparison across display types are reported with limited detail.

1.1   Immersive Environments and Decision-Making

Decision-making tasks, such as battlefield intelligence analysis or optimal route planning for tactical operations, are two areas where virtual or augmented reality may enable Warfighters to better perform their roles. For example, individuals who manipulated visualized social media data in a fully-immersive and motion-tracked virtual environment reported that they learned more about the data than when it was viewed in a traditional setting [6]. Often, though, subjective metrics may not be externally valid. It has also been shown that overlaying virtual information may dramatically improve performance and task engagement [7, 8]. MR can also be used to overlay the virtual hands from an expert user to a novice, guiding them through a complex scenario remotely [9]. In a military context, an analyst in VR at a forward operating base could assist a solider at the tactical edge by highlighting known enemy positions and display that information on a tablet or through an augmented reality HUD integrated with their helmet.

Prior work has shown that augmenting data displays may provide some benefit to understanding and decision-making. In a recent study by [10], the authors compared the effectiveness of immersive AR (HoloLens) and tablet VR to traditional desktop use by measuring completion time and error in a point cloud estimation tasks. The immersive AR environment was reported as best for tasks involving spatial perception and interactions with a high degree of freedom, but subjects were generally faster on the desktop where interactivity was already familiar to them. As suggested by Bellgardt et al. [11], it is critical that mixed reality systems are designed in such a way that integration with existing workflows is seamless.

Finally, from a military perspective, the time and resource cost associated with travel across the battlefield, construction and deployment of command and analyst tents, and upkeep to meet constantly changing mission demands make fluid collaboration across the battlefield challenging. Virtualizing some elements of mission command and intelligence operations may help to reduce this difficulty. For example, Fairchild and colleagues built a VR telepresence system which allowed scientists in Germany and the U.K. to collaborate remotely and in real-time on data from a Mars mission [12]. The VR system tracked gaze, facial expressions, and user positions to maximize the scientists' nonverbal communication over the wire. GraphiteVR, a project by Gardner and Sheaffer [13], allows multiple remote users to visualize high-dimensionality social media data and manipulate it in a shared virtual space.

2   Experiment Design

2.1   Study Objectives

The goal of this work is to determine how different display technologies and data visualization techniques affect decision-making in a tactical scenario. Although prior research [2, 3] has demonstrated some evidence that visualization of spatial information is easier when viewed through a stereoscopic-display, there is limited work showing such enhancement in tactical decision-making scenarios. For this study, the scenario will involve the perception and analysis of both spatial and non-spatial information from a fictional military operation to breach a hostile building and secure a specific item. Information pertinent to execution of this operation will be presented either in 2D slices on a desktop monitor, as a full 3D model on a desktop monitor, or as a 3D model presented in virtual reality. These conditions will enable us to empirically determine how differences in display type and data visualization method affect the speed and confidence of decision-making, and the usability and comfort of the display medium.

The inclusion of the 3D model condition is essential because it allows us to determine if any changes in behavioral performance in the VR condition are truly because of immersive qualities produced by stereoscopy, and not simply because of the presence of depth information in the scene.

2.2 Questionnaire

The System Usability Scale (SUS) [14] a reliable, low-cost usability scale that can be used for global assessments of systems usability. It is a is a simple, ten-item scale giving a global view of subjective assessments of usability. The SUS is generally used after the respondent has had an opportunity to use the system being evaluated, but before any debriefing or discussion takes place. Respondents should be asked to record their immediate response to each item, rather than thinking about items for a long time.

2.3 Task and Stimuli

This experiment uses a between-subjects design, with three separate interfaces as the independent variable. In Condition 1 (2D Desktop), users will view task information as 2D images on a desktop monitor. In Condition 2 (3D Desktop), users will view task information as a 3D model rendered on a desktop monitor. In Condition 3, users will view task information as a 3D model displayed in virtual environment inside an Oculus Rift HMD. Screenshots of the task environment are shown in Fig. 1.

The task information displayed across all three conditions is spatial data from a fictional two-story building with various rooms, entrances, and objects. On the inside of the building, one room contains a bomb which the forward operators must safely navigate to for extraction. A visual legend is shown in the display in each condition which indicates whether or not a particular entrance of the building is either open (green marking), breachable by the forward operating team (yellow marking), or not breachable by the forward operating team (red marking). Across the outside of the building, three possible initial entry points are highlighted and given a text label. The user's task is to explore all of the information about the building and choose which initial breach point will maximize successful navigation to the target room, while minimizing risk to the forward operating team.

Users are given as much time as they would like to consider all options and explore the provided information. When ready, they must select which of the three initial breach points they think is most optimal be selecting its label on the experiment interface. Once selected, they will be prompted to select how confident they are in that decision, using a -2 to $+2$ Likert scale. Finally, they are told whether or not their selection was indeed the most optimal choice.

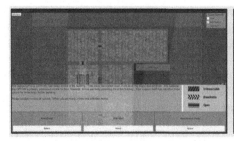

Fig. 1. Example scenes showing the scenario building from the 2D Desktop (left) and 3D Desktop/VR (right) experimental conditions. (Color figure online)

2.4 AURORA-VR

The virtual environment in all three experimental conditions is displayed through AURORA-VR, a research and development sandbox created by the Army Research Laboratory and Stormfish Scientific as the VR component of the AURORA (Accelerated User Reasoning: Operations, Research, and Analysis) project in the Battlefield Information Processing Branch. Real-time user interaction, position, and decision data are captured through the system and sent to Elasticsearch for online visualization in Kibana or offline analysis in MATLAB.

2.5 Data Analysis

Our hypotheses are motivated by prior research that has suggested it may be easier for humans to understand spatial information when observing a display that includes depth information (e.g. three dimensions or stereoscopy). Critically, we also expect that interacting with this spatial information through an immersive HMD will provide users with a better understanding of the layout and properties of the building. Therefore, we anticipate that actual and perceived task performance will be worse in the 2D Desktop condition, better in the 3D Desktop condition, and best in the VR condition.

To test this hypothesis, we will compare metrics recorded across experimental conditions. These data include the time spent on each of three introduction screens, the time spent exploring the virtual environment until a decision is made, the time spent deciding the level of decision confidence, the number of times the user switched which floor to display in the building, and how long the user spent observing each floor. Condition-specific metrics will also be analyzed to observe differences between subjects within that condition. In the 2D Desktop condition, metrics include the total variability of camera zooming and panning and the variability of these actions with respect to which floor was displayed. In the 3D Desktop condition, metrics include the total variability and magnitude of camera zooming and rotational panning (yaw, pitch) and the variability and magnitudes of these actions with respect to which floor was displayed. For the VR condition, position information about how the user moved around the virtual environment (forward-backward, right-left, up-down) will be analyzed over the duration of the experiment and with respect to which floor was viewed.

3   Pilot Results

Nine members of the research and development team pilot tested the environment. Data were acquired through custom software connecting Unity to Elasticsearch and offline analyses were carried out in MATLAB v2017b. Time dependent information were sampled at a rate of 5 Hz. Because a limited number of pilot data were acquired for the purpose of feasibility testing, statistical comparisons are not reported. All error bars represent one standard error (se) of the mean.

3.1   Questionnaires Data

The System Usability Scale is a ten-item scale giving a global view of subjective assessments of usability. Scores range from 0 to 100. For the 2D Display condition, the average score was 41.7 (se = 4.41). For the 3D Display condition, the average score was 48.3 (se = 0.83). For the VR Display condition, the average score was 48.8 (se = 1.25).

3.2   Behavioral Data

Across Condition Metrics
We first analyzed data to report metrics that were common to all three experimental conditions (2D, 3D, VR). Figure 2 shows that in the 2D and 3D conditions, one user chose the Side Entry point, and two users chose the Roof Entry point. For the VR condition, one user chose the Floor Entry point and another chose the Roof Entry point. As the optimal selection was the Roof Entry, performance was best for 2D and 3D displays.

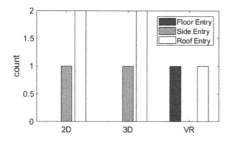 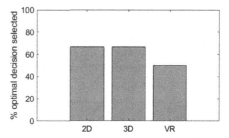

Fig. 2. Breach decision selection count (left) and percent optimal selection (right), with respect to display type.

The average time users spent reading over the introduction screens is shown in Fig. 3. Generally, the data trend to show that less time was spent on subsequent screens for all display types.

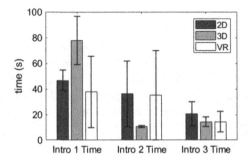

Fig. 3. Average time in seconds spent observing each intro screen, with respect to display type.

The average time users spent interacting with the breach environment information is shown below in Fig. 4 for each display type. The data trend to show that users spent more time examining information in the 3D than 2D condition, and the most time in the VR condition.

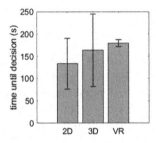

Fig. 4. Average time interacting with the VE until a decision was made, with respect to display type.

The left subplot of Fig. 5 shows that, on average, users trended to spend more time deciding how confident they were in their decision after viewing the breach environment in VR. Generally, the data trend to show that less time was spent on subsequent screens for all display types. The right sub-plot shows that generally users reported the same level of confidence across display types, with the highest variability in the 3D condition.

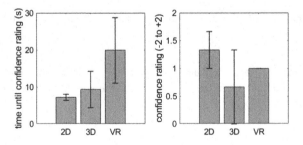

Fig. 5. Average time (left) and rating (right) for confidence input, with respect to display type.

On average, users trended to spend the most time looking at information on the first (ground) floor of the building, where the objective room was located (see Fig. 6). Generally, the data trend to show that less time was spent on subsequent screens for all display types. The right sub-plot of Fig. 6 shows that generally users reported the same level of confidence across display types, with the highest variability in the 3D condition.

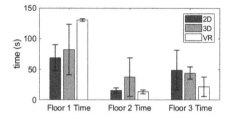
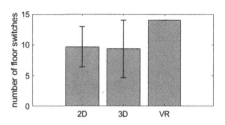

Fig. 6. Average time observing each floor (left) and total number of floor switches (right), with respect to display type.

2D Specific Metrics

In the 2D display condition, users zoomed in and out of the environment only when the 3rd Floor was being viewed (see Fig. 7). More left-right and up-down panning activity was observed when the 1st and 2nd floors were being viewed, as shown in the Fig. 7 center and right subplots.

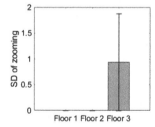
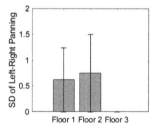
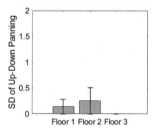

Fig. 7. Average variability in zooming activity (left), left-right camera panning (center), and up-down (right) camera panning activity, with respect to highest visible floor.

3D Specific Metrics

Users on average zoomed in and out of the 3D environment only while viewing the 1st and 2nd Floors of the building (see Fig. 8A). The data trend to show that users rotated the camera along the yaw direction more while viewing the 3rd Floor, as shown in Fig. 8B and D, whereas users pitched the camera up and down similarly while viewing all floors, as shown in Fig. 8C and E.

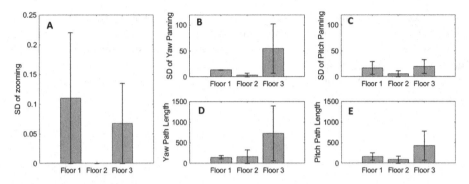

Fig. 8. Variability of zooming activity (A), panning in the yaw direction (B), and panning in the pitch direction (C), total path length in the yaw direction (D) and pitch direction (E).

VR Specific Metrics

Data from the VR display condition where analyzed with respect to mo variability in the cardinal directions. Figure 9A and D show that head movement in the left-right direction was greatest when users viewed the 1st Floor of the building. Figure 9B and E shows that users trended to have greater forward-back head movement variability and much greater distance traveled when viewing the 1st Floor. Figure 9C shows that the head movement variability in the up-down direction was similar when viewing all floors, but Fig. 9F shows a trend that users moved their head up and down more when viewing the 1st Floor of the building.

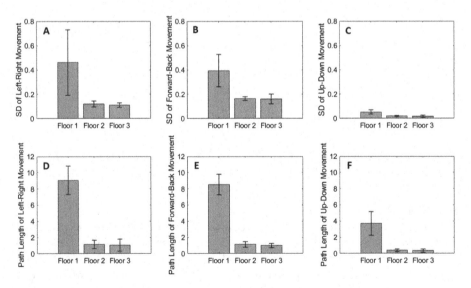

Fig. 9. Variability of head left-right movement (A), forward-backward movement (B), up-down movement (C), total path length of movement in the left-right (D), forward-backward (E), and up-down (F) directions.

4   Conclusions and Future Work

In this paper, we presented the design and pilot results of a study to examine qualitative and quantitative differences associated with viewing spatial tactical information rendered as 2D information on a flat-screen display, as 3D information rendered on a flat-screen display, and as 3D information rendered in an immersive virtual environment viewed through an Oculus Rift HMD. As a shift away from other work in the field that has primarily focused on high-level and broad comparisons between display types and tasks, our goal was to focus on extracting interaction and behavioral metrics that were common across all three experimental conditions and those that were unique to each. Critically, this allows for a much finer grain comparison of how users chose to interact and thus perceive information from the environment.

The inclusion of the 3D Display condition, namely where tactical information was rendered as a 3D model on a flat-screen display, is necessary to tease apart behavioral effects related to depth information from those potentially arising from the user being immersed in the virtual environment. This is important because although viewing the task environment in an HMD may be more enjoyable or captivating to the user, as has been previously reported in the literature (citation), VR may not provide any tangible benefit over simply viewing the same depth information on a traditional desktop display.

Individual differences in prior exposure to virtual reality technology and performance on spatial information are important to consider when doing any comparison between non-immersive and immersive systems. For this pilot study, all users had prior exposure to VR and thus may not represent the average population. The full version of this study will include the Visualization of Viewpoints and Spatial Orientation [15] pen-and-paper surveys to assess differences in 3D orientation skills of users before they interact with the VE. It is critical to ensure enough data are collected such that performance on these tests is not significantly different across condition groups.

We first analyzed the behavioral data with respect to metrics common across conditions. Users spent about the same time viewing the introduction screens for each display condition, with less time spent on subsequent screens (see Fig. 3). Figure 2 shows that generally most users chose the correct answer, which was entering the building from the roof. This answer was optimal as the floor entry was in line of sight of the enemy, and the side entry ended in a door that was not breachable by friendly forces, as denoted by symbology present in user interface for all display conditions. Users in each condition also took about the same amount of time to come to a decision about which breach point they thought was optimal, although the data trend to suggest users may have spent more time interacting with the environment when it was viewed in VR. Additionally, users showed the same trend when deliberating on the confidence rating associated with that choice (see Fig. 5), with data trending to show more time taken in the VR condition. The magnitude of confidence ratings ranged from neutral, to very confident, with the greatest variation from users in the 3D display condition. Lastly, the System Usability Scale results demonstrated that on average, users felt about the same for each of the display conditions, with perhaps slightly less favorable scores for the 2D Display condition. Users likely had to perform more actions to view the same information, this could have led to feelings of frustration which might be the reason for the lower score.

The tactical information in this experiment's design was presented across three different floors, so interaction behavior was analyzed with respect to which floor the user was currently viewing. Figure 6 shows that across display conditions, most users spent most of their time observing the bottom floor of the building. This may have been because two of the breaching options were on this floor. The data also show that typically, users switched between floors about ten or so times during a run.

The 2D Display condition allowed the user to navigate the presented environment by clicking and dragging the camera left and right or up and down. It also allowed the user to zoom in and out of the building from a top-down perspective. Users in this condition showed the greatest zooming activity when floor three was presented (see Fig. 7). This is likely because floor three was visible at the start of the run, and users zoomed in and out to a view they preferred and then kept the camera at this distance for the rest of the run. Panning left and right appears to have occurred more than panning up and down, however more data are needed in a full study to confirm this statistically.

In the 3D Display condition, users could navigate the environment by zooming in and out of the 3D building model, or rotating the camera along the yaw and pitch axes. Here, we saw the most zooming activity when floors one and three were visible (see Fig. 8). Additionally, users may have moved the camera along the yaw axis more than they pitched the camera up and down. This makes sense as the camera was positioned at approximately 45° from the ground which may have already been an acceptable position for most users to view the 3D model.

For the VR Display condition, we tracked how users moved their head in 3D space around the virtual environment. Figure 9 shows that users primarily showed the most movement along the left-right and forward-backward directions. Minimal movement was shown in the up-down direction, which was likely caused by head bob from walking, or perhaps some tilting to look down into the building model. This matched our expectations as to completely view the environment, a user would have to walk around the horizontal plane.

Our results suggest the current experimental design may be useful for evaluating immersive and non-immersive interfaces for tactical decision-making. For the full experimental study, it is clear that a large number of users is necessary in each display condition to ensure that individual differences in VR experience, aptitude in spatial data navigation, and underlying bias are accounted for. We also plan to record four minutes of resting EEG collection, with two minutes of eyes-open and eyes-closed respectively. These EEG signals will be examined for time-frequency changes in power at individual and coherence across groups of electrodes. Prior research examining resting cortical activity has been predicative of differences in cognitive performance [16], visuo-motor learning [17], and related inversely to the default-mode network [18].

Finally, the current design allows for only one decision selection to be made at the end of the interaction. The full iteration of this study may benefit from users making multiple decisions in larger-scale tactical operation across multiple buildings. For example, the user could make a breach choice, receiving feedback in real time, and then continue making decisions until the final objective is reached. Here, their "score" could be tracked based on optimality of decision selection, and then tallied at the end of the session. This may allow for a richer outcome measure with which to correlate the quantitative and qualitative metrics described in this paper.

References

1. Moran, A., Gadepally, V., Hubbell, M., Kepner, J.: Improving big data visual analytics with interactive virtual reality. In: 2015 IEEE High Performance Extreme Computing Conference (HPEC), pp. 1–6 (2015)
2. McIntire, J.P., Havig, P.R., Geiselman, E.E.: What is 3D good for? A review of human performance on stereoscopic 3D displays, p. 83830X (2012)
3. McIntire, J.P., Liggett, K.K.: The (possible) utility of stereoscopic 3D displays for information visualization: the good, the bad, and the ugly. In: 2014 IEEE VIS International Workshop on 3DVis (2014)
4. Dan, A., Reiner, M.: EEG-based cognitive load of processing events in 3D virtual worlds is lower than processing events in 2D displays. Int. J. Psychophysiol. **122**, 75–84 (2016)
5. Donalek, C., et al.: Immersive and collaborative data visualization using virtual reality platforms. In: IEEE International Conference on Big Data, pp. 609–614, October 2014
6. Royston, S., DeFanti, C., Perlin, K.: A collaborative untethered virtual reality environment for interactive social network visualization, April 2016
7. Frank, J.A., Kapila, V.: Mixed-reality learning environments: integrating mobile interfaces with laboratory test-beds. Comput. Educ. **110**, 88–104 (2017)
8. Dascalu, M.-I., Shudayfat, E.A.: Mixed reality to support new learning paradigms. In: 2014 18th International Conference on System Theory, Control and Computing, pp. 692–697, October 2014
9. Huang, W., Alem, L., Tecchia, F., Duh, H.B.L.: Augmented 3D hands: a gesture-based mixed reality system for distributed collaboration. J. Multimodal User Interfaces **12**, 77–89 (2017)
10. Bach, B., Sicat, R., Beyer, J., Cordeil, M., Pfister, H.: The hologram in my hand: how effective is interactive exploration of 3D visualizations in immersive tangible augmented reality? IEEE Trans. Vis. Comput. Graph. **24**(1), 457–467 (2017)
11. Bellgardt, M., Pick, S., Zielasko, D., Vierjahn, T., Weyers, B., Kuhlen, T.W.: Utilizing immersive virtual reality in everyday work. In: 2017 IEEE 3rd Workshop on Everyday Virtual Reality, pp. 1–4 (2017)
12. Fairchild, A.J., Campion, S.P., Garcia, A.S., Wolff, R., Fernando, T., Roberts, D.J.: A mixed reality telepresence system for collaborative space operation. IEEE Trans. Circuits Syst. Video Technol. **27**(4), 814–827 (2017)
13. Gardner, M.R., Sheaffer, W.W.: Systems to support co-creative collaboration in mixed-reality environments. In: Liu, D., Dede, C., Huang, R., Richards, J. (eds.) Virtual, Augmented, and Mixed Realities in Education. SCI, pp. 157–178. Springer, Singapore (2017). https://doi.org/10.1007/978-981-10-5490-7_9
14. Brooke, J.: SUS-a quick and dirty usability scale. Usability Eval. Ind. **189**, 4–7 (1996)
15. Kyritsis, M., Gulliver, S.R.: Gilford Zimmerman orientation survey: a validation. In: Proceedings of the 7th International Conference on Information, Communications and Signal Processing, ICICS 2009 (2009)
16. Manuel, A.L., Guggisberg, A.G., Thézé, R., Turri, F., Schnider, A.: Resting-state connectivity predicts visuo-motor skill learning. Neuroimage **176**, 446–453 (2018)

17. Wu, J., Srinivasan, R., Kaur, A., Cramer, S.C.: Resting-state cortical connectivity predicts motor skill acquisition. Neuroimage **91**, 84–90 (2014)
18. Scheeringa, R., Bastiaansen, M.C.M., Petersson, K.M., Oostenveld, R., Norris, D.G., Hagoort, P.: Frontal theta EEG activity correlates negatively with the default mode network in resting state. Int. J. Psychophysiol. **67**(3), 242–251 (2008)

Virtual Nature: A Psychologically Beneficial Experience

Laura M. Herman[1,2(✉)] and Jamie Sherman[3]

[1] Department of Psychology, Princeton University, Princeton, USA
lmherman@princeton.edu
[2] Adobe, San Jose, USA
[3] Intel Corporation, Santa Clara, USA

Abstract. This study sought to determine which, if any, of the benefits conferred by experiences in nature are conferred by an equivalent Virtual Reality (VR) experience. To this end, previous VR users were immersed in a virtual forest environment. Post-immersion, participants were measured on a variety of metrics including stress level, relaxation level, and directed attention abilities – metrics that have been shown to be significantly modulated by exposure to physical nature. Our results indicate that experiences in virtual nature afford much the same psychological benefits of exposure to physical nature, but they did not show the same kinds of attentional benefits. Experiencing nature in VR significantly decreased self-reported anxiety levels.

Keywords: Virtual Reality · Nature · Directed attention · Stress reduction · Immersive environments · Attentional fatigue

1 Introduction

Virtual Reality (VR), as implied in the name, immerses users in digitally created or captured environments. Enthusiastically embraced by the world of gaming, entertainment, and marketing, the relationship between "really real" and "virtually real" experiences is not yet fully understood. In addition, ethnographic research has found that non-gamer consumers were interested in VR, but they struggle to see the benefits of this technology (Sherman 2016). Aside from being "cool," what can VR really accomplish?

Experimentation and literature exploring the relationship between virtual and physical reality offerings is growing, and largely divides into three bodies of work. One body of work explores psycho-social aspects of VR and addresses how VR and similar technologies can be used to change users' social attitudes by placing them in new kinds of virtual social roles, physical bodies, or exposing them to immersive documentary material (Maister et al. 2013; Maister et al. 2015; Peck et al. 2013; Tettegah et al. 2006). A second body of work explores the cognitive relationship between virtual and physical realities with a primary focus on spatial cognition (Bohil et al. 2011). Finally, an emerging third body of work documents psycho-therapeutic benefits enabled by VR. Experiments have looked at the uses of VR for treating mental health, phantom limbs, chronic pain, Alzheimers, and even remapping for neuromuscular pathways of paralyzed patients (Lugrin et al. 2016; Serino et al. 2017; Tsirlin et al. 2009). This study contributes

© Springer Nature Switzerland AG 2019
J. Y. C. Chen and G. Fragomeni (Eds.): HCII 2019, LNCS 11574, pp. 441–449, 2019.
https://doi.org/10.1007/978-3-030-21607-8_34

to the latter two bodies of work by exploring the extent to which exposure to nature in VR mirrors the well-documented effects of being in nature in the physical world.

A plethora of studies document the beneficial effects of human exposure to nature. Many of these studies have focused on the psychological benefits, including increased relaxation and diminished stress and anxiety levels (Ulrich et al. 1991; Brown et al. 2013; Keniger et al. 2013; Tennessen and Cimprich 1995). Nature has been shown to significantly decrease stress according to many measures: whether qualitative or quantitative, biometric or participantive (Keniger et al. 2013). In a thorough review of the nature literature, Keniger et al. also noted that many studies demonstrated increased academic performance, increased ability to perform mentally challenging tasks, decreased mental fatigue, and increased attentional resources (Herzog et al. 1997; Keniger et al. 2013; Taylor et al. 2002; Berman et al. 2012; Cimprich et al. 1992).

Such research has led to the "Attentional Restoration Theory" (ART). The basis of this theory is that nature relieves one's focusing overload, thus restoring directed attention, which is used to perform highly-focused and detail-oriented tasks, such as proof-reading (Herzog et al. 1997; Atchley et al. 2012). Certain experiences replenish one's ability to perform these highly-attentive tasks. The underlying cause of such restoration is involuntary fascination, by which an individual's attention is naturally– rather than consciously– directed. Furthermore, environments that offer "soft" involuntary fascination, where one's focus may wander (i.e. on a nature walk) are even more restorative than situations that evoke "hard" involuntary fascination, where one's focus is more specific (i.e. a racecar race). Neuroscientists suggest that soft involuntary fascination relieves the pre-frontal cortex, which is responsible for directing an individual's attention (Herzog et al. 1997).

Indeed, Hartig et al. demonstrated that nature is particularly evocative of soft involuntary fascination, and also especially effective at attentional restoration. Participants were assigned to either urban, nature, or relaxing indoor environments. Participants' self-reported levels of fascination with their surroundings were highest for the nature condition participants. The nature condition participants also scored the highest on a directed attention task (in this case, a proof-reading task), as ART would predict (Hartig et al. 1991).

Additionally, Tennessen and Cimprich showed that students who were simply placed in dorms with a nature view likewise scored higher on directed attention tasks than their non-nature-facing peers (Tennessen and Cimprich 1995). One of these tasks was the Necker Cube Pattern Control Task– or NCPCT– which sought to deduce student's level of top-down control of bistable perception. In other words, students attempted to "hold" the amount of times that a bistable illusion flipped in their view.

Similarly, Atchley et al. demonstrated that four days of full nature immersion yields a full 50% increase in performance on creativity and problem-solving tasks, which utilize directed attention (2012). The question remained open: was this outcome spurred by the increase in exposure to nature or the decrease in exposure to technology? ART would predict that a technology-absent, nature-present environment would improve attention relative to a technology-absent, nature-absent environment. What about a technology-present, nature-present environment? The present study directly addresses this case by incorporating nature within a technological experience.

2   Methods

In previous literature on the effects of nature, participants were (a) exposed to a stressful experience, surveyed about their mood, immersed in nature, and then asked about their mood again or (b) immersed in nature and then given directed attention tests, the results of which were compared to participants who were not immersed in nature. This study replicated such methodologies.

We controlled for experience with VR; all participants were first-time users of VR. Additionally, we controlled for gender: half of our participants were female, while the other half were male. Similarly, all participants were in the same age range: between 18–25 years old. Lastly, we controlled for general technological experience and daily exposure to screens: all participants were generally familiar with technology, and self-reported high levels of comfortability using devices such as smartphones and computers. All participants held day jobs that consisted of 5+ h of screen time; in this way, we sought to control for daily levels of screen exposure across participants.

First, participants were subjected to a "stressful experience" intended to mimic equivalent experiences utilized in previous studies that examined the effect of nature on the psyche. In many of these psychological experiences, "It Didn't Have to Happen," a workshop safety video, was used to induce stress. We used a modern version that depicts driver safety, which we believed to be more relevant to our participants.

After this stressor, an 8-question survey was administered. Utilizing a Leickert scale, participants were asked to indicate how stressed, happy, busy, relaxed, tired, and anxious they felt, among other questions. We clarified that the participants should answer the questions on the basis of "how they are feeling today," rather than basing their answers on how the video clip made them feel. It is important to note that we were primarily interested in participants' relaxation and anxiety levels, and the other self-report measures (e.g. happiness, business, tiredness, etc.) acted as distractor measures.

Next, participants in the experimental condition were fitted with an HTC Vive headset. Using SteamVR, NatureTreks VR was launched. In NatureTreks VR, participants are able to explore a natural VR environment via armswinger locomotion; thus, they progress through the natural experience in a simulation that feels as if one is walking. We limited the participants' options to five specific environments, all of which resembled forest-like landscapes so as to ensure the level of foliage and greenery touted in previous nature studies. Amongst these five options, we allowed participants to choose the experience that most interested them. The primary difference between the experiences was time of day: some experiences occurred at dawn, others during the daytime, and others at sunset.

During this phase, control participants read simple, short biographies on a computer screen indoors. The reading task and VR task were planned so as to occupy the same length of time and the same physical location. In both situations, the participants were looking at a screen, albeit at different distances.

After the experimental or control experience, participants were administered the same set of qualitative questions about their mood and stress levels. Again, the participants were instructed to indicate how they were feeling "today," such that the answers would be expected to be identical, unless a large shift had occurred. The participants responded to each question using a Leickert scale, and the questions were re-ordered to reduce memory effects.

Finally, participants were given a battery of directed attention tests. First, participants completed the Necker Cube Pattern Control Task (NCPCT). Participants received a blank sheet with a line drawing of a three-dimensional cube. They were told that their perspective of the cube would shift, with the front and back faces of the cube reversing their relative positions. Once they familiarized themselves with this property of the Necker cube, they were instructed to look at the cube and tap audibly on a hard surface when the pattern reversed. We counted the number of reversals that occurred during two consecutive 30-s "hold" periods during which the participant was to focus on one pattern for as long as possible. Reversals that occur despite the effort to hold a pattern are thought to be due to attentional fatigue (Kaplan 1995). We used the average number of reversals across the two hold periods as a dependent variable in our analyses (cf. Tennessen and Cimprich 1995). The NCPCT has been shown in previous studies to be a sensitive measure of restored attention due to natural environments (Cimprich 1993; Tennessen and Cimprich 1995).

Next, participants engaged in a Backward Digit Span task. The participants were given series of numbers, asked to hold them in their memory, and then instructed to repeat the numbers aloud in reverse order. The series of numbers increased in length and difficulty as the task continued. We recorded the maximum digit span that participants were able to correctly repeat, as well as their accuracy level across numerical series of all lengths. This task involves active attention to retain the numbers in working memory and directed modification of memory in order to reverse the order of the numbers upon recall. Therefore, it fits well within a battery of highly-focused directed attention tasks.

Finally, participants were given a Remote Association Test, as created by Bowden & Beeden. Participants were given a multitude of triplets of words and asked to find the linking word amongst as many triplets as possible. This linking word, for example, would be "cheese" for "cottage, swiss, cake;" it is the one word that can be cohesively added to the beginning or end of each word in the triplet. We recorded the number of triplets that each participant was able to accurately complete in a two-minute timespan. Across participants, the triplet prompts and task length were kept constant.

3 Results

3.1 Psychological Effects

Data analyses indicate a significant decrease in anxiety ratings for experimental participants– those who had been immersed in virtual nature– compared to control participants, who completed a reading task. We performed a one-way ANOVA between experimental and control groups' change in anxiety pre-to-post task (Δ anxiety). The results demonstrated a significant effect of the VR experience as compared with the control experience: $F(1, 8) = 7.0$, $p = 0.0294$ (Fig. 1).

Change in Anxiety Levels

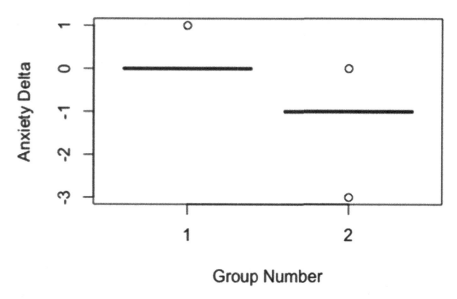

Fig. 1. This graph shows the anxiety level delta for both groups. Group 1 is the control group, who completed a reading task. Group 2 is the experimental group, who participated in a Virtual Reality nature experience. The anxiety level delta (on the y-axis) represents the difference between participants self-reported anxiety levels before and after their experience: either reading or being in VR. As demonstrated, participants who experienced virtual nature experienced a significant decrease in anxiety.

Surprisingly, the data did not show a significant change in relaxation levels between experimental and control participants. A one-way ANOVA between experimental and control groups' change in relaxation levels demonstrated an insignificant effect of the VR experience as compared with the control experience: $F(1, 8) = 0.615$, $p = 0.455$ (Fig. 2).

Participants' self-response ratings of their happiness, business, and tiredness showed no effect of the experience. As expected, these distractor measures were unchanged, in contrast to the change in anxiety for experimental participants.

Change in Relaxation Levels

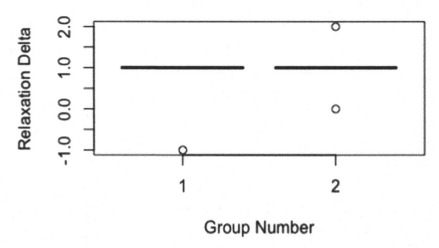

Fig. 2. This graph shows participants' changes in relaxation before and after the experiment. Group 1 represents the control group, whose experience included reading biographies on a screen; Group 2 represents the experimental group, who participated in a Virtual Reality nature experience. The relaxation delta (on the y-axis) indicates the participants' change in relaxation levels before and after their experience. As demonstrated, participants in both groups experienced an increase in relaxation, without a significant difference between groups.

3.2 Directed Attention Effects

Additionally, there were negligible differences in success between experimental and control participants on all three directed attention tasks. In fact, for one task, control participants outperformed experimental participants, albeit by an insignificant margin.

For the Necker Cube Pattern Control Task (NCPCT), a one-way ANOVA between the experimental and control groups' respective "number of flips" during a 30-s top-down "hold" period revealed an insignificant effect of group: $F(1,8) = 0.435, p = 0.528$.

Within the digit span task, there were not significant results for either the digit span achieved or for the digit accuracy achieved. A one-way ANOVA between the experimental and control groups' respective "digits missed" during the digit span task revealed an insignificant effect: $F(1,8) = 0.021$, $p = 0.89$. Similarly, a one-way ANOVA between the experimental and control groups' respective "maximum digit span" revealed a whoppingly insignificant effect: $F(1,8) = 0$, $p = 0.1$. As shown in the plot below, the two groups performed nearly identically on this task (Fig. 3).

Lastly, a one-way ANOVA between experimental and control groups' performance on the Remote Association Test, measured by the number of triplets correctly completed, showed an insignificant effect of group: $F(1,8) = 0.036, p = 0.854$. According to this data, it is clear that none of the directed attention tasks showed an effect of group.

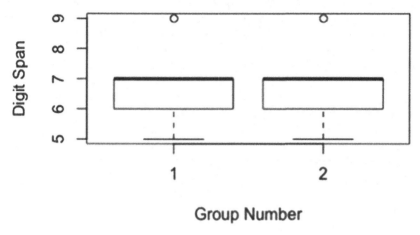

Fig. 3. This graph represents the maximum number of numerical digits that participants were able to hold in active memory and subsequently recite. Group 1 represents participants in the control group, who read biographies on a screen. Group 2 represents the experimental participants, who participated in a Virtual Reality nature experience. As represented by this graph, the two groups performed quite similarly on this task: that is, there were able to remember similar amounts of numerical digits after their respective experiences.

4   Discussion

This study shows that virtual nature reduced anxiety in a way that mirrors exposure to physical nature. However, unlike exposure to physical nature, the VR nature experience did not produce the attentional restoration that others have observed after exposure to physical nature.

This presence of one set of benefits (reduced anxiety levels) and the absence of the other (increased attentional resources) is surprising and somewhat puzzling. It raises a series of questions as to why this is so, and indeed raises questions about what facets of physical nature effectively restore attention. Is it that the novelty of VR promotes "hard" rather than "soft" fascination? Could current VR display technologies, known to induce visual fatigue, be at fault? Would light field or other technologies that more closely mimic physiological properties of spatial vision enable the attentional benefits of nature in VR? Are the attentional tests themselves part of the problem; would attentional tasks less dependent on a visual system potentially taxed by compensatory processes induced by current VR display technologies show different results? Or perhaps the answer lies in other sensory or cognitive aspects of being in physical nature– perhaps UV spectrum, wind, or smell contribute to attentional improvement. Further, it may be the case that mindful recognition of the vastness of nature in comparison to the smallness of one's individual existence enhances fascination levels, which in turn restore attentional capacity. Certainly, the results of this study suggest that further research is needed to fully understand the relationship between nature and attentional restoration, as well as how virtual experiences relate to physical experiences.

It is particularly interesting that– while anxiety levels significantly decreased for those in the experimental condition– relaxation levels were not different across the two groups. In previous experiments on the psychological benefits of nature, reduced anxiety levels co-varied with increased relaxation levels. Perhaps this fine-tuned difference is informative in and of itself: though nature maintains its anxiety-reducing abilities in VR, it loses its soft, calming effect. This may contribute both to the lack of relaxation effects as well as to the lack of soft fascination, which subsequently contributes to the minimal attentional restoration found in this study.

Here, it is important to note a limitation of our research: as mentioned previously, all participants were new to VR. It is likely, therefore, that they were eagerly adjusting to their new environment. As they explored their new perceptual space, it is quite possible that they were excited. Excitement would certainly diminish relaxation levels and could lead to "hard" fascination, rather than the requisite soft fascination necessary for attentional restoration. A future study with avid VR users may address this discrepancy.

Such limitations aside, this study clearly demonstrates that virtual nature carries one of the most substantial benefits of physical nature: anxiety reduction. In a world of increasing urban density and development, immersion in nature can be challenging at best, involving significant investments in time and access to transportation resources. In addition, there are many for whom physical mobility is a considerable challenge. For those with limited access to nature, whether due to time, money, or physical limitation, the benefits of accessing nature in VR could be a significant benefit. Even for those with greater access, the immediacy of VR is an advantage. Simple 10-min sessions of immersion in virtual forests at work, at home, or clinical settings could be used to effectively and reliably reduce anxiety.

References

Atchley, R.A., Strayer, D.L., Atchley, P.: Creativity in the wild: improving creative reasoning through immersion in natural settings. PLoS ONE 7(12), e51474 (2012)

Berman, M.G., Jonides, J., Kaplan, S.: The cognitive benefits of interacting with nature. Psychol. Sci. 19(12), 1207–1212 (2008)

Berman, M.G., et al.: Interacting with nature improves cognition and affect for individuals with depression. J. Affect. Disord. 140(3), 300–305 (2012)

Bohil, C.J., Alicea, B., Biocca, F.A.: Virtual reality in neuroscience research and therapy. Nat. Rev. Neurosci. 12(12), 752–762 (2011)

Bratman, G.N., Hamilton, J.P., Hahn, K.S., Daily, G.C., Gross, J.J.: Nature experience reduces rumination and subgenual prefrontal cortex activation. Proc. Natl. Acad. Sci. 112(28), 8567–8572 (2015)

Brown, D.K., Barton, J.L., Gladwell, V.F.: Viewing nature scenes positively affects recovery of autonomic function following acute-mental stress. Environ. Sci. Technol. 47(11), 5562–5569 (2013)

Cimprich, B.: Attentional fatigue following breast cancer surgery. Res. Nurs. Health 15(3), 199–207 (1992)

Cimprich, B.: Development of an intervention to restore attention in cancer patients. Cancer Nurs. **16**(2), 83–92 (1993)

Faber Taylor, A., Kuo, F.E.: Children with attention deficits concentrate better after walk in the park. J. Atten. Disord. **12**(5), 402–409 (2009)

Hartig, T., Mang, M., Evans, G.W.: Restorative effects of natural environment experiences. Environ. Behav. **23**(1), 3–26 (1991)

Hartig, T., Mitchell, R., De Vries, S., Frumkin, H.: Nature and health. Annu. Rev. Public Health **35**, 207–228 (2014)

Herzog, T.R., Black, A.M., Fountaine, K.A., Knotts, D.J.: Reflection and attentional recovery as distinctive benefits of restorative environments. J. Environ. Psychol. **17**(2), 165–170 (1997)

Kaplan, S.: The restorative environment: nature and human experience. In: Role of Horticulture in Human Well-Being and Social Development: A National Symposium, pp. 134–142. Timber Press, Arlington (1992)

Kaplan, R.: The nature of the view from home: psychological benefits. Environ. Behav. **33**(4), 507–542 (2001)

Keniger, L.E., Gaston, K.J., Irvine, K.N., Fuller, R.A.: What are the benefits of interacting with nature? Int. J. Environ. Res. Public Health **10**(3), 913–935 (2013)

Lugrin, J.L., Polyschev, I., Roth, D., Latoschik, M.E.: Avatar anthropomorphism and acrophobia. In: Proceedings of the 22nd ACM Conference on Virtual Reality Software and Technology, pp. 315–316. ACM, November 2016

Maister, L., Sebanz, N., Knoblich, G., Tsakiris, M.: Experiencing ownership over a dark-skinned body reduces implicit racial bias. Cognition **128**(2), 170–178 (2013)

Maister, L., Slater, M., Sanchez-Vives, M.V., Tsakiris, M.: Changing bodies changes minds: owning another body affects social cognition. Trends Cogn. Sci. **19**(1), 6–12 (2015)

Peck, T.C., Seinfeld, S., Aglioti, S.M., Slater, M.: Putting yourself in the skin of a black avatar reduces implicit racial bias. Conscious. Cogn. **22**(3), 779–787 (2013)

Serino, S., et al.: A novel virtual reality-based training protocol for the enhancement of the "Mental Frame Syncing" in individuals with alzheimer's disease: a development-of-concept trial. Front. Aging Neurosci. **9**, 240 (2017)

Tennessen, C.M., Cimprich, B.: Views to nature: effects on attention. J. Environ. Psychol. **15**(1), 77–85 (1995)

Tettegah, S., Taylor, K., Whang, E.W., Meistninkas, S., Chamot, R.: Can virtual reality simulations be used as a research tool to study empathy, problems solving and perspective taking of educators?: Theory, method and application. In: ACM SIGGRAPH 2006 Educators Program, p. 35. ACM, July 2006

Tsirlin, I., Dupierrix, E., Chokron, S., Coquillart, S., Ohlmann, T.: Uses of virtual reality for diagnosis, rehabilitation and study of unilateral spatial neglect: review and analysis. Cyberpsychol. Behav. **12**(2), 175–181 (2009)

Ulrich, R.S., Simons, R.F., Losito, B.D., Fiorito, E., Miles, M.A., Zelson, M.: Stress recovery during exposure to natural and urban environments. J. Environ. Psychol. **11**(3), 201–230 (1991)

White, M.P., Alcock, I., Wheeler, B.W., Depledge, M.H.: Would you be happier living in a greener urban area? A fixed-effects analysis of panel data. Psychol. Sci. **24**(6), 920–928 (2013)

Effects of Weight and Balance of Head Mounted Display on Physical Load

Kodai Ito$^{(\boxtimes)}$ ⓘ, Mitsunori Tada ⓘ, Hiroyasu Ujike ⓘ,
and Keiichiro Hyodo

National Institute of Advanced Industrial Science and Technology,
2-3-26 Aomi, Koto, Tokyo, Japan
kodai.ito@aist.go.jp

Abstract. Recently, VR technology has advanced rapidly, and many Head Mounted Displays (HMD) are sold by companies all over the world. In order to have good experiences in VR environment, comfortability of wearing HMD is essential. However, few studies investigated the feelings of fatigue on commercially available HMDs. In this research, we focused on the effects of weight and balance of HMD on physical load. We performed experiment with 188 participants using shooting game played under different weights and balances. After playing the game, the participants were asked to answer a questionnaire to assess the level of physical loads that they perceived. As the results, we clarified that the weight of HMD affects the feelings of fatigue, and its degree varies depending on the position of the center of gravity. The results suggest the joint torque at the neck can be an indicator of the physical load of HMD. Our results will be highly suggestive for designing new HMD.

Keywords: Head Mounted Display · Physical load · Product design

1 Introduction

Recently, rapid advances in VR technology enables us to immerse into VR world more easily [1, 2]. In order to have good experiences in such environment, comfortability of wearing Head Mounted Display (HMD) is essential. Weight and balance of HMD are two dominant factors that affect head movements and physical loads of HMD users. Therefore, these factors must be taken into account to improve the comfortability of HMD.

Previous research [3] clarified that physical loads of users reduced when wearing lower-weight HMD. Research [4] investigated the effects of both weight and balance of HMD on physical workload using a professional-grade HMD. However, it weighs about 800 g and has head-worn attachment made of plastic resin. On the other hand, many consumer-grade HMDs with lighter weight are becoming available. For example, Oculus Rift CV1 with 468 g weight [5] as well as various smartphone-based HMDs [6] are in the market. These lightweight HMDs have elastic belts as head-worn attachments. Therefore, they should also be investigated as their weight and balance might improve the comfortability of HMDs.

© Springer Nature Switzerland AG 2019
J. Y. C. Chen and G. Fragomeni (Eds.): HCII 2019, LNCS 11574, pp. 450–460, 2019.
https://doi.org/10.1007/978-3-030-21607-8_35

This research aims to clarify the relationship between the physical loads, weight, and balance of HMD for consumer use. For this purpose, we asked the participants to play shooting game wearing HMD with different weight and balance. After playing the game, the participants were asked to fill out a questionnaire to assess the level of physical loads that they perceived.

2 Experimental Method

2.1 Devices

We employed the following devices for this experiment:

- Notebook PC: ALIENWARE13 (DELL)
- HMD: Oculus Rift CV1 (Oculus)

2.2 Shooting Game

We developed a shooting game for our experiment. Figure 1 shows the example scene. In this game, participants were asked to shoot 20 targets which appear at random position and posture within the field of view. The aim of the gun moves along with the roll, pitch and yaw angle of the head. To shoot out the target, players have to keep aiming at the target for one second.

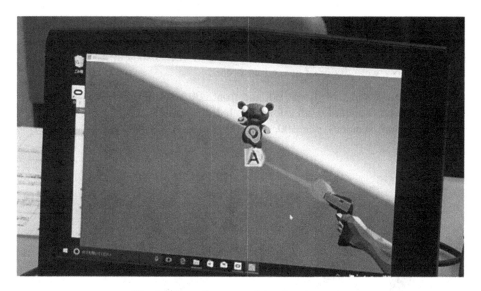

Fig. 1. Example scene of the shooting game

2.3 Experimental Setup

To change the weight and balance of HMD, we prepared lead weights that can be attached to the front and rear of the HMD (Figs. 2 and 3) with hook-and-loop fastener. We prepared seven conditions of weight and balance as shown in Table 1.

"Front", "both", and "rear" in this table indicate the place where the lead weight is attached. The subsequent numerical values indicate the weight of the lead weight. For example, "Both 100" indicates that the HMD is attached with 100 g lead weights both at the front and rear sides. "Standard" indicates that no additional weight is attached to the HMD. The original balance index was set to zero. The minus values indicate that the center of gravity is moved to the rear side, while the plus values indicate that the center of gravity is moved to the front side.

Table 1. Weight and balance conditions

Weight [g]	Balance index						
	−4	−3	−2	−1	0	1	2
200	Rear 200		Both 100				Front 200
100		Rear 100		Both 50		Front 100	
0					Standard		

We divided the participants into three groups for the three positions of lead weights: "front", "both", and "rear". For each group, one of the three positions was assigned, and for each position, three conditions of weights (i.e. standard, 100 g, 200 g) as described below were assigned at random order.

- "Front" group: standard, front 100, and front 200 conditions.
- "Both" group: standard, both 50, and both 100 conditions.
- "Rear" group: standard, rear 100, rear 200 conditions.

Fig. 2. Lead weights for front (left) and rear (right)

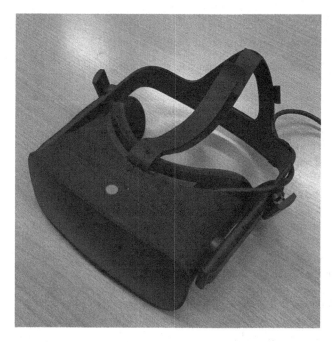

Fig. 3. Oculus Rift CV1 with hook-and-loop fastener

2.4   Participants

We performed the experiment with 188 participants who were 13 to 85 years old (96 males and 92 females). Table 2 shows number of participants grouped by gender, age and positions of weights.

Table 2. Number of participants grouped by gender, age and positions of weights

Gender	Group	10 s	20 s	30 s	40 s	50 s	60 s	70 s	80 s	Total
Male	Front	5	5	4	8	5	4	4	1	36
	Both	3	5	2	7	5	4	4	0	30
	Rear	3	6	1	7	5	4	4	0	30
Male total		11	16	7	22	15	12	12	1	96
Female	Front	3	8	3	7	5	3	5	0	34
	Both	3	6	2	5	4	4	4	0	28
	Rear	3	7	3	6	3	4	4	0	30
Female total		9	21	8	18	12	11	13	0	92
Total		20	37	15	40	27	23	25	1	188

2.5   Evaluation Method

We measured the following data from each participant:

- Physical properties (visual and muscle strengths)
    - Pupillary distance
    - Visual acuity (self-declared)
    - Grip strength
- Log data from HMD
    - Position and posture of the target and corresponding head movement (roll, pitch and yaw angles)
    - Time until the game completion
- Questionnaire for physical load
  The participants answered this questionnaire immediately after the game completion for each condition. They answered the following questions using 5-point Likert scale:
    Q1. Was the HMD fixed to your head?
    Q2. Did you see the graphics clearly?
    Q3. Did you feel a physical load from the graphics?
    Q4. Did you feel a physical load from the weight?
    Q5. Did you feel a physical load from the balance?
- Questionnaire for residual effect
  The participants answered this questionnaire 15 min after finishing the last game. They answered the following questions using 5-point Likert scale.
    Q1. Do your eyes feel uncomfortable?
    Q2. Did your eyes feel more uncomfortable after taking off the HMD?
    Q3. Does your head feel uncomfortable?
    Q4. Did your head feel more uncomfortable after taking off the HMD?
    Q5. Does your neck feel uncomfortable?
    Q6. Did your neck feel more uncomfortable after taking off the HMD?

3   Experimental Results and Discussion

3.1   Grip Strength

Figure 4 shows the results of grip strength measurement. Basically, male participants had stronger grip strength than female participants. In addition, 40 to 50 years male subjects had the strongest grip strength.

We compared the results of questionnaire between participants group with strong grip strength and with weak grip strength. However, we could not observe significant differences among them. Therefore, in the following analysis we divide the participants into two groups by their age for both males and females: young (10 to 49 years old) and elderly (50 to 89 years old).

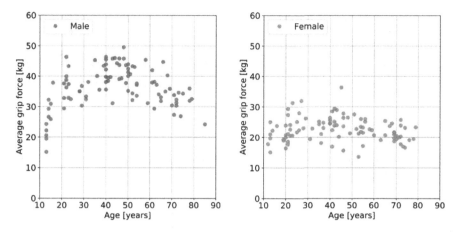

Fig. 4. The results of grip strength measurement

3.2 Elapsed Time to Clear the Game

Figure 5 shows elapsed times to clear the game for male participants. Figure 6 shows the results for female participants. In each figure, we plotted the results for the "front", the "both", and the "rear" groups. In addition, as explained above we separated the results into the young (10–49 years old) and the elderly (50–89 years old) groups.

The elapsed times to clear the game were not significantly different among the weight conditions. On the other hand, the elderly group took longer time to clear the game than the young group. This is speculated because they were less familiar with playing video games. Therefore, the effects of familiarity with playing games may have strong effects on the elapsed time to clear than the weight and balance of the HMD.

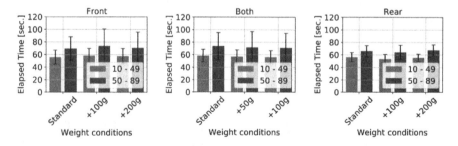

Fig. 5. The elapsed times to clear the shooting game (Males, Left: "Front" group, Center: "Both" group, Right: "Rear" group)

3.3 Questionnaire Results for Physical Load

The questionnaire results (subjective scores) are shown for "front" group (Figs. 7 and 8), "both" group (Figs. 9 and 10), and "rear" group (Figs. 11 and 12).

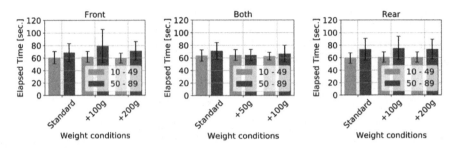

Fig. 6. The elapsed times to clear the shooting game (Females, Left: "Front" group, Center: "Both" group, Right: "Rear" group)

From the results of Q1 and Q2, HMD fixation to the head and sharpness of the graphics is about 4 on average (slightly agree). Most participants did not feel uncomfortable about these two conditions.

From the results of Q3, some participants felt fatigued by vision. However, the feelings of fatigue by vision were not different among the weight conditions and the position of weights.

From the results of Q4 and Q5, there were tendencies that the feelings of fatigue increased with additional weights. In the "front" group results, as weight increased, the feelings of fatigue increased. The "both" group results were similar but showed few significant differences. In addition, the gradient of the feelings of fatigue as weight increased was less than that of the "front" group. The "rear" group results showed no significant differences. In particular, the results of young female group showed opposite gradient of graphs to those of the "front" group. It suggests a possibility that the feelings of fatigue become smaller with additional weights on the rear side.

Since the original center of gravity is in the front of HMD, it moved to the center of the head by adding weight on the rear side which reduced the physical load. We need further investigation why only the results of young female group show this tendency markedly.

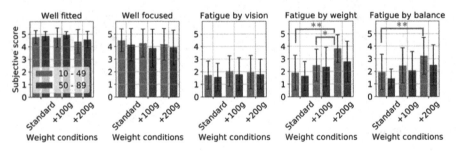

Fig. 7. The questionnaire results ("Front" group, male, From the left, Q1 to Q5)

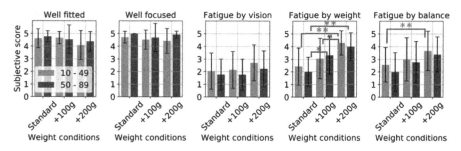

Fig. 8. The questionnaire results ("Front" group, female, From the left, Q1 to Q5)

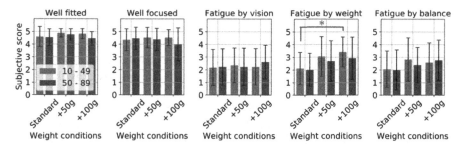

Fig. 9. The questionnaire results ("Both" group, male, From the left, Q1 to Q5)

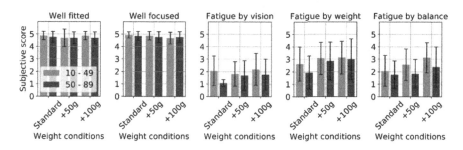

Fig. 10. The questionnaire results ("Both" group, female, From the left, Q1 to Q5)

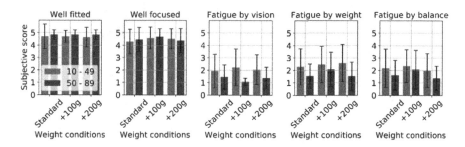

Fig. 11. The questionnaire results ("Rear" group, male, From the left, Q1 to Q5)

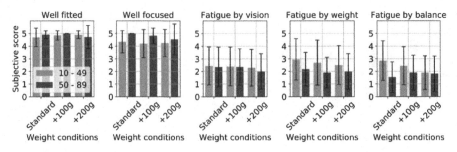

Fig. 12. The questionnaire results ("Rear" group, female, From the left, Q1 to Q5)

Figure 13 shows plots of the average fatigue scores as an isosurface on a two-dimensional space composed of weight axis and balance axis.

The results show even if the weight was the same, the fatigue score increased as the balance index increased (the center of gravity moved to the front side). In addition, even if the balance index was the same, the fatigue score increased as the weight increased.

The contour line forms an inverse proportional hyperbolic curve. It indicates that the feelings of fatigue will be constant if the product of weight and balance (distance from the center of gravity) is constant. The product of weight and balance indicates the torque required to hold the HMD. These results suggest the joint torque at the neck can be an indicator of the physical load of HMD.

In the guidelines on helmet-mounted displays [7], similar results are shown for the relationship between weight, balance and feelings of fatigue. Helmet-mounted display and head-mounted display have some common features. Therefore, our results can be considered reasonable and appropriate. They will contribute to creating comfortable HMD standards.

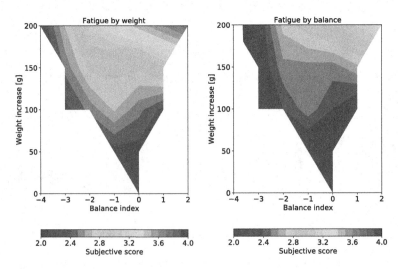

Fig. 13. Variation in feelings of fatigue by weight and balance (Left: fatigue by weight, Right: fatigue by balance)

3.4 Questionnaire Results for Residual Effect

Figures 14 and 15 shows the results of questionnaire answered 15 min after finish playing the game for all three conditions. The average scores of residual effects to the eyes, the head, and the neck were less than 2 (slightly disagree) as well as the results of the increase in discomfort. These results indicate few subjects had residual effect after playing the game.

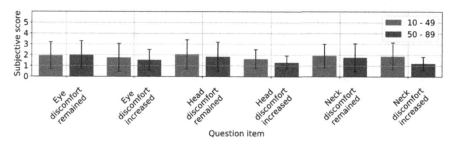

Fig. 14. The results of questionnaire answered 15 min after finish playing the game (Males, From the left, Q1 to Q6)

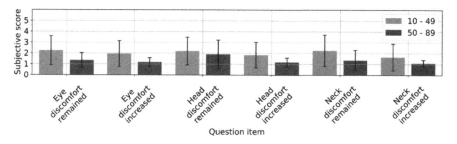

Fig. 15. The results of questionnaire answered 15 min after finish playing the game (Females, From the left, Q1 to Q6)

4 Conclusion

We focused on the effects of weight and balance of HMD on physical load. We performed experiment using shooting game with various weights and balances. After playing the game, the participants were asked to answer a questionnaire to assess the level of physical loads that they perceived.

As the results, we clarified that the weight of HMD affects the feelings of fatigue, and its degree varies depending on the center of gravity. The product of weight and balance indicates the torque required to hold the HMD. Our results suggest the joint torque at the neck can be an indicator of the physical load of HMD.

To improve comfortability of HMD, it is necessary to take into account weight balance as well as weight reduction. Our results will be highly suggestive for HMD design.

References

1. "2016: The Year of VR? - Virtual Reality" Virtual Reality Society. https://www.vrs.org.uk/news/2016-the-year-of-vr. Accessed 1 Feb 2019
2. Chryssolouris, G., Mavrikios, D., Fragos, D., Karabatsou, V.: A virtual reality-based experimentation environment for the verification of human-related factors in assembly process. Robot. Comput. Integr. Manuf. 16(4), 267–276 (2000)
3. Yan, Y., Chen, K., Xie, Y., Song, Y., Liu, Y.: The effects of weight on comfort of virtual reality devices. In: Rebelo, F., Soares, M.M. (eds.) AHFE 2018. AISC, vol. 777, pp. 239–248. Springer, Cham (2019). https://doi.org/10.1007/978-3-319-94706-8_27
4. Chihara, T., Seo, A.: Evaluation of physical workload affected by mass and center of mass of head-mounted display. Appl. Ergon. 68, 204–212 (2018)
5. Oculus Rift: VR Headset for VR Ready PCs. https://www.oculus.com/rift/. Accessed 1 Feb 2019
6. Steed, A., Julier, S.: Design and implementation of an immersive virtual reality system based on a smartphone platform. In: 2013 IEEE Symposium on 3D User Interfaces (3DUI), pp. 43–46 (2013)
7. U.S. Army Aeromedical Research Laboratory: Helmet-mounted Displays: Sensation, Perception, and Cognition Issues, Biodynamics Guidelines and Recommendations (2009)

The Impact of Motion on Individual Simulator Sickness in a Moving Base VR Simulator with Head-Mounted Display (HMD)

Mara Kaufeld[(⊠)] and Thomas Alexander

Fraunhofer Institute for Communication,
Information Processing and Ergonomics FKIE,
Zanderstraße 5, 53177 Bonn, Germany
mara.kaufeld@fkie.fraunhofer.de

Abstract. Simulators are increasingly used for training applications. Therefore, it is essential to consider negative side effects like simulator sickness. Influencing factors of simulator sickness are related to the individual, to the system, or to the training design. Our empirical study investigates some of these factors in a 30-min virtual helicopter flight with HMD. 30 subjects (M_{age} = 19.3 years; SD = 4.02) completed the MSSQ (motion sickness susceptibility questionnaire) and the SSQ (simulator sickness questionnaire) before exposure and the SSQ after exposure. The participants received the same treatment on two consecutive days: One day without real motion and the other day with real motion realized utilizing a motion platform. Results show that symptoms of simulator sickness significantly increased directly after VR-exposure. One hour after exposure, the symptoms of simulator sickness are comparable to symptoms before exposure. A difference between the two conditions with real motion and without could not be observed after exposure. Individual motion sickness susceptibility has been identified as a predictor for experiencing simulator sickness. Implications of our findings for the training of helicopter crews and theoretical implications in terms of simulator sickness are discussed.

Keywords: Virtual reality · Virtual training · Helicopter · Simulator sickness · Motion cueing · Moving base simulator · Motion platform

1 Introduction

Advances in Virtual Reality (VR) provide new technical capabilities for advanced education and training. Particularly, costly and inaccessible contents can be trained more effectively and efficiently with VR-HMDs (Head-Mounted Displays). Training of helicopter crews is an example for this. The crew members need special skills to identify and evaluate critical situations especially for difficult rescue missions. This includes the identification of dangerous situations and special risks in the environment. In general, VR provides a natural immersion in a computer-generated environment and, thus, a close link to training content. VR is a promising technology, which has the ability to immerse users and, thus, creates a sense of presence. Nevertheless, negative side effects like simulator sickness are still present and limit practical applicability.

© Springer Nature Switzerland AG 2019
J. Y. C. Chen and G. Fragomeni (Eds.): HCII 2019, LNCS 11574, pp. 461–472, 2019.
https://doi.org/10.1007/978-3-030-21607-8_36

2 Related Work

Simulator sickness is a special form of motion sickness. Both forms have in common that negative after-effects occur. However, after-effects are triggered through different components of the human sensory system. Motion sickness is evoked through the movement of a vehicle, ship, aircraft or any other moving object. The movement stimulates the human's vestibular system. In contrast to motion sickness, simulator sickness is not necessarily triggered by the movement of the body, but by a conflict between the vestibular system and the visual system. Unpleasant symptoms can also occur due to visual stimulation in a fixed base simulator [1]. Hence, the symptoms are rather induced visually.

2.1 Measuring and Predictors of Symptoms

Symptoms of motion sickness and simulator sickness are quite similar and implicate symptoms like eyestrain, headache, sweating, disorientation and nausea [2].

Kennedy et al. [3] analyzed the occurrence of simulator sickness symptoms in VR systems and found that symptoms can be split in three symptom groups: oculomotor stress, nausea, and disorientation. Based on their findings they developed a simulator sickness questionnaire (SSQ) [2], which has since then become the most popular instrument to gather data about symptoms experienced after simulator exposure. Several attempts to develop instruments that are capable to measure symptoms during exposure did not achieve satisfactory results. Changes in psychophysiological indicators such as heart rate, skin conductivity, stomach activity and blinking are also likely to occur with increased sickness [4, 5]. However, the direction of change for most physiological measures of simulator sickness differs among individuals [6]. A great need for research and development of cost-effective and objective physiological measures still persists [7].

Different factors contribute to adverse health effects of using virtual environments. Factors influencing simulator sickness include system factors, application design factors and individual user factors [6]. Examples for system factors are latency, calibration, field of view, refresh rate or the use of motion systems in simulators. Application design refers to the training design of virtual reality applications like the duration or frequency of training or the movement in VR, e.g. head movement, standing/walking vs. sitting. Individual user factors include for instance gender, age, mental models, and health. Another individual user factor is the prior history of motion sickness, which is known as the best predictor for experiencing simulator sickness in simulator-based training [8]. The motion sickness susceptibility questionnaire (MSSQ) predicts individual differences in motion sickness caused by a variety of stimuli in the user's past experiences [9].

2.2 Theories of Simulator Sickness

Three common theories exist in literature referring to the causes of simulator sickness: the poison theory, the postural instability theory, and the sensory conflict theory [10]. These three theories had originally been developed for motion sickness and later transferred to simulator sickness. The poison theory by Treisman [11] attempts to explain sickness symptoms from an evolutionary point of view. It holds that the adverse stimulation of vestibular and visual system triggers mechanism that evolved to prevent poisoning. Hence, unpleasant symptoms are caused by alleged poisoning. The postural instability theory developed by Riccio and Stoffregen [12] states that symptoms are caused by a loss of postural control. The duration of the postural instability influences the severity of symptoms. The sensory conflict theory is the most popular theory. Many authors agree that simulator sickness is caused by a mismatch of senses. The theory has been originally developed by Reason and Brand [10]. An example for a sensory conflict can be found in virtual reality applications in general: Wearing a VR-HMD - flying with a virtual helicopter - and sitting on a stationary chair at the same time, induces a sensory conflict. The user is moving in the virtual environment, but not in the real world.

Thus, the movement is induced visually and not vestibular. The optical flow patterns of the surrounding landscape passes by and creates a sense of self-motion. Visually induced illusory self-motion is known as vection, which is a precondition for simulator sickness [13]. To sum up, visual stimulation is present in virtual reality applications while vestibular stimulation might be absent. According to the sensory conflict theory the discrepancy between what is seen and what is felt triggers unpleasant symptoms.

2.3   Impact of True Motion on User's Simulator Sickness

Since the sensory conflict theory is the oldest and most influential theory, our work focuses on how to reduce simulator sickness within the framework of sensory conflicts. To reduce sensory conflicts the usage of motion simulators is a suitable option. A combined system of VR-HMDs and a motion platform is capable to provide corresponding visual and vestibular input.

Casali was the first researcher who introduced motion platforms to reduce simulator sickness [14]. However, he reported that in some cases real motion can be helpful to reduce the severity of symptoms and in other cases it is not. This is in line with other studies conducted in the last century that provides ambiguous findings. In past studies, users suffered from simulator sickness symptoms, although motion platforms were used [15, 16]. A possible explanation is that the motion platforms were not aligned correctly with the visual input. Another explanation is true motion sickness. This means that the sickness is motion-induced and not a result of sensory conflicts [10].

Nevertheless, anecdotal evidence from practice exists, that pilots and instructor operators agree that flying with the motion system turned off induced more sickness [17, 18]. In another study (Miller and Goodson, 1958) [cited by 19] the authors found that 75% of experienced pilots suffered from simulator sickness symptoms when the motion platform was turned off whereas 10% reported symptoms when the motion platform was turned on. The authors implicate that these effects might be only true for experienced pilots since they are used to motion.

More recent studies provided evidence that an activated motion system is able to reduce simulator sickness symptoms [20, 21]. These results are still discussed, since the same authors also found contradictory result [21]. Moreover, the validity of Curry's study is limited, because two simulators were compared that also differed in other features than motion [20].

Stein and Robinski compared different simulators and found that simulators with motion platforms are more likely to evoke simulator sickness symptoms [22].

McCauley draws the conclusion that there is no reliable evidence that using motion platforms prevent simulator sickness. Nonetheless, true motion contributes to the realism of the simulation and, therefore, positively influences the pilot's acceptance of simulators [23].

The scientific evidence for the sensory conflict theory is far from clear. Continuous research in this field is essential, since research results are ambiguous and the rapid technology progress limits a simple transfer of results from older studies. Furthermore, new investigations are crucial because above-mentioned studies did not analyze the impact of virtual reality HMDs as a COTS technology in combination with motion platforms.

2.4 Temporal Aspects of Simulator Sickness

Many studies explored the occurrence and the increase and decrease of simulator sickness symptoms over time. When studying the impact of motion on the severity of symptoms it is also important to examine the impact before and after exposure. It is important to check whether simulator sickness symptoms occur before analyzing if motion affected symptoms. Moreover, it is interesting to know when the symptoms will disappear. Examining the severity of symptoms over the time can also be beneficial for detecting interaction effects between motion and point of time.

An article by Dużmańska et al. reviews 39 different studies about temporal aspects of simulator sickness [24]. They found that severity of the simulator sickness increases with time of exposure. Likewise, the persistence of the symptoms varies between 10 min and even 4 h depending on the individual studies and the duration of VR exposure. Although there is a clear connection between duration of exposure and persistence of the symptoms, it is impossible to develop a single, universal pattern for this effect. Thus, the authors recommend to test time courses for each VR technology separately. For example, a study with a ship motion simulator, participants received a 30-min simulator exposure [25]. Within one hour, most participants fully recovered from the simulator sickness symptoms.

2.5 Study Objectives

The current study examines the impact of motion on individual simulator sickness in a moving base VR simulator. We use modern virtual reality HMDs for a novel investigation of the sensory conflict theory. Furthermore, we analyze the time course of the simulator sickness decline and the prediction of simulator sickness through motion susceptibility history.

3   Method

We conducted an empirical study to examine the impacts of different variables on simulator sickness. This section describes sample, procedure and design as well as materials and measures.

3.1   Sample Description

30 subjects, 28 men and 2 women, volunteered in our study with a mean age of 19.3 years (SD = 4.02). Most of the subjects were particularly interested in video games (28). 18 subjects stated that they play video games several times a week. They had no experience in helicopter flying and little VR experience. Analyzing the motion sickness susceptibility by the MSSQ revealed that participants had an average score of 4.74, which is a relatively low score compared to the norms Golding [9] reported (M = 12.9, SD = 9.9). A necessary precondition was a normal or a corrected to normal vision, which was tested beforehand. All subjects participated in both conditions (motion, no motion).

3.2   Procedure

Prescreening took place on the first day and consisted of eyesight testing, ratings of the SSQ and the MSSQ. After prescreening subjects received a 5 min VR-training followed by the 30-min exposure. The SSQ was used to collect data on simulator sickness symptoms before and directly after and one hour after VR-exposure. The interval of one hour was chosen because based on the findings of [25] it was likely that the symptoms would have disappeared one hour after VR-exposure. The Motion Sickness Susceptibility Questionnaire (MSSQ) was administered to detect individual vulnerabilities. During VR-exposure, the participant is in the right rear part of the virtual helicopter. While looking out from the helicopter's side door, participants completed visual search- and working memory tasks. In the real world the subject knelt on a motion platform and pressed buttons on an input device (see Fig. 2). The participants received the same treatment on two consecutive days: One day without real motion and the other day with real motion realized using a motion platform. We named these conditions: motion vs. no motion. Conditions were counterbalanced for the two days. On the second day, the subjects were asked after exposure which condition they preferred either motion or no motion. The entire procedure is illustrated in Fig. 1.

3.3   Experimental Design

Two independent variables were defined for a 2×3 repeated measures ANOVA. The first independent variable was motion with two levels (motion/no motion). The second was point of time (before, after, and 1 h after). Besides analyzing the focal independent variables, we also examined the effect of motion sickness susceptibility (MSSQ) as a predictor for simulator sickness. Altogether, we analyzed how motion, point of time, and motion sickness susceptibility influences the dependent variable simulator sickness.

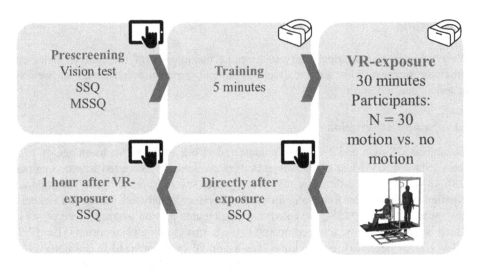

Fig. 1. Illustration of the experimental procedure.

3.4 Apparatus and Measures

Technical Specifications of the Apparatus

For our experiment, we set up an experimental demonstrator including a motion platform, a VR-HMD and the virtual simulation itself. The construction on the motion platform was self-built (see Fig. 2). The virtual simulation was developed using the software VBS3 from Bohemia Interactive Simulations [26]. For displaying the simulation, the Oculus Rift CV1 was used as a popular low-cost VR-HMD [27]. The motion base *6 DoF Electrical Motion System* by Brunner [28] was used to provide real motion analog to the virtual simulation.

The motion system provides heave, pitch, roll, yaw, surge, and sway movement, as well as a combination of all of them. Movement information were transferred from simulation framework to the motion base with a transfer rate of 60 Hz. Scientific experience indicates that, in practice, it is not necessary to update faster than 60 Hz [29]. Testing our experimental demonstrator for any physical thresholds in terms of velocity and acceleration shows that the motion system is able to perform 97 to 99.5% of all the movements timely and correctly. In pretests subjects stated that they did not recognize any mismatches between visual and vestibular input.

Questionnaires

SSQ scores were calculated according to Kennedy et al. [2]. 16 different somatic symptoms were rated from *none* to *severe*, which corresponds to values from 0 to 4. The single symptoms and their severity ratings (0, 1, 2, 3) were sorted into subscales: nausea, oculomotor distress, and disorientation. Values for each subscale were summed up and weighted. The total score was calculated by multiplying the summed subscale values by 3.74.

The short form of the MSSQ, which was applied, asks for the previous sickness occurrences in cars, buses, trains, aircrafts, small boats, large ships, swings,

Fig. 2. Picture of the experimental demonstrator with subject.

roundabouts in playgrounds, and leisure park attractions. Subjects can rate their experiences by ticking one of these options: not applicable/never travelled, never felt sick, rarely felt sick, sometimes felt sick, and frequently felt sick. It asks separately for childhood experiences before age 12 and the experiences over the last 10 years. Calculation of the total scores followed the instructions of Golding [9]. In his initial sample the median score was 11.3, 25th percentile was 5.5, and 75th percentile was 19.0.

4   Results

In the following sections statistically significant results are marked with * for $p < .05$, ** for $p < .01$, and *** for $p < .001$. SSQ scores were found not to be normally distributed due to a broad range of individual symptom severity. Nonetheless, parametric analyzing methods were applied since ANOVAs are relatively robust to violations of normality [30]. The reported degrees of freedom were corrected according to the Greenhouse-Geisser procedure.

4.1   Impacts of Motion and Point of Time

Results of a repeated measures ANOVA revealed a significant main effect of point of time for the SSQ total score, $F(1.41, 39.33) = 19.00$, $p < .001$, $\eta^2 = .40$, for the subscale nausea, $F(1.59, 44.36) = 11.91$, $p < .001$, $\eta^2 = .30$, for the subscale oculo-motor, $F(1.41, 39.55) = 16.06$, $p < .001$, $\eta^2 = .36$ as well as for disorientation, $F(1.65, 46.05) = 11.61$, $p < .001$, $\eta^2 = .29$. Follow-up pairwise comparisons are depicted in Fig. 3.

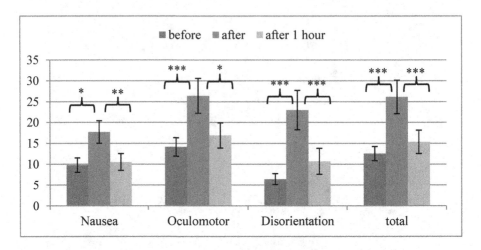

Fig. 3. Means and standard errors of simulator sickness symptoms before, after and 1 h after VR-exposure.

Neither a main effect of motion nor an interaction effect of motion and point of time was found to be significant. Hence, we could not detect any significant differences between motion and no motion in any of the SSQ scales (see Fig. 4).

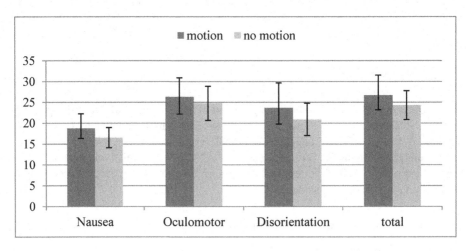

Fig. 4. Means and standard errors of simulator sickness symptoms for motion and no motion.

The evaluation of the subject's preference showed that 26 subjects (87%) favored the condition which included real motion generated by the motion system. According to most subjects the simulation felt more realistic when the motion system was applied.

4.2 Motion Sickness Susceptibility

A moderated regression was conducted to examine whether the predictors motion susceptibility and motion, or their interaction influence total SSQ scores. Predictors were mean-centered to reduce multicollinearity and z-transformed. The assumption of homoscedasticity was graphically checked. The overall model revealed to be significant, $F(3, 56) = 6.52$, $p > .001$, $R^2 = .26$. MSSQ scores were found as a significant predictor of simulator sickness scores, $\beta = .48$, $p < .001$ (see Fig. 5).

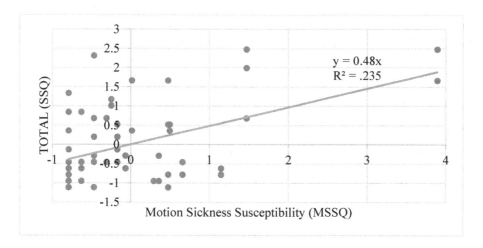

Fig. 5. Predicted simulator sickness symptoms as a function of motion sickness susceptibility.

Regarding the contribution of each individual predictor, motion revealed to be a non-significant predictor, $\beta = -.10$, $p = .653$. The interaction of both predictors does not explain a significant portion of the variance over and above the criterion, $\beta = -.29$, $p = .209$.

To sum up, individual motion sickness susceptibility was found as a predictor for experiencing simulator sickness. We could not find any evidence for a moderating function of motion on simulator sickness.

5 Discussion and Conclusions

The objective of the current study was to investigate the impact of motion on individual simulator sickness in a moving base VR simulator. We could not find any differences in simulator sickness for applying or not applying a motion platform. Thus, we cannot provide evidence for the sensory conflict theory. Past studies provided ambiguous results for using a motion platform to reduce simulator sickness as described in Sect. 2.3. Most of these studies are only partially comparable to our approach due to the age of the studies and other technical specifications of the simulator systems. That is why we discuss our results in a theoretical framework. Assuming the sensory conflict theory holds there are some possible explanations why we did not find differences between motion and no motion. One reason might be that our motion platform was not aligned correctly with the visual input. This should not apply to our simulation as explained in Sect. 3.4. Another explanation for the occurring sickness could be *true motion sickness [10]*. To test this explanation we intend to include real helicopter crews for our future research. They are familiar with real helicopter movements and may suffer less from motion sickness. Nonetheless, it should be emphasized that the real movement through the motion platform did not show any negative effects on simulator sickness. Moreover, the subject's preference clearly indicates advantages for the use of motion platforms in training. Since our results did not provide any evidence that real motion leads to increased severity of sickness the application of the used system is recommended with an activated motion system.

Furthermore, we detected that one hour after exposure the simulator sickness symptoms decreased to normal. It is pointed out that these results only apply to our simulation and thus are not transferable to other simulators. Further research can analyze the exact course of time for the sickness decrease by asking for the symptoms at shorter intervals. In general, it is highly recommended to measure the duration of simulator sickness decline for every new simulator in order to adapt the training design.

Motion sickness history is known to be one of the best predictors for simulator sickness [8, 9]. This is in line with our findings that motion sickness susceptibility is a predictor for simulator sickness symptoms right after VR-exposure. We could not detect any moderating function of motion for the relation between motion sickness susceptibility and simulator sickness. Thus, in our study an individual factor explains most of the variance in simulator sickness.

We conclude that interindividual variability seems to outweigh the effect of motion as system factor. Since interindividual factors are not adaptable, further research is needed in areas of system and training factors. It would be especially interesting to learn under which circumstances real motion is beneficial for the prevention of simulator sickness.

References

1. Hettinger, L.J., Riccio, G.E.: Visually induced motion sickness in virtual environments. Presence Teleoperators Virtual Environ. **1**(3), 306–310 (1992)
2. Kennedy, R.S., Lane, N.E., Berbaum, K.S., Lilienthal, M.G.: Simulator sickness questionnaire: an enhanced method for quantifying simulator sickness. Int. J. Aviat. Psychol. **3**(3), 203–220 (1993)
3. Kennedy, R.S., Lane, N.E., Lilienthal, M.G., Berbaum, K.S., Hettinger, L.J.: Profile analysis of simulator sickness symptoms: application to virtual environment systems. Presence Teleoperators Virtual Environ. **1**(3), 295–301 (1992)

4. Dennison, M.S., Wisti, A.Z., D'Zmura, M.: Use of physiological signals to predict cybersickness. Displays **44**, 42–52 (2016)

5. Kim, Y.Y., Kim, H.J., Kim, E.N., Ko, H.D., Kim, H.T.: Characteristic changes in the physiological components of cybersickness. Psychophysiology **42**(5), 616–625 (2005)

6. Jerald, J.: The VR Book: Human-Centered Design for Virtual Reality, 1st edn. Morgan & Claypool, New York (2016)

7. Davis, S., Nesbitt, K., Nalivaiko, E.: A systematic review of cybersickness. In: Proceedings of the 2014 Conference on Interactive Entertainment, pp. 1–9. ACM, New York (2014)

8. Johnson, D.M.: Introduction to and Review of Simulator Sickness Research. Army Research Institute for the Behavioral and Social Sciences, Fort Rucker (2005)

9. Golding, J.F.: Predicting individual differences in motion sickness susceptibility by questionnaire. Personality Individ. Differ. **41**(2), 237–248 (2006)

10. LaViola Jr., J.J.: A discussion of cybersickness in virtual environments. ACM SIGCHI Bull. **32**(1), 47–56 (2000)

11. Treisman, M.: Motion sickness. An evolutionary hypothesis. Science **197**(4302), 493–495 (1977)

12. Riccio, G.E., Stoffregen, T.A.: An ecological theory of motion sickness and postural instability. Ecol. Psychol. **3**(3), 195–240 (1991)

13. Hettinger, L.J., Berbaum, K.S., Kennedy, R.S., Dunlap, W.P., Nolan, M.D.: Vection and simulator sickness. Mil. Psychol. **2**(3), 171–181 (1990)

14. Casali, J.G.: Vehicular Simulation-Induced Sickness. Volume 1. An Overview. Virginia poltechnic institure and state university Blackburg dept of industrial and system engineering (1985)

15. McCauley, M.E., Sharkey, T.J.: Cybersickness: perception of self-motion in virtual environments. Presence Teleoperators & Virtual Environments **1**(3), 311–318 (1992)

16. Sharkey, T.J., McCauley, M.E.: Does a motion base prevent simulator sickness? In: Proceedings of the AIAA Flight Simulation Technologies Conference, pp. 21–28. American Institute of Aeronautics and Astronautics, Washington, DC (1992)

17. Gower Jr., D.W., Fowlkes, J.: Simulator sickness in the AH-1S (Cobra) flight simulator. Army Aeromedical Research Laboratory, Fort Rucker (1989)

18. Gower Jr., D.W., Fowlkes, J.: Simulator Sickness in the UH-60 (Black Hawk) Flight Simulator. Army Aeromedical Research Laboratory, Fort Rucker (1989)

19. McCauley, M.E.: Research issues in simulator sickness. In: Proceedings of a Workshop. National Academies, Washington, DC (1984)

20. Curry, R., Artz, B., Cathey, L., Grant, P., Greenberg, J.: Kennedy SSQ results: fixed-vs motion-based FORD simulators. In: Proceedings of Driving Simulation Conference, Paris, France, pp. 189–300 (2002)

21. Watson, G.: A synthesis of simulator sickness studies conducted in a high-fidelity driving simulator. In: Proceedings of Driving Simulation Conference, Paris, France, pp. 69–78 (2000)

22. Stein, M., Robinski, M.: Simulator sickness in flight simulators of the German armed forces. Aviat. Psychol. Appl. Hum. Factors **2**(1), 11–19 (2012)

23. McCauley, M.E.: Do Army Helicopter Training Simulators Need Motion Bases?. Army Research Institute for the Behavioral and Social Sciences, Fort Rucker (2006)

24. Dużmańska, N., Strojny, P., Strojny, A.: Can simulator sickness be avoided? a review on temporal aspects of simulator sickness. Front. Psychol. **9**, 1–14 (2018)

25. Bos, J.E., MacKinnon, S.N., Patterson, A.: Motion sickness symptoms in a ship motion simulator: effects of inside, outside, and no view. Aviat. Space Environ. Med. **76**(12), 1111–1118 (2005)

26. Bohemia Interactive Simulations Homepage. https://bisimulations.com/products/virtual-battlespace. Accessed 07 Jan 2019
27. Oculus Rift Homepage. https://www.oculus.com/rift/. Accessed 07 Jan 2019
28. Brunner Homepage. https://www.brunner-innovation.swiss/. Accessed 07 Jan 2019
29. Casas, S., Alcaraz, J.M., Olanda, R., Coma, I., Fernández, M.: Towards an extensible simulator of real motion platforms. Simul. Model. Pract. Theory **45**, 50–61 (2014)
30. Norman, G.: Likert scales, levels of measurement and the "laws" of statistics. Adv. Health Sci. Educ. **15**(5), 625–632 (2010)

Communicating Information in Virtual Reality: Objectively Measuring Team Performance

Shannon Moore[1]([✉]), Michael Geuss[1], and Joseph Campanelli[2]

[1] The U. S. Army Research Lab, Aberdeen Proving Ground, Adelphi, MD, USA
shannon.m.moore43.ctr@mail.mil
[2] DCS Corporation, Alexandria, VA, USA

Abstract. It is unknown whether teams communicate more effectively in virtual spaces than when using more traditional technologies due to a lack of objective measures of team performance. Social psychology research shows that teams struggle to share information and suggests the absence of certain social cues in virtual reality (VR) would making sharing information more difficult. We developed a methodology to assess objective performance of communication during an information-gathering task. In this study, using a within-subjects design, 24 pairs of participants examined maps of cities both in VR, using a head-mounted display, and on desktop monitors. For each map, pairs worked together to read the maps, identify patterns amongst variables, and make predictions beyond the given data. In VR, the only cues from one's partner were speech and the ability to point out places on the map with a laser. In contrast, when working on the desktop monitors, partners were also able to view one another. Because groups struggle to share unique information, we anticipated a task providing partners with unique variables and requiring pairs to exchange information in order to solve problems would create a sufficiently challenging situation and be an effective way to measure team performance. Overall, performance in VR did not suffer, as pairs were just as fast and equally accurate at identifying patterns and predicting future events. Pairs performed better at reading the maps when in VR but did have better recall of the information viewed on the desktop monitors.

Keywords: Team performance · Telecommunication ·
Virtual reality for command and control · Collaborative virtual environments

1 Introduction

Virtual reality (VR) technology has advanced considerably in recent years, renewing interest in utilizing virtual reality for multiple applications including military, commercial, and telecommunication. While using virtual reality for teleconferencing boasts many potential positives (e.g., shared visual space) that may aid team problem solving, it is unknown whether teams work together more effectively in virtual spaces than when using non-immersive display technologies, such as a desktop computer. The utility of virtual reality to improve team-performance is inconclusive because previous

© Springer Nature Switzerland AG 2019
J. Y. C. Chen and G. Fragomeni (Eds.): HCII 2019, LNCS 11574, pp. 473–489, 2019.
https://doi.org/10.1007/978-3-030-21607-8_37

studies have largely utilized subjective measures of team performance or satisfaction [1–3]. Specifically, participants have been asked their opinions on different aspects of the virtual experience like presence [e.g., 2] or researchers rely on informal assessments [e.g., 3]. Virtual reality technology allows users to communicate within a common visual space when in different physical locations, which may aid collective problem solving on spatial tasks [2]. However, when evaluating potential benefits of using VR on human performance, subjective reports are often not correlated with objective performance [e.g., 4].

In this paper, we describe an approach to objectively measure team communication and performance. Specifically, individual team members each had access to unique geospatial information and were asked questions pertaining to the geospatial information that either required them to identify information (e.g., how many low-income neighborhoods?), identify relationships across variables accessed by different team members (e.g., please determine the pattern to these recent robberies), or make predictions beyond but based off of available data [5]. Using this methodology, there were no negative impacts on performance when working in VR compared to when teams worked on desktop monitors. When using VR, participants performed just as quickly and were equally skilled at determining patterns to events and predicting future events. However, team members were better able to identify information when in VR. We believe that this measure is useful for assessing team performance in virtual reality environments because the ability to read, understand, and utilize displayed information is essential to many tasks. In addition, we believe the results from using this methodology are generalizable to other tasks where exchanging information is essential to success.

1.1   Objectively Measuring Performance in Virtual Reality

Very little work exists studying team performance in virtual reality [6, 7], and not all of the available work allows for conclusions to be drawn as to whether working in VR affects objectively-measured team performance. Older works have focused on solely describing the system [e.g., 8] or have provided informal observations of others using the system [e.g., 3]. For example, Greenhalgh and Benford [3] provided "a rough and ready summary of what happened" [3, pp. 175] when individuals used the system to hold a laboratory meeting. Such setups do not provide adequate experimental control as there is no comparison to performance using other displays. Additionally, even when participants do interact with others in VR in a true experimental design, the manipulated variable may not be the environment in which teams perform [e.g., 9]. Thus, overall there is a lack of experimental studies that focus on team performance in VR compared to team performance using non-immersive displays.

Another consideration is that many of the outcomes that have been measured in order to examine group performance in VR are not indicative of the effectiveness or accuracy of human teams. Research on teams or groups in virtual reality may choose to focus on participants interacting with virtual humans instead of examining all-human teams [10, 11]. Recently, outcomes examined have included self-reported individual understanding, cognitive load, shared understanding, consensus, response time [7], reactions to the training (e.g., perceived value), learning, and knowledge transfer to a complex task [1]. These measures lean toward subjective measures of performance (e.g., understanding) or task-specific measures that may not apply to other situations (e.g., reactions to training).

Related research on virtual teams also does not point to a clear, generalizable measure of team performance. Specifically, virtual teams are teams working together in different locations on a shared task and using technology to communicate. In their meta-analysis on performance in virtual teams, Ortiz de Guinea et al. [12] defined "performance" in the following way: "Performance represents the effectiveness of the outcome with respect to the specific task or project at hand. Researchers have included measures such as project outcomes (e.g., met requirements, within budget, within schedule) and confidence in the decision reached by the group" [12, pp. 303]. They included studies in their analysis where outcomes were labeled as performance as well as studies with labels related to performance, such as "creativity of the solution" [12]. More specifically, virtual teams research has focused on measures of project quality, decision quality, time to arrive at a decision, and the number of unique ideas generated [6]. Overall, the performance of virtual teams has been studied in varied ways, though there is still a preponderance of subjective measures, such as confidence and creativity, and task-specific concerns, such as budgets and schedules. We propose a method to objectively measure team performance in virtual reality that does not require task-specific knowledge. Instead, it only requires participants to have the ability to read information and communicate it to their team member, which are skills that underlie multiple tasks.

1.2 Teams in Immersive Virtual Environments

Recent work on team performance suggests that performance in immersive virtual environments may be no worse than in the real world. Specifically, some qualities of real life social interactions, such as interpersonal distance and eye gaze norms, can translate into the environment [13]. Additionally, replicating a real life finding, participants were more persuaded by and had greater liking for avatars (i.e., digital representations of human bodies) that mimicked their head movements, even knowing the avatar was controlled by a computer [9]. Furthermore, team members also perceive themselves as performing better in immersive virtual environments, indicating they felt they made fewer mistakes and were more effective [2]. And there is some objective support for this feeling: related work has tested memory in ecological settings and found that individuals are better able to remember items when items are naturally presented [14]. This finding could suggest that 3D environments would be more effective than working with 2D displays on a desktop monitor. Some basic social functions can be implemented in VR, making it a more realistic environment for teamwork than relying on desktop computers or email.

However, Van der Land et al.'s [7] study further illustrates the complexity of team performance in virtual reality. Teams performed better in terms of shared understanding and group decision making when working with static 3D environments (e.g., a 3D scene viewed on a desktop monitor that could be rotated) compared to when participants could navigate the 3D room from a first-person perspective. They suggest that, in addition to coordinating with teammates, working in this 3D scenario may have been overwhelming for participants. These findings suggest that social norms and theories are applicable to virtual reality and that the more ecological presentation of information may improve performance. However, it is less clear how teams would function in virtual reality when unable to see one another. It may be possible that avatars are unnecessary and teams are able to function equally well without them, but the findings are not conclusive.

1.3   Barriers to Sharing Information in Virtual Reality

Research suggests that working in virtual reality would cause difficulties for teams, as participants would be working in an environment that lacks cues, norms, and regulatory feedback. It is well established that sharing information in groups can be difficult [e.g., 15]. Research shows that people struggle to share unique information when working in groups [16], and of concern to virtual teams, this may be especially true when we introduce technology to the situation [17, 18]. Stasser and colleagues have studied hidden profiles, where information is distributed to group members and some of that information is unique to only one individual. Groups are tasked with making a decision, and to make the best decision, that unique information must be shared. Unfortunately, groups are likely to focus on information they have in common instead [15]. Specifically, one study found that while groups discussed 46% of the information that the group shared, they discussed only 18% of the information that was distributed to a single person [16]. "Group decisions and postgroup preferences reflected the initial preferences of group members even when the exchange of unshared information should have resulted in substantial shifts of opinion" [15, pp. 1476]. While sharing unique information can be vital to team success, groups may also struggle to establish mutual knowledge. The failure to establish mutual knowledge has been found to result in poorer decision quality and lower productivity, as well as interpersonal problems or difficulties [19]. Being strangers [20] and experiencing relationship conflict [21] appear to be two specific barriers to sharing information.

Another barrier to sharing information effectively may be the technology used to communicate. Hightower and Sayeed [17, 18] found that when participants used computers to communicate with one another, their discussions were less effective at exchanging information versus when groups were face-to-face. Thus, even when the performance of a group would benefit from doing so, sharing information doesn't appear to be easy for teams, for a variety of reasons. The identification and communication of unique information is an underlying factor in achieving success in many team activities. Therefore, in this study, we created a task that required teams to identify unique information and share it with their partner to answer questions about the presented information, making it a task with results that are applicable to a wide range of situations. However, additional research shows that teams working together in VR are likely to face many barriers in their attempts to work together successfully.

It appears the absence of certain cues in virtual reality makes sharing information even more difficult. This may be why Ortiz de Guinea et al.'s [12] meta-analysis overall concluded that virtualness, or communication environments that do not relay normal social information, was related to poorer team performance. Cramton [19] acknowledges that it can be challenging for people in dispersed locations to have a clear understanding of the context their colleagues are operating within (e.g., features of their equipment, commuting time, etc.). This could also be true when teams are working with HMD's, where certain information, or cues, involving one's teammates are absent.

The literature suggests there would be an absence of social norms in VR. Kiesler et al. [22], when examining the rising popularity of computers, pointed out that it can take decades for a new type of media to develop a code of etiquette. As a new method of communication, there may be both a lack of social context and few existing norms [22]. With the introduction of new ways to interact with others, people must then learn how to act toward one another. Thus, in addition to completing an assigned task and interaction in VR, people also have to learn how to behave toward one another in a virtual environment.

Using HMD's, we also expected a lack of regulating feedback in VR. When we perceive social cues, such cues can cause us to make a cognitive interpretation and experience a related emotion, as we adapt our reactions in response [23]. "In traditional forms of communication, head nods, smiles, eye contact, distance, tone of voice, and other nonverbal behavior give speakers and listeners information they can use to regulate, modify, and control exchanges" [22, pp. 1125]. However, in this case, using the HMD's provided our participants with only tone of voice, thus eliminating many other types of nonverbal cues that can aid interactions. The results of Kiesler et al.'s [22] study found that a new mode of communication (e.g., computers) took longer and involved less communication, though the groups were equally task oriented. A possible explanation that was proposed was the absence of informational feedback. Because people did not know if others understood or agreed with them, they spent more time and effort attempting to be understood [22].

Relatedly, the loss of social cues should have consequences for the quality of interactions. It has been suggested that nonverbal cues are more honest and reliable because they tend to be unconsciously emitted [24]. Thus, they may be more useful than behaviors that are more closely monitored. Possessing only weak information can alter the perceivers' behavior. "When social context cues are weak, people's feelings of anonymity tend to produce relatively self-centered and unregulated behavior" [23, pp. 1495]. Indeed, a feeling of social anonymity can encourage people to act more assertively, which is illustrated in work on cyberbullying [25]. Sproull and Kiesler [23] also found that using the new type of communication tool (i.e., email) was associated with people overestimating their own contribution to the conversations. Thus, when working in VR, a lack of social cues could create a situation that fosters a focus on oneself that would be detrimental to effective teamwork.

While the various considerations listed above may be the reason a meta-analysis [12] found that virtualness was negatively related to team performance, this is not conclusive. Sharing information is both important and challenging. As we reviewed, in a scenario where teammates work together in VR using HMD's, there are qualities of such a situation that the literature suggest would make it even more difficult to exchange information. It may not be as easy to understand a teammate's perspective, the social environment lacks established norms and protocols, while missing cues make the interactions more challenging and eliminate modes of regulatory feedback. However, there are also some reasons to expect that teams can work together in VR effectively.

1.4   The Present Study

In this study, our goal was to assess team performance objectively by measuring teams' ability to identify, understand, and utilize technology. Building upon the established importance, and difficulty, of teams exchanging information, we created a task that required teammates to share information with one another in order to reach the correct answer. In this study, using a within-subjects design, 24 pairs of participants examined maps of cities both in VR, using a head-mounted display (HMD), and on desktop monitors. While they viewed a map of the same city and focal events (i.e., robberies), each participant had access to unique sociocultural information, such as political and religious information, that their partner did not. For each map, pairs answered three types of questions: (1) Teams were asked to read the map and identify information. In this case, only one partner had access to the relevant variable; (2) Pairs were asked to examine a common focal variable (i.e., attacks in the city) and determine the pattern to these events. Here, each partner had access to one unique, relevant variable. Partners had to share their information to reach the correct answer; and, (3) Teams again had to determine the pattern to a focal event. However, they then had to predict where the next event would occur based on that pattern. Probing participants' knowledge of presented information using these 3 levels (identification, relation, and prediction) was adapted from Galesic and Garcia-Retamero's [5] evaluation criteria of graph literacy, or ability to read information representations. In VR, the only cues from one's partner were speech and the ability to point out places on the map with a laser. In contrast, when working on the desktop monitors, partners were also able to view one another and use a familiar device. Because groups struggle to share information, we anticipated a task providing partners with unique variables and requiring pairs to exchange information in order to solve problems would create a sufficiently challenging situation and be an effective way to measure team performance. We used the objective measures of decision quality, response time, and memory for information viewed to assess team performance. It was predicted that, because of the missing cues, context, and norms in VR, pairs would answer fewer questions correctly and take more time when working in VR. However, it was predicted that information viewed in VR would be better recalled due to the more natural presentation of information [14].

2   Method

2.1   Participants

A power analysis was conducted for an F test using G*Power. Conducted for a repeated measures, within-between interaction ANOVA, we assumed a small medium effect ($f = .25$). Using the questions posed when reading the maps as the outcome example (24 measurements) and with the power set to .80, we determined that we would need 24 pairs to participate in this study.

We recruited participants from the Aberdeen Proving Ground (APG) civilian workforce, the Army Research Lab participant pool, and the Army Research Lab dispatch. APG employees participated during their normal duty hours and did not receive any compensation other than their normal pay. Participants were required to be

18 years of age or older, have normal or corrected to normal vision, able to fuse stereo images, and have normal color vision. Forty-eight individuals participated in this study (i.e., 24 pairs). Participants consisted of 37 males and 11 females. Participants ranged in age from 18 to 50 ($m = 27.15$, $sd = 7.49$).

2.2 Design

A 2 Display Condition (Head-Mounted Display, Desktop Monitor) by 2 Display Order (HMD first, Desktop Monitor first) $\times$ 3 Type of Question (Identification, Relation, Prediction) design was implemented with all factors except Display Order being manipulated within-subjects. Pairs were semi-randomly assigned to either the HMD first or Desktop Monitors first order so that after 24 pairs, half of the pairs were intended one or the other order. Presentation of the geo-spatial maps and associated information was designed so that the same pair did not see the same information in the HMD as they did in the Desktop Monitor.

2.3 Instrumentation and Facilities

The experiment took place in the Systems Assessment and Usability Laboratory (SAUL) in building 459, APG [26]. When participants were working in Virtual Reality, they viewed virtual stimuli through an HTC Vive HMD. The resolution within the HTC Vive is 2160×1200 with a 90 Hz refresh rate and $110°$ field of view. Participants were seated in a desk chair and viewed themselves in front of a desk with the map on top. The questions posed to them were on the wall in front of them as were the types of information they could choose to view. Using the hand control, they were able to toggle different variables on and off. When looking at the computer monitors, participants sat facing one another at a table, each with a desktop computer monitor in front of him or her. A participant's screen was not visible to his or her partner. Each presentation and organization of information on the maps and legend were designed to fit each display.

Four cities were chosen (Hamburg, Germany; Salt Lake City, USA; Cape Town, South Africa; Tokyo, Japan) to use for the maps in our task. We strove to include cities that had landmarks (e.g., bodies of water, bridges) to introduce variety and that participants could point to throughout their task. Teams viewed two maps in VR and the other two maps on the desktop monitors. The maps viewed on VR differed among teams. Team members always had access to four shared variables, while unique information varied from three to seven variables per partner.

2.4 Procedure

Participants agreeing to participate in the study were placed into pairs. After arriving at the SAUL, all participants completed informed consent and then completed the stereo images and color vision tests. These tests ensured that participants could discriminate colors and fuse stereo images. Both abilities were needed in order to properly view stimuli in Virtual Reality. They were also asked if they were hearing impaired, as this could hinder their ability to complete the task. Participants were then placed on opposite sides of the room to complete their surveys in order to ensure confidentiality.

Participant pairs were required to answer a set of six questions for each of the four maps. Participants had access to the same map and the same data on incidents: recent locations of bombings, attacks, robberies, and assumed gang headquarters. This was the common information both participants shared. However, the additional information available to each partner differed. See Image 1. For example, for one map, Person 1 also had the option to view economic information, gang territories, locations of school "A", locations of school "B", and marked traffic circles. In contrast, Person 2 had the option of viewing dock locations, grocery and retail stores, population data, the locations of religions "A" and "B", and train stops. Two questions per map asked the participants to identify information that was presented on one or the other partner's map. Two questions per map asked the participants to cross reference information presented on each partner's map. Two questions asked participants to cross reference information presented on each partner's map and then, as a pair, make a prediction beyond the information presented. This was repeated for three different maps, for a total of four maps, with six questions per map. Participants using the computer monitors were able to see the movement of their partner's mouse, enabling them to point to areas about which they referred. They were also able to view their partner, and thus see their

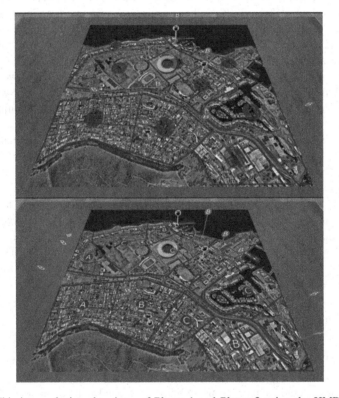

Image 1. This image depicts the views of Player 1 and Player 2 using the HMD. The green markings represent bombings in the city (a shared variable), while blue and pink markings indicate players' unique sociocultural variables.

posture, facial expressions, etc. Those in VR were able to see their partner's controller which was held in his/her hand. Participants' controllers served as a pointer. When they pressed the button on the controller, a laser appeared that they could use to point to specific areas on the map. While in VR, participants were only able to see their partners' laser pointer, and they could hear their voice. No other cues (e.g., an avatar) were visible. Participants completed two maps in VR and two maps on the computer monitors while in the same room, the order of which was counterbalanced. They then completed the memory task. Participants' performance was assessed through their ability to accurately answer the questions and the amount of time required to submit a response. Following each map task in VR, participants were asked to rate their motion sickness. At the end of the experiment, participants indicated their prior experience in VR and were debriefed. The average length of the experiment was between 90 and 120 min (Image 2).

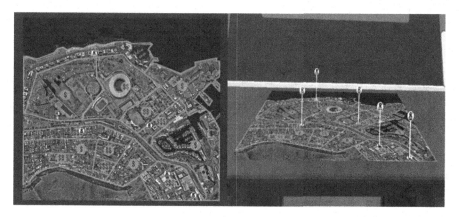

Image 2. This image depicts the desktop monitor display (left) compared to the display visible using the HMD.

2.5   Measures

Prescreening. The Random Dot-E test [27] was used to determine whether participants could fuse stereo images. The test required participants to identify a letter in a random-dot stereogram. The letter was only perceptible if participants were able to fuse stereo images. The Color Dx test [28] was used to determine if participants had normal color vision. The test required participants to identify shapes that were drawn in one color and surrounded by other colors. If participants could accurately identify the shapes, it indicated that they had normal color vision. Participants were excluded if they failed either the test of stereo vision or test of normal color vision as these abilities were necessary to properly view stimuli in the HMD condition. We also asked participants to self-report if they were hearing impaired as this could have hindered their ability to successfully complete the task.

Outcome Variables

Decision Accuracy. Participant pairs were required to, as a pair, answer a set of six questions for each of the four maps. Two questions per map asked the participants to identify information that was presented on one or the other partner's map. Two questions per map asked the participants to cross reference information presented on each partner's map. Two questions asked participants to cross reference information presented on each partner's map and then, as a pair, make a prediction beyond the information that was presented. The questions were designed so that there was only one correct answer per question.

Response Time. During the study, participants received questions to read before they were able to view their maps. We measured the length of time between participants' indication that they had read each question and the pair's unanimous decision as to the answer of said question. Doing so allowed us to determine if one condition led to faster decision making.

Memory. Participants' memory of the information they saw on the maps during the experiment was also assessed. During the experiment, participants viewed maps of urban areas. To assess their memory of the information presented on their maps, participants were shown the map with information marked that matched what they had seen previously and another map with incorrect information which they had not seen previously. The order of presentation for incorrect and correct maps was counterbalanced. Participants were asked to indicate whether the map they viewed was identical to the map they used during the experiment. For each map, participants received 12 such questions assessing memory. Across all four maps, there were a total of 48 questions assessing memory. As each question had only one correct answer (yes/no), participants' memory scores were able to range from 0–48.

Potential Covariates

Virtual Reality Variables. Participants' level of experience playing videogames and being in virtual reality was also assessed. Specifically, participants were asked to self-report what type of games they normally played and for how long. It was possible that those with more experience would perform better on the tasks.

Participants periodically rated their level of simulator sickness using the Fast Motion Sickness Scale (FMS) [29]. The FMS required participants to rate experienced motion sickness on a scale 0 (no sickness at all) – 20 (frank sickness) verbally. Prior to beginning the task in VR, participants were asked to verbally rate their initial motion sickness. They rated this again verbally after each of the map tasks. The experimenter said "Please rate your existing feelings of motion sickness on a scale of 0 (no sickness at all) – 20 (frank sickness)." Participants were given the chance to take a break after each map. In addition to potential discomfort, it was possible that the experience of simulator sickness would negatively affect participants' performance.

3   Results

3.1   Response Time

Response time was defined as the time between participants indicated having read the question and the time that they indicated they had an answer. We first ran a 2 Display Condition (Virtual Reality, Desktop Monitor) × 2 Display Order (VR first, Desktop first) × 3 Type of Question (Identify, Relate, Predict) repeated measures ANOVA to determine whether response time differed when in VR versus when working on desktop monitors. Display condition and type of question were within-subjects variables while display order was a between-subjects factor. There was no main effect of display condition, $F(1, 21) = 1.65$, $p = .213$. Teams were just as quick to answer questions in the VR condition ($m = 1258.98$ s, $sd = 895.55$ s) as they were in the desktop condition ($m = 1104.78$ s, $sd = 514.48$ s). There was a main effect of Type of Question, $F(2, 20) = 40.30$, $p < .001$, such that as questions increased in complexity from identifying information ($m = 292.03$, $sd = 91.29$) to determining patterns to how variables related ($m = 566.63$, $sd = 254.31$) to predicting future events ($m = 775.54$, $sd = 369.01$), pairs took longer to answer. Lastly, there was no significant interaction between Display Condition and Type of Question, $F(2, 20) = 1.28$, $p = .290$.

3.2   Accuracy

Accuracy was examined for three types of questions: identifying information individually, determining how variables related to events, and by predicting future events based on existing patterns.

Accuracy for Identifying Information. We first ran a 2 Display Condition (Virtual Reality, Desktop Monitor) × 2 Display Order (VR first, Desktop first) × 4 Question repeated measures ANCOVA, with experience in VR as the covariate, to determine if pairs were more or less accurate at identifying information in VR compared to on the desktop monitors. Condition and questions were within-subjects variables, while order was between-subjects. There was a main effect of display condition, such that pairs were slightly better at identifying information in virtual reality than on the desktop monitors, $F(1, 20) = 3.86$, $p = .063$. Identification questions required participants to count the number of items present or to estimate the percentage of the map covered by a group/landmark. Teams were more likely to report answers further away from the correct value when on the desktop monitors ($m = 1.97$, $se = .38$) compared to when in VR ($m = 1.20$, $se = .22$). There was not a significant interaction between display condition and experience in VR, $F(1, 20) = 1.43$, $p = .246$. See Fig. 3.

Accuracy for Relating Information. We repeated this test to compare accuracy between the two display conditions on questions that required pairs to determine how variables related to one another. Specifically, participants were required to focus on a specified shared variable, and determine the other variables that predicted that event, based on which variables spatially overlapped. Since participants could select from several different variables (some that were predictive of the outcome and some that were not), we computed a measure of participants sensitivity (d'). D' allows us to

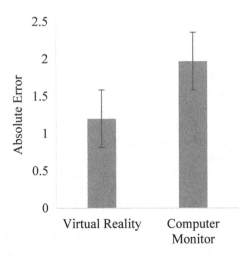

Fig. 3. Absolute error is plotted for each display condition. Lower values indicate answers closer to the correct value. Participants in the VR condition performed significantly better than those in the computer monitor condition.

analyze participants' ability to correctly identify important variables while correctly ignoring variables that were not predictive of the outcome. D' was calculated using the following formula [30]:

$$d' = \ln\{[H (1 - FA)]/[(1 - H)FA]\}$$

D' is interpreted such that higher values indicate greater sensitivity, or participants' ability to correctly identify important variables and ignore distractor variables. There was no main effect of display condition, $F(1, 20) = 1.98$, p = .175. Pairs were equally skilled at determining the patterns to events when working in VR (m = 10.07, se = .685) as they were when working on desktop monitors (m = 11.12, se = .48). There was not a significant interaction between display condition and experience in VR, $F(1, 20) = .000$, p = .994. See Fig. 4.

Accuracy for Predicting Events. Finally, we examined accuracy for the questions pairs answered that involved predicting future events. Teams again had to determine the variables that spatially overlapped with a focal event, and then predict where a future event would occur based on that pattern. There was no main effect of display condition for this type of question, $F(1, 20) = .007$, $p = .936$. Pairs were just as accurate in VR ($m = .74$, $se = .06$) as they were using the desktop monitors ($m = .72$, $se = .06$). There was not a significant interaction between display condition and experience in VR, $F(1, 20) = .374$, $p = .548$. See Fig. 5.

Memory of Information. Memory for information viewed was defined as whether participants could identify the information they had viewed previously when presented with two maps that were marked (correctly and incorrectly) with one of their socio-cultural variables. Therefore, if participants purely guessed, we would expect them to

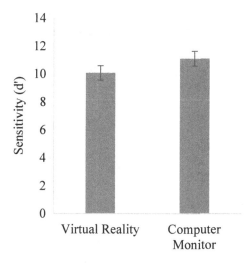

Fig. 4. Sensitivity scores are plotted for each display condition. Higher values indicate that participants were better able to select relevant variables while ignoring irrelevant information. There was no main effect of display condition on participants' ability to relate information.

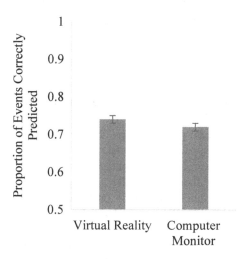

Fig. 5. The proportion of events that were correctly predicted is plotted for each display condition. Participants' ability to predict beyond the data did not differ between conditions.

answer 50% of the questions correctly. We ran a paired samples t-test that compared memory for information viewed in VR to memory for information viewed on the desktop monitors. This difference was significant, $t(43) = -2.68$, $p = .010$. Specifically, participants' were able to remember more information that had been presented on the desktop monitors (69%) than information that had been viewed in VR (63%). It is also important to note that the amount of information remembered from each display condition was significantly greater than chance (p's < .001). This suggests that participants were able to recall the information they had viewed, even though they were not told they needed to do so. See Fig. 6.

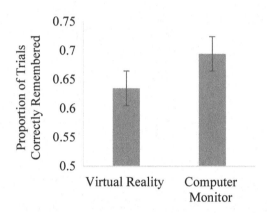

Fig. 6. The proportion of trials correctly remembered is plotted against display condition. In both conditions, participants were able to remember a significant proportion of the maps. In addition, participants remembered more of the information in the computer monitor condition than the virtual reality condition.

4 Discussion

The goal of the current study was to investigate whether team performance was influenced by the display media through which team members communicated. Despite the predicted lack of social context in virtual environments and findings that virtualness is associated with poorer team performance [12], our findings suggest that team performance did not suffer when pairs used virtual reality to communicate. Team members performed equally well when relating information across variables and when predicting beyond the data in VR as they did on the desktop monitor. Team members also answered questions just as quickly in VR as on the desktop monitor. This is encouraging, as team performance in VR remained strong despite the fact that the environment was expected to lack norms, regulatory feedback [e.g., 22], and social cues [e.g., 23], as well as basic familiarity with the device. This is important as it provides evidence that VR could be an effective tool for teams to communicate and to use so that they can train or work together regardless of their physical distance.

Interestingly, team members were better able to identify information in VR. This was the simplest measure of accuracy, where only one participant had access to the variable of interest and was required to read that information correctly and communicate it to his or her partner. Because this measure of accuracy did not involve higher level thinking (i.e., such as deducing a pattern between two variables) and did not require involved collaboration with one's partner, it could suggest that information is more easily identified when reading from a 3D graph in VR. This may be because the more natural display of information in 3D [e.g., 14] and participants' perception of greater effectiveness [e.g., 2] lead to better performance in virtual reality. It is worth noting that this is the only type of question that did not require team interaction to reach an answer. So while this provides evidence that VR may aid basic information identification, it may not improve team performance. Future research should independently investigate the influence of using VR on ability to read information and communicate information. In addition, future work could integrate more social cues in the virtual environment using this scenario and assess whether performance in VR then improves beyond that seen using the desktop monitors. This would help further deduce whether the method of display or the lack of social context are the cause of these differences.

We had also anticipated that representing sociocultural information in 3D would be associated with a better ability to remember information viewed in VR. Previous work has shown that participants are better able to remember the location of objects in a room when the object locations are viewed through a head-mounted VR headset [31]. Pausch and Proffitt [31] argued that better memory of objects was the result of better encoding from self-movement associated with scanning the room. Our results did not replicate their findings, as participants remembered more information in the desktop condition than the VR condition. This suggests that field of view may interact with self-motion to influence memory of objects.

In addition, we adapted a measure of graph literacy [5] to test team members' ability to collectively measure ability to identify information, communicate it to their teammate, and solve problems together. We built this paradigm around the established finding that it is challenging for groups to share information with one another, be it unique information [16] or even mutual knowledge [19]. This difficulty sharing information often comes at the price of decision quality [15, 19]. Furthermore, there is reason to believe that the introduction of technology to such a situation makes teams even less effective at exchanging information [17, 18]. These skills—reading comprehension, communication skills, and shared problem solving ability—are ones that would be useful for teams on a variety of tasks and in a variety of situations. We argue that this task and methodology are useful measures of team performance that could be used to evaluate multiple different communication technologies.

References

1. Bertram, J., Moskaliuk, J., Cress, U.: Virtual training: making reality work? Comput. Hum. Behav. **43**, 284–292 (2015)
2. Bosch-Sijtsema, P.M., Haapamäki, J.: Perceived enablers of 3D virtual environments for virtual team learning and innovation. Comput. Hum. Behav. **37**, 395–401 (2014)
3. Greenhalgh, C., Benford, S.: Virtual reality tele-conferencing: implementation and experience. In: Marmolin, H., Sundblad, Y., Schmidt, K. (eds.) ECSCW 1995, pp. 165–180. Springer, Dordrecht (1995). https://doi.org/10.1007/978-94-011-0349-7_11
4. Smallman, H.S., John, M.S.: Naïve realism: misplaced faith in realistic displays. Ergon. Des. **13**(3), 6–13 (2005)
5. Galesic, M., Garcia-Retamero, R.: Graph literacy: a cross-cultural comparison. Med. Decis. Making **31**(3), 444–457 (2011)

6. Gilson, L.L., Maynard, M.T., Jones Young, N.C., Vartiainen, M., Hakonen, M.: Virtual teams research: 10 years, 10 themes, and 10 opportunities. J. Manage. **41**(5), 1313–1337 (2015)

7. Van der Land, S., Schouten, A.P., Feldberg, F., van den Hooff, B., Huysman, M.: Lost in space? cognitive fit and cognitive load in 3D virtual environments. Comput. Hum. Behav. **29**, 1054–1064 (2013)

8. Rickel, J., Johnson, W.L.: Virtual humans for team training in virtual reality. In: Proceedings of the Ninth International Conference on Artificial Intelligence in Education, vol. 578, p. 585 (1999)

9. Bailenson, J.N., Yee, N.: A longitudinal study of task performance, head movements, subjective report, simulator sickness, and transformed social interaction in collaborative virtual environments. Presence Teleoperators Virtual Environ. **15**(6), 699–716 (2006)

10. Van Loon, A., Bailenson, J., Zaki, J., Bostick, J., Willer, R.: Virtual reality perspective-taking increases cognitive empathy for specific others. PLoS ONE **13**(8), e0202442 (2018)

11. Kim, K., Maloney, D., Bruder, G., Bailenson, J.N., Welch, G.F.: The effects of virtual human's spatial and behavioral coherence with physical objects on social presence in AR. Comput. Animation Virtual Worlds **28**(3–4), e1771 (2017)

12. Ortiz de Guinea, A., Webster, J., Staples, D.S.: A meta-analysis of the consequences of virtualness on team functioning. Inform. Manage. **49**, 301–308 (2012)

13. Yee, N., Bailenson, J.N., Urbanek, M., Chang, F., Merget, D.: The unbearable likeness of being digital: the persistence of nonverbal social norms in online virtual environments. Cyber Psychol. Behav. **10**(1), 115–121 (2007)

14. Robinson, A., Triesch, J.: Task-specific modulation of memory for object features in natural scenes. Adv. Cogn. Psychol. **4**, 1 (2008)

15. Stasser, G., Titus, W.: Pooling of unshared information in group decision making: biased information sampling during discussion. J. Pers. Soc. Psychol. **48**(6), 1467–1478 (1985)

16. Stasser, G., Taylor, L.A., Hanna, C.: Information sampling in structured and unstructured discussions of three- and six-person groups. J. Pers. Soc. Psychol. **57**, 57–67 (1989)

17. Hightower, R., Sayeed, L.: The impact of computer-mediated communication systems on biased group discussion. Comput. Organ. Behav. **11**(1), 33–44 (1995)

18. Hightower, R., Sayeed, L.: Effects of communication mode and prediscussion information distribution characteristics on information exchange in groups. Inform. Syst. Res. **7**(4), 451–465 (1996)

19. Cramton, C.D.: The mutual knowledge problem and its consequences for dispersed collaboration. Organ. Sci. **12**(3), 346–371 (2001)

20. Gruenfeld, D.H., Mannix, E.A., Williams, K.Y., Neale, M.A.: Group composition and decision making: how member familiarity and information distribution affect process and performance. Organ. Behav. Hum. Decis. Process. **67**(1), 1–15 (1996)

21. De Wit, F.R., Greer, L.L., Jehn, K.A.: The paradox of intragroup conflict: a meta-analysis. J. Appl. Psychol. **97**(2), 360–390 (2012)

22. Kiesler, S., Siegel, J., McGuire, T.W.: Social psychological aspects of computer-mediated communication. Am. Psychol. **39**(10), 1123 (1984)

23. Sproull, L., Kiesler, S.: Reducing social context cues: electronic mail in organizational communication. Manage. Sci. **32**(11), 1492–1512 (1986)

24. Pentland, A., Heibeck, T.: Honest Signals: How They Shape our World. MIT Press, Cambridge (2010)

25. Lowry, P.B., Zhang, J., Wang, C., Siponen, M.: Why do adults engage in cyberbullying on social media? an integration of online disinhibition and deindividuation effects with the social structure and social learning model. Inform. Syst. Res. **27**(4), 962–986 (2016)

26. Geuss, M.N., Campanelli, J.A.: User guide: How to use and operate virtual reality equipment in the systems assessment and usability laboratory (SAUL) for conducting demonstrations. Army Research Lab-Technical Note-0839 (2017)
27. Simons, K.: A comparison of the Frisby, Random-Dot E, TNO, and Randot circles stereotests in screening and office use. Arch. Ophthalmol. **99**(3), 446–452 (1981)
28. Clark, J.H.: The Ishihara test for color blindness. Am. J. Physiol. Optics **5**, 269–276 (1924)
29. Keshavarz, B., Hecht, H.: Validating an efficient method to quantify motion sickness. Hum. Factors **53**(4), 415–426 (2011)
30. Snodgrass, J.G., Corwin, J.: Pragmatics of measuring recognition memory: applications to dementia and amnesia. J. Exp. Psychol. Gen. **117**, 34–50 (1988)
31. Pausch, R., Proffitt, D., Williams, G.: Quantifying immersion in virtual reality. In: Proceedings of the 24th Annual Conference on Computer Graphics and Interactive Techniques, pp. 13–18. ACM Press/Addison-Wesley Publishing Co. (1997)

Quality of Experience Comparison Between Binocular and Monocular Augmented Reality Display Under Various Occlusion Conditions for Manipulation Tasks with Virtual Instructions

Ming Qian[✉], John Nicholson, and Erin Wang

Lenovo Research, 7001 Development Dr, Morrisville, USA
{mqian,jnichol,ewang}@lenovo.com

Abstract. Using optical head-mounted display (HMD) devices, users can see both real world and Augmented Reality (AR) content simultaneously. AR content can be displayed to both eyes (binocular) or in one eye (monocular).

For a binocular display, users benefit from (a) using both eyes to focus on the same content, and (b) having depth perception. However, the vergence-accommodation conflict can negatively impact the time and accuracy of fusing the views. For a monocular display, users benefit from (a) easy and quick focal depth switches between the virtual content and the physical world, and (b) having a larger virtual information overlay in one eye while also seeing the real-world in the other eye.

In this study, users performed manual tasks by following real-time, step-by-step instructions for 2D tasks (drawing cartoon characters) and 3D tasks (assembling plastic bricks). The instructions were presented on an AR HMD through various occlusion conditions, after which we compared the users' Quality of Experience (QoE) feedback.

Our investigation found that users commonly chose to separate the AR content display from the physical working area, placing them adjacent in the field of view and shifting their attention between them. The overwhelming majority of users preferred the binocular display. For a monocular display, users need to balance the benefits of depth perception (for 3D tasks) and the annoyance of binocular rivalry. While most users can tolerate binocular rivalry, a significant subset have a low tolerance for binocular rivalry and prefer to mask or close the eye without the virtual display.

Keywords: Augmented Reality (AR) · Binocular · Monocular ·
Quality of Experience (QoE) · Head-mounted device (HMD) · Focal depth ·
Virtual content · Virtual instruction overlay · Attention switch ·
Binocular rivalry · Stereoscopic display · Binocular interaction ·
Binocular fusion

© Springer Nature Switzerland AG 2019
J. Y. C. Chen and G. Fragomeni (Eds.): HCII 2019, LNCS 11574, pp. 490–499, 2019.
https://doi.org/10.1007/978-3-030-21607-8_38

1   Introduction

1.1   AR Content Display

Augmented Reality (AR) is a technology used to project artificial visual content into the real world. Using an optical head-mounted display (HMD), users can see both the real world and the superimposed AR content simultaneously without turning their head or moving their eyes to a different display. AR content can be displayed to both eyes (binocular) or one eye (monocular, left or right eye).

1.2   Binocular Display

When a binocular display is used, users benefit from (a) being able to use both eyes to focus on the same content, avoiding binocular rivalry [1, 2] or eye dominance concerns [3]. Binocular rivalry is a phenomenon of visual perception in which perception alternates between different images presented to each eye. Eye dominance is the tendency to prefer visual input from one eye over the other. Another user benefit of binocular displays is (b) the possibility of depth perception.

On the other hand, the vergence-accommodation conflict [4], a well-known problem for head-mounted stereoscopic displays that force the user's brain to unnaturally adapt to conflicting depth cues, increases the fusion time of views while simultaneously reducing fusion accuracy.

1.3   Monocular Display

Previous research indicates that switching focal depth between virtual content and the physical world is easier and faster when monocular displays are used [5]. Additionally, with a monocular view it is possible to have a larger virtual information overlay in one eye while also not occluding or blocking the view of real-world surfaces and objects in the other eye.

1.4   Study Objectives

In this study, we focus on the quality of experience (QoE) of users performing manual tasks by following real-time, step-by-step instructions for 2D tasks such as drawing cartoon characters and 3D tasks. In these tasks, the instructions are presented in an AR HMD through various occlusion conditions (binocular, monocular while masking the other eye, and monocular without masking the other eye). For these tasks, the participants need to switch their attention between the virtual instruction overlay (the displayed instructions) and the real-world 2D surface or 3D object (on which they perform the drawing and assembly tasks). We then compare the QoE described by users for various occlusion conditions.

2   Methodology

2.1   Participants

Testing sessions are conducted in the Lenovo Research Lab located in RTP, North Carolina, USA. Twelve adults between 23–61 years of age, with normal or corrected-to-normal vision, participated in this study.

2.2   Tasks

Participants performed a 2D task of drawing cartoon characters (Mickey Mouse or Goofy) on a piece of paper by following real-time, step-by-step instructions [7, 8]. The participants also performed a 3D task of assembling LEGO bricks [9]. In both tasks, the instructions are presented in an AR HMD (ODG R-7 Smartglasses) through various occlusion conditions (binocular, monocular while masking the other eye, and monocular without marking the other eye) (Figs. 1 and 2).

Fig. 1. 2D task – drawing cartoon characters

Fig. 2. 3D task – assemble a kit of plastic building brick pieces

2.3   Procedures

The procedure begins with the user preference for configuration of the size and placement of the virtual AR content in the HMD display. The ODG R-7 Smartglasses have a display resolution of 1280 × 720 pixels per eye, and the user was allowed to choose the AR content size between the native full-screen resolution (1280 × 720 pixels), large (960 × 540 pixels), medium (640 × 360 pixels) and small (320 × 180 pixels). For sizes other than full-screen, they were further allowed to choose the placement of the AR content in the HMD display (upper-left, upper-middle, upper-right, center-left, center-middle, center-right, lower-left, lower-middle, or lower-right). In addition, for the monocular display the user chose which eye they preferred to see the display (left or right). While the participant was selecting their preferences, they were watching a portion of YouTube instruction videos for the tasks.

The participant was then instructed to perform the 2D drawing task, following the drawing instructions. Participants were instructed to draw Mickey Mouse using one display format (monocular or binocular) and then to draw Goofy using the other display format. The order of display formats was randomly selected for every participant. For the monocular display, participants started with both eyes open, and half-way through the task, participants were asked to mask the eye without a display by wearing an eye patch [10], shown in Fig. 3.

Fig. 3. Eye mask used in experiment

For the 3D assembly task, participants randomly started with one display format (monocular or binocular) and switched to the other display format in the middle of the assembly. Again, for the monocular display, participants started with both eyes open, and after enough assembly steps were executed, participants were asked to mask the eye without a display.

The instruction video for the 3D task ran at a fast pace even after lowering the play speed down to 25% of the normal speed. When a participant's physical assembly fell behind the instructions, he or she was allowed to request a pause or rewind of the instructional video.

After the tasks were completed, the participants were asked to answer the following QoE questions:

1. Do you prefer binocular or monocular AR display in terms of the experience of performing the tasks? Why?
2. For monocular AR display, do you prefer to have the other eye masked or unmasked? Why?

3   Results and Discussion

3.1   Results

Table 1 lists the QoE (user preference) responses for binocular vs. monocular views. Table 2 lists the QoE (user preference) responses for using the mask for the monocular view.

Table 1. Participants' QoE responses for binocular vs. monocular view.

Subject No. (Gender, Age)	2D Drawing Task		3D Assembly Task	
	Binocular	Monocular	Binocular	Monocular
1 (Male, 23)	Preferred		Preferred	
2 (Male, 24)	Preferred		Preferred	
3 (Male, 49)	Preferred		Preferred	
4 (Female, 24)	Preferred		Preferred	
5 (Male, 39)	Preferred		Preferred	
6 (Female, 61)	Preferred		Preferred	
7 (Male 42)	Preferred		Preferred	
8 (Male, 48)	Preferred		Preferred	
9 (Male, 23)		Preferred	Preferred	
10 (Female, 35)	Preferred		Preferred	
11 (Male, 48)	Preferred		Preferred	
12 (Male, 31)		Preferred	Preferred	
Summary	10 (83%)	2 (17%)	12 (100%)	0 (0%)

Table 2. Participants' QoE responses for with or without mask in the monocular view.

Subject No. (Gender, Age)	2D Drawing task		3D Assembly Task	
	W/out Mask	With Mask	W/out Mask	With Mask
1 (Male, 23)		Preferred	Preferred	
2 (Male, 24)		Preferred	Preferred	
3 (Male, 49)	Preferred		Preferred	
4 (Female, 24)	No preference	No preference	No preference	No preference
5 (Male, 39)	Preferred		Preferred	
6 (Female, 61)		Preferred	Preferred	
7 (Male 42)		Preferred		Preferred
8 (Male, 48)		Preferred	Preferred	
9 (Male, 23)	Preferred		Preferred	
10 (Female, 35)		Preferred		Preferred
11 (Male, 48)		Preferred	Preferred	
12 (Male, 31)		Preferred		Preferred
Summary	3 (25%)	8 (67%)	8 (67%)	3 (25%)

For both 2D and 3D tasks, the majority participants (83% for the 2D task, and 100% for the 3D task) rated the binocular display as the best experience. They provided the following reasons:

- "Two eyes have better viewing quality."
- "Both eyes can focus on the same spot. That is more relaxing."
- "Two eyes provide a much better experience."

For the 2D task, the majority of the participants (67%) rated the experience of using the monocular display with the other eye masked better than the experience of using the monocular display without masking the other eye. They listed the following reasons:

- "With the mask, there is no competition between the two eyes." (no rivalry)
- "With the mask, the eye seeing the display feels more comfortable."
- "There is a better focus with the mask on."
- "With the mask, I was able to see the bottom part of the Mickey Mouse better, while without the mask the whole drawing area is positioned lower so I cannot see."
- "Without mask, I got a very serious duplicated view, and the eye without the display is not comfortable."
- "With mask, I have much clear view compared to the view without mask."

For the 2D task a small subset of participants (25%) rated the experience of using the monocular display without masking the other eye as better than the experience of using the monocular display with the other eye masked. They listed the following reasons:

- "To wear the mask made my eyes hurt, and I had watering eyes quickly after starting the task."
- "When the other eye was blocked, the eye being used felt very tired, two eyes were not coordinated and focused together. That made me feel uncomfortable."
- "For single-eye with the mask, the video's position sometimes blocks my drawing hand, maybe a smaller video display might resolve this problem."

On the other hand, for the 3D task the majority of the participants (67%) rated the experience of using the monocular display *without* masking the other eye better than the experience of using the monocular display with the other eye masked. They listed the following reasons:

- "For 3D task, I needed depth perception so seeing different contents in each eye can be tolerated because of the gain for depth perception." This comment was given by multiple participants.
- "Without the mask, I can find the LEGO parts faster."
- "With the mask on, I lost depth perception, so I could not pick up pieces very well, even confused on the colors of the LEGO pieces."
- "With the mask on, the eye behind the mask started to see some statics, like snow flakes on a TV channel without broadcast program, ..."

For the 3D task, another small subset of participants (25%) who preferred the experience of using the monocular display with the other eye masked over the experience of using the monocular display without masking the other eye. They listed the following reasons:

- "I experienced serious duplicated view. That made me feel very uncomfortable in the other eye where there was nothing to display."
- "Without mask, the image becomes very blurred and the single most important factor is that I cannot live with that vision quality and with the mask, the quality is much better and clear."
- "Without mask, the view becomes blurred. With mask, it is much better."

We had one participant (8%) who rated the two monocular experiences (with and without mask) as the same for both the 2D and 3D tasks. She stated the following reason:

- "Single eye with or without mask feels the same for me. My left eye has better vision than the right eye. That maybe a factor."

3.2 Discussion

For the experiments performed in reference [5, 6], AR images covered background figures displayed on the monitors, and observers were asked to trace star-shaped frame patterns on the background figures. For these experiments where AR images and background images overlapped onto each other, the superiority of the monocular AR presentation was demonstrated through the wider UFOV (Useful Field of View) and better tracing accuracy.

For our experiments, all participants reported that they chose to separate the AR content display area and the working area where they drew the cartoon characters or assembled plastic building pieces by tilting their head so that both views could be seen without any overlap or occlusion. Most participants chose to shift their visual attention back and forth in this way between the working area and the AR overlay area, as depicted in Fig. 4.

However, we did have one subject who wanted to overlap the instructions with his workspace, and asked if we could change the brightness of the AR display window so he could better see the working area through the HMD display.

Given the fact that nearly all participants naturally chose to position the AR display at a non-overlapping but close position to the working area, the majority of them found the binocular display to be the best because they can avoid binocular rivalry. The vergence-accommodation conflict is also minimized because the two attention centers (the AR content area and the drawing/assembling areas) do not overlap or interact in any way.

The experiment comparing monocular display with or without the mask provided interesting results. This experiment tests whether the user prefers to avoid the binocular rivalry problem, or to have their depth perception of the physical space. A majority of participants (75%) preferred to include the mask for the 2D task since depth perception isn't particularly helpful for this task, while at the same time a similar majority (67%)

Fig. 4. A depiction of placing the virtual content adjacent to the physical workspace. Nearly all participants chose to arrange the content in this non-overlapping manner.

preferred not to wear the mask for the 3D task since the need for depth perception outweighed the annoyance of binocular rivalry. However, a significant subset (25%) of participants could not tolerate the "pain" of the binocular rivalry and were willing to give up the benefits of depth perception.

Table 3 in the appendix listed additional User Experience (UX) comments given by 12 test subjects. As we can see, users have very diversified reactions and preferences over the visual experiences.

4   Conclusion

While performing manual tasks by following real-time, step-by-step instructions for 2D tasks such as drawing cartoon characters on a piece of paper and 3D tasks such as assembling plastic building pieces, participants naturally chose to separate the AR content display from the physical workspace and put them in adjacent locations in the field of view. By shifting the attention between the AR content display and the drawing/assembling area, participants preferred binocular display on the head mounted devices. For a monocular display, participants need to balance the benefit of the monocular display and the annoyance of binocular rivalry. While a majority of users can tolerate binocular rivalry, a significant subset of users has a low tolerance of binocular rivalry and prefer to mask or close the other eye.

Appendix

Table 3. Detailed comments on user experiences given by test subjects.

Subject No. (Gender, Age)	Comments on User Experiences
1 (Male, 23)	"...Changes to one eye makes the overlay look much bigger for me. In that case, to reduce the overlay size from [full screen] to [large] is better"
2 (Male, 24)	"By masking one eye, the glass wearing becomes uncomfortable. But the mask does help me to focus better"
3 (Male, 49)	"To mask one eye irritates my eyes, my eyes started to feel sour and tearing immediately and constantly afterwards. So to mask one eye is definitely not an option for me. It feels like torture" "Attention switch is not a problem for binocular display. But it is a problem for monocular display"
4 (Female, 24)	"For 2D drawing task, I would rather to look at a computer screen, not an AR glass. It is very intuitive to draw with one hand, and look away for the screen and come back. For 3D task, both hands were occupied, smart glass makes more sense because I need to look more closely to coordinate both hands constantly" "My left eye has better vision than the right eye. That maybe why I do not feel any difference with or without wearing a mask"
5 (Male, 39)	"I hate the mask because the blocked eye gets tired without coordination with the other eye. Also I need to roll up my eyes to see the video in the AR glass, which feels like watching movie on the first row in a cinema [too close and uncomfortable!]"
6 (Female, 61)	"My eyes compensate with each other. One watched near while the other watched far. That is why I felt better about the two-eye view" "The 2D task is fairly easy and very intuitive" "The 3D task, on the other hand, is not that natural because I need to look at the videos and do the lego task at the same time. Without depth perception, I would rather look at a screen instead of the smart glass"
7 (Male 42)	"I experienced serious duplicated views" "With the mask on, the eye behind the mask started to see some statics, like snow flakes on a TV channel without broadcast program, ..." "I wear a pair of heavy glasses already, so it is hard to have the AR glass on top of my own glasses. It is way too heavy"
8 (Male, 48)	"Video quality in the AR glass is not good. For 3D task, there is a color confusion problem for me (the lego pieces in the video look like different colors compared to the real pieces). I have to take off the AR glass to verify the real color"
9 (Male, 23)	"I like to change the brightness of the video display so I can look through and overlay the video on top of the work space. I actually like to overlay the AR video on top on the working area"
10 (Male, 48)	"It is intuitive to have two attention centers and I can switch my attentions between them"

(continued)

Table 3. (*continued*)

Subject No. (Gender, Age)	Comments on User Experiences
11 (Female, 35)	"I will always select two-eye approach because of the vision quality is much better. Any other factors are secondary"
12 (Male, 31)	"I always like to operate with one-eye. It is much relax and clear for me. Both eyes are needed for the 3D task because I need the depth to pick up the pieces"

References

1. https://en.wikipedia.org/wiki/Binocular_rivalry. Accessed 14 Feb 2019
2. Laramee, R.S., Ware, C.: Rivalry and interference with a head-mounted display. ACM Trans. Comput.-Hum. Interact. **9**(3), 238–251 (2002)
3. https://en.wikipedia.org/wiki/Ocular_dominance. Accessed 14 Feb 2019
4. Kramida, G., Varshney, A.: Resolving the vergence-accommodation conflict in head mounted display, a review of problem assessments, potential solutions, and evaluation methods. IEEE Trans. Visual Comput. Graphics **22**(7), 1–16 (2015)
5. Kitamura, A., Naito, H., et al.: Distribution of attention in augmented reality: comparison between binocular and monocular presentation. IEICE Trans. Electron. **E97-C**(11) (2014)
6. Kitamura, A., Kinosada, Y., et al.: Superiority of monocular augmented reality when continuous viewing is required. In: SID Symposium Digest of Technical Paper (2018)
7. https://www.youtube.com/watch?v=TSCZIDrBtNs. Accessed 14 Feb 2019
8. https://www.youtube.com/watch?v=Nh4JhXMcfYY. Accessed 14 Feb 2019
9. https://www.youtube.com/watch?v=LGOBClXeUWw. Accessed 14 Feb 2019
10. https://www.amazon.com/gp/product/B0768FJHGL

Cybersickness and Postural Sway
Using HMD Orientation

Lisa Rebenitsch[(⊠)] and Breanna Quinby

South Dakota School of Mines and Technology, Rapid City, SD 57701, USA
lisa.rebenitsch@sdsmt.edu

Abstract. Virtual reality (VR) systems have become widespread in recent years. However, feelings of motion sickness-like symptoms, or cybersickness, is a significant concern. Currently, there is no reliable, objective method to dynamically monitor cybersickness in consumer systems. This longitudinal study expands on prior postural stability research to permit fewer disruptions. The motivation is to find objective measures for monitoring that is applicable in a wide variety of consumer head mounted displays (HMD). This study's results suggest that postural sway is correlated with cybersickness even without the restriction of the Tandem Romberg stance using HMD location data. To accomplish this, the correlation of cybersickness to the movement of the HMD without suspending VR use was examined. As in past studies the HMD horizontal variance correlates with simulator sickness questionnaire (SSQ). Other significant correlations were found in the HMD fore-aft translation, HMD pitch, and HMD roll. These results reveal that measuring postural sway could lead to warning VR users if they are at risk for becoming ill.

Keywords: Cybersickness · Vision induced motion sickness (VIMS) ·
Virtual Reality · Postural instability · Simulator sickness

1 Introduction

With the increasing usage of Virtual Reality (VR) systems comes an increasing population of users with motion-sickness-like symptoms, or cybersickness. Ideally, a warning system should be employed so that consumers are notified when they are at risk of becoming ill. There are a few issues with this, however, as current methods of measuring illness typically include stopping and/or special equipment. This makes it difficult to create marketable, dynamic, consumer-level warning systems. Early tracking systems failed to provide sufficient tracking sensitivity, and normal usage with continuous movement produces noise in postural sway. The hypothesis is that using a modern head mounted display (HMD) to track position with their improved tracking sensitivity could solve this problem. This provides a ready solution as HMDs are already worn during system use and there is no pausing of game-play.

Using postural stability as an objective measure of illness has been a goal in cybersickness research for a few decades. Past research has found consistent correlation between the two [1–9]. Unfortunately, past studies typically use specialized hardware, and required pausing usage at regular intervals to attain specific stances during VR

© Springer Nature Switzerland AG 2019
J. Y. C. Chen and G. Fragomeni (Eds.): HCII 2019, LNCS 11574, pp. 500–509, 2019.
https://doi.org/10.1007/978-3-030-21607-8_39

immersion. The hardware requirement of a sensor taped to the torso is not available in consumer systems and would likely not be accepted. The stance typically employed is the Tandem Romberg stance, which is an eyes-closed, arms folded, and heel to toe position. This stance is used as it encourages sway and therefore is easier to detect. This is unnatural and requires stopping use every few minutes, which would also not be tolerated.

To achieve consumer usability, specialized hardware was not used. Instead this method used the equipment already required for the game system. Moreover, immersion was not stopped at regular intervals to attain the Tandem Romberg stance. Instead, a longitudinal study was performed with a relatively sedentary VR application. This application allowed limited, but continuous, normal movement. This served as a step to confirm postural stability can still be used without special hardware and stances, at least in some contexts.

This research expands on prior research by tracking both the top of the torso and head. The head moves substantially more than the neck during VR usage, which generates more noise in the postural data. Historically, the sharp movement of the head made tracking position via the HMD unreliable due to both low accuracy refresh rates in the equipment, but this has changed with recent devices. The HMD used allowed refresh rates of 60–100 Hz.

As in past studies the horizontal variance correlated with the simulator sickness questionnaire (SSQ) [10]. In our study, it also correlated with HMD horizontal variance. The SSQ score had correlations with HMD variance with a $p < 0.00002$. There was also a correlation in the fore-aft HMD variance with the SSQ. The SSQ had a correlation with HMD fore-aft variance with $p < 0.01$. Roll had not previously been tracked as it's measure is unique to the HMDs tracking. HMD roll was correlated to the SSQ-Total with $p < 0.007$. These results reveal that measuring sway along the HMD horizontal and fore-aft axes(s) and the roll rotation could lead to warning VR users if they are at risk for becoming ill. These results suggest that this method could lead to adding software to consumer equipment that would warn a user if they were soon to become ill without interference of normal usage.

2 Background

Cybersickness is a maladaptation to visual stimuli resulting in motion sickness-like symptoms. It is highly individual as it is polysymptomatic (many symptoms) and polygenic (symptoms manifested differ from individual to individual) making it a difficult illness monitor. The biological causes of cybersickness have not been firmly established and the common theories are sensory mismatch, postural instability, poison, and rest frame theory. Sensory mismatch and postural instability are the most common.

Sensory mismatch states that if the stimulus from the outside environment is being perceived differently by different senses, it will induce cybersickness. Rest frame theory is based on the direction the user believes is "up" in relation to actual gravity. Poison theory is rarely used in cybersickness research, but states a person feels ill within an incorrectly perceived environment if the perception could have been due to poison in the past.

The current experiment is built on the postural instability theory which states that if a person is unable to maintain a posture necessary given the stimulus from the outside environment, it will induce cybersickness. It suggests that the more unstable the posture, the more ill a participant will become. As such, postural instability can be viewed as a more restricted form of sensory mismatch, since it focuses on the vestibular systems' inability to cope with the stimulus to attain proper posture.

Given the wide variety of theories and symptoms, there are also a variety of measurement systems. The most common measurement system in cybersickness studies is the simulator sickness questionnaire (SSQ) developed in 1993 by Kennedy et al. [10]. Even when postural testing or physiological testing is used, the SSQ is often used to determine their accuracy. The SSQ consists of several questions asking for the severity of symptoms on a scale of 0–3. Scores are computed for three categories of nausea (e.g. stomach awareness, nausea, etc.), oculomotor (e.g. headache, eyestrain, etc.), and disorientation (e.g. difficulty focusing, vertigo, dizziness, etc.). The categories are abbreviated as N, O, and D, respectively.

Since cybersickness is highly individual, the average susceptibly can skew the results. Gender is the most common demographic cited with cybersickness with females typically having higher scores [11–14], but there are some studies that show no difference [5, 13]. To better determine susceptibility, a susceptible questionnaire may be employed. One is the revised motion sickness susceptibility questionnaire (MSSQ) by Golding which shortened and simplified the scoring of the Reason and Brand Motion Sickness Susceptibility Questionnaire [15]. The MSSQ analyzes the frequency an individual has become ill from motion in the past.

Unfortunately, questionnaires are subjective, time consuming, and disrupt VR use. Movement of the user is an objective alternative. Studies have focused on postural sway, which has been consistently correlated with symptoms. Bos, Bles, and Groen have proposed that cybersickness and related illnesses should use postural instability as the sole measurement of severity of symptoms [16]. Countering this is that while postural stability is well associated with illness it can occur without illness [17], and the amounts vary from system to system [18]. In addition, most postural studies separate according to sick versus well, rather than a continuous scale.

Current postural instability research typically measures the changes in fore-aft and horizontal movement, and typically shows the fore-aft axis resulting in the greatest change with cybersickness. Prior studies have found correlations with horizontal velocity [1–6], variance in fore-aft and horizontal axes [3, 7, 8], and discriminant functions [9]. Villard et al. found the standard deviation of head position in the fore-aft and horizontal axes were greater for the participants that stayed well [3]. Dong and Stoffregen and Dong, Yoshida, and Stoffregen partially agreed with these results [7, 8]. Bos, Ledegang, et al. instead employed a Nintendo Wii Balance Board© when examining postural instability after watching a stereoscopic movie [4]. They found there was a significant increase on average in standard deviation in both horizontal and fore-aft directions. Chardonnet, Mirzaei, and Merienne found correlations with area, length, horizontal length, fore-aft length, slope, and speed variance of the center of gravity [19].

In practice, postural instability detection is neither continuous nor does it leave the participant undisturbed. Postural instability detection typically requires that a specific standardized stance be taken every few minutes, resulting in greater interference than one-question scales, and only the position data recorded during the stance is used for analysis.

To address the fact that postural instability interferes with virtual environment interactions in recent years, there has been an exploration of "bio-signals" or "physiological signals" measurement of cybersickness. Physiological signals such as the heart rate and blood pressure are analyzed to determine their correlations with cybersickness [20, 21]. The disadvantages of the method are that wearing the sensors is often uncomfortable and costly.

3 Methodology

The main purpose of this study was to examine the potential of a low interference, objective, monitoring system on consumer VR devices. Users want to be able to plug in and play. Therefore, a noninvasive process is needed, but the process must still allow the ability to monitor the user and warn them if they are at risk for becoming ill.

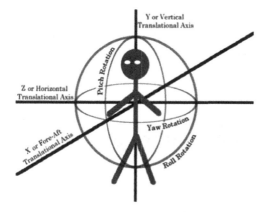

Fig. 1. Rotational and translational axes

The first hypothesis was that it was possible to monitor a person's wellbeing via the HMD position alone. The second hypothesis was that the improvement of tracking accuracy would make the Tandem Romberg stance unnecessary for correlation. Therefore, the postural features most correlated in prior research should still show significance if the hypotheses were correct.

This study took postural stability data recorded from a prior experiment [22] which involved testing HMD weight, HMDs versus large screens, and perceived screen sizes. The navigation scheme was the same throughout, allowing postural comparison. There were approximately 150 trials lasting up to 24 min. The head positions in the x, y, and z axes and the pitch, roll and yaw rotations were collected. These axes were as noted in Fig. 1. The top of the torso positions in the x, y, z axes were also collected. History of motion-sickness was also recorded via the MSSQ as an estimate of the susceptibility of the participants. For safety purposes, participants were asked for their feeling of wellness on a 1-point scale every three minutes. This caused limited interference as many participants answered before the question was complete.

The interaction with the environment was always performed when standing. Participants were permitted a step to the side, forward, or backward. Longer distance movement and selection were done with an X-Box controller.

The initial and ending postural sway were then tested within-subject to determine if there was change as previously found in prior literature. All six degrees of freedom were included as this was a longitudinal study. Those features that showed significance were then tested for correlation.

3.1   Environment

To generalize the results, the experiments required an environment that could be seen in the home. Specifically, the environment needed to be interactive, fully 3D, have at least some effects of gravity (no flying), and could not be made with the intention to encourage cybersickness. A treasure hunt game was created to meet these conditions. The virtual environment consisted of five to nine rooms, two of which were simple mazes. The rooms were varied for each session, but always included one rectangular maze, and one curved wall maze. The object of the game was to locate all the items given in a left-hand menu as quickly as possible. Examples of screen shots are provided in Fig. 2. The environment was created to scale, if possible, and most objects were approximately 80 cm from the floor.

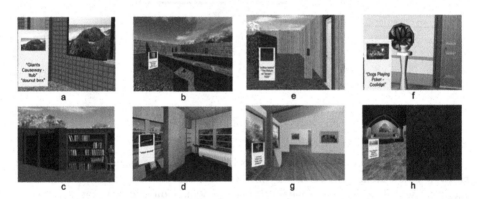

Fig. 2. Screen shots from the experiment virtual environment

To offset the learning effects, a different set of rooms and treasure lists were provided in each session. Later analysis with the Kruskal test (the Kruskal test is a non-parametric variant of ANOVA) displayed no effect based on the choice of room set ($p < 0.75$).

3.2   Hardware

The virtual environment was presented using Vizard 3.0 with 3-sample antialiasing and a 4:3 aspect ratio. Tracking was done with an Intersense IS900 which has a specified latency of 4 ms. Formal tracker-to-display latency calculations were not performed. If stereo was used, the software IPD was 6 cm. The two different display technologies were a Sony Glasstron LDI-D100B HMD and tracked 3D projector. The HMD had an 800×600 resolution, fixed interpupillary distance, and a 35° diagonal FOV, and a refresh rate of 60 Hz. The projector had a maximum resolution of 1600×1200 and a refresh rate of 100 Hz due to the shutter glasses. Postural samples were done at the same rate as the refresh rate.

The Shapiro normality test determined that the populations were non-Gaussian. Therefore, the Wilcoxon test (a non-parametric equivalent of the t-test) was used, $p < 0.05$ meant statistically significant and $p < 0.10$ meant a trend. The results are listed in Table 1. HMD horizontal and roll variance demonstrated significance or trends, with ill individuals. The same feature had high p-values of over 0.4 for well individuals, as expected. This suggested that there was an effect when people got sick, and no effect based on movement when people were not sick. This filtered what would be checked for correlations in the next step.

Those features that showed a difference in ill participants were then tested for correlation using all participants. The non-parametric Spearman test was used for correlation testing.

Table 1. Wilcoxon

	x	y	z	Pitch	Yaw	Roll
H-MSSQ	0.057*	0.457	0.091*	0.215	0.098*	0.447
H-Nausea	0.861	0.727	0.408	0.367	0.920	0.842
H-Disorientation	0.789	0.705	0.022**	0.573	0.304	0.017**
H-Oculomotor	0.855	0.715	0.153	1.000	0.296	0.035**
H-Total	0.582	0.960	0.053*	0.380	0.689	0.105
T-MSSQ	0.013**	0.352	0.242	NA	NA	NA
T-Nausea	0.803	0.173	0.053*	NA	NA	NA
T-Disorientation	0.638	0.239	0.015**	NA	NA	NA
T-Oculomotor	0.426	0.542	0.068*	NA	NA	NA
T-Total	0.408	0.027**	0.002***	NA	NA	NA

*legend * < 0.10, ** < 0.05, *** < 0.01*
H is Head and T is Torso

Table 2. Head roll Spearman results

	Final SSQ-N	Final SSQ-D	Final SSQ-O	Final SSQ.T	Initial MSSQ	Final MSSQ
p-value	.0117**	0.218	0.1206	0.007***	0.001***	0.18
ρ	0.247	0.137	0.214	0.214	0.318	0.132

legend: ** < 0.05, ***< 0.01

Table 3. HMD Z (horizontal) Spearman results

	Final SSQ-N	Final SSQ-D	Final SSQ-O	Final SSQ.T	Initial MSSQ	Final MSSQ
p-value	0.000***	0.022**	0.000***	0.000***	0.014**	0.242
ρ	0.332	0.289	0.348	0.341	0.272	0.0458

legend: ** < 0.05, ***< 0.01

Table 4. HMD X (fore-aft) Spearman results

	Final SSQ-N	Final SSQ-D	Final SSQ-O	Final SSQ.T	Initial MSSQ	Final MSSQ
p-value	0.049**	0.436	0.014**	0.010***	0.047**	0.353
ρ	0.190	0.162	0.246	0.222	0.232	0.051

legend: ** < 0.05, ***< 0.01

4   Results

Table 1 holds the results from the Wilcoxon tests. The tests were within-subject, with the variance taken from the postural data of the first and last three minutes of immersion. If the first hypothesis was correct, there should be statistical significance in ill individuals as the participants postural sway should change. For those that stayed well, there should be high p values as there should be limited changes in postural sway. The cutoff used to determine separate populations was an SSQ score of 50. After viewing a histogram, it became evident that this is where the difference between non-ill users and those with moderate to severe symptoms appeared. This left 26 trials to be used.

These results repeat past literature findings for the torso (neck) horizontal and fore-aft movement. It is not surprising that head sway on these axes is a factor due to the consistency in past literature for sway along the torso in the same direction. The new feature found is the HMD roll postural sway. It also shows statistically significant differences in sick participants. Roll is not trackable in a torso sensor, so this was a discovery. Although background demographics were not a focus of the study, the MSSQ correlation was included. The MSSQ has been correlated with the SSQ in the past, so in theory, it may also be correlated with postural sway. This will be evaluated further later.

As a result of the initial test on populations, the HMD roll, HMD horizontal variance, and HMD fore-aft variance were included in the correlation tests.

Table 2 documents the correlations found in HMD roll variance. There is significant correlation in the final minutes of variance and the final reported SSQ-T scores. The results cannot determine if illness causes the participant to change their head's roll as a coping mechanism, or if the head's movement causes the change in sickness. The SSQ-N seems to be the most frequent symptom correlated to head roll. This may allow direct monitoring of nausea in the future.

Table 3 contains the result of the final head variance along the Z axis (horizontal). As expected, the HMD Z axis remains correlated with both overall well-being for the entire population, despite using postural data collected with natural standing posture, and not the Tandem Romberg stance.

The fore-aft HMD correlation results are found in Table 4. While the only positive Wilcoxon results in the X direction came from MSSQ populations, past literature has frequently found a correlation in fore-aft variance and user well-being. Also, noteworthy is the MSSQ Wilcoxon results consistency in both torso and HMD trackers indicating its useful measure if it is known whether a participant had past motion sickness. The small p-values found in the Spearman results confirm past literature's findings and suggest a correlation between fore-aft movement and user illness.

Lastly, correlation is seen with the MSSQ and initial variance. This is an unanticipated, but useful result. If the MSSQ is consistently correlated with initial postural sway, the MSSQ may be used as an object susceptibility measure in the future.

5   Discussion

This project examined if the Tandem Romberg stance is necessary to detect a correlation between postural sway and cybersickness. The motivation was to ascertain if a lower interference method may be available to monitor participants during use.

These results suggest that it could be possible to dynamically monitor a user's wellbeing in consumer HMDs. There remained significant correlation along the horizontal and fore-aft axes using the HMD alone with normal standing postures. The addition of rotation required examination of three more degrees of freedom. While using the HMD introduced more noise into the data, statistically significant results were found with HMD roll. Monitoring these variances could lead to warning a user when they are at risk for becoming ill in the future. Individuals that are prone to illness will have an aid in determining their safe VR duration. It also may help heavy users to adapt more easily to the system.

The risk in performing a wide variety of correlations is the possibility of false positives. Therefore, this longitudinal study's results will be compared against a new experiment. The application used for this experiment did not have much yaw variation in its navigation. However, with the observed statistically significant difference in populations based on MSSQ found in Wilcoxon testing, it is possible yaw is also correlated with illness and will be tested in future apps that include more yaw variance. Other future work includes examining path length and discriminate functions as features, and the development of a prediction model using verbal scores over time. Although not a focus of the study, initial variance in many features correlated with the MSSQ with p-values all under 0.05 which could prove to be an objective measure of susceptibility.

The results of the study suggest several future directions. The first is to examine if the postural sway can be used to dynamically monitor a participant over time rather than only detect correlation with changes between the start and end of immersion. The source experiment included verbal illness score every three minutes, and this analysis is currently in progress. The second is to further consider the ability to objectively measure susceptibility with postural sway. This will require additional participants and a wide range of systems. The third is to confirm the results with a new set of participants and other VR systems. Prior literature had shown different levels of changes in postural with different systems. This has made it difficult to transfer the results to a new system. Ideally, a wide variety of systems should be used to determine the average change in postural sway or find the average change in postural sway in particular varieties of VR systems.

References

1. Kennedy, R.S., Stanney, K.M.: Postural instability induced by virtual reality exposure: development of a certification protocol. Int. J. Hum.-Comput. Interact. **8**(1), 25–47 (1996)
2. Chang, C.-H., Pan, W.-W., Tseng, L.-Y., Stoffregen, T.A.: Postural activity and motion sickness during video game play in children and adults. Exp. Brain Res., 1–11 (2011)
3. Villard, S.J., Flanagan, M.B., Albanese, G.M., Stoffregen, T.A.: Postural instability and motion sickness in a virtual moving room. Hum. Factors J. Hum. Fact. Ergon. Soc. **50**(2), 332–345 (2008)
4. Bos, J.E., Ledegang, W.D., Lubeck, A.J., Stins, J.F.: Cinerama sickness and postural instability. Ergonomics **56**(9), 1430–1436 (2013)
5. Hakkinen, J., Vuori, T., Paakka, M.: Postural stability and sickness symptoms after HMD use. In: International Conference on Systems, Man and Cybernetics, pp. 147–152, October 2002
6. Koslucher, F., Haaland, E., Stoffregen, T.A.: Sex differences in visual performance and postural sway precede sex differences in visually induced motion sickness. Exp. Brain Res. **234**(1), 313–322 (2016)
7. Dong, X., Yoshida, K., Stoffregen, T.A.: Control of a virtual vehicle influences postural activity and motion sickness. J. Exp. Psychol. Appl. **17**(2), 128–138 (2011)
8. Dong, X., Stoffregen, T.A.: Postural activity and motion sickness among drivers and passengers in a console video game. Proc. Hum. Factors Ergon. Soc. Annu. Meet. **54**(18), 1340–1344 (2010)
9. Smart, L.J.J., Otten, E.W., Stoffregen, T.A.: It's turtles all the way down: a comparative analysis of visually induced motion sickness (2007)
10. Kennedy, R.S., Lane, N.E., Berbaum, K.S., Lilienthal, M.G.: Simulator sickness questionnaire: an enhanced method for quantifying simulator sickness. Int. J. Aviat. Psychol. **3**(3), 203–220 (1993)
11. Jaeger, B.K., Mourant, R.R.: Comparison of simulator sickness using static and dynamic walking simulators. In: Proceedings of the Human Factors and Ergonomics Society, Santa Monica (2001)
12. Stanney, K.M., Hale, K.S., Nahmens, I., Kennedy, R.S.: What to expect from immersive virtual environment exposure: influences of gender, body mass index, and past experience. Hum. Fact. J. Hum. Factors Ergon. Soc. **45**(3), 504–520 (2003)
13. Harm, D.L., Taylor, L.C., Bloomberg, J.J.: Adaptive changes in sensorimotor coordination and motion sickness following repeated exposures to virtual environments, League City (2007)
14. Stanney, K.M., Kennedy, R.S., Drexler, J.M., Harm, D.L.: Motion sickness and proprioceptive aftereffects following virtual environment exposure. Appl. Ergon. **30**(1), 27–38 (1999)

15. Golding, J.F.: Motion sickness susceptibility questionnaire revised and its relationship to other forms of sickness. Brain Res. Bull. **47**(8), 507–516 (1998)
16. Bos, J.E., Bles, W., Groen, E.L.: A theory on visually induced motion sickness. Displays **29**(2), 47–57 (2008)
17. Dennison, M.S., D'Zmura, M.: Cybersickness without the wobble: experimental results speak against postural instability theory. Appl. Ergon. **58**, 215–223 (2017)
18. Munafo, J., Diedrick, M., Stoffregen, T.A.: The virtual reality head-mounted display Oculus Rift induces motion sickness and is sexist in its effects. Exp. Brain Res. **235**(3), 889–901 (2016)
19. Chardonnet, J.-R., Mirzaei, M.A., Merienne, F.: Visually induced motion sickness estimation and prediction in virtual reality using frequency components analysis of postural sway signal. In: Artificial Reality and Telexistence Eurographics Symposium on Virtual Environments, Kyoto, Japan (2015)
20. Roberts, W.K., Gallimore, J.J.: A physiological model of cybersickness during virtual environment interaction. Proc. Hum. Factors Ergon. Soc. Annu. Meet. **49**(26), 2230–2234 (2005)
21. Kim, Y.Y., Kim, H.J., Kim, E.N., Ko, H.D., Kim, H.T.: Characteristic changes in the physiological components of cybersickness. J. Appl. Signal Process. **2004** (2004)
22. Rebenitsch, L., Owen, C.: Evaluating factors affecting virtual reality display. In: Lackey, S., Chen, J. (eds.) VAMR 2017. LNCS, vol. 10280, pp. 544–555. Springer, Cham (2017). https://doi.org/10.1007/978-3-319-57987-0_44

Author Index

Printed in the United States
By Bookmasters